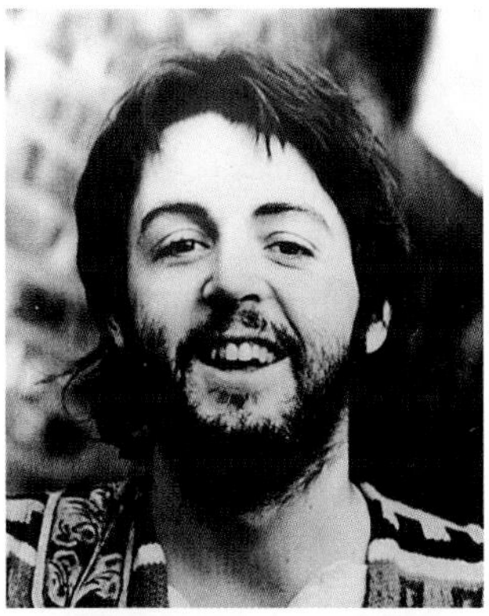

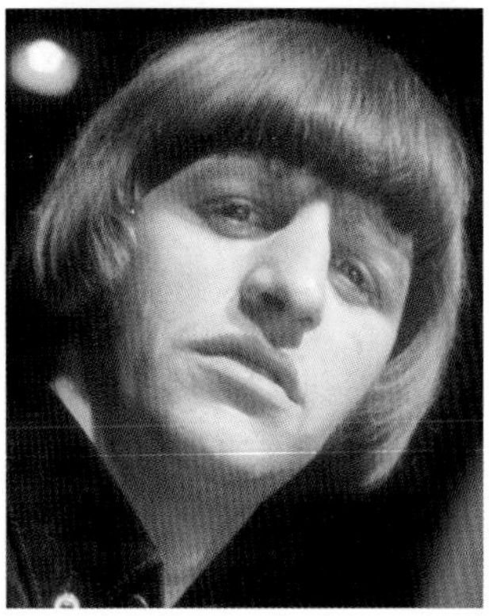

The Beatles

Ten Years That Shook The World

THE
BEATLES

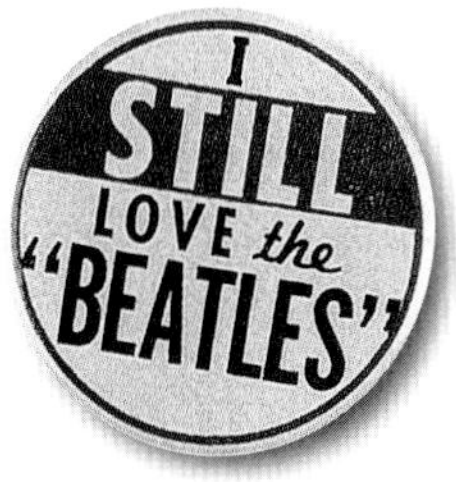
I
STILL
LOVE the
"BEATLES"

The Beatles

Ten Years That Shook The World

Editor-in-Chief: Paul Trynka

DK

LONDON, NEW YORK,
MUNICH, MELBOURNE, DELHI

DORLING KINDERSLEY
Senior Editor Becky Alexander
Project Art Editor Mark Cavanagh
Managing Editor Adèle Hayward
Managing Art Editor Karen Self
Digital Publishing Manager Mark Bracey
Production Controllers Heather Hughes & Jane Rogers
Category Publisher Stephanie Jackson

MOJO
Editor-in-Chief Paul Trynka
Editor Chris Hunt
Executive Editor Pat Gilbert
Art Editor Lora Findlay
Production Manager Simon McEwen
Picture Editor Susie Hudson
Designers Isabel Cruz, Dani Golfieri, Miles Johnson, Carol Briggs & Nigel Truswell
Publishing Director Maddy Ballantyne
Managing Director Marcus Rich

First published in the USA & Great Britain in 2004 by
Dorling Kindersley Limited, 80 The Strand, London, WC2R 0RL.

A Penguin Company

2 4 6 8 10 9 7 5 3 1

All timelines in this book are supplied by Johnny Black's
Rocksource database

A Cataloging-in-Publication record for this book is available
from the Library Of Congress
(US) ISBN 0-7566-0670-5

A CIP catalog record for this book is available from
the British Library (UK) ISBN 1 4053 0691 2

Reproduction by Rival Colour
Printed and bound by Star Standard in Singapore

**See the complete Dorling Kindersley catalogue at
www.dk.com**

**For more information about MOJO magazine go to
www.mojo4music.com**

MOJO
The Music Magazine
Mappin House, 4 Winsley St,
London W1W 8HF

REDFERNS (3), TERENCE SPENCER, REX, ATLANTIC, TOPHAM, HULTON, CAMERA PRESS

Contents

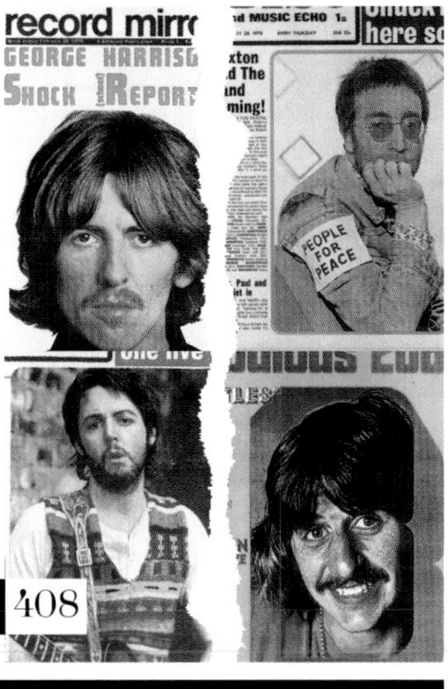

Editor's letter

THE ORIGINAL STORY IS A DISTANT memory for some of us, but there can be few people whose lives haven't been affected by The Beatles. Their influence on the world of music is pervasive; the effect they've had on popular culture is profound.

Looking from today's vantage point, over four decades on from when The Beatles first came to the world's attention, we might think that the story is complete, that there's nothing more to be said. We'd be wrong. Eric Burdon, the gravel-voiced singer with The Animals, expressed it as well as anyone: "there is something beyond time about The Beatles, something fairy tale. I think people will still be talking about them 100 years from now, like we discuss the Bible, or Shakespeare." Burdon has made his share of great records – but he recognised that, with The Beatles, the story is about much more than the records.

At MOJO magazine, we're lucky to be surrounded by an unending supply of new music, of new bands to enthuse about, or rediscovered gems that are new to us or our readers. But The Beatles are always there. Many of the staff weren't even born when Paul McCartney dissolved the band in London's High Court, but when a new cache of photos is discovered, or another piece of their story is unearthed, it's still as exciting as hearing the latest demo by a bunch of 23-year-olds. Their charisma leaches through every artefact – incredibly, after eight years of looking through stashes of photos, it's still impossible to find one where they don't look cool.

This epic tome that you're holding now is a product of that enthusiasm. Conceived over lunch just by the old Speakeasy club in London, it's taken nearly four years to complete, aided by the greatest team of music writers who've ever worked on a book devoted to a single act. MOJO is fortunate to have probably the widest roster of contributors of any music magazine, but it was nonetheless a shock to find out how many leapt at the chance to write about The Beatles, each of them confident there were new insights to be shared, or new facts to be unearthed.

The structure of this book is simple: a timeline that tells you what The Beatles were doing over 10 years, with every major event pulled out and discussed in greater detail. You will learn about their music, their lives, their times, and how they changed the world. And you will listen to their music all over again.

Space is too tight to thank everyone involved in this mammoth project, but I must pay tribute to the sterling work of Chris Hunt, who edited the magazines on which much of this book is based, and Pat Gilbert, MOJO's then editor, who helped develop the concept. I'd also like to bid a fond farewell to Ian MacDonald, who's generally acknowledged as the greatest writer on The Beatles' music. Ian's contributions to this book were probably the last major pieces he wrote on The Beatles before his untimely death, and I'm proud to feature them here.

Paul Trynka, Editor-in-Chief

Foreword

by Brian Wilson

I CAN STILL REMEMBER the first time I saw The Beatles. It was on the Ed Sullivan show. The sound of the girls screaming was like nothing we had ever heard before. It was an unbelievable sound. The first time I'd heard them was on the radio, with I Want To Hold Your Hand. I flipped. It was like a shock that went through my system.

It was amazing that they were getting such a big sound from so few instruments. In those days, The Beach Boys onstage had the same instrumental line-up plus Mike as lead singer, but we certainly weren't making as much rock'n'roll noise as The Beatles. We watched the Ed Sullivan show at Marilyn's [Brian's first wife] parents' house. I was jealous. I was jealous of their electricity… the magnetism they had. They were such electrical performers. Paul is the most versatile singer ever. He can rock like Little Richard and sing a ballad as sweet as anybody. And John had an amazing voice. So powerful… and so full of pain.

PHOTO: CAPITOL

In 1964 and 1965, I knew that it was up to me to keep The Beach Boys competitive. Each time The Beatles released a record, it inspired me to try something new. Sometimes, like with Girl Don't Tell Me on our *Summer Days (And Summer Nights!!)* album, I even tried writing a Beatles song. The "you'll wri...i...ite" part that Carl sings came about after I heard Ticket To Ride. They definitely influenced the writing of that song.

I don't think that at the time I thought about Paul and John's contrasting songwriting styles. To me, it was Beatles music, and with albums like *Rubber Soul*, they were blowing my mind. The thing that appealed to me about their writing was that album after album was filled with great songs. The first time I heard *Rubber Soul* I was at my house on Laurel Way. I was stoned on marijuana. I absolutely flipped. I think I listened to it four times in a row. I was so blown out, I couldn't sleep for two nights. It was the first time in my life I remember hearing a rock album on which every song was really good.

Hearing *Rubber Soul* was really a challenge to me. And it was after I heard *Rubber Soul* that it all started. I told Marilyn that I was going to make the greatest rock album ever. That's how blown out I was over The Beatles. *Rubber Soul* got to my soul, and I wanted to do something as good as that. I didn't care about sales. I just cared about the artistic merit of it. And while I had already recorded some tracks for what would become *Pet Sounds*, it wasn't until after I heard *Rubber Soul* that I brought Tony Asher [the primary lyricist on *Pet Sounds*] on board. I knew what I wanted to say; I just needed somebody who could help me say it in a more complex way.

England really embraced *Pet Sounds* immediately. I was constantly hearing how some pretty heavyweight musicians loved the record. That really cheered me up. And when I heard that Paul McCartney said that God Only Knows was the most beautiful song ever written, well... actually, I didn't really believe it. Of course, in the years since then, I've met Paul and he's told me how much that record means to him. I can't even begin to express how much his support of *Pet Sounds* means to me. It makes me want to continue to make music. And Sir George Martin told me that when The Beatles heard *Pet Sounds* and Good Vibrations, it really caused them some concern as to how they were going to top our productions. That was pretty good stuff for the ego, I have to admit.

"Unbelievable": The Beatles with Ed Sullivan, February 9, 1964

PHOTOS: REDFERNS/ RETNA

They broke our hearts: the last days of The Beatles, August, 1969.

When I heard the *Sgt Pepper* album, I knew that The Beatles had found a way to really take rock in a new direction. A psychedelic direction. It was brilliant. I love With A Little Help From My Friends and that last chord on A Day In The Life scared the heck out of me.

Some of my favourite Beatles songs are Tell Me Why (I love Paul's bass line), Michelle, With A Little Help From My Friends and Let It Be. Paul's version of The Long And Winding Road too, I absolutely love. All You Need Is Love is brilliant. And I love the humorous horn arrangement that George Martin did. In some ways, the 1960s seem so long ago, but in others, I feel like we need that spirit more than ever.

I have always subscribed to the idea that "All You Need Is Love," so like everybody else, it broke my heart when The Beatles broke up. I was really sad. Of course, being from a group, I can understand how there comes a time when everybody needs to go their separate ways. But that doesn't make it easy. Every time I sit at my piano and play Let It Be, I get in touch with how Paul felt when The Beatles were coming to an end. That song heals me; it's saved my life a bunch of times.

Since the 1960s, like The Beatles, The Beach Boys have gone their own ways. I've lost my brothers Dennis and Carl, and Paul and Ringo have lost their brothers John and George. My favourite John song was Across The Universe; that blew me out. And I've played My Sweet Lord at the piano a lot in the last couple of months. I love that song.

People will listen to the music of The Beatles forever. The British Invasion and that moment I first heard them may have been 40 years ago, but their music is so deep in our souls that it will always be part of us.

Love & Mercy,

Brian Wilson
Los Angeles
March 2004

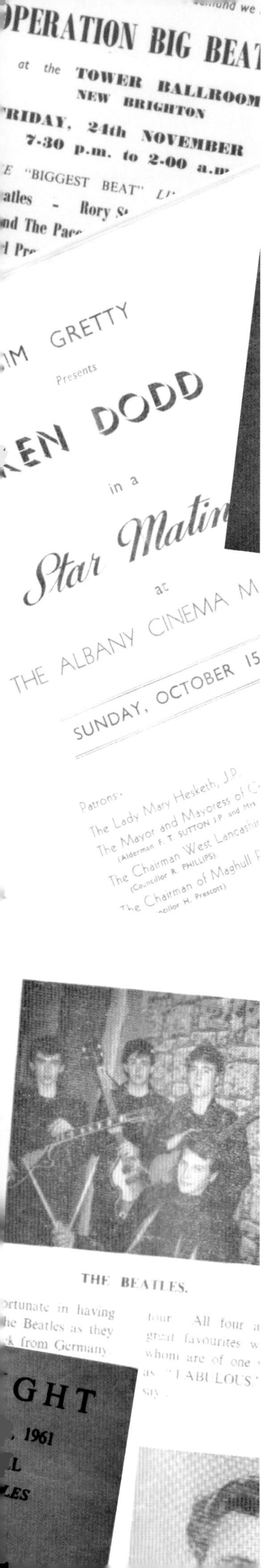

1961

In 1961 The Beatles were regarded at best as one of Liverpool's four top acts, well behind Rory Storm, The Big Three and Gerry And The Pacemakers. But in that crucial year they honed their live act in Hamburg, recorded their first single, found a manager who owned a chain of local record stores – and acquired distinctive new haircuts...

g them
an we

MEET THE BEATLES

every Saturday at

AINTREE INSTITUTE

(BUSES 20, 21, 22, 30, 61, 91, 92, 93, 95, 96 & 500 TO BLACK BULL, NEXT DOOR)

YES ! PAUL, JOHN, GEORGE AND PETE

will be playing for you exclusively at A

every Saturd

You m

Come ea

Jiving from 7-30

Aintree Institut

presents

STAR MATINEE

compere ARTHUR SCOTT introducing . . .

10. The Beatles

11. Dennis Horton

12. Jackie Owen and

Bell

etty

merdon

ODD

etty

LOOK !

THREE TOP GROUPS AGAIN

NEXT WEDNESDAY NIGHT

AT HAMBLETON HALL

Page Moss, Huyton

What a terrific line up for

WEDNESDAY, 25th JANUARY 1961

- The Sensational Beatles
- Derry & The Seniors
- Faron & The Tempest Tornadoes

YES! You must come along early and bring your friends !

PAY AT THE DOOR 2/6 before 8 p.m. 3/- afterward

NOTE ! No admission after 9-30 p.m.

JIVE TO-NIGHT

FRIDAY, 15th SEPTEMBER, 1961

AT KNOTTY ASH HALL

TO THE FABULOUS BEATLES

AND THE BIG THREE

Bus Routes 75, 74, 10, 61, 9

Admission 3/6 [2/6 with this ticket before 8-30]

BE EARLY

Beatles - Rory Storm a

The Pacemakers -

the Tem

BIG BEAT SESSIONS

EVERY FRIDAY at the

TOWER BALLROOM, NEW BRIGHTON

FRIDAY, 1st DECEMBER 1961

Another Great Six Band Line Up -

THE BEATLES - - RORY STORM AND THE HURRICANES

DALE ROBERTS AND THE JAYWALKERS - DERRY AND THE SENIORS

KINGSIZE TAYLOR & THE DOMINOES - STEVE DAY & THE DRIFTERS

First Heat "Mr. Twist" Competition

7-30 p.m. to 1-00 a.m. Licensed Bars (until 11-30 p.m.)

LATE TRANSPORT (Liverpool, Wirral and Cheshire)

Excursions Leaving St. John's Lane (Lime Street) 7-30 p.m. to 9-00 p.m.

TICKETS 4/6

ENTS
eturn)
p.m.
hways C
E TRA
room to th
r Trip to
Seacombe
easowe, Mo
ort, ETC.

THE BEATLES.

We are fortunate in having secured the services of The Beatles as they have only just arrived back from Germany. They are in England for only a short time before embarking upon another European tour ... great ... whom are ... as "FABULOUS ... say

When we were

PHOTOS: CAMERA PRESS; HULTON ARCHIVE; TRACKS

Their chemistry was unique – and so were their childhoods. Bill Harry, a long-term friend of the band, goes back to the very beginning of The Beatles.

very young

The Quarry Men, July 6, 1957; John plays guitar, centre, with Eric Griffiths (guitar), Rod Davis (banjo), John's friend Pete Shotton (washboard) and Len Garry (bass). Paul McCartney was in the audience...

Reared beneath the blue suburban skies in the leafy middle-class village of Woolton, he was no working class hero, nor was he born during an intense air raid as he liked to imagine – nor did his father desert him as his Auntie Mimi alleged. In fact, John Lennon's early life was not just comfortable, it was a happy childhood. He had a group of close friends – Nigel Wally, Ivan Vaughan, Pete Shotton – an intimate family group of aunts and uncles and happy relationships with his many cousins, particularly Stan Parkes and Liela Harvey.

It was an upbringing which contrasted sharply with that of little Ritchie Starkey, who was born in the tiny bedroom of a small terraced house in Dingle, one of the poorest areas of Liverpool. Deserted by his father at the age of three, struck down by numerous illnesses including a ruptured appendix, peritonitis and chronic pleurisy, Ritchie spent so many of his early years in hospital (including two months in a coma) that when he returned to school they didn't even know who he was. The fact that he was still alive, against all odds, inspired the other kids to nickname him 'Lazarus.' His mother Elsie took a job as a barmaid to support them both, but their dire economic straits forced a move into even smaller accommodation.

Ritchie's lack of looks were compensated for by the fact that he was witty, generous, kind-hearted and well liked. In contrast, John, with his relatively affluent background, would prove to be acerbic and menacing – when he could get away with it.

George Harrison was also born in the bedroom of a tiny two-up, two-down terraced house, this time in Wavertree, with the only toilet situated outside in a small paved yard. The lack of a bathroom meant that the baby was initially bathed in the kitchen sink and later, like the rest of the family, in a tin bath.

"I used to beat them up if they were small enough, but I'd just use long words and confuse them if they were bigger."

Paul McCartney's mother had been a nursing sister at Walton Hospital; hence Paul, her first son, was born in a private ward there. Her job as a midwife meant that council house accommodation was provided and the family moved to various parts of Liverpool, ending up in Speke, a newly-built district outside the city. The Harrison family ended up there too – which meant that Paul and George shared the same 92 bus, when the two of them were attending the city's grammar school, The Liverpool Institute.

John Lennon, meanwhile, had started Quarry Bank School in September 1952. He is reported to have deliberated, "I looked at all the hundreds of new kids and thought, Christ, I'll have to fight my way through all this lot." Whether he genuinely thought up this piece of bravado is open to question, although John had been expelled from Mosspits Infants School, reportedly for bullying a little girl, Polly Hipshaw. By the time he got to Dovedale Primary his technique was more versatile: "I used to beat them up if they were small enough but I'd just use long words and confuse them if they were bigger."

Did Lennon's tough outer shell cover a much softer centre? At one of the first appearances by his group The Quarry Men, in Rosebury Street, Dingle, John was heckled by two boys. He escaped into one of the houses followed by his group, and a policeman was called who escorted them safely to the bus stop. At Wilson Hall, Garson, two teddy boys threatened to beat him up and he fled to a bus with the boys running after the vehicle. Despite any claims made by future biographers, it wasn't John's physical aggression which frightened people; rather it was his verbal abuse, which was backed up by his powerful charisma.

The crucial early cultural influence on John, Paul, George and Ringo was not American. What inspired them to make music was the success of

Scottish musician Lonnie Donegan with Rock Island Line. Donegan's distinctive version of the 1930s Leadbelly song made him one of the few British artists to have a major hit across the Atlantic; the single went to Number 8 in the US, selling over a million copies in the process.

When he was 16, John bought a 78rpm version of Rock Island Line and played the song until it was nearly worn out, then sold it to Rod Davis, a friend who would later join Lennon's skiffle group, The Quarry Men. When Donegan played the Liverpool Empire in 1956, Paul McCartney was in the audience; he was so impressed he would sneak down to the theatre during school lunchtimes to catch a glimpse of the great man. The Empire show sparked Paul's desire to own a guitar; Paul's father, Jim, bought him one for £15. It was a fateful change of musical direction. A Fred Astaire fan, Paul loved Broadway musicals, and was so inspired by his musician father that his initial instrument of choice was the trumpet. The discovery that he might develop a lip callus – and possibly spoil his looks – soon put paid to the notion.

George Harrison, too, was ensnared by skiffle: "Lonnie Donegan was appearing at the Empire and of course George just had to go," recalled George's brother Harry. "In fact, he borrowed the money from our parents so that he could see every single show! Anyway, he found out where Lonnie was staying, which happened to be in a house in Speke, so George went round and hammered on the door until he came out and gave George his autograph."

The skiffle music that Donegan championed was a godsend to youngsters throughout the British Isles because it didn't require expensive musical instruments – all they needed to equip a band was an acoustic guitar, home-made tea-chest bass, washboard and harmonica. "Lonnie and skiffle seemed made for me," George Harrison would later point out. "It was easy music to play if you know two or three chords; you'd have a tea chest as bass and a washboard and you were on your way."

Ritchie Starkey, meanwhile, had formed his own outfit, The Eddie Clayton Skiffle Group, with his next door neighbour Eddie Miles. Rather than a mere washboard, Ritchie had managed to buy a drum kit for £10, funded by his recently-acquired stepfather (whom Ritchie, with his memorable ability to subvert the English language, referred to as his "step ladder"). Ritchie later joined the Darktown Skiffle group before becoming a member of the Raving Texans – who would later change their name to Rory Storm & the Hurricanes and emerge as one of Liverpool's leading rock'n'roll bands.

But skiffle wasn't the future Beatles' only musical influence. Like George Harrison, John also loved the music of George Formby, a Lancashire film and recording artist famous in Britain for his innuendo-packed songs and expertise on the banjulele. John's grandfather George Stanley and his mother Julia used to play Formby tunes on a banjo; Julia taught John how to play one, too.

ON SATURDAY, JULY 6, 1956, JOHN'S school band, The Quarry Men, played their most crucial date. It was at the Woolton Village Church Garden Fete. By now, The Quarry Men's skiffle repertoire, of songs like Rock Island Line, Cumberland Gap, Freight Train, Midnight Special, Worried Man Blues, was augmented with the Del Vikings' hit Come Go With Me. The date was a crucial one because a mutual friend, Ivan Vaughan, had lured Paul McCartney to the performance with the promise there would be lots of girls to chat up. Later, in the village hall, Paul was introduced to John. The 15-year-old Paul made an impression because he could tune a guitar and knew the lyrics to songs – he even wrote out the words to Be-Bop-A-Lula and Twenty Flight Rock for John.

"I had a group, I was the singer, I was the leader," John would say of their meeting. "Meeting Paul meant making a decision about having him in the line-up. Was it good to make the group stronger, by bringing in someone better than the ones we had, or to let me be stronger? The decision was to let Paul in and make the group stronger."

Via his friend and fellow Quarry Man Pete Shotton, John put out the call. "Pete saw me cycling one day and shouted that John wanted me to join the band," said Paul. "It was as simple as that."

In those early days, John used to bring Paul over to his mother Julia's house and she taught them both some numbers. "Oddly," said Paul, "one of them was Wedding Bells Are Breaking Up That Old Gang of Mine, while another was definitely Ramona. Much later, during the Beatle years, John and I attempted to write a few songs with a similar feel, with Here, There And Everywhere coming to mind."

The two were soon drawn closer together by a tragic event, when Julia was killed in a road accident on July 15, 1958.

Paul's mother had died of breast cancer on October 31, 1956. "He lost his mum when he was 17," Paul would say many years later. "That was one of the things that brought John and me very close together. It was a bond between us, quite a big one. We came professionally together afterwards. And, as we became a writing team, I think it helped our intimacy and our trust in each other. Eventually, we were pretty good mates – until The Beatles split up and Yoko came into it."

New member Paul was actually away on a scouting trip when The Quarry Men made their Cavern Club debut on Wednesday, August 7 1957. Rock'n'roll was banned at the jazz club, although skiffle was tolerated. However, during the performance John decided to play some Elvis Presley numbers, singing Hound Dog and Blue Suede Shoes. His flagrant transgression of the club's rule upset owner Alan Sytner so much he sent a note to him on stage, saying "Cut out the bloody rock!"

As American rock'n'roll became the inspiration, skiffle numbers were dropped from The Quarry Men's set. Lennon liked Elvis Presley, McCartney performed Little Richard numbers, although Buddy Holly songs made up a substantial portion of their repertoire.

On the bus to school one day George told Paul that he'd just played his first gig with his own band, The Rebels. Impressed, Paul decided to persuade John to let George join The Quarry Men. John was against the idea; he regarded George as just a 'little kid' – an attitude that arguably persisted for many years. He finally bowed to the pressure after George brought along a guitar and played him the rock'n'roll instrumental Raunchy on the top deck of a bus after a Quarry Men gig at Wilson Hall.

George's abilities on lead guitar helped him fill a crucial vacant slot. When Paul made his debut with The Quarry Men at New Clubmoor Hall on October 18, 1957 he was the group's lead guitarist. However, he made such a hash of playing Arthur Smith's Guitar Boogie that he was forbidden to play lead again.

On Saturday, July 12, 1958, The Quarry Men decided to make a record at Percy Philips' studio in Liverpool's Kensington district. They performed Buddy Holly's That'll Be The Day and an original number, In Spite Of All The Danger, credited to Harrison/McCartney. The session ➳

John and Paul, with 'little kid', George – destined to be a junior partner for years.

PHOTOS: REX FEATURES; HULTON ARCHIVE

would be the summit of The Quarry Men's career. They played their last gig together, at the Woolton Village club, and then went their separate ways – John and Paul to work at becoming a songwriting team, while George joined the Les Stewart Quartet.

Later, The Beatles' combination of recording and songwriting – now commonplace – would be regarded as startlingly innovative. Yet, over this period, John and Paul essentially dropped the former role, to concentrate on writing songs. The two youths cut school on numerous occasions to meet at Paul's house in Forthlin Road, while his father was away working at the Cotton Exchange. The two would spend their time around Jim's piano in the small front parlour, filling exercise books full of lyrics to the songs they composed. Paul recalled that the first number they wrote was called Too Bad About Sorrows, followed by Just Fun.

Throughout this period, John and Paul had visions of becoming a major song writing team, who would compose for famous stars like Frank Sinatra. Paul wrote a song with Sinatra in mind, which he called Suicide. Many years later, when the Lennon and McCartney 'brand' almost guaranteed a hit record, Sinatra requested a song from them. Paul sent him a demo of Suicide. Sinatra felt insulted, commenting "Is this guy having me on?"

"When we started off, we were uncertain as to exactly where our writing would take us," recalled Lennon. "Paul was a rocker with one eye on Broadway musicals, vaudeville, and shit like that. I, on the other hand, was inspired by Buddy Holly's songwriting and was determined to show I was as capable as any Yank. To me Buddy was the first to click as a singer-songwriter. His music really moved and his lyrics spoke to us kids in a way no one ever bothered before."

The two were to exaggerate the number of songs they wrote during that period, telling the Mersey Beat newspaper they had written more than 100, while the real amount was closer to twenty.

For the most part, the great majority of their songs were written individually. Rather than sitting down to write each song together, they used each other as a catalyst. It was during this time that they made a vow: whoever wrote the biggest part of a song would have his name first. Depending on the individual contribution to a number, it would be credited to McCartney/Lennon or Lennon/McCartney (although, curiously enough, their first single, Love Me Do, written mainly by Paul, was credited to Lennon/McCartney while Please Please Me, written mainly by John, was credited to McCartney/Lennon). They were forced to abandon this equitable arrangement by Brian Epstein and music publisher Dick James, who thought a standard Lennon/McCartney credit would simplify matters.

"Paul and John's bond superseded Lennon's relationship with Stuart – which was close, but not as close as some have suggested."

THE NEXT ACT OF THE drama opens in August 1959. A new club, the Casbah, was opening in the West Derby area of Liverpool. The Les Stewart Quartet were offered the residency, having been tipped off by George's girlfriend Ruth Morrison. Stewart didn't take up the residency – he was in a pique because guitarist Ken Brown had been missing rehearsals to help prepare the Casbah for the opening. Brown suggested to George that they form another group and go for the residency; so George contacted John and Paul. Mona Best, who ran the Casbah, gave them the job and they revived the name The Quarry Men. But for this turn of events, George would have gone his separate way, and The Beatles would never have existed.

The first photo of Paul and John performing together, at the Casbah, 29 August, 1959.

The continuing dispute over Brown meant The Quarry Men's residency didn't last long, but they continued as a trio, changing their name to Johnny & the Moondogs and appearing at the Carol Levis talent competition at the Empire Theatre. Then, in January 1958, John Lennon realised his band needed a bass guitarist.

John had entered the Liverpool College of Art, age 16, in September 1957. I was also a student there, and was able to introduce John to Stuart Sutcliffe, whose best friend was Rod Murray. Stuart and Rod had recently moved into a flat in Gambier Terrace. Somehow, during the move from nearby Percy Street, one half of a large painting of Stuart's was lost. Stuart entered the remaining half in John Moore's Exhibition at the Walker Art Gallery. Moore, a millionaire whose exhibitions were a celebrated event in the contemporary art scene, bought Stuart's painting for £60.

Arthur Kelly, a friend of George's, was the band's first choice as bassist. But Arthur couldn't afford to buy a bass guitar, so John informed both Rod and Stuart, without telling the other, that the job of bass player was up for grabs. Rod began actually making a bass – which he owns to this day – but by selling his painting Stuart won the race and put a deposit on a Hofner guitar at the local music store, Frank Hessy's.

The Liverpool Institute and the College of Art adjoined each other, so George and Paul joined John and Stuart to rehearse in the college; I would book them for our college dances. At the time I simply referred to them as "the college band" because they still hadn't settled on a name.

John had moved into Gambier Terrace with Stuart and Rod, and one evening there was a discussion about potential band names. Stuart suggested that as they played a lot of Buddy Holly numbers they should find a name similar to Holly's backing group, the Crickets. Once it was decided to use the name of an insect, Beetles became an obvious choice. During the next few months there were various changes: the Beatals, the Silver Beats, the Silver Beetles, the Silver Beatles and finally, in August 1960 they became, simply, The Beatles.

Following an audition for impresario Larry Parnes on May 19, 1960, the band were booked on a short tour of Scotland to back singer Johnny Gentle, taking with them drummer Tommy Moore. Local club-owner Allan Williams started acting as part-time agent for local groups and booked them for some gigs at his Jacaranda coffee bar and two venues on the Wirral. Williams booked another local group, Derry & The Seniors, into the 2 I's coffee bar in London; this attracted a season's booking at the Kaiserkeller club in Hamburg. Club-owner Bruno Koshmider contacted Williams for another group; Williams tried Rory Storm &

All friends together: John, George and Paul with Stuart Sutcliffe, far left, Pete Best, far right and German friend, third from left.

The Hurricanes, but they were booked for a summer season at Butlins. Next he tried Gerry And The Pacemakers, who turned him down. Almost in desperation he turned to The Beatles.

By this time Moore had left the line-up, to be replaced by Norman Chapman, who left in turn after his National Service call up. Then the group dropped into the Casbah club and noticed Mona Best's son, Pete, with his brand new drum kit. Paul phoned Best asking him to join them. He auditioned, and The Beatles set off for Hamburg.

IN THOSE EARLY DAYS, MY OWN IMPRESSION OF JOHN AND Paul was that Paul was the hungry one while John had a more laissez-faire attitude. John loved digging into his pockets to pay for classified adverts in Mersey Beat, the magazine I founded in 1961, but it was Paul who went out of his way to help me with coverage of The Beatles. He brought photos by Astrid Kirchherr from Hamburg for me to publish and gave me the first record they'd made in Germany to review. He also wrote me letters when he was travelling, packed with information on their burgeoning career, such as backing a stripper, making their Hamburg debut, or the time he travelled to France with John. He even bought extra copies of Mersey Beat with our poll forms in, anxious that The Beatles be voted Number 1 group.

John and Paul's personal relationship seemed to deepen along with their professional partnership. I regularly spotted John and Cynthia and Paul and his girlfriend Dot Rhone double-dating together. Walking along Slater Street I'd often see both couples huddled in a doorway necking.

It was a friendship they cemented by going off together on short trips. During the Easter holidays in April 1960, John and Paul hitch-hiked down South and stopped off at the Fox and Hounds pub in Berkshire, where the new tenants were Mike and Elizabeth Robbins – 'Beth' was Paul's cousin. When Paul and John turned up, Mike suggested they perform at the pub and gave them the name the Nerk Twins (Paul and his brother Mike had called themselves the Nurk Twins when performing for family members). The two performed sitting on stools playing acoustic guitars in the tap room on the evening of April 23 and during lunchtime the following day.

In October 1961, when John received £100 from his Aunt Elizabeth as a 21st birthday present, John and Paul set off for Spain together, although they ended up in Paris and remained there during their brief holiday. During this stay they were given a stylish haircut by their friend Jurgen Vollmer, which became the basis for the famous Beatles moptop. On their return they stopped off in London and bought Cuban-heeled boots from Anello & Davide – which would one day start a fashion trend.

Although Stuart Sutcliffe was not as bad a guitarist as history has it, Paul wanted him out of the group. Paul had been central to the plot to rid The Quarry Men of guitarist Eric Griffiths so he could replace him with his pal George, and he continually provoked Stuart, virtually edging him out of the band (it was also mainly Paul who plotted with George to oust Pete Best, against the wishes of Brian Epstein and a reluctant John).

The McCartney/Lennon bond superseded John's relationship with Stuart – which was close, but not as intense as some have suggested. Stuart's best friend at art college was Rod Murray, not John, and when Stuart remained in Hamburg with his girlfriend at the end of 1960, John actually offered Chas Newby the position of Beatles bass guitarist.

In hindsight, Paul's determination to hone the group was crucial, and these changes would help make up the right chemistry for what would be a unique quartet. For all his tough guy image, John shied away from the unpleasant task of ousting people. He got on well with Pete Best. The two used to hang around together in Hamburg and at one time when John suggested they do some mugging to earn extra money, the others shied away, but Pete joined John in a disastrous episode in which the mugging 'victim' had the two fleeing in fright as he fired a gas pistol at them!

When Pete finally came to be ousted from the band, John was quite open in saying that Pete's sacking was a disgraceful episode and that they were "cowards" to do it. The arrival of Brian Epstein, and the departure of Pete, started a process that would effectively change The Beatles from John's group, to Paul's group. As John hinted, the process of letting Paul in had made the band stronger. It would also change popular music forever. ■

PHOTOS: SAM LEACH. REX FEATURES

JANUARY 61

5 The Beatles earn £7 10s for a gig at Litherland Town Hall, Liverpool.

6 The Beatles earn £6 10s for a gig at St John's Hall, Bootle, Liverpool, with Johnny Sandon and the Searchers.

FEBRUARY 61

9 The Beatles debut at Liverpool's Cavern Club with a lunch-time session. Bob Wooler (DJ): "From January 1961 to February 1962, I introduced The Beatles at the Cavern Club 292 times. For that first lunch-time session they got £5. For the last one they got £300."

14 John Lennon is knocked to the floor by girl fans at the Valentine Dance, Litherland Town Hall, who storm on stage when one 'wins' a kiss from Paul McCartney.

24 The Beatles play their first gig on the other side of the Mersey, at the Grosvenor Ballroom, Wallasey.

MARCH 61

13 The Beatles play at The Cavern Club (below) and later at the Liverpool Jazz Society; they play another lunchtime Cavern session the next day.

15 Beatles' bass-player Stuart Sutcliffe returns to Hamburg to be with Astrid Kirchherr.

16 The Beatles play at The Cavern Club, Liverpool.

17 The Beatles play at Mossway Hall, Moss Way, Croxteth, Liverpool, and later at Liverpool Jazz Club.

19 The Beatles play at The Casbah Coffee Club, Liverpool.

20 The Beatles play at The Cavern, and later at Hambleton Hall, Huyton, Liverpool.

21 The Beatles play their first evening show at The Cavern, supporting The Bluegenes.

APRIL 61

1 The Beatles return to Hamburg for 92 nights at the Top Ten Club.

20 Having learned that The Beatles plan to stop paying his agency commission, Liverpool-based promoter Allan Williams threatens to have them deported from Germany.

MAY 61

1 The Beatles continue their 92 day residency at The Top Ten Club.

12 Tony Sheridan and The Beatles sign a one-year recording contract with Bert Kaempfert of Polydor Records in Hamburg, Germany.

JUNE 61

1 The Beatles continue their 92 day residency at The Top Ten Club.

22 The Beatles record over two days with Tony Sheridan for Polydor.

JULY 61

1 The Beatles play their final gig at the Top Ten Club, Hamburg.

6 The Beatles' college friend Bill Harry launches Mersey Beat.

13 The Beatles start a run of Liverpool shows, at St John's Hall, Tuebrook. Over the next two weeks they will play a further 24 shows in the area.

What: Recording My Bonnie
Where: Friedrich Ebert Halle school
When: 22 June 1961

SCHOOL OF ROCK

How The Beatles made their recording debut in a Hamburg infants' school, tutored by a man with the ultimate CV. By Patrick Humphries.

AROUND THE VILLAGE HALLS AND ballrooms of the Merseyside circuit, there was little to suggest The Beatles had any more to offer than their beat contemporaries – indeed, for a time, the smart money was on the Big Three or Rory Storm & The Hurricanes. But soon after their return from Hamburg in July 1961, The Beatles were moving up the ladder: they had cut a record.

That first single wasn't a Lennon and McCartney original – wasn't even a rock'n'roll song – and it didn't have the group's name on the label. But it was a record…

The last of the famously unfortunate princes and kings of the Stuart line, Bonnie Prince Charlie had fled Scotland after the failure of the 1745 rebellion, inspiring a raft of tributes over the years, including Charlie Is My Darling; Will Ye No Come Back Again?; and My Bonnie. But although it started out as a 19th Century sentimental ballad, the song eventually entered the realms of easy listening. And during the '50s rock'n'roll era, pepping up family favourites was a familiar device – Conway Twitty did Danny Boy; Lord Rockingham's XI, Loch Lomond; and Gene Vincent, Over The Rainbow.

A few years later in Hamburg, The Beatles also became adept at pillaging everything and anything to fill those endless all-night sets. So desperate were they for songs, that they used show tunes, ballads, film themes… "In Hamburg, we even used to do The Harry Lime Theme," Paul McCartney told me, "John used to play that. He'd learned it as a little party piece, so we said, Let's do it, we need material!"

Also in Hamburg at the time was orchestra leader Bert Kaempfert, who, in his role as Polydor talent scout, was on the look-out for "authentic" rock'n'roll acts – and the one he found was Tony Sheridan, who had been playing in Hamburg since 1960. Impressed by the dynamism of Sheridan's performance, Kaempfert invited him to a recording session – and, on Sheridan's recommendation, enlisted the five-man Beatles as backing group for the recording.

And so it was, that on 22 June 1961, after another exhausting all-night session of sex and drink and rock'n'roll, The Beatles made their first visit to a professional recording studio.

The "studio" turned out to be an infants' school hall, the Harburg Friedrich Ebert Halle, but the Liverpool teenagers were still impressed. Bert Kaempfert was, after all, a bona-fide star. Earlier that year he had scored an American Number 1 with Wonderland By Night, and he would later secure a place in musical history as the man who wrote Wooden Heart for Elvis and gave Frank Sinatra Strangers In The Night – his only Number 1 of the '60s.

The facilities were primitive, but Polydor's mobile studio did at least allow the luxury of recording on two-track stereo. With Sheridan on vocals, John and George on guitars, Pete on drums, Paul on bass, and the group's "real" bassist Stuart Sutcliffe as an observer, the session yielded seven songs, including: My Bonnie, Tony Sheridan's own Why, another rocked-up oldie, When The Saints Go Marching In, Hank Snow's maudlin Nobody's Child (which George would return to decades later with the Traveling Wilburys) and Jimmy Reed's Take Out Some Insurance On Me Baby.

Excited by their first contact with a legitimate producer, Lennon and McCartney suggested some of their own songs to Kaempfert. He was pretty underwhelmed, but did allow them to record a version of the hoary old Ain't She Sweet (with John on lead vocal), and the Lennon-Harrison instrumental Cry For A Shadow.

Re-named the Beat Brothers for the occasion (because "The Beatles" sounded too much like the German slang for "penis"), they each received a flat fee of 300 marks for their recording debut.

On the evidence of the seven songs from that session, there really was nothing to suggest a future for The Beatles – and by the time Polydor released My Bonnie in August 1961, The Beatles had already returned to Liverpool. But, just in case the record did prove to be a hit, Kaempfert asked the group to supply their CVs; John Lennon ("Leader") noted that he had "written a couple of songs with Paul".

The performances on My Bonnie were leaden, the vocals uninspired, the playing pedestrian; but, though musically undistinguished, the single (credited to Tony Sheridan & the Beat Brothers) did make its mark on the German charts and – by virtue of being the record that first alerted Brian Epstein to The Beatles – won a lasting place in rock history. But, ever the gentleman, Bert Kaempfert played his part in their next record deal.

Kaempfert asked the group for their CVs. John Lennon noted he'd "written a couple of songs with Paul."

In February 1962, discovering that his protegés had signed a contract with Kaempfert, Epstein wrote to Germany asking for them to be released. Kaempfert replied: "I do not want to spoil the chance of the group getting recording contracts elsewhere…"; but he did have one last crack while they were still under contract to him. This last Kaempfert session happened in April 1962, while the four-man Beatles were playing a residency at Hamburg's Star Club. Once again they tackled standards (Sweet Georgia Brown and Swanee River); and once again, Hamburg, Liverpool and the world passed.

After that, Bert Kaempfert – the only man to link The Beatles, Elvis Presley and Frank Sinatra – let them go. And within two months The Beatles were auditioning at Abbey Road.

Photo: K&K ARCHIVES/REDFERNS

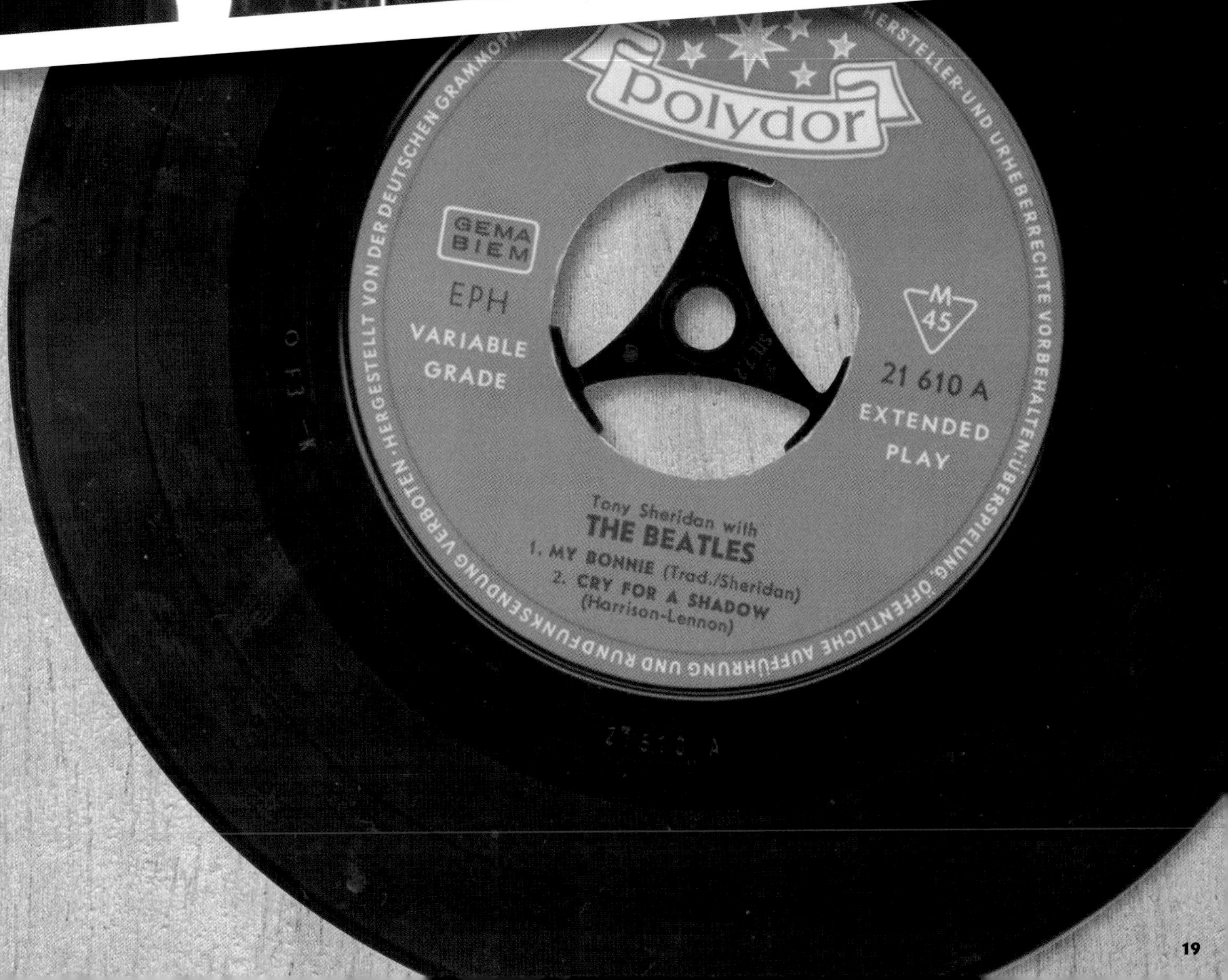

The Beatles with Tony Sheridan and, below, the band's debut single, re-released under their own name. Opposite, musical maestro Bert Kaempfert.

The elusive Raymond Jones – and the man he told about The Beatles (right).

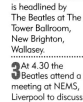

What: Raymond Jones orders My Bonnie
Where: The NEMS store, Liverpool
When: October 1961

NOWHERE MAN?

According to legend, Raymond Jones inspired Brian Epstein to track down The Beatles. But is the legend true? Spencer Leigh investigates.

The name Raymond Jones has always been a significant one in The Beatles' story. For Raymond was the man who reportedly walked into the NEMS record store and asked for a copy of My Bonnie, and therefore was responsible for that truly seminal moment when Brian Epstein first decided to find out about The Beatles. Yet for many years, fans have argued about the role of Raymond Jones – and even whether he ever existed. Living in Liverpool, I determined to reach the truth about this matter.

In 1961, The Beatles recorded My Bonnie with Tony Sheridan in Hamburg. The single made Number 32 on the German charts but was not released in the UK. Pete Best: "We gave a copy of My Bonnie to [Cavern DJ] Bob Wooler and asked him to play it, either at the Aintree Institute or Litherland Town Hall. It sounded good to hear our record coming out of the speakers alongside the American stuff." Local fans thus could hear the record – and would of course want to buy a copy. A key element in The Beatles' story is that an 18-year old called Raymond Jones went into Brian Epstein's record store, NEMS, in Liverpool's Whitechapel in October 1961 and asked for My Bonnie, which would have to be imported.

Alistair Taylor worked for Brian Epstein at NEMS as his personal assistant. He wrote his autobiography (Yesterday – The Beatles Remembered) in 1988, and apparently didn't take issue with the Raymond Jones story. Then, in 1997, Raymond Jones was announced as one of the guests at the Penny Lane Beatles Festival – and who should stand up but Alistair Taylor and say, "I am Raymond Jones!" Alistair has repeated this story on several occasions since, notably a Brian Epstein Arena documentary on BBC TV. According to Alistair, the public was asking for My Bonnie but Brian wouldn't stock the record until he had a definite order with a deposit. Alistair claimed, "It was me. I ordered The Beatles' record and put down the deposit." But if Alistair didn't know The Beatles at the time, there was no valid explanation for this subterfuge.

I was at that Penny Lane Festival with legendary Cavern DJ Bob Wooler, who said, "Let's all do this. Let's all say, I am Spartacus, and claim to be Raymond Jones." "Why are you so sure he's wrong?" I said. "Because I knew Raymond Jones," said Bob, "and I can assure you that I wasn't talking to Alistair Taylor."

Sam Leach also believed he was the inspiration for the Raymond Jones story. In Leach's book, The Rocking City, Sam claimed he was the one who told Brian about The Beatles, but Brian didn't want to acknowledge his presence. Sam said, "If I was the reason Brian went to see the lads for the first time, he would never admit it. He would invent a fictitious character instead – and my opinion is that Raymond Jones was a figment of Brian's imagination."

Following a trail provided by Bob Wooler, it became apparent that Raymond Jones does exist. Bob Wooler knew Raymond's friend, Ron Billingsley, who soon put us onto Raymond himself. Raymond owned a printing company in Burscough, which is now run by his son and daughter; Raymond has now retired and lives in a farmhouse in Spain. I spoke to him and learnt that he was a shy person – who is horrifed that people are claiming to be him. He says, "I never wanted to do anything to make money out of The Beatles because they have given me so much pleasure. I saw them every dinner-time at the Cavern and they were fantastic. I had never heard anything like them. Everybody had been listening to Lonnie Donegan and Cliff Richard and they were so different. Ron Billingsley had a motorbike and we would follow them all over the place – Hambleton Hall, Aintree Institute and Knotty Ash Village Hall."

How did he come to be talking to Brian Epstein? "I used to go to NEMS every Saturday and buy records by Carl Perkins and Fats Domino because I heard The Beatles playing their songs. My sister's ex-husband, Kenny Johnson, who played with Mark Peters and the Cyclones, told me that The Beatles had made a record and so I went to NEMS to get it. Brian Epstein said to me, 'Who are they?' and I said, 'They are the most fantastic group you will ever hear.' No one will take away from me that it was me who spoke to Brian Epstein and then he went to the Cavern to see them for himself. I didn't make them famous, Brian Epstein made them famous, but things might have been different without me." When Brian published his autobiography which told the story of how he came across The Beatles, his staff wrote to Raymond Jones in order to send him a copy, thanking him for the tip – the note is conclusive proof of Raymond's crucial role in The Beatles' history. Brian Epstein knew The Beatles' name through the headlines in Mersey Beat, but he had not shown any interest in them before. Although Raymond Jones was heterosexual, no doubt Eppy was intrigued that such a good-looking boy should be following The Beatles and he determined to find out about them for himself.

Many Beatles sites have been turned into shrines, but not NEMS, the site of this crucial meeting. There is nothing to suggest that it was ever there. It is now a branch of an Ann Summers sex shop which, considering Brian's sexual predilections, is one of the best jokes in Liverpool. It's also right by a shop called Beaver Radio.

"Brian Epstein said to me, Who are they? I said, They are the most fantastic group you will ever hear!"

AUGUST 61

2 Fast becoming Liverpool's favourite band, The Beatles begin an intensive month's residency at The Cavern Club, plus other shows across the city.

3 The Beatles play at St John's Hall, Tuebrooke, Liverpool. Brian Epstein begins writing a weekly column in Mersey Beat.

17 At St John's Hall, Tuebrook, Liverpool, Johnny Gustafson of The Big Three plays bass with The Beatles, allowing Paul McCartney to roam among the crowd, singing through a hand-held microphone.

18 At a lunch-time Cavern session, Ringo Starr plays with The Beatles for the first time. Ringo Starr: "What a laugh it turned out to be. We knew the same numbers, but did them differently and I didn't fit in at all well..."

SEPTEMBER 61

1 The Cavern residency continues, with other shows around the city, including the Town Hall, Litherland, the Aintree Institute, and St John's Hall, Tuebrook, Liverpool and several shows at the Village Hall, Knotty Ash.

OCTOBER 61

1 John Lennon and Paul McCartney begin a two-week holiday in Paris, France, during which they re-style their hair in a fashion similar to their friend, photographer Jurgen Vollmer.

14 John Lennon and Paul McCartney return to Liverpool.

15 The Beatles appear on the same bill as comedian Ken Dodd at a St John's Ambulance Brigade fundraiser in the Albany Cinema, Maghull, Liverpool.

28 Raymond Jones asks Brian Epstein for the German recording of My Bonnie by The Beatles in NEMS Record Store, Liverpool.

NOVEMBER 61

9 Brian Epstein visits The Cavern Club, Liverpool, UK, to see The Beatles for the first time, on a lunchtime session. Bob Wooler (Cavern DJ) :"He said he was there 'because I've ordered copies of My Bonnie, which people keep asking for'."

10 At the Tower Ballroom, New Brighton, Wallasey, The Beatles top the bill of Operation Big Beat, a Merseybeat spectacular also featuring Rory Storm and the Hurricanes, Gerry and the Pacemakers, Kingsize Taylor and the Dominoes, and The Remo Four.

DECEMBER 61

1 A five-and-a-half-hour, six group marathon entitled Big Beat Sessions is headlined by The Beatles at The Tower Ballroom, New Brighton, Wallasey.

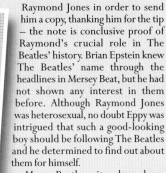

3 At 4.30 the Beatles attend a meeting at NEMS, Liverpool to discuss Brian Epstein managing the group.

6 At a second meeting, Brian Epstein offers to become their manager. John Lennon accepts on behalf of the group.

9 The Beatles play their first gig in the south of England at the Palais Ballroom, Aldershot, Hampshire, UK, to an audience of 18 teenagers.

13 Mike Smith of Decca Records goes to see The Beatles at The Cavern, Liverpool, where they're performing throughout December. Smith invites them to a formal audition in London.

30 The Beatles close the year with a Cavern show, with the White Eagles Jazz Band.

WHERE DID THEY GET THAT SOUND FROM?

A TALE OF TWO CITIES

JOHNNY BLACK ASSESSES HOW THE PECULIAR CULTURAL CIRCUMSTANCES OF TWO NORTHERN TOWNS, LIVERPOOL AND HAMBURG, SHAPED THE SOUND AND THE STYLE OF THE BEATLES

PHOTO: REDFERNS

"Liverpool and Hamburg had a lot in common in the early '60s," muses Gibson Kemp. "They're both sea ports, they're both on the same line of latitude – 56 degrees North – and they were both full of teenagers who were looking for something new."

These days, Kemp is landlord of the George And Dragon pub in the quiet Wiltshire village of Potterne, but he led a very different existence in the early '60s. After a brief period as Ringo Starr's replacement on the drum stool in Rory Storm And The Hurricanes, a top-ranking Liverpool band of the time, 17-year-old Kemp jumped ship to Kingsize Taylor And The Dominoes. Almost immediately, he found himself pounding his skins in the Star Club, Hamburg. Barely out of school, he had joined the throng of Northern rockers who, in the slipstream of The Beatles, were exporting Scouse-inflected rock'n'roll to the Reeperbahn.

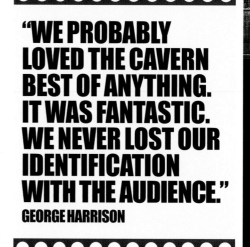

The Mersey tunnel: The Cavern (above) and (left) resident DJ Bob Wooler.

"The way Liverpool's take on rock'n'roll came about was from hearing records on Radio Luxembourg," remembers Kemp, "and records brought in from America by sailors. If you knew someone whose dad was a sailor, you'd know as soon as he got home if he'd brought back any American records, and you'd go round their house and play them to death. The problem was that, in trying to imitate them, our skills were not as great as the musicians on the records, so we had to simplify what we heard. And the kids in Hamburg loved it as much as the kids in Liverpool."

Kemp reckons that the Liverpool bands came as something of a revelation to Hamburg's teenage population. "The local radio station, MDR, played *volksmusik* – German folk music, and *schlagers*, which was German MOR pop. They were aware of blues but, in those days, blues was lumped in with jazz. Folk was around, but it was even more underground than rock. Until we arrived, the only rock they heard would have been on jukeboxes, or if they happened to live near an American military base where the soldiers would have American records. So when they heard us playing live they were drawn to it as something that was much more exciting to them."

> **"WE PROBABLY LOVED THE CAVERN BEST OF ANYTHING. IT WAS FANTASTIC. WE NEVER LOST OUR IDENTIFICATION WITH THE AUDIENCE."**
> **GEORGE HARRISON**

Nice and sleazy: the Hamburg Reeperbahn – musical home to The Beatles and many more during the early '60s.

Kemp was sufficiently smitten with the city and its culture that he lived there for many years, married to Astrid Kirchherr, the local photographer often credited with transforming The Beatles from a gang of greasy-quiffed rockers playing in sleazy clubs into the quartet of loveable moptops who went on to conquer the world. But before they ever got to Hamburg, they had to pay their dues and learn a few tricks rather closer to home.

Like all children, The Beatles' earliest exposure to popular music came at the knees of their parents. Ringo's first musical memory, for example, is of singing cowboy Gene Autry yodelling South Of The Border (Down Mexico Way). "That was the first time I really got shivers down my backbone," he says. "It was just a thrill to me."

Similarly, George Harrison owned up to very early recollections of warbling the folk song One Meat Ball by Josh White, and popular Hoagy Carmichael standards from the heyday of the crooners, adding, "I would say that even the crap music that we hated – the late-'40s, early-'50s American schmaltz records like The Railroad Runs Through The Middle Of The House, or the British I'm A Pink Toothbrush, You're A Blue Toothbrush – even that has had some kind of influence on us."

McCartney's father, Jim, steeped in ragtime and music hall, had led his own bands, the Masked Melody Makers and Jim Mac's Band, and his influence on the Beatles bassist was profound. "My main roots are in singalong stuff like When The Red Red Robin Comes Bob-bob-bobbing Along and Carolina Moon," McCartney told Liverpool broadcaster Spencer Leigh on his BBC Radio Merseyside show. "It's only later that I found out about Leadbelly, Arthur 'Big Boy' Crudup and all the black guys. It's all down to them really."

But even before they'd learned the

Inspirations: (left) Gene Vincent with The Beatles; (below, l-r) Jerry Lee Lewis, Lonnie Donegan, Arthur 'Big Boy' Crudup, Little Richard, Elvis and Buddy Holly.

Kraut rock: the Star Club where The Beatles learned their trade.

name of Arthur 'Big Boy' Crudup, he was already having an indirect impact on The Beatles, via po' white trash rocker Elvis Presley's recording of his song That's All Right. Lennon and Harrison both cited Presley as the one who initiated them into the mysteries of rock'n'roll, and Lennon's half-sister, Julia Baird, has described how John and his mother would jive together to Presley records.

Although largely raised by his Aunt Mimi, Lennon had grown closer to his natural mother, Julia, towards the end of her life, and she contributed significantly to his musical education. "The very first tune I ever learned to play was That'll Be The Day," he remembered. "My mother taught me to play it on the banjo, sitting there with endless patience until I managed to work out all the chords."

If Elvis provided the impetus, the attitude and much of the performing technique, it was Buddy Holly, composer of That'll Be The Day, who inspired them to write. "The big attraction with somebody like Buddy," McCartney has said, "was that he wrote his own stuff and it was three chords. For people looking at the idea of writing their own stuff, it was great, because we didn't know more than four or five chords."

Within a year of Elvis's breakthrough in 1956, rock'n'roll had exploded with a wide range of exciting new stars. Apart from Buddy Holly and Bill Haley, the front-runners were Eddie Cochran, Jerry Lee Lewis, Carl Perkins and Gene Vincent, whose Be-Bop-A Lula was the first single bought by McCartney.

Lennon, however, was about to discover that although country music was a huge influence on all of those young white men, there was a hitherto unsuspected additional element that made rock'n'roll so special. John had a school friend who, "said he'd got this record at home by somebody called Little Richard who was better than Elvis. Elvis was bigger than religion in my life. We used to go to this boy's house after school and listen to 78s. The new record was Long Tall Sally. When I heard it, it was so great I couldn't speak."

A whole new world of possibilities opened up. From Little Richard, The Beatles quickly progressed to Lloyd Price, Chuck Berry, Bo Diddley and, lest we forget, Arthur 'Big Boy' Crudup.

The first distinctively British music to have an impact on them was skiffle. A kind of home-grown halfway house between folk-blues, jug band music and rock'n'roll, skiffle was typified by acoustic guitars, single-string tea-chest basses and washboards employed as rhythmic percussion devices. And the undisputed King Of Skiffle was Lonnie Donegan.

On November 11, 1956, McCartney went to see Donegan in concert at The Empire, Liverpool, and was blown away. "He was great, Lonnie. He was the man at one time, and he was highly instrumental in making us buy guitars. After we saw him and the skiffle groups, we just wanted guitars. He kind of started the English scene in many ways."

The first band in which Lennon and McCartney played together, The Quarrymen, was effectively a skiffle combo but, just before that soon-to-be legendary pairing came together in the summer of 1957, an event occurred which gave Liverpool a home for its own burgeoning group scene.

On January 16, 1957, a near neighbour of Lennon's, local businessman Alan Sytner, rented a Mathew Street cellar for 50 shillings a week and started to promote jazz gigs. He called his new club The Cavern ➳

PHOTOS: POPPERFOTO/REDFERNS

and, despite his original all-jazz policy, by the late summer he had begun to realise that skiffle and rock were making significant inroads into the affections of local teenagers.

So it was that on August 7, 1957, The Quarrymen ambled onstage at The Cavern. "They went down all right, but it was hardly a discerning audience," says Sytner. "I thought they were pretty useless, just a bunch of kids going through their apprenticeship, doing poor imitations of current pop, Buddy Holly and the like."

"The Cavern was a small, smelly cellar, that looked like a train tunnel, basically," explains Gerry Marsden, leader of another local band of young hopefuls, Gerry And The Pacemakers. "It was great. All the kids came down and it stank of disinfectant because they used to clean it out with tons of the stuff. It was a great place to play in."

On a more personal level, John Lennon's best friend and greatest influence as the '50s waned was his college mate Stuart Sutcliffe. "They were on the same wavelength but they were opposites," opines Lennon's first wife, Cynthia. "Stuart was a sensitive artist and he was not a rebel, as John was. He wasn't rowdy or rough. But they complemented each other beautifully. John taught Stuart how to play bass. He wasn't a musician, but John wanted Stuart to be with him."

"I looked up to Stu," is how Lennon subsequently expressed it. "I depended on him to tell me the truth… Stu would tell me if something was good and I'd believe him." Although Stu lacked any significant playing ability, he was drafted into The Quarrymen in January 1960 as their bassist, and it was he who came up with a new name, The Beatals, which after briefly morphing into The Silver Beetles, settled down as The Beatles.

The Beatles first played at The Cavern during a lunch-time session on February 9, 1961. "We probably loved The Cavern best of anything," said Harrison years later. "It was fantastic. We never lost our identification with the audience. We never rehearsed anything, not like the other groups who kept on copying The Shadows. We were playing to our own fans who were just like us. They would come in their lunch-times to hear us and bring their sandwiches to eat. We would do the same, eating our lunch while we played."

In the early '60s, The Cavern was joined by The Iron Door, The Casbah, The 527 Club and many others, outposts of a rapidly expanding local scene which now boasted literally hundreds of bands. As they racked up gigs around town, The Beatles were developing their stagecraft. Neil Foster, sax-player in The Delacardoes, points out, however, that it took some time before they became the biggest fish in that little pond. "The hierarchy in Liverpool at that time," says Foster, "probably had The Big Three at the top, then Rory Storm And The Hurricanes with Ringo on drums, then Gerry And The Pacemakers. The Beatles were a long way down the list. Musically I'd never been impressed by them. Their singing was generally good but their instruments were often out of tune and yet they'd just keep on playing regardless."

While The Beatles were striving to build a local following, several hundred miles east along the line of 56 degrees N, another British rocker was doing the groundwork that would transform them from enjoyable semi-pro entertainers into the best band in town.

Inevitably, when Hamburg's contribution to rock is discussed, the first name mentioned is The Beatles, but Horst Fascher, manager of the Star Club, remembers that it was, in fact, Norwich-born Tony Sheridan who blazed the way for all the others to follow. "He was wild onstage and he'd sweat all over. Within five minutes he looked as though he'd come out of the baths, and we liked him very much. He did *mach schau*." *Mach schau*, roughly translated as 'make a show', would become a very significant phrase to The Beatles.

On August 17, 1960, when The Beatles played their first Hamburg gig, at the Indra club, just off the Reeperbahn, Sheridan was already ripping it up at The Kaiserkeller, just down the road on Grosse Freiheit. Naturally, as Rob Young of the Beat Brothers points out, the new arrivals were keen to check out the opposition. "John and George – you'd always see them there in the front watching Tony's every move, you know. They'd copied him. They really did copy a lot of his moves: styling; the way of playing; you know, the stand; and John especially stood just like Tony."

"IT WAS AS THOUGH THE BEATLES HAD GONE TO HAMBURG AS AN OLD BANGER AND HAD COME BACK TO LIVERPOOL AS A ROLLS-ROYCE."
JOHNNY HUTCHINSON, THE BIG THREE

Within days, The Beatles found that the set they'd played in Liverpool would not be enough to satisfy Hamburg's red light district audiences. Before long, ballads were being ousted from the running order in favour of cranked-up rock tunes. And as McCartney recalls, there were other more mercenary factors to be taken into consideration. "Hamburg was our real introduction to the world of show business. People would appear at the door of the club, and our job was to convince them to come in and see us so that they would buy beer from the guy who was paying us. So this is obviously very important when it comes to show business. You're basically there as a means to sell beer."

At this point, The Beatles' drummer was still Pete Best, and he well remembers the punishing schedule attached to the beer-selling business. "We'd play six, seven hours a night. Unbeknownst to yourselves, you'd become tight, your sound changes. We suddenly found ourselves tight, everyone was reading what everyone else was doing."

One vital element that quickly evolved was Best's legendary Atom Beat, which he developed as a means to pump up the volume and excitement levels of the music. "To project this and get a real powerhouse sound, a real rocking sound, I started to use the bass drum a lot. I worked with something which would pump it out."

At the end of their season at the Indra, instead of returning home, The Beatles moved into The Kaiserkeller, which is where they were first seen by a young magazine illustrator, Klaus Voormann. Drawn inside by that newly honed powerhouse sound, he was impressed enough to note that, "Paul stepped up to the microphone and started speaking to the audience. '*Guten taag*'. He spoke quite a lot of German."

When Voormann returned with some friends, McCartney also took note of them.

"They looked very cool, quite mysterious. I seem to remember them dressed in black – as they called it 'Exi' – existentialist."

With Voormann and the other Exis on that second visit was photographer Astrid Kirchherr. "We were influenced by the French actors, writers and musicians. Our favourite film-maker, writer and painter was Jean Cocteau, which inspired us to dress in black, but also Juliet Greco and the whole Sartre movement."

As a group, the Exis stood out a mile in The Kaiserkeller. "A lot of the kids that came in were rockers," says McCartney, "with the leather, the quiff, the rock'n'roll hairdo, but their hair wasn't the same. It was sort of down at the front, like The Beatles' was later. They were the inspiration for that."

A mutual admiration society soon evolved, a cross-pollination of the ideals and dreams of the young working-class Brits with the more intellectually-inclined Hamburg teen intelligentsia. "I invited them to my place," remembers Astrid. "My mother used to cook for them, egg and chips, steak and kidney pie – and they'd look through my books and my records."

Although Astrid's books and records undoubtedly provided much food for thought, it was probably the steak and kidney pie that the band needed most because their lifestyle was decidedly unbalanced. "We drank during the shows and after," says Best. "Most of the day we'd sleep. Some used to drink more than others, but what we found over there, the German way of showing their appreciation to us was to send booze to us. So, you know, you're thirsty, you're drinking. You'd find that the crowd, if you played a ➳

PHOTOS: REDFERNS

The fab three: (from left) Sutcliffe, Lennon and Harrison onstage in Hamburg, 1960.

Booze explosion! – at the Star Club the audience would line up beers onstage for The Beatles.

request or they wanted a request played or something like that, you knew they'd send booze up. There was a constant supply coming up onstage."

And, of course, it wasn't just booze. "They had to work so hard, for over eight hours a night," remembers Voormann. "To stay alive and be able to get through this you had to think of something, and those people in the clubs had the right stuff to make them feel good." The right stuff, most of the time, was Preludin, an amphetamine-based slimming pill, supplied by the club's cleaning lady.

Tony Sheridan, meanwhile, was living the same life. "It takes its toll," he admits. "We didn't eat right, drank too much, didn't sleep enough, but sometimes we were taking five or eight of these pills and not sleeping for two nights."

Given their living conditions, not sleeping might have seemed like a very attractive proposition. "I saw the terrible conditions they lived in," said Voormann in a Swedish TV documentary. "They lived in little rooms that weren't really rooms – just little concrete boxes. They had no windows, just a bare light bulb, no wardrobe, and not even a hook to hang their stuff on."

For McCartney, that first Hamburg trip was "A baptism of fire. It's amazing we could sing so well. Lots of booze, cigarette smoke, lots of fights would break out, you'd see people getting thrown out. It was a very grown-up world for us – we looked at it wide-eyed, like kids in a toy shop."

When they returned to Liverpool, the difference was immediately noticeable. John McNally of The Searchers recalls seeing them at St John's, Bootle, shortly after their return from Hamburg.

"Most of the bands were playing very controlled, rhythmic bass drum patterns, but Bestie was playing straight fours. It was thump, thump, thump all the time, which was really unusual at the time."

As well as making them musically tighter and more dynamic, Pete Best reckons that the Hamburg experience had another unforeseen side-effect. "When you've been used to playing six or seven hours a night, six or seven nights a week, if someone asks you to play an hour a night, it's like a breeze."

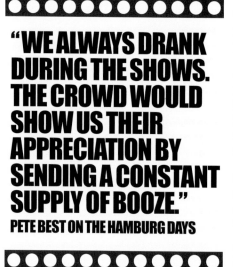

"WE ALWAYS DRANK DURING THE SHOWS. THE CROWD WOULD SHOW US THEIR APPRECIATION BY SENDING A CONSTANT SUPPLY OF BOOZE."

PETE BEST ON THE HAMBURG DAYS

Johnny Hutchinson, drummer with The Big Three, sums it up neatly. "It was as though The Beatles had gone to Hamburg an old banger and had come back as a Rolls-Royce."

It was now that Stuart Sutcliffe exerted what was possibly his greatest influence on The Beatles. In March of 1961 he hung up his bass and left the band to live with his new soulmate, Astrid Kirchherr, in Hamburg. Reluctantly, McCartney switched from rhythm guitar to bass and, in so doing, brought a new coherence to their sound.

But they didn't hang around long enough in Liverpool to capitalise fully on their new-found skills because, on April 1, 1961, The Beatles returned to Hamburg for the second time, contracted to play 92 nights at the Top Ten Club.

It was during this trip that German orchestra leader and record producer Bert Kaempfert of Polydor Records dropped in to see their show. Kaempfert's idea was to record Sheridan with The Beatles as his back-up band. Although the session didn't give The Beatles much opportunity to do more than belt out sturdy rocked-up cover versions of such standards as My Bonnie, Ain't She Sweet and The Saints, they did manage to slip in one of their own compositions, the Harrison-led instrumental Cry For A Shadow, copped largely from the well-established style of Cliff Richard's hit-making backing group, The Shadows.

My Bonnie, chosen as the single, became the first record to feature The Beatles. Hal Fein, owner of the publishing company Roosevelt Music, and an associate of Kaempfert's at the time, recalls that, "When the record was released, the initial sales were about 180,000 copies, a fair-sized hit for Germany. Due to its success in Germany, it was played on Radio Luxembourg – one of the most powerful stations in Europe, beaming in all directions – into Germany, into England, and south into the continent."

And, as legend has it, it was the European success of My Bonnie that convinced future Beatles manager Brian Epstein to go and check out the band at The Cavern during their next stay in Liverpool. The Top Ten residency ended on July 1, 1961 and, this time, it would be almost 10 months

PHOTOS: REDFERNS

before they would return to Hamburg again. Now, finally, they could establish their supremacy on their home turf.

Bookings were now easy to get, with the band in such demand that they would sometimes be required to perform two or even three shows a day at different venues. The Cavern, however, was soon established as The Beatles' 'home'. Bob Wooler, the MC at The Cavern, was a man with impeccable taste, and his choice of music certainly played its part in shaping The Beatles' ever-expanding repertoire. According to Gerry Marsden, "Bob was the first DJ in Liverpool. He didn't actually invent the Mersey Beat, but he had a hell of a lot to do with it. He was into the young bands, and helped us out a lot."

One specific example of Wooler's influence came about when he acquired a new American release, Hippy Hippy Shake by Los Angeles rocker Chan Romero. "I played it at a lunchtime session at The Cavern, and Paul McCartney asked me about it. He always fancied himself as a high-voiced singer. I lent him the record, and The Beatles started doing it." As if that weren't enough, it was Wooler's own copy of Hippy Hippy Shake from which The Swinging Blue Jeans learned the song, and subsequently took it to Number 1 in the UK.

Get smart: (above, Star Club) the Fabs ditch the early leather-boy look (below, The Cavern).

Before The Beatles returned to Hamburg, an even more significant Liverpudlian began his association with them. Local record store owner Brian Epstein popped into The Cavern on November 9, 1961, to catch The Beatles in a lunchtime session.

Bill Harry, a good friend of Lennon and, by this time, proprietor of the city's pop paper, Mersey Beat, explains, "He phoned me up and said, 'This Beatles group, I'd be interested in seeing them. I notice in Mersey Beat they're on at The Cavern. I've never been there. Can you fix me up to go?' So I phoned up The Cavern and said, Mr Brian Epstein of NEMS is coming down. Can you fix him up? You know, a VIP thing. Though it was only a shilling entrance, I wanted to fix it for him because he wanted to see them."

With Epstein that day was his assistant, Alistair Taylor, who recalls that, "We looked out of place in white shirts and dark business suits. The Beatles were playing A Taste Of Honey and Twist And Shout, but we were particularly impressed that they included original songs. The one that sticks in my mind is Hello Little Girl." So it was that Epstein saw them, loved them and, on December 13, 1961, signed them up to a management deal.

Once Epstein had them under his wing, his influence was profound. "We were in a daydream til he came along," is how Lennon later explained it. "We'd no idea what we were doing. Brian was trying to clean our image up. He said unless we did, we'd never get past the door of a good place."

It was of course Epstein who negotiated their EMI deal, and simultaneously negotiated them out of their old Polydor deal, but it was also Epstein who completed the image transformation begun by Astrid Kirchherr's assault on their greasy quaffs. "The leather gear was a bit old hat and we decided that we looked a bit ridiculous dressed in all-leather," says McCartney. "We got the impression we looked like a gang of idiots. Brian Epstein suggested we wear suits, so we got rid of the leather gear."

"We respected his views," said Lennon. "We stopped champing at cheese rolls and jam butties onstage. We paid a lot more attention to what we were doing. Did our best to be on time."

"Wake up Stuart!" Sutcliffe and Astrid Kirchherr.

Nobody present at Heswall Jazz Club on March 24 could have any doubts that Epstein was now running the show. The venue's manager, Bob Ellis, likes to tell the story of how, "With The Beatles in full flow, Epstein looked down at his wrist watch, then raised his arm to signal to The Beatles to stop playing. They had fulfilled the allotted time they had been paid for and Epstein signalled to them that their time was up." This was the new regime. The Beatles were now professionals.

On April 10, 1962, just three days before The Beatles started their third Hamburg residency, Stuart Sutcliffe died of a brain haemorrhage. Tragic though the loss was, the band had little choice but to get on with the business of selling beer at the Star Club. The major innovation for this trip was that, as well as playing their own sets, the band could now rub shoulders with visiting American stars like Little Richard, Ray Charles and Gene Vincent. It was Little Richard who had the most direct effect on the band.

"I remember how excited The Beatles were to meet Richard," recalls the Georgia Peach's keyboardist Billy Preston. "He had been their idol for years. In Hamburg they'd always be with him, asking him questions about America, the cities, the stars, the movies, Elvis, and all that."

Little Richard himself has told of how, "They'd come to my dressing room and eat there every night. They hadn't any money, so I paid for their food. I used to buy steaks for John. Paul would come in, sit down and just look at me. He wouldn't move his eyes. And he'd say, 'Oh, Richard! You're my idol. Just let me touch you'. He wanted to learn my little holler, so we sat at the piano going, 'Oooooh!' until he got it."

It was during this third sojourn in Hamburg that Brian Epstein secured the recording contract with Parlophone which would, in very short order, lift The Beatles out of the Liverpool-Hamburg axis forever. Many have argued, however, that the group, as performers, had learned everything they needed to know by then, and would never surpass the intensity of those early shows. "Our peak for playing live was in Hamburg," Harrison has said. "At the time, we weren't famous and people came to see us simply because of our music and the atmosphere we created."

By the time of their fourth Hamburg trip in November 1962, their first single, Love Me Do, was already in the UK charts, and their sights were now set far higher than the sweaty night spots which had been their stomping ground for so long. When they returned to the UK on November 15, they found their world had changed. The routine of endless lunchtime gigs at The Cavern was replaced by interviews with Radio Luxembourg, features in Record Mirror and auditions at the BBC.

One final Star Club residency had been scheduled and they went, reluctantly, to fulfil a contractual obligation to play over the Christmas and New Year period. The band had moved on from Hamburg – as they soon would from Liverpool.

When The Beatles appeared at The Cavern for the last time on August 3, 1963, it was obvious that they'd outgrown the scene that had nurtured them. Neil Aspinall, their road manager at the time, describes how, "We all gradually moved to London. They would keep going home and still play the leftover dates at The Cavern, but it quickly became far more practical to live in London."

Ringo, however, summed it up rather more poignantly. "By the end of 1963," he said, "it was impossible to go home." ■

PHOTOS: REDFERNS

1962

In 1962 The Beatles finally got everything they'd ever wanted – they secured a record deal with EMI and released their debut single. And while they lost drummer Pete Best, they acquired Ringo Starr and scored their first Top 20 hit with Love Me Do. Plus they played their last residency in Hamburg, and John Lennon got himself hitched...

PTING ORDERS FOR
EATLES
ON PARLOPHONE
HAVE A BALL!
AT
LITHERLAND
TOWN HALL
SHANE FENTON
JOHN
LENNON
PAUL
McCARTNEY
oducing
THE BEATLES
EATLES
HESWALL
JAZZ CLUB
BARNSTON INSTITUTE BARNSTON ROAD, HESWALL
NOTE THE DATE - -
TUESDAY 25th SEPTEMBER,
Special Mid - Week Attractio
7-30 p.m. — 11-0 p.m.
Disc Jockey
Derek Jeffery
introdu
The North's TOP ROCK CO
The Fabulous
BEATLES
(Parlophone Record
and MR. PERSONALITY
GERRY AND THE Pa
plus the Week's
Admission by TICKET
AT THE DOOR
Note the Da
RECORDING FOR THE PARLOPHONE LABEL
HOTROD
HAVE A BALL!
AT
LITHERLAND
TOWN HALL
SHANE FENTON
AND THE FENTONES
ODD
SPOT
CLU
89 BOLD STRE
LIVERPOOL

JANUARY 62

1 The Beatles are auditioned by Decca Records in London.

3 The Beatles play at The Cavern Club, supported by Johnny Sandon and The Searchers.

5 My Bonnie is released in the UK to good reviews.The band plays a lunchtime show at The Cavern. More Cavern shows follow through the month.

7 The Beatles play at The Casbah, West Derby, Liverpool.

24 In Liverpool, at the home of Pete Best, The Beatles sign a contract with Brian Epstein.

26 A busy day for The Beatles, who play twice at The Cavern Club, Liverpool and once at the Tower Ballroom, New Brighton, Wallasey.

27 The Beatles play at the Aintree Institute, Aintree, Liverpool, UK.

29 The Beatles play at The Kingsway Club, Southport.

FEBRUARY 62

1 The Beatles play at the Thistle Cafe, West Derby, 10 miles from Liverpool, for a fee of £18.

2 The Beatles play at the Oasis, Manchester. Rick Dickson (co-owner, The Oasis): "It was a total disaster. There were 37 people and none of them were very impressed."

8 While in London seeking a recording contract, Brian Epstein arranges endorsement deals for Vox amps and Ludwig drums.

10 The Beatles play at St Paul's Church Hall, Birkenhead.

12 The Beatles audition for BBC Radio at Broadcasting House, Manchester and are approved to perform on Teenager's Turn.

20 Brian Epstein writes to Bert Kaempfert asking Polydor to release The Beatles from their contract.

24 The Beatles are booed off the stage when they play at the YMCA in Birkenhead, The Wirral, Liverpool.

MARCH 62

1 The Beatles play at The Storyville Jazz Club, Liverpool.

2 The Beatles play two shows in one day – first at St John's Hall, Bootle, Liverpool and later at the Tower Ballroom, New Brighton, Wallasey.

7 The Beatles record the BBC radio show Teenager's Turn, and sing Dream Baby, Memphis Tennessee, Please Mr Postman and their own composition, Hello Little Girl, at the Playhouse Theatre, Manchester. Bill Harry (editor, Mersey Beat): "We had coachloads of fans travelling together... Everybody was going berserk over Pete Best. So the rest of us had to leave in the coach and drive around and leave him behind."

8 The Beatles BBC radio session of the previous day is broadcast across the UK at 5.00pm, without Hello Little Girl.

16 The Beatles play at The Cavern, Liverpool. They will play at various venues across Liverpool every remaining day in March, bar one day off on the 27th.

24 At Heswall Jazz Club, in the Barnston Women's Institute, Wirrall, Cheshire, The Beatles' manager Brian Epstein demonstrates his control over his now smartly dressed protegés. Paul McCartney: "The leather gear was a bit old hat, so Brian Epstein suggested we wear ordinary suits."

What: Unsuccessful Decca audition
Where: West Hampstead, London
When: 1 January 1962

THE WRONG HORSE

How Decca Records decided to pass on The Beatles, and elected to sign The Tremeloes instead. By Peter Doggett.

ON THE EPIC CANVAS THAT IS THE Beatles' story, there are villains as well as heroes. Among the unfortunates, few have suffered as much, for as little cause, as Dick Rowe – who went to his grave as The Man Who Turned Down The Beatles. As the head of Decca Records' A&R department in 1962, he was a major powerbroker in the British music industry. Rowe signed dozens of successful artists and masterminded countless hits. In 1963, he left his mark indelibly by giving the Rolling Stones their first record deal. But until his premature death in 1984, Rowe was destined to be remembered for one financially disastrous decision. At least one of The Beatles never forgave him."(Rowe) must be kicking himself," a journalist said to John Lennon at the height of Beatlemania. "I hope he kicks himself to death", Lennon is said to have retorted.

The cause of Rowe's notoriety was a 30-minute audition held on a freezing New Year's morning in 1962 – an event at which the unlucky A&R chief wasn't even present. The cast included an exhausted quartet of Liverpudlians, their over-anxious manager and an admittedly hung-over junior A&R executive. What happened has been a subject of contention ever since.

It wasn't musical talent that won The Beatles their shot at an audition with arguably Britain's biggest label, but business leverage. The group's newly acquired manager, Brian Epstein, was also a record retailer and one of Decca's major clients in the North of England. Desperate to prove himself to The Beatles, Epstein had visited fellow Liverpudlian, Tony Barrow. The future Beatles press officer was then working for Decca as a sleeve-note writer. Barrow alerted the label's marketing department that an important client was shopping around a new group, and soon the chain reached the desk of Dick Rowe.

It was Rowe's corporate duty to consider Epstein's group, at the very least, and to that end his assistant, Mike Smith, was dispatched to Liverpool to meet and charm The Beatles. In return, Epstein's boys worked their magic on Smith. "I was very excited by what I saw The Beatles do on stage," he told The Beatles Book years later, "and on the strength of their stage show and the reaction from their local fans, I had no hesitation in telling Brian that we'd fix an audition as soon as possible."

New Year's Day wasn't a bank holiday in 1962, but it was still a short straw for both The Beatles and Mike Smith. With Rowe on an extended festive break, his junior was once again left to entertain Epstein and his group. The Beatles endured a painfully slow and snowbound trip from Liverpool to the West End, arriving just in time to watch the capital celebrating the chimes at midnight.

The next morning, they reported for duty at Decca's HQ in West Hampstead, where Mike Smith – his journey disrupted by the snow – kept them waiting for the best part of an hour, while Brian Epstein silently fumed. Nervous and unsettled, they finally trooped into Decca's hallowed recording studio, and set up their battered equipment. Eventually, the tapes began to roll, and the group ran through a less than sparkling sample of their repertoire – carefully selected by Epstein to demonstrate their virtuosity as entertainers rather than their raw rock'n'roll power, with material like Three Cool Cats.

Smith was politely enthusiastic, though he later admitted: "In the studio, they were not good, and their personalities didn't come across." Still, Barrow, who doubled as a pop pundit for the Liverpool Echo, told his eager readers: "Decca disc producer Mike Smith tells me that he thinks The Beatles are great. He has a continuous tape of their audition performances that runs for over 30 minutes, and he is convinced that his label will be able to put The Beatles to good use."

It was time for Rowe to make his fateful entrance. Smith auditioned another group that month, Brian Poole & the Tremeloes, and wanted to add both combos to Decca's roster. Rowe told him he must choose between them – and Smith opted for the Trems. They sounded more professional in the studio, and subsequently rewarded his faith with a run of eight hits, including a Number 1. As Smith revealed, Rowe hadn't even bothered to weigh up the two audition tapes: "He didn't express any opinion. He left the decision to me." With that, he settled the fate of his reputation.

Epstein was shattered by the decision. He briefly toyed with closing his store's account with Decca, before commercial common sense triumphed. Six months later, he was able to use the same financial stick to beat EMI into signing the group, and the Decca debacle was – almost – forgotten. Meanwhile, The Beatles' lacklustre audition tape festered in the company vaults. Legend has it that employees would stage annual wakes, when the tape would be dusted down and they would drink to the profits that they had lost.

"Decca staff staged annual wakes; the tape would be dusted down and they would drink to the profits they'd lost"

At Christmas 1971, when the pair were supposedly at loggerheads, Lennon sent Paul McCartney a gift: a bootleg LP containing what he believed was the long-lost Decca audition. It wasn't – it actually featured some early BBC recordings – but eventually the elusive tape did leak, and by the late '70s fans could judge Smith's judgement for themselves via underground releases on the cruelly titled Deccagone label. Would The Beatles have triumphed a year earlier at Decca? Or were they not yet ready to seize the attention of the world? The debate lingers on, just as Dick Rowe continues to be cited as the man who made the most disastrous decision in the history of the music business.

PHOTOS: TRACKS, TERRY RAWLINGS, REX

Brian Poole (top) and The Tremeloes. More successful than many contemporaries; rather less successful than The Beatles. Left, the 'guilty' man: Dick Rowe (in glasses) with the Small Faces.

A portrait of the artiste, Stuart Sutcliffe, with George in the foreground, Hamburg, 1960.

What: Stuart Sutcliffe dies
Where: Hamburg, West Germany
When: April 10, 1962

IN HIS LIFE

Even after 40 years Stuart Sutcliffe's life and death remain shrouded in mystery. Joe Cushley goes in search of the man that even John looked up to.

STUART SUTCLIFFE – THE BEATLES' ex-bass guitarist, and John Lennon's best friend – died of a brain haemorrhage in Hamburg on April 10, 1962. The next day the band – minus George, delayed by illness – flew in to start an engagement at the city's Star Club. These are undisputed facts.

All the following have been mooted as possible causes of Sutcliffe's tragically early death. A kicking administered by Liverpudlian teddy boys after a gig at Lathom Hall; a congenital blood-supply defect; a fall at his fiancée, Astrid Kirchherr's home; a kicking administered by Lennon in a Hamburg street in May 1961; years of little sleep and food, and lots of hard work, "Prellies", cigarettes and alcohol. To this day, some friends of the band doubt whether a couple of these events actually ever occurred. As is often the case with the Fabs, the myths multiply with the passage of time.

There is no debate, however, that Sutcliffe was a phenomenally talented artist, and that his influence on John's attitudes when they met at the Liverpool College of Art in late 1957, was instant and profound. One of Sutcliffe's sisters, Pauline, has written a book which has courted controversy for its claims that the beating which Lennon, on balance, probably did dish out, led directly to Stu's death; and that John and Stuart had at least one homosexual encounter.

Probe Into Mystery Death Of City Student

Mother In Germany: Father Cannot Be Told

An investigation into the mystery death of a 21-years-old Liverpool art student, Stuart Sutcliffe, who died in a German ambulance with his fiancee by his side, was being held to-day.

Mrs. Millie Sutcliffe, aged 54, of 37 Aigburth Drive, Aigburth, flew to Hamburg after a telegram told her of her son's death. His father, Mr. Charles Sutcliffe, a second engineer, sailed for South America on Sunday and cannot be told of the death for at least three weeks.

"He has a weak heart and we cannot radio his ship to tell him. He will be told when he reaches port," said his daughter, Joyce, aged 20.

Stuart went to Germany 18 months ago with a Liverpool skiffle group ...

"On the surface they seemed an unlikely pair," recalls Pauline Sutcliffe, "but I think it was a friendship based on the not-quite-consciously-formed idea of the performing arts being linked to other forms of creative art. Stu was into the transference between high and low art, early on. There was a painting of Elvis, à la Picasso, which he did when he was 17, for example. John was intrigued that such a fine artist and intelligent person should love rock'n'roll, I think it validated and legitimised his own love of the music."

It wasn't until early 1960 though – after Stu had sold a painting to Liverpudlian arts benefactor John Moores – that he was invited to join The Quarry Men. Sutcliffe invested the money in a 'brunette' Hofner President bass and started to learn to play: another contentious subject as it transpired. Sutcliffe made another contribution by suggesting a new group name, 'The Beetles' (as a play on Buddy Holly's Crickets, not after a motorcycle gang in Brando's The Wild One as is sometimes said). The band set out in late May on their first tour, backing Johnny Gentle around Scotland; and then in August their manager, Allan Williams, secured their first stint in Hamburg. Stu's tutors were aghast as he apparently turned his back on a potentially brilliant art career. Pauline, on the other hand, was – "delighted, that he was going. I was a Cavern girl! It was great that he was in a band."

Klaus Voormann, who befriended The Beatles in Hamburg, designed the cover of *Revolver* and later played on various solo Beatle projects, remembers the impact the band had. "I first saw Rory Storm & The Hurricanes that night, but they were more of a show-band. The Beatles had a much larger repertoire, they were really communicating… all those voices, and of course, they could play better. Stuart was a heavy rock'n'roller. Rock'n'roll is an art form, and Stuart had the feel and the taste. They weren't playing anything very complicated, and taken as a whole – feeling it and playing those few notes – Stuart was a really, really good bass player."

Paul McCartney never agreed, but John was adamant, so Sutcliffe stayed. "You could feel that John was always looking up to Stuart," explains Voormann. "If you read all those letters between them, there was almost this inferiority thing with John. Stuart was so open and interested in anything new, and a very quick learner. He was a very wise person."

Thinking back to the opening of an exhibition – Stuart Sutcliffe: From The Beatles To Backbeat – at the Rock & Roll Hall Of Fame, Pauline Sutcliffe concurs with Klaus's evaluation.

"I could see this big photograph of Stuart juxtaposed with one of John, and Stuart's was looking up at John's, finally. This was John's gig, the Rock & Roll Hall of Fame, but Stuart had made it as well."

Klaus introduced his then girlfriend, Astrid Kirchherr to the band, and she and Stuart soon fell in love. Both Astrid and Klaus possessed a continental artistic savvy, which influenced Stuart certainly, and through him, John and the rest of the band. The Beatles haircut was a mirror of the 'Exi' (existentialist) style barnet affected by Klaus and his bohemian friends. Astrid, a former fashion student, also persuaded the band to wear tight black leather trousers, and designed a prototype Beatles suit for Stuart. She also, of course, took some of the most famous band photos in history.

John and Stu play in the sand, the Baltic, 1961.

However influential their Hamburg stay – aesthetically, as well as in terms of the sheer unit-honing hours onstage – they had to return to Britain to progress. Stuart, though, was now determined to follow his first love, art; and stay with his new love, Astrid. Klaus recalls his own bid to be a Beatle.

"After Stuart left I had the cheek to ask John Lennon if I could play bass in the band. He gave me a very careful reply. 'Sorry, mate. Paul has already bought a bass. We're going to stay as four people'."

Sutcliffe is remembered poignantly in Lennon's lyric for In My Life as one of his "lovers and friends" and there can be little doubt that he was ever far from Lennon's mind. A willingness to explore was perhaps the major hallmark of The Beatles throughout their career, and Stuart was certainly an explorer. His reputation as an artist is now secure, but he was also a Beatle. And that's a fact.

PHOTOS: REDFERNS

APRIL 62

1 The Beatles play The Casbah Coffee Club, West Derby, Liverpool.

2 An intensive week of gigs at The Cavern, in addition to Liverpool's Casbah and the Pavilion Theatre.

8 The Beatles play The Casbah (right), and head for Hamburg, Germany.

10 Former Beatles bassist Stuart Sutcliffe dies of a brain haemorrhage, aged 22.

11 John, Paul and Pete arrive in Hamburg on their third German trip to begin a residency at the newly-opened Star Club.

12 George Harrison arrives in Hamburg following a short illness.

13 The Beatles start a seven-week residency at The Star Club.

MAY 62

7 Brian Epstein arrives in London seeking a recording deal.

9 Epstein meets with EMI producer George Martin at Abbey Road Studios, London.

31 Mersey Beat newspaper reveals that The Beatles have secured a contract with Parlophone Records.

JUNE 62

2 The Beatles fly back to the UK.

3 The band rehearse in The Cavern.

4 A provisional contract is signed, to record demos for EMI.

6 The Beatles audition for George Martin at EMI's Abbey Road, Studio 3.

9 A record-breaking homecoming gig at The Cavern, playing to 900 ecstatic fans. A week of lunchtime and evening shows at the venue follows.

21 Supporting visiting US vocalist Bruce Channel at the Tower Ballroom, New Brighton (above).

22 A busy eight days starts with five gigs at The Cavern and then shows at Heswall, St Helen's, Birkenhead, New Brighton and Northwich.

JULY 62

1 A hectic two weeks in the North West supporting Gene Vincent at The Cavern. The band continue with gigs in St Helen's, Birkenhead and Wallasey.

14 The Regent Dansette, Rhyl, North Wales.

15 The beginning of an almost solid run of gigs at The Cavern for 11 days. They also play in St Helen's, Birkenhead, Warrington, New Brighton, Southport and venture out to McIlroy's Ballroom in Swindon on the 17th.

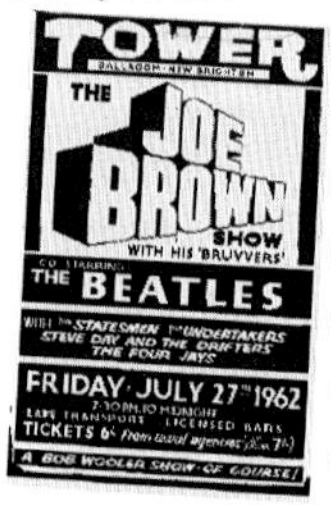

26 Cambridge Hall, Southport, supporting Joe Brown.

27 Tower Ballroom, New Brighton, supporting Joe Brown.

28 Two shows, first at The Cavern, then at the Majestic, Birkenhead.

29 Lunchtime at The Cavern, then an evening show at the Majestic, Birkenhead.

30 A lunchtime gig at The Cavern, followed by an evening show at St John's Hall, Bootle.

AUGUST 62

1 Two shows at The Cavern: a lunchtime performance then an evening gig with Gerry & The Pacemakers and The Mersey Beats.

3 The Beatles play the Grafton Rooms, Liverpool.

4 The band play a show at the Victoria Hall, Wirral.

5 Three gigs in two days at The Cavern.

8 A show at the Co-op Ballroom, Doncaster, Yorkshire.

9 The Beatles play a lunchtime show at The Cavern.

10 Supporting Johnny Kidd & The Pirates aboard the MV Royal Iris, sailing down the Mersey River.

11 The band play the Odd Spot Club, Liverpool.

12 A nightime show at The Cavern.

13 A lunchtime gig at The Cavern, followed by a show at the Majestic Ballroom, Crewe, in the evening.

14 Brian Epstein approaches Ringo Starr of Rory Storm & The Hurricanes to see if he'd like to replace Pete Best as drummer in The Beatles.

15 Last performance with Pete Best, at The Cavern.

16 Brian Epstein informs Pete Best in his office that he is fired, and is to be replaced by Ringo Starr. In the mean time, Johnny 'Hutch' Hutchinson of The Big Three joins The Beatles as drummer for their show at the Riverpark Ballroom, Chester.

17 Two shows: the Majestic Ballroom, Birkenhead (above), and the Tower Ballroom, New Brighton.

18 Ringo Starr drums for the first time as an official member, at Hulme Hall, Birkenhead.

19 Pete Best fans shout rowdy support for the sacked drummer when Ringo drums with The Beatles at The Cavern.

20 The Beatles play the Majestic Ballroom, Crewe.

22 The Beatles are captured on film for the first time at The Cavern. The band perform two songs, Some Other Guy and Kansas City, for Granada TV show Know The North. On the same day, John Lennon tells his Aunt Mimi that he is marrying his girlfriend, Cynthia Powell.

What: The sacking of Pete Best
Where: Brian Epstein's office, Liverpool
When: August 16, 1962

THE AXE FILES

Mystery surrounds the real reason why drummer Pete Best was booted out of The Beatles. Spencer Leigh investigates this perennial 'whodunnit'.

WHEN PETE BEST AWOKE ON THE morning of Thursday, August 16, 1962, he put on his T-shirt and jeans and asked his lodger – Beatles roadie, Neil Aspinall, who shared the house with Best and his mother, Mona – to come into the city centre with him. Arriving at the North End Road Music Stores (NEMS) record shop at 12-13 Whitechapel, Liverpool, Pete went into Brian Epstein's office while Neil looked through the new releases. Pete thought they would be discussing future bookings, but 'Eppy' had a surprise for him. "The lads don't want you in the group any more," he said, as though distancing himself from the decision.

No reason, no explanation, but the phone rang on Brian's desk. It was Paul, and Brian said, "I can't talk now. Peter's here". Outside on the street, Pete met up with Neil and they bumped into Lu Walters from The Hurricanes. He was on a short visit from Butlin's at Skegness where he was playing with Ringo Starr. He wouldn't be doing that any more.

The sacking of Pete Best is still a mystery worthy of Agatha Christie, but although the ex-Beatle has now written his autobiography three times, when you are being sacked, you can never fully be certain 'whodunnit'. As it would appear that no single issue sealed the drummer's fate, what was it about Pete Best that John, Paul, George, Brian Epstein and George Martin found so unacceptable?

Look at the early Beatles and you are drawn immediately to Pete's face. The consensus is that Best was sacked because he was too handsome and the others were jealous. Pete had plenty of girlfriends, but the others did well too and John was to marry the gorgeous Cynthia Powell on August 23. Girls cried out for Best and camped on his lawn, but this could only benefit the group. Epstein would have been pleased and although Best said no to his manager's sexual advances, it wouldn't have bothered Brian as he had faced rejection many times before (by the same argument, Epstein would never have recruited Billy J Kramer).

Was it that Best just didn't fit? He was quiet, but so was George, and in any event, you can't have four garrulous members in one group – the Stones didn't sack Charlie Watts. Best had been with The Beatles for two years, including several months in Hamburg, and had no inkling that anything was wrong. He didn't have a Beatles haircut but then Astrid Kirchherr couldn't do anything with his curly locks – hardly his fault.

A more substantial reason was his drumming. Best was fine on their 1961 single, My Bonnie, but he played the same pattern, either slow or fast depending on the arrangement. John didn't stray from rock'n'roll, but Paul was trying show songs and may have noticed Pete's limitations, particularly as bass and drums are acutely bonded. The Cavern DJ Bob Wooler recalled one incident that demonstrated Paul's frustrations with the situation. "The Beatles played The Cavern at lunchtimes and sometimes they would stay behind and rehearse. One afternoon I found Paul showing Pete how he wanted the drums to be played for a certain tune, and I thought, That's pushing it a bit."

On the recording The Beatles did for their Parlophone audition in June, Best sounds as if he is playing bin-lids. If this is all George Martin heard, no wonder he wanted to use a session drummer; the fact that Best might spoil John and Paul's success certainly would have counted against him. Ringo was George's best friend – but nobody was certain he would fare much better, as Rory Storm & The Hurricanes were essentially a novelty band. But at least Ringo would be enthusiastic. Pete often looked simply bored, which must have irritated the super-ambitious Paul.

Before Brian Epstein, The Beatles' bookings had been handled by Best's mother, Mona. She wanted Epstein to do all he could for the group and especially for her son, often letting the new manager know what she had in mind for the group's development. Maybe Epstein had had enough of Mona's 'best intentions' for the band?

Bob Wooler has also said: "It was very wrong of The Beatles to state on the Anthology video that Pete Best was unreliable. The most unreliable Beatle was Paul, although he was not consistently late."

The Beatles asked Epstein to do their dirty work because they didn't want to face Best – John was distracted by his wedding so Paul seized the moment. Even though The Beatles came across Best at subsequent shows, they didn't speak, and haven't done so since.

"The consensus is that Pete Best was sacked because he was too handsome and the others were jealous."

Confusingly, there may be other factors. When The Beatles returned from Hamburg in June 1962, Neil Aspinall left his accountancy job and became their full-time roadie in July. He made Mona Best pregnant and she had their son, Roag, on July 21, 1962. When Best was sacked, he told Aspinall to leave their house if he was to continue as the band's roadie. As a result, Aspinall was effectively being deprived of seeing his son. This must have further soured an already fragile relationship.

Bill Harry, editor of Mersey Beat, was so enamoured with Epstein that he accepted his explanation and on August 23, 1962 told his readers, "Pete Best left the band by mutual agreement. There were no arguments and this has been an entirely amicable decision."

Years later, Best worked for the Restart employment scheme. When someone who had lost their job came to the Restart offices, they would be told, "Pete Best will see you now." "Whatever they'd been through," said Best later, "they knew I'd been through it as well."

PHOTO: K&K/REDFERNS

Was it the haircut? Pete Best and unruly locks at Hamburg's Star Club; inset, the classic leather-clad Best-era Beatles line up

The nervous-looking new boy, in regulation Beatles suit and hair-cut; inset, right, Ringo with Rory Storm (third from left) & The Hurricanes.

What: Ringo Starr joins The Beatles
Where: Hulme Hall, Birkenhead
When: August 18, 1962

STARR QUALITY

Lured away from Kingsize Taylor by a fiver a week, Ringo was guaranteed a baptism of fire when he joined The Beatles. By Alan Clayson.

AFTER ARRIVING JUST IN TIME FOR A two-hour rehearsal, Ringo Starr made his debut as an official Beatle in front of an audience of around 500 at a Horticultural Society function in Birkenhead. The opportunity had come when Starr had reached something of a crossroads. At 22 there didn't seem to be much of a future for him as a professional drummer beyond the treadmill of local bookings, Butlin's holiday camp residencies and rare side-trips overseas with Rory Storm & The Hurricanes. In January 1962 he'd quit the group to back Tony Sheridan in Hamburg for £30 a week – a huge fee for the time – plus use of a flat and a car. However, Ringo became disenchanted with Tony, who, on closer acquaintance, was given to provoking arguments, sulking and launching impetuously into songs not in the modus operandi.

After having more than his fill of both Sheridan and Hamburg, Starr was reinstated in The Hurricanes. They got into trim for a short series of mess dances for US airmen in France – and a summer at Skegness, the largest camp in the Butlin's network. Ringo promised to see out the contract with – so Rory had assured Mersey Beat – "the only group to make the grade in Butlin's for three years in succession".

Yet, as mother Elsie and stepfather Harry reminded him, it wasn't too late for him to resume his apprenticeship as a joiner at Henry Hunt & Sons, an engineering firm where he'd worked before throwing in his lot with Rory in 1959. While taking stock, Starr also contemplated moving to America, going so far as to write to the Chamber of Commerce in Houston, simply because it was in the heartland of the Wild West, and the nearest city to Centerville, birthplace of Lightnin' Hopkins, the bluesman to whose grippingly personal style an enthralled Ringo had been introduced by Tony Sheridan.

Ringo's reply from Houston was heartening, but the thickness and aggressive intimacy of the application forms for emigration were too off-putting. Hunt's seemed to be beckoning still but, while removed from parental pressure in Skegness, Starr received a letter from Kingsize Taylor offering £20 per week for him to fill the drum stool in The Dominoes. As Taylor was a bandleader of steadier stamp than either Storm or Sheridan, Ringo gave tentative assent to be a Domino as soon as he was free. Nevertheless, he was to decamp mid-season after John Lennon and Paul McCartney had driven through a windy night to rouse him at 10am on an August Tuesday, offering a fiver a week more than Kingsize Taylor.

Two years earlier, Ringo had known The Beatles only by sight as riff-raff that frequented the Jacaranda Coffee Bar in Liverpool. Only on noticing George Harrison in his basement teaching Stu Sutcliffe the rudiments of bass guitar had Starr understood that they were an actual group.

Conversely, when Rory Storm & The Hurricanes were working split-shifts with The Beatles at Hamburg's Kaiserkeller in autumn 1960, Harrison had been particularly indifferent, even antipathetic, towards Ringo, "the nasty one with this little streak of grey hair". Into the bargain, the newcomers were on a higher wage than The Beatles. Nevertheless, the ice melted, and, according to Pete Best, "that's when their friendship with Ringo began" – when, from that unfavourable first impression, George especially found him a bit of a card.

Starr, Lennon, McCartney and Harrison would be on hand to accompany Lou Walters, a Hurricane who could swoop elegantly from bass grumble to falsetto shriek in the space of a few bars, at a recording date in the Akustik Studio near Hamburg's main railway station. There was also a joint conspiracy between Beatles and Hurricanes to render the Kaiserkeller's rickety stage irreparable via an excess of stamping and jumping, on the assumption – erroneous, as it turned out – that proprietor Bruno Koschmider would be obliged to get a new one.

Back on Merseyside, such *esprit de corps* was evidenced by a jam session at the Zodiac Club by personnel from The Hurricanes and The Beatles – with The Big Three and Gerry & The Pacemakers – which was enlivened by the unveiling of a stripper. Of more portent was that, although Ringo didn't feel he yet knew them well enough to invite to his uproarious 21st birthday party, he became closer to The Beatles during a second visit to Hamburg, deputizing for Pete Best when the latter was poleaxed with bronchitis and on later occasions.

After Ringo graduated from Best's deputy to his successor, the Horticultural Dance proved to have been the quiet before the storm. At The Cavern the following night, there was a near-riot when The Beatles entered. Harrison, his principal champion, was punched in the face, while Starr tried to ignore bawled abuse from incensed Best devotees.

"The fans loved Pete [Best]. Why get an ugly-looking cat when you already have a good-looking one?" Ringo Starr

Three days later, the crew of ITV's Know The North lugged cumbersome television cameras into The Cavern to film The Beatles performing in uniform waistcoats. At the end of the opening Some Other Guy, there was a cry of "We want Pete!" from the crowd as further proof that, as Starr lamented, "They loved Pete. Why get an ugly-looking cat when you already have a good-looking one?" To be fair, Ringo had shaved off his scrappy beard and re-sculpted his hair to a heavy fringe that, after a decade of quiffing, wouldn't cascade into a moptop for about a year.

Elsie might have approved of this shorter style, but when a photo of her son was printed with The Beatles in Mersey Beat, it took a while for readers to become accustomed to this changeling. "It will be difficult for a few weeks," said Harrison, "but I think the majority will soon be taking Ringo for granted." Other than turn from The Beatles altogether, there was nothing for fans to do but to accept the situation – and by November they were already yelling for Ringo to sing a number.

PHOTO: BETTMANN/CORBIS- PICTORIAL PRESS

AUG 23 - OCT 2, 1962

23 Lennon marries Cynthia in a secret ceremony at Mount Pleasant Registry Office, Liverpool, with Paul McCartney as his best man. Evening gig at Riverpark Ballroom, Chester.

24 Two gigs, first at The Cavern, then at the Majestic Ballroom, Birkenhead.

25 A show at the Marine Hall Ballroom, Fleetwood.

26 Mersey Beat newspaper reports that The Beatles are finding a wider audience, via bookings in parts of England as far afield as Manchester, Swindon, Rhyl, Crewe, Chester and Warrington. The band play an evening show at The Cavern.

28 The Beatles play an evening show at The Cavern.

29 Floral Hall Ballroom, Morecambe, supported by Rory Storm & The Hurricanes.

30 Two shows, first at The Cavern, then the Riverpark Ballroom, Chester.

31 The Beatles perform at the Town Hall, Lydney, Gloucestershire.

SEPTEMBER 62

1 The band play the Subscription Rooms, Stroud, Gloucester.

2 An evening show at The Cavern.

3 A lunchtime show at The Cavern followed by a performance at the Queen's Hall, Widnes.

4 During their first proper EMI recording session at Abbey Road, The Beatles record a version of Love Me Do.

5 Three gigs in two days. One at the Rialto Ballroom (right) and two at The Cavern.

7 The Beatles play Newton Dancing School, Irby, Cheshire.

8 Two shows: one at the YMCA, Birkenhead, and then the Majestic Ballroom, Birkenhead.

9 An evening show at The Cavern, with Clinton Ford and Billy J Kramer.

10 A lunchtime show at The Cavern followed by an evening gig at the Queen's Hall, Widnes.

11 The Beatles, with session drummer Andy White standing in for Ringo, record Love Me Do, P.S. I Love You and Please Please Me at Studio 2, Abbey Road, London.

12 An evening show at The Cavern. Freddie & The Dreamers also play.

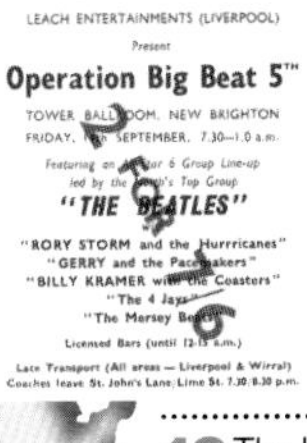

13 Two gigs: first at The Cavern, followed by a show at the Riverpark Ballroom, Chester.

14 The Beatles play Tower Ballroom, New Brighton.

15 A gig at the Memorial Hall, Northwich.

16 The band keep up the pace for the remaining two weeks of the month with eight gigs at The Cavern and five others in Widnes, New Brighton, Birkenhead, Heswall and Manchester.

OCTOBER 62

1 Brian Epstein signs The Beatles to a five-year management contract.

2 The band start the first of three days' gigs at The Cavern.

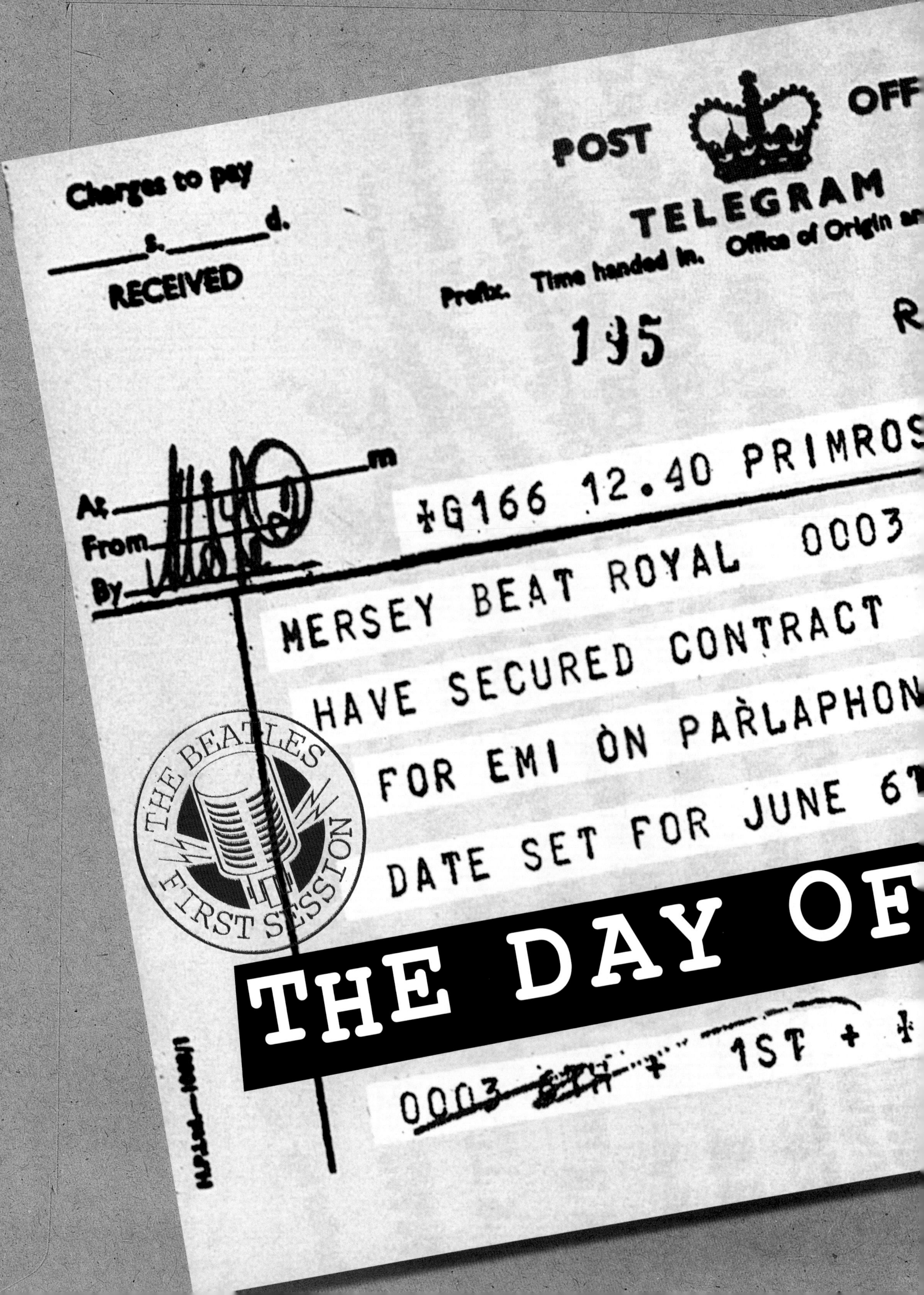
Charges to pay
s. d.
RECEIVED
POST OFF
TELEGRAM
Prefix. Time handed in. Office of Origin an
195
R
At
From
By
m
+G166 12.40 PRIMROS
MERSEY BEAT ROYAL 0003
HAVE SECURED CONTRACT
FOR EMI ON PARLAPHON
DATE SET FOR JUNE 6T
0003 1ST +
THE BEATLES FIRST SESSION

THE DAY OF

0033

TS 26

LIVERPOOL=

FOR BEATLES TO RECORDED

LABEL 1ST RECORDING

BRIAN EPSTEIN +:

RECKONING

When The Beatles first visited Abbey Road studios on June 6, 1962, it would be the biggest day in their lives. But were they there for an "artist test" or a proper recording session? Mark Lewisohn examines the evidence.

"We heard last week from our manager that we now have a contract with EMI for Parlophone records, and we will be doing our first recording on June 6 before we play our welcome home thing at The Cavern... We are all very happy about Parlophone, as it is a big break for us. We will just have to work hard and hope for a hit with whatever we record. [We don't yet know what the producer will want.]"

Letter from George Harrison to a fan, Margaret, sent from Hamburg. Dated simply 'Thursday', it would have been written mid-May 1962. The square brackets are Harrison's.

A romanticist might reflect that Wednesday, June 6, 1962 was The Beatles' date with destiny. Down in London, their first session at the EMI recording studio on Abbey Road, was their first meeting with the man who, as producer of the astonishing music soon to wash the world, would become nearly as famous as they.

Such is the profit of hindsight. And yet it's clear that, for The Beatles, what happened this day was recognised as pivotal even at the time. The session led forward, and we all know where. Had it not, disenchantment may soon have taken hold, and their new manager Brian Epstein may have been forced to yield to his father's increasing pressure: to stop messing around with a silly pop group and buckle down once more to the family business. In Ray Bradbury's A Sound Of Thunder the killing of a butterfly 60 million years back in time alters every aspect of the present; today's popular culture, life, would be unrecognisable if The Beatles had flunked June 6, 1962.

A date with destiny, then. And, urged on by Epstein, The Beatles must have felt it. Having just completed their third Hamburg season, they flew Lufthansa to London Airport on June 2, caught a connecting flight to Manchester and were driven to Liverpool, Epstein pressing home the importance of the imminent EMI session. While the jury remains out, even 40 years later, about whether this was a contract-seeking audition or their first nerve-racking session under a just-signed contract (more on this later), Epstein will have left nothing to chance. Having kept The Beatles' diary free of bookings, he had them rehearse solidly over the next two days, privately at The Cavern, no-one else in the house. Then, a day early, on Tuesday June 5, Neil Aspinall loaded up the van and they drove south to London.

It was a long journey: 200 miles, no motorway until Birmingham, halts and hazards in every town. Long-haul travelling in Britain was as much an unfunny joke 40 years ago as now, only the encumbrances have changed. Radio would have done little to alleviate the crammed-together tedium: the BBC's Light Programme, with its pop monopoly, broadcast less than two hours of it this day, otherwise it was Housewives' Choice, Workers' Playtime, Mrs Dale's Diary and Wilfred Pickles asking Where Are You Now?.

Where The Beatles stayed the night isn't known, nor how they spent the following daytime. On the 16th anniversary of D-Day this was another: Derby Day at Epsom, but The Beatles had scant interest in sport. With an unofficial London Transport bus strike adding to the road traffic, and considering the rage he had flown into when The Beatles had arrived late at Decca, Epstein – for whom punctuality was an obsession – would have had them setting off to Abbey Road in ample time for their 7-10pm date in Number Two studio.

"They pulled into the car park in an old white van," says Abbey Road doorman John Skinner, straight-backed and strait-laced in worsted uniform and polished war medals. "They all looked very thin and weedy, almost under-nourished. Neil Aspinall, their road manager, said that they were The Beatles, here for a session. I thought, What a strange name."

It wasn't only the name that raised eyebrows. "We'd seen a few long-haired groups, a few weirdos," recalls balance engineer Norman (later Hurricane) Smith, "but nothing like The Beatles. It was a double-take job: you'd look and have to look again."

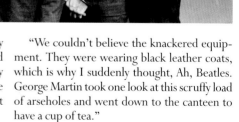

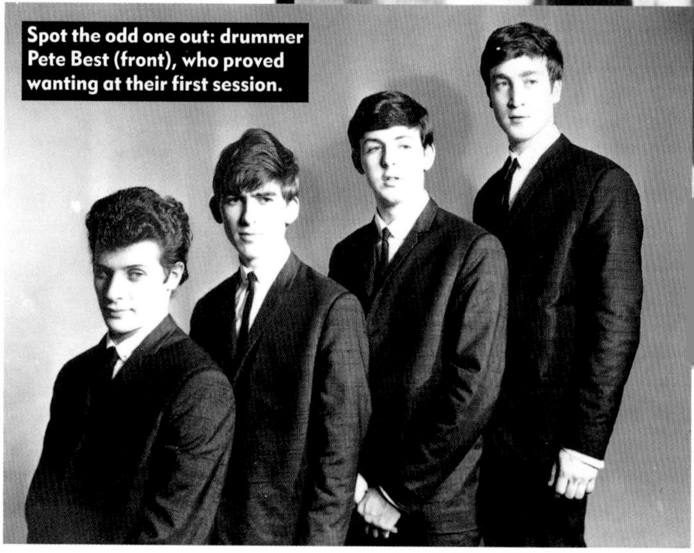
Spot the odd one out: drummer Pete Best (front), who proved wanting at their first session.

In a white lab-coat, de rigueur for Abbey Road technical staff in those days, Ken Townsend was assigned to take care of any electronic problems arising: "The Beatles dressed a bit differently and had what we thought was very long hair, though looking back now on the old photographs it's very hard to believe. And they had broad Liverpool accents – we didn't have many people from Liverpool recording at Abbey Road."

Tape operator ('button-pusher') Cris Neal remembers: "We had a common room at Abbey Road and anyone not on a session used to hang around in there – Norman Smith was a shit-hot draughts player. Our worksheets for the week were posted up on the wall and it said '7pm: The Beatles'. I thought, 'Some typist has buggered up again'.

"We couldn't believe the knackered equipment. They were wearing black leather coats, which is why I suddenly thought, Ah, Beatles. George Martin took one look at this scruffy load of arseholes and went down to the canteen to have a cup of tea."

George Martin's role at The Beatles' first session has been queried since 1983 when Abbey Road revealed that the tape library log named his assistant, Ron Richards, as Artiste Manager (ie, producer). "Some sessions I'd say, Right, Ron, you take that because I'm up doing such-and-such," Martin explains. "When it came to doing artist tests, which this was – this

"So which one's the singer?" George Martin learns to think differently with The Beatles.

"WE'D SEEN A FEW LONG-HAIRED GROUPS, A FEW WEIRDOS, BUT NOTHING LIKE THE BEATLES. IT WAS A DOUBLE-TAKE – YOU'D LOOK AND HAVE TO LOOK AGAIN." NORMAN SMITH, ENGINEER

was just looking at four berks from Liverpool – it didn't mean anything in our lives at all. I said, OK, Ron, get it organised, I'll pop in and see what they're like. It's as simple as that."

"I used to work with lots of George's artists," says Richards. "I was more au fait with rock'n'roll than he was. He'd had some success with Jim Dale but he'd been through a period of doing comedy records and I suppose he thought I'd be better starting it off. I rehearsed The Beatles in the studio beforehand. Pete Best was on drums and it was me who said to George, He's useless, we've got to change this drummer. Poor old Pete, but he wasn't very good."

Matters worsened when Norman Smith began to test The Beatles' gear. "They had such duff equipment," he recalls, "ugly unpainted wooden amplifiers, extremely noisy, with earth loops and goodness knows what. There was as much noise coming from the amps as there was from the instruments. Paul's bass amp was particularly bad." Paul's 'coffin' amp, made for him by Adrian Barber of the Liverpool band The Big Three, was a signature of The Beatles' live appearances, where it could blast the bass to the back of the Aintree Institute. It was not designed for studio use.

Ken Townsend tried to make good with a soldering iron but the amp wouldn't produce a decent sound.

"It looked like we would have to write the entire session off," he says. Then the white-coated engineer had one of his regular eureka moments. "As there was no demand that night for echo chamber one, down in the basement, Norman and I fetched a very large, very heavy Tannoy speaker from there and I soldered a jack socket on to the input stage of a Leak TL12 amplifier. We were soon back in business."

And so The Beatles began to play: John his Rickenbacker, George his Duo-Jet, Paul his Hofner and Pete his Premier kit. As Paul would reflect, it was a testing moment – Number Two studio at EMI had "those great big white studio sight-screens, like at a cricket match, towering over you. And up this endless stairway was the control room. It was like heaven, where the great gods lived, and we were down below. Oh God, the nerves!"

In advance of the session, George Martin had told Brian Epstein that he would want to evaluate the merits of each Beatle as a singer (save for Pete, who sang only on rare occasions). The producer was hoping to identify the 'leader' for recording purposes. There was Cliff Richard & The Shadows, Johnny Kidd & The Pirates, Shane Fenton & The Fentones – would it be, perhaps, Georgie Harrison & The Beatles?

Martin's request must have caused a ➳

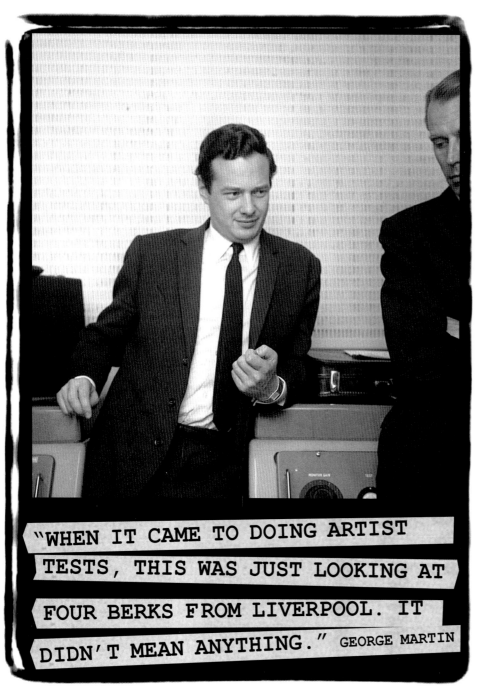

"WHEN IT CAME TO DOING ARTIST TESTS, THIS WAS JUST LOOKING AT FOUR BERKS FROM LIVERPOOL. IT DIDN'T MEAN ANYTHING." GEORGE MARTIN

sticky moment for The Beatles' manager, being that John Lennon had criticised his song selection for the Decca audition. With or without consultation this time around (and we may never know which) Epstein suggested The Beatles launch themselves at EMI with a three-song medley, to spotlight each singer in turn. The segued Besame Mucho/Will You Love Me Tomorrow/Open (Your Lovin' Arms) – Paul, John and George covering The Coasters, The Shirelles and Tex-Mex warbler Buddy Knox respectively – was very likely the first Beatles music to be heard at Abbey Road.

Among 13 further numbers that Epstein suggested Paul should sing at EMI were five which he informed George Martin were "original compositions" – Love Me Do, P.S. I Love You, Like Dreamers Do, Love Of The Loved and Pinwheel Twist. The last of these – the only one of these songs never recorded by anyone, and so unknown – was a new piece written to capitalise on the twist boom; The Beatles soon dropped it. Paul's eight other songs were covers: If You Gotta Make A Fool Of Somebody (James Ray), Your Feet's Too Big (Fats Waller – "That was Paul's dad's influence," George mused in the Anthology book), Hey! Baby (Bruce Channel), Dream Baby (Roy Orbison) and four designed to spotlight the more mellow side of The Beatles' repertoire – Till There Was You (Peggy Lee), Over The Rainbow (Gene Vincent), September In The Rain (Dinah Washington) and The Honeymoon Song (Marino Marini).

Epstein detailed 10 further songs that John might perform, including two original compositions: Ask Me Why and Hello Little Girl. The others reflected the singer's hefty penchant for R&B: Baby It's You (The Shirelles), Please Mr Postman (The Marvelettes), To Know Her Is To Love Her (The Teddy Bears – Phil Spector), I Just Don't Understand (Ann-Margret), Memphis, Tennessee (Chuck Berry), A Shot Of Rhythm And Blues (Arthur Alexander), I Wish I Could Shimmy Like My Sister Kate (The Olympics) and Lonesome Tears In My Eyes (The Johnny Burnette Trio).

Not yet a writer of original compositions, George had seven additional songs in his possible repertoire this day: A Picture Of You, The Sheik Of Araby and What A Crazy World We're Living In (all Joe Brown & The Bruvvers), Three Cool Cats (The Coasters), Dream (Cliff Richard), Take Good Care Of My Baby (Bobby Vee) and Glad All Over (Carl Perkins).

The Beatles are likely to have focused on these 33 songs in the closed Cavern rehearsals but which ones they performed at EMI was never documented. Just four were printed to two-track mono tape, presumably after a wider selection had been whittled down – Besame Mucho, Love Me Do, P.S. I Love You and Ask Me Why. "The four were chosen to reflect the fact that we wrote our own songs," remembers Pete Best, "and that if we did do a cover version – like Besame Mucho – we did it in our own unique way." Only two are known to have survived: Besame Mucho, which turned up in the 1980s, and Love Me Do, which surfaced in 1994 during production of *Anthology*. (Encouraged to sort through a pile of acetate discs, literally in his attic, George Martin found one whose label had Love Me Do scrawled in yellow chinagraph.)

It was Love Me Do that fetched George Martin up from the canteen. As Cris Neal recalls, "They ran through a couple of tunes which Norman and I were not all that impressed with and then they did Love Me Do and all of a sudden there was this raunchy noise which struck a chord in our heads. Norman said to me, 'Oi, go down and pick up George from the canteen and see what he thinks of this'."

Martin's interest, too, was piqued. "I picked up on Love Me Do mainly because of the harmonica sound," he says. "I loved wailing harmonica – it reminded me of the records I used to issue of Sonny Terry and Brownie McGhee. I felt it had a definite appeal."

No example of Love Me Do exists prior to this first EMI session so it isn't clear when it was decided that John should add this harmonica to the sound – the instrument almost certainly being the one he stole from a music shop in Arnhem, Holland, in 1960, when The Beatles first made their way by road to Hamburg. The current (first time round) hit Hey! Baby by Bruce Channel, prominently featuring Delbert McClinton's harmonica, was among the 33 songs prepared for the EMI session so John would have had the instrument with him anyway. But whenever it was, its addition to Love Me Do presented a problem unforeseen by The Beatles in private rehearsal, as Paul McCartney has recalled.

"We started playing it, [*singing*] 'Love, love me do/you know I love you' and I'm singing harmony, then it gets to the 'pleeeaase'. STOP.

PHOTOS: REX FEATURES

John goes 'Love me…' and then puts his harmonica to his mouth: 'Wah, wah, wahhh'. George Martin went, 'Wait a minute, wait a minute, there's a crossover there. Someone else has got to sing "Love me do" because you can't go "Love me wahhh". You're going to have a song called Love Me Wahhh. So, Paul, will you sing, 'Love me do'?

"God, I got the screaming heebie-jeebies. I mean, he suddenly changed this whole arrangement that we'd been doing forever, and John was to miss out that line: he'd sing, 'Pleeeeease', put his mouth-organ to his mouth, I'd sing, 'Love me do', and John would come in 'Wahhh-wahhh-wahhhh'. We were doing it live, there was no real overdubbing, so I was suddenly given this massive moment, on our first record, no backing, where everything stopped, the spotlight was on me and I went, [*in quivering voice*] 'Love me do-oo'. And I can still hear the shake in my voice…"

Released on *Anthology*, this Love Me Do is marred by some eccentric changes in tempo which do little to enhance the past and present drumming reputation of Pete Best, and probably helped cement the Richards/Martin view that he was for the chop, studio-wise. However, to be fair, these variations were adhered to by all four Beatles, suggesting – erratic though it is – that this was the song's current arrangement. All told, it is a much slower, even more bluesy, much less assured version than the two subsequent remakes.

The 1940s tune Besame Mucho (Spanish for 'kiss me much') had been in The Beatles' repertoire since The Coasters had issued their cover version in 1960. John and George usually added a flavoursome 'Cha-cha-boom' backing – they did this at Decca and in a BBC radio broadcast – but at EMI they were restrained: Paul 'Cha-cha-boom'-ed alone. This song would soon be jettisoned from The Beatles' repertoire but their affection for it shows unconfined in the Let It Be film, shot in 1969, when they perform a spirited rendition.

According to Pete Best, The Beatles felt the session went well. "We were even a little bit blasé," he says, a shy man still. "We were a lot more confident at EMI than we were at Decca, there was a far more relaxed atmosphere. All of us had felt nervous at Decca, and when we listened to the playback it sounded a lot better than Decca. We thought it was good."

After the session had finished, the band had a chat with George Martin which has become part of Beatles lore. Having invited them upstairs to the control room to hear the four recordings, George Martin began addressing the group, discussing technicalities and what he would require of them as Parlophone recording artists.

"George was giving them a good talking to," recalls Ken Townsend, "explaining about the studio microphones being figure-of-eight – in other words, you could stand on either side of them as opposed to stage mikes which were one-sided." All this time, says Norman Smith, The Beatles kept quiet.

"They didn't say a word back, not a word. They didn't even nod their heads in agreement. When he finished, George said, 'Look, I've laid into you for quite a time, you haven't responded. Is there anything you don't like?'"

"I just looked at him and said, Well, I don't like your tie for a kick-off!" George told Q years later. "I nearly got killed by the rest of the band… The others were like, 'Oh no! We're trying to get a record deal'. But he [George Martin] had a sense of humour."

As well he did. Martin has often said that it was The Beatles' personalities that really persuaded him these were people he could work with. They, in turn, were pleased to meet the producer of the Peter Sellers and Spike Milligan recordings they so much admired. Before either side realised quite what skills the other could bring to the party, The Beatles and their producer met at head level and found the experience an agreeable one.

"What I recall about George Martin the first time we met him was his accent," George Harrison declared in the Anthology book. "He didn't speak in a Cockney or a Liverpool or a Birmingham accent, and anyone who didn't speak like that we thought was very posh. He was friendly, but school-teacherly, we had to respect him, but at the same time he gave us the impression that he wasn't stiff – that you could joke with him."

Harrison concluded, "It [the session] went not too badly. I think George Martin felt we were raw and rough but that we had some quality that was interesting."

On their way out of Abbey Road, The Beatles cut along to see Mr Mitchell, studio cashier (evening shift), who handed out chittys and paid them their Musicians' Union session fees, £7 10s [£7.50] each, a cash sum over and above any royalties that might accrue. Ken Townsend's recollection that the staff were unfamiliar with Liverpudlians is borne out by Mr Mitchell's befuddled comprehension of the four fringe-haired Scallys standing before him: in the mumbled confusion he prepared payment cards denoting G Harrison as 'Bass Guitar', JP McCartney as 'E Guitar' and 'JW Lewnow of 251, Mew Love Ave., Liverpool???'.

The next day, the remnants of £30 in their pockets, The Beatles slowly motored back to Liverpool. But was the session on June 6, 1962 an artist test – an audition – the outcome of which, subject to George Martin's say-so, would determine whether or not The Beatles would be granted a record deal? Or were they already under contract, making this their first session proper?

Paul McCartney, Neil Aspinall, George Martin, Norman Smith and Cris Neal have described the session as an ➽

PHOTOS: REX FEATURES

THE NORTH'S OWN ENTERTAINMENTS PAPER

MERSEY BEAT

FRANK HESSY

BEATLES RECORD FOR EMI
story inside

artist test. Drawing a distinction between an artist test and a commercial test – the former designed to see if an act was worth signing, the latter an initial recording after a contract has already been drawn up – Ken Townsend is adamant that the session was a commercial test.

Memories are fallible, contemporary paperwork not so. What information pertains? George Martin's personal diary for 1962 cites a meeting with 'Bernard Epstein' on Tuesday, February 13.

Various items of Brian Epstein correspondence in March allude to an impending contract with a recording organisation he does not identify.

On Monday, May 7, Epstein wrote to Neil Aspinall: "You will be interested to hear that I am going to London this week to see EMI and very sincerely hope that when I see you on Friday I'll have good news." (The letter is reproduced in The Beatles – The True Beginnings by the brothers Roag, Pete and Rory Best.)

On May 9, Epstein sent two telegrams from the Post Office closest to Abbey Road. One, to Mersey Beat, read: "Have secured contract for Beatles to recorded [sic] for EMI on Parlaphone [sic] label. 1st recording date set for June 6th." The other, to The Beatles in Hamburg, said (paraphrased by Pete Best in the Hunter Davies biography), "Congratulations boys. EMI request recording session. Please rehearse new material." [It was after receiving this news that George Harrison wrote his letter to Margaret.]

On May 18 George Martin sent an 'Application For Artiste Contract' form to EMI's administration department, giving the precise details and terms with which the department was to draw up a 'period contract' for 'the Beattles' [sic] – a one-year agreement, with options for three annual renewals, to commence on June 6.

On May 24 the typed contract was sent to Martin for despatch to Epstein.

June 4 was the date of the contract – again, the first year set to begin on June 6.

On June 5, Martin forwarded to EMI administration the signed contract he had just received back from Epstein.

Especially persuasive is the internal-EMI 'red form', signed by George Martin, which set out, in advance, details of the June 6 session. Interesting in several respects, it states: 'Type of contract: Period', and 'Royalty: 1d', this being the paltry penny that was The Beatles' initial EMI emolument. Artists merely given an audition were not paid.

Ten years ago, when completing my research for The Complete Beatles Chronicle, I spread all these papers before George Martin and suggested to him that The Beatles were already under contract when the June 6 session took place. Though he couldn't refute the documents, the conclusion – that he had signed The Beatles before he saw them – struck him as utterly ludicrous. "So I must have seen them before June 6," he declared. "I don't think so, they had been in Hamburg since 13th April," I said, feeling sorry for the knighted producer whose long-established version of history – his own, too – was being challenged by an upstart still in short trousers when the events took place.

"I must have seen them in February or March, then," he insisted.

Well, the EMI and Abbey Road paperwork is not lacking and it betrays no indication of this. Also – something of a clincher – I've asked Pete Best how many times he met George and how many times he went to Abbey Road and the answer was the same on both counts: "Once." George then confirmed that he had indeed met Pete Best on one occasion only.

"So why on earth would I have signed a group before I even saw them? I would never have done that, it's preposterous," George Martin concluded. "I don't know, George, it beats me, too." Even the suggestion (made by me, among others) that the contract was drawn up early, so that Martin could either add his signature or rip the whole thing up after seeing The Beatles, is effectively disproven by the 'red form' – the session clearly took place under a contract.

However, signed to Parlophone they were. And The Beatles expected their debut single to be taken from the June 6 session. An article in the May 31-June 14 1962 issue of Mersey Beat, the information doubtless fed by Brian Epstein, stated "their first disc... is released in July". (The same piece also invited readers to suggest the songs they would most like The Beatles to record for this first 45, urging them to "write in immediately... the closing date will be next Wednesday, June 6th.")

And in a letter dated June 29, Epstein declared to EMI's general marketing manager Ron White – with whom, as a record retailer, he had regular dealings – "I am very much looking forward to the issue of the group's first disc which I expect should be towards the end of August – although I have not heard from George Martin recently."

It seems that the producer was still mulling his options, wondering which of The Beatles to make leader. Says Ron Richards, "George and I were walking up Oxford Street one day trying to work out whether it should be Paul – the good looking one – or John, who had the big personality. Neither of us could make up our minds."

Eventually, Martin realised that the group was a balanced unit and should not be disturbed. Well, with one exception. As Paul McCartney recalls, "When we first came down in June 1962, George [Martin] took us aside and said, 'I'm not happy about the drummer'. And we all went, 'Oh God, well I'm not telling him. You tell him!'" This change was hinted at in a letter dated June 26 from Ron White to Brian Epstein: "George Martin tells me that he has been suitably impressed with them [The Beatles] and has made certain suggestions to you which in his view may improve them still further and it is for this reason that he has offered a contract." (That last bit further remuddles the chronology, note.)

Explaining the long delay between The Beatles' first Abbey Road session and their next, on September 4, and also the non-appearance of the debut single until October, George Martin reflects, "I was looking for the first single but knew that the Love Me Do we did in June wasn't good enough. I wasn't in any desperate hurry. I mean, I had signed the group and I knew we had to get it right if we were going to issue a record. I knew too that we had to remake Love Me Do, and that we would do so with a different drummer." (He would also find them another song, of course, How Do You Do It, which would come very close to being The Beatles' debut.)

For Pete Best, his studio performance was a significant addition to the growing movement that would result in his dismissal. For John, Paul and George, and for Brian Epstein and George Martin, life-altering events of a different hue were but a Beatle breath away. ■

PHOTOS: REX FEATURES

New boy: Ringo debuts in an Astrid Kirchherr press shoot, November 1962.

5 The Beatles release their first single, Love Me Do/P.S. I Love You.

6 A show at a Horticultural Society Dance, Hulme Hall, Birkenhead.

7 An evening gig at The Cavern, supported by The Bluegenes.

8 At EMI's headquarters in Manchester Square, London, The Beatles record their first appearance on the influential Radio Luxembourg.

9 The Beatles visit the offices of Record Mirror, Shaftesbury Avenue, London, to be interviewed about their first single.

10 A week of North-West gigs, taking in The Cavern as well as dates in St Helen's, Birkenhead, Runcorn and New Brighton's Tower Ballroom where they support Little Richard.

17 Lunchtime and evening shows at The Cavern. The Beatles' first TV appearance is recorded live on People And Places, a Granada TV show broadcast only in the Manchester area.

19 The Beatles play The Cavern at lunchtime.

20 The band play the Majestic Ballroom, Hull, Yorkshire.

21 An evening gig at The Cavern, Liverpool.

22 A show at Queen's Hall, Widnes, supported by The Merseybeats.

24 Brian Epstein writes to London booking agent Tito Burns, giving him details of The Beatles' availability and rates for live performances.

25 Another session is recorded for BBC radio show Here We Go, in Manchester. During an interview for Cleaver & Clatterbridge Hospital Radio, Wirral, Lancashire, Paul says, "John Lennon is the leader of the group".

26 The Beatles play two shows, one at the Public Hall, Preston, Lancashire and the other at The Cavern.

27 The band perform at Hulme Hall, Birkenhead (above).

28 The Beatles support (and back) Little Richard again at Liverpool's premier venue, The Empire (right).

29 Another appearance is recorded for Granada TV show People And Places in Manchester.

30 The Beatles fly off to Hamburg, Germany.

NOVEMBER 62

1 The first of a two-week residency, sharing the bill with Little Richard, at The Star Club, Hamburg.

10 Brian Epstein writes to UK promoter Larry Parnes quoting a rate of £230 per week for a Beatles tour.

17 The band plays at Matrix Hall, Coventry, Warwickshire.

18 The band play The Cavern, supported by The Merseybeats.

19 A busy day for The Beatles with a lunchtime show at The Cavern, followed by two evening gigs, one at the Baths Ballroom, Smethwick, and one at the Adelphi Ballroom, West Bromwich.

20 The Beatles play two shows at the Floral Hall, Southport.

What: John marries Cynthia
Where: Mount Pleasant, Liverpool
When: August 23, 1962

A SLIGHT HITCH

Despite bad weather and a pneumatic drill conspiring to ruin their big day, John remembered his marriage to Cynthia as "a laugh". By Chris Ingham.

THEY BOTH WENT TO LIVERPOOL College of Art in 1957 but they had nothing in common. Cynthia Powell was a polite, shy, tweedy twin set from Hoylake, John Lennon was an anti-establishment leather jacket apparently more interested in creating hilarity and disruption in class than studying Lettering.

She initially found him uncouth and his constant borrowing of her equipment irritating. Then she found herself looking forward to the Lettering class they shared until one lecture she thought she saw a friend stroking Lennon's hair and as the frisson of jealousy overcame her, Cynthia realised she'd fallen for him.

(Top) Paul, John and Cynthia and (above) the Lennons' wedding certificate.

A connection of sorts was made later when they were able to share a laugh over their respective short-sightedness. However, when John asked her to dance at an art school lunchtime party during summer 1958 and enquired as to her availability, Cynthia blurted in a panic that she was engaged. "I didn't ask you to marry me, did I?" snorted Lennon.

Later that afternoon, retiring to Stuart Sutcliffe's bedsit, John and Cynthia became lovers. They spent as much of the summer break together as they could, lying to their respective guardians about where they were. When they returned to art college in autumn 1958, they were an established, if unlikely couple.

Cynthia soon discovered a couple of things about being involved with John. Firstly, she would sometimes have to share her time with him with his young music pals Paul and George who attended the Liverpool Institute next door to the art college. Sixteen-year-old George especially would appear from nowhere and tag along, gawkily unaware of his gooseberry status (and later intimated to John, helpfully, that while Cynthia was "great" she had "teeth like a horse").

Secondly, John had ferocious mood swings and an intimidating jealous temper when things didn't suit him. Living in a state combining excitement and trepidation, she wrote later that she was "terrified of him 75 per cent of the time". But she was involved and empathised with the pain of a teenager who had only recently lost his mother in tragic circumstances (Cynthia had lost her father early, to cancer).

Changing her appearance to suit Lennon's tastes, she had already evolved from "secretary bird to bohemian" as she put it and now took the bottle blonde/tight black sweaters/fishnet stockings route. However, she continued to feel awkward not to say positively threatened by the tough Liverpool girls who were turning out in greater numbers to stare at her boyfriend onstage.

When The Beatles hit Hamburg for months at a time, Cynthia was less concerned about the good-time girls of the Reeperbahn (she remained oblivious to Lennon's extra-curricular activities throughout their relationship – "I think I must have had a mental block," she reflected) than an "Astrid" John kept mentioning in his regular letters. Meeting and staying with Astrid Kirchherr when she visited John in Hamburg in spring 1961, she was impressed but reassured and the two became friends.

The same didn't quite happen when, upon the emigration of her mother to Canada, Cynthia moved in to lodge with John's Aunt Mimi; "two women loving the same man… an impossible situation," Cynthia said.

By summer 1962, Brian Epstein's efforts on behalf of The Beatles were paying off in the form of better quality work and recording sessions for EMI in London. Also, it was clear Pete Best's days were numbered. It was in this atmosphere of exhilaration and upheaval that a tearful Cynthia told John she was pregnant. "There's only one thing for it, Cyn," she remembers as his stunned reply. "We'll have to get married."

John told his Aunt Mimi who was bitterly disappointed. Though she would have nothing to do with the wedding, she later gave John £10 for a ring. Brian calmly advised John on a special registry office licence for a quick appointment and the date was set for August 23, 1962. Cynthia's mother was sailing back to Canada the day before and didn't change her plans.

Present at Mount Pleasant Registry Office that morning were three nervous Beatles (a newly recruited Ringo was not even told, let alone invited), Cynthia's brother Tony and sister-in-law Margery as witnesses and Brian Epstein as best man. No-one from John's family attended. Cynthia wore a purple and black check two-piece with a frilly shirt given to her by Astrid. As a wedding present, Brian gave the couple free and unlimited use of his unoccupied flat on Faulkner Street (a venue usually used for his own discreet assignations) as living quarters.

The ceremony itself quickly descended to low farce with a nearby pneumatic drill obliterating the sound of the Registrar's voice and the couple struggling to keep their faces and minds straight. When the relieved wedding party spilled back onto Hope Street, a torrential downpour greeted them. Adjourning to Reece's Café, the gathering waited for a free table, had a chicken lunch, paid for by Brian, and toasted the couple with water. "It was all a laugh," Lennon remembered later.

On their wedding night, The Beatles played the Riverpark Ballroom in Chester and Cynthia moved her belongings into Faulkner Street. As the group's career took off, the marriage remained an undercover (until late 1963) and undernourished affair. "I did feel embarrassed, walking about, married," Lennon said later. "It was like walking about with odd socks on, or your flies open."

PHOTOS: PICTORIAL PRESS, SAM LEACH

The odd couple: John and Cynthia Lennon, now "officially married", depart for America, Heathrow, August 1964.

Breaking the Tin Pan Alley monopoly: Paul McCartney, composer of Love Me Do, in 1962.

What: Love Me Do is released
Where: UK
When: October 5, 1962

LOVE UNLIMITED

Written by a 16-year-old Paul "trying to do the blues", the Fabs' debut single ended up sounding like it came from another planet. By Martin O'Gorman.

EXCITED AT THE PROSPECT OF HEARING his debut single on the radio for the first time, 19-year-old George Harrison kept a lonely vigil by the wireless one night in October 1962. His mother, a steadfast Beatles supporter, had long since crept off to bed, only to be woken by her son yelling, "We're on!" "The first time I heard Love Me Do on the radio, I went shivery all over," he recalled. "I listened to the lead guitar work and couldn't believe it."

Even allowing for Radio Luxembourg's notoriously fuzzy reception, compared to the rest of 1962's pop output Love Me Do sounded like it had been beamed in from another planet. With its raw harmonica and flat Northern vowels, the record exuded the same spirit of social change that had already spawned the satire movement and the "kitchen sink" drama.

Squeezed between Better Luck Next Time by Johnny Angel and Nicky Hilton's Your Nose Is Gonna Grow on Parlophone's schedules, Love Me Do was released on Friday, October 5, 1962. The following day, The Beatles signed copies at a shop in Widnes, giving the record publicity that wasn't forthcoming from EMI – when George Martin had unveiled his new signings to his bosses, they thought The Beatles were another of the producer's Goon jokes. "Then when I played it for them," Martin recalls, "they thought I'd gone slightly mad."

Despite such obstacles, Love Me Do sneaked onto the Record Retailer chart at Number 49 on October 11, reaching its peak position of 17 some 11 weeks later. But it was suggested in some quarters at the time that the single's success had little to do with public enthusiasm, and more to do with the unusually high order placed by the NEMS record shop in Liverpool, managed by a Mr Brian Epstein.

NEMS' Peter Brown later claimed that Epstein had "unblinkingly" ordered 10,000 copies, but newly-hired Beatles press officer Tony Barrow thinks it was less than that. "Brian bought more copies than he normally would," he says today. "But if he was saying that his band was going to be bigger than Elvis, he had to put his money where his mouth was."

As "Disker", Barrow was the Liverpool Echo's record reviewer and an ideal choice to write The Beatles' first press release. Declaring The Beatles "rhythmic revolutionaries", it was, Barrow says, "More explanatory than anything. When I first read the word 'Beatles', I thought it was a typo. So, the first thing to do was clarify that it wasn't a typo, it was actually spelt B-E-A."

More significantly, Barrow promoted the fact that Love Me Do and its Shirelles-inspired B-side, P.S. I Love You, were penned by John Lennon and Paul McCartney, heralding the eventual demise of Tin Pan Alley. Written back in 1958, Love Me Do was the 16-year-old McCartney "trying to do the blues". Adding a harmonica line influenced by Bruce Channel's contemporaneous hit Hey Baby, The Beatles eased Love Me Do into their live set in the spring of 1962 and would later air the song at their EMI audition in June.

However, unimpressed by their originals, George Martin searched for a suitable song from a professional writer, finding it in the innocuous How Do You Do It by Mitch Murray. The Beatles weren't convinced, but Epstein insisted the group learn the song for their first recording session on September 4. "Brian gave us a warning," says McCartney. "He said, 'It doesn't matter if you don't like it, just do it.' We said, 'We can't take that song home, we'll get laughed at!"

Dispatching a deliberately perfunctory performance of How Do You Do It, Lennon and McCartney cajoled George Martin into giving Love Me Do another listen. He agreed, rearranging the song to accommodate Lennon's harmonica part and handing McCartney the lead vocal – much to the chagrin of Lennon. Martin "looked very hard" at The Beatles' version of How Do You Do It, before leaving Gerry And The Pacemakers to take it to Number One in April 1963. "In the end, I decided to go with Love Me Do," he admits. "It was John's harmonica which give it its appeal."

Despite winning that battle, The Beatles had more problems to deal with – Martin misinterpreted Starr's intuitive playing on the off-beat as mere sloppiness. McCartney later speculated that the producer was accustomed to show drummers who "locked in" their bass drum with the bass guitar. "We weren't bothered with that," he says. "Ours was very four in the bar – that's what became known as the Mersey Beat."

Martin called The Beatles back to Abbey Road a week later, leaving them with his assistant Ron Richards, who had, unknown to the group, hired session drummer Andy White to sit in. Starr therefore dejectedly shook a tambourine on both Love Me Do and P.S. I Love You. "I was shattered," he remembered. "I thought, They're doing a Pete Best on me. How phoney the record business was – getting other musicians to make your records for you."

"The first time I heard Love Me Do on the radio, I went shivery all over – I couldn't believe it!" George Harrison

In retrospect, the situation was blown out of all proportion – the single ultimately bore the "Ringo version", although Andy White could still be heard on the flip. Over three decades later, Starr still grumbled about Martin, claiming, "I hated the bugger for years".

But the loose "Mersey Beat" only accentuated the blunt, earthy appeal of Love Me Do. As the single garnered airplay, The Beatles' fame began to spread without any contrived hype. When the record broke the Top 20, Brian Epstein declared, "What could be more important than this?"

NOV 21 - DEC 31, 1962

21 Lunchtime and evening sessions at The Cavern.

22 A show at the Majestic Ballroom, Birkenhead.

23 The Beatles audition for Light Entertainment Auditioner Ronnie Lane of BBC TV at St James' Church Hall in London to assess their TV potential. Four days later Brian Epstein receives a rejection letter from the BBC. The band play the Tower Ballroom, New Brighton.

24 The group play at the Royal Lido Ballroom, Prestatyn, Wales.

25 An evening session at The Cavern.

26 The band record Please Please Me, Tip Of My Tongue and Ask Me Why at EMI Studios, Abbey Road, London. George Martin tells the band: "Congratulations, boys! You've got yourself your first Number One."

27 The Beatles record first BBC radio session in London for the Talent Spot show at Paris Studio, Regent St.

28 Two evening shows: at The Cavern and the 527 Club, Liverpool.

29 The Beatles play the Majestic Ballroom, Birkenhead.

30 A lunchtime show at The Cavern is followed by an evening gig at the Town Hall, Newton-le-Willows.

DECEMBER 62

1 The Beatles play two shows, one at the Victory Memorial Hall, Northwich, and the other at the Tower Ballroom, New Brighton.

2 Playing the Embassy Cinema, Peterborough, The Beatles' egos are dented by a very unfavourable reception.

3 The Beatles play live on TV show Discs A Go Go, at TWW Studios, Bristol.

4 The band make their London-area TV debut on the children's show, Tuesday Rendezvous.

5 Over the next week The Beatles play at The Cavern five times. On the 9th George Martin watches them play there with a view to producing a live album. The band also find the time to perform in Southport, Runcorn, New Brighton and Manchester.

13 The Beatles stand in for Joe Brown at the Corn Exchange, Bedford.

14 Music Hall, Shrewsbury, supported by Gary B Goode.

MERSEY BEAT
present
A GRAND MIDNIGHT MATINEE
The Mersey Beat Poll Awards, 1962
at THE MAJESTIC BALLROOM
CONWAY STREET, BIRKENHEAD
SATURDAY, 15th DECEMBER, 1962
12-30 a.m. to 4 a.m.
ADMISSION BY TICKET ONLY - 7/6
The entire proceeds will be donated to Charity
EVENING DRESS OPTIONAL ★ BUFFET ★ LICENSED BAR APPLIED FOR
AWARDS WILL BE PRESENTED BY THE EDITOR OF MERSEY BEAT, W. HARRY

15 The Beatles play the first Mersey Beat Poll Awards Show at the Majestic Ballroom, Birkenhead.

17 A third appearance is recorded on Granada TV show People And Places, in Manchester.

18 A 14-night residency marks The Beatles' fifth and last season at The Star Club, Hamburg.

28 During tonight's show at the Star Club in Hamburg, John Lennon appears onstage with a toilet seat draped around his head to show his displeasure with the venue's manager.

31 The Beatles' final Star Club show.

1963

In 1963 The Beatles released their first album, had their first Number 1 hit and, as Beatlemania set in, turned the country crazy for a song called She Loves You. They made friends with the Stones and went on tour with Helen Shapiro and Roy Orbison. And within the space of three months, they said goodbye to The Cavern and played in front of the Queen Mother at the Royal Variety Performance. Truly, the Fab Four had arrived.

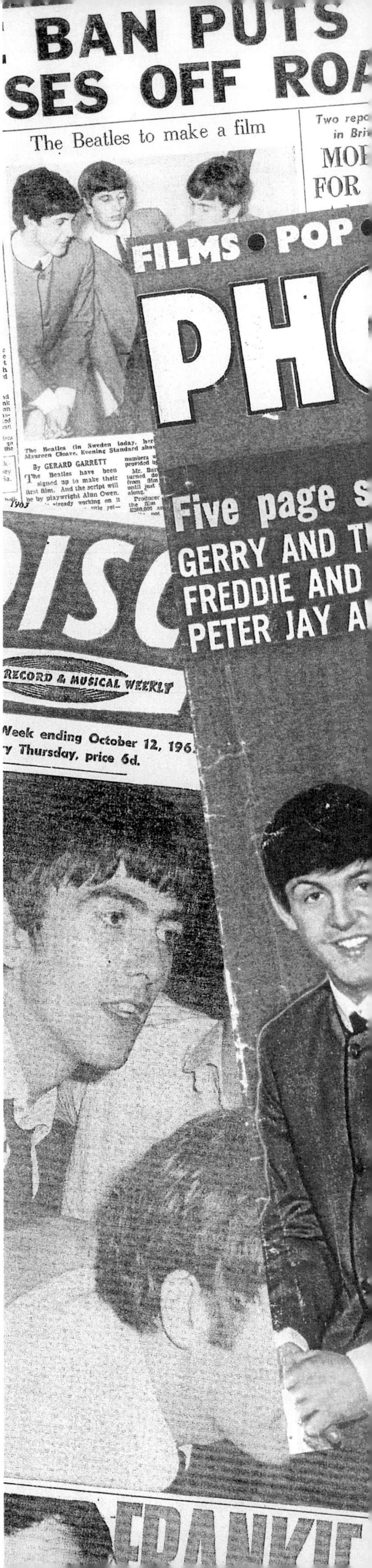

BEATLES-T
D-J VERR
honey
New People '63
NOVEMBER 1963 1'6
DISCS
TOPLAY
lement on THE GROUPS
full colour portrait.
ACEMAKERS—
DREAMERS
HE JAYWALKERS
THE BEATLES
LITTLE LESS SWIM SUIT
OFFER
Romeo
BEATLES
DEC. 21, 1963 EVERY TUESDAY 6d
ONE NIGHT STAND
TOMMY TOMS
PAULI
THE DAY THE beatles CAME TO TOWN
see page 4

JANUARY 63

1 The Beatles fly from Hamburg, Germany, to London Airport.

2 At the start of a five-day tour of Scotland, The Beatles fly out from London, but their plane is diverted from Edinburgh to Aberdeen because of bad weather. Their show at the Longmore Hall, Keith, Banffshire is cancelled.

3 The band kick off their tour at the Two Red Shoes Ballroom, Elgin, Scotland.

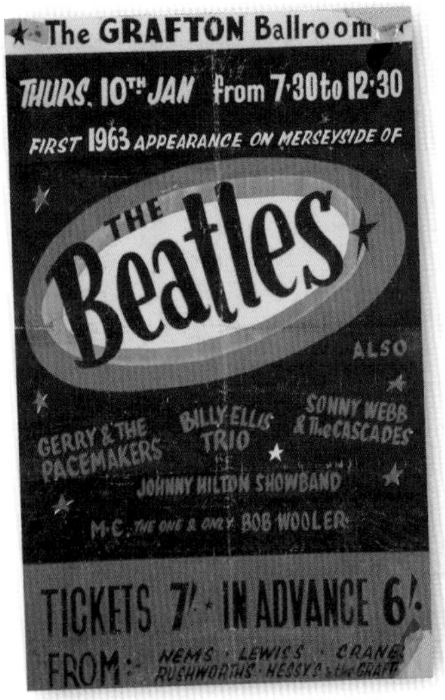

10 The band return to Liverpool for a show at the Grafton Rooms (above).

11 The second single, Please Please Me/Ask Me Why, is released in the UK. On the same day, The Beatles play a lunchtime show at The Cavern, followed by an evening gig at the Plaza Ballroom, Old Hill, Staffordshire.

12 A show at the Invicta Ballroom, Chatham, Kent.

13 A performance of Please Please Me is recorded for ABC/ITV show Thank Your Lucky Stars at Alpha Television Studios, Birmingham.

16 The band appear live on the TV show People And Places at the Granada TV Centre, Manchester.

17 The Beatles play a lunchtime show at The Cavern, then at the Majestic Ballroom, Birkenhead, in the evening.

19 Thank Your Lucky Stars' broadcast of Please Please Me gives The Beatles their first national UK TV exposure.

21 An appearance is recorded for Radio Luxembourg show The Friday Spectacular, at EMI House, London.

22 Five songs are recorded for the BBC radio show Saturday Club at the Playhouse Theatre, London.

24 A show at the Assembly Hall, Mold, Flintshire.

25 Brian Epstein signs a contract with Vee-Jay Records to release Beatles recordings in the US.

26 The Beatles play the El Rio Club, Macclesfield, followed by another at King's Hall, Stoke-on-Trent.

27 A show at the Three Coins Club, Fountain Street, Manchester.

28 The Beatles play the Majestic Ballroom, Newcastle-upon-Tyne.

FEBRUARY 63

1 They play the Assembly Rooms, Tamworth, followed by Maney Hall, Sutton Coldfield, Warwickshire.

2 Helen Shapiro opens her UK tour at The Gaumont Theatre, Bradford, with The Beatles among the supporting acts.

4 The Beatles play their last lunchtime session at The Cavern.

5 The Helen Shapiro tour continues at the Gaumont Theatre, Doncaster.

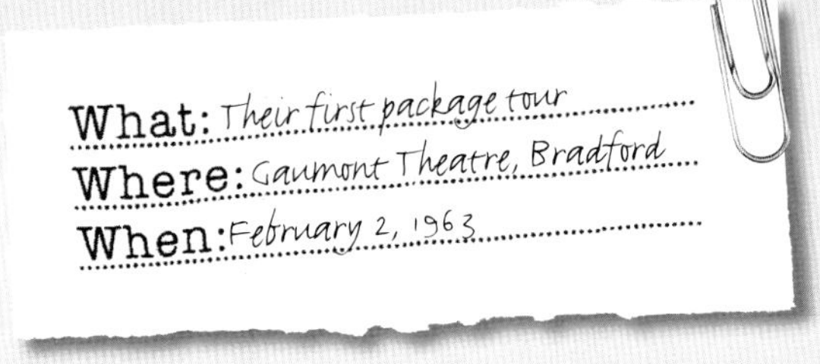

NICE PACKAGE!

The Beatles began 1963 playing support on a series of national tours. But before long they were outshining the star acts. By Johnny Black.

Although the rock'n'roll industry had yet to see out its first decade, by the time The Beatles began attracting national attention with Love Me Do, there was already a recognisable career development structure in place. It was, essentially, a ladder whose lowest rung was the poorly paid local club gig and whose giddiest height – in a world where stadium rock was yet to be invented – was topping the bill at The London Palladium.

In between lay the package tours, the seaside summer seasons and, given that rock was clearly just a passing phenomenon, the inevitable shift into the grown-up world of cabaret. On February 2, 1963, The Beatles took their first step up the ladder that would lead them away from The Cavern, when they joined headliner Helen Shapiro as the humble opening act on a month-long package tour, setting off from the Gaumont Theatre, Bradford, along with Danny Williams, Kenny Lynch, The Honeys, The Kestrels, the Red Price Orchestra and, as MC, comedian Dave Allen.

"Beatlemania hadn't really started," remembers Tony Bramwell, their assistant roadie. "The only change in their act was that they were doing less numbers in their slot than they'd normally do in a full night's gig, and they bowed at the end of each song, which was something Brian Epstein had suggested."

Having been big fish in the small pools of Liverpool and Hamburg, they now found themselves back at the bottom of the feeding chain. "Helen was the star," Ringo recalled later. "She had the telly in her dressing room and we didn't have one. We had to ask her if we could watch hers."

A seasoned pro, Shapiro noticed how quickly the Northerners adjusted. "I watched them adapt themselves and polish up their act – refining the songs in the set and turning the volume down. Not too much polish though – I was glad that they kept some rawness."

Kenny Lynch, for his part, recalls one memorable innovation that they introduced during that tour. "I remember John and Paul saying they were thinking of running up to the microphone together and shaking their heads and singing, 'Whoooo!'. I said, You can't do that. They'll think you're a bunch of poofs!"

On February 22, Please Please Me hit Number 1 on the British charts and, by the end of the tour on March 3, The Beatles had been promoted to a more prestigious slot – closing the first half. It was a move that set a precedent for every subsequent package tour on which they appeared.

Barely pausing to draw breath, The Beatles lurched into another package on the 9th, headlined this time by visiting US stars Tommy Roe and Chris Montez, plus homegrown attractions The Viscounts, Debbie Lee, Tony Marsh and The Terry Young Six. Bramwell remembers these as "the best shows The Beatles ever played. They were at their peak as a performing band and you could actually see and hear them. The intense, prolonged screaming hadn't really started, but Beatlemania was getting under way, and I think the Americans were quite baffled by them."

Like Shapiro, Chris Montez soon realised he was facing stiff competition. "They would get the show going and I would close the show. I would watch them every night and they had such energy and power."

In Liverpool, on the 24th, his co-star Roe acknowledged the inevitable. "I said, This is your town, you close the show, I'm not the headliner here. They were impressed that I went on before them."

After that night, The Beatles headlined every date. "It was embarrassing as hell for him *[Montez]*," admitted McCartney subsequently, "I mean, what could you say to him? Sorry, Chris? He took it well."

On May 18, The Beatles faced their biggest package challenge yet, the start of a tour supporting Roy Orbison, a bona fide rock'n'roll pioneer, admired and respected by them all. "He'd slay them and they'd scream for more," says Ringo. "In Glasgow, we were all backstage, listening to the tremendous applause he was getting. He was just standing there, singing, not moving or anything. As it got near our turn, we would hide behind the curtain whispering to each other – 'Guess who's next folks, your favourite rave'. But once we got on the stage, it was always OK."

"Having been big fish in Liverpool and Hamburg, The Beatles were now at the bottom of the feeding chain."

Sufficiently OK, in fact, that once again The Beatles leap-frogged the headliner and were soon closing the show. "They could, by this time, have actually earned more by doing individual one-nighters," points out Bramwell, "but the exposure of a package tour was very valuable to them."

Their fourth and last package outing, starting on November 1 at the Cheltenham Odeon, was titled The Beatles' Autumn Tour, with support acts including Peter Jay And The Jaywalkers and The Brook Brothers.

With The Beatles empire expanding daily, Bramwell was by now promoted to admin at Brian Epstein's NEMS organisation, but he still got out to see the boys every Friday. "I'd drive out from Liverpool and take them their wages in a little envelope with a blue Kalamazoo wages slip inside. They were earning £300 a night, but much of that was swallowed up in administration and touring costs, so they ended up with £50 each, pretty good money at the time." In the space of one year, The Beatles had reached the top of the package tour tree, and would never again play second fiddle to anybody.

PHOTOS: REDFERNS

"Imagine John, your band's even bigger than Kenny Lynch!" Helen Shapiro grabs a quick dance with the support act.

The Immaculate Inception

Please Please Me didn't just launch the Fabs' album career – it started a new era and created a phenomenon. Richard Williams examines the 14 songs that helped change popular music.

For a generation then in its teens, *Please Please Me* provided an introduction to the world of the long-playing record, and the first taste of a long-playing addiction. Before that time the world had revolved at 45rpm. Older brothers and sisters might have had a wire rack next to the Dansette, holding copies of *Ella Sings Gershwin*, the *West Side Story Soundtrack*, *Chris Barber Bandbox Vol 1*, perhaps Bill Haley's *Rock Around The Clock* LP; but at the beginning of the '60s proper, 12-inch LPs were usually beyond the means of the demographic group that would become the most economically powerful the world had ever known. By the time *Please Please Me* came around, however, teen spending power had reached critical mass and was ready to explode.

It arrived in the shops on Friday, March 22, 1963, just as the sales of the single from which it took its name were starting to tail off. Five and a half months earlier Love Me Do had edged into the Top 20, giving no indication that a phenomenon was being born. But as winter gave way to spring, Beatlemania took shape. And whatever the Tin Pan Alley machinations that may or may not have assisted its launch, in youth clubs and bedrooms around the nation the acceptance was practically instantaneous, virtually unanimous and entirely organic. An appetite had been created, and now a 14-song LP arrived to satisfy it.

"In youth clubs and bedrooms around the country, the acceptance was instantaneous and virtually unanimous."

Not that it offered any revolutionary new formula. Those 14 songs were selected and sequenced to package the hits and demonstrate the versatility of these new artists. Superficially, the programme echoed the recipe – two hit singles plus quickly-recorded miscellaneous filler material – which had already become the conventional way to exploit the potentially short-lived success of new chart stars. If one factor marked it out, it was the inclusion of eight original songs by John Lennon and Paul McCartney. What this album was doing, although no-one yet knew it, was announcing the arrival of the age of the self-contained group whose members created their own material. The addition of six cover versions reflected not only the composition of their stage act but probably an uncertainty at A&R level over the ability of their songwriting talent to sustain a whole LP (albeit one that contained only 32 minutes of music).

But even when you saw it in the shop window, there was something different about it, just as there had been something different about the sound of the harmonica on Love Me Do or even the very name "Beatles", and it was a quality that seemed to come from somewhere other than the processed world of the pop music industry. The cover photograph, taken by Angus McBean in the stairwell of the foyer at EMI's headquarters in Manchester Square, set the mood: the clues were in the jaunty expressions, the pink tab-collar shirts, and most of all the hair combed forward (although Ringo still had the vestige of a quiff). The environment of a post-war block seemed modern and informal and definitely unshowbizzy. The four musicians looked like cheeky office juniors, not at all the smouldering Elvis wannabes turned out by the star-making factories of Larry Parnes and Joe Meek.

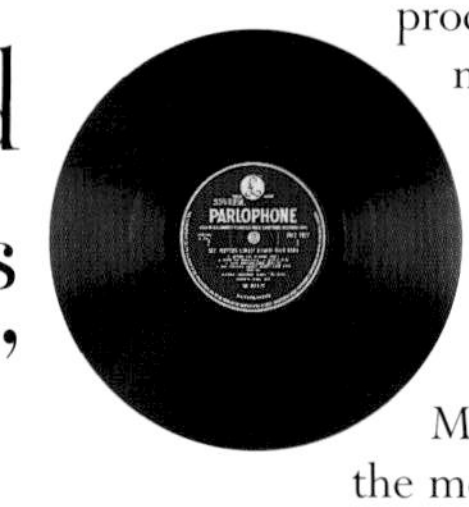

The first of George Martin's brilliant production decisions on behalf of The Beatles was to allow their debut album to open with the hoarse shout of "One-two-three-FOUR" that announced I Saw Her Standing There – as dramatic an introduction as the

PHOTO: CAMERA PRESS

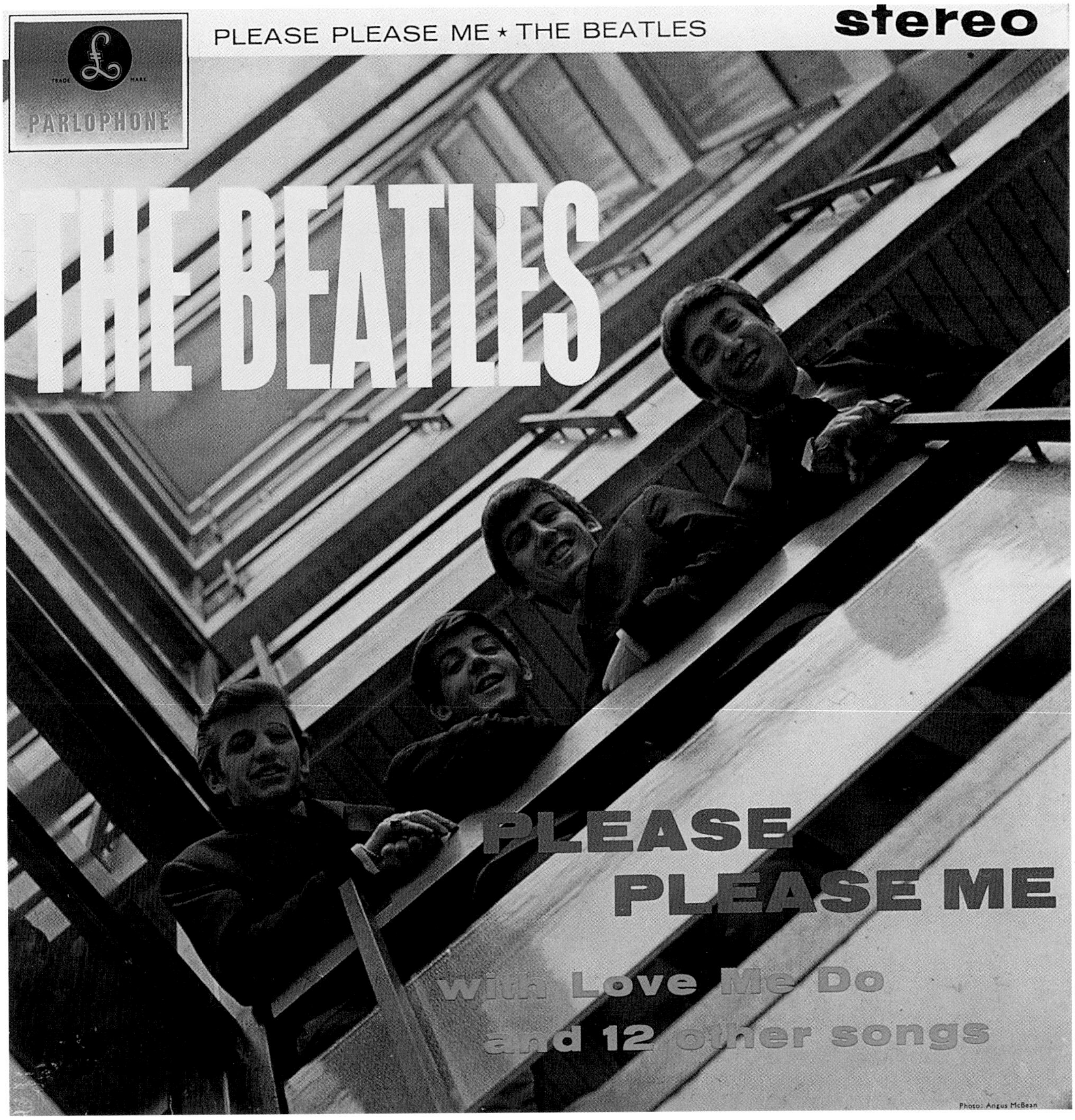

"Well it's a-one for the money, two for the show, three to get ready and go, cat, go!" with which Elvis had opened his own first album seven years earlier. Their new audience was only beginning to learn about their background, but at once, whether Martin intended it that way or not, the world knew that The Beatles were a real performing band.

No less significant, in the opening seconds of the opening track, was the tone of John Lennon's high-slung, low-riding rhythm guitar. Recorded flat (no echo) and played with tightly focused energy but without inflection or affectation, it became the signature sound of the whole beat boom.

Bursting with kinetic energy, I Saw Her Standing There got the album off to an exhilarating start. Written in 20 minutes by John and Paul several years earlier on an afternoon stolen from school, it sounded like the product of a band that had already

TRACK LISTING

A-SIDE

1. I Saw Her Standing There
Lennon/McCartney
Sung by McCartney

2. Misery
Lennon/McCartney
Sung by Lennon & McCartney

3. Anna (Go To Him)
Alexander
Sung by Lennon

4. Chains
Goffin/King
Sung by Lennon, McCartney & Harrison

5. Boys
Dixon/Farrell
Sung by Starr

6. Ask Me Why
Lennon/McCartney
Sung by Lennon

7. Please Please Me
Lennon/McCartney
Sung by Lennon

B-SIDE

8. Love Me Do
Lennon/McCartney
Sung by McCartney

9. P.S. I Love You
Lennon/McCartney
Sung by McCartney

10. Baby It's You
Bacharach/David/Williams
Sung by Lennon

11. Do You Want To Know A Secret
Lennon/McCartney
Sung by Harrison

12. A Taste Of Honey
Marlow/Scott
Sung by McCartney

13. There's A Place
Lennon/McCartney
Sung by Lennon

14. Twist And Shout
Medley/Russell
Sung by Lennon

PLEASE PLEASE ME

WHAT THE PAPERS SAID...

Please Please Me "whipped up a storm" in 1963.

"Fourteen exciting tracks, with the vocal instrumental drive that has put this Liverpool group way up on top. Please Please Me and Love Me Do are well known, but there are 12 other thrillers, including John Lennon's singing of a torrid Twist And Shout; Boys, with drummer Ringo Starr shining; and a pippin of a duet of Misery by John and Paul McCartney."

Allen Evans, NME, April 5, 1963

"I Saw Her Standing There is one of the fastest things the boys have ever recorded. Typical bluesy backing on the rather wistful type number that is good enough to be a single. Loud and long – the fans can go mad to this. Boys has some great instrumental stuff – the singer this time being drummer Ringo, who probably has more genuine talent as a blues shouter than the others. There's A Place has a wistful flavour; not a standout track. Twist And Shout, a frantic R&B song, has the whole group whipping up a storm...

For a debut LP it's surprisingly good and up to standard – a goodly number of tracks on this could be issued as singles and maintain the boys' chart standard."

Norman Jopling, Record Mirror, March 30, 1963

NEW RECORD MIRROR, Week-ending March 30, 1963

GUESS WHAT!

The Beatles L.P. is called 'Please Please Me!'—Here's a review in depth . . .

TO date, the Beatles have had two disc releases. One was "Love Me Do", the other "Please Please Me". And now comes a third. In the shape of a rather bigger disc also entitled "Please Please Me". But this time there happens to be fourteen songs on it.

Including both sides of both singles — that still leaves ten new sides from the Beatles. So here in depth are ten reviews of ten new songs ... on the debut LP "Please Please Me".

I SAW HER STANDING THERE, penned by Paul McCartney and John Lennon, it's one of the fastest things the boys have recorded. Typical bluesy backing with the boys singing together on the rather wistful type number that is good enough to put out as a single. Loud and long — the fans can go mad to this one.

MISERY

MISERY. The number that the boys penned for Kenny Lynch — they've included on their LP. Lucky for Kenny they haven't issued it as a single. But seriously the boys take the plaintive tuneful number at a medium tempo pace — it's one of the best ballads on the disc and there's the usual distinctive group backing on it, plus the boys singing in the "Please Please Me" style.

ANNA (GO TO HIM). In the States lives a great exponent of Rhythm and Blues named Arthur Alexander. He wrote and recorded this number some months ago, and the Beatles take it at the same slow pace with a very unusual piano riff in the background, the same [illegible] Arthur employed. One lead voice this [illegible] — it's John Lennon. The boys [illegible] beautifully on the slow [illegible] which works out in a terribly atmospheric way.

CHAINS will be familiar to almost everyone. A hit in the States, and a minor one here for the Cookies. Sounds slightly unusual on the first play, when you hear a male vocal group singing it. Medium tempo, insistent and repetitive, exciting and tuneful. Good guitar work on the backing.

BOYS

BOYS. Faster beat, and some great instrumental stuff on this one, the flip to the Shirelles great hit "Will You Love Me Tomorrow". Very Ray Charles-ish it moves along at a fast pace, the lead singer this time being drummer Ringo who probably has more genuine talent as a blues shouter than the other members of the group. Exciting and stimulating with a polish that doesn't usually occur on LP material.

ASK ME WHY and PLEASE PLEASE ME will of course be familiar to everybody, as will be the first two tracks of side two — LOVE ME DO and P.S. I LOVE YOU.

The other tracks on side two are as follows:

BABY IT'S YOU is considered by many to be the best disc the Shirelles have made. Certainly I think it is and by the way the Beatles gently interpret it I should think they do too. It's a slowish ballad with perhaps more atmosphere than any other track on the LP. The boys "Sha-La-La" all the way through with John leading vocal, and it's a faithful copy of the original — they do it well enough not to spoil the enchantment of the song.

[illegible]ANT TO KNOW A[illegible]

SECRET is a medium tempo lilter with George Harrison on the lead voice and the others giving him a little choral support. An original composition it's tuneful and slightly off-beat. Not outstanding but pleasant enough.

A TASTE OF HONEY. Vocal version of the Acker Bilk hit first brought out vocally by Lenny Welch. Gentle and almost leaves a honey flavour in your mouth. The only [illegible] in this number — and it's Paul McCartney singing on his own. Gentle and sweet with a great tune, and a sympathetic backing.

PLACE

THERE'S A PLACE. Harmonica once more on this side. It's a typical type number with John and Paul singing on it. Rather a wistful flavour with a definite beat on the backing. Not a standout track but one with plenty of appeal.

TWIST AND SHOUT. Just as the disc begins with a fast number it ends with a frantic one. It's the Isley Brothers U.S. hit of last summer and is a frantic R & B song with plenty of opportunity for shouting and screaming. Fastish tempo, with the whole group doing a power of work whipping up a storm on the commercial blues number both vocally and instrumentally.

That's the lot then. If you own this LP you'll own all the Beatles discs [illegible] date. And for a debut LP it's surp[illegible] good' and up to standard — [illegible] goodly number of the tracks on [illegible] could be issued as singles and mai[illegible] the boys' chart standard. A good [illegible] and excellent sleeve notes [illegible] a worthwhile LP in all [illegible] word.

[illegible]RMAN

SLEEVE NOTES

The music was great, but the cover was "crap", reckoned George.

The Beatles' debut album may have heralded an exciting musical revolution, remaining at the top of the album charts for a remarkable 30 weeks, but the sleeve artwork certainly did not. The information listed on the sleeve – the title of the LP, unimaginatively taken from The Beatles' first Number 1 hit single, the inclusion of their debut 45 Love Me Do plus the byline "and 12 other songs" – was given equal precedence to the photograph of the band pictured on the front.

As for what the band should actually be doing on the cover, well no-one could quite decide. Brian Epstein wanted to go with photographer Dezo Hoffman's wacky shot of the quartet goofing around outside Abbey Road studios, while George Martin had an entirely different idea. "I was a fellow of London Zoo and, rather stupidly, thought that it would be a great idea to have The Beatles photographed outside the insect house," he recalls in Mark Lewisohn's The Recording Sessions. "But the people from London Zoo were very stuffy indeed and decided against it. I bet they regret their decision now."

In the end, Angus McBean, a talented theatrical photographer, was hired to shoot the band. The photograph was taken from below, with The Beatles looking out from the EMI headquarters balcony in London's Manchester Square. While George Harrison was none too impressed with the results – he declared the sleeve "crap" – it pulled the right strings with John Lennon, who invited McBean back to the scene six years later to repeat the session. Originally planned as the cover for the band's then proposed *Get Back* album (which later developed into *Let It Be*), the session was finally utilised on the covers of the 'red' and 'blue' compilations, *The Beatles 1962-66* and *1967-70*, released in 1973.

Lois Wilson

"The four musicians on the cover looked more like cheeky office juniors than the usual Elvis wannabes."

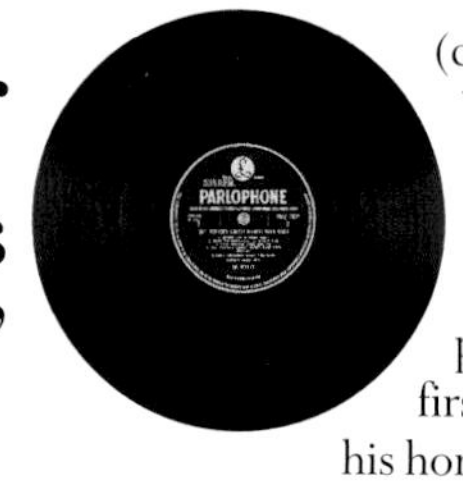

found its groove and its voice. From Paul's rockaboogie bassline to his falsetto screams, it formed a rock'n'roll manifesto that was immediately contradicted by Misery, another original, with its out-of-tempo introduction and its rather formal piano figures (overdubbed by George Martin several days after the original session). But, as we were to learn, The Beatles could be relied on not to do the obvious.

Anna (Go To Him), a perfectly respectable cover of the Arthur Alexander song, stated their R&B credentials for the first time. In Liverpool and Hamburg they had been listening to the new sounds from Detroit, Chicago and New York – to the embryos of soul music, and to the girl groups. From The Cookies they borrowed the next track, Carole King and Gerry Goffin's loping Chains, and from The Shirelles they took the sweet Baby It's You, an early Bacharach and David song (co-written with Barney Williams), and Boys, the B-side of Will You Love Me Tomorrow, a raucous rocker which provided Ringo with the first of many showcases for his homespun vocals.

In an interview with Mark Lewisohn, McCartney once pointed out that their early songs were written as if directly to their fans: the consistent use of personal pronouns – "you", "me", "I" – was another factor in their unusually direct appeal to a new generation of girl fans. Confirming his perception, and lying at the heart of the album, are the two singles, along with their respective B-sides, Ask Me Why and P.S. I Love You, a pair of melodic ballads gently propelled by the kind of watered-down Latin rhythms then almost ubiquitous in pop music. McCartney's lead vocal on P.S. I Love You is impressively poised and polished, particularly his little improvised asides between the lines of the last verse. John's lead on the subsequent Baby It's You lacks Paul's precision but has a rougher, more genuinely soulful edge.

George Harrison makes his slightly wobbly singing debut

Well pleased: The Beatles and George Martin – at the album launch, April 5, 1963 – receive their first silver disc for the Please Please Me single.

on Do You Want To Know A Secret, a workmanlike pop tune destined to propel Billy J Kramer And The Dakotas, fellow protégés of Brian Epstein, towards their big moment in the spotlight. McCartney's romantic side returns to the fore in A Taste Of Honey, a heavily echoed ballad on which they switch back and forth between waltz-time and a jazzy 4/4 without any apparent discomfort.

When John and Paul wrote There's A Place, they must have heard a hit single in the making. How easy would it have been to release this 1-minute 49 second beat-music template, with its keening Everlys-style harmonies and jolting triplets from Ringo's drums, as the follow-up to Please Please Me? But then She Loves You came along, with the "yeah yeah yeah" hook that somehow defined the whole of Beatlemania.

But, as they were often to do in the future, they saved the most significant and exhilarating moment for the very end of the album. Twist And Shout, a song borrowed from The Isley Brothers, had virtually become their theme song at The Cavern. A simple variation on the immortal three-chord formula of La Bamba and a thousand other songs, with a lead vocal delivered by a hoarse Lennon at the end of a long day, its extended screaming crescendos became for millions the soundtrack to their very first rave-up.

PHOTO: HULTON ARCHIVE

FIRST LOVE

Lemmy pays tribute to *Please Please Me*, the album that got him hooked on rock'n'roll.

"The first band I ever saw was The Beatles at The Cavern when I was 16. They were fuckin' wild. It was mad. I lived in Anglesey and this girl from Liverpool was staying on her holidays and drew a beetle with six legs on my garage wall. I didn't have a clue what she was up to. That was the first time I had ever heard of them. She played me them and I thought they were fantastic. They were a revolution. All we'd had then was Bobby Darin, Perry Como and Frankie Avalon so when they came along it was just so very exciting. It was something I understood.

"When they played live there were screaming girls pissing themselves at the sight of them. They were seen as very rebellious at the time. My parents hated them. They really didn't approve of me listening to their music and playing my guitar. We lived on a farm and they made me practise in the barn. At least I was allowed a guitar I suppose.

"I'd play along to *Please Please Me*, working out the chords. I stole my attitude from them too. John was my favourite. He was the most bastard of them all. The most sarcastic. I'm a great fan of sarcasm and he most definitely had it. *Please Please Me* has the best tracks on it – Twist And Shout is pure rock'n'roll, Anna, Baby It's You, Boys is hilarious. Would I ever consider covering The Beatles? No, I couldn't make their songs sound any better, so why bother?"

Lois Wilson

I wanna be your Fan

Even when it came to their fans The Beatles proved to be something new. Mark Lewisohn charts the amazing rise of Beatlemania.

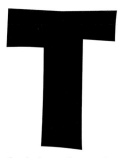

The images persist: four guys in suits or smart raincoats being chased by hundreds of fans, girls frenzied at their merest glimpse, sloping Bobbies – arms-linked, teeth-gritted, straining to hold back the throng, heels dug as deep as the grins on their faces; John with a black comb for Hitler's moustache, sieg-heiling to the massed crowds.

Beatlemania is a collective global warming 40 years and counting. Social commentators were baffled and psychologists waffled out half-baked rationale: "The girls are subconsciously preparing for motherhood; their frenzied screams are a rehearsal for that moment," one analyst helpfully informed the News Of The World. To this day, Beatlemania remains a slippery subject, hard to pin down and not much easier to explain. But its history, at least, is clearer, and no less exciting.

Beatlemania – the word – was the invention of the (then still Fleet Street-based) national press, and they certainly found the subject an inexhaustible source of fun and good humour. Yet Beatlemania itself was no media gadget, no record company hype, no Popstars. British teenagers were not stirred to fever pitch by hyperbole. This was a natural phenomenon, an all too rare – unique apart from Elvis – coincidence of a particular talent striking the people in its purest form. While the press revelled in rather than reviled it, the public also wanted Beatlemania.

There were lots of groups around in 1963 and yet it wasn't Brian Poole And The Tremeloesmania. The Beatles had the complete package: a kaleidoscope of attraction that included good looks, uplifting songs, a great 'sound' (to use the vernacular of the day), inquisitive, intelligent and unfettered minds, wit, impudence, arrogance, indomitable personalities and an extraordinary, innate ability to play the media. And on top of this heady brew was the miracle that none – scarcely the fans yet and certainly not Fleet Street – could foresee: The Beatles had a genius for timing and an instinctive ability to surprise and be ruthlessly original.

Mass adulation wasn't new. A once popular British humorist, Gale Pedrick, wrote in 1957, "Fan-worship in its nastier form – hysteria, mob frenzy and utter lack of good taste – is completely foreign to Britain's traditional sang-froid... [and] it is all the more remarkable that we started it."

The romantic actor-manager Lewis Waller had a fan club in the early 1900s, after which film stars Rudolf Valentino, Ramon Novarro and Carl Brisson had invoked screams in the 1920s and singers Johnnie Ray and Frank Sinatra likewise in the 1950s. After 1957 came rock'n'roll, which rejuvenated idolising – many girls had screamed at Cliff Richard since Move It and some even screamed quite a bit at Jess Conrad, whose attributes may well have been extensive but they ran some way short of spot-on tuneful singing. Such idols were marketed as movie stars by the ageing Variety/showbiz establishment, which ran the British music business until late into the 1960s.

For The Beatles, a form of genuine mania was present long before the nation knew them. Some (though, not all) of those who witnessed their December 27, 1960 performance at Litherland Town Hall, claim that Beatlemania was born that night, when this band of unknown locals mostly from the south of the city – John, Paul, George, Pete and the temporary and much overlooked Chas (Newby) – unleashed their Hamburg know-how on an unsuspecting crowd of drainpiped and creped North Liverpool jivers. It is said there was a sudden, mad rush to the front of the hall, with screaming.

Over the next two years The Beatles continued to attract a local reception which was certainly an embryonic Beatlemania. As early as August 1961 the sagely and articulate Bob Wooler – DJ at The Cavern and several other venues – wrote an article in Mersey Beat expressing his gratitude at "the opportunities of presenting them to fever-pitch audiences". The Beatles were "the stuff that screams are made of," Wooler declared.

In 1963, with interest in The Beatles spread by the rather curious, ear-grabbing Love Me Do and by hundreds of gigs planned by Brian Epstein in an ever-wider sweep beyond Lancashire, the same picture emerged on the national canvas. Fleet Street editors didn't cotton on until the autumn – they were actually *well* late – yet some perceptive individuals were quick off the mark. The first important piece of journalism

"For The Beatles, a form of genuine mania was present long before the nation knew them."

about The Beatles was an article by Maureen Cleave published in the London Evening Standard. Based on an interview conducted on January 10 or 11 (Please Please Me was released on the 11th) it was titled 'Why The Beatles create all that frenzy'.

Just under two weeks later, on January 22, The Beatles hosted a press round-robin in between and after recording lunchtime, afternoon and evening BBC radio shows in London. Writing in the Peter Cook-funded arts magazine Scene, Gordon Williams remarked on how "The little girls cheer The Beatles in a frantic way", and added, "...outside, a hundred or so of the same infants try to tear the door off the taxi in which the four boys are going to travel to a West End hotel to have some more interviews."

Williams also noted that Brian Epstein, "hears the screaming of the assembled infantitude and agrees that owning The Beatles does, indeed, feel something like sitting on a bomb which will soon go off in a mushroom of money."

The adulation gathered pace solidly through the spring of 1963. Please Please Me hit Number 2 and in April they had their first Number 1 with From Me To You. The Beatles did a score of press interviews and photo-shoots when they had a spare couple of hours, which wasn't often: from January to April they appeared in 12 TV shows, 16 live and recorded radio sessions, cut their debut album and second Number 1 single, and performed 95 gigs; on the few dates in between the nationwide, nightly package tours with Helen Shapiro, Tommy Roe/Chris Montez and Roy Orbison, Brian Epstein had them booked into ballrooms from Southsea to Sunderland.

"Fantastic. I've never known anything like it." That was the verdict of Ron Stoten, harassed manager of the State ballroom, Kilburn, on Tuesday evening. He had spent an exhausting evening trying to hold back hundreds of hysterical teenagers who had flocked to see (and hear) the fabulous Beatles.

Kilburn Times (headline: Screaming Teenagers Flock To Hear The Beatles), April 1963

Beatlemania was underway. Ironically, after the twist boom had peaked and Chubby Checker lay panting in the wings, The Beatles had wondered what the next pop fad would be. Latin-beat, perhaps? Calypso-rock? They hadn't imagined that they would be it, let alone that in their wake a shipload of their Liverpool mates would suddenly be dominating the charts. On the BBC Top 20, unveiled to an eager teen nation from four until five o'clock every Sunday afternoon in Pick Of The Pops, British acts accounted for the Number 1 spot in all 52 weeks in 1963. In the second half of the year, Liverpool groups spent five months at the top. The Beatles own tally for 1963 was 18 weeks at Number 1, more than a third of the year.

If Beatlemania surprised The Beatles, and they often said it did, they took it fully in their stride. As George revealed in the Anthology book, sex was at least one of the bonuses. "We would pull

PHOTOS: REX FEATURES/HULTON ARCHIVE/TERRY SPENCER/CAMERA PRESS

The Beatles for sale: the new wave of mania was a merchandising godsend for Britain and America.

up at the gig and run through them [the girls] to the stage door. And if you could quickly suss out the ones who looked half decent you could push them in through the door with you, slam it behind, and then they'd come up to the room…"

> **"Around 50 hysterical girls were carried backstage, where they lay dazed after fainting… the girls, many of whom were shaking from head to toe and crying, were laid on the floor. It looked like a battlefield. It is a sight I never want to see again."**
> *Nelson Leader (headline: Beatles On The Battlefield), May 1963*

It wasn't too long before the mania began to infringe The Beatles' personal freedom. For ever-dependable aide and roadie Neil Aspinall, Beatlemania was certainly a right pain in the backside. Hassled to hell as he laboured to offload equipment out of the van and into the halls, then hassled to hell again afterwards and thwarted in his speedy getaway attempts by deflated tyres (one up for the girls) and souvenir-hunted windscreen wipers that would anyway have merely smeared the tableau of lipsticked love messages.

> **Rock Boys Flee Screaming Mob As Teenagers Go Wild**
> *Romford Times headline, June 1963*

> **Girl Bites Steward At Leeds Dance**
> *Yorkshire Evening News headline, June 1963*

Beatlemania got The Beatles into some very unusual scrapes, and they enjoyed quite an interest surveying the madness around them ("You could make a film, just showing how idiotic everybody else was whenever The Beatles came to town" – George in Anthology again) yet they were also maddened when the sound of screaming began to obscure the sound of music. Coinciding as this did with a sudden slashing of their stage time – from what had been, at one extreme, six hours a night in Hamburg, to 10 or 15 or 20 minutes twice-nightly on the package tours, "a snack instead of a meal," John once described it – dissatisfaction with live performances quickly set in. Ballrooms were the last place where punters would have seen The Beatles play for anything like a decent amount of time, usually two half-hour sets in an evening, but with the riotous scenes at such gigs Epstein quickly realised The Beatles' lives were in danger and no longer booked ballrooms. From autumn 1963 until their last tour date in December 1965, The Beatles only played in Britain in theatres or cinemas with stages.

> **"I suddenly realised why pop records sell so well. The fans buy them so they can listen to the words at home, then they know where to scream when they see their idols on the stage."**
> *Bournemouth Evening Echo, August 1963*

If Beatlemania was cooking in the summer of 1963, then She Loves You brought it to the boil. The Beatles had introduced the Little Richard-inspired "Oooooh" into From Me To You, then noticed that when they sang it and shook their heads the girls went absolutely wild; repeating the phrase in She Loves You provided a sense of continuity even though the song dispensed with the harmonica sound that had hallmarked Love Me Do, Please Please Me and From Me To You. Moreover, the "yeah yeah yeah" lyric – an inspired blend of postwar urban British chic and glamorously appealing Americana – immediately became a catchphrase for the young, every bit as much as their elders (betters?) had their music hall, radio and TV heroes' catchphrases.

Released two weeks before schools went back, the summer holidays over, She Loves You thumped straight into the BBC chart at Number 7 and then leapt to Number 1 a week later. As sales proceeded to go through the roof the British music business was agog. Record companies, record distributors, record shops, music publishers and their army of pluggers, sheet music salesmen, club owners, managers, agents, promoters – everyone was suddenly winning; pop music had come alive.

British popular culture, groundbreaking (and no longer necessarily so good-natured) satire, a thriving pop art movement, and a cultural drift northwards with Look Back In Anger, A Taste Of Honey and Coronation Street, now let loose. A generation of postwar children, raised on rationing, kept healthy by free school milk and the socialist National Health Service, educated at state-funded schools and colleges of art and liberated by the abolition of national service, had money to splash and a strong (albeit still mostly unspoken) desire to live life more fully than their parents. Record sales had already been steadily increasing, from a spend of £15m in 1960 to £17.4m in 1962: the people wanted to buy. And it all took off with She Loves You. Stuck in the 1930s for 30 years, Britain came roaring up to speed in the few seconds it took John Lennon, Paul McCartney and George Harrison to harmonise "yeah yeah yeah".

Such was the timing, and the dynamic impact, The Beatles quickly began to permeate even establishment bastions, whose then-sniffy attitude to pop had always been in absolute contrast to their complete embracing of it today. On September 12, the BBC's still rather august listings journal Radio Times printed an exclusive full-page photo of The Beatles in its weekly series Portrait Gallery. Readers were invited to send a two-shilling postal-order in return for which they would receive a glossy print. The usual take-up was around 10,000; more than 250,000 applications deluged the magazine's office.

The mayhem at the gigs, the fantastic record sales, the surge in all-round interest – the head of steam was ever building... and it was at this point that Fleet Street jumped on board. Newspapermen too loved the ride – it did wonders for circulation – and the immortal word Beatlemania was born. Suddenly, a trendy vicar of the kind spoofed in Beyond The Fringe wanted them to sing Oh Come All Ye Faithful Yeah Yeah Yeah as a Christmas carol; parents – suddenly definable as old fogies or trendy – were either pleased or furious that headmasters were sending boys home for sporting "long Beatles hair"; there were questions in Parliament about the cost of The Beatles' police protection; they were the subject of TV, radio and night club comedy sketches and songs; a Beatles ballet was announced for the West End; their first feature-film contract was sealed, as was the BBC's plan to devote an hour of prime-time television to them in December; and Conservative MP Anthony Barber – later the Chancellor of the Exchequer – became the first politician of the modern era to shove his progeny (his Beatles-mad daughter Josephine) into the limelight in order to court publicity. Newspapers ran all these and more daily good-time stories. Screaming girls, struggling policemen, a constable's helmet rolling on the floor: "It's those Beatles again!" When they returned to London from a week's tour of Sweden and faced their first 'airport reception' the BBC Home Service sent along a news journalist to report on the cheerful mayhem, Reg Abbiss shouting in stentorian tones, "What confusion here!"

Hindsight has revealed that Fleet Street was not going to spoil the fun. Although continuously hungry for Beatles stories – they quickly found and splashed the Beatle Wife, the Beatle Child, the arty Dead Beatle and the Dumped Ex-Beatle Drummer – they unanimously failed to remind readers that, as recently as June, John had beaten up Bob Wooler at Paul's 21st birthday party. The story had made the Daily Mirror at the time but this was before the press's Beatlemania bandwagon had begun to roll. The Mirror's piece would have been topmost in any Beatles cuttings file in Fleet Street and beyond; a Beatle had committed grievous bodily harm to a long-time acquaintance and supporter – a headline of this nature could have damaged The Beatles severely. But the papers held off; they would only begin to get nasty when The Beatles began transgressing their unwritten laws. And still Beatlemania escalated. Sunday Night At The London Palladium gave The Beatles blanket headlines for days, the Royal Variety Show even more. These and the daily scream stories from around the country then combined to produce the single most phenomenal moment in the rise of the British music industry: She Loves You shot back to Number 1 at the end of November. It had spent five weeks at the summit in September and then held firm at 3, 3, 3, 2, 2 and 2. Now it returned to the top. The Beatles were still adding scores of thousands of new fans every week – She Loves You had already sold an industry-boggling three-quarters of a million before these fresh converts were pushing it into seven figures. And at this very moment, just four weeks before Christmas, with everyone connected to the music and relevant retail industries already lying prone in paroxysms of unimaginable delight, EMI pulled the trigger and released I Want To Hold Your Hand to over a million advance orders.

And then it was bloody pandemonium. People said they'd "never seen the like" and they hadn't. In Britain, The Beatles, if not yet bigger than Jesus, were already bigger than Elvis.

The Beatles' Autumn Tour – 68 shows at 34 nationwide venues in November and December,

"One trendy vicar wanted the band to sing O Come All Ye Faithful Yeah Yeah Yeah."

No, not even Cliff Richard could match this: The Beatles slay Vancouver, August 1964.

their fee £300 a night – was the pinnacle of British Beatlemania. The screaming, the fainting, the drama, the disguises, the getaways – here was a media orgy for all-comers.

The Beatles Come To Town, the eight-minute Pathé colour newsreel (*newsreel!*) shot at the ABC Cinema in Ardwick, Manchester on November 20, is the primary relic of the period. Although garish and oddly and poorly shot, with some very close close-ups, the excitement remains almost touchable.

The year ended with, as the London Evening Standard reported in a special supplement, the word Beatles "engraved upon the heart of the nation", and The Times breaking ground with its first serious journalistic take on pop music, a critic's article praising the freshness and excellence of songwriters Lennon-McCartney – a piece that the pair loved to send up. In 1963, The Beatles had gone from a beat-up van to an Austin Princess, and revolutionised British popular culture in the space of three singles. The cinema venues (and undeveloped British music industry) prevented them from being a stadium act in their home country but The Beatles Christmas Show – at the Finsbury Park Astoria from December 24 to January 11, 1964 – was an equivalent: The Beatles played to 70,000, but it took 30 performances over 16 nights to do it.

"In Britain, The Beatles, if not yet bigger than Jesus, were already bigger than Elvis."

Had The Beatles story ended here they may still be in the history books, though only the British ones. But Beatlemania went on to become a worldwide love affair. In January 1964, while – pfouf! – the French held out against embracing Les Beatles, and Fleet Street temporarily and unintelligently picked at the fabric by suggesting that The Dave Clark Five had stolen their mantle ("the Tottenham sound crushes the Liverpool sound"), America capitulated in about four weeks. This was the clincher.

It is often said that The Beatles were the first British act to break into America. This is factually wrong (Vera Lynn, Eddie Calvert, Lonnie Donegan, Laurie London, The Tornados) but actually right. These people had enjoyed freak hits; Cliff Richard, meanwhile, had the humbling American experience of being booked a long way down the bill on a January/February 1960 Frankie Avalon and Freddie Cannon tour, the quaint 'British rock'n'roll star'.

Paul McCartney says The Beatles informed Brian Epstein they wouldn't subject themselves to such ignominy. But such resolve never had to be tested: I Want To Hold Your Hand flew virtually straight to Number 1 on all the US charts – Billboard, Cashbox and Record World – and was in every sense to America in 1964 what She Loves You had been to Britain in 1963.

The arrival of Beatlemania US-style had been assisted by a tremendous run of coincidences. I Want To Hold Your Hand was still selling dynamically when the group arrived in New York to appear on The Ed Sullivan Show, booked long before the record's release. The band were backed by a Capitol Records publicity blitz, a campaign that saw The Beatles truly hyped for the first time. And the breakthrough was perhaps assisted by the nation's quest for good cheer in the aftermath of Kennedy's assassination only two months earlier. (Some say this is psychobabble but it does make sense.)

All the same, it was The Beatles everyone wanted, and they did not flinch. Their handling of the first American press conference was consummate: articulate and witty Beatles in best switched-on bright and breezy mode. So the American press went along with the fun just as Fleet Street had done.

After this, Beatlemania is more or less down to statistics. The biggest gigs were in America, Shea Stadium setting a world record, the most rigorous policing was in Japan, the biggest trouble was in the Philippines and the biggest crowds outside hotels were in Australia, where George asked Derek Taylor to wave his hand through a curtain because he was too spent by the experience to do it himself. Ringo mostly enjoyed it, it seems; Paul has said that he loved most of it most of the time; John in 1970, angry after primal therapy, would remember "the most humiliating experiences".

And all this time on, all these decades later, Beatlemania endures, the soundtrack to the first half of seven whirlwind, world-altering years... still invigorating, still bringing a smile to the face. ■

PHOTOS: REX FEATURES

Mick takes the mike,
The Crawdaddy Club,
Surrey, 1963.

What: Meeting the Stones
Where: The Crawdaddy Club, Surrey
When: April 14, 1963

PLEASED TO MEET YOU

Although they would later become great adversaries, when the Stones first met The Beatles there was a mutual admiration. By Mark Paytress.

BY MID-APRIL 1963, THE BEATLES HAD just come off their first proper nationwide tour, *Please Please Me* was ripping up the album charts and From Me To You was poised to give the group their first Number 1 hit single. While all eyes were fixed on Liverpool, keenly awaiting the group's next challengers, The Beatles themselves paid a low-key visit to a small, sweat-drenched club in a quiet corner of south-west London. They didn't know it at the time, but the unknowns playing onstage that night were to become their greatest rivals.

The Rolling Stones had been playing a weekly residency at The Crawdaddy Club, in a back room of the Station Hotel, Kew Road, Surrey, every Sunday night since February 24. Alighting the train on April 14, 1963, they rushed into a local newsagents, where they eagerly read their first press write-up, published in that weekend's local paper. Their manager, Giorgio Gomelsky, returning from Teddington Studio Centre four miles away, had even better news for them.

As the R&B hopefuls refuelled on beer and sandwiches, Gomelsky walked in. "That's when I told them, Hey, something nice might happen today. The Beatles might come…" he remembered. Gomelsky had visited the TV studios to discuss the possibility of securing The Beatles' involvement in a new, Goons-inspired musical, but The Beatles, who were miming From Me To You for Thank Your Lucky Stars, only truly perked up when the bearded Russian enthused about The Rolling Stones. "I said, You've got to come and see this band when you finish recording the show."

Unlike The Beatles, who'd become a crowd-pleasing rock'n'roll variety act, the Stones had grown out of the dissident jazz scene and were playing what the local reporter described as the "deep, earthy sound of R&B". Young and iconoclastic, they wore their hair "Piltdown-style, brushed forward from the crown like The Beatles". Early that evening, just as the joint was starting to rock, Britain's latest pop sensations were silently ushered through the doors of the Station Hotel.

Pat Andrews, mother of Brian Jones' son Julian, remembers that when Jones mentioned The Beatles might drop by, she told him to "stop talking soft". Her disbelief was suspended when she saw "this leather cap coming round the door. I think it was Ringo. They were all dressed in black leather overcoats and blended in with the atmosphere. I ushered them into the shadows. It was one of the scariest moments of my life." Of Brian's, too, insisted Gomelsky. Even Jagger was mildly intimidated, recalling later that his celebrated judges resembled "a four-headed monster" that evening.

"They stood at the left-hand side of the stage and watched," recalled James Phelge, who was living with Mick, Keith and Brian at the time. "Very soon the word spread around the hall: The Beatles are here."

What the Liverpudlians witnessed was an exhilarating mix of rhythm and blues (Jimmy Reed and Bo Diddley covers) and Chuck Berry-inspired rock'n'roll. George Harrison was particularly impressed. "It was a real rave," he enthused. "The audience shouted and screamed and danced on tables. They were doing a dance that no-one had seen up 'til then, but we now all know as The Shake. The beat the Stones laid down was so solid it bounced off the walls and seemed to move right inside your head. A great sound."

After the show, The Beatles waited around while the Stones packed away their equipment. Both bands then headed off back to the Stones' infamous first-floor flat at 102 Edith Grove on the seamier side of Chelsea.

Back at Edith Grove, the six Stones (pianist Ian Stewart was still a member), four Beatles and a smattering of associates congregated in the living-room. Pat and two other girls made the coffees while the bands debated the merits of various R&B artists. One, Jimmy Reed, provoked an unexpected reaction from John Lennon, who remarked, "What's this? I think it's crap". Essentially, though, the mood was convivial, with Brian obtaining a signed photo before The Beatles left in the early hours. "There was no Beatles versus Stones then," says Pat. "That was the newspapers."

Four days later, at The Beatles' invitation, Mick, Keith and Brian had front row seats for their show at the Royal Albert Hall. Afterwards, Brian was mobbed by a group of fans. Turning to Giorgio Gomelsky, he deadpanned: "That's what I want." By the autumn, Jones' wish had come true, thanks in part to another act of Beatles generosity. Judging a beat contest in Liverpool, George advised Decca A&R man Dick Rowe to sign the Stones. "As I had turned down The Beatles, I didn't want to make the same mistake again," Rowe recalled. He saw the Stones in Richmond on May 6 and signed them immediately.

"Mick Jagger recalled later that his celebrated judges resembled 'a four-headed monster' that night."

The Stones take it to the stage, The Crawdaddy, 1963.

In the wake of the band's debut Decca 45, Come On, in June, Brian Jones was asked about "the Liverpool-London controversy". "It's all a load of rubbish," he insisted. "We are on very friendly terms with the Northern beat groups and there's a mutual admiration between us."

Mick Jagger didn't see it quite that way, as he reminded The Beatles in January 1988, at their induction to the Rock'n'Roll Hall Of Fame. "When the Stones were first together, we heard there was a group from Liverpool with long hair, scruffy clothes and a record in the charts with a bluesy harmonica riff. The combination of all this made me sick." He was, of course, only half-joking.

11 Ten new tracks for their debut album, *Please Please Me*, are recorded in Studio 2, Abbey Road Studios. The session lasts 585 minutes.

12 The Beatles resume solo dates with two shows: the Arena Ballroom, Sheffield, and the Astoria Ballroom, Oldham.

16 The Beatles appear on the cover of a national music paper, Record Mirror, for the first time.

20 A live BBC session is broadcast from the Playhouse Theatre, London, for radio show Parade Of The Pops, followed by a show at the Swimming Baths, Doncaster.

21 A show at the Majestic Ballroom, Birkenhead.

22 A new publishing company, Northern Songs, is set up to handle Lennon and McCartney's songs. The band play the Oasis Club, Manchester.

23 When the Helen Shapiro tour resumes at the Granada Theatre, Mansfield, the artists are trapped inside by hundreds of screaming Beatles fans.

25 The Beatles' first US release is Please Please Me/Ask Me Why on Vee-Jay Records.

28 On the Helen Shapiro tourbus from York to Shrewsbury, John and Paul write From Me To You. The Beatles play Granada Cinema, Shropshire.

MARCH 63

1 The Beatles appear today and tomorrow on regional TV show ABC At Large, recorded at Didsbury Studio Centre; they later play the Odeon, Southport.

2 A show at City Hall, Sheffield.

3 The final gig of the Helen Shapiro tour, at the Gaumont Cinema, Hanley.

7 The Beatles head the first Mersey Beat Showcase at the Elizabethan Ballroom, Nottingham.

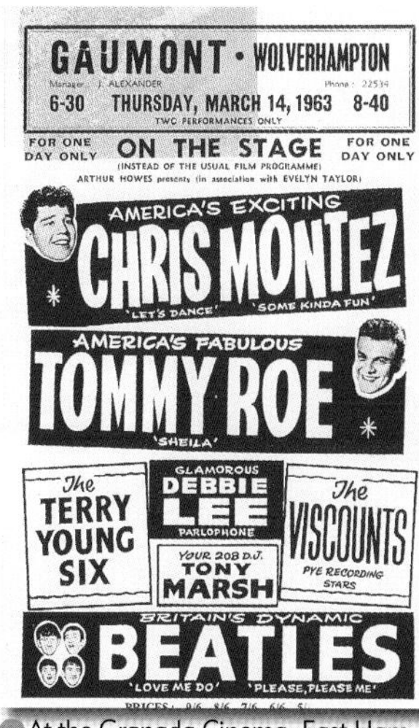

9 At the Granada Cinema, East Ham, London, The Beatles start a UK tour, billed as supporting Chris Montez and Tommy Roe (see above, March 14 gig) but immediately usurp the headliners and become the closing act.

10 The Beatles play the Hippodrome Theatre, Birmingham. To avoid crowds of fans, the band are smuggled into the venue disguised as policemen.

12 A gig at the Granada Cinema, Bedford. Lennon is absent, allegedly suffering from a cold, so the band play as a trio for the next three nights.

16 A show at the City Hall, Sheffield. Then on to record the first BBC Saturday Club at Broadcasting House, Portland Place, London.

21 The tour continues at the ABC, West Croydon. Then on to record the first BBC radio session for On The Scene at the Piccadilly Studios, London.

22 The Beatles' debut album, *Please Please Me*, is released in the UK, while the Roe/Montez package continues at the Gaumont, Doncaster.

31 The Roe/Montez tour ends at the De Montfort Hall, Leicester.

APRIL 63

1 Live sessions are recorded for BBC radio show Side By Side at Piccadilly Studios, London.

4 Another Side By Side radio session is recorded at the BBC's Paris Studio, London (above).

5 The Beatles are awarded their first Silver Disc, for the single Please Please Me, at EMI House, London.

8 Cynthia Lennon gives birth to a boy, Julian.

9 As well as a live show at the Gaumont, Kilburn, London, The Beatles cram in one BBC radio and ITV appearance during the day, Pop Inn and Tuesday Rendevous respectively.

12 The Beatles release their first chart-topper, From Me To You/Thank You Girl, in the UK. The band play an evening show at The Cavern.

13 The Beatles record an appearance on BBC TV's The 625 Show at Lime Grove Studios, West London.

14 The Beatles nip down to the Crawdaddy Club in the Station Hotel, Richmond, to check out up-coming band The Rolling Stones, then join them at their Edith Grove, London, flat.

16 An appearance is recorded for Granada TV show Scene At 6.30 in Granada TV Centre, Manchester.

18 The Beatles play at the Swinging Sound '63 show at the Royal Albert Hall, London. During rehearsals, Paul McCartney meets actress Jane Asher, soon to become his girlfriend. She was writing a piece about them for the Radio Times.

21 The Beatles play to 10,000 people as part of the 14-act NME Poll Winners' Concert, Empire Pool, Wembley.

23 A show at the Floral Hall, Southport.

24 The band play the Majestic Ballroom, Finsbury Park, London.

25 A gig at the Fairfield Hall, Croydon.

26 The Beatles play the Music Hall, Shrewsbury.

27 A show at the Memorial Hall, Northwich.

28 John Lennon and Brian Epstein fly to Spain on holiday, while the other Beatles head for Tenerife.

MAY 63

2 From Me To You reaches Number 1 in the UK singles charts.

What: Paul meets Jane Asher
Where: Royal Albert Hall
When: April 18, 1963

BRIMFUL OF ASHER

When the Fabs met Jane Asher they "all tried to pull her". But it was Paul who made the strongest play for the 17-year-old actress. By Barry Miles.

DESPITE THEIR NATIONAL SUCCESS THERE was at first a great reluctance on The Beatles' part to move down to London. Paul: "They'd said, 'You'll never make it from Liverpool', which had kind of angered us a bit, so we stayed up in Liverpool a lot, we didn't just all move down here. We tried to kind of prove ourselves from Liverpool. Hamburg, Liverpool, the North, you know, 'Fuck you!' And we did, we had our original success up in The Cavern."

But as the engagements became more numerous, The Beatles found themselves spending more and more time trundling up and down to London in their old van. This was the old route, via Brownhills in Staffordshire before the motorway was built, and it was a long and tiring ride. Often they would only have one night in Liverpool before having to return to London for TV or a concert or a meeting at EMI. They grew familiar with the cheap hotels around Russell Square, then, as the fans became more problematic, the more upscale accommodations of the Royal Court Hotel on Sloane Square.

This was where they were staying on April 18, 1963 because they had a concert that day at the Royal Albert Hall. It was a typical early-'60s line-up: Del Shannon, The Springfields, Shane Fenton & The Fentones, Kenny Lynch, Lance Percival, Rolf Harris, George Melly and The Vernon Girls. The concert was in two parts, with the second part broadcast live on the BBC as Swinging Sound '63 – yes, the BBC was really switched on in those days. The Beatles performed Please Please Me and Misery in the first part and Twist And Shout and From Me To You in the second. The big finale consisted of the entire cast singing Kurt Weill's Mac The Knife.

This type of show had to be well rehearsed, so The Beatles were at the hall all day. Seventeen-year-old child-actress Jane Asher was reviewing the concert and writing a celebrity piece about The Beatles for the Radio Times. The BBC photographer posed her with the group, with her mouth open, screaming like a fan. She watched the show from the audience but afterwards went backstage. The Beatles knew who she was, of course. Paul: "She was the rather attractive, nice, well-spoken chick that we'd seen on Juke Box Jury." Jane was a well-known actress and had been one of the celebrity guests on the panel that reviewed new singles each week. "We all thought she was blonde because we'd only ever seen her in black and white on television, and we went mad for blondes."

John and Paul in particular had a thing about Brigitte Bardot to the extent that John made Cynthia dye her hair blonde to make her look more like the celebrated sex symbol. Fortunately Paul's girlfriend at the time was a natural blonde. Paul: "I remember us talking and saying, Yeah, well, the more they look like Brigitte, the better off we are, mate! Jane's hair was long, straight and centrally parted like Brigitte's but she was not a blonde, she had richly coloured red hair which was even better. Paul: "We all immediately tried to pull her."

They all returned to the Royal Court Hotel and hung around there for a little while, then went on to NME journalist Chris Hutchins' apartment on the nearby King's Road. "It was all very civilised, and we were all there. But at the end of all of that, I ended up with Jane, because I'd maybe made the strongest play or maybe she fancied me, I don't know what. But I ended up with her. All very innocent and stuff, so from then on I made strenuous efforts to become her boyfriend."

Jane Asher was educated at Queen's College in Harley Street, and appeared in her first film, Mandy, playing next to Mandy Miller, at the age of five. She was the youngest actress until then to play Wendy in the 1960 West End production of Peter Pan and had also starred in Greengage Summer by the time she met Paul. "Paul was obviously as proud as a peacock with his new lady," observed Cynthia Lennon. "For Paul, Jane Asher was a great prize. The fact that she was an established actress of stage and screen, very intelligent and beautiful gave an enormous boost to Paul's ambitious ego."

Brian Epstein rented a flat at 57 Green Street, Mayfair, as a pied-à-terre for the group whenever they had to stay over in London. It was unfurnished but for some reason no-one in Epstein's office did anything to make it habitable for them. They had beds but nothing else. The Beatles didn't have time to buy furniture or supplies. They couldn't even make a cup of tea because there was no tea, no kettle, and no table to put it on. Paul hated it and to compound his misery John, George and Ringo got in first, and took the good rooms leaving only a very small room at the back for Paul.

> **"Jane was this rather attractive, nice, well-spoken chick that we'd seen on Juke Box Jury." Paul McCartney**

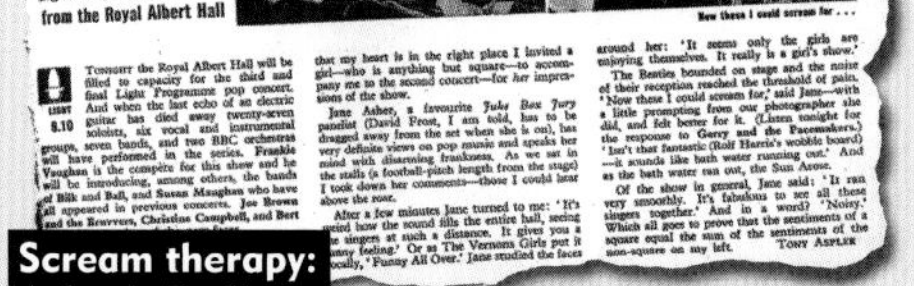
POPS for everyone

The final concert in the Light Programme series—from the Royal Albert Hall

Now these I could scream for . . .

Tonight the Royal Albert Hall will be filled to capacity for the third and final Light Programme pop concert. And when the last echo of an electric guitar has died away twenty-seven soloists, six vocal and instrumental groups, seven bands, and two BBC orchestras will have performed in the series. Frankie Vaughan is the compère for this show and he will be introducing, among others, the bands of Bilk and Ball, and Susan Maughan who have all appeared in previous concerts. Joe Brown and the Bruvvers, Christine Campbell, and Bert

that my heart is in the right place I invited a girl—who is anything but square—to accompany me to the second concert—for *her* impressions of the show.

Jane Asher, a favourite *Juke Box Jury* panelist (David Frost, I am told, has to be dragged away from the set when she is on), has very definite views on pop music and speaks her mind with disarming frankness. As we sat in the stalls (a football-pitch length from the stage) I took down her comments—those I could hear above the roar.

After a few minutes Jane turned to me: 'It's weird how the sound fills the entire hall, seeing the singers at such a distance. It gives you a funny feeling.' Or as The Vernons Girls put it vocally, 'Funny All Over.' Jane studied the faces around her: 'It seems only the girls are enjoying themselves. It really is a girl's show.'

The Beatles bounded on stage and the noise of their reception reached the threshold of pain. 'Now these I could scream for,' said Jane—with a little prompting from our photographer she did, and felt better for it. (Listen tonight for the response to Gerry and the Pacemakers.) 'Isn't that fantastic (Rolf Harris's wobble board) —it sounds like bath water running out.' And as the bath water ran out, the Sun Arose.

Of the show in general, Jane said: 'It ran very smoothly. It's fabulous to see all these singers together.' And in a word? 'Noisy.' Which all goes to prove that the sentiments of a square equal the sum of the sentiments of the non-square on my left.

TONY ASPLER

Scream therapy: Asher's Radio Times article.

He spent as much of his time as possible with Jane and her family at their huge house at 57 Wimpole Street. He particularly liked Jane's mother: "Very nice mumsy type woman, great cook, nothing was too much for her. For a young guy who likes his home comforts, boy did she spoil me." Sometimes it would get late and he would stay the night in one of the spare rooms. Then came the offer he couldn't refuse. In November Jane suggested: "You know you could stay here if you hate Green Street so much. And mum will let you have the attic room." As Paul told it later: "See this was what Green Street was missing, Green Street was very cold, this was the opposite, because Mrs Asher was a very warm person and Jane being my girlfriend, it was kind of perfect, you know!" He stayed three years.

PHOTOS: HULTON ARCHIVE/ATLANTIC/PICTORIAL PRESS

Not Brigitte Bardot, but... Paul and Jane Asher get cosy, 1963.

Hooking up: Epstein once described Lennon as "the only important one" in The Beatles.

What: John goes on holiday with Brian
Where: Barcelona, Spain
When: April 28, 1963

IT'S ONLY LOVE

When John Lennon and Brian Epstein went on a 10-day holiday to Spain, it was the culmination of an intense relationship. Chris Ingham investigates.

BRIAN EPSTEIN LOVED THE BEATLES. BUT then so did Sir George Martin. "The Beatles were number one in Brian's life always," Sir George has said, "as they became my number one." The difference is, of course, Brian's homosexuality made his devotion to the group a little more complex. He couldn't help wanting them too.

Or some of them. He wasn't especially drawn to Harrison's fresh-faced youth or Paul's prettiness. "He never hit on me at all," McCartney has said, "there was never any question of it." He did, however, hit on 'moody, magnificent' Pete Best. In a car one night with John and Cynthia in the back and Pete Best riding up front with Brian, Epstein invited the drummer to spend the night with him. "No," said Pete, unperturbed but firm, trying to ignore the giggles from the back. "You've got the wrong guy." Pete remembers getting a "little smirk" from John later.

He loves you: Brian's thoughts on Ringo remain unknown, however.

Even John's friend Pete Shotton tells of Brian, within hours of first meeting him in early 1962, inviting Pete (a self-described "scruffy layabout") back to Epstein's apartment. Brian accepted Shotton's rejection with good grace for which Shotton remembers Epstein with great affection, calling him "the perfect gentleman". And Shotton maintains Brian was only interested in him in order to get closer to his true love, John Lennon.

Peter Brown (an assistant of Brian's at NEMS) remembers Brian being so fascinated by John's cruel wit, looks and talent, he was hardly able to look at Lennon when the Beatle spoke, nervous of revealing his feelings. And when wooing The Beatles' parents, Brian assured John's Aunt Mimi that "John is the only important one", a judgement with which Mimi would have enthusiastically concurred.

Lennon affected a typical roughneck response to Epstein's homosexuality in public. "If he lays a finger on me I'll punch his lights out," Best remembers him saying. But gradually, realising the hold he had over this gentle, helplessly besotted man who after all, only wanted to make The Beatles bigger than Elvis, Lennon's response to his manager developed more nuance.

In the frequent visits John made to the Epsteins' house (Brian still lived at home) in late 1961 and early 1962 to discuss the marketing of the group, John and Brian developed what Brian's brother Clive described as "a mental contact that was perfect". McCartney sees the situation more prosaically and has called Lennon "a smart cookie… he wanted Brian to know who he should listen to in this group, and that was the relationship."

According to Peter Brown, Brian purchased his flat in Faulkner St with the purpose of seducing John there but when invited, John would always have another Beatle in tow. Brian made a standing offer to take John for a weekend to Copenhagen, which The Cavern coterie soon got wind of and teased Lennon about.

Lennon would continue to unleash his barbed tongue on Brian, which would often leave his manager in fits of private tears. Blaming their rejection by Decca on Epstein's showy tune selection, when Brian offered a later opinion on their music, Lennon snarled, "You stick to your percentages Brian, we'll make the music". Yet in April 1963, in the wake of the success of Please Please Me, John at last agreed to accompany Brian on a 10-day holiday to Barcelona.

John informed Cynthia in hospital on his first visit to see mother and newly-born baby of the arrangement and Cynthia, agreeing he deserved a break, oblivious to the implications and quietly stunned at being further neglected, wearily acquiesced.

In Spain, Brian and John attended bullfights, shopped and clubbed. They would sit in cafés and discuss Epstein's homosexuality, chatting about what he found attractive about passing men. Lennon enjoyed it, "thinking like a writer all the time," he said later, "I am experiencing this."

John said later their relationship was "almost an affair" that was "never consummated", but given later anecdotal accounts, that their relationship became physical at some point seems likely. Pete Shotton recalls John telling him that after Brian had kept "on and on" Lennon eventually said, "Oh, for Christ's sake, Brian, just stick it up me fuckin' arse then". Brian had apparently demurred, preferring to masturbate the Beatle ("What's a wank between friends?" shrugged Shotton).

"Given later accounts, it seems likely that Brian and John's relationship became physical at some point."

In restrained contrast, Peter Brown has written that Brian told him John allowed Epstein to make love to him. Albert Goldman, not one to shirk from details, asserts that Peter Brown meant oral sex. (But then, Goldman also speculates that Brian and John continued an affair for years, for which there appears to be no evidence. And Peter Brown, by the time a documentary on Brian was filmed in 1999, contritely decided "it's wrong to discuss something when I only know one side of the picture.")

John endured some light-hearted insinuations on his return to Liverpool, but at Paul's 21st birthday party he drunkenly beat up Cavern DJ Bob Wooler, when Wooler's comments went too far. Brian, as ever, smoothed things over, dissuading Wooler from suing with £200 compensation.

"He was in love with me," John said of Brian in 1980. "It's interesting and will make a nice Hollywood Babylon someday about Brian Epstein's sex life, but it's irrelevant, absolutely irrelevant."

PHOTOS: LONDON FEATURES, REX

11 The Beatles' debut album, *Please Please Me*, hits the UK Number 1 spot. The band play the Imperial Ballroom, Nelson, Lancashire.

12 Another Thank Your Lucky Stars appearance is recorded at Alpha TV Studios, Birmingham.

14 The Beatles play the Rink Ballroom, Sunderland.

15 The band perform at the Royal Theatre, Chester.

16 An appearance on BBC TV show Pops And Lenny is recorded at Television Theatre, Shepherd's Bush, London.

17 A London photo session with Dezo Hoffman is followed by a gig at the Grosvenor Rooms, Norwich.

18 A 21-date tour with Roy Orbison starts at the Adelphi Cinema, Slough, Bucks, with The Beatles as supporting act, but they quickly assume the headlining position.

19 The Beatles play the Gaumont, Hanley, Staffordshire.

21 A live performance is recorded for BBC radio show Saturday Club at the Playhouse Theatre, London.

22 The band play the Gaumont, Ipswich.

23 A show at the Odeon, Nottingham.

24 The first edition of a 15-week BBC radio series, Pop Go The Beatles, is recorded at Aeolian Hall, New Bond Street, London.

25 The Beatles play City Hall, Sheffield.

26 A show at the Empire Theatre, Liverpool.

27 The Beatles play the Capitol Cinema, Cardiff.

28 The band play the Gaumont Cinema, Worcester.

30 A gig at the Odeon Cinema, Manchester.

31 Another show at the Odeon Cinema, Southend-On-Sea.

JUNE 63

1 Two further editions of Pop Go The Beatles are recorded at the BBC's Paris Studio, London. The band play the Granada Cinema, Tooting, London.

2 The Beatles play the Hippodrome Theatre, Brighton.

3 A show at the Granada Cinema, Woolwich, London.

4 The BBC broadcasts the first edition of Pop Go The Beatles.

5 A show at the Odeon Cinema, Leeds.

7 Another show at the Odeon Cinema, Glasgow.

8 The Beatles play a gig at City Hall, Newcastle-Upon-Tyne (above).

9 The Roy Orbison tour ends at King George's Hall, Blackburn.

10 A return to one-nighters, starting with the Pavilion, Bath.

12 The Beatles play the Grafton Rooms, Liverpool, a charity gig in aid of the NSPCC.

13 Shows at the Palace Theatre Club, Stockport, and Southern Sporting Club, Manchester.

15 The band play City Hall, Salisbury. The Beatles' fee is £300.

16 The Beatles perform at the Odeon Cinema, Romford, Essex.

17 Another Pop Go The Beatles is recorded in Maida Vale Studios, London.

18 Paul celebrates his 21st birthday twice. First there's an official party at Abbey Road, then another one later with family and friends in a marquee in an aunt's back garden in Huyton, Liverpool. John rather spoils the happy occasion by getting into a fight with Cavern DJ Bob Wooler, who implied that Lennon was gay. The Beatles play the Aldelphi Theatre, Slough with Roy Orbison (above).

19 The band play the Playhouse Theatre, London, recording for the BBC radio programme, Easy Beat.

20 The Beatles form a company, Beatles Ltd, to handle their income, with Brian Epstein as a director.

21 The band play the Odeon Cinema, Guildford, Surrey.

22 John Lennon pre-records an appearance for BBC TV show Juke Box Jury (voting every record a "miss") in London, then flies by helicopter to join the group for a show in the Town Hall, Abergavenny.

23 At Alpha TV Studios, Birmingham, The Beatles record a special all-Liverpool edition of Thank Your Lucky Stars.

24 Another Saturday Club appearance is recorded at the Playhouse Theatre, London.

25 A show at the Astoria, Middlesbrough.

26 The Beatles play the Majestic Ballroom, Newcastle-Upon-Tyne. Lennon and McCartney compose She Loves You in their hotel room. George also helps but will receive no credit.

27 Paul flies to London to see Billy J Kramer recording Bad To Me and I Call Your Name at Abbey Road.

28 The Beatles play the Queen's Hall, Leeds.

29 The band appear on BBC radio show Saturday Club.

30 The band play the ABC, Great Yarmouth.

JULY 63

1 The Beatles record She Loves You and I'll Get You at Abbey Road, London.

2 The first edition of Pop Go The Beatles is recorded at the BBC's Maida Vale studios, London.

3 An appearance on BBC radio's The Beat Show is recorded at the Playhouse Theatre, Manchester.

What: The final gig at The Cavern.
Where: Liverpool
When: August 3, 1963

GOING OVERGROUND

When they played their 274th and final gig at The Cavern, The Beatles had had two Number 1 singles and were ready to move on. By Mark Lewisohn.

IN MARCH 1961, WHEN FOR £5 THE BEATLES made their night-time debut in The Cavern, the jazzy Swinging Bluegenes had a blazing row with club owner Ray McFall, accusing him of sullying what was supposed to be their "guest night" with a rock'n'roll group. Twenty-eight months later, The Swinging Blue Jeans, restyled and pop personified, were in the singles chart alongside several other exponents of "the Mersey Sound", and The Beatles – who started and were cresting this musical tsunami – were about to make their 274th and final appearance at the underground club with which they had become synonymous.

Yet by the bank holiday weekend that kicked off August 1963, The Beatles hadn't performed in Liverpool for two months and hadn't played The Cavern for four. The fear of their dedicated local fans was made manifest – with their two Number 1 singles and the Number 1 album, The Beatles had become so popular that the country at large had grabbed them. During a four-month period the previous summer, heading towards the release of Love Me Do, The Beatles played The Cavern 70 times.

All the same, their addition to The Cavern's crowded Saturday, August 3 bill was scarcely altruistic. "It only came about because Brian Epstein couldn't pull them out of a booking at the Grafton Ballroom the night before," the clerkly Cavern DJ Bob Wooler remembered shortly before his death. Arranged back in January, the Grafton contract prevented The Beatles from performing within a 10-mile radius in the preceding fortnight but left Epstein clear to arrange anything afterwards. It seems likely that Epstein, upset by the Grafton promoter's refusal to cap the ballroom's capacity to ensure The Beatles' safety, hoped to keep the numbers down by arranging a rival date. "I rather resented this," Wooler remarked.

It seems too that there was no great desire on The Beatles' part to venture back to their old stomping ground. As John would later reflect (though not necessarily speaking solely about this gig), "We couldn't say it at the time but we really didn't like going back to Liverpool. Being local heroes made us nervous. When we did shows there they were always full of people we knew. We felt embarrassed in our suits and being very clean. We were worried that friends might think we had sold out. Which we had, in a way."

Added to a bill already crowded by The Mersey Beats, The Escorts, The Road Runners, The Sapphires and the rather worryingly named Johnny Ringo & The Colts, The Beatles were paid their now current £300 fee, a 5,900 per cent increase on their initial Cavern fiver. When Epstein also insisted the attendance be limited to 500 (900 had once packed into the former fruit and vegetable warehouse to see them) the club was bound to lose money on the arrangement. At 10 shillings apiece the maximum take was £250 and still the other groups had to be paid. Tickets sold out in 30 minutes on July 21.

With Friday/Saturday bookings in Liverpool, a Sunday show in Blackpool and a Monday gig in Manchester, at least The Beatles were able to spend a rare weekend at home, to enjoy a lie-in and eat a leisurely eggs and bacon breakfast in their own kitchen. Paul returned to his dad's council house in Allerton, Ringo to his mum and step-dad's two-up, two-down council house in the Dingle and George to his parents' new council house in Hunts Cross. Only John was denied such familiar and familial comforts. Pro tem, home was 'over the water' in rural Hoylake, where Cynthia had secretly retreated with four-month-old baby Julian. The villa at 18 Trinity Road was the residence of her mother, the redoubtable Mrs Lil Powell, with whom John rarely got along. The Grafton, The Cavern, Blackpool, wherever – John was probably glad to get out of the house.

Too big for their roots: The Beatles outgrow The Cavern.

While history claims August 3, 1963 as The Beatles' last Cavern appearance, this wasn't appreciated at the time. The gig merited no coverage in any of the pop weeklies, the Liverpool Echo or even Mersey Beat. No recording was made and no cameras preserved the moment. There isn't even a set-list to provide details of The Beatles' final Cavern repertoire, though it's likely that the beaty strains of the William Tell Overture would have sounded as they arrived onstage, Bob Wooler spinning Piltdown Rides Again, the 45 he had long ago chosen as their Cavern entrée. "The Beatles were very professional that night," Wooler recalled, tellingly but without detail. "There was no larking around and they got on with it."

"We didn't like going to Liverpool. Being local heroes made us nervous. The shows were full of people we knew." John Lennon

For Ray McFall, The Beatles' departure was inevitable: "I expected that eventually we would lose them, and Brian would have come to the same conclusion. He didn't want them to be playing this kind of venue any more. The combined smell of the snack bar, cigarettes, body odour, the cleaners' detergent fluid and urine from the toilets was pretty atmospheric." The night literally went with a bang for McFall when, for neither the first nor last time, The Cavern electricity blew. "The place was steaming," he says. "The humidity was so great that the lights blew. While The Beatles were talking to the girls on the front row I had to do a quick job on the fuse, but after I'd fixed it and was flicking the switch it went again: there was a blue flash and I copped it in my left hand.

"That burned hand was my memento of The Beatles' last Cavern performance," remembers McFall. "It was a momentous night – then all of a sudden they finished and were gone."

PHOTOS: HULTON ARCHIVE/ATLANTIC/PICTORIAL PRESS

The Beatles have left the building: an electricity blow-out helped make the Fabs' last Cavern gig a suitably dramatic finale.

"Mmmm, this music really sends me!" DJ and presenter Annie Nightingale relaxes with a copy of *With The Beatles*, Brighton, December 1964.

What: With The Beatles photo session.
Where: Palace Court Hotel, Bournemouth
When: August 22, 1963

SNAPPER'S DELIGHT

Through his half-shadow image for *With The Beatles*, lensman Robert Freeman began a quiet revolution in LP sleeve design. By John Harris.

BOURNEMOUTH'S STAKIS HOTEL SITS opposite the town's Pavilion Ballroom, on Westover Road. Its exterior suggests nothing more remarkable than a bolt-hole for visiting conference delegates and holidaying OAPs – yet it was here, when it was the altogether more raffishly-named Palace Court Hotel, that The Beatles posed for one of the most iconic portraits of their career.

On August 22, 1963, they were mid-way through a six-night stand at the town's Gaumont Cinema, timed to coincide with the release of She Loves You. So it was that Robert Freeman was summoned to take the photograph that would adorn the sleeve of their second album, most of which had been completed the previous month. The Beatles wanted to avenge the all-grinning naffness of the *Please Please Me* sleeve – "crap", in George Harrison's estimation – and try something very, very different. Freeman's brief was so different from standard showbiz portraiture as to be positively avant-garde, a point only underlined by the simplicity of the photo shoot.

"Neil Aspinall arranged for them to arrive at midday wearing their black polo-necked sweaters," Freeman later recalled. "It seemed natural to photograph them in black and white wearing the dark clothing they were into at the time. There was no make-up, hairdresser or stylist: just myself, The Beatles and a camera."

Freeman posed them in the Palace Court's dining room, in front of a maroon curtain, with their faces half-lit by a nearby window. Mindful of an album sleeve's restrictive dimensions, he arranged the group according to their in-built hierarchy; as usual, Ringo came fourth. "They had to fit in the square format of the cover," said Freeman, "so rather than have them all in a line, I put Ringo in the bottom right corner, since he was the last to join the group. He was also the shortest, although he still had to kneel on a stool to get in the right position."

In Freeman's account, the *With The Beatles* picture was aimed at capturing the same boho moodiness that he had brought to his photos of jazz musicians. Students of The Beatles' Hamburg period, however, will instantly recognise the apparent influence of Astrid Kirchherr, who used the half-lit technique in portraits of John, George and Stuart Sutcliffe. In that sense, *With The Beatles* – replete with readings of such Kaiserkeller staples as Roll Over Beethoven, You Really Got A Hold On Me and Money (That's What I Want) – represents a canny repackaging of their early '60s incarnation: Hamburg shorn of Prellies and leather, and sold to their public as a mixture of accomplished rock'n'roll and art-house cool.

In 1995, during the hoopla that surrounded the release of Backbeat, Kirchherr was asked about the picture's obvious links with her own work. "The Beatles loved the half-shadow bit when I did their first pictures, because it looked moody," she said. "I can imagine they told Bob Freeman, 'We want those pictures like Astrid did, with the half-shadow'. Maybe that's how the cover came together."

Upon delivery of Freeman's portrait, Brian Epstein was well aware of the implied break with record business etiquette: visitors to his home would be anxiously quizzed about whether The Beatles were going a little too far. The question was hardly misplaced: to EMI's disquiet, Epstein and the band initially aimed at printing the shot full-bleed, with no logos or lettering. That plan was understandably overruled, though – with the help of George Martin – Freeman's picture was eventually accepted. He also managed to bump up his fee from the standard £25 to a then-mind-boggling £75.

The success of *With The Beatles* – repackaged in the US as *Meet The Beatles*, and with an almost identical sleeve – proved that EMI's jitters had been rather misplaced. Moreover, the sleeve marked a watershed in album design: from hereon in, groups could hold out against the more cartoonish aspects of pop photography, citing *With The Beatles* as incontestable proof that the market was not nearly as dumbed-down as had once been assumed. In 1964, Andrew Loog Oldham proved the point, forcing Decca into accepting what EMI had rejected: an album cover uncluttered by any typography at all. The Rolling Stones' self-titled debut album thus oozed all the tradition-shredding nerve that oozed from their rebellious brand of rock'n'roll.

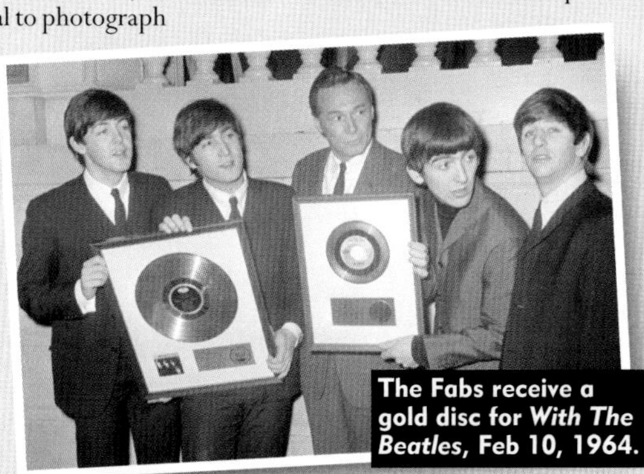
The Fabs receive a gold disc for *With The Beatles*, Feb 10, 1964.

"The final record sleeve, in the English version, looked like four white faces in a coal cellar." Photographer Robert Freeman

The change quickly became unstoppable: by the end of 1964, the days of fun-for-all-the-family cover shots, replete with hucksterish reminders of the band's last couple of singles, were long gone. The aftershocks of *With The Beatles* continued to ripple down the decades: one can arguably recognise its influence in all manner of iconic sleeve designs, from Lou Reed's *Transformer* to Patti Smith's *Horses*, and on to the stark, no-nonsense approach to design that was cemented by punk.

Freeman had, in effect, pulled off a quiet revolution, though any triumphalism was slightly offset by his problems with the quality of his picture's reproduction. "The printing of the sleeve turned out much darker than I expected, so a lot of the textured quality was lost," he lamented. "The final sleeve, in the English version, looked like four white faces in a coal cellar."

PHOTOS: HULTON ARCHIVE/ATLANTIC/PICTORIAL PRESS

JULY 5 - AUG 5, 1963

5 The Beatles play a show at the Plaza Ballroom, Dudley.

6 Prior to a gig at the Memorial Hall, Northwich, Paul crowns the local carnival queen (above).

7 The band play a show at the ABC Theatre, Blackpool.

8 The Beatles begin a six-night residency at the Winter Gardens, Margate.

10 Two more editions of Pop Go The Beatles are recorded at the Aeolian Hall, London.

12 The Twist And Shout EP is released in the UK.

15 In his absence, Paul McCartney is fined £17 for a speeding offence, at Birkenhead Magistrates Court.

16 Three more editions of Pop Go The Beatles are recorded at the BBC's Paris Studio, London.

17 An appearance on BBC radio's Easy Beat is recorded at the Playhouse Theatre, London.

18 The Beatles start work on their second album, *With The Beatles*, at Abbey Road Studio, London.

19 The band play two consecutive nights at the Ritz Ballroom, Rhyl.

21 The Beatles play a show at the Queen's Theatre, Blackpool.

22 *Introducing The Beatles* is released as their first US album and a six-day season begins at the Odeon, Weston-super-Mare.

23 Guest artists on Pop Go The Beatles are Carter Lewis & The Southerners. An evening show at the Odeon Cinema, Western-super-Mare.

26 The *Introducing The Beatles* album is released in the US by Vee-Jay Records.

28 The Beatles play a show at the ABC Cinema, Great Yarmouth.

30 The band record Please Mr Postman and It Won't Be Long at Abbey Road. The band do an interview on Non Stop Pop, a session for the Saturday Club and, in the evening, continue working on the *With The Beatles* album.

31 The Beatles perform at the Imperial Ballroom, Nelson.

AUGUST 63

1 The first edition of The Beatles Book, a monthly fan club magazine, is published. The band record two shows at the Playhouse Theatre, Manchester, for the Pop Go The Beatles programme.

2 The band play their last show at the Grafton Rooms, Liverpool.

3 The Beatles appear at The Cavern for the last time and achieve their first US chart entry when From Me To You enters the Billboard chart at Number 116.

4 At the Queen's Theatre, Blackpool, the band is lowered into the venue through the roof to avoid fans outside.

6 The band play the Springfield Ballroom, St Saviour, Jersey, the first of four nights in the Channel Islands.

9 The Beatles play two nights at the Springfield Ballroom, St Saviour, Jersey.

11 The band return to the UK to perform at the ABC Cinema, Blackpool.

12 The Beatles play the first of a six-night residency at the Odeon Cinema, Llandudno (above).

14 The band record two songs for Granada TV show Scene At 6.30 in Manchester.

18 Another appearance on Lucky Stars (Summer Spin) is recorded at Alpha TV Studios, Birmingham.

19 Five days of shows begin at the Gaumont Cinema, Bournemouth, Hants.

22 Halfway through their Bournemouth residency, The Beatles are photographed in the Palace Court Hotel by Robert Freeman for the cover of their second album, *With The Beatles*. In the afternoon, the band record an appearance on Southern TV's Day By Day.

23 The Beatles' fourth single, She Loves You, is released in the UK. The band play the Gaumont Theatre, Bournemouth.

24 The band are awarded a silver disc for the Twist And Shout EP.

25 The band play another show at the ABC Cinema, Blackpool.

26 Cilla Black makes her first major concert appearances, supporting The Beatles, during a six-night residency at the Odeon Cinema, Southport.

27 The Beatles are filmed playing at a small theatre in Southport for BBC TV's Mersey Sound.

SEPTEMBER 63

1 An appearance on TV show Big Night Out is recorded in Didsbury Studio Centre, Manchester.

3 The last three episodes of radio show Pop Go The Beatles are recorded in Aeolian Hall, London.

4 The Beatles play a show at the Gaumont Cinema, Worcester.

5 The band perform at the Gaumont Cinema, Taunton.

6 The Beatles' Hits EP is released in the UK.

7 The Beatles record an appearance for Saturday Club at the Playhouse Theatre, London and in the evening perform at the Fairfield Hall, Croydon.

8 The Beatles play a gig at the ABC Theatre, Blackpool (see ticket stubs, right).

11 The Beatles record tracks for the next album in EMI Studio 2, Abbey Road, London.

12 She Loves You reaches Number One in the UK singles chart.

What: She Loves You is released
Where: United Kingdom
When: August 23, 1963

A GOOD YEAH!

She Loves You was more than just a rock'n'roll record, argues Mark Ellen, it was the perfect synthesis of what made the Fabs great.

SHE LOVES YOU, A PIVOTAL MOMENT IN the ascent of The Beatles' fortunes, came together in just five days, in the wake of The Profumo Affair and just before The Great Train Robbery. It was written in a Newcastle hotel room after playing The Majestic Ballroom on June 26 and recorded the same week, and in a world where market research was fast and hard-won and took place on the killing floors of steaming dancehalls, it was the perfect synthesis of all that made The Beatles so great.

For boys it was about the massive backbeat and the light shining off their guitars, for girls it was as much about the way they clicked their heels together as they approached a mikestand, and their hair, and the divisions of their personality, and how whenever the drummer thrashed the big cymbal it was your cue to start shrieking. Compressed into two minutes and 17 seconds was every hallmark, every signature, every meticulous detail that made The Beatles so electrifying, and the result was more than a single, it was the soundtrack to a movie that played in the nation's head.

"John and I wrote it together," McCartney remembers. "There was a Bobby Rydell song out at the time [*presumably Forget Him, a chart hit in May '63*] and, as often happens, you think of one song when you write another. We were in a van up in Newcastle-Upon-Tyne. I'd planned an 'answering song' where a couple of us would sing 'she loves you' and the other one answers 'yeah yeah'. We decided that was a crummy idea but at least we then had the idea for a song called She Loves You. So we sat in the hotel bedroom for a few hours and wrote it – John and I, sitting on twin beds with guitars."

"We wrote it in a few hours in a hotel bedroom in Newcastle. John and I, sitting on twin beds with guitars." Paul McCartney

"It was Paul's idea," John Lennon conceded. "Instead of singing 'I love you' again, we'd have a third party. That kind of detail is still in his work. He'll write a story about someone. I'm more inclined to write things about myself."

Crucially there was no danger of missing your favourite lead vocalist here as they *both* jointly sang every note from start to finish, veering apart into shivering harmonies and converging in unison, occasionally in octave, to make it impossible not to join in. And, magically, George Harrison joined in too, adding only one note, a delicious sixth to the first and final climactic chord. "We took that to George Martin, that little tight sixth cluster," McCartney again, "and he said, 'It's very corny, it's like the old days'. But we said, 'It doesn't matter, we've got to have it, it's the greatest harmony sound ever'. It's good that we could override a lot of his so-called professional decisions with our innocence. We never listened to any rules."

She Loves You was also an extraordinary balance of major and minor chords, a bold manoeuvre when the charts at the time radiated the tireless gleaming optimism of Bobby Vee, Cliff Richard and Gerry & The Pacemakers. And the arrangement was utterly peerless, so blindingly confident that it started with the chorus – a ruse The Beatles were to repeat many times: Can't Buy Me Love, Help!, A Hard Day's Night, Paperback Writer – and with every characteristic high in the mix, George's guitar figure that echoed the vocal refrain, Ringo's swooning fills and tom-tom rolls and, most significant of all, George and Paul's head-shaking harmonies around a single mike that caused the audience to fall apart like a cheap suit. Even the phrase 'yeah' on national radio was controversial at the time, seen in some quarters to hail the imminent collapse of civilised society. McCartney's father begged him to change it as "there's enough Americanisms around", but its swaggering confidence was the icing on the cake.

She Loves You rocketed to the toppermost and took up a staggering 31-week residency on the Top 40. The broadcaster Brian Matthew pronounced it "banal" in the Melody Maker – though none of The Beatles knew what it meant ("What's that, soppy? Too rebellious?") but next week was backpedalling furiously on the cover – "at first I thought it was a little banal... but it grows on you!". You felt the might of its influence immediately: the crooners, matinee idols, Brylcreemed family entertainers, laundered rock'n'rollers, jazz tradsters, even the beehived girls in frocks, all began to feel like a shower of frauds, charlatans and geriatrics.

Four months after its release, the singles setting the chart alight were by the Stones, The Ronettes, Dave Clark and The Hollies, artists without a bus pass and many of them writing their own material. It's no coincidence, too, that The Beatles' barrelling performance of She Loves You as the climax of their televised set on Sunday Night At The London Palladium was officially acknowledged as the start of Beatlemania, the moment even your parents caved in. The same song soon hot-wired the group into Europe and, when screened by Jack Parr in January '64, finally broke down the door to America.

PHOTOS: PICTORIAL PRESS, HULTON ARCHIVE

Just say yes: DIY chic was all the rage back in '63.

By royal appointment: the Fabs take a curtain call at the Prince Of Wales Theatre, London, November 4, 1963.

What: The Royal Variety Performance
Where: Prince Of Wales Theatre, London
When: November 4, 1963

WE MEAN IT, MA'AM

They may have been reticent about cosying up to the establishment, but the Fabs' RVP show proved to be their best career move yet. By Phil Sutcliffe.

"THE PEOPLE IN THE CHEAPER SEATS CLAP your hands. The rest of you, if you'll just rattle your fookin' jewellery," said John Lennon. Brian Epstein howled, "John! No!" Lennon grinned, pleased with himself that he got the manager panicking yet again.

It was the evening of October 12, 1963, at NEMS' office, 13 Monmouth Street. The Beatles were rehearsing for their two biggest shows to date. The following day they were headlining ITV's Sunday Night At The London Palladium, live to 15 million viewers. On Monday, November 4, it was the Royal Variety Performance – the reason why Lennon was winding Epstein up about "fookin'" in front of their Majesties.

When they got the invitation in late August the whole band said "reject it". They were working-class, anti-establishment. As former Daily Mirror showbiz correspondent Don Short recalls: "They didn't want to be seen as soft and cuddly. But Brian argued it was a great honour, great publicity, and they agreed in the end."

While still goading Epstein, they actually adjusted their royal set to please him when they included Till There Was You, the ballad from The Music Man. "That was typical Brian," says Beatles publicist Tony Barrow, who was at the rehearsal. "He said, 'You're dealing with *class*'. He wanted to push their family entertainer side."

Which was ironic. Because next day, outside the Palladium, gaudy home of old-fashioned variety, up to a thousand screaming girls jammed the street. The Daily Mirror christened it "Beatlemania".

On November 4, overwrought fans were already gathering in front of the Prince Of Wales Theatre, Coventry Street, when The Beatles arrived at 10.30am, rather frazzled after playing Leeds the night before. Effectively trapped backstage, they had little to do apart from a brief run-through. So they carefully examined every corner of the labyrinthine dressing-room area, idly star-spotting – Tommy Steele, Harry Secombe, Steptoe & Son, Pinky & Perky... They noted the red carpet leading from bill-topper Marlene Dietrich's dressing-room to the stage, but hardly saw her except when she slid between George and Ringo at the photocall and linked arms. Still, they found one kindred soul in Susan Maughan, of Bobby's Girl renown, the only other representative of British pop. She sat with them in the hospitality suite "gossiping and drinking tea". The gallant Ringo, she remembers, bought her egg and chips (price 1s 3d).

The Queen being pregnant (with Andrew), the Queen Mother, Princess Margaret and Lord Snowden arrived after a police cordon of 500 had pressed 3,000 Beatles fans back from the theatre entrance. When they saw the royal party, they interrupted chants of "We want The Beatles!" to cheer loyally.

The Beatles were on seventh of 19 acts and were keen to make an instant impact, playing From Me To You before the curtain went up. As the closing harmony hung in the air an ultra-Scouse McCartney hollered "How are yer – all right?". After She Loves You, introducing Till There Was You, he played cutely to the middle-aged crowd with "This one's been covered by our favourite American group – Sophie Tucker" (for younger readers: a fat lady who sang). When they came to Twist And Shout and Lennon twinkled, "For our last number I'd like to ask for your help...", he didn't say "fookin' jewellery".

In the royal box, said The Daily Express, "Princess Margaret led the applause" while "the Queen Mother smiled broadly". And in the wings, says Barrow, "Brian bathed in it all. Acceptance by royalty was huge for him."

On the night, even The Beatles admitted to a thrill or two. When Short nabbed them backstage, Ringo enthused, "It's too good to be true", and McCartney gushed, "It was fantastic. We never dreamed of this!"

Around midnight, Susan Maughan stood next to them in the presentation line-up. "They were very polite," she says. "'Honoured to be here, ma'am', and all that." One of those oddly legendary royal dialogues ensued. "Where are you playing next?" asked the Queen Mother. "Slough Adelphi, ma'am," said George Harrison. "Oh that's near us," she said. In 2002 this "quip" regularly featured in her obituaries, a signifier of her "common touch".

Next morning in the The Daily Mirror, Short hailed it "their greatest triumph yet. The Beatles were on their own and they made it".

"Recorded highlights of the show pulled 26 million viewers – half the population of the United Kingdom."

The Queen Mother mixes with her loyal subjects.

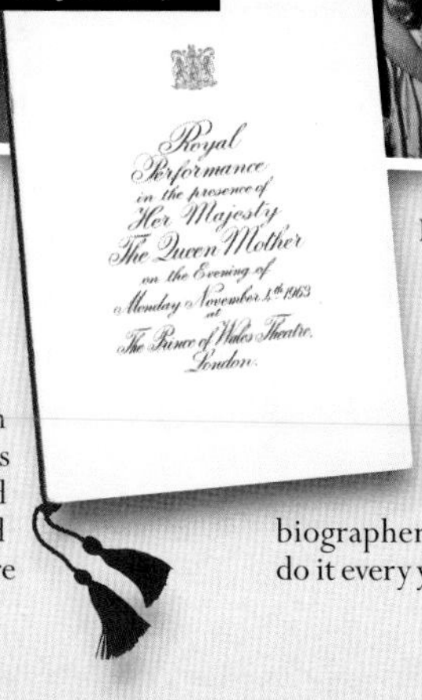

Recorded highlights of the show pulled 26 million viewers – half the population – for ITV the following Sunday. On The Beatles' 31-date winter tour, for their physical safety, group transport arrangements moved upscale from Transit vans to limos with police escorts. When their second LP, *With The Beatles*, came out on November 22 it went straight to Number 1. Unsurprising then that Don Short reckons the Royal Variety Performance "career-wise, was one of the best moves they made in terms of momentum and publicity".

But they never shook off their unease about the event's cosying-up-to-the-establishment implications. As Lennon told biographer Ray Coleman, "We were asked discreetly to do it every year after that but we always said 'Stuff it!'."

13 The Beatles play the Public Hall, Preston. Paul judges a beauty contest afterwards at the Imperial Ballroom, Nelson.

14 After a day of press interviews in Liverpool, a gig at Memorial Hall, Northwich.

15 The Beatles play the Great Pop Prom, Royal Albert Hall, London.

16 George becomes the first Beatle to set foot on American soil, visiting his sister, Louise, in Benton, Illinois. John sets off on holiday to Paris, France, with Cynthia, while Paul and Ringo head for Greece. She Loves You/I'll Get You is released in the US by Swan Records.

24 The final edition of Pop Go The Beatles is broadcast.

30 George Martin records additional keyboard parts for Money and I Wanna Be Your Man in Abbey Road.

OCTOBER 63

2 The Beatles arrive back in London from their holidays abroad.

3 The band record at Studio 3, Abbey Road, London.

4 The Beatles' debut appearance on TV show Ready Steady Go! is recorded at Studio 9, Television House, Kingsway, London.

5 A mini-tour of Scotland begins at Carnegie Hall, Glasgow.

9 A BBC radio appearance is recorded for the Ken Dodd Show, at Paris Studio, London.

11 The band play The Ballroom, Trentham Gardens, Stoke-on-Trent, Staffordshire.

12 Rehearsals in London for the next night's appearance on UK TV show Sunday Night At The London Palladium.

13 Fifteen million viewers see The Beatles on Sunday Night At The London Palladium.

14 Brian Epstein receives an invitation for the band to appear on the Royal Variety Performance. Daily UK papers, reporting on the Palladium show, coin the phrase "Beatlemania".

15 The band play the Floral Pavilion, Southport.

16 A session is recorded at the Playhouse Theatre, London, for BBC radio show Easy Beat.

17 In EMI Studio 2, Abbey Road, London, The Beatles record I Want To Hold Your Hand, This Boy and their first Christmas disc for distribution to their fan club members.

18 An appearance on TV show Scene At 6.30 is recorded at Granada TV Centre, Manchester.

19 The Beatles play the Pavilion Gardens, Buxton.

20 A performance for TV show Thank Your Lucky Stars is recorded at Alpha Television Studios, Birmingham (above).

Across The Universe

Recorded just at the onset of Beatlemania in Britain and released just in time for their explosive impact on America, Paul Du Noyer analyses why *With The Beatles* was the album that would break the Fabs worldwide.

November 22, 1963, was the 9/11 of its era – a day of abrupt, shocking catastrophe. Driving through Dallas in his open-topped limousine, President John F Kennedy was shot dead. On that same day, in London, Parlophone Records released the first great album of the decade. Had it been a record by anyone else the bleak coincidence of its release date would be irrelevant. But this LP was *With The Beatles*, and it stands, in the history of its times, as an event of no mean significance. Where the killing of Kennedy suggested the crushing of youthful hope and the onset of a morbidly pessimistic age, the arrival of The Beatles in the global imagination would herald the very opposite.

The magic began at Abbey Road in mid-July. Having three self-written hits to their credit, the group kicked off their new album sessions with a growing confidence as composers. (Soon there would be a fourth triumph, She Loves You, becoming their second chart-topper: its "yeah yeah yeah" refrain would capture the nation's imagination that summer and must have pushed morale inside the EMI studios to astronomic levels). This time around the LP's original tracks would outnumber the cover versions. The only snag was that their own songs weren't written yet. To get the juices flowing they used the initial days to record cover versions, most of which had been road-tested at The Cavern and elsewhere.

> "The cover showed their four faces hung like brand new planets, half-lit in inky blackness, full of promise."

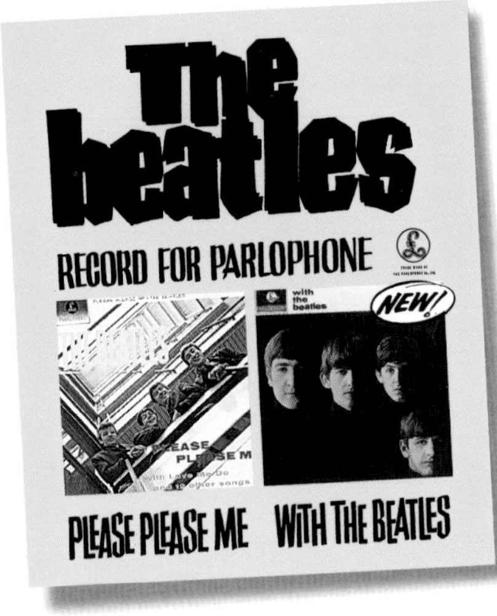

Foremost among the covers must be John Lennon's Motown trilogy, comprising Smokey Robinson's You Really Got A Hold On Me, The Marvelletes' Please Mr Postman and Barrett Strong's Money. In common with most of their Liverpool peers, The Beatles weren't really blues scholars like their London counterparts in The Rolling Stones and Yardbirds, but they were among the first young Britons to recognise the genius of Berry Gordy's Detroit label. And Smokey Robinson, of The Miracles, was their songwriting idol.

It's one of the clichés of rock'n'roll history that white performers stripped the sex and danger out of black material and cleaned up in the process. That may be true of Pat Boone covering Little Richard, or Bill Haley doing Big Joe Turner, but it was not the case with Elvis and nor was it true of Lennon's Motown covers. For better or worse, he turns the yearning submission of Smokey's song, You Really Got A Hold On Me, into a smouldering declaration of sexual impatience. Please Mr Postman becomes almost violent, the passive chant of its girl-group original replaced by John's aggressively demanding bark. And Money, at the album's close to supply the same blazing finale that Twist And Shout had given the first LP, is absolutely hardcore. Written by Gordy himself, the song was intimidating enough when sung by Strong, who invested his request ("I need money, that's what I want") with macho menace; in Lennon's hands it becomes one long howl of desperation. A soul connoisseur could argue that The Beatles' Motown covers lost the sophistication of the originals, but they are not wanting in passion.

Paul McCartney had yet to emerge as a composer of plangent, romantic ballads (a reputation he would soon establish with And I Love Her on *A*

PHOTO: HULTON ARCHIVE

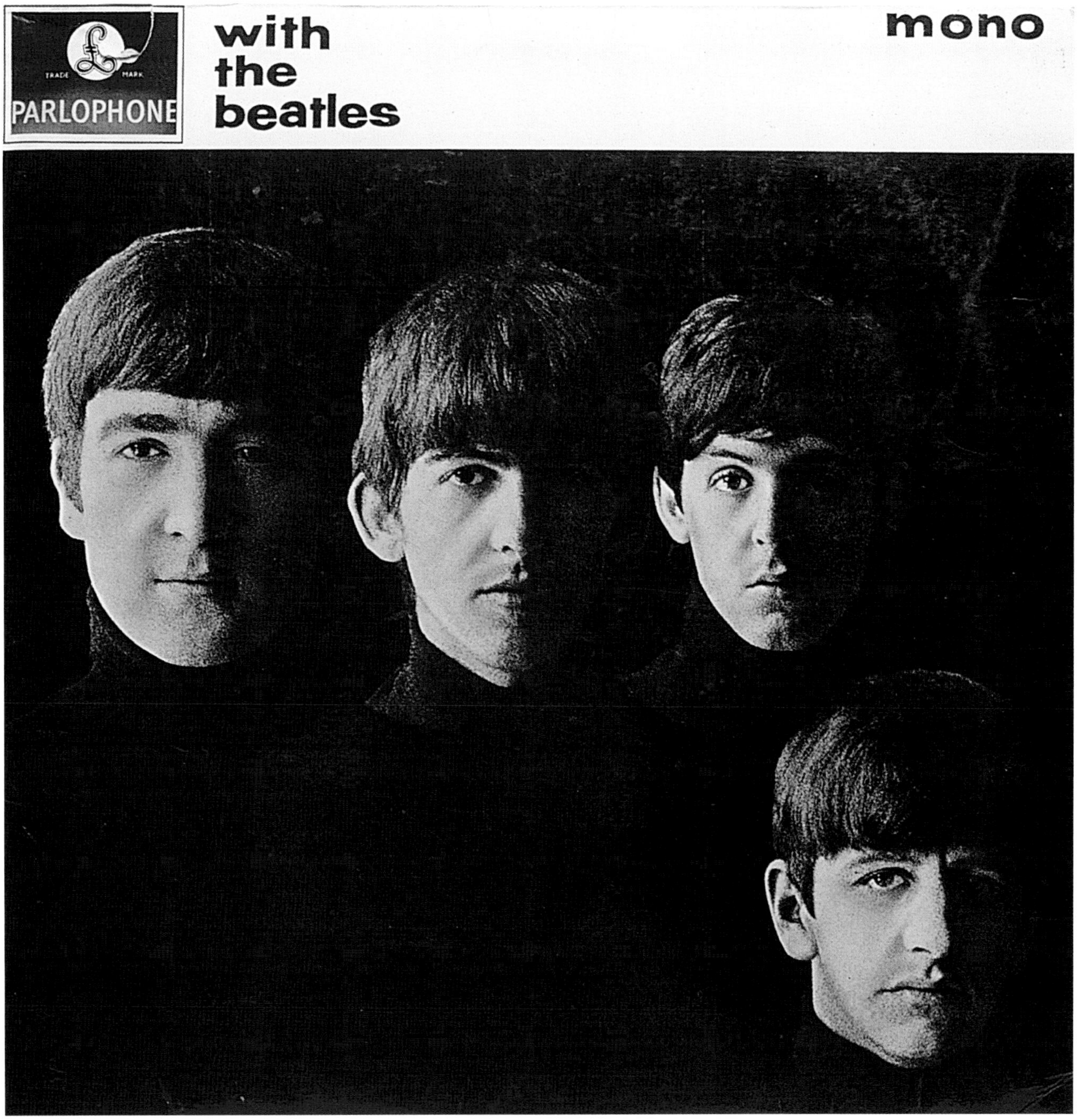

Hard Day's Night). Here, however, was another of the songs he evidently honed that craft upon, namely Till There Was You. The number had been around for a few years, first aired in Broadway show The Music Man, but it was Peggy Lee's single of 1961 that brought the song to McCartney's attention. His reading takes a step back from Lee's huskily intimate delivery, and there may have been a sense that such a track was slightly square. But it remained for a while a staple of their live performances, offering a dash of that "versatility" required of any act with claims to being all-round entertainers.

George Harrison is well represented on *With The Beatles*. He chalks up his first songwriting credit with the slight but attractive Don't Bother Me; he takes the lead vocal on Chuck Berry's Roll Over Beethoven (itself a lead guitarist's showcase) and effects a gender switch for yet another girl-group

TRACK LISTING

A-SIDE

1. It Won't Be Long
Lennon/McCartney
Sung by Lennon

2. All I've Got To Do
Lennon/McCartney
Sung by Lennon/McCartney

3. All My Loving
Lennon/McCartney
Sung by McCartney

4. Don't Bother Me
Harrison
Sung by Harrison

5. Little Child
Lennon/McCartney
Sung by Lennon/McCartney

6. Till There Was You
Meredith Willson
Sung by McCartney

7. Please Mr Postman
Holland/Bateman/Gordy
Sung by Lennon

B-SIDE

8. Roll Over Beethoven
Chuck Berry
Sung by Harrison

9. Hold Me Tight
Lennon/McCartney
Sung by McCartney

10. You Really Got A Hold On Me
Smokey Robinson
Sung by Lennon/Harrison

11. I Wanna Be Your Man
Lennon/McCartney
Sung by Starr

12. (There's A) Devil In Her Heart
Richard B Drapkin
Sung by Harrison

13. Not A Second Time
Lennon/McCartney
Sung by Lennon

14. Money (That's What I Want)
Gordy/Bradford
Sung by Lennon

WITH THE BEATLES

WHAT THE PAPERS SAID...

It was unanimous – *With The Beatles* was a hit.

BEATLES tell the SECRETS behind their GOLDEN TRACKS

to Alan Smith

Chuck Berry

"The highlight of *With The Beatles*? To my mind, All My Loving. This John Lennon/Paul McCartney original has an instantly recognisable melody line, taken at mid-tempo... Remember Boys, the number with which Ringo made his debut on the *Please Please Me* album? It turned out to be so successful that there was almost a demand for him another vocal. John and Paul obliged by writing one for him – I Wanna Be Your Man. Ringo handles the insistent rhythm with more polish, in fact, than in Boys. He shows signs of becoming a first-rate beat vocalist.

"No mention of this terrific album could go by without including Chuck Berry's Roll Over Beethoven. It's an out-and-out rocker... and George makes one of his rare vocal appearances on this one, duetting with himself, while the others add to the exciting atmosphere by clapping in time

"If there are any Beatles-haters left in Britain, I doubt they'll remain unmoved after hearing With The Beatles. It's a knock-out. I'll even go this far: if it doesn't stay at the top of the NME LP chart for at least eight weeks, I'll walk up and down Liverpool's Lime Street carrying an 'I Hate The Beatles' sandwich-board!"

Alan Smith, NME, November 15, 1963

"Titles range from the jaunty All My Loving – easily the standout track with a haunting quality – to the plaintive Till There Was You. A great album, with variety of tempo and a raw style that puts the Beatles unmistakably at the top of the beat tree."

Melody Maker, November 23, 1963

SLEEVE NOTES

How everyone's favourite cheeky Scousers got all mean'n'moody.

The brainchild of lensman Robert Freeman, the *With The Beatles* sleeve artwork was a landmark in pop photography, transforming the one-time grinning mop tops into cool, serious musicians. As a photographer working for The Sunday Times, Freeman had snapped Khrushchev in the Kremlin. He'd also worked on the first Pirelli calendar but it was his black and white photos of John Coltrane taken at a London jazz festival that convinced The Beatles that he was the right man for this job.

The photo session took place on August 22 in Bournemouth's Palace Court Hotel at noon – the band were midway through their six-date residency at the Gaumont in Bournemouth – and took just one hour to complete. With his trusty Pentax SLR with its 180mm telephoto lens, Freeman set up shop in the hotel's dining room. "There was a broad sidelight from the windows and a deep maroon curtain that could be pulled behind them to create a dark background," he explains in his book, A Private View. "It seemed natural to photograph them in black-and-white wearing the dark clothes they were into at the time." Because of the composition's square format Freeman decided to "put Ringo in the bottom right corner since he was the last to join the group. He was also the shortest, although he still had to kneel on a stool to get into the right position and be comfortable!" Deemed too radical by the EMI establishment and Brian Epstein – because the band weren't smiling – it was George Martin who finally convinced the record company to use the photo. Yet Freeman remains critical of his own work. "The printing turned out much darker than I expected so a lot of the textured quality in the reproduction print was lost. The final sleeve looked like four white faces in a coal cellar."

Lois Wilson

"Not A Second Time had the classical music critic of The Times making comparisons to Mahler."

number, The Donays' Devil In His Heart. And Ringo Starr, in the tradition initiated by Boys on *Please Please Me*, is given his own romp in the spotlight on I Wanna Be Your Man: Paul and John had begun to write the song with their drummer's limited range in mind, but they finished it sitting in the corner of a Rolling Stones session, in a comradely response to an appeal for material. (The juddering Bo Diddley rhythm has always seemed more right for Jagger and co, and their recording was soon their first Top 20 hit.)

There was, at any rate, one new Lennon and McCartney number already available for the second album. Hold Me Tight had been attempted in the course of that heroic one-day session for the first album, just a few months earlier. Somehow the song failed to gel that time, and it was resurrected now for a fresh effort. Yet there is still an impression of unfinished business in Hold Me Tight: it's an efficient little rocker but there's a general unsteadiness of pitch in Paul's vocal: the glitches in his approach to the two middle eights, in particular, are probably the biggest boobs in The Beatles' official catalogue. The leisurely days of endless retakes were not yet at hand: the pressures of time and money meant the old dictum "close enough for rock'n'roll" ruled even a figure as fastidious as George Martin.

A few of the other new compositions are hardly in the front rank of Lennon and McCartney's work – Little Child is anonymous, while All I've Got To Do is more evidence of Lennon's apprenticeship at the schools of Smokey Robinson and Arthur Alexander. Few would now nominate Not A Second Time as one of The Beatles' greatest songs, but it claims the strange distinction of having prompted the classical music critic of The Times to hail that celebrated "Aeolian cadence" and make cautious comparisons to Mahler. Valid or not, the comments opened a generation of well-stocked minds to the possibility of real art arising in a pop music disguise.

The outstanding additions to John and Paul's portfolios are It Won't Be Long and All My Loving. Each abounds with the respective partners' signature characteristics: urgency and ten-

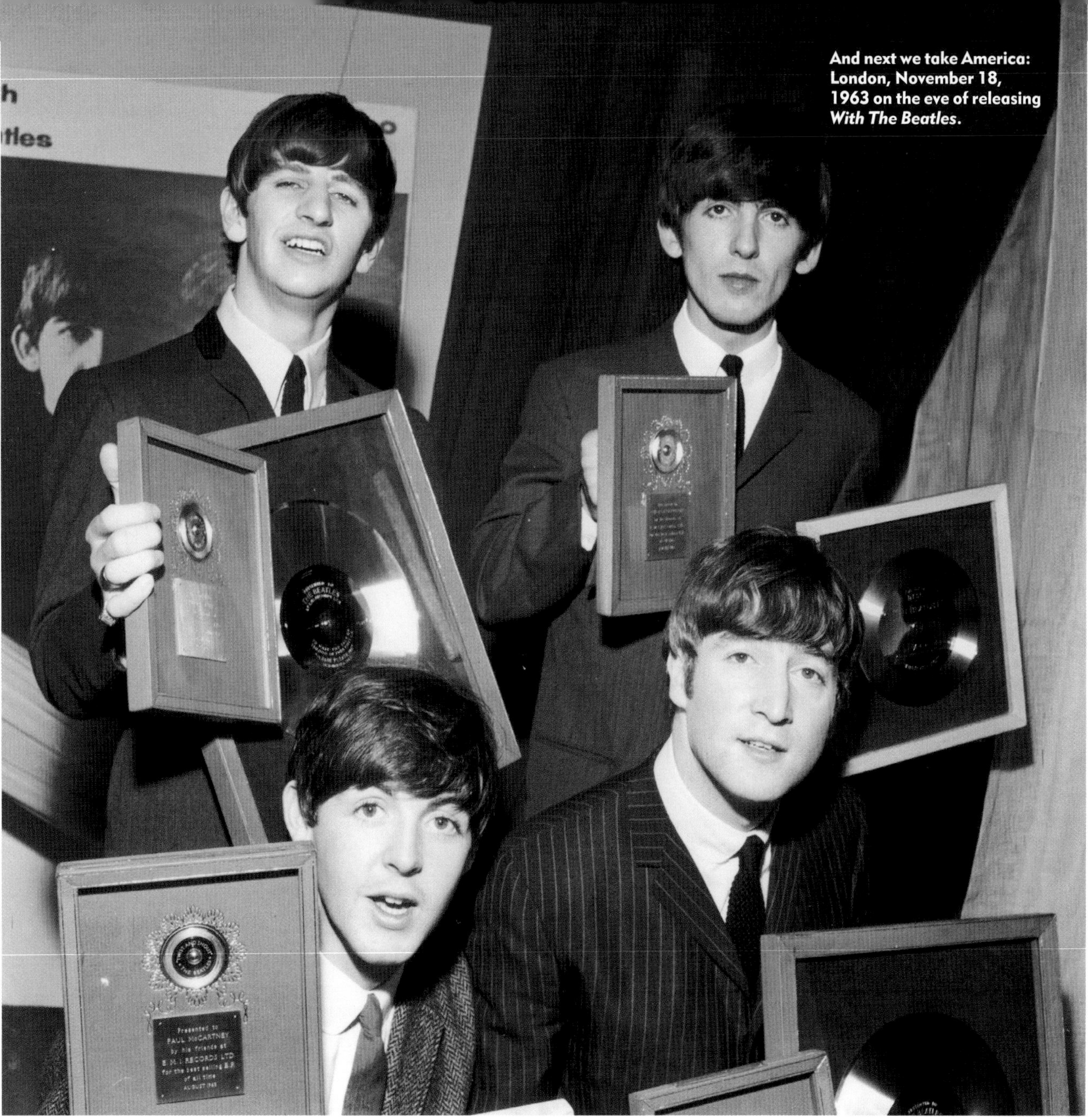

And next we take America: London, November 18, 1963 on the eve of releasing *With The Beatles*.

PHOTO: HULTON ARCHIVE

sion in Lennon's song ("You're coming home! You're coming home!"), optimism and consolation in Paul's ("I'll pretend that I'm kissing the lips I am missing"). Although they were developing their melodic and harmonic powers by the day, their lyrical ideas were still off-the-peg. Just as they understood the potency of personal pronouns and stock scenarios (Love Me Do, From Me To You, She Loves You), so they were aware of radio listeners' devotion to the "missing you, darling" songs of Two-Way Family Favourites, forever stocked by tremulous requests from lovelorn soldiers in Cyprus, sorrowing sailors in Valparaiso and homesick emigrants in Australia.

In between the sessions' end and the LP's release, the British newspapers invented a new word, Beatlemania, while the Queen and courtiers were invited to "rattle their jewellery" at the Royal Command Performance. Within a week of the appearance of *With The Beatles*, just in time for a million missives to Santa Claus, the boys unleashed I Want To Hold Your Hand and America's surrender was imminent. But for now, all that mattered in British homes was getting a copy of this album. It looked so well on the low-slung stereogram that had just replaced the wind-up gramophone in the corner. And the cool, strangely austere artwork hinted at something deeper and darker to emerge from these funny young men. Their four faces hung like brand new planets, half-lit in the inky blackness of space, full of a wonderful promise.

CHILDISH PLEASURES

He may wish that Ringo had been lead singer, but Billy Childish still loves *With The Beatles*.

"I first heard The Beatles when I was four years old. Up until then it had been Dusty Springfield and some other scary stuff. I sat in front of the TV staring as they played She Loves You, and afterwards me and my big brother practised miming in the living-room mirror. Back then The Beatles were still fans of a style of music, rather than fans of themselves. You've Really Got A Hold On Me, is still elemental. Money – that's a good version, and George does great on Roll Over Beethoven. George is my favourite Beatle – very disciplined and conscientious in writing his parts. I like Till There Was You, it suits Paul McCartney better than Sir Paul's later disco rubbish.

"It seems that The Beatles could hammer anything into their style. Hear them on *Live! At The Star-Club* doing Marlene Dietrich's Falling In Love Again like you never will again. I Wanna Be Your Man would have been better with its original Bo Diddley beat. To annoy real Beatles fans I suggest that the Fab Four should've brought Ringo out from behind the drums permanently as lead singer – give the job to the person least suited and increase the punk rock factor!

"It Won't Be Long and All My Loving are OK for pop songs – pleasant and upbeat without degenerating into total hell. For me, The Beatles were about believing you could do it yourself with toy guitars and plastic wigs. It made you feel part of something bigger and more exciting. This was as big an influence in doing my own stuff as punk was in '77. In 1965 our next door neighbour, Big Caroline (aged 11) went to see The Beatles play Canterbury. For some inexplicable reason, my parents wouldn't allow me to go. I've never forgiven them."

Joe Cushley

A Design For Life

When Terence Spencer first shot the Fabs for Life magazine, John Lennon invited him to join them on the road. Here he tells Lois Wilson some of the stories behind the pictures.

"You're a bloody nuisance. I can't stand the sight of you!' – those were the first words John Lennon ever uttered to me," reflects photographer Terence Spencer. "But then he said, 'If you're that interested in The Beatles, why don't you come up to Liverpool and we'll give you a real story?' It was all the impetus I needed and I didn't leave the band's side for the next four months."

That was back in November 1963. Spencer had just returned from Africa where he'd been taking photos for American magazine, Life. It was his 13-year-old daughter Cara who tipped him off about the band ("At first I thought she was talking about a plague of insects!") and, eager to get a piece of the action, he and Life magazine's chauffeur and photo assistant Frank Allen followed the band to Bournemouth where The Beatles were playing the Winter Gardens. "At first it was difficult to infiltrate their inner circle, but after a couple of days I became a part of their lives. We soon got on like a house on fire. They didn't even notice I was taking photographs of them."

Spencer was used to adapting to new situations. As a fighter pilot in World War II he'd been a prisoner of war twice and still holds the record for the lowest authenticated parachute jump. Taking snaps of The Beatles was easy in comparison. Although getting Life magazine interested in the story wasn't. "The Beatles were yet to make it big Stateside and the editor reluctantly gave me two pages to fill. By the end of the project The Beatles had appeared on The Ed Sullivan Show and were such a huge phenomenon they not only made the biggest showbiz story in the magazine ever – running at eight pages – but the cover too."

▶ THE BEATLES PARIS, JANUARY 1964

"This is one of the few posed pictures that I shot of the band and, I have to say, they *hated* posing for the camera. But Life magazine insisted we get a cover shot of the group all together on their trip to Paris. If you look closely you can see the Eiffel Tower in the background. The Beatles enjoyed their stay in France because they could wander around on their own and not be recognised by anyone. They weren't big stars over there yet – they could sightsee and stay in swish hotels. In England they were so famous they felt like prisoners."

◀ JOHN AND FRIENDS LONDON, NOVEMBER 1963

"Here John is lounging backstage somewhere. To alleviate the boredom between performances the band would invite their friends around. They couldn't actually venture outside because their fans would follow them everywhere they went. In fact, they had to hide from the public. The actress Sandra Caron and Brian Epstein are also in the room. Can you see how bored they all look? They used to play chess, or play with their Scalextric and toy trains to pass the time."

ALL PHOTOS: TERRY SPENCER/ CAMERA PRESS

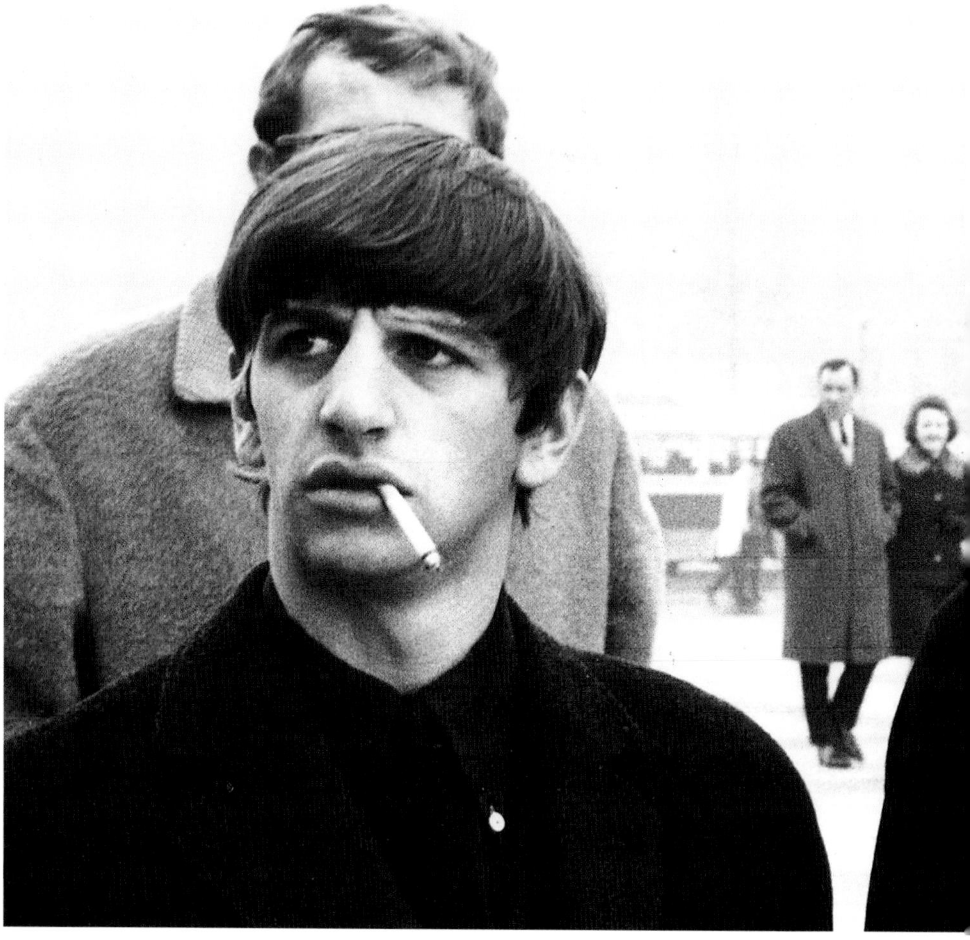

▶ THE BEATLES
PARIS, JANUARY 1964

"I wanted to encapsulate the moment. Four friends relaxed and strolling around the city centre. The Beatles always went around together. They were proper pals. Here you can see they're out on a day trip with their press officer, Brian Somerville and road manager, Mal Evans. It's an off the cuff shot. By this time they were oblivious to my camera but I had to remember never to use a flash, however dark it was. I didn't want to arouse attention."

◀ THE BEATLES NOVEMBER 1963

"What's unusual here is that although The Beatles were already incredibly popular they always did their own make-up and styled their own hair. It was always just the four of them backstage getting ready and having a joke and a laugh together. They didn't wear much make-up, just a dusting of powder to offset the glare of the bright lighting."

◀ RINGO AND JOHN LONDON, DECEMBER 1963

"Ringo and John are checking out the front stage area before their series of Christmas shows at the Astoria in London. I was crouched down on the side of the stage to get the shot. John is wearing sunglasses even though we're inside and it's quite dark. The shows ran from Christmas Eve to January 11. They were spectacular. Girls were screaming – they were actually having orgasms and the medics had to be on standby because some girls would lose consciousness with all the excitement. I'd never seen anything like it!"

▲ RINGO AND PAUL
COVENTRY, NOVEMBER 1963

"They used to smoke incessantly. It helped pass the time although they didn't smoke pot, just tobacco. They weren't big drinkers either. I never once saw them drunk. They seemed to prefer tea and Pepsi Cola. They really were very polite boys in complete contrast to The Rolling Stones who cultivated a very rebellious, naughty image. They always used to be watching television. In all the time I was with them I never once heard them play music. I don't think they even had a record player with them."

▲ JOHN
COVENTRY, NOVEMBER 1963

"Here's John on his own backstage in Coventry. I caught him totally off-guard by calling out his name. If you look closely you can see he's got a camera around his neck. You can see the strap over his shoulder. To stop some of the boredom they all got cameras like my Nikon 35mm and I taught them how to photograph properly. They couldn't go out and buy the cameras themselves, of course, they couldn't step foot outside. But they got their road manager to buy them and soon they all became avid picture-takers. They'd snap anything – each other, friends, myself. And because I'd leave my cameras lying around they would often pick them up and have a go on them too. Some of these photos could actually have been taken by The Beatles themselves."

▲ RINGO AND THE POLICE LONDON, DECEMBER 1963

"The Beatles weren't allowed to go anywhere without a police escort. Although they missed their freedom to walk around on their own they made the best of any situation they found themselves in and always had a lot of fun. Here they'd just finished playing one of their Christmas shows at the Astoria. At the end of the concert three of the policemen jumped onstage, grabbed Ringo and lifted him up to the ceiling then carried him backstage as a jape. Ringo got them back by showering them with hundreds of pieces of torn-up paper. 'It's snowing!' he cried."

▶ GEORGE AND JOHN LONDON, NOVEMBER 1963

"With all of my pictures of The Beatles I wanted to convey what they were really like – basically four very clean, nice, pleasant boys. This is my favourite picture actually. I think it captured their innocence and their humour at that time. John was the wittiest but he could also be the most abrasive. They found it very difficult being cooped up backstage before a performance for so long. They had to make their own entertainment. Of course, they didn't really cut their own hair – they're just pretending. They had their own barber and a tailor too, to make their suits."

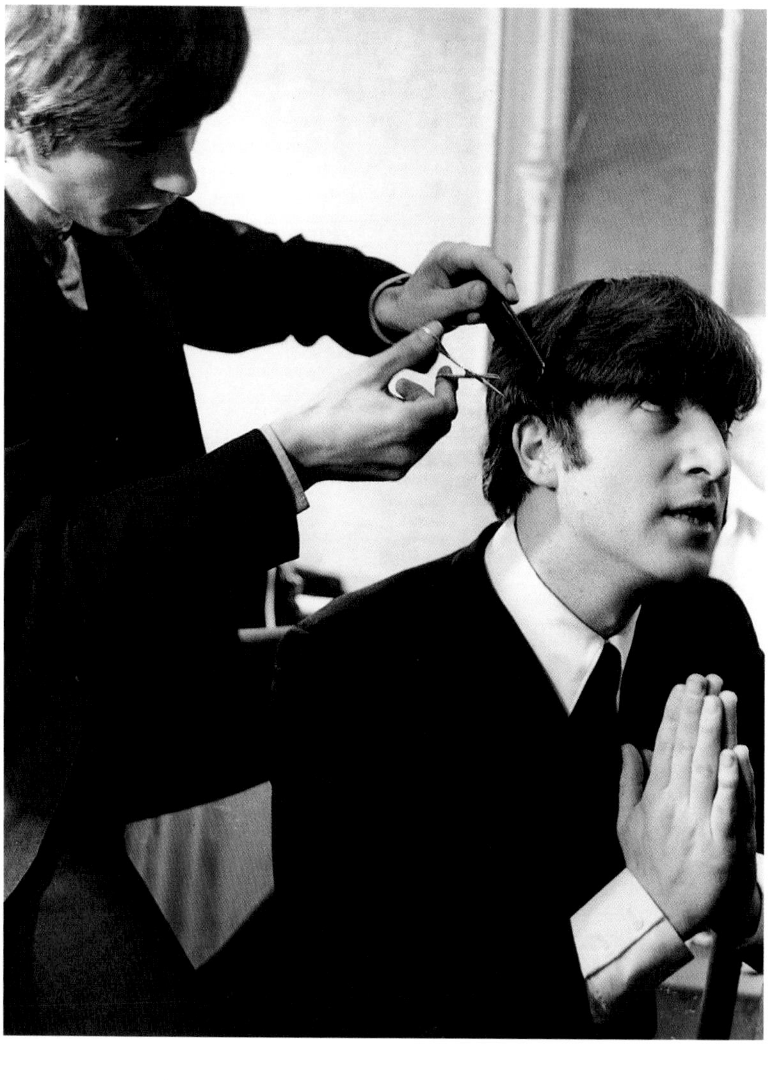

ALL PHOTOS: TERRY SPENCER/ CAMERA PRESS

▲ THE BEATLES
PARIS, JANUARY 1964

"When The Beatles went to Paris they took their Austin Princess with them. Here they are leaving a hotel being chased by autograph-hunters. I'm in the car behind – a Mercedes Benz limo – with Frank Allen of The Searchers. I took it from the right-hand front seat with the lens right up against the glass of the window so as not to get a reflection. Sometimes, John would play his guitar while they were in the car, though I don't think he's doing that here!"

◀ BRIAN EPSTEIN
MANCHESTER, NOVEMBER 1963

"Brian was a keen gambler and he loved nothing more than going to the casino. I had to take this picture surreptitiously because you aren't actually allowed to take photos inside a casino. When I was about to leave the manager came over and said, 'I'd better have a copy of that picture you took'. He wasn't angry but he'd spotted me through one of the cameras that was placed over the croupiers to spy on them. I used a tiny SP Nikon, which is like a Leica and has a very quiet shutter. I slipped it under my jacket and snuck it in."

23 A brief recording session at Abbey Road is followed by a flight to Sweden for their first foreign tour.

24 After a press call at the Hotel Continental, the Swedish visit begins with a live radio concert at Karlaplanstudion, Karlaplan, Stockholm.

25 The Beatles' Swedish tour continues at Nya Aulan, Sundsta Laroverk, Karlstad.

27 Three shows in one day at Lorensberg Circus, Gothenburg.

29 Brian Epstein concludes an agreement with United Artists to make the first Beatles film. Meanwhile, The Beatles play the Sporthallen, Hamngatan, Eskilstuna, Sweden.

30 The Beatles end their Swedish tour at Narren-teatern, Grona Lund, Stockholm.

31 At Heathrow Airport, thousands of screaming fans welcome The Beatles back from their Swedish tour.

NOVEMBER 63

1 At The Odeon Cinema, Cheltenham, The Beatles begin their first headlining UK tour.

2 The UK tour continues at the City Hall, Sheffield.

3 The band play the Odeon Cinema, Leeds (right).

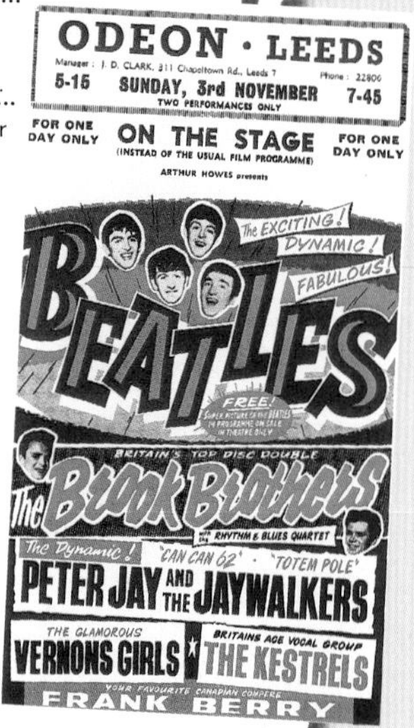

4 The Beatles appear on the Royal Variety Command Performance at the Prince Of Wales Theatre, London, along with Tommy Steele, Marlene Dietrich, Joe Loss & His Band, Buddy Greco and Harry Secombe.

5 Brian Epstein flies to New York City with Billy J Kramer, to make plans for The Beatles' first visit.

7 The Beatles fly to Eire for a show at the Adelphi Cinema, Dublin.

8 The Beatles play the Ritz, Belfast.

12 Paul McCartney collapses with gastric flu during rehearsals for a show at The Guildhall, Portsmouth.

13 The Beatles' tour continues at the ABC Cinema, Plymouth.

18 A presentation of several Silver Discs is made to The Beatles at EMI House in London.

20 Another performance at the ABC Cinema, Manchester. Parts of the show are filmed for Pathé News' Beatles Come To Town newsreel.

22 The band's second album, *With The Beatles*, is released in the UK.

25 The band spend the afternoon at Manchester's Granada Studios filming for Scene At 6.30, they are interviewed with Ken Dodd by Gay Byrne.

26 The Beatles' UK tour continues at the Regal, Cambridge.

29 The Beatles release I Want To Hold Your Hand/This Boy – their first single to achieve advance sales of more than one million. The band play the ABC Cinema, Huddersfield.

30 A show at the Empire Theatre, Sunderland. Backstage, they meet aspiring politician Jeffrey Archer, who persuades them to be photographed as part of an Oxfam fund-raising appeal.

What: The Beatles meet Jeffrey Archer
Where: Empire Theatre, Liverpool
When: December 7, 1963

CAMPAIGN SUPERNOVA

When Jeffrey Archer conned the Fabs into being pictured with an Oxfam poster, it triggered one of 1963's biggest charity campaigns. By Johnny Black.

DYNAMIC, GOOD-LOOKING JEFFREY ARCHER, (alleged) Oxford undergraduate and president of the University Athletic Club, was clearly a young man going somewhere. Overflowing with boundless energy, he was never short of ideas. Towards the end of 1963, young Jeffrey took on the task of running the Oxford end of Oxfam's latest campaign – to raise £1m. And, of course, he knew just how to do it. He would get The Beatles to front the campaign. The fact that he didn't know the Fabs or anyone remotely connected with them, was neither here nor there. He would find a way.

A visit to Oxford by Geoffrey Parkhouse, universities correspondent of The Daily Mail, provided a starting point. Archer button-holed Parkhouse and pitched the idea at him, astutely suggesting that the Mail could become involved. His timing was perfect. Every newspaper in the land was desperate to find new angles on the Fab Four, and the opportunity to tie in with their first charitable venture would be hard to resist.

On his return to London, Parkhouse presented the idea to his bosses, who proved to be very interested indeed, but only if Archer could provide solid evidence to back up his claim of Beatles involvement. This, of course, Archer did not have.

Undaunted, he approached their press officer, Brian Sommerville. Up until that moment, Sommerville's boss, Brian Epstein, had politely but determinedly turned down every single approach made by charity organisations hoping to secure the direct involvement of The Beatles in a campaign, fearing that to accept even one would be to open the floodgates. But Archer's luck was in. Epstein was in America and, after an initial refusal, he secured one tiny concession from Sommerville. Far from agreeing to become involved, Sommerville merely suggested that if Archer could make his way to Liverpool's Empire Theatre on December 7, he might be able to get The Beatles' autographs.

That was all he needed. At the appointed time, Archer presented himself at The Empire and was ushered into the presence of The Beatles. In a bravura masterstroke, rather than simply asking for autographs, he unfurled an Oxfam banner and presented them with collecting tins. Before they had time to think, a Press Association photographer had taken the shot that gave Archer everything he needed.

"We didn't know who he was," recalls Tony Bramwell, the band's aide at the time. "This was a particularly frantic day, with a live fan club show at The Empire in the afternoon, a TV recording for Juke Box Jury, and a regular gig in the evening at the Odeon. Somewhere in the middle of all this, the photograph with Archer was taken. In those days, The Beatles were used to being herded into rooms to have a picture taken with the Lord Mayor, another picture with the Chief Constable, and if someone stuck a collecting tin and an Oxfam poster in their hands, they'd get photographed with that too, but it didn't necessarily mean that they'd agreed to take part in a fund-raising campaign."

For Archer, however, it was enough. The photograph was all he needed to convince Oxfam and The Daily Mail that he had secured their involvement. Then, in a brilliant flourish, he used everything he'd finessed so far to convince former Prime Minister Harold Macmillan – who happened to be Oxford's University Chancellor – that he too should get on board the Oxfam-Beatles-Daily Mail bandwagon.

When The Daily Mail began running the campaign story, complete with the picture that 'proved' The Beatles' involvement, Brian Epstein hit the roof. Nothing had been signed and nothing agreed, but he was well aware of the damage potential of the inevitable adverse publicity that would attach itself to his loveable moptops if they seemed to be pulling out of such a worthy cause.

Paul and George hobnob with Archer, Brasenose College, Oxford, 1964.

Reluctantly, he came to an agreement with Oxfam that The Beatles would do the minimum necessary to be seen to be supporting the campaign. Throughout the month of December 1963, The Daily Mail championed Oxfam and, by the start of the new year, the £1m target was clearly in view. One top Oxfam executive, Richard Exley, subsequently noted that Archer had "muscled in and made a lot of money and, in my view slightly exaggerated things. The Beatles did blow-all… all they actually did was hold up a poster and say, 'Great thing, guys'."

"Jeffrey Archer struck me as the kind of bloke who would bottle your piss and sell it." Ringo Starr

But the story was still not quite at an end. Part of Epstein's damage limitation agreement was a promise that The Beatles attend a dinner with Harold Macmillan in London, where they would present an autographed poster to the child who had raised the most for Oxfam. However, American commitments meant they were unable to fulfil this obligation. The fall-back plan was to present the poster at a dinner in Oxford's Brasenose College on March 5, 1964, during a break from filming of A Hard Day's Night.

That was the moment when one Beatle took the opportunity to put his feelings about Archer into words. The writer and broadcaster Sheridan Morley was then a student at Oxford and he remembers, "There was a dinner and I went along. In the course of the evening I went to the toilet, and there beside me was Ringo Starr. He asked if I knew this Jeffrey Archer bloke. I said everyone in Oxford was trying to work out who he was. Then Ringo said: 'He strikes me as a nice enough fella, but he's the kind of bloke who would bottle your piss and sell it'."

PHOTOS: PA PHOTOS/POPPERFOTO/HULTON ARCHIVE

Don't do it, John! Future Conservative politician and jailbird Jeffrey Archer nabs his Beatles "photo op" backstage at Liverpool's Empire, December 7, 1963

Well, it beats panto: the Finsbury Astoria, London, 1963, venue for The Beatles' Christmas show.

What: The Beatles' Christmas show
Where: The Astoria, Finsbury Park
When: December 24, 1963

FROM ME TO YULE

In 1963 The Beatles decided to offer their fans a little something extra with a Christmas show. They soon regretted it. By Chris Hunt.

FROM HIGH UP ON THE FRONT OF THE Finsbury Park Astoria, four giant Beatle faces grin down on the screaming girls below. December 24, 1963, and the streets are jammed for the first night of The Beatles Christmas Show. John, Paul, George and Ringo have been inside for the last couple of hours, spirited into the theatre early to avoid the chaos that their arrival would cause this close to showtime.

In the dressing room of the opening act, The Barron Knights take a look out of the window and are taken aback. The streets around the theatre are rammed as far as the eye can see, a bold 'All Seats Sold' sign above the entrance testifying to the band's popularity, all 100,000 seats having been snapped up within days of going on sale.

In his bid to consolidate the position of the acts in his NEMS management stable at the heart of the nation's show business establishment, Brian Epstein had been looking beyond the pop charts, setting his sights on film, TV, and on that traditional cornerstone of British family entertainment, the pantomime. On the same night that Epstein had Gerry & The Pacemakers opening at the Hanley Gaumont in his co-production of Babes In The Wood, The Beatles were debuting what they hoped would be a rather more alternative slice of seasonal fare. "Something different," they had suggested when pushed by 'Eppy' to outline their ideas, "with sketches and things".

"We didn't like the idea of doing a pantomime," George explained the next year, "so we did our own show – like a pop show, but we kept appearing every few minutes, dressed up... for a laugh."

Always eager to deliver value for money, and wanting to offer fans something more than a pop concert draped in tinsel, Epstein had brought in a seasoned veteran of the 'Christmas show' to add fine detail to the band's broad brushstrokes. "I'm changing the concept of the pantomime," director Peter Yolland had bravely announced, as he set about cobbling together as many scream-proof visual gags as he could muster in the incredibly short rehearsal time offered to him.

"The Beatles were never much for rehearsing," says PR man Tony Barrow. "That never really mattered as far as songs were concerned, but the fact that they were so bad at doing the sketches was an added extra for the show – it was organised chaos but it was very funny chaos."

The Beatles dashed on and off-stage between support acts – The Barron Knights, The Fourmost, Tommy Quickly, Billy J Kramer & The Dakotas, Cilla Black – woodenly performing their short 'humorous' skits with winning Scouse charm. A Victorian melodrama, a quick 'doctor' sketch, whatever they did, rehearsed or not, the Fabs would be greeted with uncontrollable hysteria. "Let's face it," said Paul McCartney, "they would have laughed if we just sat there reading the Liverpool telephone directory."

Their novelty turns might have proved popular, but nothing could compare to the reaction that greeted their closing rock'n'roll set. Rolf Harris was in position to experience this nightly wall of noise close-up – as the show's compere, he filled the 15-minute slot prior to The Beatles, busking while the band's equipment was being set-up behind the curtain. "After my spot I'd say, Last night nobody heard a word these boys sang and it's such a waste because they are fantastic. Have a listen to the wonderful music of The Beatles," recalls Rolf. "But a scream went up and it lasted for the whole of their act – they might just as well have been miming, you couldn't hear a single note."

Ducking to avoid the jelly beans flying at them from out of the blinding glare of the spotlight, The Beatles kicked off with Roll Over Beethoven, and exactly 25 minutes later, with the last chords of Twist And Shout still echoing around the auditorium, they were already gone, "otherwise they'd never have got out," recalls Rolf.

"The big trick was to get them out of the theatre before the national anthem had finished," explains Barrow. "The audience dutifully stayed, chanting, 'We want The Beatles', by which time they were in their car and away."

After their opening night success, the Liverpool members of the cast – everyone but Rolf and The Barron Knights – were flown home to their families in a private Viking aircraft, chartered for £400 by Epstein. Returning for the first show of Boxing Day, the 'organised chaos' could then start over again – until the curtain fell on the 30th and last performance on January 11, 1964, the same day that I Want To Hold Your Hand entered the American charts.

With their first US Number 1 only a matter of days away, The Beatles had good reason to wonder whether such revue-style shows were in the best interest of a serious rock'n'roll band. "As the run went on I think they realised that it wasn't really working," says Barron Knight, Pete Langford. "They wanted to be songwriters and pop stars, they didn't want to be actors."

Brian Epstein succeeded in booking the band into a 38-show run at the Hammersmith Odeon for Another Beatles Christmas Show in December, '64, but on August 2, 1965, when he announced the NEMS artists who would be in pantomime that year – Cilla Black (Little Red Riding Hood), Gerry & The Pacemakers (Cinderella) and Billy J Kramer & The Dakotas (Mother Goose) – there was no mention of The Beatles.

Two weeks later, facing a press conference in Toronto, the Fabs were asked whether they would be performing in a third Christmas Show.

"Ask Mr Christmas Epstein," sniped Lennon.

"Mr Epstein," chipped George, "may have a Mr Epstein Christmas Show."

For The Beatles the era of all-round family entertainment had come to an end. Rock'n'roll was moving in other directions – and the acts that stayed in panto that year were the acts that rock left behind.

PHOTOS: TERENCE SPENCER, PICTORIAL PRESS

DECEMBER 63

1 The Beatles play the De Montfort Hall, Leicester.

2 An appearance on the Morecambe & Wise Show is recorded at Elstree Studio Centre, Borehamwood. The Beatles perform a charity show at the Ballroom, Grosvenor House Hotel, Park Lane.

6 The first Beatles Christmas Record begins arriving at homes of Beatles Fan Club members across the UK.

7 In London, The Beatles appear on Juke Box Jury as the entire panel. On the same day, a Silver Disc is awarded to I Want To Hold Your Hand.

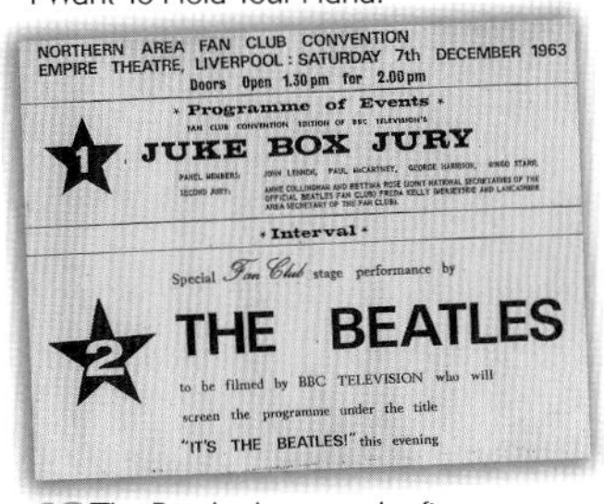
NORTHERN AREA FAN CLUB CONVENTION
EMPIRE THEATRE, LIVERPOOL : SATURDAY 7th DECEMBER 1963
Doors Open 1.30 pm for 2.00 pm
* Programme of Events *
FAN CLUB CONVENTION EDITION OF BBC TELEVISION'S
1 JUKE BOX JURY
PANEL MEMBERS: JOHN LENNON, PAUL McCARTNEY, GEORGE HARRISON, RINGO STARR
SECOND JURY: ANNE COLLINGHAM AND BETTINA ROSE (JOINT NATIONAL SECRETARIES OF THE OFFICIAL BEATLES FAN CLUB) FREDA KELLY (MERSEYSIDE AND LANCASHIRE AREA SECRETARY OF THE FAN CLUB)
* Interval *
Special Fan Club stage performance by
2 THE BEATLES
to be filmed by BBC TELEVISION who will screen the programme under the title "IT'S THE BEATLES!" this evening

12 The Beatles become the first act ever to knock themselves off the top of the UK singles chart when I Want To Hold Your Hand replaces She Loves You. The band play the Odeon Cinema, Nottingham.

14 The band perform at a Southern Area Fan Club concert at the Wimbledon Palais.

15 The Beatles record an appearance on an all-Liverpool episode of Thank Your Lucky Stars, at Alpha Television Studios, Birmingham.

17 A live appearance is recorded for the Christmas edition of BBC radio show Saturday Club, at the Playhouse Theatre, London.

18 A two-hour long Beatles radio special, From Us To You, is recorded at the BBC's Paris Studio, London.

20 In the NME Annual Readers' Poll, The Beatles win World Vocal Group and British Vocal Group categories.

21 A performance in the Gaumont Cinema, Bradford, is described by Peter Jones of Record Mirror as "pretty much a shambles". The gig was effectively a dress rehearsal for the upcoming Beatles' Christmas Show.

22 The second dress rehearsal at the Empire, Liverpool, is much improved.

23 A new 15-minute Radio Luxembourg series, It's The Beatles, has its first transmission.

24 The Beatles' Christmas Show opens at the Astoria Cinema, Finsbury Park, London.

25 The Beatles fly to Liverpool (above) to be with their families for at least part of Christmas Day.

29 The Sunday Times music critic, Richard Buckle, describes Lennon and McCartney as "the greatest composers since Beethoven".

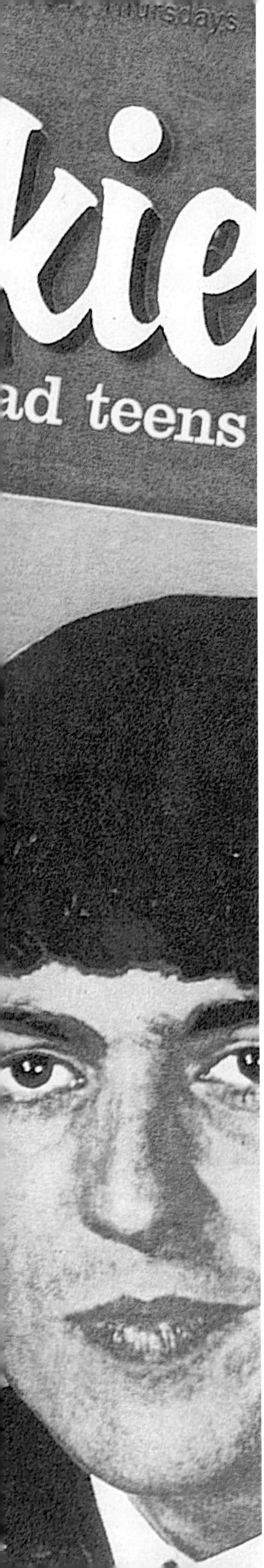

1964

By 1964 The Beatles went supernova worldwide. They released their first movie, A Hard Day's Night, exported Beatlemania to the States by way of a memorable appearance on The Ed Sullivan Show, and then totally dominated the American charts before the end of the year by scoring 19 hit singles. They even managed to find time to meet Harold Wilson and Cassius Clay!

beatles
Australia 1/6 · New Zealand 1/3 · South Africa 15 cents
Rhodesia 1/9 · East Africa 1·60 cents · West Africa 1/6
9th MAY 1964
COLOUR COLOUR COLOUR
bulous
S INTO HAMBURG
IZE FULL COLOUR PIN-UPS
S GERRY RATTLES BACHELORS ETC
HOWTIME
NEW FILM MONTHLY
Star-Club
Gerry and the Pacemakers
Hier Gastierten:
Tony Sheridan
Bo Diddley
Brenda Lee
TOMMY ROE
Ray Charles
Bill Haley
Dee Dee Sharp
THE BEATLES
Joe Brown
Fats and his Cats
VINCE TAYLOR
Jerry Lee Lewis
WITH THE BEAT
en, the man who wrote the
TLE BAT
Test cricketer's family killed

One was loud, passionate and sardonic; the other urbane, ambitious and optimistic. Together, the formidable songwriting partnership of Lennon and McCartney sparked a musical revolution that changed popular culture for ever. By Ian MacDonald.

A Perfect Match

When the songwriting partnership of Lennon and McCartney walked into the Studio 51 jazz club in Great Newport Street, Soho, London on Tuesday, September 10, 1963, they seemed, to James Phelge, early friend of The Rolling Stones, like "two well-heeled businessmen in dark coats and suits". According to Andrew Loog Oldham, the Stones' co-manager, who'd just met the pair in the street outside and been hailed by them as an old cohort, "John and Paul looked fabulous in their three-piece, four-button bespoke Dougie Millings suits. With Paul in lighter and John in darker shades of grey, their gear was a mod variation of the classic Ted drape jacket, set off by black velvet collars, slash pockets and narrow, plain-front trousers."

PHOTOS: JANE BOWN/CAMERA PRESS

The Beatles were then in the middle of recording their album *With The Beatles*, and had three smash hit singles to their name, their current Number 1 being She Loves You. They were already enjoying the wealth that Beatlemania had brought them and, in showbiz terms, were a made act, having just been guests of honour at a Variety Club lunch at The Savoy. Within a month, they would top the bill on ATV's Sunday Night At The London Palladium, the official recognition of Beatlemania as a national phenomenon.

The Stones listened respectfully while Lennon and McCartney finished writing I Wanna Be Your Man, before Brian Jones speculatively added a slide guitar part. The two expensively dressed Beatles then departed – established stars descending briefly from on high to offer assistance to some scene friends as yet to hit the big time. (The Stones quickly recorded I Wanna Be Your Man and went to Number 12 in the UK chart with it, the next stage in their career before it finally exploded with Not Fade Away.)

By then, of course, the Lennon-McCartney franchise was an exclusive friendship. Proven hit-writers, they were a team in more ways than one: best mates as well as mutually respectful musicians. Yet only a few years earlier, Lennon's loyalties had been somewhat divided between McCartney and his art school contemporary and ex-Beatle Stuart Sutcliffe. Lennon, who was two years closer to Sutcliffe than McCartney, admired his older friend's Fine Arts savoir faire and Existentialist chic. McCartney had no answer to either quality and must have seemed a bit of a kid in comparison. Yet the musical bond between Lennon and McCartney had been strong since they first met at Woolton fête on July 6, 1957. They'd both been writing, or trying to write, songs for at least the last five years. Music was what was ultimately important to Lennon. In any event, when Sutcliffe died, on April 10, 1962, the last obstacle to Lennon's commitment to McCartney as a creative equal had disappeared.

Not that the Lennon-McCartney trademark was functionally operational by April 1962. A list of early Beatles songs sent by Brian Epstein to George Martin on June 6, 1962, shows Lennon and McCartney's "original compositions" under their respective authors rather than as the product of a partnership. (McCartney: Love Me Do, P.S. I Love You, Like Dreamers Do, Love Of The Loved; Lennon: Ask Me Why, Hello Little Girl.) Moreover, the partnership was referred to in the credits for the *Please Please Me* album, released in the UK on March 22, 1963, as "McCartney/Lennon". Indeed, "Lennon-McCartney" did not emerge until The Beatles' fourth single, She Loves You, released here on August 23, 1963, only a fortnight before the duo met The Rolling Stones at the Studio 51 club and gave them I Wanna Be Your Man. In Barry Miles's Many Years From Now (1997), McCartney complains that he could never see why "Lennon-McCartney" was better than "McCartney-Lennon", but says nothing about the process by which this trademark became changed in August 1963.

What's more certain is that, in their initial stage as public property, The Beatles seemed to be 'led' by Lennon, the most physically imposing and loud of the group. He, of course, always regarded The Beatles as, in an inspirational sense, his, having formed the germinal group and thence recruited McCartney to his cause. Likewise symbolic was the band's line-up with Lennon alone at his own mike to stage right, and McCartney stage left at a mike shared with Harrison. Lennon also sang the band's two early rabble-rousing set-enders, Twist And Shout and Money. There was more than a subliminal sense that Lennon, and others around him and The Beatles, believed him to be in some unspecified way the leader of The Beatles in the first year of their career. This changed with *With The Beatles*, when McCartney's creative profile was upped by All My Loving. A more balanced view of the two partners resulted – but not before the group's writing trademark had been altered to give Lennon priority.

Joined at the hip: Paul and John, playing in Germany in 1963.

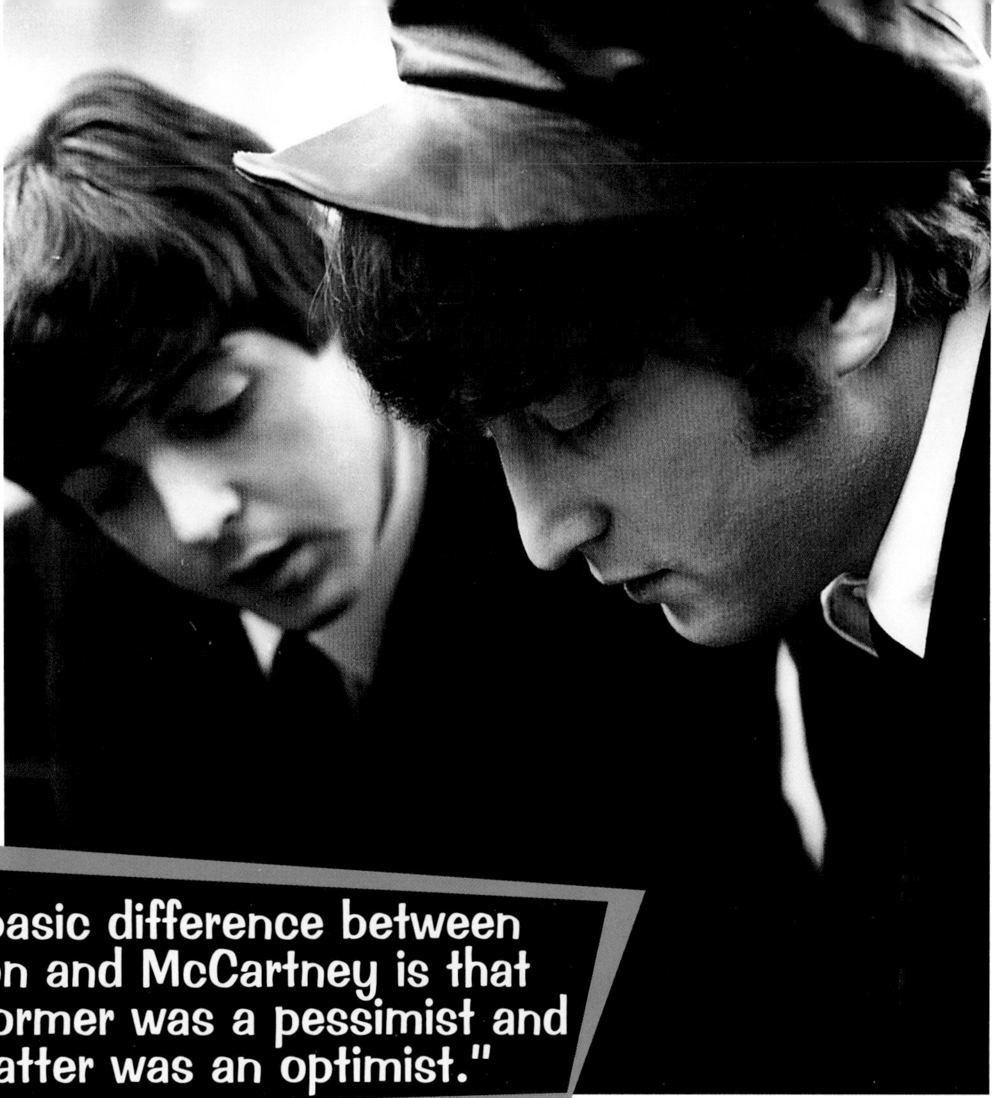

By April 1962, what's known of the products of what later became called the Lennon-McCartney partnership was uneven, albeit already developing. Some of what they were writing (eg, One After 909) was frankly crude, while Love Me Do has a bleak 'Northern' simplicity about it that seemed quite radical in the context of the more softcore UK singles chart of the time. It wasn't until September 1962, when Lennon and McCartney wrote Please Please Me and I Saw Her Standing There, that the partnership came into full swing as a recognisable voice of real originality. By then, the two of them were into a firm, businesslike partnership, taking their writing craft seriously, intent on not merely staying competent at it but getting better all the time.

"The basic difference between Lennon and McCartney is that the former was a pessimist and the latter was an optimist."

They also very soon cottoned on to the fact that they could place their songs with other 'artistes' if they wrote in a way which suited them. On *Please Please Me*, P.S. I Love You is a perfect formula song for sale, while Do You Want To Know A Secret, written for Harrison's voice, was taken up by Billy J Kramer & The Dakotas, and Misery, written for Helen Shapiro, was covered by Kenny Lynch. There's evidence of a quid pro quo fairness going on between Lennon and McCartney at this time: Paul got the B-side of Love Me Do with his P. S. I Love You, John got the B-side of Please Please Me with his Ask Me Why.

Apart from I Saw Her Standing There and the title track, the outstanding original on *Please Please Me* was There's A Place, a 50-50 co-composition done at McCartney's home in 20 Forthlin Road, Liverpool, and, as such, the model for a way of working – bar by bar, "one on one, eyeball to eyeball" writing – which carried on for the next six months: From Me To You, Thank You Girl, She Loves You, I'll Get You. The raw intensity of There's A Place made it sound especially original, almost as if it already existed in a version by some other artist, as their R&B and Motown covers did. The Lennon-McCartney partnership proceeded very closely between The Beatles' first and second albums, but as the time to record *With The Beatles* arrived, they began to work more independently again. Lennon took the lead with It Won't Be long, Not A Second Time and All I've Got To Do, showing the last to McCartney in the studio just before it was recorded. McCartney was responsible for Hold Me Tight and All My Loving. Only Little Child and I Wanna Be Your Man were 50-50 co-composed.

The climax of the 50-50 style was The Beatles' fifth single, I Want To Hold Your Hand, recorded on October 7, 1963, during the fourth of the six weeks in which She Loves You was Number One on the UK singles chart. The Beatles' sixth single, however, made during January-February 1964, was entirely composed by McCartney, being The Beatles' first A-side not to be a collaboration between John and Paul. Can't Buy Me Love must have come as something of a shock to Lennon, who can only have been taken by surprise by the situation. Its B-side (which we can assume to have been written by Lennon during the month between the two dates for Can't Buy Me Love) was You Can't Do That, which, title and all, appears to have been the opening shot in a campaign to make sure he kept a leader's grip on the The Beatles' songwriting. On *A Hard Day's Night*, he wrote the title track, plus I Should Have Known Better, Tell Me Why, Any Time At All, I'll Cry Instead, When I Get Home, and, of course, You Can't Do That, as well as co-writing If I Fell, I'm Happy Just To Dance With You, and I'll Be Back, on the last of which he was the dominant voice. McCartney, by contrast, added to Can't Buy Me Love only And I Love Her and Things We Said Today.

Lennon 'got' the next Beatles A-side, too – I Feel Fine – adding No Reply and I'm A Loser to *Beatles For Sale*. McCartney countered with I'll Follow The Sun, Every Little Thing and She's A Woman. Baby's In Black, Eight Days A Week, I Don't Want To Spoil The Party and What You're Doing were co-written. Lennon would go on to claim the next two Beatles A-sides (Ticket To Ride and Help!). Indeed McCartney would not begin fully to recover his position as an equal partner until summer 1965.

Thus the 1,000 days between April 1, 1962 and December 31, 1964 were marked by a distinct rivalry within the Lennon-McCartney partnership during which Lennon may have prevailed upon Brian Epstein to alter the original "McCartney/Lennon" credit while also being stung into accelerated action as an independent writer by the appearance of Can't Buy Me Love, an A-side in which he had had no consultation. This rivalry between John and Paul was the secret of the continuing upward trend in the quality of the work ascribed to "Lennon-McCartney". They worked together as usual on 50-50 co-compositions but also made sure they strove to match each other independently, at which effort Lennon, seemingly by design, was demonstrably more effective for about 12 months (ie, February 1964 to February 1965). Thereafter, McCartney came increasingly into his own, eventually dominating the partnership in terms of quantity of compositions, whether independently or collaboratively done.

PHOTOS: REX/TERRENCE SPENCER

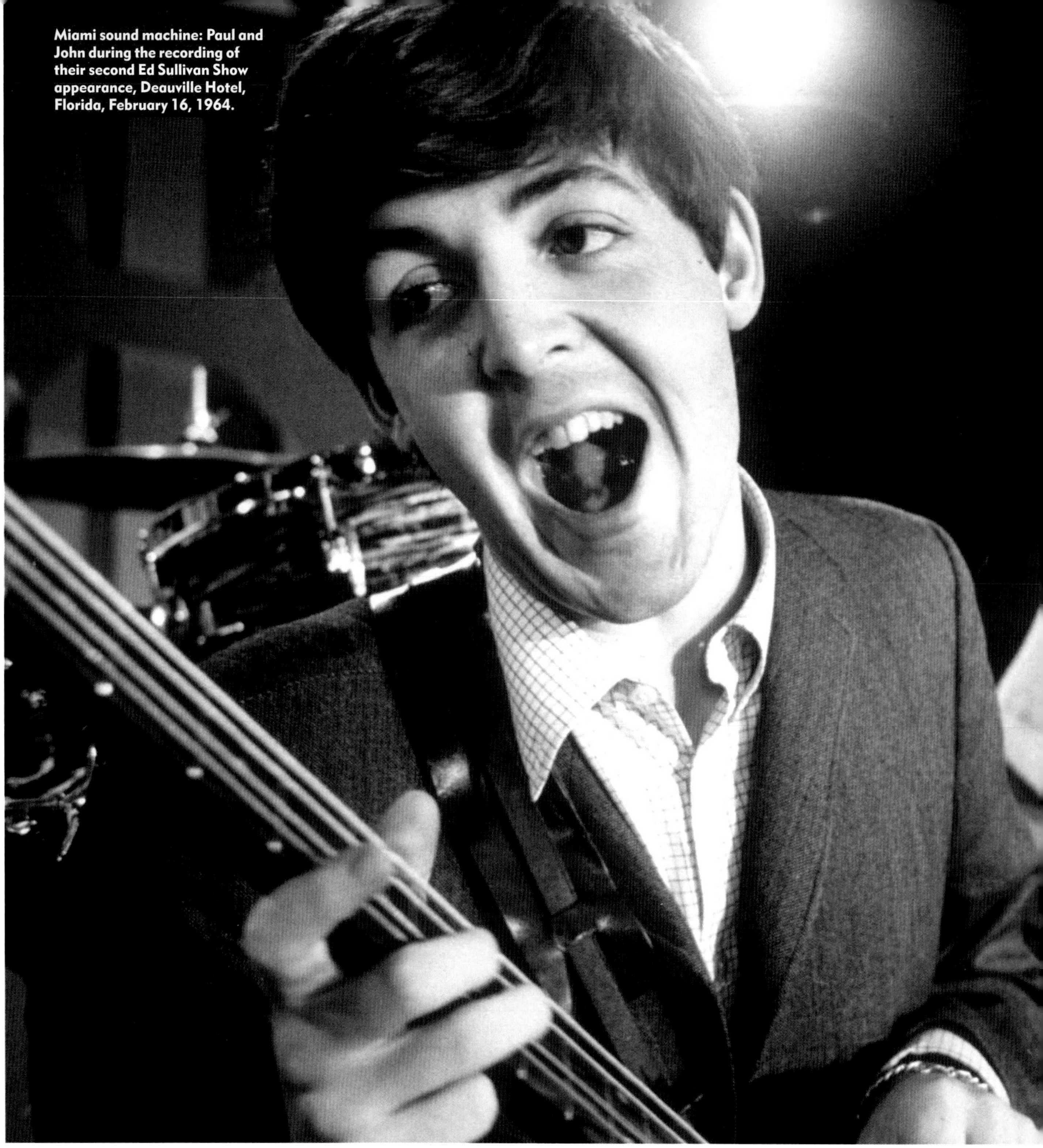

Miami sound machine: Paul and John during the recording of their second Ed Sullivan Show appearance, Deauville Hotel, Florida, February 16, 1964.

PHOTO: REX

Behind the urbane and affluent facade of the Lennon-McCartney partnership which The Rolling Stones saw at the Studio 51 club on September 10, 1963, was an ongoing more-or-less-friendly tussle between two contrasting stylists, each intent on getting his input into The Beatles (and/or the repertoire of other artists who wished to take a ride to success on their material). Lennon and McCartney wrote fluently together when the mood or the situation took them, but they wrote at least as much, and sometimes more, apart from each other. Moreover, the differences between their independently conceived songs embodied the distinct contrast between them as individuals – a contrast which Norman Smith, The Beatles' engineer between 1962 and 1966, saw, by the time of *Rubber Soul*, as an "obvious clash" of personalities.

More naturally musical than Lennon, McCartney expressed his breezy, optimistic character in wide-striding melodic steps which range freely over the stave to create tunes that need no harmonic support, making sense on their own. Lennon's lazy, sardonic nature comes through in the smaller range of his melodic intervals, closer to the intonations of speech than song. Without their chordal accompaniment, many of his tunes are less eloquently hummable than McCartney's, although in harmonic context they regain their force of expression. The essential difference between the two as writers is one of temperament. Lennon's allegiance to truth over beauty reflects in the close correspondence between his lyrics and his melodies, the music expressing the feeling evoked in the mood of the song as a whole. McCartney, by contrast, could let his natural facility create music more loosely constrained by the sentiment of the lyric, although at his best he could be every bit as musically expressive as his partner.

The simplest reduction of the differences between Lennon and McCartney would be that the former was basically a pessimist and the latter basically an optimist. There are exceptions to this rule in the work of both partners. Lennon, for example, became more optimistic during The Beatles' LSD period; McCartney's songs about Jane Asher were often tense with unresolved disagreements. Fundamentally, though, Lennon's caustic humour was based on a view of life conditioned by his experiences as a boy and a youth, periods in which he lost several

"No other songwriting partnership has ever outstripped Lennon & McCartney in terms of consistency of quality or sheer aural fantasy."

people close to him, including, most significantly, his mother. This left him with a brusque intolerance of the false or sentimental. McCartney, while he shared with Lennon the loss of his mother during his teens, was more susceptible to softness and sentimentality. He was also, though, more energetic and inquisitive than Lennon, while his general attitude to his work as a songwriter and musician was firmly realistic and hardheaded.

United by their love of rock'n'roll, Lennon and McCartney took a businesslike view of their songwriting partnership, working assiduously on weaknesses in their songs and always checking back over recent work to make sure that they were up to scratch in what they were producing. The three-hour "writing sessions" they began to adopt after their first album were based on the three-hour recording sessions then standard in the British pop industry. They felt that if they treated their songwriting with the same regularity and intensity of input that they devoted to recording, the results would naturally maintain a high standard. They sought to keep their noses to the grindstone by whatever means best suited them – a methodology derived from their shared sense of ambition.

A key aspect of the Lennon-McCartney partnership was the sense of history the two had. They set out to surpass what had gone before them in youth-oriented popular music, but also had a conception of songwriting as a craft older and more widely established than what had immediately preceded The Beatles. They were, for example, far more catholic in their pop music taste than the Stones, who started, not as a rock'n'roll group, but as a blues and R&B band, and whose notion of precedence for what they were doing began as a focus on the urban black music of Chicago. The Beatles, schooled in the demanding night-long sets expected of them in Hamburg's bars, incorporated not only rock'n'roll, but folk music, Broadway ballads, and the new black pop emanating from Detroit. As songwriters, John and Paul had no snobbery, drawing on a variety of traditions without creative compromise. On the contrary, The Beatles' strength in songwriting very much depended on the fertile mixture of inspirations their rough Hamburg upbringing had inculcated in them.

While Lennon and McCartney's achievement in almost single-handedly sweeping away the songwriting incumbency of Denmark Street is as easily underestimated as their role in promoting the English language around the world, the most remarkable single thing about them, particularly by the standards of today, is that, for nearly five years they got better and better at what they did. Young rivals attempting to keep up with Lennon and McCartney in original material in 1963 would have been astonished to foresee what heights their models would have ascended to by the end of 1966. The creative trajectory between Love Me Do and, for example, the Strawberry Fields Forever/Penny Lane single shows the musical conceptions of the main songwriting Beatles moving between almost entirely different imaginative worlds. The gain in articulacy and ambition is quite vertiginous; nor was the fall-off thereafter very marked. Lennon and McCartney remained productive until The Beatles' career ended.

The fact that the Lennon-McCartney songbook, musically and lyrically, so rapidly improved in scope and expression is only one facet of the partnership's achievement. Lennon and McCartney also led a revolution in the very ethos of songwriting which consisted in seeing the song as a part of something larger: the record. The duo started as songwriters who, with two other partners, made records, spending most of their time outside the recording studio. By early 1966, they were record-makers who wrote songs, and most of their time was spent inside Abbey Road, working continuously for months at a time. They did not invent this trend. Pioneers like Phil Spector were early luminaries in the process. But it was The Beatles, and especially Lennon and McCartney, whose development as songwriters pushed the revolution through.

Identifiable as upward jumps in the ascending arc of Lennon and McCartney's output between April 1962 and the end of 1964 are songs/records like She Loves You, I Want To Hold Your Hand, A Hard Day's Night and I'm A Loser – each acquiring greater expressive force or articulacy than that with which the partnership had operated before. (The sequence thereafter continues with Ticket To Ride, Yesterday, In My Life, Tomorrow Never Knows, Strawberry Fields Forever/Penny Lane, A Day In The Life and I Am The Walrus.) Other groups shadowed this revolution – in particular The Beach Boys and The Byrds in America, the Stones and The Kinks in Britain – but no other songwriting/record-making set-up outstripped Lennon-McCartney in terms of consistency of quality or sheer aural fantasy. They were, and remain, the measure of popular music in their time – and, by genealogical descent, of music in our time, too. ■

We have lift-off: The Beatles charm 73 million Americans with a little help from Ed Sullivan (second left).

What: Playing The Ed Sullivan Show
Where: Studio 50, Broadway, New York
When: February 9, 1964

BEST IN SHOW

When fate brought The Beatles and Ed Sullivan together, 73 million people tuned in and rock'n'roll changed overnight. By David Fricke.

IN OCTOBER, 1983, I SAT IN A DRESSING room at the Ed Sullivan Theater in New York, on Broadway at 53rd Street, interviewing the members of REM. They were there to play on a TV show, a children's music programme on the Nickelodeon channel. "You know," guitarist Peter Buck said, gesturing at the make-up mirror, "this was The Beatles' dressing room."

Maybe it was. Later, I heard that stage-hands there liked to tease visitors, telling everyone in any of the tiny, changing spaces backstage that they were in The One – the room John Lennon, Paul McCartney, George Harrison and Ringo Starr used on Sunday, February 9, 1964, when they made their live American television debut on The Ed Sullivan Show and transformed the nation, popular music and the future of rock on TV, all at once. I don't remember if there was a number on REM's door; I should have checked. According to an original Sullivan production memo, the Fab Four had two rooms: 52 and 53.

In fact, the entire building is hallowed ground. Now the home of Late Night With David Letterman, Studio 50 – as it was originally known – was Sullivan's throne during his quarter-century reign as "Mr Sunday Night", from 8 to 9pm on the CBS network. A stern fireplug of a man who spoke in a strange chuckling cadence with his chin tucked down on his chest as if he had no neck, Sullivan literally broadcast the rock'n'roll revolution as it happened. Elvis Presley's three appearances in 1956 and '57 capped his meteoric rise from hellcat to king. And all through the 1960s, Sullivan booked only the hottest young hit-makers for his variety hour. The Rolling Stones, The Supremes, The Byrds, Smokey Robinson and The Doors were just some of the legends who sang for Sullivan, between comics, crooners and trapeze acts, before he went off the air in 1971.

But nabbing The Beatles was Sullivan's great triumph, the gold seal on his genius as a showman. Rock'n'roll was already a staple on network TV, in sanitized form: on Dick Clark's ABC after-school dance party, American Bandstand; in Ricky Nelson's singing spots on his parents' sitcom, The Adventures Of Ozzie And Harriet. Sullivan was not the first guy to put The Beatles on TV in the US. On January 3, 1964, a week after Capitol Records issued I Want To Hold Your Hand, Jack Parr broadcast BBC footage of the group singing She Loves You on his NBC talk show.

On The Ed Sullivan Show, however, the country saw Beatlemania, live, up close and uncompromised, for the first time. The five songs The Beatles performed on February 9 – All My Loving, Till There Was You and She Loves You in the opening segment; I Saw Her Standing There and I Want To Hold Your Hand in the finale – perfectly compressed the electricity they had invented and honed at The Cavern and the Star Club. The cameras' repeated cutaways to the screaming teenage girls in the studio audience, leaping in their seats and crying in ecstasy, made sure no-one at home missed the physical and sexual energy flying between band and fans. (Things could have turned out a lot differently. Harrison, feeling ill, missed a rehearsal that morning; Beatles assistant Neil Aspinall was used as a stand-in while the cameramen set their positions.)

"We were new," Lennon crowed in triumph years later. "When we got here, you were all walking around in fuckin' Bermuda shorts with Boston crew cuts and stuff on your teeth." He was right. Still reeling from the murder of its youngest President, John F Kennedy, three months earlier, psychologically stuck in the surface white-bread calm of the 1950s, America was ripe for blindsiding. The Beatles did the rest. But Sullivan gave them the air time.

The impresario happened to be in London, at the airport with his wife Sylvia on October 31, 1963, when The Beatles returned from a Swedish tour to the usual lunatic reception. "I asked someone what was going on," Sullivan recalled, "and he said, 'The Beatles!' Who the hell are The Beatles?" Two weeks later, Sullivan was back in New York, negotiating with Beatles manager Brian Epstein. Epstein pressed for top billing. Sullivan claimed there was no such thing on his show: He was the star.

Epstein won in principle, if not fact. Sullivan typically paid top stars $7,500 for a single appearance, but Epstein accepted a more modest total fee of $10,000 for two live broadcasts on February 9 and 16, the latter from the Deauville Hotel in Miami, and a third pre-recorded segment on February 23. The real pay-off was astounding. Seventy-three million people watched the February 9 show, a record-breaking audience for a single telecast. In Miami, The Beatles played six songs, dropping Till There Was You and adding This Boy and From Me To You. For February 23, the group did Twist And Shout, Please Please Me and, once again, I Want To Hold Your Hand. And The Beatles remained loyal to Sullivan. They played live again in August, 1965, and returned, via film clips, in '66, '67 and '70.

Almost 40 years later, there is more rock'n'roll on TV than Sullivan or The Beatles could have ever imagined. The magnetism is harder to find: awards shows are scripted to death; concert films are edited into confetti; most documentaries are airbrushed valentines. In 1964, The Beatles merely had to be themselves; Sullivan had the eyes of America. Together, they made it possible for rock'n'roll to change an entire nation – overnight.

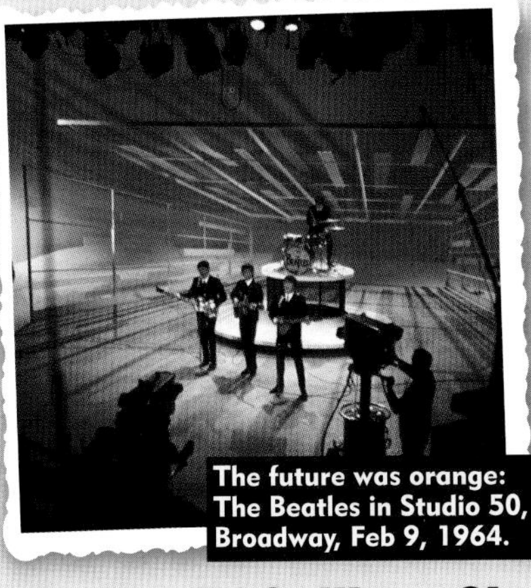

The future was orange: The Beatles in Studio 50, Broadway, Feb 9, 1964.

"On The Ed Sullivan Show the US saw Beatlemania up close, live and uncompromised for the first time."

PHOTOS: ALPHA, POPPERFOTO, PICTORIAL PRESS

JANUARY 64

4 The Beatles' Christmas Show (see programme, right) continues at the Astoria Cinema, Finsbury Park, London, for another 11 nights.

8 The band's first appearance on American TV is a film clip on the Jack Paar Show, in which they are seen performing in Bournemouth.

4 US trade magazine Billboard reviews The Beatles' new single, I Want To Hold Your Hand, as "a driving rocker with surf-on-the-Thames sound and strong vocal work".

5 Pre-production work begins on the first movie starring The Beatles, A Hard Day's Night.

7 A live session is recorded for BBC radio show Saturday Club, at the Playhouse Theatre, London.

11 The Beatles' Christmas Show comes to the end of its run at the Astoria, Finsbury Park, London.

12 The Beatles make their second appearance on TV show Sunday Night At The London Palladium.

14 John Lennon, Paul McCartney and George Harrison arrive in Paris to begin a three-week season at the L'Olympia Theatre.

15 Capitol Records is granted an injunction in Chicago, Illinois, to prevent Vee-Jay Records from distributing or marketing any more recordings by The Beatles. (Vee-Jay was the first US company to release material by The Beatles, but the group later signed to Capitol).

16 The three-week season begins at L'Olympia, Paris.

17 I Want To Hold Your Hand reaches Number 1 in the US charts.

20 The Beatles' first US album, *Meet The Beatles*, is released.

29 The band record a session at Pathé Marconi studios in Paris. They record Can't Buy Me Love and also make German-language versions of She Loves You and I Want To Hold Your Hand.

30 Vee-Jay Records re-release Please Please Me in the US, backed by From Me To You.

FEBRUARY 64

3 A US Gold Disc is awarded to the band for the *Meet The Beatles* album.

4 The season at L'Olympia, Paris, comes to an end.

5 The Beatles fly back to London from Paris.

7 On Pan-Am flight PA-101, The Beatles fly into New York City's Kennedy Airport for their first US tour. They're greeted by 5,000 screaming fans (above).

8 Brian Epstein asks New York City attorney Walter Hofer to take care of The Beatles' US fan-mail. His first batch consists of 37 sacks.

9 In the evening, 73 million Americans tune in to watch the Fabs' first US TV performance on The Ed Sullivan Show.

10 New York Times critic Theodore Strongin notes that, "The Beatles have a tendency to build phrases around unresolved leading tones. This precipitates the ear into a false modal frame that temporarily turns the fifth of the scale into the tonic, momentarily suggesting the Mixolydian Mode. But everything always ends a plain diatonic all the same."

11 The Beatles make their first live concert appearance (right) in the US at The Coliseum, Washington DC, headlining over Tommy Roe, The Righteous Brothers, Jay & The Americans, The Chiffons and The Caravelles. For the first time, they are pelted with jelly beans. They attend a party at the British Embassy. US President Lyndon B Johnson tells former British Prime Minister Sir Alec Douglas-Home, "I like your advance party but they need a haircut."

12 When The Beatles arrive at Pennsylvania Station, New York, their carriage is detached from the train and brought in to an inconspicuous side-platform, enabling the group to be smuggled past the waiting crowds. That night they play two shows at Carnegie Hall.

13 The Beatles arrive at Miami Airport where 4,000 fans riot by breaking down doors, smashing windows and trampling police officers. The band were hoping for a brief break in their hectic tour schedule.

14 More rehearsals for a second Ed Sullivan Show appearance.

15 Billboard magazine reveals that The Beatles have five songs climbing the US Hot Hundred and three LPs on the albums charts.

16 Seventy million Americans watch the band's second performance on The Ed Sullivan Show, live from the Deauville Hotel, Miami, Florida.

17 A new single, All My Loving, is released in the US. A rest day is spent water ski-ing and fishing.

18 A meeting with boxer Cassius Clay is arranged at his Florida training camp.

19 Two more rest days are spent on Miami Beach.

21 The Beatles fly out of Miami, making a brief stop in New York.

22 The Fabs arrive at Heathrow Airport, London (above).

23 Another appearance on TV show Big Night Out is taped at Teddington Studios.

24 Ringo Starr makes a visit to his family in Liverpool.

25 George Harrison celebrates his 21st birthday on the same day that The Beatles begin recording tracks for their first movie, A Hard Day's Night. The first two songs taped are Can't Buy Me Love and You Can't Do That.

26 The Ministry of Aviation states that, following disruption to services at Heathrow Airport caused by crowds of airline staff flocking onto the tarmac to see The Beatles landing on the 22nd, they will investigate arrangements for VIP arrivals at the airport.

What: *The Beatles meet Cassius Clay*
Where: *Fifth Street Gym, Miami*
When: *February 18, 1964*

SECONDS OUT!

Getting The Beatles in the ring with Cassius Clay was a risk, but the five pulled it off to produce a memorable publicity stunt. By Merrell Noden.

IN THE MARTINI-SWILLING BOYS' CLUB THAT was Sports promotion in the early '60s, Harold Conrad was definitely a maverick. He actually preferred marijuana to Martinis and was, in the words of Ali biographer David Remnick, "an all-star pothead before the invention of rock'n'roll". Hired to do the thankless job of hyping a seemingly one-sided fight between two men nobody liked – the thuggish ex-con champion, Sonny Liston, and the pretty boy challenger with the non-stop mouth, Cassius Clay – Conrad was visited by one of his most brilliant ideas. The Beatles, who had just hit the top of the US charts with I Want To Hold Your Hand, were in Miami that week, killing time after appearing on The Ed Sullivan Show – throw the charming Beatles together with the witty Clay. Who knew what sparks would fly?

Conrad was right on the money. The meeting worked then, yielding a priceless photo of a bug-eyed Clay landing a right on George Harrison's cheek, with the other Beatles lined up behind him, domino style, and it works today.

In February of 1964 Clay was many years and many controversies away from becoming the beloved figure he is now. A few days after the fight, he would acknowledge that he had joined the Black Muslims, and if that didn't alienate a mainstream America still reeling from the assassination of President Kennedy, his later name change and refusal to fight in Vietnam would make him one of the most reviled men in America, a lightning rod for vitriol. All that was still in the future, but the vast majority of Americans did not need those excuses to despise the 22-year-old boxer. What infuriated them was his mouth, which spewed doggerel, insults and boasts in a non-stop torrent of verbiage. Good athletes, not to mention good negroes, were supposed to be humble and quiet.

He was not the first boxer The Beatles would encounter that week. Appearing on The Ed Sullivan Show with them was the man everyone was sure was going to give Clay the whupping of his life, the surly Sonny Liston. "A couple of minutes after The Beatles started singing," recalled Conrad, "Sonny sticks his elbow in my ribs and says, 'Are those the motherfuckers what all the people are screaming about? My dog plays better drums than that kid with the big nose'."

The Beatles showed up at the Fifth Street Gym at 10.30am on February 18, one week before the fight. Clay wasn't there, so Ringo began introducing the band, deliberately mixing them up. This schtick might have charmed elsewhere, but not with the assembled pack of cynical beat writers. "I thought they were a pain in the ass," admits sportswriter Hank Kaplan.

The Beatles were not exactly short on attitude themselves. As the minutes ticked by and Clay still hadn't shown up, they grew increasingly mutinous. "Where the fuck's Clay?" complained Ringo.

"Let's get the fuck out of here," said Lennon.

They tried to leave but found their path blocked by two hulking Florida state troopers. Who knows what might have ensued had not a voice boomed from the doorway. "Hello there, Beatles. We ought to do some road shows together. We'll get rich."

It was Clay, of course, framed in the doorway. It was a first sight of the boxer in the flesh, not only for The Beatles but also for a reporter from the New York Times named Robert Lipsyte. "The Beatles gasped and so did I because that first glimpse of Cassius Clay was thrilling," recalled Lipsyte. He was so beautiful and so perfectly proportioned. You could never really tell from the photographs and from television just how big he was. He filled the doorway – six-foot three and over 200 pounds – and he was carrying a big staff like a prophet. He'd been up the beach, harassing Sonny Liston. And there was a wonderful, hushed moment when the five of us just looked at this gorgeous creature from another planet."

How much either party knew about the other is questionable, though Clay's trainer, Angelo Dundee, insists that The Beatles were huge fight fans and may have met Clay earlier, when he was in England to fight Henry Cooper. One thing they certainly had in common was their taste in music. According to Howard Bingham, Ali's closest friend, Clay "loved Little Richard: Good Golly Miss Molly and Tutti Frutti. And Lloyd Price."

Everyone knew what to do when the cameras were on. Though The Beatles were probably at the gym for less than an hour, it was enough for some inspired horseplay. At one point, Clay ordered, "Get down, you little worms!" and down went all four Beatles on the canvas. At another, he picked up Ringo as if he weighed ounces. "Clay mesmerised them," said Harry Benson. "He completely controlled them."

Well, not quite. Clay employed a stock line he still uses today: "Hey, you guys aren't as dumb as you look!"

"No," said Lennon, staring him in the eye, "but you are."

"After The Beatles left the gym, Cassius Clay was heard whispering, 'So who were those little faggots?'"

The awkwardness of that moment was swept aside, though after The Beatles had left, Clay turned to Lipsyte and whispered, "So who were those little faggots?"

One week later Clay would stun the world by so completely befuddling Liston that he refused to answer the bell for the seventh round. From there, he would become the most famous face in the world, a martyr whose loyalty the establishment could never quite be sure of. Like The Beatles, he was a sign of the revolution to come, and that scared the old guard silly.

PHOTOS: POPPERFOTO/HULTON ARCHIVE/PA PHOTOS

ords of the ring: Clay
ells the Fabs to, "Get
own, you little worms!"

Wearing their "Purple Hearts" on their sleeves: John and Ringo receive their Variety Club awards from Harold Wilson, Dorchester Hotel, Park Lane, London

What: Harold Wilson meets The Beatles
Where: Dorchester Hotel, Park Lane
When: March 19, 1964

POLL POSITION

When Harold Wilson seized a photo opportunity with the Fabs, he wasn't the first politician to jump on The Beatles bandwagon. By John Harris.

IN EARLY 1964, BILL DEEDES – AN OLD Harrovian, Conservative Cabinet member – gave a speech to the City of London branch of the Young Conservatives. Given that The Beatles were freshly successful in America, it was perhaps not surprising that his speech paid tribute to them; what was truly remarkable was that Deedes seemed to see the group as the leaders of some kind of national renaissance.

"They herald a cultural movement among the young which may become part of the history of our time," he said. "For those with eyes to see it, something important and heartening is happening here."

Within a month, Alec Douglas-Home, the Tory Prime Minister since October 1963, had seen fit to join in. The Fabs, he claimed, were "our best exports" and "a useful contribution to the Balance of Payments". Not long after that, the New Statesman published an infamous essay by Paul Johnson entitled The Menace Of Beatlism, in which he claimed that "Conservative candidates have been officially advised to mention The Beatles whenever possible in their speeches". Reeling from the Profumo Scandal, and clearly atrophying after 13 years in power, the Tories seemed to be making a last-ditch grope for some reflected glory.

In the Club: the Fabs accept their VC awards.

The response of Harold Wilson, Leader Of The Opposition and the MP for the Liverpool constituency of Huyton, was perhaps predictable: "The Conservative Party," he privately fumed, "are trying to make The Beatles their secret weapon." It is some token of the speed at which the group had snared Britain's affections that, a mere 16 months after the release of Love Me Do, they were assuming enough importance to fleetingly become a political football.

"John seized on the shape and colour of the awards and said, 'Thanks for the Purple Hearts, Harold'."

On March 19, mid-way through the filming of A Hard Day's Night, The Beatles were scheduled to appear at the annual Variety Club Awards, to accept their gong for Showbusiness Personalities of 1963. Wilson, even then famed for his wiliness, saw his chance: putting in a call to Sir Joseph Lockwood, the Chairman of EMI, he suggested that he would be the perfect man to make the presentation. No matter that Wilson's roots were in Yorkshire; he assured Lockwood that he was "a fellow Merseysider".

And so what the modern political vernacular terms a "photo-opp" came to pass. Pictures of the event show The Beatles marking the occasion with the behaviour they had long since perfected in the presence of local dignitaries: wearing stick-on smiles, while managing to affect just enough cheeky irreverence to live up to expectations. Wilson, however, looks very pleased with himself indeed. In the words of Philip Norman's Shout, "His face, in the double-page newspaper spreads, wore the smile of one who had discovered a great secret".

There are two accounts of the group's brief acceptance speeches. In one, John Lennon – apparently unsure of who Wilson was, and doubtless in a hungover fug after another night at the Ad-Lib – confused the Leader Of The Opposition with the Variety Club's Chief Barker, thought of Barker & Dobson toffees and mumbled, "Thank you, Mr Dobson". In another, altogether more legendary version, John seized on the shape and colour of the Variety Club's awards and smirked, "Thanks for the Purple Hearts, Harold".

Whatever, Wilson's appearance was enough to turn The Beatles-related political debate on its head: soon enough, the Conservatives were accusing the Labour Party of cynically manipulating the group for political ends. Wilson's response was his craftiness in excelsis: while rebutting the charge, he managed to sustain the idea that he and The Beatles were somehow riding the same wave. "As a Merseyside Member of Parliament," he said, "I have to ask – is nothing sacred?"

As evidenced by the political stampede to The Beatles' door, 1964 was election year – and though they were recurrently asked about their sympathies, they yielded to showbiz etiquette and never gave any real hint one way or the other. On October 15, the night of the General Election, they were in Stockton-On-Tees, where they played a show at the Globe Cinema and gave an interview to North East Newsview. "Good stuff, this election stuff," smirked Paul. When asked if they had voted, John claimed that they "were having dinner at the time". Ringo implored Wilson not to increase the duty on cigarettes; George, serving notice of one of his key '60s obsessions, asked him to "cut surtax a bit".

Nonetheless, Wilson managed to build himself into The Beatles' story: it barely needs mentioning that his one *coup de grâce* was the recommendation that The Beatles should receive MBEs for Services To The British Economy. He also sporadically popped up in their creative endeavours: in the last verse of Taxman, and in Commonwealth (aka No Pakistanis), Paul's slack satire on the race debate that found its way on to tape during the *Let It Be* sessions. There was also The General Erection, a delightfully garbled essay in A Spaniard The Works that satirised the 1964 General Election and proved that John had a little more political nous than he let on.

Six years after the Variety Club Awards came decisive proof that, thanks to the supernatural forces of history, the fates of Wilson and The Beatles were intertwined. The former's '60s tenure as Prime Minister ended with his defeat by Ted Heath in June 1970: two months after Paul McCartney had formally announced the band's demise.

PHOTOS: POPPERFOTO/LFI/PICTORIAL PRESS

27 In continuing recording sessions at Abbey Road, work is completed on And I Love Her, If I Fell and Tell Me Why.

28 Peter & Gordon release a new single, A World Without Love, written by Lennon and McCartney. The Beatles record a second From Us To You special for BBC radio at 201 Piccadilly, London.

29 *Introducing The Beatles* peaks at Number 2 in the US album charts, held off the top by *Meet The Beatles*.

MARCH 64

1 More recording takes place at Abbey Road Studios.

2 At Paddington Station, London, The Beatles set off for the West Country to begin filming their first, as-yet-untitled, movie. The first six day's shooting would take place on a train.

3 During this day's filming, George Harrison meets the model Patti Boyd (above, far left).

4 George asks Patti Boyd out on a date.

5 In a break from filming, The Beatles dine with Jeffrey Archer at Brasenose College, Oxford, as part of the Oxfam campaign they are supporting.

6 Filming continues between London and Minehead.

9 The last day of train-based filming is completed between London and Newton Abbot – The Beatles have travelled 2,500 miles in the past week.

10 Filming takes place at the Turk's Head pub, Twickenham – where in the film Ringo plays darts and almost takes out a closely-perched parrot.

11 A train guards' van sequence is filmed at Twickenham Studios, in which The Beatles perform I Should Have Known Better.

12 Peter & Gordon enter the UK charts with the Lennon-McCartney song, A World Without Love. The band continue filming at Twickenham studios.

13 Closing scenes are filmed by helicopter at Gatwick Airport.

14 A new single, Twist And Shout, is released in the US.

16 Can't Buy Me Love is released in the US, with advance orders of 2.1 million copies. Ringo films his canteen sequence for A Hard Day's Night at Twickenham.

17 Filming at Les Ambassadeurs Club, Hamilton Place, London.

18 Further filming takes place at Twickenham Studios.

19 British Prime Minister Harold Wilson presents The Beatles with their Show Business Personalities Of The Year (1963) Award at the Dorchester Hotel, London.

20 Can't Buy Me Love is released in the UK and The Beatles appear again on Ready Steady Go!.

21 A UK Silver Disc is awarded to the All My Loving EP as She Loves You reaches Number 1 in the States.

You need
ventilation
STEEL

Empire Building

Welcome to the messy rise of The Beatles' business empire featuring dodgy dealings and missing millions. Peter Doggett explains all.

"Money, that's what I want", John Lennon sang in 1963. Four months later, Paul McCartney countered: "Money can't buy me love". Yet as Beatlemania spread around the world, money became as central to The Beatles' myth as the music for which they were famous.

PHOTO: NORMAN PARKINSON/CORBIS

"So much of the media coverage about their early success hinged around how much they were earning," says Beatles chronicler Mark Lewisohn. "Every time they met the press, someone would be bound to ask them whether they were millionaires yet." Under that scrutiny, it's not surprising that money, and especially the magic million mark, loomed large in the group's consciousness in 1963 and 1964. "I don't know if I'll ever be a millionaire," George told the Daily Mirror on his 21st birthday in February 1964. "We only get two bob [10p] from every £1 we earn, and that's split four ways – sixpence each."

Even though the basic equation was correct – the British government did indeed claim up to 90 per cent of their unsheltered income in tax – George's mental arithmetic let him down on one important point. Their share of the cake was divided not into four but five. The spare fifth was claimed by the man who, legitimately as well as mathematically, was the only contender for the title of the Fifth Beatle: Brian Epstein.

"That's it, we're finished," John Lennon thought to himself when Epstein died in 1967. Brian had been their mentor and protector since the end of 1961, the man who had steered them from Liverpool's clubland to Shea Stadium and beyond. Utterly trusted by his charges, he had erected a management organisation which handled all of their financial and contractual negotiations, their dealings with the media, even their legal hassles with paternity and broken promise suits. Urbane and passionately committed to his 'boys', he was acclaimed by both the group and the outside world as the man responsible for their scarcely believable ascent to fame.

Yet by 1970, Lennon's mood had changed. "Brian was a nice guy," he told Jann Wenner, "but he knew what he was doing, he robbed us. He fucking took all the money and looked after himself and his family." A few months later, he repeated his verdict: "Brian ripped us off. We never got anything out of it – Brian did."

Nearly three decades on, Paul McCartney's confidant and official biographer Miles delivered a similar verdict on behalf of a second Beatle: "For the most part Brian's arrangements with The Beatles were very unfair, even by prevailing showbiz standards. The Beatles had only agreed to them because they didn't know any better… John and Paul's music publishing was set up in the same way that Brian's management contract was handled. They had no legal advice, trusted him, and were screwed."

Lennon and McCartney's disillusionment has undermined Epstein's posthumous reputation as the initial architect of The Beatles' business empire. Philip Norman's Beatles biography Shout! in 1981 aided the demolition job with his exposé of Epstein's shortcomings, particularly in relation to the sorry tale of US merchandising rights for Beatle-related novelties in 1964. In Norman's account, Epstein was entirely culpable for the legal farrago which pitted the group and their US agents against each other in a three-year court battle. Norman concludes: "The total business lost among the lawsuits, in that one year alone, must be close to $100 million."

Even allowing for 10-fold exaggeration, such a sum is surreal in relation to the £10 and £20 fees which Epstein had been negotiating for the group's services a couple of years earlier. A troubled, sensitive man with vague artistic leanings, a desperately secretive personal life, and business experience only as manager of Liverpool's most profitable record store, Epstein tumbled into pop management like an infatuated teenager.

He was stunningly naive about financial showbiz etiquette, yet within a year he had secured The Beatles a record contract; and within two he had overseen the founding of their own music publishing company, signed them up for a feature film, and negotiated bill-topping appearances on America's top TV variety show.

He had also built himself a substantial personal fortune, much of which he poured straight back into his work. By the start of 1965, he and The Beatles were directly or indirectly responsible for an array of companies: The Beatles Ltd, NEMS Enterprises, The Beatles Film Productions Ltd, Subafilms, Northern Songs, Lenmac Enterprises Ltd, Maclen (Music) Ltd, Harrisongs Ltd – not to mention Ringo Starr's home decoration and construction business, the Brickey Building Company Ltd. Tax authorities in Britain and America were vying for the right to lay their hands on The Beatles' income. Music publisher Dick James had taken out £500,000 life insurance on Lennon and McCartney, aware that without his two most lucrative clients, his business was doomed.

So many golden eggs were being laid that Epstein could scarcely find nests broad enough to hold them. But the wider he diversified, and the faster he expanded his NEMS empire, the more difficult it became for one trusting Liverpool businessman to maintain control. He put himself at the tender mercy of a small team of advisers, none of whom had ever been confronted with anything on such a vast scale.

"He robbed us. He fucking took all the money and looked after himself and his family." *John Lennon on manager Brian Epstein*

At times, The Beatles' financial organisation must have looked like the cast of an Ealing comedy. "The one I remember," says Tony Barrow, who acted as press officer for both The Beatles and NEMS Enterprises during the '60s, "was Walter Strach – Dr Strach, as we were supposed to call him. He was the accountant who looked after the group's financial partnership, The Beatles Ltd. He reminded me of Peter Sellers in Dr Strangelove, not physically but the manner. Then there was Brian's lawyer, David Jacobs. Like Brian, he was Jewish and gay, a very smooth operator. I always thought the character of Jeremy Boob in Yellow Submarine was based on him."

Despite their collective experience in law and showbusiness, Epstein's team rapidly began to flounder. "It's almost impossible to convey how overwhelming the whole thing was," notes Barrow. "In merchandising terms, the only possible comparison was Walt Disney. In pop, nothing had ever been that big. We were all very naive. It was our strength, particularly in Brian's case. It meant that he didn't have to stick to the accepted rules, because he didn't know what they were. He brought totally fresh thinking to every problem. But it also left him open to being exploited by businessmen with more experience and less honesty."

The latter quality is the most enduring memory of Epstein in the eyes of those who worked with him. "He was totally straight in his dealings with his artists," Tony Barrow insists, "and also with the rest of the music business. The Beatles trusted him completely, and justifiably, and that freed them to concentrate on their music."

Yet McCartney spokesman Miles aired a different interpretation of Epstein's dealings with The Beatles: "The expenses deducted from their share of the income were enormous, not least because Brian himself had very refined tastes in hotels, wine and food, all of which The Beatles paid for. By taking 25 per cent of the gross, Brian made at least twice as much as any individual Beatle."

Epstein's 25 per cent cut of The Beatles' pre-tax income (officially paid to his NEMS

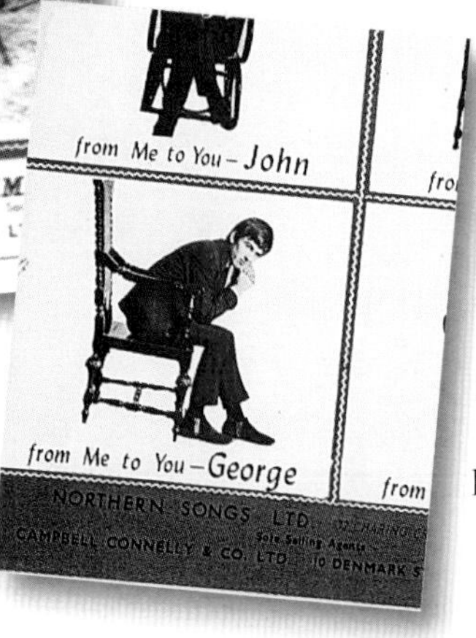

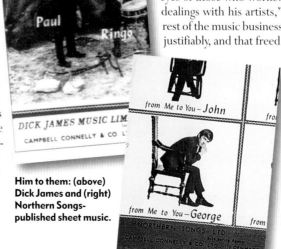

Him to them: (above) Dick James and (right) Northern Songs-published sheet music.

The money trap: (main pic) The Beatles discuss percentages with Brian Epstein in 1963. (Left) Some joker tries to tell Epstein and Dick James something.

Enterprises company) was not uniquely high. The 50-50 split agreed by Elvis and the Colonel was mirrored when Gordon Mills began to handle Tom Jones, while pioneering UK rock'n'roll manager Larry Parnes sometimes took a similar fee. Conversely, many managers took no more than 10 per cent of their artists' earnings, but recouped by removing every possible business expense – including the services of top-flight accountants, PR organisations, stylists and musical directors – from the artist's share.

In Epstein's eyes, he was much more than The Beatles' booking clerk: "I act as manager as well as agent. Most acts have one of each – to whom, by the way, they pay separate commissions." He stressed that NEMS offered the full gamut of showbiz services to its clients: "We direct and guide and shape careers. We have our own experts. We run our own public relations division. These things cost a fortune if they are done in the right way. One's profits from that 25 per cent are not really as fantastic as people imagine. Critics often forget that we have hefty outgoings just like any other firm." The fine wines and five-star hotels were merely a necessary signal to his business contacts of his success and clout.

Yet some areas of The Beatles' career were beyond his control. Epstein has often been criticised for accepting what, in retrospect, seems a laughably unrewarding record contract with Parlophone in 1962. For each double-sided single The Beatles sold, they received one old penny (240 to the pound). This penny was then split five ways. When a single such as She Loves You sold a million copies, Epstein and the individual Beatles pocketed merely £833 each. Millionaire status was still a long way off. It's true that the record contract allowed for four one-year options, each adding an extra farthing (one-quarter of a penny) to the royalty. But at best this raised the group's individual income for a million-seller to £1,666 by 1967.

Such (literal) penny-pinching was the norm in the early '60s, however. All new signings were subjected to the same extortionate deal, regardless of who their manager was. As an indication of the way in which EMI treated its artists and staff, it was only in March 1965 that George Martin – the producer of chart-topping hits by The Beatles, Gerry & The Pacemakers, Billy J Kramer and Cilla Black – was allowed a minuscule pay rise over his 1962 salary, despite the fact that he had been personally responsible for the explosive rise in the company's earnings during that period.

More damaging to Epstein's reputation is the claim made by Lennon's schoolfriend Pete Shotton: "In 1966, while renegotiating their recording deals with Capitol and EMI, [Epstein] stuck in a clause stipulating that 25 per cent of The Beatles' royalties through to 1976 were to be automatically siphoned on by his own company, NEMS. Unaware of the implications of this fine print, The Beatles affixed their signatures to the dotted line."

The allegation has proved impossible to verify, and the documents in question remain concealed in EMI's archives. If true, this subterfuge meant that even after Epstein's death, NEMS would have continued to receive its 25 per cent – long after the company's management deal with The Beatles had expired.

Record royalties and fees for live performances formed the bulk of The Beatles' collective income during 1963 and 1964. For two of the group, however, even more substantial sums were raised by their status as songwriters, in the form of music publishing receipts and broadcast royalties. "Ringo and I are constantly being reminded that John and Paul make so much more money than us," George Harrison noted sourly in 1965. Epstein wasn't unaware of the problem: "It bothers me. I look for extra income for the two who aren't collecting such rich rewards. For George, I was able to fix up a daily fee from a newspaper during the Paris visit in January [1964]. I'd like to think we can market drum kits in Ringo's name."

Meanwhile, Lennon and McCartney basked in their financial status as the most successful songwriters in the history of British pop. Inevitably, they weren't the only beneficiaries from their success. Epstein had allowed EMI's in-house publisher, Ardmore & Beechwood, to handle the Love Me Do single in 1962. But he was unimpressed by their blasé attitude, in an era when publishers were expected to boost their clients' careers by securing cover ➸

PHOTOS: POPPERFOTO/REX

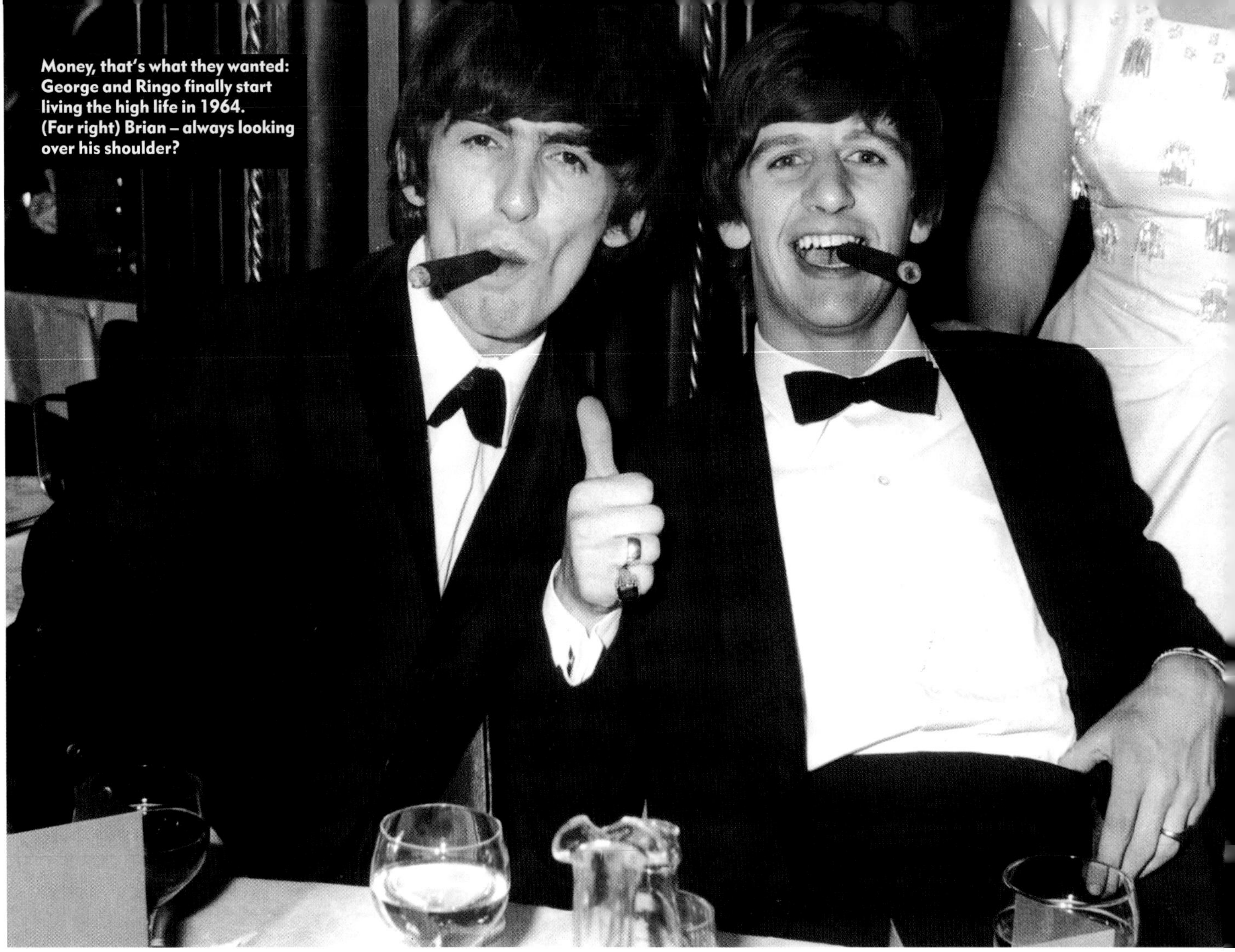

Money, that's what they wanted: George and Ringo finally start living the high life in 1964. (Far right) Brian – always looking over his shoulder?

versions of their songs, and even arranging radio and TV broadcasts.

George Martin recommended that Epstein should contact an old friend of his, a newly established independent publisher called Dick James.

"He'll work his arse off for you," Martin promised. Duly warned of Epstein's imminent arrival, James greeted The Beatles' manager with a neatly arranged coup whereby he phoned the producer of TV's prestigious pop show, Thank Your Lucky Stars. While Epstein looked on amazed, James talked the producer into booking The Beatles onto the show to promote their second single. When the call was over, James turned to Epstein and said, "Now, can I publish your boys' songs?"

In the rogues' gallery of Beatles advisers, Dick James has long occupied a more prominent place than Brian Epstein. As ever, Lennon established the tone: "He's another one of them people, a bit like George Martin, who think they made us, and they didn't. I'd like to hear Dick James's music, please, just play me some."

With his overt preference for McCartney's ballads over Lennon's eccentricities, the unashamedly middle-aged James had long since aroused Lennon's contempt. But his music had been heard on the airwaves a decade before The Beatles. In 1948, the young Dick James (or Isaac Vapnick) had become the first British male singer to breach the US charts, with You Can't Be True, Dear. By the early '50s, he had been signed by George Martin at Parlophone, and in 1956 the two men scored a hit with the theme tune to the TV series Robin Hood – a ditty that was still familiar enough at the start of the '70s to be parodied by the Monty Python team.

As rock'n'roll supplanted jaunty old-time pop, and James began to shed his hair, he moved into music publishing, starting in business on his own in 1961 with a £5,000 loan from his accountant, Charles Silver. When he first met Epstein in November 1962, James was a hungry hustler with a reputation for straight dealing and financial probity. Epstein signed over the publishing rights to Please Please Me without a qualm, and felt validated when it reached Number 1.

To Epstein's surprise, James refused to add Lennon and McCartney to the small roster of Dick James Music. Instead, as James recalled, he "suggested that what I would like to do is set up a company in which John, Paul and Brian would make 50 per cent and my company would make 50 per cent. John and Paul would be exclusively signed to that company. I said, Considering you're all from the North, perhaps it should be called Northern Songs."

It was a staggeringly far-sighted offer, which gave Lennon and McCartney a larger share of the cake than they would have received from a more conventional deal, but also tied them to Dick James for the long term. James had six months to prove himself, after which another three-year deal would be signed. Eventually, the two Beatles signed contracts linking them to Northern until 1973.

Although Dick James recalled that Lennon and McCartney "had been advised by their advisers that it was a very good idea," McCartney's memory of the deal is hazy but altogether less rose-tinted. "We just showed up, went into this dark little house, and signed this thing," he told Miles, "not really knowing what it was all about, that we were signing our rights away for our songs. That became the deal

"The Beatles' accountants searched for investment opportunities – Lennon set up schoolfriend Pete Shotton in a supermarket."

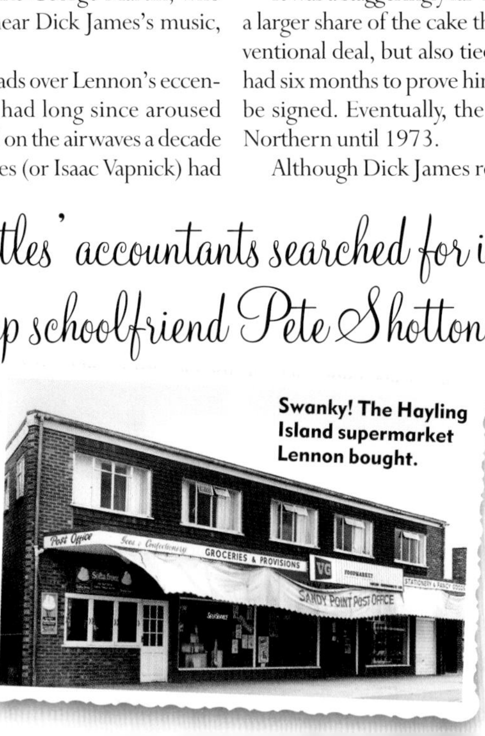

Swanky! The Hayling Island supermarket Lennon bought.

and that is virtually the contract I'm still under. It's draconian!"

McCartney claims not to have understood the very basis of the deal: "We said to them, Can we have our own company? They said, 'Yeah'. We said, Our own? They said, 'Yeah, you can. You're great'. So we really thought that meant 10 per cent owned. But, of course, it turned out to be 49 per cent to me and John and Brian, and 51 per cent to Dick James and Charles Silver. There was always this voting share that could beat us. We could only muster 49; they could muster 51."

The deal was actually more complicated than that – and over the next three years it grew more tangled still. Of the original 98 shares in Northern, James took 49, Lennon 19, McCartney 20, and Epstein (via NEMS) 10. Beyond that, Dick James Music Ltd took 10 per cent of Northern's income off the top for 'administering' the account. In April 1964, Epstein set up a company called Lenmac Enterprises Ltd, entirely to collect their share of the Northern income. Lennon and McCartney owned 40 per cent each of the new concern; Epstein 20 per cent. A similar firm, Maclen (Music) Ltd, was established in the USA.

So far, so good. But by late 1964, The Beatles' accountants were desperately searching for investment opportunities into which The Beatles' earnings could be poured – the alternative being that the Chancellor of the Exchequer would continue to collect 90 per cent of their international riches. Ringo put capital into a friend's building company; George took part share in a London discotheque; Lennon set up Pete Shotton in a supermarket on Hayling Island.

For Lennon and McCartney, however, their publishing income required a wider dispersal of their assets. One of Epstein's financial advisers, Jim Isherwood, suggested that Northern Songs should be floated as a public company on the stock exchange. Not only would individual investors be able to buy shares in The Beatles' future success, with the added City of London kudos that entailed, but Lennon and McCartney's tiny number of Northern shares could be converted into hundreds of thousands of public shares – which might, if the hits kept coming, rise in value overnight and keep on rising. A mid-'60s government loophole meant that this transaction could be carried out without the instant profits being subject to capital gains tax. It was, literally, money for nothing.

So The Beatles moved into stock market speculation. Five million Northern Songs shares were issued, at a nominal value of five shillings (25p) apiece. Dick James and Charles Silver were given their half; the rest were split between John, Paul and Brian, as before. A few weeks later, the stock exchange flotation took place, with two million shares (each party having relinquished 40 per cent of their holding) on offer to the public at 7s 9d (39p) each. The price dipped sharply for a while, then steadied, and gradually rose, adding significantly to Lennon and McCartney's assets on paper. Along the way, Isherwood chipped in and bought both George and Ringo 25,000 shares each, to make them feel as if they had a stake in the company.

This (to The Beatles) baffling set of financial manoeuvres was accompanied by two more sleights of hand. First, to reassure the public, but also keep Dick James's golden eggs within reach, Lennon and McCartney were persuaded to extend their exclusive deal with Northern Songs until February 1973. The contract applied not only to joint compositions, but also to their solo work – a clause which had ramifications years later when both John and Paul claimed to be writing songs with their wives, who definitely weren't signed to Northern.

At the same time, Lenmac Enterprises, the holding company which had been collecting the group's Northern royalties, was bought up by Northern for the way above market value sum of £365,000. Eighty per cent of this cash went immediately into the hands of Lennon and McCartney, and the deal was presented to them as a financial coup. What the two Beatles didn't realise was that along with Lenmac, they had lost the rights to the first 56 Lennon/McCartney songs handled by Northern, including several of their biggest early hits, such as She Loves You and I Want To Hold Your Hand. These were now owned outright by Northern, which was fine as long as Lennon and McCartney remained shareholders of the company. Once they pulled out, during the fracas in the late '60s when Dick James sold Northern to Sir Lew Grade without their knowledge, they lost all their earning potential from this material. To this day, McCartney and Lennon's estate earn literally nothing in airplay royalties for those 56 songs from 1963 and 1964.

Ironically, it was the third Beatle signed to Northern Songs in 1963, George Harrison, who attempted to keep pace of these bewildering business shenanigans. As early as January 1964, Brian Epstein had told the world: "George is most aware of business detail and likes to talk to me about fees and percentages." Tony Barrow recalls: "George wanted to know how much he was getting – and particularly how much Brian was getting."

"I'm not really the most-interested-in-money Beatle," Harrison protested in 1965, "I'm just the only one interested in what's happening to it. I like to know where it's going. I can't understand why the others aren't so bothered. We sit at accountants' meetings and we are told that we have got two-and-a-half per cent of this and four-and-a-half-per cent of that, and that is confusing and boring and just like being back at school. After a year or so of The Beatles making records and doing well, I started trying to find out what was happening and where it was going. John and Paul were equally interested, but they gave in. I didn't."

As Tony Barrow notes, however, "George wasn't very well educated. He wasn't a business genius in academic terms. So although he tried to work it out, he was soon as confused as the others were." As events in America had already proved, his confusion was no disgrace. The Beatles' vertiginous success had already overwhelmed the mental and legal capacities of Brian Epstein and his trusty advisers to an extent which even now is difficult to imagine, and impossible to calculate.

"We're musicians, not salesmen," The Beatles regularly told Epstein when he asked them to endorse articles of clothing or toys bearing their name. "Brian was adamant that the Official Beatles Fan Club, which was run out of the NEMS office, would not act as a shop for Beatles-related merchandise," says Tony Barrow, who oversaw the club as part of his PR duties. "You could say that he was missing out on an obvious business opportunity, but he saw it from the other side, that he didn't want the club to ➻

PHOTOS: HULTON ARCHIVE/POPPERFOTO/PICTORIAL PRESS

exploit the fans. There was only one exception to that rule. A couple of his cousins ran a firm which manufactured sweaters, and they talked him into offering fan club members a black polo neck sweater with a Beatles badge sewn on the front. It was very high quality, and it was offered to fans at Christmas 1963. He never did it again."

"Dick James is a fascist bum!" George Martin and James enjoy some impromptu Fabs.

Other entrepreneurs weren't so shy. "As early as spring 1963," Barrow recalls, "we would go on tour with The Beatles, and after the concerts there would be people selling cheap cash-in photo booklets. Some of them were purely about The Beatles; some covered all sorts of artists, but the vendors would turn it to The Beatles' picture to attract the fans."

By late summer 1963, when the group were established as Britain's leading pop attraction, it was obvious even to Epstein that some sort of control had to be exerted on Beatles-related product. In October, he set up a licensing system, with two rules: he had veto over every item issued under The Beatles' name, and The Beatles themselves wouldn't endorse any of them. Initially he attempted to issue the licences from NEMS, but the demand threatened to swamp the company's daily business, so the responsibility was passed to one of his socialite friends: Nicky Byrne, who headed a consortium of well-heeled Chelsea denizens under the name of Stramsact.

By Christmas 1963, the British shops were awash with Beatle dolls, wallpaper, toy guitars, moptop wigs, and much more besides – most of it bearing the NEMS logo, but a significant percentage still unauthorised. "Brian tried to chase the early offenders through the courts," Tony Barrow explains, "but soon there were just too many of them."

British exploitation of The Beatles' fame was soon overshadowed by the rapaciousness of American businessmen. Nicky Byrne established an American subsidiary company, Seltaeb ('Beatles' backwards), to handle the flood, working from a New York office. He was besieged with requests, on a financial scale far exceeding anything he had met in the UK. One company allegedly sold a million Beatles T-shirts within three days of the group's arrival in New York. Chains such as Woolworth's were transformed into Beatles department stores, where rabid American fans could purchase everything from Beatles bubblegum to full-size cardboard portraits for that dreamy midnight moment.

Money flooded into Seltaeb, and to a lesser extent Stramsact as well, but little found its way to The Beatles. Epstein had given his lawyer, David Jacobs (not the disc jockey of the same name), carte blanche to negotiate a royalty split with Byrne. The cocky young businessmen offered Jacobs and NEMS 10 per cent of the cut; Jacobs accepted, on the basis that it was better than nothing. "Merchandising can be profitable, but figures of millions of pounds in royalties from America are undistilled nonsense," Epstein said that summer, speaking more truth than he realised.

Eventually another pop manager suggested to Epstein that he was being robbed. Blaming Byrne and himself in that order, he renegotiated the Seltaeb deal, to give the Beatles 46 per cent of the income; and then launched the first in a series of lawsuits against the company which was working to make money for him and The Beatles.

With Byrne and Epstein now concentrating on sniping at each other, the merchandising business was allowed to fester. Major retailers cancelled their orders rather than risk becoming embroiled in a legal saga; some manufacturers were able to evade the licence procedure entirely. The result was a financial disaster for Byrne, Epstein and The Beatles. At one point, NEMS were fined several million dollars for failing to keep appointments at court hearings. That demand was eventually dropped, and a settlement was reached whereby Byrne received a one-off cash payment, and Epstein – in a fit of guilt – paid The Beatles' legal fees entirely out of his personal fortune.

The episode was most ruinous to The Beatles themselves, however, who lost an incalculable amount of potential income. Philip Norman's figure of $100 million is the most dramatic; he also suggested in Shout! that the fiasco may have inspired underworld figures to murder Epstein, an idea dismissed as ludicrous by those who worked in The Beatles' organisation.

Yet, as rock historian Johnny Rogan noted in his managerial study, Starmakers And Svengalis, the Seltaeb deal proved more lucrative for the group than it might have done. Some commentators have jibed that even the 54/46 split between Byrne and The Beatles was unfairly biased against the group. But so desperate were manufacturers to capitalise on The Beatles' success that Byrne was able to negotiate a 15 per cent cut of their income – far higher than previous deals for Elvis Presley merchandising. This offered some compensation for the inadequacy of Epstein's contracts with Seltaeb.

"The Beatles didn't get involved in any of this business at all," says Tony Barrow. "They didn't understand merchandising, or like it. They would get upset when a photographer they trusted, such as Dezo Hoffman, would publish a book of his Beatles photos. He'd immediately be refused access in the future. The famous quote from John to Brian about 'We'll look after the music, you look after the percentages', was entirely true. With the possible exception of George, they didn't want to know what was happening."

It was only in 1969, when Allen Klein entered the group's circle and began looking for evidence of past mismanagement, that The Beatles gradually became aware that many of Epstein's decisions had been naive or simply wrong. Yet, as Tony Barrow points out, their own instincts were no more trustworthy: "Look what happened when they started Apple: they put their faith in people like Alexis Mardas [*aka Magic Alex, infamous hippy crank*] and the Fool [*a Dutch team of designers*]. That's some indication of their own ongoing naivety, I think."

Even before then, George Harrison led The Beatles into ever more jaundiced comments on the subject of money. In 1964, the group's American accountant, Walter Hofer, was faced with a demand for US income tax on money which was already being taxed in Britain. "We are not at all resisting the tax," he said politely, "but we don't want to have to pay it twice." Asked at a press conference in 1964 how America could repay Britain for sending them The Beatles, Harrison quipped: "Just let us off the income tax". Two years later, the *Revolver* song Taxman encapsulated his feelings towards the Inland Revenue.

It was Harrison too who provided the most eloquent commentary on the Northern Songs saga. While Lennon called Dick James a "pig" or "fascist bum" to his face when the publisher dared to attend Beatles recording sessions, Harrison channelled his distaste into music. "It doesn't really matter what chords I play", he wrote in 1967, "cos it's only a Northern Song". And within two years, Northern Songs – and its peerless catalogue of Lennon/McCartney and, indeed, Harrison songs – had been snatched out of The Beatles' reach forever. By then, commercial innocence was no longer an option. But the band must have looked back wistfully at the early years when they knew nothing about their financial affairs – and cared less. ■

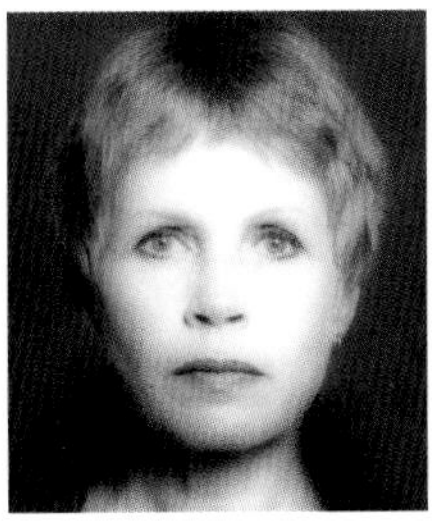

"I Was There"

Her photos immortalised their Hamburg years. In return, The Beatles taught Astrid Kirchherr about bravery and a nice cup of tea.

The first word that comes to mind is breathtaking. Klaus Voormann took me to the club that night and I was a bit frightened, but then I saw these wonderful people on the stage. They looked so wild and yet so innocent. Stuart caught my attention first. He was so absolutely cool. He was wearing his sunglasses, standing with his legs crossed, playing the bass and smoking a cigarette. He'd stepped out of my dreams as far as I was concerned. Then I noticed the rest of them were pretty impressive as well. Just the way John used to stand at the microphone, and my darling little Georgie, looking all lost – but when he played the guitar... Germany just didn't have any music like that. I'd heard rock'n'roll before, but Elvis Presley didn't look 'real' to me, and these boys were *real*.

I was working for a photographer, Reinhart Wolf, and my main interest was in portrait photography. I'd seen American photographers such as Richard Avedon and their pictures of Marlon Brando, and here were these five young English boys looking individually beautiful, and on top of that playing incredibly exciting music. After a week or two I asked if I could photograph them, and they immediately said yes. Then afterwards I took them to my home, and my mother would make them all the English food they missed – steak, mashed potato, 'a nice cup of tea', the whole lot! They could have a bath, for a change, and they used to sit around and look at my books and records. It was nice for them to sit in a decent place. I used to go and see them play all the time, especially when they moved to the Top Ten Club. We became great friends very quickly.

> "I'd heard rock'n'roll before, but Elvis Presley didn't look real to me, and these boys were *real*."

It was always a giving and taking between us. They taught me the meaning of bravery, of sticking to an idea. They had to survive in situations in Hamburg when they were penniless, which were disgusting. I tried to help them, and our different influences changed each other. Theirs came from America, and they taught me about Chuck Berry – and mine came from France and they learned about Sartre or Juliette Greco. It was an equal thing. And they liked my knowledge as far as fashion was concerned. But all this rubbish about 'the haircut' is nothing to do with what The Beatles really were.

Nobody could dream of the success they were going to have, but you just knew they were going to make their way. Paul with his music, John because he was multi-talented, and George – you could feel his love of the music.

People say John was a so-and-so, he was so sarcastic, he was always fighting. But that's a *Schablone*, as we say in German. That's putting someone in a box. We were just mates, and we had a laugh. He was a revolutionary from the start, and, yes, he pretended to be the tough guy – but he was full of humour and love, and he comforted me so beautifully after Stuart died. And he and Stuart together – I cannot describe the depth of their wit and humour and intelligence.

George became my closest friend after that. He has always looked after me, right up to the time he had to go. I stayed at George and Ringo's flat in Green Street when I came over to do some photography for Stern magazine, during the filming of A Hard Day's Night. They had to put a bit of cardboard over the letter-box, because fans kept shouting through it. George was dying to show me his new car – a Jaguar – but we couldn't go outside until three in the morning, and there were still fans out there screaming.

I felt very sorry for them. They had missed their youth in some way. I could see that in their eyes. But their attitude towards me never changed; and they were still very, very strong together – just like brothers. They moaned and groaned, but you could feel the love which had developed into something wonderful. They still seemed to have their pleasure in making music and being together.

When they came to Hamburg on tour in 1966 they looked very tired – exhausted. They were booked into a castle outside the city – and it was, out of the gig, guitars in hand, and "straight to the bleedin' castle", where we all had dinner. They would have loved to go to the Reeperbahn and seen the old places, but they just couldn't, because of the fans.

I didn't even have a camera when George talked me into doing the cover of *Wonderwall Music*. I had taken other pictures besides The Beatles, some of which I thought were better, but no-one was interested, and I began to feel unsure. Am I really good enough? But George never ever changed, he still believed in me.

I know that even if they hadn't become famous we would still have been friends. I gave them my love. I always trusted their friendship, and they trusted mine, and that's all that matters. I'm terribly, terribly proud of them.

Astrid Kirchherr
Hamburg
October 2002

PHOTOS: REDFERNS

"Beat that, Paul!": Lennon shows off his warped literary debut in 1964.

What: In His Own Write is published
Where: UK
When: March 23, 1964

SYNTAX MAN

John reckoned it was "about nothing" while others considered Lennon's first book a dystopian trip through the Beatle's imagination. By John Harris.

IN ADDITION TO THEIR STANDARD RETINUE, the touring party on The Beatles' Autumn 1963 trek around the UK contained one new face: Michael Braun, an American journalist whose time with the group would form the substance of Love Me Do, a book that still stands as one of the most intelligent accounts of their ascent. John Lennon was sufficiently comfortable with Braun's company to show him the sheaves of poems, prose and drawings that he used to fill his quieter hours; Braun was impressed enough to slip some of them to Tom Maschler, his editor at Jonathan Cape. The result was a £1,000 advance, the eventual publication of John's first book, and his instant portrayal as the literary Beatle.

The roots of all this are etched into Beatles lore: the schoolroom satire John poured into The Daily Howl, the out-there prose he wrote for Mersey Beat's 'Beatcomber' column, the flatly strange personal ads he took out in the same paper's classified pages. The Hamburg-era letters he wrote to both Stuart Sutcliffe and Cynthia Powell also fit the bill: scanning these, one gets the sense not only of a frenziedly creative mind, but a need to use words and pictures to exorcise his mind's darker aspects.

Such was In His Own Write, presented to the public on March 23, 1964. Its more breathless reviews suggested a rib-tickling collection of nonsense verse, yet within its pages lurked rather more pointed words. In No Flies On Frank, a fantasia set around a suburban breakfast table, "not even his wife's battered face could raise a smile on poor Frank's head". The Fat Growth On Eric Hearble ended with Eric losing his job "teaching spastics to dance", a fate explained thus: "Were [*sic*] not having a cripple teaching our lads". Little Bobby turns out to be an amputee, given a prosthetic hook for his birthday. If anyone sought to draw lines between all this and John's life as a Beatle, to cite his lyrics seemed to be missing the point: much of In His Own Write seemed of a piece with those moments onstage when John would break into "spastic" faces.

"It's about nothing. If you like it, you like it. There's nothing deep in it. It's just meant to be funny." John Lennon

And that's Ringo on the right: one of Lennon's illustrations.

The drawings only furthered the sense of something being not quite right. John drew human beings as lumpy grotesques: when he sketched out an orgiastic party scene ("Puffing and globbering they drugged theyselves rampling or dancing with wild abdomen"), the result was surprisingly unsettling. All told, for all In His Own Write's undoubted hilarity, his imagination also seemed to be a deeply dystopic kind of place.

Inevitably the book prompted all kinds of inquiries about where such visions came from. "It's about nothing," John responded, rather disingenuously. "If you like it, you like it, if you don't, you don't. That's all there is to it. There's nothing deep in it, it's just meant to be funny. I put things down on sheets of paper and stuff them in my pocket. When I have enough, I have a book." When asked on BBC2 if he made conscious use of onomatopoeia, John replied, "Automatic pier? I don't know what you're on about, son."

However, just as Ringo found his hungover solo scene in A Hard Day's Night compared to Charlie Chaplin, and The Times' music critic discerned "aeolian cadences" in the early Beatles love songs, so In His Own Write was mentioned in the same breath as James Joyce. "He seems to take the general format for his stories, fables, playlets and poems from a British humorist named Spike Milligan," wrote Tom Wolfe. "But the underlying bitterness of much of what Lennon writes about marriage and family life, for example, as well as his Joycean excursions into language fantasies, are something else altogether. The intimations of Joyce – the mimicry of prayers, liturgies, manuals and grammars, the mad homonyms, especially biting ones such as 'Loud' for 'Lord', which both use – are what have most intrigued the literati here and in England."

A year later, one John Wain repeated the point in the American magazine New Republic. "The first thing any literate person will notice on reading through Mr Lennon's book is that it all comes out of one source, namely the later work of James Joyce," he claimed. By way of illustrating his point, Wain quoted a passage from Ulysses: "Night we were in the box. Trombone under blowing like a grampus, between the acts, other brass chap unscrewing, emptying spittle. Conductor's legs too, bagstrousers, jiggedy jiggedy. Do right to hide them." For all the apparent similarities, John was unfamiliar with Joyce; when he got round to reading his work, it was, he said, "like finding Daddy".

Other readers of In His Own Write were less impressed. On June 19, 1964, Mr Charles Curran, the Conservative MP for Uxbridge, quoted from Deaf Ted, Danoota (And Me) in a parliamentary debate. "I quote that poem not because of its literary merit, but because one can see from it, as from other poems and stories in the book, two things about John Lennon: he has a feeling for words and storytelling and he is in a pathetic state of near-literacy," he seethed. "He seems to have picked up bits of Tennyson, Browning and Robert Louis Stevenson while listening with one ear to the football results on the wireless."

Curran seemed to be a minority of one: within 10 months, In His Own Write had sold 200,000 copies, and the next year, A Spaniard In The Works – arguably a yet-more warped compendium – was published. Ten years later, the BBC included an In His Own Write poem entitled I Sat Belonely in an anthology of poetry for schools. If John found out, we can only assume that he allowed himself a very sarcastic kind of laugh.

PHOTOS: HULTON ARCHIVE/ TERENCE SPENCER

22 The Beatles are heard interviewing each other on the BBC radio programme The Public Ear.

23 In His Own Write, a book of writings and drawings by John Lennon, is published in the UK, while Do You Want To Know A Secret is issued in the US by Vee-Jay. The band are filmed at the Scala Theatre, London.

24 Wax replicas of The Beatles are put on display at Madame Tussaud's Waxworks, London (above). Filming continues at the Scala.

25 The Beatles mime to Can't Buy Me Love for their first Top Of The Pops appearance. Filming continues at the Scala.

26 Former Beatles drummer Pete Best flies to America to appear on the TV show I've Got A Secret.

27 George and John spend Easter weekend with Cynthia Lennon and Patti Boyd at Dromolan Castle Hotel in Ireland. Ringo spends the weekend at Woburn Abbey, while Paul remains in London.

29 Pirate station Radio Caroline begins broadcasting. The first track played is Can't Buy Me Love.

30 The BBC radio special From Us To You is broadcast.

31 A concert sequence for A Hard Day's Night is filmed at the Scala Theatre, London. In the evening, The Beatles record a session for BBC Light Programmes' Saturday Club.

APRIL 64

1 At the NEMS office in London, John Lennon meets with his estranged father Freddie. Filming continues at the Scala.

2 Filming continues at the Scala Theatre, London.

3 A trailer for the film A Hard Day's Night is shot at Twickenham Studios, featuring all four Beatles in prams.

4 Billboard reports that The Beatles now hold all of the Top Five positions in the American singles chart, with Can't Buy Me Love at Number 1.

5 At Marylebone Station, London, the opening sequence for A Hard Day's Night is filmed.

6 Filming continues at Twickenham for the next couple of days.

9 Ringo's solo sequence in A Hard Day's Night is filmed on the towpath of the River Thames, Kew, Surrey.

10 The Beatles' *Second Album* is released in the US. The Beatles continue filming for the next few days at Twickenham.

12 Further filming takes place at Marylebone Station.

13 A US Gold Disc is awarded to *The Beatles' Second Album*.

14 While filming continues at Twickenham, John and Paul put finishing touches to the song, A Hard Day's Night.

15 Paul is interviewed by David Frost for the BBC TV show A Degree Of Frost.

16 Filming moves to Notting Hill Gate, London, and the song A Hard Day's Night is recorded at Abbey Road.

17 The name of The Beatles' film is publicly revealed as A Hard Day's Night.

18 Rehearsals for a Rediffusion TV special, Around The Beatles, are held in the Hall Of Remembrance, Flood Street, Chelsea, London.

19 The Beatles' musical contributions to Around The Beatles are recorded at IBC Studios, London.

20 Paul is filmed today and tomorrow at a dance school in Notting Hill, but the sequence is not used in the film.

21 Petula Clark declares in Melody Maker that, "Cliff Richard is a name more universally powerful than The Beatles. The French don't like The Beatles, as so many people here believe. And in Romania, they're hardly known!"

22 Location filming takes place in Hammersmith, Shepherd's Bush and Notting Hill.

23 John is guest of honour at a Foyle's Literary Lunch (above) in the Dorchester Hotel, London. Somewhat tired and emotional, his speech is brief – "Thank you very much. You've got a lucky face".

24 The final day of filming takes place in Ealing, West London.

25 Peter & Gordon knock Can't Buy Me Love off the UK Number 1 slot with World Without Love, a Lennon-McCartney composition.

26 The 1964 NME Poll Winners' Concert at Wembley (right) in London features The Beatles, The Rolling Stones, The Searchers, The Hollies, Manfred Mann, The Animals, Gerry & The Pacemakers, Brian Poole & The Tremeloes, Dave Clark Five, Cliff Richard & The Shadows, Billy J Kramer & The Dakotas, The Merseybeats, The Fourmost, Joe Brown, Big Dee Irwin and more. That evening, The Beatles attend Roy Orbison's 28th birthday party.

27 Love Me Do is issued in the US by Tollie Records.

28 The hour-long TV special Around The Beatles, directed by Jack Good, is taped at Wembley Studios.

29 The Beatles' chartered de Havilland Dove touches down at Turnhouse Airport, Scotland. The band play the ABC Cinema, Edinburgh. At the press conference Lord Provost Duncan Weatherstone surprises The Beatles by asking them for a £100,000 contribution to the Edinburgh Festival fund.

30 The Beatles perform at the Odeon Cinema, Glasgow.

MAY 64

2 As The Beatles' second album knocks *Meet The Beatles* off the US Number 1 slot, the Fabs go on holiday. John and George head for Hawaii while Paul and Ringo fly to the Virgin Islands.

What: John is reunited with his father
Where: NEMS, Argyle Street, London
When: April 1, 1964

MEET THE PARENT

John Lennon had last seen his father in 1946, but the huge success of The Beatles ensured a reunion – whether he wanted it or not. By Peter Doggett.

WITH TYPICAL TENACITY, IT WAS THE British media who ferreted out the story. Every day in 1964, the popular press competed to offer a new angle on the increasingly surreal success of The Beatles. They were innocent times, and there were no Murdoch tabloids to offer thousands to seduced barmaids and abandoned groupies. Instead, Fleet Street's finest began to investigate the one gaping hole in the group's personal history – John Lennon's parentage.

The absence of his mother, Julia, was easy to explain; she had been run down and killed by an off-duty policeman in 1958. Quizzed about his father, however, Lennon admitted that he hadn't seen him for nearly 20 years, and could barely remember a shared holiday in Blackpool in 1946.

The hard-nosed hacks breezed into action, floating the theme with a variety of "Beatle abandoned at birth" tales. Then The Daily Express struck gold. "Beatle's dad washes dishes at Greyhound pub in Hampton Court", they announced proudly.

Lennon had made no attempt to use his wealth to track down his errant dad. He had been raised by his Aunt Mimi on stories of the irresponsibility of Alfred 'Freddie' Lennon. Mimi had never thought that the sailor was good enough for her younger sister, Julia, and she had been the first to say, "I told you so" when Freddie failed to return home from the war to reclaim his wife and small son.

The Blackpool visit had been a rare meeting between father and boy, but any hope of a belated relationship was soon dashed. The vacation ended in a row between Freddie and Julia, during which John was offered a stark choice: leave with his father for New Zealand, or remain at home with his mother. He chose safety over adventure, and heard no more of his father's exploits until the press found Freddie in London.

Kitchen sink drama: Freddie washes up in the Greyhound.

Brian Epstein grew alarmed at the potential for bad publicity if the media were allowed to collar Freddie before he'd been defused and disarmed. So he sent a polite and elegant invitation: if Alfred Lennon would care to visit Epstein's NEMS offices next to the Palladium in central London on April 1, 1964, then he would be sure to meet up with his long-lost son.

Freddie duly arrived, and was shown into a plush office, where he found not only the suave Mr Epstein exuding courtesy and good manners, but also no fewer than three members of The Beatles. Unwilling at first even to exchange a few words with the man who, he felt, had abandoned him years before, John Lennon was only persuaded to go through with the meeting on the understanding that he could call on the others for mutual support. During a break in filming A Hard Day's Night at the Scala Theatre half a mile away, Lennon, Harrison and Starr were ferried to NEMS, and prepared for the inevitably uncomfortable encounter.

Initial conversation was stilted, verging on abrupt. Brian Epstein endeavoured to find uncontroversial ground; George Harrison was his usual polite but laconic self; Alfred Lennon attempted to make up for years of neglect with a few friendly words; John Lennon mumbled sarcastic responses. Eventually, the two Lennons were left alone for a few minutes, until Epstein re-entered the room, and explained that John and the others were required back at the theatre for another film scene.

The brief father and son reunion passed unmentioned in the papers, until Freddie Lennon sniffed out the possibility of some quick cash, and sold his story to The Daily Herald. Once again, Epstein intervened, suggesting that John should send his dad a cheque for £30 as a filial gift, and then a weekly stipend of £12 to dissuade Freddie from offering too many more exclusives to the newspapers.

The money itself meant nothing to the newly-rich John, but the gesture merely increased his sense of bitterness and betrayal. When his father turned up at his stockbroker belt mansion the following year, John greeted him tersely: "Where have you been for the last 20 years?" The question illustrated just how lacking in intimacy the earlier encounter at NEMS had been. Cynthia Lennon politely invited her father-in-law to stay, but after three days John threw Freddie out of the house, accusing him of having turned up purely in search of cash. Their relationship wasn't improved at the end of 1965 when the elder Lennon attempted to launch his own pop music career with a single. Rumours persist that Brian Epstein exerted pressure on Freddie's record label to have the single withdrawn from the shops.

And so the burden of guilt remained balanced between Freddie and John, who was already starting to transfer his distorted parental views onto his own son, Julian.

Subsequent events did little to reduce the strain. Freddie and John continued to enjoy sporadic if uneasy contact during the mid-to-late '60s, and the elder Lennon occasionally saw his son at the newly opened Apple offices in Savile Row in 1968. There he proved that the old charm which had seduced Julia 30 years earlier was still intact, as he wooed and soon married one of the Apple secretaries – a young woman barely a third of his age.

John's response to this romance was ungracious, to say the least, and it was only when he heard that Freddie was terminally ill in the mid-'70s that he relented and made a concerted attempt to make it up with his father. The reunion was carried out by phone, as John remained in New York, and Freddie in Brighton, Sussex. But when Freddie died on April 1, 1976, he did so with the consolation that he had finally succeeded in making peace with his son.

"Brian told John to send £12 a week to Freddie to dissuade him from offering more stories to the papers."

PHOTOS: POPPERFOTO

Heeeere's Freddie!:
John's old man holds up his debut 45, January 4, 1966.

CAN'T BUY ME LOVE
(John Lennon-Paul McCartney)
Northern Songs Music, Ltd.
ASCAP—2:12
5150
Recorded in England
Capitol RECORDS
THE BEATLES
tollie RECORDS
63-3194
Robert Mellin Inc., & Progressive Music-BMI
TWIST AND SHOUT
(Medley-Russell)
THE BEATLES
Tollie-9001
Swan
"SHE LOVES YOU"
THE BEATLES
I WANT TO HOLD YOUR HAND
(Lennon-McCartney)
Duchess Music Corporation
BMI-2:24
5112
Recorded in England
1-134
Capitol RECORDS
THE BEATLES
VJ VEE-JAY RECORDS
63-2967 Vocal
Concertone Songs ASCAP TIME: 2:00
PLEASE PLEASE ME
(J. Lennon-P. McCartney)
THE BEATLES
VJ 581
I SAW HER STANDING THERE
(Lennon-McCartney)
Walter Hofer
2:50
5112
(45-X44772)
Recorded in England
1-134
Capitol RECORDS
THE BEATLES
VJ VEE-JAY RECORDS
63-3218 Vocal
Gil Music Corp. BMI TIME: 1:49
FROM ME TO YOU
(McCartney-Lennon)
THE BEATLES
VJ 581
VJ VEE-JAY RECORDS
63-3191 Vocal
Metric Music BMI
DO YOU WANT TO KNOW A SECRET
(McCartney-Lennon)
THE BEATLES
VJ 587
ALL MY LOVING
(Lennon—McCartney)
W. Hofer
2:05
72144
(7XCE 17560A)
Capitol RECORDS
RECORDED IN GREAT BRITAIN
THE BEATLES
YOU CAN'T DO THAT
(John Lennon-Paul McCartney)
Northern Songs Music, Ltd.
ASCAP-2:33
5150
(45-X44913)
Recorded in England
3-304
Capitol RECORDS
THE BEATLES
ROLL OVER BEETHOVEN
(Chuck Berry)
Arc Music Corp.
2:40
72133
(CC1-72133)
Capitol RECORDS
RECORDED IN GREAT BRITAIN
THE BEATLES
VJ VEE-JAY RECORDS
63-3219 Vocal
Conrad Pub. BMI
THANK YOU GIRL
(McCartney-Lennon)
THE BEATLES
VJ 587

What: 12 hits in the US charts
Where: America
When: April 4 1964

HITSVILLE USA

When The Beatles cracked America they did it in style, notching up an amazing 12 singles on the Billboard chart. By Dave DiMartino.

One document and one document alone pinpoints the exact moment The Beatles first captured the hearts and minds of mid-America. And that would be the Hot 100 chart published by the US music trade magazine Billboard for the week ending April 4, 1964. For on that very chart, published less than two months after the Fabs' famed appearance on The Ed Sullivan Show, a total of 12 Beatles tracks were perched merrily on the influential hit list – five of which, astonishingly, were at the very top. One might say the lads had taken America. And back then, one did. Repeatedly.

Certainly no record company in its right mind would ever allow so many tracks to cannibalize each other's chances for sales, airplay and promotion – but then, who's talking about one record company? The same wayward American label politics that saw the band's earliest singles emerging on smaller independents rather than EMI's American affiliate Capitol Records allowed for this surplus of Beatle hits. Here's the tally: aside from chart-topper Can't Buy Me Love, Capitol also had claims to I Want To Hold Your Hand, I Saw Her Standing There, and You Can't Do That. In a show of North American/ EMI synergy, the Billboard charts also bore All My Loving and Roll Over Beethoven courtesy of Capitol Of Canada. The smaller Vee-Jay record label offered Please Please Me, From Me To You, Do You Want To Know A Secret, and Thank You Girl. She Loves You came via Swan Records, and Twist And Shout showed up on the comparatively unsung Tollie label.

Not excessive enough? How about The Carefrees' We Love You Beatles, slotted at Number 42 that week, and The Four Preps' A Letter To The Beatles, that week's Number 85 entry, courtesy of, er, Capitol Records.

"It was one of the most exciting moments in my career," recalls Alan Livingstone today, who, as president of Capitol Records during most of the '60s, had a bird's-eye view of The Week That Was. "It represented a success not based on anything that anybody else did – and not based on anything that had to do with my career. It was a result of The Beatles having been turned down by every major record company, including Capitol."

Livingstone recalls the day "the man who had the responsibility to review records" had told him The Beatles were no big deal. "He came in and said, 'They're a bunch of long-haired kids, they're nothing, forget it'. RCA then got a crack at them, turned them down, CBS got a crack at them and turned them down, and Decca turned them down. And they were forgotten. I had never listened to them – they were an English group and English records weren't selling, so I didn't pay too much attention.

"Then I got a call one day from Brian Epstein in London," continues Livingstone. "I didn't know who he was, but I soon learned when I picked up the phone. He said, 'I don't understand, Mr Livingstone, why you don't sign The Beatles'. And I said, Well, I haven't *heard* them. And he said, 'Well, will you please listen and call me back?'"

Livingstone did, of course, and agreed to bring the band on-board – but not before Epstein asked for $40,000 for promotion to "get them started" following their relative flop singles on Vee-Jay and Swan. "We decided on the first record and I took it home to play to my wife, Nancy. And she said, 'I want to hold your *hand*? Are you kidding?' And I thought, Well, maybe I made a mistake. But I went forward with it, and, of course, the rest is history."

One man who recalls that history very well is Bobby Vinton, the enormously successful American pop singer whose four-week stint at Number 1 with There! I've Said It Again came to an end via I Want To Hold Your Hand. Vinton would enjoy a total of five Top 40 hits in 1964; newcomers The Beatles, however, managed 19. "Times were changing. I couldn't believe it," says Vinton today. "I was in Miami at the Fontainebleau Hotel and Murray the K called me and said, 'There's The Beatles here – we're playing their records, they're taking over the industry, what do you think of them?'. And I said, Well, it sounds like The Everly Brothers – there's two guys singing two-part harmony. And I wasn't all that impressed, to be honest with you. I thought, Gee, they won't be around long, that's a dumb song, 'She loves you, yeah yeah yeah'.

Britannia rules the airwaves: the Fabs occupy the Top 5.

> **"Of the 12 Beatles tracks perched merrily on the influential hit list – five were astonishingly at the very top."**

"I was a musician. I had big bands – if you listen to my early records, There! I Said It Again, Blue Velvet, they all had advanced chords. And even though they were commercial, they were a quality type of songs. So I was kind of saying I think music is going to get *better*, it's not going to come down with less chords and less lyrics. I had no idea that it would have such an impact."

Vinton still recalls the time a DJ from a prominent Philadelphia station phoned him, asking advice. "He said, 'You're Number 1 here with My Heart Belongs To Only You, but we're getting calls from The Beatles' fans saying, 'You better take that Bobby Vinton off and make The Beatles Number 1, or we're going to slash your tyres'. He says, 'What do I do?'. So I wasn't basically too thrilled about what was happening out there."

Neither were other artists at Capitol, adds Alan Livingstone. "They didn't like it too much, because they felt that our pressing plants were saturated with Beatles product, and a lot of them – particularly the newer artists – were being hurt. But I couldn't help it."

Was this the true peak of American Beatlemania, then?

"No," he insists. "It all happened so very fast that it *didn't* peak. From the very first record, they were a smash, smash hit – and they stayed that way year after year after year. There was not a peaking of *anything* from then on."

PHOTOS: PICTORIAL PRESS/ PETE NASH

4 On holiday in Honolulu, Hawaii, John and George are obliged to remain indoors for all but 20 minutes due to besieging fans on their private beach.

5 The first pictures of baby Julian Lennon appear in the UK press.

6 The television special Around The Beatles (above) airs in the UK.

8 The Strangers and Mike Shannon release a new single in the UK, One And One Is Two, written by Lennon and McCartney.

10 The Beatles' NME Poll Winners' performance is shown on ITV in the UK.

11 An EP, Four By The Beatles, is released in the US.

18 BBC TV show A Degree Of Frost broadcasts its interview with Paul.

21 Sie Liebt Dich is issued in the US by Swan Records.

24 A pre-recorded Beatles interview is broadcast on The Ed Sullivan Show.

26 John and George return from their holidays.

27 Peter & Gordon release a new single in the UK, Nobody I Know, written by Lennon and McCartney. On the same day, Paul and Ringo return from their holidays.

30 Love Me Do hits Number 1 in the US.

31 The Beatles play the Prince Of Wales Theatre, London.

JUNE 64

1 Carl Perkins – a big influence on the band – visits a recording session in Abbey Road where The Beatles lay down the non-soundtrack side of the *A Hard Day's Night* album.

2 Recording continues at Abbey Road Studios, London.

3 With Ringo collapsing from tonsillitis and being taken into hospital, substitute drummer Jimmy Nicol is drafted in at the last minute for the start of their world tour.

4 The Beatles' first world tour starts at KB Hallen, Copenhagen, Denmark.

5 John is photographed crawling out of an Amsterdam brothel. The Beatles record a TV special for VARA-TV at the Treslong Café, Vosselaan.

6 The Beatles play the Exhibition Hall, Blokker, Holland.

7 The band flies from Amsterdam to Hong Kong via London.

8 John attends the Miss Hong Kong pageant in the President Hotel, Kowloon, Hong Kong.

9 A show at the Princess Theatre, Kowloon, Hong Kong.

11 The Beatles touch down in Darwin, Australia, just as Ringo is discharged from hospital in London.

12 It is reported that 100,000 fans line the six-mile route from Adelaide Airport to the town centre when The Beatles arrive to play two nights at the Centennial Hall.

JUNE 13 - JULY 14, 1964

13 When violence erupts among female Beatles fans in Cleveland, Ohio, who have been waiting all night to buy tickets for the band's upcoming concert, the police have to be called in to quell the public disturbance.

14 A crowd of 250,000 fans gather to meet The Beatles as they arrive in Melbourne, Australia. Ringo, now recovered, rejoins the others.

15 The first of three nights at the Festival Hall, Melbourne.

18 A 13-year-old girl is caught by police on the outside of the eighth floor of The Beatles' Sydney hotel, trying to climb up to their penthouse suite.

19 The Long Tall Sally EP is released in the UK, and The Beatles play at Sydney Stadium.

20 The band play a second night at the Sydney Stadium.

21 The Beatles fly to Auckland, New Zealand.

22 The first of two nights at the Town Hall, Wellington.

24 The first of two nights at the Town Hall, Auckland.

26 The band play the 4,000-seater Town Hall, Dunedin.

27 Their last New Zealand show, at the Majestic Theatre, Christchurch.

28 The Beatles fly to Brisbane, Australia, via Auckland and Sydney.

29 The first of two shows at the Festival Hall, Brisbane.

JULY 64

1 With the tour over, The Beatles fly home from Australia.

3 The Pete Best Four release a new single, I'm Gonna Knock On Your Door.

4 The Beatles attend a preview of A Hard Day's Night.

6 The world premiere of A Hard Day's Night takes place at the London Pavilion. It is reported that the soundtrack album has sold 1.5 million copies in nine days, making it the fastest-selling album in UK history.

7 An appearance is taped for Top Of The Pops at Lime Grove Studios, London.

8 The Top Of The Pops appearance is transmitted by BBC TV.

10 An estimated 150,000 people line the streets when The Beatles return to Liverpool (above) for the hometown premiere of A Hard Day's Night. On the same day, a new single and LP, also both called A Hard Day's Night, are released.

11 A live appearance on TV show Lucky Stars (Summer Spin) at Teddington Studio Centre.

12 The Beatles begin a five-night stint at the Hippodrome, Brighton.

13 The single, A Hard Day's Night, is issued in the US by Capitol.

14 A live session is recorded for a new BBC radio show, Top Gear, at Broadcasting House, London.

What: Jimmy Nicol joins The Beatles
Where: London
When: June 3, 1964

JIM'LL FIX IT

Who was the fifth Beatle? When Ringo contracted tonsillitis on the eve of a world tour, it was Jimmy Nicol who came to the rescue. By Lois Wilson.

RINGO HAD BEEN FEELING UNWELL FOR a couple of days but when he awoke on Wednesday, June 3, 1964 with a sore throat and drenched in sweat, The Beatles' sticksman knew he should really go and see a doctor. But instead he headed straight for the Saturday Evening Post offices in Barnes where John, Paul and George were already waiting to take part in a photo session for the newspaper. On his arrival, the photographer began snapping away. Suddenly, Ringo fell to the floor. Panic ensued – the band were due to leave for Denmark for the first part of their world tour the following day – and Ringo was rushed to the nearby University College Hospital where upon arrival he was diagnosed with tonsillitis and pharyngitis, registering a temperature of 103 degrees. Obviously Ringo was in no fit state to board a plane. George wanted to cancel, "If Ringo's not going," he told Brian Epstein, "then neither am I." But Brian had other ideas. He suggested they find a replacement. "It was a very last minute decision," recalls Tony Barrow, The Beatles' press officer. "Frankly I didn't think the tour would happen. It wasn't a multimillion-dollar money-spinner but Brian saw it as the lesser of two evils. Cancel the tour and upset thousands of fans or continue and upset The Beatles."

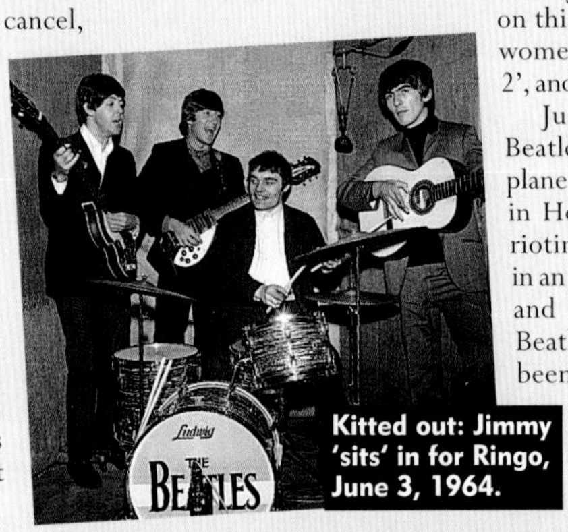

Kitted out: Jimmy 'sits' in for Ringo, June 3, 1964.

Ringo in particular was very disappointed with the decision. "He felt terrible," relates Barrow. "He felt so guilty. You see, Ringo was so much more than just The Beatles' drummer. I remember when he first joined the band I asked John what the difference was between him and Pete Best. John just said, 'Pete Best is a great drummer but Ringo's a great Beatle'. They all knew how important Ringo was. He set the whole rhythm, the whole tempo of a concert. He wanted to be there to drive them and they wanted him to be there too."

"I felt like an intruder, as though I had wandered into the most exclusive club in the world." Jimmy Nicol

Brian called a meeting and several names were bandied about but only one stuck: that of Jimmy Nicol. He'd just finished working with George Martin on a session with Georgie Fame And The Blue Flames so The Beatles' producer knew all too well what the then 24-year-old Londoner was capable of. "Jimmy was also in Georgie Fame's live band," explains Tony Bramwell, then part of The Beatles' entourage. "We used to see him play all the time. He seemed the obvious choice."

Jimmy had also appeared on the Koppykats' cash-in Beatles album, *Beatlemania*, so was already well acquainted with keeping time on the Fab Four's material.

Nicol explained at the time: "I was having a bit of a lie down after lunch when the phone rang. It was George Martin. He asked, 'What are you doing for the next four days? Ringo is ill, and we want you to take his place on The Beatles' tour'. I couldn't get there fast enough."

Before flying off though, Jimmy went to Abbey Road Studios to rehearse through the night in front of a hopeful Epstein, Martin and band.

"It was very strange for them," explains Barrow. "The Beatles didn't really rehearse. They didn't need to, only when they'd written a new song."

Boarding the flight from London the next day, Jimmy knew he had to do it for real in front of an audience of 4,500 screaming fans at Cogenhagen's Tivoli Gardens. There wasn't even time for him to get his own outfit. Instead he took the stage wearing Ringo's gear and blazed through the opening number, I Want To Hold Your Hand, with no problems. The set – 10 instead of the usual 11 songs because Ringo's star turn, I Wanna Be Your Man, was dropped – went down a storm. Only Paul had reservations: "It was the first time that we'd had this new drummer because Ringo was sick, and he was sitting up on this rostrum, just eyeing up all the women. We'd start She Loves You, '1, 2', and nothing. '1, 2' and still nothing."

Just 11 days after first meeting The Beatles, Jimmy found himself on a plane home. Having played further gigs in Holland – where he experienced rioting fans and spent an alleged night in an Amsterdam brothel – Hong Kong and Australia, his time as the fifth Beatle had come to an end. Ringo had been given a clean bill of health and had rejoined the band in Melbourne. Jimmy didn't even get a chance to say goodbye. As the band slept he made his way to the airport. "I became the deputy Beatle," he said on his return to England. "The only outsider to get on the inside of the group. John, Paul and George made me feel welcome from the start. But the funny thing is that I felt like an intruder, as though I had wandered into the most exclusive club in the world. They have their own atmosphere and their own sense of humour. It's a little clique and outsiders just can't break it."

Brian Epstein gave him a pat on the back, a £500 cheque and an inscribed gold Eternamatic watch for his troubles. But it wasn't to be the last time Jimmy played with The Beatles. On July 12, 1964, he performed with his band, The Shub Dubs, on the same bill with them and The Fourmost at Brighton's Hippodrome. Just nine months later he declared himself bankrupt with debts of £4,066. "Standing in for Ringo was the worst thing that ever happened to me," he confessed several years later. "Up until then I was feeling quite happy turning over £30 to £40 a week. I didn't realise it would change my whole life. Everyone in the business said I couldn't miss. But after the headlines died, I began dying too."

He then disappeared and now earns a living as a painter and decorator based in South London.

PHOTOS: POPPERFOTO/CORBIS/LIVERPOOL POST AND ECHO

I wanna be you, man: Jimmy takes on Ringo's Beatles role with relish.

Oz fest: The Beatles receive a ticker-tape reception in Melbourne, June 16, 1964.

What: The Beatles' Australasian tour
Where: Adelaide, Australia
When: June 12, 1964

AUSSIE RULERS!

They may have had eggs thrown at them, but the Fabs' only tour 'down under' soon reached Nuremberg-style proportions. By Keith Badman.

ON THURSDAY, JUNE 11, JUST 48 DAYS after filming their last scenes for the A Hard Day's Night movie, The Beatles were in Sydney, Australia, right in the middle of a tropical rainstorm. It was a part of their travels on their 27-day 'world tour', which had so far taken in Denmark, Amsterdam and Hong Kong. After the brief stop for fuel, The Beatles and their entourage flew on to Adelaide arriving on June 12. It was The Beatles' first and only time in Australia and Beatlemania was at its height, giving all concerned little time for rest and relaxation.

Police reports suggested that over 30,000 people had lined the 10-mile route of their motorcade from Adelaide airport to the city centre. The Beatles' first port of call was City Hall, where at least 300,000 fans – half the population of Adelaide – had converged in King William Street and the surrounding area. It was quite a reception. As John commented later, "The reception that Adelaide gave us will stick in our memories." At the City Hall, The Beatles were presented with toy koala bears. Later that evening, the group gave two performances at the Centennial Hall. The promoter of the tour was Ken Brodziak, who had booked the group through Brian Epstein back in June 1963. He had agreed to pay the group just £2,500 a week. For that, they were entitled to perform 12 shows a week, two shows a day. As Brodziak later admitted, "That sum was absolute peanuts! They were earning far more at this time."

The following day saw two further sold out shows at Adelaide's Centennial Hall and on June 14, Ringo, who had just been discharged from London's University College Hospital, arrived in Sydney to be greeted by the obligatory screaming fans and clamouring press. Ringo and Brian Epstein flew on to Melbourne – and more screaming fans – and immediately headed off to the Southern Cross Hotel where another large crowd greeted them. The other Beatles arrived later at Melbourne's airport to be welcomed by a crowd that had now swollen to 5,000.

John, Paul, George and Jimmy then set out for the Southern Cross. Protected by 12 motorcycle outriders, the entourage arrived at the hotel at 4pm, where they were greeted by the sight of 300 police and 100 members of the military battling with the large excited crowd. Subsequent activities resulted in cars being crushed and fans breaking bones after falling from nearby trees. It was therefore suggested that, to relieve the immense pandemonium, The Beatles show themselves to the assembled hordes. The group duly obliged and waiting fans were treated to the unusual sight of five parading Beatles, who appeared waving to the crowd on the first floor balcony of the hotel. The roar from the crowd was so loud that it resembled the sound heard at a Nuremberg rally, prompting John to give the crowd a Nazi-style salute and shout, "Sieg Heil", even holding his finger to his upper lip as a Hitler-style moustache. The Fab Five then assembled inside the hotel where they faced another press conference. But this duty was to be Jimmy's last as a Beatle and, on June 15, he slipped from The Beatles' hotel and sank into obscurity. Brian Epstein accompanied Jimmy to the airport and presented him with a cheque for £500 and an inscribed gold watch.

Later that night, The Beatles played the first of their six performances at the Festival Hall. They also played Sydney Stadium before they headed off to New Zealand on June 21, to be greeted at the airport by some 7,000 fans. There, the group received a traditional Maori welcome at the airport, complete with affectionate nose-to-nose rubbing from women dressed in native costumes. John Lennon quipped, "My wife will kill me when she finds out."

Performances at the Town Halls in Wellington, Auckland and Dunedin followed. But the primitive sound equipment The Beatles were forced to use marred the first concert on June 22. It transpired that, due to a fear of damaging the equipment, the PA operator had never before fully turned the speakers up and was scared to do so. Afterwards, John screamed, "What the fucking hell is going on here?" And Paul remarked, "We have sung through worse mikes, but not very often."

On June 27, The Beatles' New Zealand tour ended with a performance in Christchurch and then, the following day, the group flew to Brisbane. Their tour down under concluded with three shows at the Festival Hall. The first night of shows was marred by the infamous egg-throwers that had, once again, managed to sneak in and ruin the concert for many fans. As George recalled, "There were six fellows. We put it in the papers that we'd like to see them and they came up to our hotel where we had a long discussion with them. And they were just typical eggheads from a university. Just as we thought, they were right schmucks and they admitted that they were being childish." Paul would recall, "We had a bit of a chat to them, more of a debate really, and we all ended up friends. We asked them why they threw eggs at us and they said they were sick of hearing our songs on the radio and sick of kids screaming at us. So John asked them why they didn't throw eggs into the crowd if it was Beatlemania they were against."

On July 1, The Beatles flew home from Sydney, arriving at London the next morning. Just four days later, The Beatles' one and only trip 'down under' was forgotten. The premiere of their first film, A Hard Day's Night, was now uppermost in their thoughts…

"John gave the crowd a Nazi-style salute, even holding his finger to his upper lip as a Hitler-style moustache."

A hard day's drive: The Beatles struggle through more fans, June 15, 1964.

PHOTOS: REDFERNS/HULTON ARCHIVE

15 John becomes the owner of a £20,000 house, Kenwood, St George's Hill, in Surrey.

19 An appearance on the ITV show Blackpool Night Out is transmitted live from the ABC Theatre, Blackpool.

20 A new US-only album, *Something New*, is released along with two new singles, I'll Cry Instead and And I Love Her, by Capitol.

23 As A Hard Day's Night hits the Number 1 single slot in the UK, The Beatles appear at the midnight charity revue, Night Of A Hundred Stars, at the London Palladium.

25 George and Ringo record appearances for BBC TV show Juke Box Jury.

26 The Beatles play the Opera House, Blackpool.

28 Two nights at the Johanneshovs Hockey Arena, Stockholm, Sweden.

30 The single A Hard Day's Night reaches Number 1 in the UK, while the album hits the top slot simultaneously in the States and Britain.

AUGUST 64

1 A Hard Day's Night reaches Number 1 in the US singles chart.

2 The Beatles play the Gaumont, Bournemouth, supported by The Kinks.

7 Time magazine in America dismisses the A Hard Day's Night movie as "rubbish to be avoided at all costs".

9 The Beatles perform at the Futurist Theatre, Scarborough.

11 Work starts on another LP at Abbey Road, London. As yet un-named, it will be released as *Beatles For Sale*.

12 As A Hard Day's Night opens in 21 New York cinemas, taking $75,000 in its first night, Brian Epstein hosts an 'At Home' party in his Knightsbridge, London, apartment. Guests include The Beatles, Mick Jagger, Judy Garland, Alma Cogan and Lionel Bart.

16 The band play the Opera House, Blackpool, supported by The Kinks and The High Numbers (who would later become The Who).

18 The band fly from London to San Francisco.

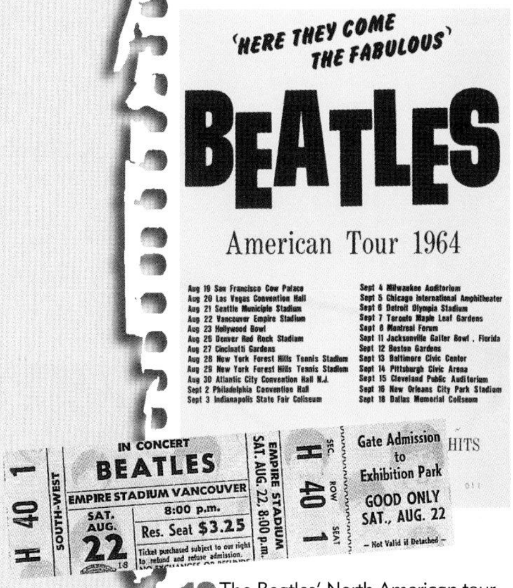

'HERE THEY COME THE FABULOUS'
BEATLES
American Tour 1964
Aug 19 San Francisco Cow Palace
Aug 20 Las Vegas Convention Hall
Aug 21 Seattle Municiple Stadium
Aug 22 Vancouver Empire Stadium
Aug 23 Hollywood Bowl
Aug 26 Denver Red Rock Stadium
Aug 27 Cincinatti Gardens
Aug 28 New York Forest Hills Tennis Stadium
Aug 29 New York Forest Hills Tennis Stadium
Aug 30 Atlantic City Convention Hall N.J.
Sept 2 Philadelphia Convention Hall
Sept 3 Indianapolis State Fair Coliseum
Sept 4 Milwaukee Auditorium
Sept 5 Chicago International Amphitheater
Sept 6 Detroit Olympia Stadium
Sept 7 Toronto Maple Leaf Gardens
Sept 8 Montreal Forum
Sept 11 Jacksonville Gaiter Bowl, Florida
Sept 12 Boston Gardens
Sept 13 Baltimore Civic Center
Sept 14 Pittsburgh Civic Arena
Sept 15 Cleveland Public Auditorium
Sept 16 New Orleans City Park Stadium
Sept 18 Dallas Memorial Coliseum
HITS
H 40 1
SOUTH-WEST
IN CONCERT
BEATLES
EMPIRE STADIUM VANCOUVER
SAT. AUG. 22
8:00 p.m.
Res. Seat $3.25
Ticket purchased subject to our right to refund and refuse admission.
SAT. AUG. 22, 8:00 p.m.
EMPIRE STADIUM
SEC. H ROW 40 SEAT 1
Gate Admission to Exhibition Park
GOOD ONLY SAT., AUG. 22
– Not Valid if Detached –

19 The Beatles' North American tour begins at The Cow Palace, San Francisco, supported by The Righteous Brothers and Jackie De Shannon.

20 The band play the Convention Center, Las Vegas, Nevada.

22 The tour continues at the Empire Stadium, Vancouver.

23 At the Hollywood Bowl, Los Angeles, the show is taped, but it is not released as a live album until 1977.

A HARD DAY'S NIGHT

Soundtrack Of Their Lives

A Hard Day's Night was more than just an accompaniment to The Beatles' first film – it heralded 'folk rock' and introduced a more delicate, relaxed side of the band, reckons Robert Sandall.

In a recording career that spanned barely seven years, The Beatles travelled so far so fast that every album they made was in some respect pivotal. In practice, though, that accolade is normally reserved for *Rubber Soul* and the psychedelic leaps and bounds that followed its release at the end of 1965. The earlier LPs are generally seen as more rushed, less intricately inspired, less complex – which to varying degrees they were. At the time they appeared, singles were still the dominant currency of the pop business and the concept of the album as an integrated body of work was unknown outside the elite circles of modern jazz and classical. Small wonder then that in the amazing story of how The Beatles conquered and changed the world, the first five albums tend to get a bit lost in the rush.

This is especially tough on number three, *A Hard Day's Night*, a highly influential record with one of the most impressive opening statements of any album ever. It began with a huge chiming chord, a sound more resonant, more electric and more, well, 'guitarry' than anything previously heard on disc. God alone knew what that chord was – G eleventh suspended fourths not having featured prominently in the work of Chuck Berry or Carl Perkins. And as for the guitar itself, electric 12-string Rickenbackers were a tremendous novelty in 1964, even to players with budgets the size of George Harrison's.

Aside from sounding great, that magnificent *drrraaeengg* announced, with no little grandeur, The Beatles' ambition to take beat music to places it hadn't been before. At the other end of the album's title track, the chime of Harrison's Rickenbacker sweetly arpeggiating to fade, signposted one of those places. In the summer of the following year there it was again, as Jim (later Roger) McGuinn's electric 12-string transformed The Byrds' version of Mr Tambourine Man. They called it folk rock.

"Not since Buddy Holly had a pop group dared to release an album made up entirely of their own songs."

The Beatles, in their own fashion, got there first. Although *A Hard Day's Night* is best known as the soundtrack of the Richard Lester movie, it is more interesting to listen to as a document of the group's recent discovery of Bob Dylan. In January 1964, Harrison came across a copy of Bob's *Freewheelin'* LP in Paris. The effect on the others, particularly Lennon, was instant and it echoed throughout the LP they began recording in earnest at the end of February.

Some of the Dylan-esque touches were, in truth, not unreservedly fab. The wheezy harmonica that ushered in the second track on side one, I Should Have Known Better, made a fairly slight, sing-song composition seem even slighter. There was nothing very Bobbish in the album's lyrics either: lurve and dating issues still predominated. But as the album progressed, so did The Beatles. They sounded more relaxed. They appeared to have picked up from Dylan one of the rudiments of boho cool: don't come on like you're trying too hard.

A new emphasis, bringing forward acoustic guitars to complement and sometimes overrule the electrics, gave their

The reel thing: fans wait for the Fabs' film debut, New York City, 14 July 1964.

PHOTO: HULTON ARCHIVE

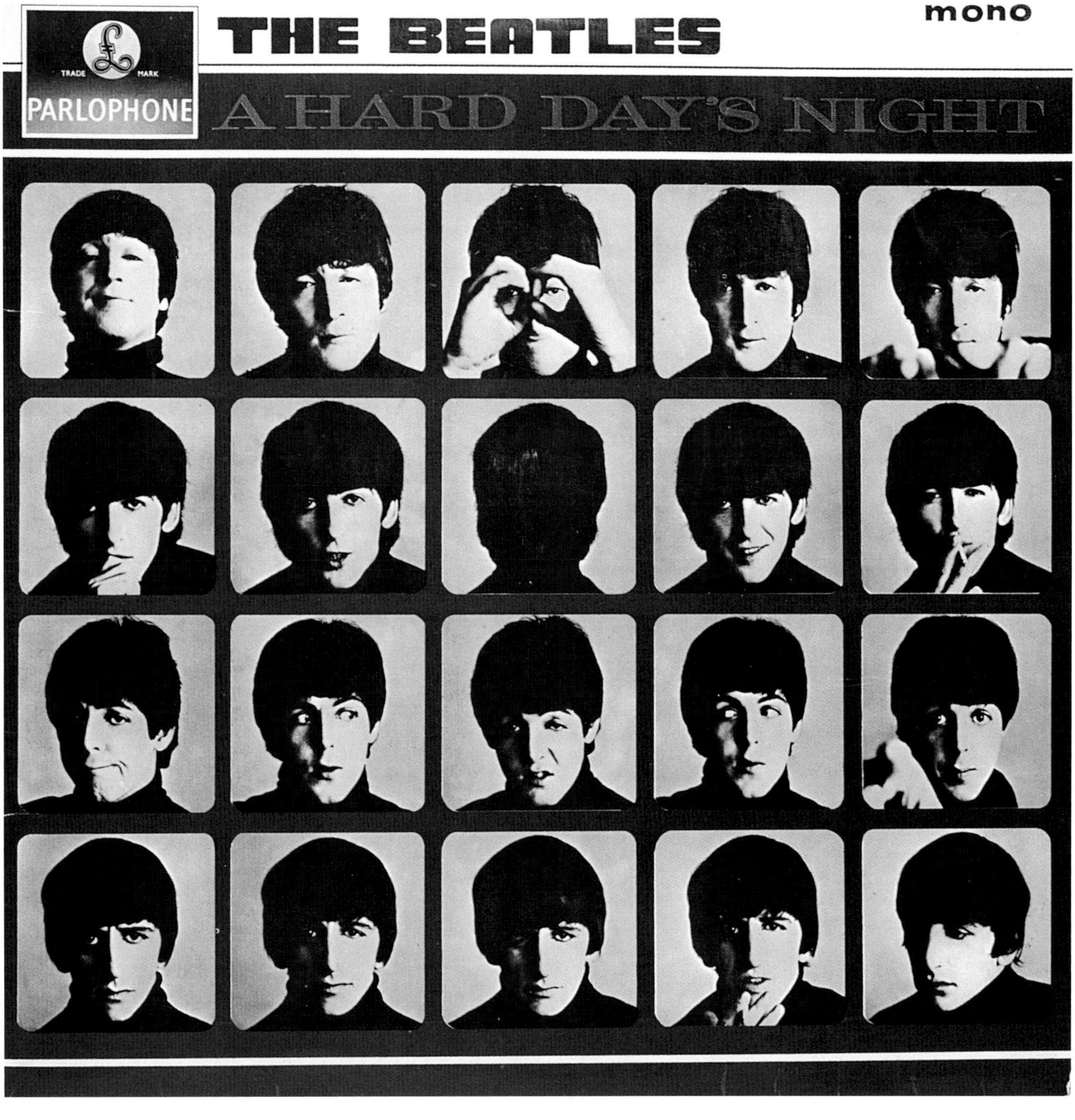

sound more intimacy, authority and depth. Delicate wasn't a quality you'd necessarily associated with The Beatles up 'til now but there was no better word to describe the airy feel of McCartney's super-sweet, Latin-tinged ballad And I Love Her. Introspective wasn't a familiar Beatles destination either but by the end of side two, there they were, carefully despatching one of Lennon's most enigmatic, and inexplicably uncelebrated songs, I'll Be Back. Swerving unpredictably from major to minor chords, never quite getting round to a chorus and relying entirely on acoustic or flamenco guitars, I'll Be Back was the early Beatles at their most prophetic. This grasp of how to colour arrangements in darker or more muted tones foreshadowed an inner journey they eventually undertook in two albums' time, on *Rubber Soul*.

It was hardly surprising, given all the other stuff that was

TRACK LISTING

A-SIDE

1. A Hard Day's Night
Lennon/McCartney
Sung by Lennon

2. I Should Have Known Better
Lennon/McCartney
Sung by Lennon

3. If I Fell
Lennon/McCartney
Sung by Lennon and McCartney

4. I'm Happy Just To Dance With You
Lennon/McCartney
Sung by Harrison

5. And I Love Her
Lennon/McCartney
Sung by McCartney

6. Tell Me Why
Lennon/McCartney
Sung by Lennon

7. Can't Buy Me Love
Lennon/McCartney
Sung by McCartney

B-SIDE

8. Anytime At All
Lennon/McCartney
Sung by Lennon

9. I'll Cry Instead
Lennon/McCartney
Sung by Lennon

10. Things We Said Today
Lennon/McCartney
Sung by McCartney

11. When I Get Home
Lennon/McCartney
Sung by Lennon

12. You Can't Do That
Lennon/McCartney
Sung by Lennon

13. I'll Be Back
Lennon/McCartney
Sung by Lennon

A HARD DAY'S NIGHT

WHAT THE PAPERS SAID...

For the press, it wasn't a hard album to swallow.

"A Hard Day's Night is the first track on the LP. It's by far the most commercial and it's also a great curtain-opener for the LP – hard swinging with George playing excellent guitar... The weird sound was produced by a special drum someone found in the effects department... Tell Me Why is introduced by John, and the others come in with good harmonies. This is the most polished Beatles number I've heard... Any Time At All is sung with great gusto all round while You Can't Do That is a much better version than the track already issued on the reverse of Can't Buy Me Love."
Jack Hutton, Melody Maker, June 27, 1964

"The opener is already passing into pop history. Double tracked vocal from John, here – this theme crops up several times orchestrally during the movie. He and Paul combine on the vocal of If I Fell. Slow ballad, with a stack of compulsive charm. I'm Happy..., has George, on lead vocal. Pushed along by Ringo's persuasive percussion, George swings amiably. Paul takes over on And I Love Her, which is not typically Beatle in sound.

"Tell Me Why gets back to normal with all the falsetto high-grabs, vocally. Unmistakably Beatlish, this – with John well to the front, aided by Paul. Can't Buy Me Love is... Oh, what's the use of saying anything more about this one... The throaty Lennon voice, leads through the medium-paced thumper Anytime At All. I'll Cry Instead is mostly John vocally – another up-tempo bit with Paul interjecting.

"When I Get Home is back to true Beatle-ism. With John apparently dislodging his tonsils as he blows the blues through the microphone."
Record Mirror, July 11, 1964

AND THEIR NEW L.P. . .

A HARD DAY'S NIGHT: A Hard Day's Night; I Should Have Known Better; If I Fell; I'm Happy Just To Dance With You; And I Love Her; Tell Me Why; Can't Buy Me Love; Any Time At All; I'll Cry Instead; Things We Said Today; When I Get Home; You Can't Do That; I'll Be Back (Parlophone PMC 1230)

Opener is already passing into pop history. Double-tracked vocal from John, here — this theme crops up several times, orchestrally during the movie. Next song is just fine. Another John vocal (just one helping this time), then he and Paul combine on the vocal of "If I Fell." Slow ballad, with a stack of compulsive charm.

"I'm Happy . . ." has George, no less, on lead vocal. He's good. Pushed along by Ringo's persuasive percussion, George swings amiably. Paul takes over on "And I Love Her," which is not typically Beatle in sound.

"Tell Me Why" gets back to normal with all the falsetto high-grabs, vocally. [illegible] Beatlish, this—with John well to the front, aided by Paul. "Can't Buy Me Love" is . . . oh, what's the use of saying anything more about this one!

The throaty Lennon voice leads through the medium-paced thumper "Any Time At All," with piano IN, solidly, George Martin, presumably. "I'll Cry Instead" is mostly John, vocally — another up-tempo bit with Paul interjecting enthusiastically.

On to "Things We Said Today." Paul, again. It's a plaintive sort of number.

"When I Get Home" is right back to true Beatle-ism. With John apparently dislodging his tonsils as he blows the blues through the microphone.

Next comes "You Can't Do That." Mid-tempo, with John mainly leading, vocally.

The closer is "I'll Be Back." This is delicately sung, by Beatle standards. Rather pleasant harmonies all the way, but the melody line [illegible] of the other [illegible]

SLEEVENOTES

How the cartoon strip-style cover art reflected the Fabs' "zany" side.

Director Richard Lester, who had previously worked with The Goons, employs every camera trick in the book from speed-ups and slow motion to silent movie captions and jump-cuts in A Hard Day's Night, Alun Owen's semi-fictionalised documentary of life on the road with The Beatles.

Robert Freeman was the man chosen to photograph and design a cover which echoed the spirit and feel of the film. This was Freeman's second time working on a Beatles album cover following *With The Beatles* (altogether he would work on five of the band's album covers up until *Rubber Soul*).

According to him it only stood to reason that the sleeve artwork for the soundtrack had to be as "animated" and "zany" as the film itself.

But when Walter Shenson, the flick's producer, finally gave Freeman a sneak preview of the United Artists' proofs for the UK film posters he was horrified.

"They were cartoon illustrations of Beatle wigs stuck on top of guitars: quite out of character," he states in his book, A Private View.

With a little help from Shenson and Brian Epstein, Freeman convinced United Artists to let him redesign the posters and came up with his famous comic strip style artwork, which was far more sympathetic to the feel of the film. "I used a studio for the portraits, shot individually with varying expressions. A white background, a soft sidelight, and The Beatles wearing black. The pictures were edited in sequence to animate their expressions, one line for each Beatle, on the same principle as polyphotos, where a person is photographed with different expressions from a fixed camera position. The grid form worked equally well for the album cover and the film poster. They used the same photo-portraits for the title sequence, which ran at the end of the film."

Lois Wilson

"The magnificent *drrraaeengg* opening chord announced their ambition to take beat music to places it hadn't been."

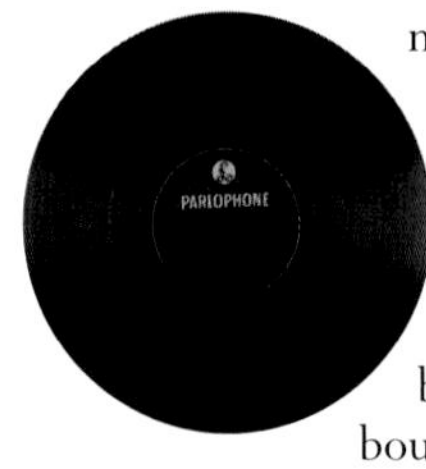

going on around them, that the group weren't quite ready yet to break the moptop mould. Most of the songs on *A Hard Day's Night* were put together during a three-month period fraught with two major distractions – filming their first movie and dealing with the sudden outbreak of Beatlemania in America. Time for writing songs was understandably short, and occasionally it showed. The country and western pastiche, I'll Cry Instead, clocking in at two minutes and six seconds, and released as a Top 30 single in the States, had the air of a piece hastily designed to appeal to a new fanbase across the Atlantic. The upbeat, lustily belted Tell Me Why could easily have been left over from their previous LP, adequate for the purposes of the film in which it featured, but hardly a classic.

Filler aside, *A Hard Day's Night* contained more than enough aces to dispel the suspicion that their dizzying fame might be inhibiting The Beatles' creativity. On the contrary, the single Can't Buy Me Love confirmed their ability to unite the generations behind a jazzy tune with a bouncy mid-tempo rhythm. This was one the mums could understand, even though McCartney kept referring to "my friend" in a way that suggested that she (or for that matter, he) was not his lover. Its B-side, the Lennon composition You Can't Do That, contradicted the genial tone with its tense threats, sexual paranoia and nagging, dragging groove. Already on this album, the pair's competitive relationship – disguised by the bland attribution of all songs to Lennon/McCartney – was beginning to make itself felt.

But only beginning. Although each of the songs on the album was subsequently revealed to have been written by one or the other, John and Paul were still, at this stage, locked in a complicated symbiotic relationship. They clearly observed, and to some degree admired and tried

It's playback time: (from left) Ringo Starr, George Martin and John Lennon during the recording of *A Hard Day's Night*, Abbey Road, 1964.

to copy, what each other was doing. If you didn't recognise the singer of If I Fell, for example, you might well have concluded that Lennon's first attempt at a ballad – with its melody leaping the octave and ardently naive lyrics – had been written by McCartney. He was, after all, head over heels in love at the time with Jane Asher.

Equally, the mood of brooding reverie in Things We Said Today conforms more closely to most people's perception of what Lennon, stuck in a failing marriage, might have been feeling at the time. Everybody now knows, however, that it was McCartney who wrote that one.

Overall, *A Hard Day's Night* ended up being the closest thing to a John Lennon album that The Beatles ever recorded. He contributed all but three of the 13 songs, including the title track. Inspired by the example of Bob Dylan, who never used any songs he hadn't written himself unless they happened to be credited to anon, Lennon went for it in 1964. Not since Buddy Holly had a pop group dared to release an album made up entirely of their own songs. He may have worked a shade too fast on occasions – putting this collection together really was a bit of 'a hard day's night' – but it was Lennon, rather than McCartney, who now sensed where The Beatles' musical future lay.

PHOTO: MAGNUM

ONE FROM THE HEART

For hopeless romantic Gary Moore, *A Hard Day's Night* was an LP to fall in love to.

"I went to see the film in a cinema in Belfast. In retrospect it was really innocent, just a group of people having fun and being stupid but at the time it marked the beginning of this huge pop explosion. You couldn't help but be affected by it. I was 11 and had just started playing guitar. I was in a band called The Beat Boys with some friends from school. We thought we were The Beatles. I was probably Ringo [*laughs*].

"We used to learn all the harmonies from that album and rehearse them in our drummer's living room. One night he threw a party. While we were playing If I Fell, I fell in love with this girl there. That's how I see this album, it's an album to fall in love to and that makes it something very special. It's very romantic. The ballads on *A Hard Day's Night* are just fantastic. Lennon and McCartney's songwriting was so simple yet so sophisticated. Lennon had a way of singing as if he were talking. He wasn't fancy with his lyrics and McCartney wrote great melodies.

"There's some brilliant guitar playing on the title track itself. Not many people could copy the guitar solo at the time and I practised over and over until I got it right. I was really chuffed. When I met George Harrison years later I went to his house and he let me play the song on his 12-string Rickenbacker. I was in my 30s but it was still a huge thrill. He played me the first chord of the song and I said, without thinking, 'Are you sure that's it? I always play it like this'. He just looked at me and said, 'Yes, I'm sure'."

Lois Wilson

24 Slow Down/Matchbox is released as a single in the US by Capitol.

26 The band plays Red Rocks Amphitheater, Denver, Colorado.

28 Two nights at Forest Hills Tennis Stadium, New York. Bob Dylan introduces The Beatles to marijuana in the Delmonico Hotel, New York City.

30 The Beatles play the Convention Hall, Atlantic City, New Jersey.

31 While staying at the Atlantic City Hotel, Paul has a telephone conversation with Elvis Presley.

SEPTEMBER 64

1 The Beatles' Monthly Book is published in the US for the first time.

2 After a show at the Convention Hall, Philadelphia, Pennsylvania, The Beatles mention on local radio that they were dismayed to see that their audience was almost entirely white, following recent race riots in the city.

3 A show at the Indiana State Fair Coliseum, Indianapolis, Indiana.

4 The band plays the Auditorium, Milwaukee. Meanwhile, the Indonesian government bans Beatle haircuts.

5 A show at the International Amphitheater, Chicago, Illinois.

7 A show at the Maple Leaf Gardens, Toronto, Canada (above).

11 The Beatles play the Gator Bowl, Jacksonville, Florida. They are assured the audience is not segregated, as they insisted in a press release on September 6.

15 At Cleveland Public Auditorium, Cleveland, Ohio, local police chief Carl Baer orders The Beatles offstage for 15 minutes so that the hysterical crowd can calm down.

16 A show at the City Park Stadium, New Orleans, Louisiana.

17 A world record fee of $150,000 is paid for The Beatles' appearance at the Municipal Stadium, Kansas City.

18 The Beatles' US tour ends at the Memorial Coliseum, Dallas, Texas.

19 On the occasion of Brian Epstein's 30th birthday, The Beatles take a one-day break at a remote ranch in Missouri's Ozark Hills. When the visit ends, their plane is prevented from taking off by a deputation of local dignitaries demanding autographs.

20 When The Beatles perform a charity show for the United Cerebral Palsy Association, at the Paramount Theatre, New York City, Bob Dylan visits them backstage.

24 Ringo starts up a building company, Brickey Building.

What: A Hard Day's Night premiere
Where: The London Pavilion
When: July 6, 1964

FOUR ON FILM

Shot for peanuts in 1964, The Beatles' film debut may have smacked of a cheap pop cash-in but it had its moments. By Charles Shaar Murray.

SSSSSHHHANNNNNNNNNNNGGGG... ONE big chord – a Gm7add11, I am reliably informed – introduces a big title song for a little movie. A Hard Day's Night was subsequently acclaimed by The Village Voice as "the Citizen Kane of jukebox movies", which sounds a trifle hyperbolic. After all, Citizen Kane is an acknowledged masterpiece of 20th century cinema, the work of a dedicated eccentric auteur, packed full of formal innovations and taking as its subject matter the nature of celebrity and power in modern America. A Hard Day's Night, by contrast, was a quick, cheap pop cash-in shot and edited in a matter of weeks on what was, by Hollywood standards, a chicken-feed budget.

The plot is a real back-of-an-envelope job: The Beatles arrive in London by train with their road managers Norm (Norman Rossington) and Shake (John Junkin), as well as Paul's (fictional) grandad Johnny McCartney (Wilfrid Brambell) to hold a press conference and perform a live transmission TV concert from what is, presumably, the BBC. Grandad winds Ringo up to the point where he walks out on the band shortly before transmission. The others have to find him in time and get him back to the studio in time to play the gig. They do. That's it.

Filmed, as much for economy as style, in grainy mock-doc monochrome, A Hard Day's Night – written by Alun Owen (with a fair amount of improv by the principals) and, of course, directed by Dick Lester – intentionally blurred the boundaries of fact and fiction. There's no attempt to depict The Beatles as anybody but themselves: though the name 'Beatles' is never spoken in the film (but it does appear on Ringo's bass-drum head and in neon lights behind the band during the closing performance sequence), there is no doubt as to whom John, Paul, George and Ringo are supposed to be.

Writer Owen, according to Ringo Starr, "came on part of our British tour, wrote down the chaos that went on all around us and how we lived, and gave us a caricature of ourselves. So A Hard Day's Night was like a day in the life; or, really, two days and two nights of our life..."

The caricature 'personalities' – John: aggressive, extrovert sarky bastard; George: deadpan, introvert sarky bastard; Ringo: insecure, lugubrious sarky bastard; Paul: bouncy, gung-ho sarky bastard – arrived in the movie through a combination of Owen incorporating aspects of real Beatles business into the script, plus his own coinings on their behalf (such as 'grotty') and the band's own variations on the dialogue they were assigned. They eventually became the templates for The Beatles' characterisations in Help!, the eponymous animated series, Yellow Submarine and, indeed, mass public perceptions of who the world's favourite boys really were. Paul McCartney was formally the least defined, almost a 'straight man' to the others and to Brambell, Steptoe And Son's 'dirty old man' reinvented as 'very clean'. Dick Lester opines that if Macca comes across as the least 'natural' in the movie, it's probably because he was always going to the theatre with Jane Asher and her family and, under this cultural influence, may actually have been trying to do some Proper Acting.

They're decidedly less clean-cut than Cliff & The Shads, or any of our contemporary boy bands. There's no boozing, shagging or drugging, but they smoke lots of ciggies, cheat at cards and lech after a posse of schoolgirls (played by a bunch of young models/actresses/whatevers, one of whom was Patti Boyd, who ended up marrying her Beatle). They also relentlessly mock the stuffy, the Southern, the bourgeoisie, each other (especially Ringo), Norm and Shake, and small-minded pettiness in all its manifestations.

The action takes place almost entirely in London, but Liverpool is ever present: The Beatles bring it with them. Liverpool's Irishness is also an undercurrent: when the future Mr Ono does his Mad Jock Lennon routine in the schoolgirls' compartment, he does so in a stage-Irish accent: when Grandad is arrested, he announces himself as 'a soldier of the republic' and starts to sing, "A nation once again". But then, as George Harrison once said, "Everyone in Liverpool thinks they're a comedian." The Beatles' press conferences were as much a masterclass in sarky-bastard deadpannery as Bob Dylan's, and hilarious in a manner which mere quotation cannot convey.

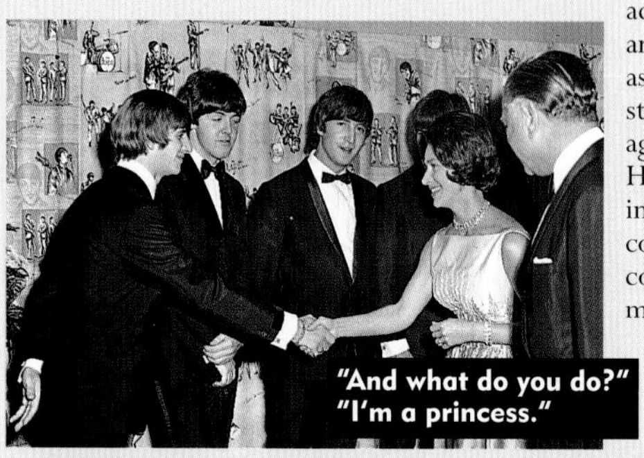

"And what do you do?" "I'm a princess."

"There's no shagging or drugging in A Hard Day's Night, but The Beatles smoke lots of ciggies and lech after schoolgirls."

We see an approximation of this in the press-launch scene, emphasising how much each Beatle was his own man.

A Hard Day's Night tempers its mock-doc feel with outbreaks of surrealism: following their encounter on the train with the pinstriped, RAF-'tached Tory Man, The Beatles suddenly appear running alongside the train, banging on the windows, and when Lennon takes a bath (wearing swimming trunks and playing submarines), he disappears beneath the bubbles and when the plug is pulled, he's not there, suddenly appearing behind the exasperated Norm. By comparison, the conventions of the Elvis or Cliff movies seem to derive from the previous century rather than merely the previous decade.

Its presentation was high style, even down to the closing credits, when Robert Freeman's 'polyphoto' images of the individual Beatles are fast-dissolved so that each Beatle morphs into one of his colleagues, emphasising both the distinctiveness of the individual personalities, and the unity of their collective identity. All for one and one for all: no wonder so many '60s kids saw the movie and wanted to be in bands. The Beatles seemed to be having more fun simply being themselves than any other four guys on the planet.

PHOTOS: CAMERA PRESS

Up in lights: A Hard Day's Night premieres in London, July 6, 1964.

Lights, Camera, Acton!

Photographer David Hurn takes Lois Wilson back to the set of A Hard Day's Night – a world of screaming girls and West London train stations.

"It could be incredibly frightening working with The Beatles," recalls lensman David Hurn. "I remember being trapped in a cab with Ringo in Piccadilly Circus. Hundreds of fans had surrounded the car and we couldn't drive on. I was scared for my life but Ringo seemed to take it all in his stride."

Hurn, now 68 and currently working on a photographic journal dedicated to the people of Wales, first teamed up with the Fab Four via friend and A Hard Day's Night director, Richard Lester. There was no brief as such. "Dick just asked me to come down to the filming and document the making of A Hard Day's Night, which is what I tried to do. It was a difficult assignment because a lot of the action took place on a train and there simply wasn't enough room for the camera and lighting crew, let alone myself to squeeze into the carriage. But I was adept at making myself invisible and still getting the shot."

This was a skill he'd had to learn very quickly on his first assignment if he were to survive. "I was asked to capture the 1956 Hungarian revolution for European Life magazine and The Observer. It was very hairy at times and I had to do a lot of thinking on my feet because I really was quite unprepared."

Over the years Hurn has snapped the likes of Jane Fonda in Barbarella, Claire Bloom and Sophia Loren, which is a far cry from his first fumble with the camera in the Royal Military in Sandhurst in 1952.

"I discovered that if you joined the photography club you had a lot more freedom in the evening because the darkrooms were situated on another campus. But of course that meant forking out for a camera, which I wasn't too happy about at first, but once I started taking pictures I was smitten."

◀ GEORGE AND PATTI BOYD PADDINGTON STATION, 1964
"Patti wasn't an actress, but George was so impressed by her that he got Dick to give her a part as a schoolgirl on the train. It was actually through me that she was there. Patti was the girlfriend of a photographer friend of mine. He boasted to her that he could get her on set via me, but he probably regretted it as once she met George she never left his side."

◀ THE BEATLES CROWCOMBE, SOMERSET, MARCH 1964
"Dick Lester had intended to shoot most of A Hard Day's Night in railway stations around London. But it soon became apparent that it wasn't always possible because the fans would discover where we'd be and disrupt the process. So we ended up shooting in out of the way places like Crowcombe. Dick was influenced by slapstick comedy and this was a typical Keystone Cops-style caper shot."

▲ JOHN
ACTON STATION, 1964

"I desperately needed a head shot of John so I asked him to pose when the day's filming had ended. Even though he was very obliging and co-operative he never really grasped the fact that a photographer needs to take time to set up the shot and then take a number of shots to get a perfect result. With all of The Beatles you had to be very quick because they wouldn't stand around waiting for you. I only had a second to get this."

◀ **TWO FANS STOP THE TRAIN**
1964

"I soon found out that taking shots from outside of the train where the filming was taking place made for a much better picture than actually being on the train itself. The two girls in this photo had been tipped off by a local station guard as to when the train would be passing through. I was crouched down on the track. It was great. The fans would often wait hours for the train even if they didn't know when it was arriving. They had parties by the station. It became a real social gathering with them all sharing their experiences."

▲ **RINGO WITH CAMERA**
1964

"This is me getting all post-modern, taking a shot of Ringo who is filming with his camera, who is in turn being shot himself. There was a lot of ad-libbing on the film set and Ringo was often at the centre of this. He'd gone out and bought a camera himself to capture some of the events. He was quite an avid photographer. The lensmen behind him are a mix of genuine photographers and extras employed by Dick Lester."

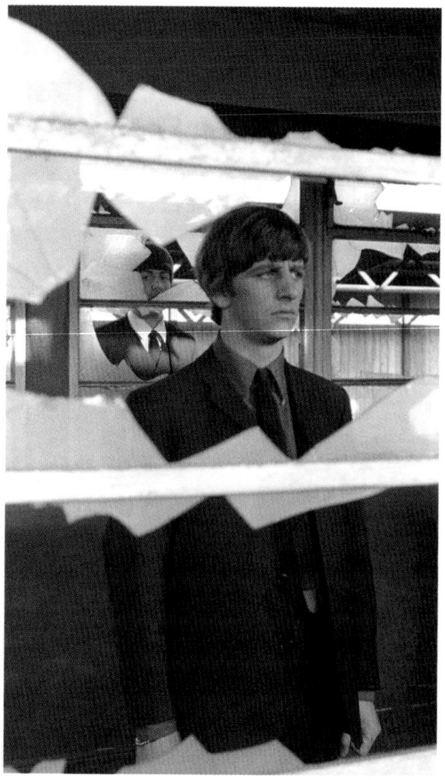

▲ PAUL, JOHN AND RINGO, ACTON STATION, MARCH 1964

"The disused railway made the perfect backdrop for the movie. Although The Beatles didn't mind posing for pictures if you asked them, they were surprisingly shy and reticent for stars. These shots behind broken glass were Dick's way of giving the pictures a sort of enigmatic meaning. It was only Ringo who seemed to be entirely comfortable with the whole proceedings. You got the impression that Paul and John were slightly removed from Ringo and George. They definitely seemed to think they were the brains of the whole operation. But it was John who was the most intelligent and this came through in his abrasive wit and eccentricities. He could be very warm but he called the shots. If he said jump that's what you did."

▶ THE BEATLES, ACTON STATION, MARCH 1964

"Getting the four of them to pose together was almost impossible. They were just never in the same place at the same time. In hindsight I think it must have been a deliberate ploy on their part but at the time it didn't occur to me. They were actually being filmed at the time I took this picture. I was positioned just behind the camera crew snapping away. There was no dialogue so I didn't have to worry about making a noise with the shutter. The actual positioning of the shot is again a ploy to make it look like there is hidden meaning behind the scene, which of course there isn't – it's just Dick Lester making it look intriguing."

ALL PHOTOS DAVID HURN/MAGNUM

◀ **THE BEATLES REHEARSING SCALA THEATRE, APRIL 1964**

"They were more at home playing their instruments than acting. They didn't like miming so actually played live for the film. Paul and John seemed to understand one another totally. There was no rivalry, just a genuine love and respect. It was great fun to watch them onstage playing. Yet despite their obvious talents they were very humble. They'd point to other musicians saying how much more able they were. Their musical limitations spurred them on."

▲ **RINGO, PAUL AND BRIAN EPSTEIN SCALA THEATRE, LONDON MARCH 1964**

"This was one of the few times that I actually got to shoot Brian Epstein. He only came down to the set for one day during filming but it was obvious from the way he interacted with The Beatles that they were all very close. He was very charming but had a firm hold on what was going on the whole time. After his death I don't think The Beatles ever trusted anyone in the music business again."

▲ **THE BEATLES ON THE PHONE MARYLEBONE STATION, 1964**

"More Keystone Cops capers with The Beatles running in and out of phone booths. They were actually filming this scene and once more I was shadowing the camera crew. You can tell by The Beatles' intense faces that the cameras are rolling. When they were rehearsing their parts they were always much more relaxed and always had a joke with those around them. This, being a long-range photo, was taken with a Canon. For my close-ups I used a Leica."

The Fabs earn their stripes Stateside, August, 1964.

What: The Fabs start first US tour
Where: Cow Palace, San Francisco
When: August 19, 1964

ALTERED STATES

The Fabs' second US tour changed both The Beatles and America. One cub reporter was lucky enough to join the ride. By Ashley Kahn.

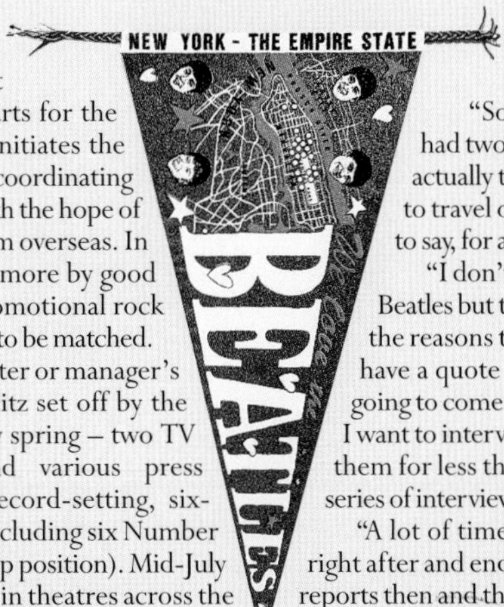

THINK OF IT: TODAY the mere hint of a local act cracking the US pop charts for the first time automatically initiates the well-practised process of coordinating publicity, marketing and touring with the hope of propelling a British band to stardom overseas. In 1964, The Beatles – less by plan, more by good timing – set the precedent for promotional rock build-up with an assault that has yet to be matched.

It was a feat beyond any promoter or manager's wildest wet-dream. The media blitz set off by the Fabs' first American foray in early spring – two TV appearances, two concerts and various press conferences – propelled their record-setting, six-month run of 17 Top 40 singles (including six Number 1s and a three-month lock on the top position). Mid-July saw A Hard Day's Night break out in theatres across the country, boosting the mid-summer mania to a fever pitch. By August all America knew the foursome on a first-name basis; the familiarity made a coast-to-coast invasion a foregone, inevitable conclusion.

It was a madcap, scream-filled, month-long, 24-city adventure that hurtled atop a tidal wave of publicity and popularity. All 26 concerts took place in venues holding anywhere from 4,000 (New York's Paramount Theater) to 28,000 (Baltimore's Civic Center) screaming or stunned fans. All shows were immediate sell-outs. Flamboyant San Francisco millionaire Charles Finley offered the group the unheard-of sum of $150,000 to add one concert to their already packed schedule. Kicking off on August 19 in San Francisco, the tour charted a course east to Las Vegas, up north to Seattle and Vancouver, down to Hollywood, east again to Denver (Finley's add-on show), Cincinnati and New York… and that was just the first week-and-a-half!

Crowds mobbed the group wherever they played or stayed. Decoy limousines and unlikely vehicles in which to smuggle the four in and out of venues (delivery vans, ambulances) became standard procedure. The lads themselves became familiar with a trapped feeling. "We just can't get out on our own," complained John. "People think fame and money bring freedom, but they don't… what can you spend on in a room?"

To ensure smooth travel, a private propeller plane was rented for the entire entourage, including The Beatles, their staff, their opening acts (Jackie DeShannon, The Righteous Brothers, Clarence "Frogman" Henry) and a few lucky journalists. One of those was Larry Kane, a cub reporter from Florida who had managed to convey an exaggerated image of his value to Brian Epstein.

"I was a radio news director in Miami – a mere 20 year old – and I had written a letter to Epstein. On my business card were seven radio stations including the one I worked for: WFUN, the one we called a general market station, while the rest were black-oriented. Brian must have thought I was a big-time American personality, and he invited me on the tour, which panicked my employees: 'How the hell are we going to pay for this?'"

"So I left in August for San Francisco and had two incredible summers with them. I was actually the only American broadcast journalist to travel on every stop in '64 and '65. Needless to say, for a young reporter it was a wild ride.

"I don't pretend to be a lifelong friend of The Beatles but they were comfortable with me. One of the reasons they did feel comfortable was – I even have a quote from Paul saying, 'Larry Kane is not going to come up here and wake me up and say, Paul, I want to interview you,' you know? I had only known them for less than a week, and they asked me to do a series of interviews for Melody Maker!

"A lot of times they would do a concert and leave right after and end up in another city at 2am. I'd file my reports then and they would still be up, real late. In 1964, the airplane used was an Electra Turboprop and we flew in this one plane from coast to coast.

"More than the hotels, that plane was our home. It was a place to sleep, a place where they truly felt comfortable, a bubble where you could get away from the crowds and let off steam. On the plane there were several things that would happen. There were pillow fights and food fights. I'm not a party animal, but I got into it too and was often a target for mischief… the favourite selections were Jello and pudding, both of which made a real mess.

"I was taking a light nap from the flight from Denver to Cincinnati and I woke up because my breathing was interrupted. Mashed potatoes and gravy were pasted over my face, and I opened my eyes to see John Lennon across the way giggling. 'A direct hit,' he said, 'smoosh, whoosh and whack'. John had a marvellous talent for creating his own vocabulary to fit the moment."

Today the memories of the music, screams and dry cleaning bills of that tour echo in Kane's soon-to-be-published, as-yet-untitled book. Since 1964, Kane established himself as a well-known TV news anchor in Philadelphia. "I've been an anchor for 37 years here, and covered kings and queens and Presidents and superstars and ordinary people who do ordinary things – everybody you can imagine. No matter where I go, the question always, inevitably pops up, 'What were The Beatles really like?'

"In truth, back in 1964, I was not a fan. I was a hard-nosed news reporter used to covering politics and government than traipsing around with a bunch of rock stars. I never thought this was going to be a story that would last well into the next century. It was the story of a lifetime."

"On the plane there were pillow fights and food fights. The favourite selections were Jello and pudding."

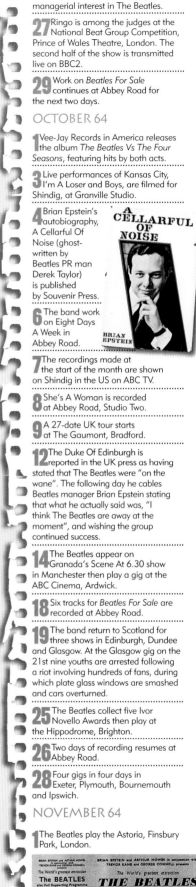

The first US date, Cow Palace, San Francisco, August 19, 1964.

PHOTOS: HULTON ARCHIVE, AP

25 Brian Epstein rejects a £3.5 million offer from an American businessman who wants to buy out his managerial interest in The Beatles.

27 Ringo is among the judges at the National Beat Group Competition, Prince of Wales Theatre, London. The second half of the show is transmitted live on BBC2.

29 Work on *Beatles For Sale* continues at Abbey Road for the next two days.

OCTOBER 64

1 Vee-Jay Records in America releases the album *The Beatles Vs The Four Seasons*, featuring hits by both acts.

3 Live performances of Kansas City, I'm A Loser and Boys, are filmed for Shindig, at Granville Studio.

4 Brian Epstein's autobiography, A Cellarful Of Noise (ghost-written by Beatles PR man Derek Taylor) is published by Souvenir Press.

6 The band work on Eight Days A Week in Abbey Road.

7 The recordings made at the start of the month are shown on Shindig in the US on ABC TV.

8 She's A Woman is recorded at Abbey Road, Studio Two.

9 A 27-date UK tour starts at The Gaumont, Bradford.

12 The Duke Of Edinburgh is reported in the UK press as having stated that The Beatles were "on the wane". The following day he cables Beatles manager Brian Epstein stating that what he actually said was, "I think The Beatles are away at the moment", and wishing the group continued success.

14 The Beatles appear on Granada's Scene At 6.30 show in Manchester then play a gig at the ABC Cinema, Ardwick.

18 Six tracks for *Beatles For Sale* are recorded at Abbey Road.

19 The band return to Scotland for three shows in Edinburgh, Dundee and Glasgow. At the Glasgow gig on the 21st nine youths are arrested following a riot involving hundreds of fans, during which plate glass windows are smashed and cars overturned.

25 The Beatles collect five Ivor Novello Awards then play at the Hippodrome, Brighton.

26 Two days of recording resumes at Abbey Road.

28 Four gigs in four days in Exeter, Plymouth, Bournemouth and Ipswich.

NOVEMBER 64

1 The Beatles play the Astoria, Finsbury Park, London.

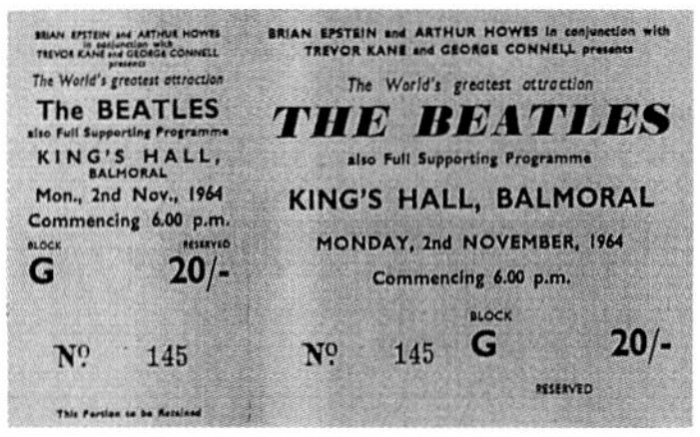
BRIAN EPSTEIN and ARTHUR HOWES in conjunction with TREVOR KANE and GEORGE CONNELL presents
The World's greatest attraction
The BEATLES
also Full Supporting Programme
KING'S HALL, BALMORAL
Mon., 2nd Nov., 1964
Commencing 6.00 p.m.
BLOCK G
RESERVED 20/-
Nº 145
This Portion to be Retained

BRIAN EPSTEIN and ARTHUR HOWES in conjunction with TREVOR KANE and GEORGE CONNELL presents
The World's greatest attraction
THE BEATLES
also Full Supporting Programme
KING'S HALL, BALMORAL
MONDAY, 2nd NOVEMBER, 1964
Commencing 6.00 p.m.
Nº 145
BLOCK G
20/-
RESERVED

2 A show at King's Hall, Belfast, Northern Ireland (above). An extra date added to the tour because of popular demand.

3 The Beatles fly back over to London from Belfast.

4 The band continue their tour, performing dates in Luton, Nottingham, Southampton, Cardiff, Liverpool and Sheffield.

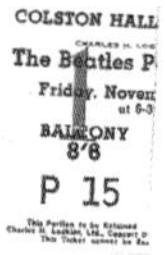

10 The Beatles' UK tour ends at Colston Hall, Bristol.

13 A tour documentary, The Beatles In America, is broadcast by CBS-TV in the States.

14 The Beatles record a four-track appearance for Thank Your Lucky Stars at Teddington Studios, London.

16 A performance for Top Of The Pops is recorded at Riverside Studios, Hammersmith, London.

17 Six songs are recorded at the Playhouse Theatre, London, for the BBC radio show Top Gear.

20 John films a scene for Peter Cook and Dudley Moore's BBC TV show Not Only… But Also on London's Wimbledon Common.

23 Four songs are recorded live for Ready Steady Go at Wembley Studio, London.

24 Paul attends his father's second wedding, to Angela Williams.

27 I Feel Fine/She's A Woman is released in the UK.

29 John records an appearance on TV show Not Only… But Also at Television Centre, London.

30 Brian Epstein is the featured guest on UK radio show Desert Island Discs. His musical choices include two Lennon/McCartney songs, She's A Woman and All My Loving.

DECEMBER 64

1 Ringo is admitted to University College Hospital, London, for a tonsillectomy.

2 During the 10.30am BBC Radio news summary, announcer Roy Williams states that Ringo Starr "has had his toe nails successfully removed".

3 Top Of The Pops features The Beatles performing I Feel Fine.

4 A new album, *Beatles For Sale*, is released in the UK.

9 *Beatles For Sale* is selling so well that it enters the singles chart at Number 28. It also enters the LP chart at Number 1.

10 The Beatles go to Number 1 in the UK with I Feel Fine.

15 The album, *Beatles '65*, is released in the States by Capitol Records.

18 Another *Beatles' Christmas Record* is mailed out to UK fan club members.

19 *Beatles For Sale* reaches Number 1 in the UK, displacing *A Hard Day's Night*.

24 Opening night of Another Beatles Christmas Show (above) at Hammersmith Odeon, London. It runs until 16 January, with support acts including The Yardbirds and Elkie Brooks.

26 I Feel Fine reaches Number 1 in the US.

What: Refusing to play segregated venues
Where: Jacksonville, Florida, USA
When: September 6, 1964

COME TOGETHER

When the Fabs said that they wouldn't play in front of segregated audiences, they gave pop music a new-found social conscience. By Bill DeMain.

"WE WILL NOT APPEAR UNLESS NEGROES are allowed to sit anywhere," announced The Beatles in a press statement on September 6, 1964. Halfway through a 23-city US tour – their first – the group was looking ahead to a date in Jacksonville, Florida, where they'd heard that blacks were confined to the balconies or upper tiers at public events such as concerts.

The next day, The Florida Times-Union, Jacksonville's daily paper, ran a disparaging editorial entitled "Beatlemania Is A Mark Of A Frenetic Era". The group was called "a passing fad, whose appearance on the scene was perfectly timed and fitted to the mores, morals and ideals of a fast-paced, troubled time". Their sound was described as "high-pitched monotone". There was no mention of segregation, but it was clear that those in the news media hardly considered these "hirsute scourges of Liverpool" intelligent enough to comment on social issues. By today's standards, their pronouncement was taken about as seriously as N'Sync's Lance Bass saying he wanted to join the space program.

"The Beatles were the first white artists to ever admit that they grew up on black music." Smokey Robinson

The music community in America felt differently. "At that time, no-one that I knew of really took the initiative to address any kind of social issues," says Mark Lindsay, lead singer of Paul Revere & The Raiders. "I can see The Beatles coming over here and being assailed by this weird, unfair policy of segregation. They were not just good musicians. They had intellect. They spoke up."

"They were really the first group to have the power to do that," says American singer Brian Hyland. "They used that platform really well. They could've just let it ride and not said anything about it. It took a lot of courage."

"We were, in many respects, just these goofy white boys," says US '60s sensation Lou Christie of the teen idol-type acts of the time. "We weren't allowed to be seen with a cigarette in our hands. We had press people watching who we went out with. The Beatles had a different attitude. They were more aggressive, they were funny and they were articulate. The minute they came to America, they literally put a halt to everything that was previously happening [in pop music]."

All three of these singers were part of Dick Clark's Caravan Of Stars, an interracial tour crossing paths with the Fabs in an America that was churning with racial tensions ("We were like a freedom bus," recalls Christie). Protesters were marching in northern cities from Seattle to Baltimore, demanding better jobs, schooling and housing for blacks. In the South, the situation was more desperate. Blacks were denied basic rights such as a place at a lunch counter or a seat in the front of a city bus. In July, President Lyndon Johnson signed the landmark Civil Rights Act, banning discrimination "on the basis of race, color, religion, sex, or national origin".

But old prejudices die hard. In the weeks after, riots broke out in Harlem and Rochester. Black churches, homes and businesses were burned in Mississippi. And there were countless incidences of violence throughout cities in the South, including Jacksonville.

Jacksonville native Don Walton, then a 16-year-old Beatle fan who was front row centre at the show, recalls, "There were some problems in our city, but we were never hardcore like Mississippi or South Carolina. Quite frankly, I know there were black kids in the audience. It was an open air concert too, which might've made it easier to have an integrated concert. With the size of the Gator Bowl, I don't think the authorities were worried about the small percentage that might've been interested that were black."

Opening the show was The Exciters, a black R&B vocal quartet from New York, best known for their hit Tell Him. Though WAPE, the local radio station promoting the concert, chose the support act, The Beatles were most likely pleased. "I don't think people connected The Beatles with their love of R&B, the way we all do now," says Walton. "It was a big influence."

In all of the press conferences they did on the '64 tour, they were certainly vocal about their reverence for black musicians. Little Richard, Chuck Berry and Fats Domino were always at the top of their major influences list (their '64 set list included Roll Over Beethoven and Long Tall Sally). When asked what they enjoyed listening to, they regularly answered, "American soul music, Marvin Gaye, The Miracles, Chuck Jackson…" And later the same year, they invited Mary Wells to join them for a UK tour.

Mixing it: The Beatles meet the locals in Florida, 1964.

"The Beatles were the first white artists to ever admit that they grew up and honed themselves on black music," says Motown main man Smokey Robinson. "I loved the fact that they did that, that they were honest and said, 'We listened to black people and this is how we groomed ourselves, and we listened to Motown'. They in fact recorded some Motown songs. I loved the fact that they did that."

The Beatles' human rights crusading would continue until the group's end and right on through their solo careers. Paul McCartney summed up their position when he told a reporter in 1966, "We weren't into prejudice. We were always very keen on mixed-race audiences. With that being our attitude, shared by all the group, we never wanted to play South Africa or any places where blacks would be separated. It wasn't out of any goody-goody thing; we just thought, Why should you separate black people from white? That's stupid, isn't it?"

PHOTOS: PICTORIAL PRESS

"We weren't into prejudice": The Beatles arrive in Jacksonville, Florida, September 11, 1964.

Some Product

Hectic touring and an even more hectic demand for new material were starting to put a strain on The Beatles. Nevertheless, their fourth album still showed signs of greatness, says Neil Spencer.

The title was sardonic and smart in the way of the satirical '60s, but also honest. The advent of Christmas, already a fixture in The Beatles' almanac, required brand new product to throw into the maw of Beatlemania. Here it was: the *Beatles For Sale* album, a hurried assemblage of left-over songs, familiar cover versions, half-written ideas completed in the studio, all strung around a handful of originals hot from the Lennon/McCartney production line.

From this unpromising inventory emerged an album that succeeds on a mixture of sheer verve and the musical adventurism that would deliver *Rubber Soul* in time for next year's Christmas market. It is a transitional album, a shrewd mix of inspiration, quick filler and loveable quirks.

As if to paper over the musical cracks, the album came in a lavish gatefold sleeve, with a cover as iconic as anything from the Fabs' short but prolific career. Robert Freeman's autumnal, soft-focus, shots showed the quartet not as grinning provincial moptops, but as rich, confident, stylish young men, their faces carrying a hint of weariness from the round of tours, reefer-heavy studio sessions and nights at the Scotch of St James. The actual title was squeezed into the corner, less prominent than the label logo.

Beatles For Sale: why not? Out there was Beatle wall-paper, jackets, wigs, boots, instruments, imitators, cover versions, mags, books, posters. Why shouldn't the originals cash in? Who knew how long Beatle madness would last?

Freeman's autumnal, soft-focus shots belonged more to chic '60s colour magazines like Nova than to the customary record cover. And that was how *Beatles For Sale* felt; like a glossy magazine, a little luxury in a society getting used to having too much rather than never enough. There had been gatefold sleeves before, but *Beatles For Sale* was the first time most people owned one. Inside were more definitive shots from Freeman, and mercurial liner notes from Derek Taylor forecasting that: "The kids of AD 2000 will draw from the music much the same sense of well-being as we do today," a truth to which every Oasis fan attests.

"*Beatles For Sale* was a transitional album, a shrewd mix of inspiration, quick filler and loveable quirks."

Paul: "Stand up you lazy buggers!" the Fabs rehearse in the BBC studios, 1964.

Beatles For Sale: Did it matter what was inside? In the short-term, no, but The Beatles were too artistically ambitious merely to cash in, even on a record they had to write and record in the midst of an ambitious foreign touring schedule. *A Hard Day's Night* had taken a heavy toll on the stockpile of Lennon/McCartney originals. Nonetheless, the group were able to open the sessions, and the album, with innovative work that led on from the downbeat moods they'd explored on *A Hard Day's Night*.

No Reply, as fine a song as Lennon wrote in the mid-'60s, was a sly, deceptive opener. Its pained, romantic scenario was familiar to any adolescent opening *Beatles For Sale* on a poignant Christmas morning; unreturned calls, boy moping outside girl's house, the stab to the heart when he sees her "hand in hand, with another man, to my face". Lennon's lyrical facility

PHOTO: REX

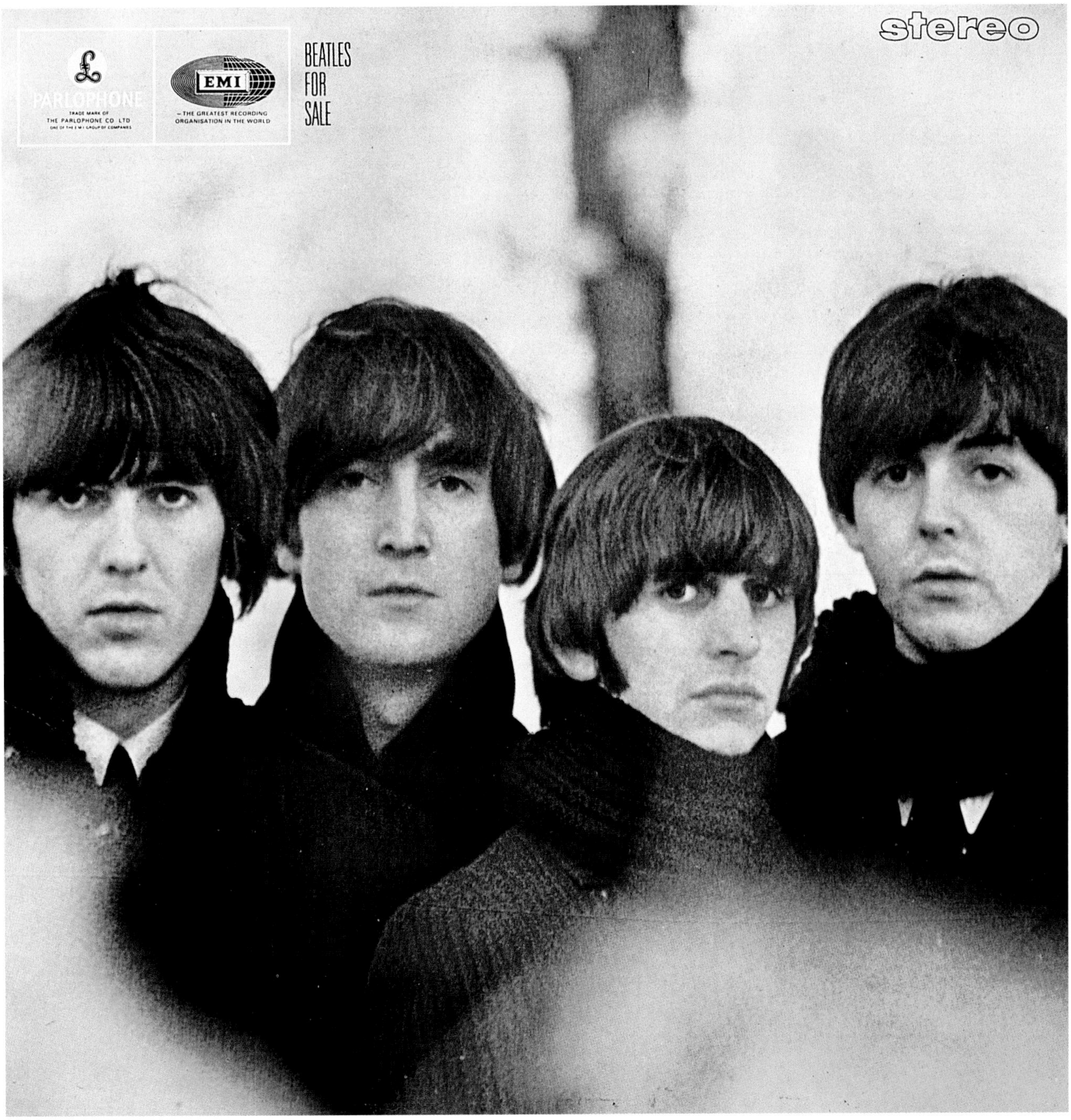

here masterfully catches the rhythms and music of common speech. The mood changes abruptly to defiance on a magnificent middle section whose storm of handclaps and multi-part harmonies has tumbled straight off a Miracles single.

stereo
PARLOPHONE
TRADE MARK OF THE PARLOPHONE CO. LTD
EMI
– THE GREATEST RECORDING ORGANISATION IN THE WORLD
BEATLES FOR SALE

The opener's shadowy ambience likewise ran through I'm A Loser – rollicking chorus, throwaway verses – and Baby's In Black, on which the Fabs use a folksy melody of Liverpool-Irish providence to court a teen widow who appears to have wandered off a 'death disc' like Tell Laura, I Love her. I Don't Want To Spoil The Party maintains the noble loser mood of No Reply with equally familiar cameos and cadences; "I've had a drink or two and I don't care".

There's more emotional complexity on Every Little Thing and What You're Doing, which explore the two sides of Paul's affair with Jane Asher. The delight of the former, a precursor to

TRACK LISTING

A-SIDE

1 No Reply
Lennon
Sung by Lennon

2 I'm A Loser
Lennon
Sung by Lennon

3 Baby's In Black
Lennon/McCartney
Sung by Lennon & McCartney

4 Rock And Roll Music
Berry
Sung by Lennon

5 I'll Follow The Sun
McCartney
Sung by McCartney

6 Mr Moonlight
Johnson
Sung by Lennon

7 Kansas City/Hey, Hey, Hey, Hey
Lieber & Stoller/Penniman
Sung by McCartney

B-SIDE

8 Eight Days A Week
McCartney
Sung by McCartney

9 Words Of Love
Holly
Sung by Lennon and McCartney

10 Honey Don't
Perkins
Sung by Starr

11 Every Little Thing
McCartney
Sung by McCartney

12 I Don't Want To Spoil The Party
Lennon
Sung by Lennon

13 What You're Doing
McCartney
Sung by McCartney

14 Everybody's Trying To Be My Baby
Perkins
Sung by Harrison

WHAT THE PAPERS SAID...

The press in '64 were sold on the Fabs' fourth LP.

★ BEATLES next album

JUST three weeks from today, the new Beatles album will be available in your local record store—in fact, it will be a case of "Beatles For Sale" on December 4. And, believe me, the latest package from the Liverpool quartet is worth every penny asked. It's rip-roaring, infectious stuff, with the accent on beat throughout By DEREK JOHNSON

There are 14 tracks, including eight new Lennon-McCartney compositions. Numbers by Chuck Berry, Carl Perkins, Buddy Holly and the Lieber-Stoller team complete the composing credits.

Rhythm ... RINGO and GEORGE

Songs ... PAUL and JOHN

"The latest Beatles package is worth every penny asked. It's rip-roaring, infectious stuff, with the accent on beat throughout. There are 14 new tracks, including eight new Lennon-McCartney compositions. The non-Beatles tracks are included for a purpose: they reflect the early years of the group because they were mostly numbers that raised screams at The Cavern in Liverpool.

"The LP is overflowing with absorbing and distinctive Beatle trademarks... Rock And Roll Music showcases Paul in his more frenzied mood. This one really moves – it's bubbling with excitement... Mr Moonlight is perhaps the most ear-catching track on the LP. It has a predominantly earthy sound, with John blues-shouting in passages, with forceful and raucous ensemble vocalising off-setting his solo... Eight Days A Week is a bouncy hand-clapper, driven along at a compulsive pace, aided by frantic cymbal bashing from Ringo. I Don't Want To Spoil The Party is one of my favourite tracks. The plaintive lyric belies the driving bounding beat. It's virtually a story-in-song, performed with absorbing counter-harmonies. Here again the melody content is strong and George is on top form."

Derek Johnson, NME, November 13, 1964

"*Beatles For Sale* is going to sell, sell, sell. It is easily up to standard and will knock out pop fans, rock fans, R&B and Beatle fans... As well as some excellent new Lennon-McCartney originals, it features belting rockers by Carl Perkins and Chuck Berry. My particular favourites are I Don't Want To Spoil The Party, Honey Don't and Rock And Roll Music. Eight Days A Week is a hand-clapping stomper and Words Of Love bows in the direction of Buddy Holly. The music is honest and again displays The Beatles' success fomula – talent."

Chris Welch, Melody Maker, November 14, 1964

SLEEVE NOTES

The *Beatles For Sale* cover was gatefold, glossy and unglamorous.

Like their music, The Beatles' albums covers were showing new sophistication.

Like the music contained within, the sleeve to The Beatles' fourth album, *Beatles For Sale*, captures the Fab Four at their most introspective and melancholic to date. Wrapped in scarves and coats, they look tired, almost surly and the very antithesis of the early-'60s pop star. The session, taken once more by Robert Freeman, was composed in Hyde Park, London, and took just one and a half hours from start to finish. Freeman readily admits it was a bit of a rush job. "There was a brief meeting with Brian Epstein and The Beatles to discuss the approach, which was to shoot in colour on an outside location towards sunset," he reveals in his book, A Private View. "We were lucky to have sunshine for the shot since there was little chance of getting them back for another session."

Freeman used the same equipment – a Pentax SLR with a 180mm telephoto lens – for the portrait as he had on his previous sleeve for the band, *With The Beatles*. Like that album there was no band logo pictured on the front cover and the title of the LP only appeared in minute type at the top of the sleeve.

The back cover was less imaginative though. "It was another colour photograph – a high angle shot of The Beatles with autumn leaves in the background, which I climbed up a tree to get. Unfortunately the pictures weren't used on the album in America. So much for climbing trees!"

But the inner picture to the gatefold sleeve, a rarity in itself, was both bold and daring with its montage comprising Jayne Mansfield, Victor Mature and Ian Carmichael amongst others, predating Peter Blake's infamous pop art sleeve to *Sgt Pepper's Lonely Hearts Club Band* by three years.

Lois Wilson

"Revisiting their rock'n'roll roots made little aesthetic sense – The Beatles were about the future."

Maybe I'm Amazed several years later, is less adventurous than the indignation of What You're Doing, both finding McCartney exploring the high end of his Hofner bass frets.

All these originals show The Beatles learning how to sculpt their songs into emotionally compelling mini-dramas, set to a musical backdrop straining for release from the past. By comparison, Eight Days A Week sounds left over from the brash, jaunty innocence of the early hits. Yet, like the rest of the originals on *Beatles For Sale*, it benefits from production that runs a sonic layer deeper than anything previously, a far less tinny sound full of chiming Gibsons and Rickenbackers of a sort soon to be heard on Ticket To Ride and from numerous West Coast bands.

McCartney's burgeoning role as acoustic balladeer deepens with I'll Follow The Sun, though it's a song, a sweet enough ditty, he'd been nursing since Hamburg days. Talking of which, here come some Star Club staples: Chuck Berry's Rock And Roll Music, still in the Fabs' live set and a blast here; the old warhorse Kansas City, capably ridden by Macca as Little Richard; and Mr Moonlight, a cultish R&B side by US group Dr Feelgood And The Interns and here made-over as proto-loungecore. A real curio.

By comparison, Buddy Holly's Words Of Love is routinely rendered. The

Dark stars: Paul and John rehearse for the Fabs' Christmas shows, shortly after the release of *Beatles For Sale*.

need for 'the Ringo song' and 'the George song' brought forth lacklustre, careless takes of Carl Perkins's Honey Don't and Everybody's Trying To Be My Baby, which round off the unexpected country stylings that pop up throughout *Beatles For Sale*.

The truth was that The Beatles had both grown out of covering other people's songs and run out of suitable originals to segue into their own stuff. Their avid championing of relatively unknown Motown and R&B imports on their first two albums made far more aesthetic sense than *Beatles For Sale*'s revisitation of familiar songs from their rock-'n'roll roots. Berry, Holly and Perkins were '50s music: The Beatles were about the future.

Beatles For Sale would have been an altogether different album if a couple of the covers had been junked in favour of two other creations from those autumn 1964 sessions – Leave My Kitten Alone, an old song fiercely delivered and destined to become a bootlegger's favourite, and She's A Woman, Macca's stoned out-take on his Little Richard legacy.

But time was tight and songs were scarce. In the wake of The Beatles' American success, their catalogue – four albums in two years, plus singles – was being released in different formats for the US. It paid to have something in the bag. And, just like the cover promised, this was, take it or leave it, *Beatles For Sale*.

PHOTO: ROBERT WHITAKER

SOLD ON YOU

Dylan, dope and lashings of attitude made *Beatles For Sale* great, says Robyn Hitchcock.

"Dylan had just been injected into their bloodstream. They had smoked pot for the first time; the speed was wearing off. *Beatles For Sale* was the dawn of Lennon's creatively-sorry-for-himself phase, and of McCartney getting aspirational. That cover said 'attitude', Stones and Dylan. Previously it was, adopt a position and grin. I prefer this LP to *A Hard Day's Night* – that was too Lennon-esque.

"*Beatles For Sale* is much shorter on original material, but I like the covers. Words Of Love is a lovely version, very simple, nearly a straight remake of Holly's original. Kansas City's got that great after-call – typical of The Beatles' vocals at this point: whoever's doing the lead vocal, the others all respond perfectly [*sings*] 'Hey! Hey! Hey!... Hey! Hey! Hey!' Or in Eight Days A Week, where they sing the lead in unison and then sheer off into harmonies; the same with the middle eight of No Reply – their best ever. Generally the studio sound seems more sophisticated, and there's more of the jangling guitars which allegedly influenced The Byrds, and the piano bodying out the middle of the sound. Even Mr Moonlight is interesting, George banging that African drum. He'd been freed up. George was hitting things he'd never dreamed of hitting before. At the same time they were still the amorphous Beatles, using the 15 words they'd rode to power on – 'Love', 'Baby', 'Friend', 'Yeah'... Things hadn't been carved up, so Paul could still write an angry song like What You're Doing. Now, we'd say – 'Oh, that must be a Lennon song', but then they were still One. But they'd taken root: they could begin to come up all over the place."

Joe Cushley

In 1964 US radio reporter Larry Kane accompanied The Beatles as they crossed America on their second US tour. This is his first-hand account of their hectic life on the road.

BEATLES OVER AMERICA

On August 19, 1964, The Beatles played the first gig of what was billed as their 'First American Tour' – 26 dates in 24 cities. Along for the ride was Larry Kane, a 20-year-old radio reporter who had managed to talk Brian Epstein into letting him travel with the band and file regular on-the-spot interviews. It was the start of a rewarding professional relationship – he was invited to visit the band in the Bahamas on the set of Help!, before once again joining them on the road for the 1965 US tour.

Today an Emmy Award-winning TV news anchor man in Philadelphia, in September 2003 Larry Kane will finally publish his first book about the period, Ticket To Ride: One Journalist's Wild Time With The Beatles (Running Press). "People will be startled by my candour in this book," says Kane. "It was electrifying – the wildest ride I've ever taken. Looking back, it is exciting to see how these first trips to America were the centre-pieces for what they would become as a band and who they would become as individuals."

Larry's on-the-road interviews with the band offer a fascinating snapshot of The Beatles on tour. Bored by the inane questioning of the press conferences and under a constant state of siege from thousands of screaming fans, more than anything they show a band killing time amidst a relentless touring schedule.

PHOTO: CURT GUNTHER

SAN FRANCISCO INTERNATIONAL AIRPORT AUGUST 18, 1964

After leaving London at midday, The Beatles flew to San Francisco International Airport via Winnipeg and Los Angeles, finally arriving at just before 6.30pm – where Larry Kane was able to spend a few minutes with the band while security matters were being rearranged. Nearby, 9,000 fans were waiting for The Beatles to make a short public appearance on a platform surrounded by a protective fence and guarded by 180 San Mateo County Sheriffs. Managing only the briefest of showings before the crowd's hysterical and repeated surging at the fence panicked the police, The Beatles were whisked off to the Hilton Hotel. Later that night John and Ringo went to Chinatown with Derek Taylor and Billy Preston, where they met cowboy actor Dale Robertson. The following night they played their first concert of the tour at the Cow Palace in front of a crowd of 17,130.

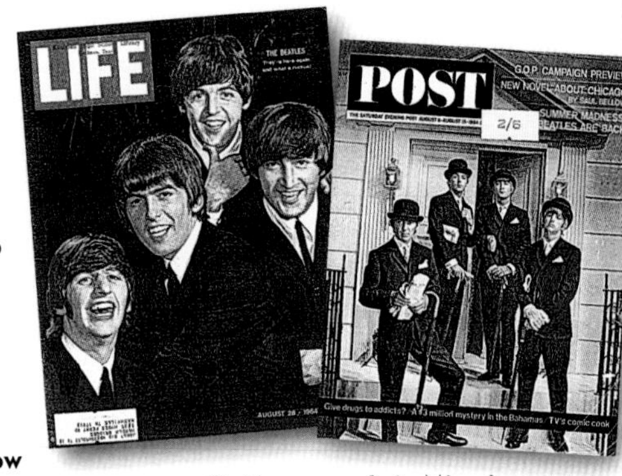

Q: This is Larry Kane, on tour with The Beatles, reporting from the San Francisco International Airport. Paul, do you find it hard to go 30 days and nights like this?
Paul: This is the first time we've tried it…
Q: I know I met you down in Miami in February, I don't know if you remember…
Paul: Yeah, sure!
Q: I'll be on your plane with you for the entire tour. Larry Kane from WFUN and I want to welcome you to the United States.
Paul: Thanks very much.
Q: John, will you say hello to everybody in Miami?
John: Hello, everybody in Miami!
Q: Tell me, when you go yachting, where do you plan to go in Florida?
John: Who said we're going yachting? Are we talking about yachting?
Q: It said yachting on the…
John: Yachting?
Q: Yachting.
John: We're not going yachting!
Q: Many people in Miami want to know when your wife's having her next baby.
John: Oh, well, y'see, you seem to have no libel laws over here, seeing as magazines write anything. One magazine called Truth – I won't name it, but it's called Truth, T-R-U-T-H – wrote a big pack of lies about how my wife broke the news to me about me baby and how she cried, and I went off, and Ringo said, 'John, you must share your wife'. It was a pack of lies, she's not having a baby!
Q: John, we'll see you on the plane. Thank you.
John: Thank you, good night, and God bless ye! Ha, ha.

Ticket to ride: Larry Kane (right) gets his press pass signed, 1964.

CONVENTION CENTER, LAS VEGAS, AUGUST 20, 1964

Having downed their instruments and left the Cow Palace in San Francisco while fans were still chanting for an encore, The Beatles headed directly to the airport and flew immediately to Las Vegas. Arriving at 1am, they were taken to the Sahara Hotel where, despite the late hour, 2,000 fans were already waiting to welcome them. With a capacity of just 8,000, the Fabs were required to perform two shows at the Convention Center – at 4pm and 9pm. Arriving for the sound check at 2.30pm, Larry Kane was left with plenty of time to chat to the band.

Q: Prior to the show, do you still get that feeling of excitement when you see the crowds?
Paul: Yeah.
Ringo: We still do, yeah.
Q: What did you think about those [fans throwing] jellybeans yesterday?
Ringo: They're too hard and they hurt. Any of you fellows get any?
Q: Did you get more at the Cow Palace than ever before?
Ringo: No, it used to be a lot worse in England. We used to get millions. The Cow Palace is so big that the people at the back haven't got a chance of reaching the stage with them. But they're too hard, so if you wouldn't mind, don't throw them jellybeans please! Give them in if we must have 'em, but don't throw 'em.
Q: Would you rather marsh mallows?
Ringo: No, I don't want anything! Streamers are marvellous. We played in Australia and they used to throw streamers, and it was a knockout because it's just like a big carnival – all streamers and balloons. And they don't hurt!
Q: Would you urge people in the other places that you're going to across the United States to throw streamers?
Ringo: Streamers.
Paul: Streamers are great, yeah, I love streamers.
Q: You want streamers, you love streamers…
Paul: Yeah, I love dem streamers, boy! They don't hurt half as much as jellybeans.
Q: Don't put anything in the streamer to weight it down.
Ringo: No, please.
Q: What about this comment that I heard about from you, Paul, concerning racial integration at the various performances?
Paul: We don't like it if there's any segregation, because we're not used to it, y'know. We've never played to segregated audiences before, and it just seems mad to me. It may seem right to some people, but to us, it just seems a bit daft.
Q: You're going to play Jacksonville, Florida. Do you anticipate any kind of difference of opinion?
Paul: I don't know, really, because I don't know what people in America are like. But I think they'd be a bit silly to segregate people, because I don't think coloured people are any different, y'know. They're just the same as anyone else, but over here there are some people who think that they're sort of animals or something, but I just think it's stupid. You can't treat other human beings like animals. I wouldn't mind 'em sitting next to me. Great, you know, because some of our best friends are coloured people.
Ringo: That's the way we all feel.
Paul: And a lot of people in England feel that way, because there's never any segregation in concerts in England, and in fact, if there was, we probably wouldn't play 'em.
Q: Sydney, Australia, was the biggest crowd that you'd ever played to before, wasn't it?
Paul: Except for last night.
Q: Before the Cow Palace?
Paul: Yeah.
Ringo: There was about 15,000, someone said.
Q: Did it give you a different kind of feeling playing before 17,000 screaming people?
Ringo: The bigger, the better for me. I love it when there's millions. It's fantastic.
Q: What do you think about all these groups doing your records, this is quite an honour for you.
Paul: Yeah. And I think Cilla Black's a very good group.
Q: What about The Animals?
Paul: Yes, they're very good.
Ringo: Great record [House Of The Rising Sun].
Paul: They're nice fellas, too.
Ringo: Marvellous. I believe it's Number 1 over here.
Q: Do you know The Rolling Stones, too?
Ringo: Yeah. Very well. They're good friends of ours.
Q: They're very personal friends of yours, aren't they?
Paul: Yeah.
Ringo: Very good friends.
Paul: In fact, most of the groups are. We hear some ridiculous rumours over here, as you know – we hear rumours like, 'The Beatles hate every other group on the face of the earth'. It's just not true, because all the English groups are friends of ours. I can't think of one group that we dislike.
Q: Last evening at the Cow Palace, the show was stopped twice to tone the crowd down.
Paul: Yeah, we hate that. It's a drag.
Q: One time right in the middle of one of your introductions to the song, the MC went out and stopped it. Did that irritate you?

Paul: Well, actually, we told him now to cut that out.
Ringo: Unless they go nuts and start ripping the place apart, which I don't think they will.
Q: Do you do a lot of reading in your spare time?
Ringo: It all depends how I feel. We have phases where we read like lunatics.
Paul: Last tour in Australia we just read every James Bond book out. Y'know, all of us did. And we were just talking 'James Bond' for the whole tour, calling each other 'M' and 'Mr X'.
Q: I imagine the tragedy of Ira Fleming [James Bond creator *Ian* Fleming died eight days earlier] was pretty close to you.
Paul: Yeah, it was a drag.
Q: Do you listen to records when you're in too.
Paul: Of course, including Cilla Black's new record, It's For You. It's not that I'm trying to plug this, but it's one of my favourite songs.
Ringo: It is, actually.
Paul: Mind you, John and I wrote it!

"WE'VE NEVER PLAYED TO SEGREGATED AUDIENCES BEFORE, AND IT JUST SEEMS MAD TO ME. IT SEEMS A BIT DAFT."
PAUL McCARTNEY

Q: Do you and John ever have any disagreements...
Paul: [*interrupting*] Remember, folks, It's For You! Pardon?
Q: Do you and John ever have any disagreements as to the lyric and the musical score of the song?
Paul: ...Remember, folks, It's For You. Pardon? Disagreements? Not really. Sometimes if we're writing a song, then one of us may think of something which is a bit corny, and the other one will say, 'That is corny'. Remember, folks, Cilla Black's It's For You. Great song, that. Not corny at all!
Q: Could you send me a copy of that record?
Paul: Yeah! I'll send you a copy.
Ringo: He needs the money.
Paul: Remember, folks, the favourite record of the moment – your favourite record, my favourite record, Cilla Black's It's For You. I'm not trying to plug this record, you realise, don't you?
Q: Now...
Ringo: ...Beatle People.
Q: I understand Pat Boone was in town last night to talk to you boys, did he see you personally?
Ringo: I understand it too, we didn't see him. He gave a message to our press officer, Mr Derek Taylor, who passed on his good wishes.
Q: How do you feel about the fact that a former teenage idol in the States now has his organisation printing oil portraits of The Beatles?
Paul: Sounds like a good idea to me. Actually, I'd never buy one, but...
Q: Why wouldn't you, Paul?
Ringo: He's got one already.
Paul: I don't know, I've never seen a good oil painting of us yet.
Q: George, before The Beatles ever came about, what ambitions did you have? Did you want to be a doctor or a lawyer?
George: I didn't want to be anything, because I was at school. I used to get my guitar out at night – and I used to neglect my work at school because of the guitar. The only thing I wanted to do was be able to play a guitar and go onstage. And as luck would have it, that's what I was able to do.
Q: Which are your favourite English groups at the moment?
George: The Animals are a great group because they have a good sound onstage. And they sound just as good as their record onstage. I like The Searchers too, because they've got good harmonies. And the Stones are good as well. In fact, there's quite a lot of groups that we like, y'know.

SEATTLE-TACOMA AIRPORT, SEATTLE, WASHINGTON AUGUST 21, 1964

With one performance scheduled for that evening at the Coliseum in front of 15,000 fans, The Beatles flew into Seattle to be greeted by the kind of scenes that were following them from city to city. Larry Kane was already on the tarmac in time to watch The Beatles step off the plane...

Q: And here come The Beatles, arriving in Seattle. They're coming down the stairs now, there's a giant squeal from a hill over here. Over on the hill, about half a mile away, are I'd say about 2,000 kids. They landed them away from the kids, primarily to keep the kids away from them, because of any danger. But everything's pretty peaceful at this time. Local photographers are taking their pictures, and, um... The Beatles are ready to walk off the plane...
Ringo: Not you again!
Q: Yes, we're here again!
Q: Ringo, were you listening to music up front?
Ringo: Yeah, we were listening to records that The Exciters were playing.
Q: The Exciters?
Ringo: Yeah.
Q: What type of records?
Ringo: Little Anthony and The Imperials, and James Brown – groovy records, man!
Q: Are you going to carry that portable tape recorder?
Ringo: Well, it's their record player, y'know, they're just good enough to play the records for us. Very nice. Made a break.
Q: Did you get any sleep on the plane?
Ringo: No, I didn't bother. I had enough last night – two and a half hours!

PHOTOS: MIRRORPIX/CURT GUNTHER

REGINALD OWENS' MANSION BEL AIR, LOS ANGELES, AUGUST 25, 1964

Two days earlier The Beatles had played at the Hollywood Bowl in front of 18,700 fans – George Martin had flown in from England to supervise the recording of the performance. The day after the concert, Alan Livingstone, the President of Capitol Records, threw a charity party for Hollywood's elite. With a few days off in LA, The Beatles spent their time in a private home in Bel Air. Larry Kane managed to get a long chat with John, while Paul and George visited the house of Burt Lancaster to watch a private screening of the second Pink Panther film, A Shot In The Dark.

Q: John, I wanted to ask you about Weyside.
John: Weyside, what's that?
Q: That's where you just bought a home, right?
John: No! It's Weybridge.
Q: Right, outside of Surrey, England, right?
John: I think it's in Surrey, I'm not sure.
Q: Out of all of the places in England you could have chosen, why did you pick Weybridge?
John: Because it was the nearest at the time when I suddenly decided I'm gonna have a house for me and me wife. Somebody said, 'There's one up there', and I said, Right, I'll have it. That's all there is to it.
Q: Do you ever find a desire to hear classical music?
John: I've enjoyed bits of classics, but I can't stand the rest, all the bits that come before it and after it. It's not worth listening to, as far as I'm concerned. Sooner just hear rock-'n'roll, because we're thick.
Q: Were you influenced in any way by American music with your genius of writing songs today?
John: Genius. Will you say that again, please, genius?
Q: Well, I say it because it's so true.
John: Oh, thank you. Everything we do is influenced by American music – mainly by American coloured music, people like Little Richard, and also by non-coloured artists like Elvis, Eddie Cochran, Buddy Holly.
Q: We had a big discussion at dinner today about the influence of country and western music...
John: I missed dinner.
Q: Right! You weren't there. Someone said that there is no country and western influence in England today, is that true? What about The Beatles, would they ever do a country and western song?
John: Well, the most country and western song we used to do ever was Honky Tonk Blues by Hank Williams. But I just couldn't sing it, y'know? I couldn't do the yodelling bits. And so we did an awful lot of Carl Perkins stuff, which we count as country and western, although he had a rock-'n'roll hit. I think he's country? Is he?
Q: What about folk music? Joan Baez and that type of thing?
John: Well, we all like Joan Baez, but we love Bob Dylan.
Q: Joan's boyfriend, there.
John: Oh, is that what it is? Well, well, Bob, you've got to watch the image, you know!
Q: John, you have a very sharp wit – we see it in the press conferences.
John: Don't believe what you read.
Q: Do you ever plan to put some comedy into your act?
John: We used to do it a bit, especially in the old Cavern days. Half the thing was just ad-lib – what you'd call comedy. We just used to mess about and jump into the audience, do anything! But now you've got to do 30 minutes of songs.
Q: Speaking of comedy, last night I had an opportunity to see for the first time the television show that you did, which has been shown in England three times, but has never been seen here in America.
John: Oh, Around The Beatles [*TV special that featured John in drag in a Shakespearean parody*].
Q: In this you include some comedy, but you were the only female, as far as your character...
John: Look, I don't like your insinuations, mister! We was doin' Shakespeare, and I had to be Thisbe, the girl!
Q: Why were you chosen to be Thisbe, the girl, John?
John: Because if anybody likes dressing up more stupid than the rest, I enjoy it, y'know. And I enjoyed doing it.
Q: Do you like Shakespearean literature?
John: As far as I'm concerned, Shakespeare's a drag.
Q: John, does your wife ever plan to join the show business fold?
John: No, not at all, no. Why should she?
Q: Of all the artists currently recording in Britain, what's your favourite group?
John: The Searchers and The Rolling Stones. It sounds daft, us liking them, but we're good friends of the Stones, so I like 'em.
Q: Do you know them from Liverpool?
John: They're not from Liverpool, you keep plugging 'em as the 'Mersey Sound' over here – they're all from London. The Searchers are from Liverpool, so we've known them for years, but the Stones are London fellas.
Q: Were the Stones influenced by you and your earlier sound?
John: I don't think they were influenced. They were probably a bit glad when we came on the scene, because they were like they are now – or almost like they are. When you see somebody doing something like you're doing - they're a bit more way out – it must be good, y'know.
Q: So far on this tour, what's been the most exciting reaction to your show?
John: Well, the one we all enjoyed most was the Hollywood Bowl, even though it wasn't the largest crowd. It seemed so important. It was a big stage, and it was great. We enjoyed that the most.
Q: What about the party yesterday afternoon that Mr Livingstone [President of Capitol Records] gave. Was that a highlight for you?
John: It was more of a job of work. It was harder than playing. You've just gotta sit on a stool and meet about 300 people of all ages.
Q: How does it feel to be sitting there and have all of these Hollywood celebrities bring their children by just to shake the hands of The Beatles?
John: Well, it feels great, but we thought we'd see more stars. We were a bit choked. We saw Edward G Robinson, Jack Palance, Hugh O'Brien... we were expecting to see more. All the kids were there, mind you.
Q: About your last picture – what did you enjoy most about it?
John: Well, all of us liked the bit in the field where we all jump about like lunatics, because that's pure film - as the director told us. We could have been anybody, but we enjoyed that.
Q: Were there many of those ad-lib moments in the film?
John: Well, there were a lot of ad-lib remarks, but in a film, you don't get to ad-lib, because you've always gotta take it eight times. You ad-lib something quite good, and everybody laughs, the technicians laugh, and then the next minute he says, 'Take it again', so your ad-lib gets drier and drier until it doesn't sound funny any more.
Q: John, outside of music, what's your favourite hobby?
John: Writing the books, I suppose they call 'em – I used to call it 'rubbish', but it's 'books' now, isn't it? Just writing, y'know.
Q: Are you a born writer?
John: I wouldn't say I was a born writer. I'm a born thinker like that. I've always been able to... at school when they want you to imagine something instead of giving you a subject, I could do that. It's the same thing, I'm just doing it, only I'm older.
Q: How did it feel going back to your hometown and see 50,000 people cheering your return?
John: It was great. I don't know how many it was, it was just enough to make it fantastic. And it was better when we were in the car, y'know, 'cause we were right near them.
Q: Did you expect that to happen?
John: No, we heard that we were finished in Liverpool, y'see, and after a bit we began to believe it. We thought, we don't want to go home, we'll just sneak home to our houses. They kept going on – people saying, 'Oh, I've been down The Cavern, they don't like you any more'. Of course, they're talking to people that didn't even know us then, anyway. And we went back, and it was... it was one of the best, ever.

"I WOULDN'T SAY I'M A BORN WRITER, I'M A BORN THINKER – I'VE ALWAYS BEEN ABLE TO IMAGINE THINGS."

JOHN LENNON

PHOTOS: CURT GUNTHER

DELMONICO HOTEL, NEW YORK AUGUST 28, 1964

After leaving New York, The Beatles played in Denver and Cincinnati, before flying into Kennedy Airport in New York at 3am on the morning of the first of two concerts at the Forest Hills Tennis Stadium. Some 3,000 fans were waiting to watch The Beatles touchdown, with several hundred more camped outside the Delmonico Hotel on Park Avenue and 59th Street. By the next day thousands more had arrived and were held back across the street by police barricades. In the chaos that ensued as The Beatles were rushed into the building, Ringo's St Christopher medallion was ripped from around his neck by eager fan Angie McGowan – who later got to meet Paul and Ringo after subsequently returning the medal.

Q: Paul, when you see a crowd outside like on Park Avenue, and you hear the screams all the time, how does it affect you. Would you like to go out there and meet 'em?
Paul: It's fantastic. People keep asking us questions, like what do you think of this, and what do you think of that, and we can only use so many words, y'know, like fantastic, marvellous. And as for going out and meeting 'em, I'd love to be able to, but it'd be impossible.
Q: There's a story going around about an experience you had at about three o'clock in the morning the last time you were in New York – trying to sneak out of the hotel, when you were chased by some teenage fans?
Paul: The only truth is we wanted to go out and see New York, so we got a car and went round – all we could do is just stick our heads out of the windows and look up at the buildings. Couldn't see anything, it just looked big, y'know.
Q: Last night?
Paul: Just went by Times Square. And then we did go to a bar for a drink, but we weren't trying to get away from anyone.
Q: When you arrived here at the hotel, I understand Ringo lost his St Christopher's medal and about half of his shirt. Did you go through any of the fracas?
Paul: No, three of us got in, y'see, but apparently one of the police didn't think Ringo was Ringo and stopped him. Everyone grabbed him and a girl ripped his shirt.
Q: Do you and John make more money than Ringo and George?
Paul: Well, on the songs we do. But actually, they make up for it in other things. George does a column in an English newspaper. Actually, none of us know how much money we're making. It's true. If we want to buy something we have to ask permission from our accountant!

"THE POLICE DIDN'T THINK RINGO WAS RINGO AND STOPPED HIM. EVERYONE GRABBED HIM AND A GIRL RIPPED HIS SHIRT."
PAUL McCARTNEY

1965

The Beatles started 1965 by making Help!, but by the end of the year they had made a huge creative leap forward with the release of *Rubber Soul*. Along the way they met Elvis, received their MBEs and played in front of a record-breaking crowd at Shea Stadium. And Paul managed to find the time to record a little number called Yesterday.

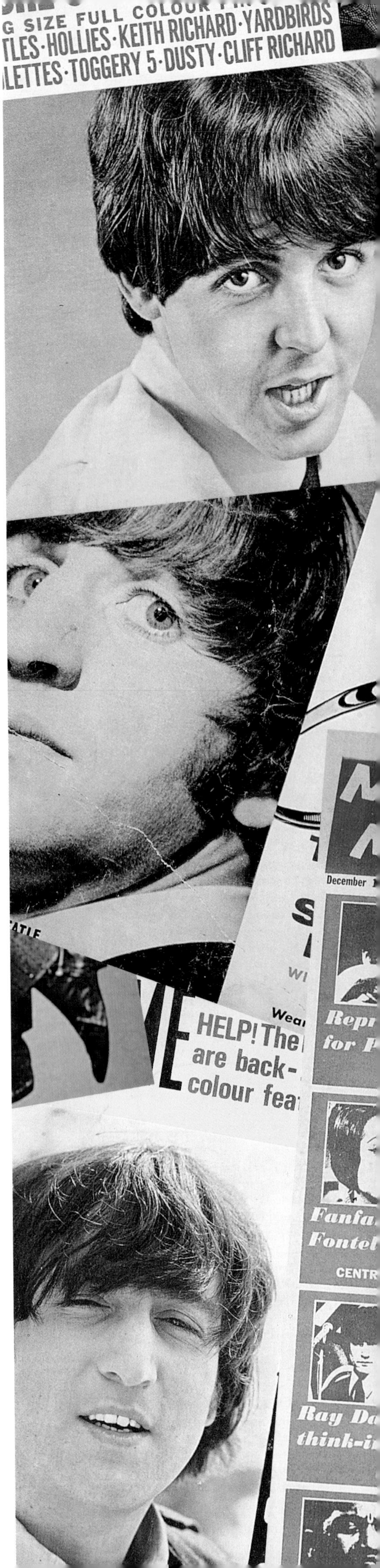

BOYFRIEND
WEEK-ENDING JULY 31st 1965 No. 319
EVERY WEDNESDAY
THE MODERN YOUNG
MAN'S MAGAZINE
COMPETITION!
WIN A REMINGTON PORTABLE TYPEWRITER.
FREE-TO-ENTER, EASY-TO-DO!
JOHN
FREE GIFT INSIDE
THURSDAYS 6d
YES! FREE FOR YOU
Melody Maker
1965
9d weekly
BEATLES BOU
r, TV, single, LP!
STEREO PLAYER
ERIC BURDON
THE OBSE VE
Melody Maker
9d weekly
FOUR FACES OF FANDOM
FIND OUT WHAT
BEATLES
Seekers, Who bloc
way to No 1 spot
WORLD'S POP STARS IN COLOUR COLOUR COLOUR
2nd JANUARY 1965
1/-
Fabulous
NEW YEAR'S HONOURS
10 KING SIZE FULL COLOUR PIN-UPS
CILLAPAULDUSTYSTONESPJJONESPJSEAN
PRIVATE EY
No. 92
Friday
25 June 65
1/6
BEATLES TO
GO ON VIETNAM
PEACE MISS

JANUARY 65

2 US-only album *The Beatles Story* reaches Number 7.

9 *Beatles '65* begins a nine week run atop the US album chart.

10 New York promoter Sid Bernstein offers to book the The Beatles into the 55,600 capacity Shea Stadium.

16 Another Beatles Christmas Show ends its 30-night season.

27 The Beatles briefly go their separate ways. John and Cynthia leave the UK for a skiing holiday in St Moritz. Paul heads for Tunisia, and George is a witness at the wedding of his brother Peter in Liverpool.

FEBRUARY 65

2 After months of deliberation, The Portuguese film censor releases The Beatles' film, A Hard Day's Night, but it is rated "for adults only".

8 The Times reports that 1,250,000 shares in The Beatles' publishing company Northern Songs will shortly be issued for sale.

9 The Times reports that Eleanor Bron has signed up as the female lead in The Beatles' as yet untitled second film.

10 A fan club is started for Cynthia Lennon, complete with its own monthly magazine.

11 Ringo Starr marries childhood sweetheart, hairdresser Maureen Cox, at Caxton Hall, London.

15 The Beatles record Ticket To Ride in EMI Studio 2, Abbey Road. More songs follow over the succeeding days.

20 The Beatles record If You've Got Trouble and That Means A Lot, neither of which are released.

22 The Beatles fly to the Bahamas and book in to the Balmoral Club, Cable Beach, to begin filming their second movie.

MARCH 65

1 The Beatles continue filming in New Providence, Bahamas.

8 Brian Epstein attends this year's Mecca Carl Alan awards, in the Empire Ballroom, Leicester Square, London. On behalf of The Beatles, he is presented with the Best Group Award by Princess Margaret.

10 The Beatles fly from the Bahamas to the UK.

13 The Beatles reach Number 1 again in America with Eight Days A Week. It will remain on top for two weeks.

13 The Beatles leave the UK to begin filming for Help! The Austrian shoot continues until the 21st.

22 The Beatles release an album, *The Early Beatles*, on Capitol in the US.

24 The Beatles begin UK filming for Help!, still titled Eight Arms To Hold You, at Twickenham Studios.

27 John Lennon and George Harrison are given LSD for the first time. Although different dates have been suggested for this event, this is the most likely day, cross-referenced with a Klaus Voormann gig John and George were supposed to attend that night.

28 The Beatles record Thank Your Lucky Stars in Alpha Television Studios, Birmingham, UK. Tom Jones: "John Lennon came up, gives me a look and sings, 'It's not a unicorn, it's an elephant' – taking the piss. He says, 'How are you doing, you Welsh poof?' I said, 'You Scouse bastard! Come up here and I'll show you...'

What: John and George drop acid.
Where: Bayswater Road, London
When: 27 March 1965

THE REAL ACID TEST

How The Beatles first experienced LSD, assisted by a dentist and a character from A Day In The Life. By Barry Miles.

On March 27, 1965, a cosmetic dentist famously spiked John Lennon, Cynthia, George Harrison and Patti Boyd with LSD. Acid was legal then, but was little known in music circles. The standard version of the story is that the dentist's girlfriend looked after the bunnies at the Playboy Club and that she had obtained six hits from Victor Lowndes, Hugh Hefner's partner in the British club. In fact the London Playboy Club didn't open until May 1966, more than a year later, but the acid could have come from Lowndes who became involved with the World Psychedelic Centre in London just a few months later.

The Beatles were not the first British rock group to take LSD. That distinction appears to go to the Daevid Allen Trio, a forerunner of the Wilde Flowers and the Soft Machine. Daevid Allen was an Australian poet; he performed sound poetry live with William Burroughs in Paris and experimented with loop tapes with Terry Riley. He had long hair, strange stainless steel glasses and had taken LSD. He turned up at drummer Robert Wyatt's mother's house in Canterbury one day in 1963, and moved in. The trio: Allen, Wyatt, and Wyatt's school friend Hugh Hopper on bass, played a few gigs in Canterbury, but spent most of their time working on tape-loops in Paris where Daevid had a houseboat on the Seine.

In 1964, two pioneers arrived from Greece: Daniel Richter, an American poet who, later in the '60s, became John Lennon's personal secretary, and New Zealander John Esam, a poet, nicknamed 'The Spider' because of his ability to involve people in his plans. John Esam moved into Nigel and Jenny Lesmore-Gordon's flat at 101 Cromwell Road, where he built a nest for himself in the corridor as there were no actual rooms available. Shortly afterwards, someone arrived from America with a large quantity of LSD for him. 101 Cromwell Road became the main acid centre of London in the early days of 1965. Chris Case, a Cambridge-educated American, who worked as art dealer Robert Fraser's assistant lived there, as did George Andrews, another American, the editor of The Book Of Grass, the first anthology of writing about marijuana. Upstairs lived Scotty, who was well known for spiking everything with acid. He and his flatmate guitarist Syd Barrett began each day with acid in their coffee and even the catfood got spiked.

The "dentist experience" as George called it, made John and George feel very close, to the point of excluding the two other Beatles, and they pressured Paul and Ringo to take it as well. George: "John and I spent a lot of time together from then on and I felt closer to him than all the others."

Paul resisted, but Ringo wanted to understand what the others had felt and took it in Los Angeles that August when they spent five days relaxing in a mansion off Mulholland Drive.

John: "The second time we had it was different. Then we took it deliberately, we just decided to take it again in California... the three of us took it, Ringo, George and I, and maybe Neil. Paul felt very out of it because we were all slightly cruel, 'We're all taking it and you're not.' It was a long time before Paul took it." It was about three months.

An alternative acid source opened its doors in September when Tim Leary sent Michael Hollingshead to London to open the World Psychedelic Centre (WPC). It was Hollingshead, an Englishman, who first turned Tim Leary onto LSD in 1961. He got off the boat wearing pink sunglasses, bringing with him 300 copies of Leary's Psychedelic Experience, 200 copies of the Psychedelic Reader and half a gram of LSD; enough for 5,000 sessions, part of an experimental batch from the Czech government laboratories in Prague.

Hollingshead rented premises on Pont Street in the heart of Belgravia; visitors included Peter Asher, Donovan, Robert Fraser, William Burroughs, 'Anti Psychiatrist' Ronnie Laing, Alexander Trocchi, Roman Polanski and Sharon Tate. John Dunbar took Paul McCartney along, warning him ahead of time "not to eat the oranges" – like 101 Cromwell, everything was spiked. Paul was curious, but didn't like to be rushed. However, a few days later he took his first trip. He had gone with a group of friends, including Viv Prince, drummer with The Pretty Things, and several girls to Tara Browne's house in Eaton Row in Belgravia.

"There was massive peer pressure. It's, Hey man, this whole band's had acid, why are you holding out?"

Paul: "Tara was taking acid on blotting paper in the toilet. He invited me to have some. I said, 'I'm not sure, you know.' I was more ready for the drink or a little bit of pot or something. I'd held off like a lot of people were trying to, but there was massive peer pressure. And within a band, it's more than peer pressure, it's fear pressure, it's fear peer pressure. It becomes trebled, more than just your mates it's, 'Hey man, this whole band's had acid, why are you holding out? What's the reason, what is it about you?' So I knew I would have to out of sheer peer pressure. And that night I thought, Well this is as good a time as any, so I said, 'Go on then, fine.' So we all did it.

"We stayed up all night. It was quite spacey. Everything becomes more sensitive... I remember John saying, 'You never are the same after it' and I don't think any of us ever were. I think it was such a mind-expanding thing."

Tara died in the early hours of the morning of December 18, 1966; his fatal car crash was the inspiration for Day In The Life.

PHOTO: BOB WHITAKER/CAMERA PRESS; HULTON; MIRROR PIX

John flying high, by Robert Whitaker. Inset, Tara Browne, the Guinness heir who launched Paul McCartney on his first acid trip.

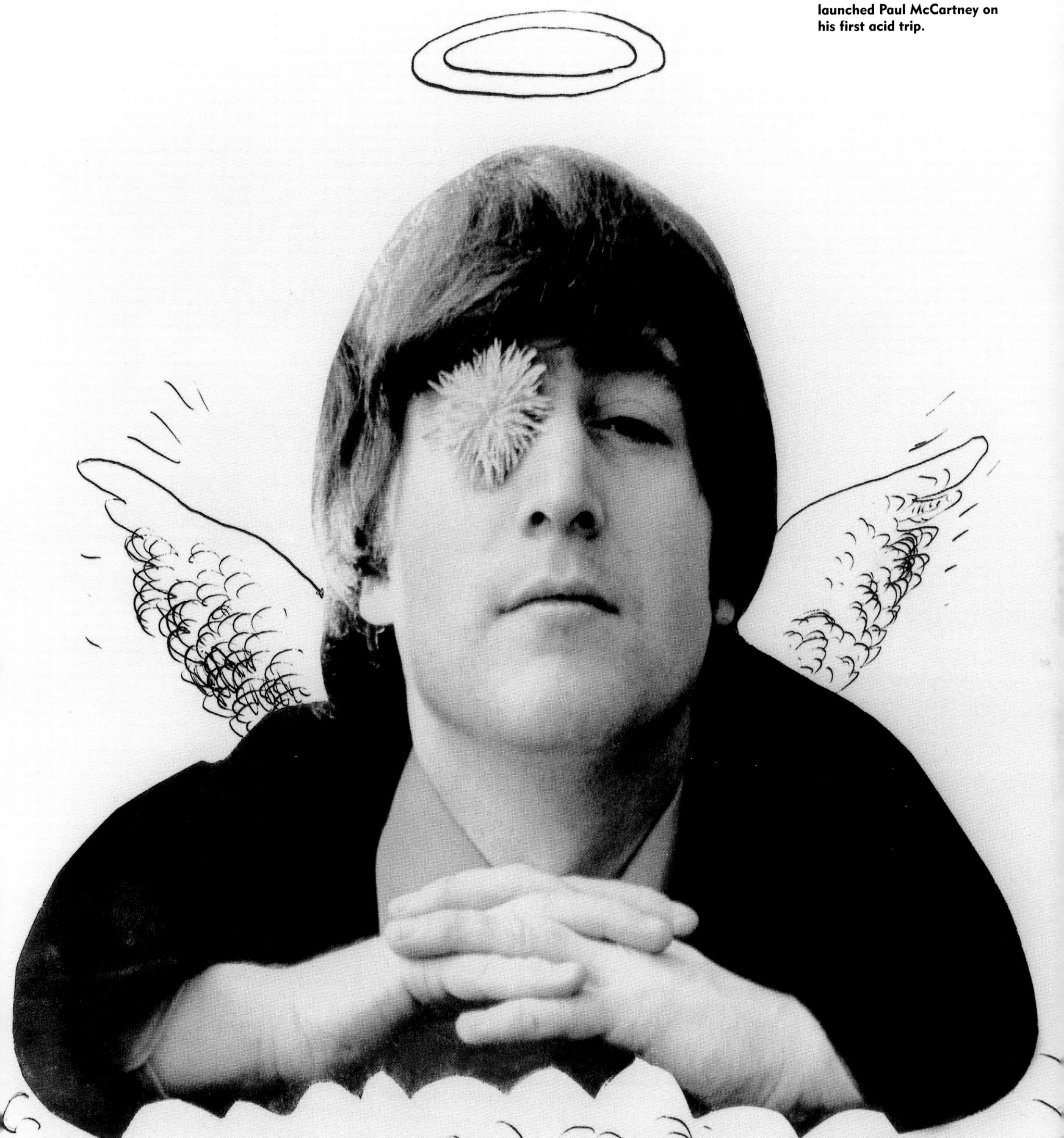

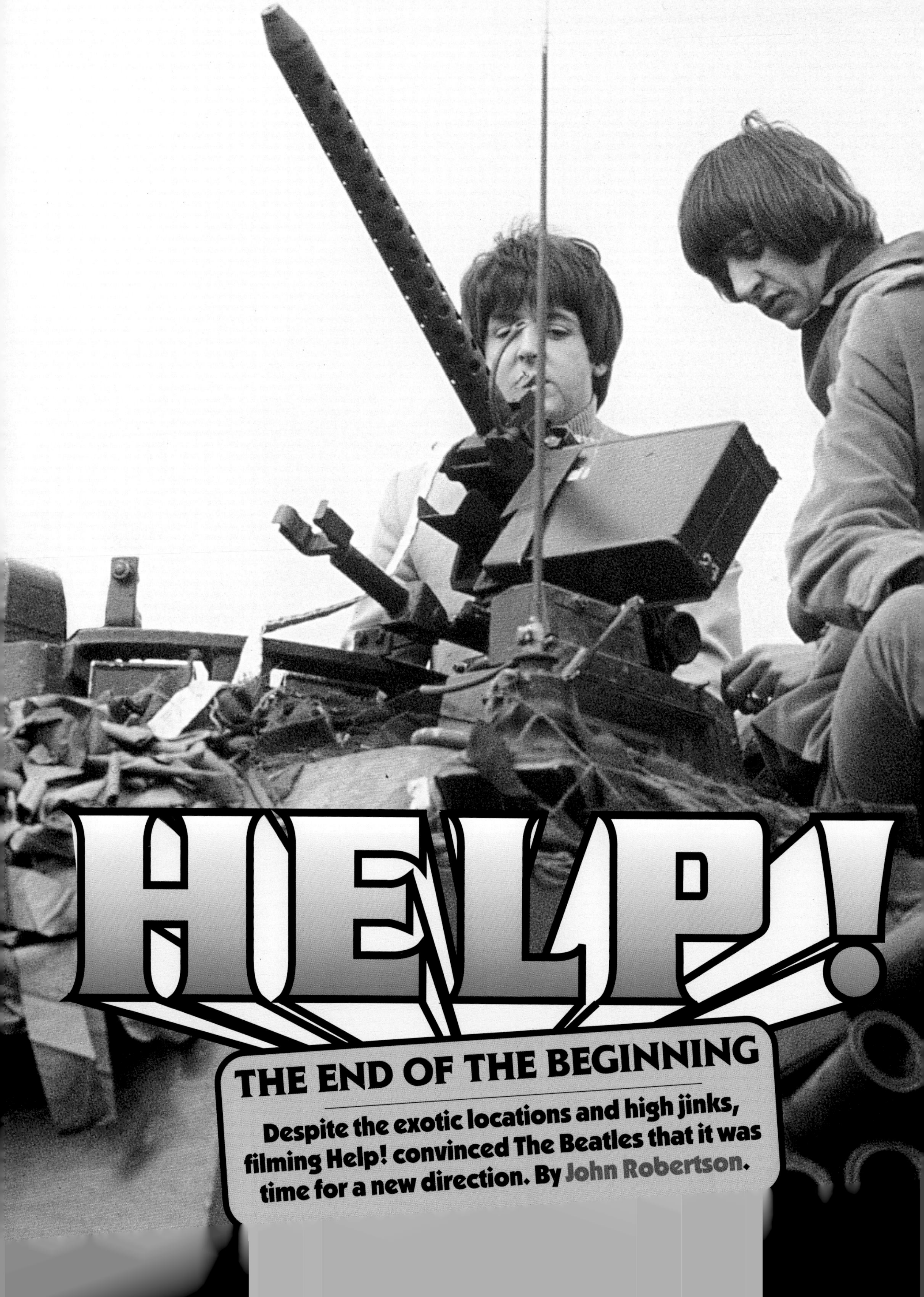

HELP!

THE END OF THE BEGINNING

Despite the exotic locations and high jinks, filming Help! convinced The Beatles that it was time for a new direction. By John Robertson.

Young gunners: the Fabs take a break during the filming of Help!, Salisbury Plain, Wiltshire, March, 1965.

PHOTO: REX

ON THE EVENING OF DECEMBER 9, 1980, BRITAIN was struggling to adapt to the news of John Lennon's murder in New York, little more than 12 hours earlier. Desperate to mark the event, BBC TV's schedulers reached for the only available footage of The Beatles, their cavalier 1965 feature film, Help!.

It threatened to be a masterstroke of bad taste, commemorating a fallen hero with a banal comedy movie. Yet for grief-stricken Lennon fans across the country, Help! provided strange relief. Far removed from reality, it conjured up a nostalgic, comforting world, in which The Beatles were still fab, still four.

It was an ironic afterlife for a movie which had been designed to prolong the initial rush of Beatlemania, but actually preserved the moment when it began to decay. The black-and-white pseudo-realism of A Hard Day's Night gave way to a Technicolor adventure in which The Beatles emerged as (in Lennon's famous phrase) "bit-players in our own movie".

A Hard Day's Night had cost £120,000 to make in spring 1964, and grossed more than $13 million worldwide. Under the circumstances, United Artists' budget for its successor, some £400,000, was still a little miserly, yet it seemed like a fortune for the production team. Producer Walter Shenson duly promised that "the film will look spectacular".

In place of Alun Owen's documentary-style script on A Hard Day's Night, The Beatles' second film was intended from the start to be a comic romp. Shenson hired the Paris-based American writer Marc Behm to write the screenplay; he obliged with a freewheeling fantasy requiring location shoots around the world.

As before, The Beatles themselves had no input into the content or design of their film. In December 1964, they were unable even to control the chaos of their Christmas Show, a mix of music and comedy skits which they performed for three weeks at the Hammersmith Odeon. Dressing up night after night for an Abominable Snowman sketch, the non-existent punchlines of which were drowned in adolescent screams, the group vowed never to become involved in something so banal again.

Exhausted after a year of international celebrity and numbing pressure, The Beatles had lost their enthusiasm for fame. The jacket of their latest LP, *Beatles For Sale*, revealed four smartly dressed, unbearably jaded faces who had witnessed the realisation of their every fantasy and discovered that both financial and physical pleasures were compulsive but empty.

"The whole Beatle thing was just beyond comprehension," said Lennon of this period. "I was eating and drinking like a pig, and I was fat as a pig, dissatisfied with myself."

None of their satiated boredom was evident to the era's pop pundits, the doyen of whom, Derek Johnson of the New Musical Express, greeted *Beatles For Sale* as "rip-roaring, infectious stuff, with the accent on beat throughout". The gulf between his ears and The Beatles' was displayed when he selected Mr Moonlight, a barely passable makeweight, as "the most ear-catching track on the LP". With even their failures acclaimed as triumphs, The Beatles could be forgiven their cynicism.

In his search for idealism, Paul McCartney landed on politics. In an era when popular entertainers rarely commented on national affairs, he made a defiant stand against racial prejudice. "It's daft looking upon coloured people as some sort of freaks," he declared that December. "Before we went to the US, someone told us that they might try to segregate the audiences. We stuck in a clause, just in case."

With the filming schedule about to be unveiled, McCartney conceived a way for this entirely frivolous project to aid the anti-apartheid movement in South Africa: "I may be putting my foot in it, but it would be an idea to give them the proceeds from the premiere of our new film."

Lennon was no less outspoken on the subject of politics, though his idealism was less easy to distinguish. He told journalist Ray Coleman that although he was a socialist at heart, he was coming to realise that he would be forced to vote Conservative at the next election. "After all," he added apologetically, "you have to look after your money, don't you?"

Cash was a common preoccupation for The Beatles that winter, not just for the newly Tory Lennon or the man popularly described as "the money Beatle", George Harrison. Having spent almost two months in America that year, the group now discovered that both US and UK authorities wanted to claim tax on their entire 1964 income. "Our position is that we await the two governments coming to a decision on the matter," noted their American lawyer and financial adviser, Walter Hofer. "We're not resisting the tax, we just don't want to have to pay it twice."

THE DECISION TO FILM THE EARLY SCENES OF HELP! IN the Caribbean – specifically the British colony of the Bahamas – may not have been made on strictly artistic grounds. The Beatles' lawyers were keen to investigate the country's status as a tax haven for British nationals, and the movie project was a perfect cover story.

While the money men wheeled and dealed, The Beatles wallowed in the rare luxury of six weeks' comparative rest. John Lennon assembled the pieces for his second book, and toyed with the idea of making a spoken-word LP of extracts from In His Own Write. Lennon, Paul and George stockpiled songs for the movie soundtrack. And Ringo married his long-time girlfriend, Maureen Cox. Collectively the group declined an invitation from the Queen to perform at the Windsor Ball. Music publisher Dick James revealed that both Lennon and McCartney had earned £1 million during 1964 from their songwriting royalties alone.

The Beatles industry purred gently into the new year, while the group prepared for the Bahamas by recording a batch of songs which would be heard in the movie – among them Ticket To Ride, You're Gonna Lose That Girl, I Need You, Another Girl and The Night Before.

One of the new songs reached further into its composer's psyche than anything The Beatles had recorded in the past. Amongst the peppy teen-beat which would fill the Help! soundtrack was Lennon's maudlin You've Got To Hide Your Love Away, an exercise in self-pity and Dylan pastiche. "It's the sort of song you sing a bit sadly to yourself, 'Here I stand, head in hand'," he reflected shortly before his death. "I started thinking about my own emotions – I don't know exactly when it started, like I'm A Loser or Hide Your Love Away or those kind of things. Instead of projecting myself into a situation, I would try to express what I felt myself, which I'd done in my books. It was Dylan who helped me realise that."

Four days after recording You've Got To Hide Your Love Away, The Beatles had to report for movie duty – a project which promised little outlet for emotional honesty. After A Hard Day's Night, which had been filmed entirely in and around London, the exotic locations on the second movie seemed to offer a welcome relief from the pressures of Beatlemania – although the group were to discover that few territories had escaped their lure. Yet these colourful settings pinpointed one inherent flaw in the venture: the dramatic realism of their first movie was being sacrificed in favour of fantasy and decorative backdrops.

"Help! was a straitjacket of a film for The Beatles," reckoned their co-star in both movies, Victor Spinetti. "They had to act out parts, and they weren't really happy about it." Not that their roles were exactly taxing: having played cartoon facsimiles of their real selves in A Hard Day's Night, they were simply required to repeat the process, this time overseas. What's more, aside from Ringo – delegated as the focus of the tenuous plot, in honour of his movie-stealing (and alcohol-fuelled) riverbank scene in A Hard Day's Night – Behm's script required nothing more difficult from The Beatles than to spiel out one-liners on cue.

Director Dick Lester had impressed The Beatles on the set of their first movie with his tales of working with the Goons, and his manic energy. Given a much larger budget second time around, he was keen to accentuate his artistic strengths, and add a madcap, surreal edge to the proceedings. This ought to have chimed with The Beatles' oddball sense of humour, but instead they felt themselves increasingly alienated ➸

Doing it for the kids: Salisbury Plain, Wiltshire, March, 1965.

"We were smoking marijuana for breakfast. The best scenes were when we were lying on the floor, unable to say a word." - JOHN LENNON

n the rocks: Macca plays
p to the camera, New
rovidence, Bahamas,
ate February, 1965.

John: on the grass, literally.

Obertauern, Austria, March 14, 1965.

from the creative process. "The movie was out of our control," Lennon moaned. "With A Hard Day's Night, we had a lot of input. But with Help!, Dick didn't tell us what it was about. Maybe that was because we hadn't spent a lot of time together since we made A Hard Day's Night."

Not that Lester claimed to be pursuing any private agenda. "You'll find nothing new about Help!," he told reporters. "There's not one bit of insight into a social phenomenon of our times."

The Beatles' half-hearted enthusiasm for the film wasn't boosted by their keen awareness of their limitations. "We can't act, you know," Paul admitted before the first day's shoot. John concurred: "Whoever cuts it makes it look as though we're nearly acting, but we're not."

Once on location, both director and stars struggled to find common ground. The Beatles found it hard to disguise their reaction to the script. "It's a mad film – at the moment, making it, it's mad," McCartney commented. Naivety and adrenalin had combined to pull the group through the tight shooting schedule for A Hard Day's Night. But, as Dick Lester recalled, "Help! took longer. We had more time, and lots more money. But during the filming, The Beatles discovered marijuana. There was lots of smiling." Lennon confessed that, "By then we were smoking marijuana for breakfast. The best scenes were those when we were sprawling on the floor, unable to say a word." Lester's early rushes suggested otherwise.

The joints were first lit on the long flight from Heathrow to Nassau, and were only extinguished when the cameras were actually rolling. To the outside world, however, Beatlemania was continuing as usual, with thousands of fans gathering at the airport to see the group off. "You couldn't hear the sound of the jet engines because of the screams of our fans," Victor Spinetti remembered. "George looked at me with a big smile and said, 'I'm so glad you're in this film with us, Vic, cos me mum fancies you'."

"Ringo emerged as the most promising in terms of screen potential. He found it easy to pull faces." - TONY BARROW, PRESS OFFICER

Also on board the plane was actress and satirist Eleanor Bron, an elegant and acutely intelligent young woman who was the star of the TV show Not So Much A Programme, More A Way Of Life. "You couldn't help being a little in awe of The Beatles," she admitted. "But they don't like that at all." The feeling was reciprocated by Lennon, who found in Bron the same qualities he also relished in folk singer Joan Baez, journalist Maureen Cleave, and ultimately Yoko Ono: emotional strength, beauty, brains and acid wit. The film script required Bron to flirt incessantly with McCartney, and for her come-ons to be intercepted by Harrison; but it was Lennon who was most entranced by her.

FILMING BEGAN THE DAY AFTER THEIR ARRIVAL, February 23, 1965, and continued without a break for the next two weeks. The Beatles were called at six every morning, splashed away their dope haze with a dip in the Caribbean, prepared a glass of fresh lime juice, and then attended to the day's filming. Between takes, they were forced to shelter beneath umbrellas, as McCartney explained: "In Nassau we had to keep out of the sun because the scenes we did out there come at the very end of the film, and it would look funny if we were all brown and tanned in the snow sequence which you see earlier on and then pale and unhealthy in the Bahamas bit."

Lack of sun wasn't the only obstacle to The Beatles' enjoyment. "The trouble with Nassau," Harrison complained, "was that spectators didn't wait until the end of each scene. They were walking up to us for autographs as the camera was still rolling." Hence his sharp response when one of the extras recruited for the movie, an 18-year-old American student called Mark Vidalis, asked George for his signature between takes. "He was a little short-tempered that day," Vidalis noted, "and he turned me down. He seemed to be rather tense."

Producer Walter Shenson reckoned that some of the tension was caused by insecurity: "The strong supporting cast bothered The Beatles. They felt that they were merely puppets being pulled around on strings and that these very fine actors, like Leo McKern, were actually the stars. I disagreed totally. It was The Beatles who made it work. Their personalities were far stronger than any of the actors. But The Beatles felt that A Hard Day's Night was their movie, and that Help! wasn't."

Already a close friend after they had made A Hard Day's Night together, Victor Spinetti was an exception to The Beatles' distrust. As he explained, there were other reasons for certain members of the group to view the Bahamas experience with mixed emotions: "The first day of filming was almost the end of the film and the end of The Beatles. We were filming on a yacht and I was playing the part of a mad scientist trying to cut the ring off Ringo's finger. He escapes me, dives off the yacht and falls 30 feet into the sea. They had a bunch of people watching the area for sharks, so Dick Lester said, 'Let's do another shot'. They dried Ringo off and he was shivering because it was out of season and very cold. We did another take and another, and after the third take, Dick said, 'Let's do another'. Ringo said, 'Do we have to?'. Dick said, 'Why?'. Ringo said, 'Because I can't swim'. Dick went white and said, 'Why on earth didn't you tell me?'. Ringo said, 'Well, I didn't like to'."

Marc Behm's script revolved around the drummer's penchant for wearing rings. The audience was required to believe that he had been sent a sacred oriental ring by an admirer, and that Indian religious fanatics were prepared to kill him to get it back. Behm had inserted some gentle satire about the Church of England, the mid-'60s "brain drain" and Britain's growing reputation for scientific incompetence, but most of this material was reserved for the professionals. The Beatles were left to make the best out of being their own caricatures.

"Ringo emerged as the most promising in terms of screen potential," reckoned the group's press officer, Tony Barrow. "He was naturally good at comic mime and found it easy to pull faces. There were elements of likeable lunacy in his personality which lent themselves to movie photography. Paul was the keenest when it came to working in front of the cameras. He was a natural actor, anyway, the one most likely to bring a dull photo session to life with a few well-timed gesticulations."

To Barrow's eyes, McCartney's enthusiasm wasn't shared by his songwriting partner: "John was restless during filming. He found it a bit tedious because it took so long to put each scene together." Lennon stated it more starkly: "It was my fat Elvis period. You can see in the movie. He – I – is very fat, very insecure, and he's completely lost himself."

Neither a natural actor nor a screen magnet, George Harrison was given the slimmest role. He was eager for distraction, but ironically the significance of what might have been his most portentous encounter in the Bahamas only became obvious to him much later.

"We were waiting for instructions," he recalled a decade later, "and Swami Vishnu Devananda walked up. He was the first Swami I met, and he obviously knew we were there. He told me years later that whilst meditating he had a strong feeling that he should make contact."

Lennon takes up the story: "This little yogi runs over to us. We didn't know what they were. He gives us a little book each, signed to us, and ➻

John and Eleanor Bron on location for Help! in Ailsa Avenue, Twickenham, April 14, 1965.

PHOTO: DAILY MAIL/ATLANTIC SYNDICATION

PHOTOS: REX

it was on yoga. We didn't look at it. We just stuck it along with all the other stuff that people give us." Harrison conceded that, "I did not look at it in detail for some time, but at a later date I found the book that he had given me all those years before, and I opened the cover, and it had a big OM on it. He was from the Forest Hills Academy in Rishikesh."

If Harrison could date the making of Help! as his accidental introduction to Indian philosophy, Lennon had less rewarding memories: "The most humiliating experience for me was sitting with the Governor of the Bahamas, and being insulted by these fucking jumped-up middle-class bitches and bastards who would be commenting on our work and our manners. I was always drunk, insulting them. I couldn't take it. It hurt me so I would go insane and swear at them. It was a fucking humiliation."

Though Lennon was commenting on his distaste for The Beatles' social duties all over the globe, his mention of the Governor – to be precise, the Governor-General – of the Bahamas wasn't accidental. One scene required The Beatles to cavort through an old army barracks, which they assumed was uninhabited. But Lennon and Spinetti peeked through the shutters of one building, and were horrified to see that it was packed with disabled children and old people, barely clothed, and living in squalor. The set for their fantasy romp was the local hospital for the mentally and physically handicapped.

Ringo and his 'sacrificial ring'.

Paul gets down with a sitar in Help!'s restaurant scene.

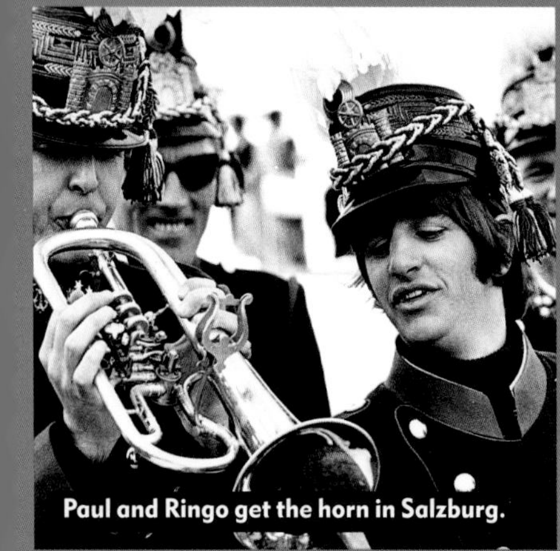

Paul and Ringo get the horn in Salzburg.

The incident roused Lennon's always ambiguous obsession with what he called "spastics". Onstage at the height of their fame, he often treated audiences to his contemptuous impression of a "spastic", pitched midway between Frankenstein's monster and a drooling baby. "Spastics" or (another favourite Lennon term) "cripples" were regularly brought to The Beatles' dressing-room before concerts, "as if they thought we could cure them", Lennon complained. The group were generally polite, while rudely mocking their disadvantaged fans as soon as they were out of earshot.

In Nassau, The Beatles were chauffeured back from the hospital to a lavish reception at the Governor-General's residence. "All these people, in their posh accents, were saying, 'Oh, which one is Ringo?'," Spinetti recalled. "'Is he the one with the nose?'. And they would push it, just to make sure it was real. Frightfully rude."

Introduced to the Bahamian Minister of Finance, Lennon's civility snapped. "We were filming today in what we thought was a deserted army barracks," he snapped at the bewildered politician, "but it turned out to be a place full of old people and spastics. It was disgusting. So how can you justify all this lavish food?" Conversation dwindled and died, as the Minister attempted to explain his role in Bahamian affairs, and Lennon, fired by wine, challenged him in increasingly vitriolic terms. "When we left the next day," Spinetti recounted, "there were headlines: 'Lennon insults the Governor-General'. We were practically thrown off the island."

ON MARCH 11, 1965, THE BEATLES RETURNED TO London; two days later, they were on another plane to Salzburg, in Austria. There they were met by 1,000 fans and a small group of Beatle-bashers wearing armbands saying: 'Beatles Go Home'. "We didn't notice they were there," Harrison told reporters during a press conference. Their media duties fulfilled, the group travelled to Obertauern, where they stayed in the Hotel Edelweiss.

To ensure their interest in the Alpine film shoot, Shenson had hired Miss Austria 1964, Gloria Makk, as The Beatles' ski instructor and translator. Beatle partners Cynthia Lennon, Patti Boyd and Maureen Starkey were compensated with their own hunky trainer, one Andy Krallinger.

Also on set were four screen doubles, for any scene which required the group to do more than ski very slowly in a straight line. So convincing were these stand-ins that they were regularly pestered for autographs, while Maureen Starkey approached Ringo from behind, threw her arms around him and planted a smacker on his cheek – only to discover that she'd embraced the fake Ringo, Hans Pretscherer.

Aside from a set piece involving the sport of curling, some girls and a fiendish bomb, the Austrian filming mostly featured The Beatles falling over in the snow. Their road manager, Mal Evans, was less fortunate: his cameo role in the movie required him to emerge from a hole in the ice clad only in his trunks, asking directions towards England. After several dips in the frosty water, he came close to losing consciousness for his art.

After hours at the Edelweiss, The Beatles made their own entertainment. An impromptu jazz trio of Lennon (guitar), McCartney (drums) and Lester (piano) was formed, while on one memorable night The Beatles marked the birthday of the movie's assistant director by playing a full two-hour set of their own hits, rock'n'roll standards and even ballads like Summertime, which they hadn't played since the Cavern. It was their only live appearance in Austria, staged solely for the cast and crew.

Meanwhile, the group's interest level continued to sag. "Paul was the only Beatle who saw any visions of a long-term movie career for himself," Tony Barrow reflected. "Ringo was delighted to find himself much closer to the centre of activity than he had ever been in the recording studio. But John and George solved their boredom problem by creeping off whenever they were not required on set."

When filming transferred to England on March 24, various distractions emerged to cloak their boredom. "We were waiting to shoot a scene in the restaurant when the guy gets thrown in the soup," Harrison recalled, "and there were a few Indian musicians playing in the background. I remember picking up the sitar and trying to hold it and thinking, 'This is a funny sound'. Then somewhere down the line I began to hear Ravi Shankar's name." Like his brief encounter with the Swami, this chance collision of cultures would have unimaginable repercussions.

The English film schedule was centred around Twickenham Studios, with brief location shoots on Salisbury Plain (where The Beatles mimed to the accompaniment of 3 Division's Centurion tanks); the stately home of Cliveden (masquerading as Buckingham Palace after Her Majesty refused to let the group inside her home); and the City Barge pub near Kew Bridge. Between scenes at Twickenham, McCartney doodled at a piano which had been installed for his benefit, vamping the same few lines over and over again – a haunting melody, matched to some banal lines about scrambled eggs. "If you play that bloody song any longer," said Dick Lester finally, "I'll have the piano taken off the stage." Only after the film was completed did the song metamorphose into Yesterday.

Ringo: Mr Tambourine Man.

By George! Harrison in Austria, March 14, 1965.

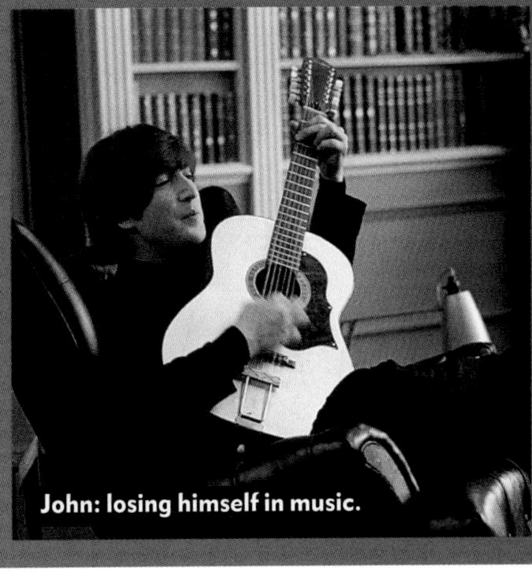

John: losing himself in music.

Titles had been a constant preoccupation among the crew and stars from the beginning. A Hard Day's Night had been slated to appear as Beatlemania until Ringo's brain coined the appropriate phrase. Late in 1964, Lennon had noted another Starr malapropism, "Tomorrow never knows", and filed it away as a potential film title. "We still have to write a title number," McCartney said before filming began, "which could be difficult because the film doesn't have a title yet." The shooting script simply called the movie Beatles Two. The group suggested High-Heeled Knickers, parodying Tommy Tucker's recent R&B hit, High-Heeled Sneakers. Shenson pushed for The Day The Clowns Collapsed. Harrison countered with Who's Been Sleeping In My Porridge, which was at least amusing. But the consensus among Shenson's staff was that the most suitable offering was Eight Arms To Hold You. When Ticket To Ride was issued as a single in the States that March, the small print boasted that the song could be heard in the movie of that name.

But Eight Arms To Hold You held no promise as a song title, and so it was with some relief that Lennon and McCartney greeted the idea of Help! – prompted, so the PR people claimed, by The Beatles' response when they first met one of their co-stars, Raja the famous man-eating tiger. As he had done with A Hard Day's Night the year before, Lennon won the race to pen the appropriate song.

Thanks to Lennon's revisionism, the creation of the song Help! has passed into Beatles mythology. "I just wrote the song because I was commissioned to write it for the movie," he said. "But later, I knew I really was crying out for help." But no one connected with the group recalls him ever mentioning anything of the kind at the time, even in private; the link only seems to have become apparent after his gruelling course of Primal Scream therapy in the summer of 1970.

A more relevant inspiration for some of the song's lyrical imagery may have been the desire to impress a strong and beautiful woman. "I remember the journalist Maureen Cleave asked me, 'Why don't you ever write songs with more than one syllable?'," Lennon revealed. "So in Help! there are two- and three-syllable words, and I very proudly showed them to her, but she still didn't like them."

However conscious or not Lennon was of his own creativity, the final weeks of filming in April and May found him exposed to a succession of unexpected stimuli. The first was his baptism into the turbulent waters of acid, in the company of his wife Cynthia and George Harrison – all of whom were inducted into the LSD community by the unlikely figure of Harrison's dentist. Almost simultaneously, Lennon was visited at home by an unwelcome reminder of the past: his long-vanished father Freddie. "Where have you been for the last 20 years?" Lennon snapped as he opened the front door. Cynthia's natural generosity secured Freddie a place in the Lennon mansion for a few days, until his father's burgeoning interest in John's finances convinced the son that this was one ghost who should be banished from the house.

"It was my fat Elvis period. You can see in the movie. He - I - is very fat, very insecure, and he's completely lost himself." JOHN LENNON

With each passing month, The Beatles slipped further away from the image they had been asked to portray in Help!. Filming ended on May 15, 1965, by which time Harrison was beginning to investigate Indian culture, McCartney was steeping himself in Ginsberg and Kerouac, and Lennon was veering between depressive self-analysis and narcotic bliss. Ten weeks later, on July 29, they attended the gala premiere of their movie in London's Leicester Square, and struggled to remember who they'd been.

Their alienation from the project wasn't helped by its downbeat reception in the press. The Daily Express was one of the few dissenting voices, announcing that "Mr Lester's direction is a joy to watch. And The Beatles are the closest thing to the Marx Brothers since the Marx Brothers."

The best-selling paper of the period, The Daily Mirror, thought differently: "The film leaned heavily on the likeable vacant grin of John Lennon, the smooth charm of Paul, the long-haired good looks of George, and the darkly villainous looks of the Long-Nosed One," proving that tabloid journalists were just as cruel in 1965 as they are today. "This was not enough to carry a movie, in my view."

The Beatles had attended a private viewing in mid-July, cushioning themselves with copious joints beforehand. "When we first saw the film, we were knocked out," Harrison said defensively, "but obviously some people weren't. The whole thing is a fast-moving comic strip, just a string of events." After the premiere, Lennon was prepared to admit his doubts: "Help! as a film was like Eight Days A Week as a record. A lot of people liked the film and a lot of people liked that record. But neither was what we really wanted. They were both a bit manufactured. The film won't harm us, but we weren't in full control." By 1980, his verdict had hardened: "It was just bullshit."

"I'm sorry John felt that way," responded the film's producer, Walter Shenson. "It would have been easy for me to defer to The Beatles on matters of taste, because I didn't want anything to offend 11- or 12-year-olds. The boys were very progressive, ahead of the average mentality. I could easily have let them make a surrealistic movie."

Help! did achieve one thing: it convinced The Beatles that they didn't want to make another lightweight buddy movie. Plans for the group to star in an adaptation of Richard Condon's western novel, A Talent For Loving, were quietly dropped. It would be two years before The Beatles appeared together in front of film cameras again; when they did, they concocted the "surrealistic movie" that had been Walter Shenson's nightmare. Meanwhile, Help! remained as the last flourish of innocent Beatlemania, the tapestry of a dream that was starting to distort and melt under the heat of change. ■

PHOTOS: CHRIS KINDHL/CAMERA PRESS/REX

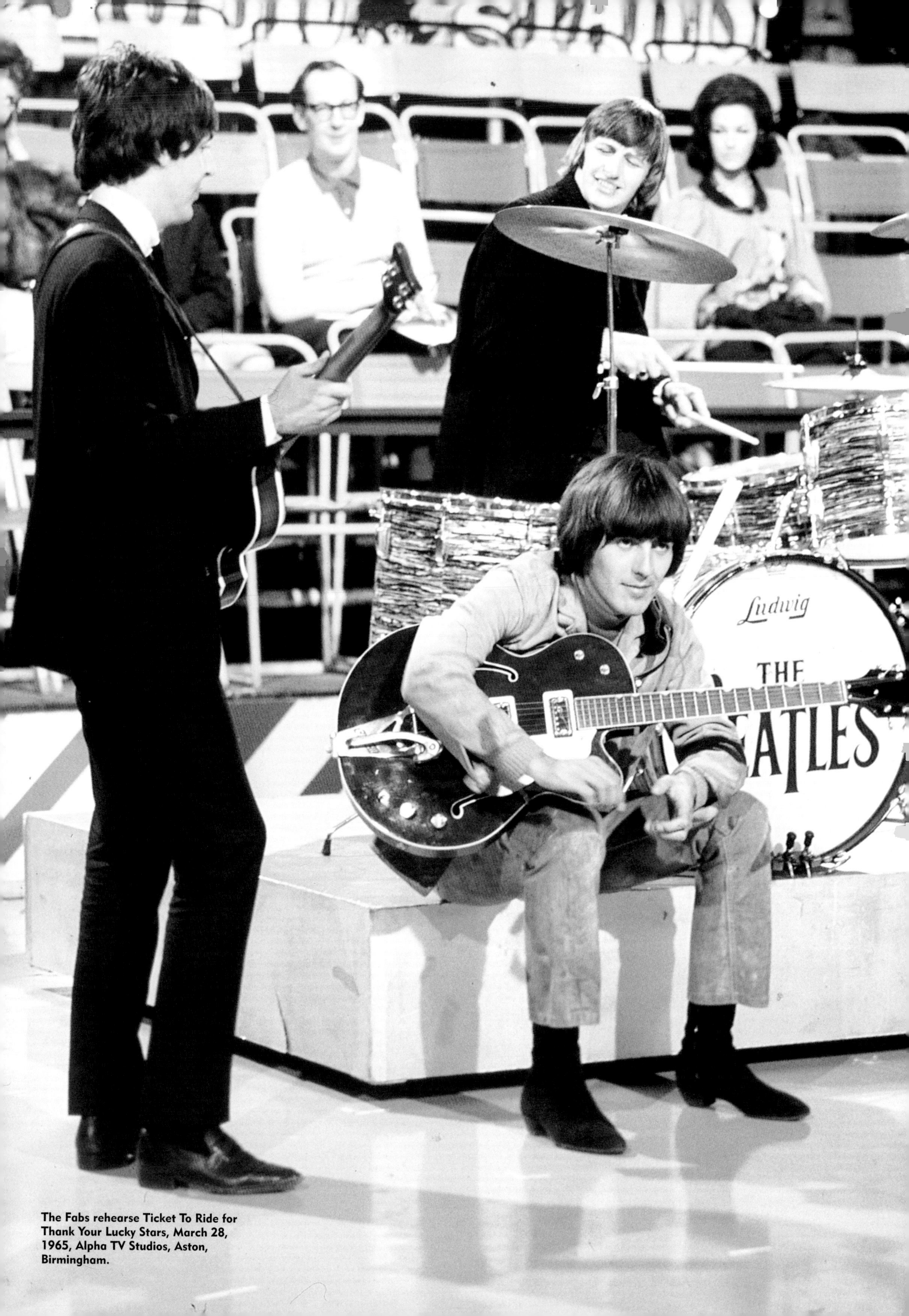

The Fabs rehearse Ticket To Ride for Thank Your Lucky Stars, March 28, 1965, Alpha TV Studios, Aston, Birmingham.

What: Release of Ticket To Ride
Where: UK
When: April 9, 1965

RIDING SO HIGH

With the melancholic Ticket To Ride, The Beatles hinted at their future sound and said goodbye to Beatlemania. By Bob Stanley.

TICKET TO RIDE IS WHERE MOPTOP Beatlemania ends and their weightless, ageless legend begins. As a musical milestone, you could make a case for the quirky squeak that starts I Feel Fine, but Ticket To Ride was full of newness, totally assimilated: a droning, melancholy wall of noise. It was the first true Beatles 'production'.

The shrill, cascading intro was a mindsnapper in itself. The Searchers had long been one of The Beatles' favourite Mersey rivals, and the 12-string chime of When You Walk In The Room was an undoubted influence. But Ticket To Ride was tougher by far – the menacing feedback of The Kinks' All Day And All Of The Night and The Who's current hit I Can't Explain were no doubt on The Beatles' minds when they entered Abbey Road in February 1965 (The Searchers would repay the compliment a few months later with the ear-shredding jingler He's Got No Love). George Harrison had first fallen in love with the 12-string guitar in early '63 when he borrowed one – presumably acoustic – from Tom Springfield, brother of Dusty. A year later on their trip to the States, George was presented with a Rickenbacker 360-12 while lying sick in his hotel bedroom. It was only the second one ever made.

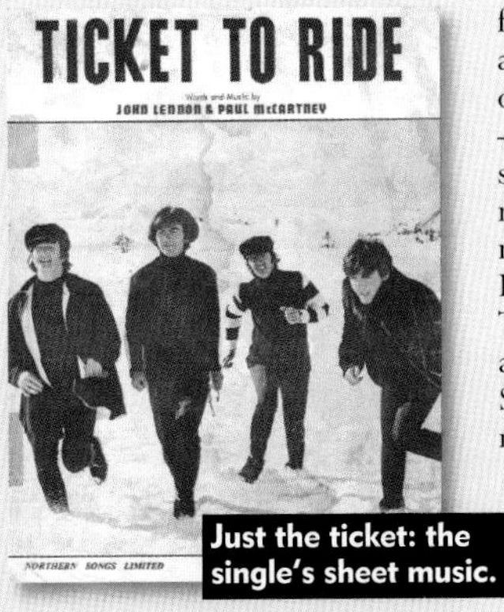

Just the ticket: the single's sheet music.

"John claimed a 'ticket to ride' was a certificate of good health that Hamburg's prostitutes had to obtain."

What could be achieved with this new machine became evident on the Hard Day's Night soundtrack. The sly intro to You Can't Do That and its abrasive, damaged break were thrilling. Jim McGuinn for one rushed out to buy a Rickenbacker straight after seeing the movie. The jet plane drone of Mr Tambourine Man would enter the US charts within a month of Ticket To Ride which, oddly, was the last record on which George used this guitar. Maybe he figured it could never be put to better use.

A Beatles single that wasn't full of boundless exuberance came as something of a shock. The dense, driving production is wholly tempered by John Lennon's cool, almost apathetic delivery. From the opening line of "I think I'm gonna be sad", the lyric is riven with doubt and shoulder-shrugging. The relentless 12-string drone finally gives way to a gorgeous chord change when John sings "...going away", and the melancholy cracks wide open. The Carpenters' cover, their debut single four years later, shows just how hopeless and helpless a song Ticket To Ride really is, stripped of Paul's peppy, tacked-on ending.

Lennon and McCartney would later do their best to out-Rutle each other in explaining away the lyric. John claimed a 'ticket to ride' was a certificate of good health that Hamburg's prostitutes had to obtain before they could go about their business. Paul's version in Barry Miles's Many Years From Now is yet more comical – the title is a pun on Ryde, the town on the Isle Of Wight where his cousin Bett ran a pub that he and John once visited. Paul's major contribution to the single ("Because John sang it you might have to give him 60 per cent of it," he told Miles) was in guiding Ringo's drum part, at once thunderous and lop-sided, and a precursor to the glory of Rain.

The troubled air of Ticket To Ride was hardly leavened by its mournful flip, Yes It Is. While the A-side looked uncompromisingly to the future, its coupling hinted at death and a past proving impossible to shake off. Structurally it resembled This Boy – and John later dismissed Yes It Is as a soundalike knock-off – but the mysterious figure in red harks back much further to the dead lovers of English folk songs like She Moves Through The Fair. Whether the apparition is his mother Julia or Stuart Sutcliffe, Yes It Is was as much a lyrical mourning for the past as Help! was musically, with its headshaking "ooooh!" on the tail. Lennon's uncertainty and his fear of irretrievably losing touch with his past, explains the cathartic, raved-up rendition of Dizzy Miss Lizzy recorded a few weeks later – a beautiful din but a strangely anachronistic last track on the *Help!* album. Still, Yes It Is sounds modern. It doesn't take a huge imaginative leap to hear it as a White Album track.

In June '65, with Ticket To Ride still in the Top 10, Fabulous magazine dedicated an issue to Liverpool. Cover stars The Searchers look "smart casual"; on the back Billy Fury holds a beach ball. Centrefold stars are The Beatles. Gathered around a telephone in a hotel lobby, they are clearly stoned out of their minds. If the new aggressive sounds of The Yardbirds, The Kinks et al were pushing The Beatles onwards, then John and George's first acid encounter at a dinner party in (probably) April '65 must have added more fuel: Ticket To Ride's clangorous density is too much of a step on from the semi-acoustic feel of *Beatles For Sale* for this to be a coincidence. This could also explain why Paul's slightly showy guitar break and near knees-up finale seem out of phase with John's haziness – possibly John and George hadn't yet shared their new discovery with him.

Ringo, back from his honeymoon the day before, went home to Maureen and their new Weybridge home at the end of the session. She cooked him Lancashire hotpot.

PHOTOS: MIRRORPIX.COM/REDFERNS

APRIL 65

1-2 Filming of Help! continues at Twickenham.

3 Broadcast of Thank Your Lucky Stars. The Beatles mime Ticket To Ride, Yes It Is and Eight Days A Week.

4 Lennon and McCartney write Help!, the title track of their next film.

5 While filming Indian restaurant scenes for Help! at Twickenham, Harrison becomes intrigued by the sitar played by a member of an Indian group.

6 A new EP, Beatles For Sale No 2, is released in the UK.

8 McCartney goes to opening of a new club, Downstairs at the Pickwick.

9 Ticket To Ride/Yes It Is released in the UK.

10 Sid Bernstein visits Brian Epstein in New York, to pay a $100,000 advance for the Shea Stadium concert.

11 Wembley's Empire Pool hosts the 1965 NME Pollwinners' Concert, featuring The Beatles and others.

13 The Beatles record Help! in Abbey Road Studios, London.

14 Filming of opening sequence of Help! in Ailsa Avenue, Twickenham.

15 Ticket To Ride clip is premiered on UK TV on Top Of The Pops.

16 John and George interviewed on Ready Steady Goes Live!.

18 Pop Gear, a film featuring The Beatles, The Animals, Spencer Davis Group, Billy J Kramer and Herman's Hermit goes on UK release.

19 Ticket To Ride is released in the US.

20 Brian Epstein is appointed a director of Harrison's publishing company, Harrisongs Limited.

21 A 'Scotland Yard' sequence is filmed at Twickenham.

22 Ticket To Ride reaches Number 1 in the UK singles chart.

24 The Times reports that the recent issue of shares in The Beatles' publishing company Northern Songs has been the 'flop sans pareil' of the year. Having been issued at 7s 9d they are now languishing at 6s 6d.

28 The Beatles are filmed being given a Grammy Award for A Hard Day's Night by Peter Sellers.

29 Jimmy Nicol (above), who stood in for Ringo when The Beatles toured Australia, is declared bankrupt.

MAY 65

3-5 Three days of filming for Help! at Knighton Down, Salisbury Plain, Wiltshire, UK.

7 Filming resumes at Twickenham, with a sequence in which McCartney is reduced to three inches in height.

9 The Beatles go to see Bob Dylan play the first of two nights at London's Royal Albert Hall.

10 Dizzy Miss Lizzy and Bad Boy are recorded in Studio 2 Abbey Road. Larry Williams attends the sessions.

12 Filming of Help! wraps up at Twickenham Studios, London.

16 Lennon attends a party for Johnny Mathis.

22 Ticket To Ride is the new US Number 1 single.

25 John and Cynthia attend the Cannes Film Festival in France.

26 A seven-song live session is recorded for BBC radio, to be transmitted under the title The Beatles (Invite You To Take A Ticket To Ride).

JUNE 65

1 A Lennon interview, filmed a week earlier at Cannes, is broadcast on the Merv Griffin Show in the US.

2 McCartney leaves for a holiday in Albufeira, Portugal, with Jane Asher.

7 The Beatles (Invite You To Take A Ticket To Ride) is broadcast by the BBC Light Programme in the UK.

8 At Abbey Road Studios, engineer Norman Smith produces a new stereo mix of I Want To Hold Your Hand for overseas compilation LPs.

11 Paul and Jane get home from holiday, denying they have married.

12 News breaks that The Beatles are to receive MBEs for their services to Britain, and ex-RAF Squadron Leader Paul Pearson returns his gong in protest.

13 Northern Songs reports that 1,337 cover versions of Beatle songs have been recorded to date.

14 McCartney records Yesterday in Abbey Road Studios. An album, *Beatles VI*, is released in the US.

15 It's Only Love is recorded at Abbey Road.

16 Lennon is interviewed for the BBC radio show The World Of Books.

17 Act Naturally and Wait recorded at Abbey Road. Yesterday is finished.

18 Lennon appears on UK TV current affairs show Tonight to promote his book, A Spaniard In The Works.

19 In a letter in The Times, Charles de Houghton defends The Beatles' MBEs, saying that they are significant earners of foreign exchange and have saved the British corduroy industry.

20 A European tour starts at the Palais Des Sports, Paris.

21 In Port Moresby, New Guinea, government official Richard Pape returns his Military Medal in protest at the award of MBEs to The Beatles.

24 A Spaniard In The Works, John Lennon's second book, is published.

27–28 Two days at the Teatro Adriano, Rome, Italy. Brian Epstein disappears without warning, not returning until the tour reaches Madrid, five days later.

29 In Jakarta, leaders of the Koes Bersaudara dance band are arrested for playing Beatles music.

JULY 65

1 *Beatles VI* is certified as a gold album in America.

4 The Beatles finish their European tour in Barcelona.

10 The Beatles' US-only album *Beatles VI*, tops the US chart.

What: The recording of Yesterday
Where: Abbey Road Studios
When: June 14 & 17, 1965

A DREAM OF A SONG

As well as becoming the most recorded song ever, Yesterday also marked the first time that any of The Beatles went solo. By Merrell Noden.

FROM THE MOMENT HE FIRST BECAME aware of it, floating around in his subconscious, Paul McCartney was wary of Yesterday. He seemed to know the changes it would bring to the Beatle camp, like some Trojan Horse whose real dangers were to be revealed in time. And his foreboding seems to have been justified, for these 124 seconds of beautifully polished rue would not only be the occasion for two important musical *firsts* for The Beatles, but also the seed of their ultimate dissolution. Even now, 37 years after its release, Yesterday continues to provoke hard feelings between McCartney and Yoko Ono.

McCartney's recollection is that the music was there in his head when he woke up one morning at the Ashers' house at 57 Wimpole Street. "I have a piano by the side of my bed and just got up and played the chords," he recalled. Sleep and dreams have always loomed large in Beatle mythology, so it's no surprise that McCartney always credited the song to his sleeping unconscious. "I dreamed it when I was staying there," he said.

For a man whose ability to crank out hit songs at warp speed was legendary, McCartney took his time with this one. Though it was recorded on June 14 and 17 of 1965, George Martin once claimed that McCartney had been working on it as far back as January of 1964, when The Beatles were in Paris. It crops up again on the set of Help! where Richard Lester grew so tired of hearing McCartney noodling away at it that he exploded, "If I hear that once more, I'll have that bloody piano taken away!"

With the music finished, McCartney sought out people who knew the songwriting canon to ask if there was any chance it was not his own, but a scrap of some standard he'd heard and forgotten. "Eventually it became like handing something in to the police," he said. "If no one claimed it after a few weeks then I would have it." Even when assured it was his, he offered it to other singers, like Chris Farlowe, Billy J Kramer and Marianne Faithfull (in the end, Matt Monro recorded the first cover version, taking it to Number 8 in the UK charts).

The song's working title was Scrambled Eggs, which seems wonderfully inappropriate until one considers how much genius was encoded here and how getting it out meant cracking the whole. McCartney worked out the final lyrics while on holiday in Portugal, as he drove to Shadows rhythm guitarist Bruce Welch's vacation home in Albufeira. Still not trusting himself, Paul asked George Martin if he thought Yesterday too corny a title. Martin did not, but told him that Peggy Lee had recorded a song called Yesterdays. McCartney didn't know it and concluded he was in the clear.

McCartney laid down his vocal and guitar track on the night of June 14. The other Beatles could think of nothing to add, though they all seemed to be getting tired of Paul's obsession with the song. "Thinks he's Beethoven!" George is supposed to have grumbled.

The testiness is understandable. Not only was McCartney obnoxiously (if justly) proud of Yesterday, it marked the first time any one of The Beatles had recorded by himself. When Martin suggested to Brian Epstein changing the credit to reflect McCartney's sole authorship, he was told emphatically no (see songbook below).

It was also Martin who suggested using a string quartet as accompaniment. The fact that McCartney was living with the cultured Ashers may have made him more receptive to this heresy. Jane's mother was an oboeist and taught at the Guildhall School of Music (indeed, she had once taught Martin). McCartney and Martin worked out the string arrangement at Martin's house, with Paul eagerly setting his mark on it by suggesting a flatted 7th in the cello's line. With Yesterday, Martin's role increased to real collaboration, and the band became eager to take chances.

For the first time, outsiders played on a Beatles track. Kenneth Essex, who played viola, recalls how quick the session was. The four studio pros were hired for two hours, for which they were paid five guineas. As it turned out, they did not need the whole two hours to record their part of what Essex today refers to as a "pleasant little song". When cellist Francisco Gabarro bumped into McCartney a few days later in the Abbey Road canteen, he was told, "I think we have a winner".

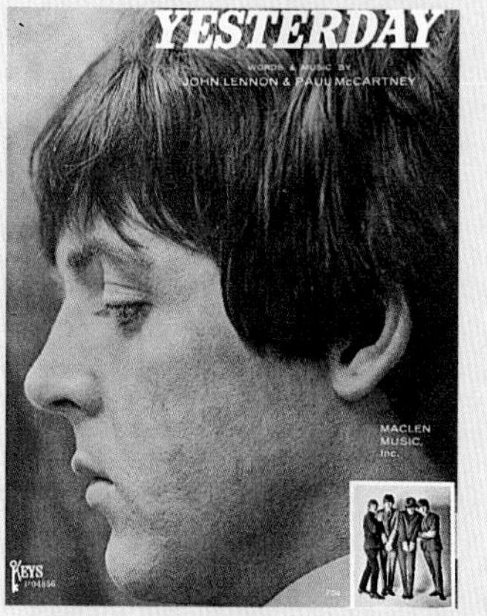

Did they ever. Not only is Yesterday the most recorded song in Beatles history, but also, according to the Guinness Book Of World Records, in songwriting history. It topped the US charts for four weeks in the summer of 1965, and was the most played song in the US for the next eight years. Even though it was certainly well known in the UK, having appeared on the album *Help!* in August of 1965, McCartney and the other Beatles decided against releasing it as a single in England, preferring to stick together as a group. It was finally released as a single in the UK in the summer of 1976 when it peaked at Number 8.

"These 124 seconds of beautifully polished rue would become the seed for The Beatles' ultimate dissolution."

Lennon biographer Albert Goldman claimed that Yesterday's extraordinary popularity was a source of ongoing annoyance to Lennon, who "despaired of ever writing anything so popular". How delighted Lennon would have been on learning that Paul was made to sing it repeatedly by his Japanese jailers during his imprisonment in 1980.

The song once again became a sore point for McCartney when, during the planning of The Beatles' compilation of Number 1s, he phoned Yoko to ask if on this one track the songwriting credit could read "Paul McCartney and John Lennon" to reflect his sole authorship. Yoko said no, underscoring once more how large Yesterday still looms in the minds of The Beatles' inner circle.

Born Yesterday: "I have a piano by my bed and I just got up and played the chords" – Paul at Jane Asher's home, London, 1965.

George run out to 55,600 screaming
Americans, Shea Stadium, New York.

What: The Beatles play Shea Stadium
Where: Shea Stadium, New York City
When: August 15, 1965

MATCHSTICK MEN

It was the biggest concert The Beatles – or any other band – had ever played. It was just a pity that no one could see or hear them... By Dave DiMartino.

IF THERE IS ONE SPECIFIC IMAGE SEARED into the collective consciousness of North America that drove home the enormity of The Beatles' fame, it may be that of the Stick Figures. The Stick Figures – as they appeared to be in the countless Polaroid snapshots still tucked away in yellowing scrapbooks the world over – seemed to be a rock combo, situated on a stage erected in the middle of a baseball field. Surveying the Stick Figures were 55,600 human beings, many screaming so loudly it remains disputed whether a single note of music was heard by anyone at all. Stick Figures included.

Yet as filmed evidence attests, on August 15, 1965, The Beatles indeed took the stage at New York's massive Shea Stadium and headlined what was, at the time, the largest rock concert in the history of humankind. To paraphrase John Lennon's celebrated remark of scant months later, witnesses recall the event as being "Louder than God". "I do not remember actually hearing anything," says Ida Langsam, who today is a music publicist in New York, but in the late '60s was known as Judee Gould, New York Area Secretary for the official Beatles Fan Club. "All I needed was one note to know what they were playing, and the rest didn't matter. Because it was all memorised in my head note for note, the way it was on the record. I played the records so many times I heard it without hearing it."

"I do not remember actually hearing anything. All I needed was one note to know what they were playing."

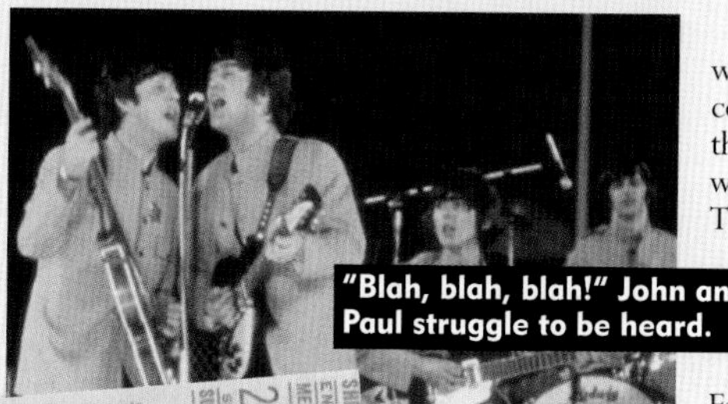

"Blah, blah, blah!" John and Paul struggle to be heard.

The event, which was filmed, titled The Beatles At Shea Stadium, and aired on BBC TV on March 1, 1966 and Stateside on ABC TV on January 10, 1967, may represent the culmination of American Beatlemania in its purest form. Present on the stage at various times were Ed Sullivan, the American TV host who'd prominently hosted the band on his show; Murray Kaufman, the WINS disc jockey known as 'Murray The K', who dubbed himself "the Fifth Beatle"; opening acts King Curtis, Brenda Holloway and Sounds Incorporated, among others; and Sid Bernstein, the American concert promoter who'd previously presented The Beatles at Carnegie Hall and would bring them back to Shea Stadium yet again a year later.

Perhaps most noteworthy in the annals of Great American Showbiz Tales was the manner in which promoter Bernstein had managed to fill the stadium to the brim without a cent of paid advertising. As charmingly recounted in Bernstein's autobiography Not Just The Beatles, Bernstein had struck a verbal agreement with band manager Brian Epstein in October 1964 to bring the band to Shea Stadium the next August, with the proviso that he not advertise the event until paying a $50,000 upfront deposit in January. Lacking that much cash, Bernstein simply spent the next few weeks spreading the word to youths in Washington Square that the Fab Four might be coming to town next August, and he had a post office box where they might send money if they wanted to buy tickets.

"I figured that I was not allowed to advertise it until I put my deposit down with Brian Epstein," Bernstein now recalls, "and so for three weekends I did this – and only The Beatles could do it. The word of mouth went around the world. I had letters from even behind the Iron Curtain. When I finally got to the post office, there were two, maybe three, huge duffel bags full of mail. I said to them, Fellas, you're giving me the wrong mail. 'No', they said, and they pulled out some sample letters that had my name on them, or that had coins rattling in the envelope. It was a phenomenon that may never again be repeated."

Thanks to an eager staff of student nurses skilled at opening envelopes, Bernstein was able to stroll into New York's Waldorf Hotel on January 10, 1965, and hand Brian Epstein a cheque for twice the amount he had promised.

Logistics? Security would be no small concern at an event of this magnitude. A plan was struck whereby The Beatles would be flown from a Manhattan heliport to the former Worlds Fairgrounds near the stadium, then transferred to an armoured vehicle and inconspicuously driven under the stands. From there, they would run across the field, climb the stage, perform their set, then do precisely the opposite.

Oddly, that is exactly what happened. Amid the screams and banners the tiny figures on the faraway stage ran through their set-list of the time (12 songs in all), plugged their new movie Help!, and enjoyed the surrealistic experience of performing onstage without the help of any monitor system. It's no small wonder that the available bootlegs of the filmed concert – both video and audio – feature a soundtrack later tweaked with overdubs and, to further puzzle historians, a version of Twist And Shout actually performed at the Hollywood Bowl two weeks later.

Though the band returned to Shea Stadium the next year, they did not sell it out. Bernstein claims this was purely the result of his misplacing a shoeboxful of tickets. "We could have sold them," he says today. "Those tickets became collectors' items, and I sold them for a fortune."

A warm fellow who, despite the title of his book, will be linked to The Beatles for the remainder of his life, Bernstein can't help looking back proudly. He recounts the time he brought Jimmy Cliff to Carnegie Hall a few years later and, at John Lennon's request, supplied the ex-Beatle with three tickets to the show. Sitting next to him at intermission, Lennon leaned over to Bernstein and confided, "You know, Sid, at Shea Stadium I saw the top of the mountain." Replied Sid Bernstein, now 83: "You know, John, so did I."

PHOTOS: HULTON ARCHIVE, REDFERNS, REX

JULY 12 - AUGUST 15, 1965

12 The Moody Blues throw a party at their house in Roehampton. Guests include Paul and Jane Asher, George and Patti Boyd and Rod Stewart.

13 At The Savoy Hotel, McCartney collects five Ivor Novello Awards, including Most Performed Work and Highest Certified British Sales, both for Can't Buy Me Love.

14 Paul goes to see Jane Asher perform in the Palace Theatre, Watford, UK.

16 Brian's plan to build a new venue, The Pilgrim Theatre in Bromley, flounders when planning permission is refused.

19 A new single, Help!/I'm Down, is released in the US.

23 Help!/I'm Down is released in the UK.

24 Ringo Starr forks out £37,000 on a house, Sunny Heights, in Weybridge, Surrey. 19

29 The world premiere of Help! is held at the London Pavilion.

29 The new single, Help!, enters the UK singles chart.

AUGUST 1965

1 Six songs are performed live on the Blackpool Night Out TV broadcast (below), from the ABC Theatre, Blackpool.

2 Paul and Jane spend an evening with The Byrds in the Scotch Of St James, London. Brian Epstein announces that there will be no more UK Beatles tours in 1965. His decision is later reversed.

3 Lennon buys a house in Poole, Dorset, UK, for his Aunt Mimi.

5 Help! hits Number 1 in the UK singles chart. Lennon and Harrison see The Byrds at Blaises, Knightsbridge.

6 The new album, *Help!*, is released in the UK. McCartney sees The Byrds at The Flamingo, London.

7 Help! enters the US singles chart at Number 41.

8 John and George go to the last day of the Fifth Annual National Jazz & Blues Festival in Richmond.

9 John produces The Silkie's version of his song, You've Got To Hide Your Love Away, at IBC Studios. Paul is on guitar and Harrison plays tambourine.

11 The movie Help! premieres in New York.

12 Lennon tries out a Mellotron at IBC Studios. Highly impressed, he declares: "I must have one." (Its distinctive tones can be heard in the opening of Strawberry Fields.)

13 The *Help!* album is released in the US, with a different track-listing. The Beatles fly from Heathrow to New York for their third US tour.

14 A performance for the Ed Sullivan Show is recorded.

15 The Beatles play to 56,000 fans in the Shea Stadium, New York. In the evening the band hang out with Bob Dylan in the Warwick Hotel.

16 The Beatles entertain visitors in their suite at the Warwick Hotel, New York, including Bob Dylan, The Supremes, Ronettes and Exciters.

17 The tour continues at Maple Leaf Gardens, Toronto, Canada.

21 At Metropolitan Stadium, Minneapolis, Minnesota, George is presented with a Rickenbacker 12-string by Ron Butwin and Randy Resnick of local music store B-Sharp Music.

22 At Memorial Coliseum, Portland, Oregon, Carl Wilson and Mike Love of The Beach Boys visit The Beatles' dressing room.

23 *Help!* is declared a gold album in the US (above).

24 Following an incident in which their plane engine caught fire, The Beatles enjoy a break from their US tour in a rented house at 2850 Benedict Canyon Drive, Hollywood, California. The Byrds and Peter Fonda attend a party with The Beatles in Benedict Canyon.

25 The Times reports that Northern Songs, having predicted a profit of £550,000 for the previous year, has in fact made £621,000.

27 The Beatles meet Elvis Presley at his house on Perugia Way, Hollywood.

28 The US tour resumes at Balboa Stadium, San Diego.

29–30 Two nights at the Hollywood Bowl, Los Angeles. BBC radio broadcast The Beatles Abroad, a 45-minute programme of interviews from the American tour.

31 The third US tour ends at the Cow Palace, San Francisco.

SEPTEMBER 65

1 The Beatles hang out with The Byrds in Los Angeles, then fly home to the UK.

2 Help! is certified as a gold single in the US.

3 A six-week break begins, with no work commitments.

4 Help! reaches Number 1 in the US singles chart.

10 It is reported that Brian Epstein is negotiating a deal for UK screenings of The Beatles' US TV cartoon series.

11 The album *Help!* reaches Number 1 in the US albums chart for the first of nine weeks.

12 The Beatles are musical guests on US TV's Ed Sullivan Show. The programme was recorded on August 14.

13 Yesterday is released in America as the new Beatles single. In the UK, it remains an album track.

15 McCartney goes to see Ben E King play in the Scotch Of St James, London.

16 Eight Days A Week is certified as a gold single in the US.

What: The Beatles meet Elvis
Where: Bel Air, California
When: August 27, 1965

'LONG LIVE ZE KING!'

There was nothing The Beatles wanted more than to meet their idol, Elvis. Then they went one better and jammed with him. By Keith Badman.

"THERE WAS ONLY ONE PERSON IN THE United States that we really wanted to meet," John Lennon recalled in 1975, "and that was Elvis. We just idolised the guy so much. When I first heard Heartbreak Hotel, I could hardly make out what was being said. It was just the experience of hearing it and having my hair stand on end. We never heard American voices singing like that. They'd always sung like Sinatra."

When The Beatles first came to Hollywood in 1964, legendary stars like Dean Martin and Frank Sinatra had all expressed a desire to meet the group, but it was The King that The Beatles really wanted to meet. They had unsuccessfully tried to meet Elvis during their first tour of the States in August, 1964. But when the group came to do a tour of America in the summer of 1965, it was discovered that The Beatles would be in Hollywood at the same time as Elvis, who was filming there. It took three days of planning to set up the get-together in Elvis's Bel Air home. "It was funny, because by the time we got near his house we'd forgotten where we were going," George Harrison recalled. "We pulled up at some big gates and someone said, 'Oh yeah, we're going to see Elvis', and we all fell out of the limo laughing."

"We hoped it would be a secret," remembered John Lennon. "But the fans and the press still got wind of it. The thought of Elvis and The Beatles being together at one time just blew the minds of some of the people... Elvis said hello in his quietly spoken way and led us into this huge circular room. I know Paul, George, and Ringo were feeling as nervous as I was. This was the guy we had all idolised for years. He was a legend in his own lifetime, and it's never easy meeting a legend."

At first, The Beatles found themselves lost for words. Paul and John sat on one side of Elvis, with Ringo on the other, George sitting cross-legged on the floor. Finally, Elvis tried to make them feel at home and broke the embarrassed silence. "If you're just going to sit there and stare at me, I'm going to bed," he joked. "Let's talk a bit, huh? And then maybe play and sing a bit?"

That seemed a fine idea to The Beatles. "That's just what we all wanted to do," recalled Lennon, "and you could feel the tension in the room begin to ease. After a bit, Elvis said, 'Somebody bring in the guitars'. One of his men jumped up, and within moments three electric guitars had been plugged into the amplifiers in the room. Elvis took a bass guitar, and I took a rhythm guitar. Elvis obviously wasn't that familiar with his instrument, so Paul gave him some instructions. George was busy looking over his instrument, and it was a few minutes before he joined in. Cilla Black's hit record You're My World was the track that we first got off together. After that I said, This beats talking, doesn't it? We had at last found a way of communicating. Only Ringo looked a bit down. He could only watch us and drum on the side of his chair. 'Too bad we left the drums in Memphis,' Elvis said."

At about 2am, The Beatles left, each with a complete set of Elvis records, a gun holster with a gold leather belt and a table lamp shaped like a wagon – gifts courtesy of The King. John: "As we were about to leave, Paul said, 'Elvis, we'd like you and the other guys to come up to the place where we are staying tomorrow night.' 'Well, I'll see,' Elvis replied. 'I don't know whether I can make it or not. But thanks all the same.' He smiled and shook our hands. It was Elvis's sense of humour that stuck in my mind. He liked to laugh and make others laugh, too. This was why I put on a Peter Sellers voice again as we walked out of the door. I said, Tanks for ze music, Elvis, and long live ze King!"

As the entourage walked to their cars, Colonel Tom Parker came across to Chris Hutchins, one of only two journalists permitted to cover this meeting between the two giants of the pop world, and said, "Tell the fans it was a great meeting". John overheard this, laughed and said, "Tell them the truth. It was a load of rubbish".

On December 21, 1970, Elvis Presley attended a meeting in the Oval Office at the White House with the then US President, Richard Nixon, during which Presley expressed his belief that The Beatles had been a real force for anti-American spirit. "I've seen those famous Nixon transcripts where Elvis actually tries to shop us," Paul later commented. "He's in the transcript saying to Richard Nixon, 'Well, sir, those Beatles, they're very un-American and they take drugs'. I felt a bit betrayed by that, I must say. The great joke was that we were taking drugs, and look what happened to him. He was caught on the toilet full of them! It was sad, but I still love him, particularly in his early period. He was very influential on me." But to John, Elvis didn't die in 1977; he died the day he joined the army. "That's when they killed him," John admitted, "and the rest was a living death."

Thank you very much: Elvis, in the doorway, says goodbye to The Beatles.

PHOTOS: CHUCK BOYD/REDFERNS/CAMERA PRESS/HULTON ARCHIVE

John Lennon: "It was Elvis's sense of humour that stuck in my mind. He liked to laugh and make others laugh, too."

HELP!

Period of adjustment

The last Beatles album produced at breakneck speed, *Help!* has its share of filler tracks – but also boasts some of John Lennon's finest moments, says Alexis Petridis. And then there's Yesterday.

Like the film it ostensibly soundtracked – the zany, U-certificate adventures of four loveable lads, performed by men so stoned they could barely stand up – *Help!* caught The Beatles in transition. At one extreme, it clearly maps out The Beatles' future. It offers a new-found emotional maturity, but also the first evidence of the polarisation between Lennon and McCartney that would characterise the band's final years: John baring his soul on the title track and You've Got To Hide Your Love Away, Paul the master craftsman, turning in the world's most popular standard, Yesterday. At the other extreme, *Help!* sounds like the death rattle of the Beatlemania era, the work of a band still being harried by their British and American record companies to come up with more material before the bubble burst (the latter in particular may have felt an involuntary shudder when Ticket To Ride, the first fruits of the *Help!* sessions, managed only one week atop the US chart).

Most famously of all, *Help!* is The Beatles' first real 'drug album': they had been introduced to marijuana by Bob Dylan the previous year, and according to whose chronology you believe, Lennon and Harrison's first LSD trip took place either just before sessions commenced, or just before they finished. In a way, *Help!* pre-empts the entire debate about the influence of drugs on pop music. Slumped beatifically in the pro-corner are tracks as good as anything The Beatles ever recorded, where their drug use audibly freed them from earlier constraints and allowed them to take pop music to places it had never been before. The glorious introspection of You've Got To Hide Your Love Away finds Lennon plumbing new emotional depths, glumly depicting dark corners of his psyche with a clarity that no British pop writer had ever managed before. Ticket To Ride is the wondrous sound of Merseybeat inhaling, a song which could be no more obviously influenced by drugs if its lyrics were about running out of Rizlas and arguing over whose turn it was to go to the all-night garage. It lumbers blearily into view, the opening lyrics seem to be unsure even of precisely how the protagonist feels (he only "thinks" he's "going to be sad"?), and its ongoing rhythmical and melodic twists mirror its indecisive emotional mood.

> "The Beatles' first real drugs album, it pre-empts the entire debate about the influence of drugs on popular music."

In the anti-corner, where drugs are held as an active hindrance to creativity, lurk those moments on *Help!* which sound dashed off by a group whose sense of quality control temporarily vanished in a puff of sweet-smelling smoke. While McCartney's I've Just Seen A Face is the album's one genuine overlooked gem – a charming English inversion of *Help!*'s much-noted Dylan influence that bowls along, midway between Greenwich Village and the more parochial sound of skiffle – many of his other contributions whiff of filler: Another Girl and Tell Me What You See are pleasant, but not pleasant enough to avoid the sensation that they are merely there to make up numbers. Lennon famously

The film shoot that inspired the LP cover; but the semaphore signals were meaningless!

PHOTO: TRACKS (2)

remarked that It's Only Love was "lousy… abysmal… the one song of mine I really hate", but there is nothing wrong with it that more time spent on the trite lyrics wouldn't have cured. Their semi-finished state is of a piece with the mess that is the double-tracked guitar line on a lacklustre version of Larry Williams' Dizzy Miss Lizzy – tellingly, the last rock and roll cover The Beatles would record until the Get Back fiasco – or the fact that Harrison's irredeemably twee You Like Me Too Much and Ringo's old Buck Owens cover Act Naturally made the cut at all. You can understand why they chose the song – its lyrics conflate cinema and doleful charm in a way that recalls Starr's celebrated 'lonely guy' sequence in a A Hard Day's Night – but the end result probably seemed more appealing at a time when Starr's acting prowess was being compared, in all seriousness, to

TRACK LISTING

A-SIDE

1. Help
Lennon/McCartney
Sung by Lennon

2. The Night Before
Lennon/McCartney
Sung by McCartney

3. You've Got To Hide Your Love Away
Lennon/McCartney
Sung by Lennon

4. I Need You
Harrison
Sung by Harrison

5. Another Girl
Lennon/McCartney
Sung by McCartney

6. You're Gonna Lose That Girl
Lennon/McCartney
Sung by Lennon

7. Ticket To Ride
Lennon/McCartney
Sung by Lennon

8. Act Naturally
Morrison/Russell
Sung by Starr

B-SIDE

9. It's Only Love
Lennon/McCartney
Sung by Lennon

10. You Like Me Too Much
Harrison
Sung by Harrison

11. Tell Me What You See
Lennon/McCartney
Sung by Lennon

12. I've Just Seen A Face
Lennon/McCartney
Sung by McCartney

13. Yesterday
Lennon/McCartney
Sung by McCartney

14. Dizzy Miss Lizzy
Larry Williams
Sung by Lennon

WHAT THE PAPERS SAID...

For the press, it was get your hankies out time...

"This album could easily be titled 'The Many Moods Of The Beatles'. Showcased in 14 tracks are ballads, rock and roll, folk, country and western and a helping of straight pop. If anyone doesn't know the title song by now they'd better have a good reason why not. You've Got To Hide Your Love Away has John in a very folksy mood; strumming guitars and tambourines are prominent throughout the sad, slow number. Flutes add to the sombre effect. George makes one of his rare vocal appearances on I Need You. The cha cha rhythm carries the song along, but it is not outstanding... It's Only Love is another slow weepie from John; he's almost in tears and you can almost imagine the wet hankies clutched in female paws as they listen to this. There's some wistful guitar work from George adding to the melodrama. And then it's hankies out again, girls, for Yesterday. Paul sings the slow, sombre and painful song and accompanies himself on guitar. An added string quartet lends a mournful quality as Paul tells how he lost his love the day before, and is very, very hurt and alone. My favourite track."

Richard Green, Record Mirror, July 24, 1965.

Mirror

Largest selling colour pop weekly newspaper
No. 228
Every Thursday 6d.
Week ending July 24, 1965
Registered at the G.P.O. as a newspaper

The sleeve of the Beatles' new album "Help," to be issued on August 25th.

'HELP!'

THIS album could easily be titled "The Many Moods Of The Beatles". Showcased in fourteen tracks are ballads, rock and roll, folk, country and western and a helping of straight pop.

The striking cover is plain white with the Beatles spelling out the word "Help" in semaphor with their arms. Their blue and black costumes contrast vividly with the background.

The title song "Help!" opens the LP. If anyone isn't familiar with it by now they'd better have a good reason why not.

Paul's slightly rusty voice takes the lead on "The Night Before", a medium-fast number. George and John provide the chorus and there's a short bluesy guitar break.

"You've Got To Hide Your Love Away" has John in a very folksy mood. Strumming guitars and a tambourine are prominent throughout the sad, slow number. At the very end, flutes add to the sombre effect.

George makes one of his rare vocal appearances on "I Need You". The cha cha rhythm carries the song ... but it is not outstanding. ... other Gir... fast

"Another chart contender is this hot soundtrack from The Beatles' forthcoming film. Included is the current hit, the film's title, and Ticket To Ride. On Yesterday, Paul goes it alone on a Dylan-styled piece of material. Backed by strings he displays a rich, warm ballad style. "

Billboard, August 28, 1965.

SLEEVENOTES

How the semaphore signals didn't quite make sense

Thanks to a budget of £400,000, director Richard Lester's second cinematic outing with The Beatles saw the Fab Four flown to such far flung locations as the Bahamas and the Austrian Alps, with their antics captured in vibrant technicolour. The sleeve for the album, which was part soundtrack, with six cuts taken from the film, was shot by one-time Sunday Times lensman Robert Freeman, who had first met the group in 1963. Never guessing their relationship would be so fertile when he was hired to take the sleeve shot for *With The Beatles*, he continued to work with the group for a further four LPs up until 1965's *Rubber Soul*. Employed as both colour consultant and title designer on the film, it was while on set that Freeman gained inspiration for his penultimate sleeve artwork for The Beatles.

"The Beatles were filming a sequence in Austria where they stood on a skyline in the snow waving their arms to a music playback. From this I had the idea of semaphore spelling out the letters HELP. But when we came to do the shot the arrangement of the arms with those letters didn't look good. So we decided to improvise and ended up with the best graphic positioning of the arms."

The snap, taken in Twickenham film studios, had the group stand on a specially constructed platform in front of a white painted background. "I used a larger format camera to get the detail on their faces because of the distance at which the shot was taken. It was a simple, graphic set-up. But I think the cover would have had more impact with just The Beatles in the white space and no lettering at all. After all, they were at the height of their fame and easily recognisable."

The back cover contained four black and white portraits of each member of the group. Freeman had chosen to capture the band in monochrome, trying to emulate the atmospheric moodiness of the classic jazz LP covers of the time.

Lois Wilson

"On the title track, Lennon felt able for the first time to emerge from behind the standard metaphors of a love song."

Before would be standard beat group fodder, were it not swathed in a disorienting swirl of reverb, which leaves it sounding infinitely more mysterious and alluring. Although Lennon appears to have dashed off the words to It's Only Love in a matter of seconds, the production is strangely futuristic: doused in shimmering effects, the lead guitar lines bear a passing resemblance to sitars, which may not be entirely accidental: a week before it was recorded, The Beatles heard Indian music for the first time on the set of *Help!*

Ultimately, however, *Help!* hinges on two pivotal tracks: one apiece from Lennon and McCartney. Lennon had expressed dissatisfaction with his lot in life before – his contributions to *Beatles For Sale* were uniformly gloomy – but on *Help!*'s title track, he felt able, for the first time, to emerge from behind the standard metaphors of a love song. Even at this distance, the force of his feelings is enough to knock you backwards. It's a testament to *Help!*'s finely-wrought melody and The Beatles' playing – the complex

that of Charlie Chaplin. As *Anthology 2* proved, there was better Lennon and McCartney material left in the can – If You've Got Trouble and a Ringo feature called That Means A Lot – but The Beatles abandoned both when they didn't immediately gel. Whether they didn't have the time to finesse them, or simply couldn't be bothered is a moot point; either way, it is *Help!*'s loss.

However, if you persevere, *Help!* can reveal hidden depths, moments which hint at The Beatles' future. Their minds expanded by marijuana (and possibly LSD), The Beatles seem to have experimented with some of their more throwaway numbers: Tell Me What You See's droning vocal coda has a hint of Rain about it. The guitar on Harrison's I Need You – fading in and out courtesy of a volume pedal – pre-empts the *Revolver*-era use of backward tapes. The Night

Everything's gone gold: Help! sold in bucketloads, but The Beatles would change tactics for its follow-up...

harmonies, Harrison's descending guitar lines, the propulsive drumming – that Lennon felt the need to point out how miserable the song was in interviews years after the event. Desperation has rarely sounded so exciting.

As for McCartney's peerless contribution, analysing Yesterday is not unlike trying to analyse Happy Birthday To You, so deeply is it ingrained in the psyche of anyone with even a passing interest in popular music. It famously came to McCartney in a dream. At the risk of sounding like a participant in the mystic "there are seven levels" gobbledegook that characterised The Beatles' and Dylan's first New York smoking session, it is as if a song that had emerged from the subconscious burrows straight back there (the Rolling Stones' Satisfaction, also literally dreamed up by Keith Richards, has a similar effect).

McCartney spent an age finessing Yesterday, playing it to anyone who would listen and asking their opinion before committing it to tape. It's hard to escape the feeling that if The Beatles had taken the same care over *Help!* as a whole, the result would have been a more satisfying album, rather than a fascinating snapshot. For whatever reason, they did not: a mistake they would not make again. Until *Let It Be*, at least...

PHOTO: TOPHAM PICTUREPOINT; REX

GLAD TO BE UNHAPPY

For legendary producer Trevor Horn, *Help* is a tour de force of emotional songwriting.

There are 12 new songs on *Help!*; 10 are Lennon and McCartney songs, and out of those it sounds like six are John's and the other four are Paul's. So John was in pretty good shape at that point – or else he was pretty unhappy and was using that for his songs: Help, You're Gonna Lose That Girl, You've Got To Hide Your Love Away and It's Only Love (one of my all-time-favourite Beatles songs, which was the B-Side to the Help single).

Help! is a great example of the contrasts in Lennon and McCartney's styles. McCartney's lyrics are good, but relatively straightforward: "we said our goodbyes, were you telling lies..." But on, say, Help!, the words are so good. I love that line, "now those days are gone I'm not so self-assured," that kind of lyric is so rare. I don't agree with the notion that Lennon was hugely influenced by Bob Dylan at this point; I honestly thought that Dylan was more influenced by The Beatles than they were by him.

Obviously, Paul wrote Yesterday; George Martin's string arrangement is lovely and Paul sings it beautifully, although it was never one of my favourite songs at the time.

I think The Beatles had a new lease of life on *Help*. On *Beatles For Sale* they sound a bit tired and battered; *Help!* is much more business-like; the six songs used in the movie, in particular, are great. I can't imagine a situation where a band today could be as prolific as they were in those days. They really were working like dogs!

Paul Trynka

Let it MBE: The Beatles pose with their medals outside Buckingham Palace, October 26, 1965.

What: The Beatles receive their MBEs
Where: Buckingham Palace
When: October 26, 1965

JOINT HONOURS

After rolling one in the bogs at Buckingham Palace, the Fabs were given their gongs. But not everyone was pleased. By Robert Sandall.

MORE THAN 30 YEARS BEFORE TONY Blair opened the doors of Number 10 to Noel Gallagher and Alan McGee, while his spin doctors talked up something called 'Cool Britannia', another Labour premier was anxiously trying to associate his party with youthful style and success.

With his white hair, plump figure and permanently smouldering pipe, Harold Wilson looked about as cluelessly 'square' as any other old pop-fearing dad. But wily politician that he was, Wilson had swiftly realised that The Beatles could assist him in sexing up a Labour party which had spent 13 years out of power. In the spring of 1964, six months before the general election, the Leader of the Opposition had turned up at The Dorchester hotel to present The Beatles with a Variety Club award. Wilson's pretext – that as member for the Huyton constituency near Liverpool, he was a fellow Merseysider – barely disguised his desire to get close to the hottest media property in the land. The fact that none of the group had the slightest idea who he was and that George Harrison mistook him for a 'Mr Dobson' (of Barker and Dobson toffee fame) didn't matter. As the following day's newspapers showed, in massive double page photo spreads, Wilson was the first senior British politician to *get* The Beatles.

Paperboy: Macca gives his MBE the thumbs up.

A year later, as the leader of a country mired in debt and a government pledged to support "the white heat of a technological revolution", he was even keener to draw attention to the beat group which had become Britain's most potent export. The Queen's birthday honours list, compiled as always by her Prime Minister, was Wilson's chosen instrument. And so on June 12, 1965, it was duly announced that, along with 182 military men, captains of industry and other elderly worthies, the four Beatles would each receive the MBE – the most junior of the orders of the British Empire.

The group, just back from their second European tour, were taken completely by surprise and they responded individually and in character. Lennon was sarky: "I thought you had to drive tanks and win wars to get the MBE". Ringo was self-deprecatingly droll: "I'll keep it to dust when I'm old". Harrison drily owned up to his ignorance that such awards could be won "just for playing rock and roll music". And McCartney, always the most eager to please and be pleased, said how marvellous it was and asked what his being an MBE made his dad?

For the next four months, the compatibility of Beatles and MBEs sparked a lively national debate with opinion divided across a recently defined 'generation gap'. Several holders of the award returned them in disgust at being joined by what one old sea dog described as "a gang of nincompoops" – a colonel resigned from the Labour party. But with the group's second feature film Help! conquering cinema box offices over the summer and attracting to its premiere the grooviest royal of the day, the Queen's sister Princess Margaret, The Beatles had pretty much won the argument by the time of their autumn investiture at Buckingham Palace .

Never had a ruling monarch been so thoroughly upstaged by a group of her subjects as was Elizabeth II on October 26. The crowds in the Mall were of coronation proportions; the cries of "God save the Beatles" were not. The arrival of four suited lads from Liverpool, all still only in their early 20s, on the long red carpet in the Palace's white and gold State ballroom was without precedent. It was also the clearest sign yet that The Beatles really had changed the world. At the press conference afterwards they waved their silver crosses and played the cheeky Scousers. McCartney called the Palace "a keen pad" and said the Queen was "like a mum". Ringo said he'd made her laugh by telling her the group had been together for 40 years.

What none of them revealed at the time, perhaps because it didn't happen, was that prior to accepting their awards they'd shared a joint in the royal washroom. The only source of this widely credited but probably apocryphal tale was John Lennon, the Beatle who later sent back his MBE as a protest at Britain's support for the American involvement in Vietnam. Whether the joint was actually present, the story's survival as myth attests to a symbolic truth: The Beatles didn't just visit the Queen's residence on that October afternoon, they took it over.

"Lennon later sent back his MBE as a protest at Britain's support for the American involvement in Vietnam."

The only party in any way injured by Wilson's cunning PR stunt was the person in The Beatles' camp to whom official recognition of this sort mattered most: Brian Epstein. Because Wilson's purpose here was to divert the lustre of the group towards himself and his government, no other intermediaries could be allowed near the event. But it must have niggled this insecure and socially ambitious man to hear Princess Margaret commenting on the newspaper headlines at the new offices of the Birmingham Post and Mail which she happened to be opening on the same day. "I think MBE must stand for Mr Brian Epstein," she remarked merrily.

PHOTOS: HULTON ARCHIVE/ATLANTIC/PICTORIAL PRESS

SEPT 20 - NOV 8, 1965

20 Former drummer for The Beatles, Pete Best, has two singles released in the US – Kansas City on Cameo Records, and I Can't Do Without You Now on Mr Maestro Records.

21 Brian Epstein's Evening of Popular Music is presented at the Royal Festival Hall, London.

25 The Beatles' Saturday morning cartoon show begins in the US.

26 At the International Film Festival in Rio, Help! wins the Grand Prix.

OCTOBER 65

2 Brian Epstein collects an Edison Award for *Beatles For Sale* at the Grand Gala du Disques, Amsterdam.

3 The Beatles consider, and reject, a script entitled A Talent For Loving, which was proposed for their next film.

4 John and Paul attend a recording of the song Eight Days A Week by singer Alma Cogan.

7 Harrison is photographed at home in Esher, Surrey for a feature in The Beatles Book magazine.

9 Yesterday starts a four-week run at Number 1 in the US. The Beatles attend a party at the home of Lionel Bart, to celebrate his musical Twang!.

11 McCartney attends the recording of Marianne Faithfull's version of Yesterday, at Decca Studios, London.

12 Recording of *Rubber Soul* begins, with Run For Your Life and Norwegian Wood.

13 Drive My Car is recorded at Abbey Road Studios. It is the first time that The Beatles record past midnight.

14 Epstein is in New York to approve the film of the Shea Stadium concert.

16 Work is carried out on Day Tripper and If I Needed Someone.

18 Work is continued on If I Needed Someone and In My Life.

19 The Beatles' Third Christmas Record is recorded.

20 Work begins on We Can Work It Out at Abbey Road. Yesterday is certified as a gold single in the US.

21 Norwegian Wood is remade and work starts on Nowhere Man.

22 Work continues on Nowhere Man.

24 Work starts on I'm Looking Through You at Abbey Road.

26 The Beatles inhale deeply in the Buckingham Palace loos before being awarded their MBEs.

28 Recording of We Can Work It Out continues at Abbey Road.

29 Beatles record new vocal track for We Can Work It Out.

NOVEMBER 65

1–2 TV special The Music Of Lennon And McCartney (left) is recorded at Granada TV Centre, Manchester.

3 Michelle is recorded at Abbey Road.

4 What Goes On is recorded at Abbey Road Studios.

6 At Abbey Road, I'm Looking Through You is remade.

8 Harrison's song Think For Yourself is recorded at Abbey Road. At 3am, the band continue to record their third Christmas record.

10 The Word and I'm Looking Through You are recorded.

11 Girl and You Won't See Me are recorded – *Rubber Soul* (being pressed, below) is now complete.

12 An Italy-only album, *The Beatles In Italy*, is released.

15 George Martin completes post-production work on *Rubber Soul*.

16 Paul goes to see Gene Pitney play in Slough.

23 The Beatles spend the day making promotional films at Twickenham.

25 Harrods is closed to the public for three hours to enable The Beatles to do their Christmas shopping.

27 McCartney goes to see Manfred Mann, The Yardbirds and The Scaffold play in East Ham, London.

29 In Aeolian Hall, London, The Beatles are interviewed for the Christmas edition of BBC radio show Saturday Club.

DECEMBER 65

2 Top Of The Pops premieres new promo films (below) for the single, Day Tripper/We Can Work It Out.

3 The single Day Tripper/We Can Work It Out, and the album *Rubber Soul* are released in the UK. The Beatles set off on their final UK tour from the Odeon Cinema, Glasgow, Scotland.

5 Day Tripper enters the UK singles chart at Number 1 and, on the same day, *Rubber Soul* hits the Number 1 spot in the album chart. The Beatles play the Liverpool Empire – it's the last time they play their home town.

6 The single Day Tripper/We Can Work It Out, and the album *Rubber Soul* are released in the US.

12 The Beatles' last UK tour ends at the Capitol Cinema, Cardiff, Wales.

15 The Beatles are seen on TV show Here Comes The Pops.

16 The Music Of Lennon And McCartney runs on TV in the London area only. It shows nationally the following night.

21 John is visited for three days by his father Alfred, who had abandoned him as a child.

24 Lennon gives his MBE to his Aunt Mimi for safekeeping. *Rubber Soul* earns a gold disc award in the US.

25 While driving to dinner in London, Harrison proposes to Patti Boyd (right). She accepts. Top Of The Pops shows clips of the group performing I Feel Fine, Help!, Ticket To Ride and Day Tripper.

26 Enjoying Christmas with his father, Paul falls off a moped and sustains a five-inch cut to his mouth.

30 McCartney gives Paul's Christmas Record, manufactured as a limited edition of four copies, to Lennon, Harrison, Starr and Jane Asher.

31 *Beatles 65* is certified as a gold album in the US.

What: Recording Rubber Soul
Where: Abbey Road Studios
When: From October 12, 1965

HIGH TIMES

It may have been the same old Fabs that went into the studio to record their 'pot record', but what came out was a whole new sound. By Mark Lewisohn.

Rubber Soul was the transition. There it sits, between the R&B-tinged pop of *Help!* and the breathtaking kaleidoscope that was *Revolver*. All three albums were released in the space of a year, a deal of work and rate of progress awesome in any context. Mop-tops no longer, at least not in their own eyes, The Beatles had become a studio band before anyone even knew what that meant. While they may have come to despise the commercial pressures put upon them by EMI (and Brian Epstein) they flourished under them, for to flinch in the face of a challenge was simply not in The Beatles' make-up.

For easy definition, *Rubber Soul* is 'the pot album'. Dylan had turned on The Beatles in 1964, and their considerable intake throughout the filming of *Help!* earlier in 1965 is well established. The cover photo – yet another revolutionary image, naturally – shows the guys standing among rhododendron bushes; leaves of a more variegated, illegal kind would have been apposite.

Ringo has since said that The Beatles preferred not to work high, but that they took their high experiences into the studio. This album is the proof. The vision, the articulation, the knowingness – all are rooted in the weed, but the manifestation is clear-headed, economical and purposeful. The Beatles were suddenly painting from an extended palette, applying new shades and textures to new sounds. The album is a particular triumph for John Lennon. Under the influence of Dylan, dope and the first few lumps of acid-imbued Tate & Lyle, his creativity was in full flow, marked by songs of maturity, depth and intelligence – Norwegian Wood, Girl, In My Life, Nowhere Man. Thanks to John himself, this later went down as his 'Fat Elvis' period.

"The Beatles said they preferred not to work high, but that they took their high experiences into the studio."

Not merely a collection of 14 songs but an entity in itself, *Rubber Soul* was a new kind of album; for lyrical wisdom and sheer savoir-faire it anticipates *Revolver* and is sometimes its better. Yet, ordained as they were by EMI to fill a million stockings at Christmas 1965, it is all the more remarkable to reflect that The Beatles didn't even begin its recording until the middle of October, by which point only a few of the songs were written. Weekend and late-night sessions – the latter soon became the Beatles' norm – were a necessity. The whole thing was polished off in under a month.

Such autumn almanac particulars aside, it is the songs and musical invention on *Rubber Soul* that still startle, and the album remains as good an indication as any of how the Lennon-McCartney partnership had evolved. Compared to the head-to-head collaborations of, say, From Me To You and She Loves You, they were scarcely writing together by this point, yet each was acutely aware of and able to contribute to the other's work. In this period, The Beatles were still tending to record songs in the order they were written, a pattern that had emerged in 1963–64 when the cover versions on several albums prove how many original songs short they were. For the fuller *Rubber Soul* experience, programme the simultaneous single Day Tripper/We Can Work It Out into the mix and follow the chronology. Now one can see that John revealed In My Life to his band-mates on a Monday, they took Tuesday off, and on Wednesday Paul brought in We Can Work It Out. John then goes home to Weybridge and comes in the following afternoon with Nowhere Man. When John pulled Norwegian Wood out of his bag, Paul's response was Drive My Car, witty and stylish and, in its own fashion, every bit as sardonic. Here were two young men about town, at their absolute coolest and each with a sibling competitive streak a mile wide, battling at the highest level. We were all winners.

Not, of course, that the other two Fabs were mere sidemen. Without frills but with a definite and unique style, and ideal temperament, Ringo was vital to the creative mix, and George's guitar work on *Rubber Soul* was excellent from first cut to last. This was the album when George's songwriting began to emerge. He'd forced only two numbers on to the preceding five albums, here he had two shots in one. It was always George's misfortune that his earliest songwriting efforts were held up to global scrutiny – and compared, too, to the by-now finessed pieces of John and Paul. While neither If I Needed Someone or Think For Yourself rivals In My Life for vision or complexity, they are at home in the setting. They were also the last Harrisongs before George, with LSD in his system and new-found spiritualism in his soul, truly found himself.

Flush with the influences of America and yet still resolutely British, and so very Scouse, *Rubber Soul* drips confidence and delicious arrogance. In My Life, such a mature piece of songwriting, ranks as close to perfection as it is possible to achieve. Girl positively aches, and yet it is also witty, with its 'tit tit tit' backing vocals and sharp intakes of breath that represented either sexual heavy-breathing or the deep inhalation of a joint, or both. The harmonies throughout *Rubber Soul* are in full flow, too, especially on Ringo's vocal track, What Goes On, one of The Beatles' best Rutles cover versions. As a rock and roll band whose musical influences were so much broader than their genre, The Beatles could also record a song like Michelle with absolute sincerity, recognising and enhancing its beauty.

In The Complete Beatles Recording Sessions I reproduced George Martin's scribbled running order ideas for *Beatles For Sale*. No such document for the other albums seems to have survived, and one gets the firm impression that with *Rubber Soul* The Beatles were, for the first time, much more closely involved in deciding how their music should be presented. It was another shift away from the 'good' old days of Tin Pan Alley, towards major freedom for all bands.

PHOTOS: HULTON ARCHIVE

Head music: (above) McCartney and Harrison play to the attentive George Martin, October, 1965; (left) John recording *Rubber Soul*.

Flowered up: Lennon photographed by Robert Whitaker (1965) and coloured by Martin Sharp.

The

Psychedelic Experience

Experimenting with drugs and oriental religion not only changed The Beatles and their approach to music, it changed them as people. As a result, the Fabs helped usher in a new Day-Glo era. By Ian MacDonald.

DURING THE LAST FIVE YEARS OF THE '60S, it seemed to many fans of The Beatles that the group was somehow above and beyond the ordinary world: ahead of the game and orchestrating things. So in tune were they with the spirit of the times that they sometimes seemed almost godlike, especially to young listeners. In fact, The Beatles, while very observant and in some ways prescient, weren't so much causing the great social and psychological changes of that era as mirroring them. The key was that they picked up on certain special ideas before most of their immediate competitors, when these ideas were still at an elite stage of development. Moreover, by selling millions of records, the group magnified what it reflected, exporting elite trends and concepts to the intelligent and enquiring side of the mainstream.

"The Beatles weren't so much causing the great social and psychological changes of that era as mirroring them."

The most striking example of this is probably The Beatles' interest in oriental religion, which turned an interest shared by only a few in the West in 1965 into a subject of discussion right across Western society within two years. The group didn't invent the Western interest in Eastern thought, which had begun as an elite pursuit in the late 18th century; however, the popular (and generally sincere) fascination with oriental wisdom which ensued in the late '60s and thereafter owes almost everything to The Beatles in their role as the cultural antennae of the mainstream. It was their absorption in Indian religion which started the spiritual revival of the late '60s, just as it was their interest in indeterminacy which took the use of randomization in avant-garde art of the time from the elite to the general audience via the chance elements in their work, some of which (eg, Revolution 9) were in themselves explicitly and uncompromisingly experimental.

Bruce Springsteen has said that Elvis liberated people's bodies while Dylan liberated their minds. The Beatles, though, did far more mind-liberating than Dylan, by virtue of their greater sales and because they worked in simpler, less essentially sceptical ways. Dylan may have opened up a university course of reference points for a non-campus audience (eg, "Ezra Pound and TS Eliot, they're fighting in the captain's tower", etc), but his Zen Absurdism encouraged people not to take these references seriously. However, when The Beatles visually namechecked their cultural icons on the cover of *Sgt Pepper*, they meant to encourage popular curiosity. When Paul McCartney dropped "Pataphysics" into the lyric for Maxwell's Silver Hammer, he was partly having a private joke but was also keen to prompt interest in the anarchic French playwright Alfred Jarry.

Dylan, furthermore, was never interested in the 'alternative society' proposed by the counter-culture of the late '60s, whereas The Beatles took a great deal of their inspiration from that source during those years. The Summer Of Love of 1967 wasn't created by The Beatles but it was certainly in part prepared by them through the medium of their barrier-breaking LP *Revolver* and, indeed, by earlier tracks like The Word and Rain. The counter-culture's sudden efflorescence from elite status in 1965 to a subject of discussion in the mainstream of Western society in 1967 was without doubt partially caused by The Beatles' mirroring interest in it at that time. Psychedelic tracks like Tomorrow Never Knows and A Day In The Life spread the idea of mind-expansion from a fringe concern to the centre of popular interest, while the psychedelic visual style was nowhere more vividly transmitted, even at second-hand, than by The Beatles in their record sleeves, clothes, hairstyles and publicity material, not to mention songs such as Lucy In The Sky With Diamonds, Being For The Benefit Of Mr Kite and I Am The Walrus.

Smokin'! The Beatles were "seasoned potheads" by the time of Help!.

While they didn't invent the counter-culture, The Beatles were certainly the first pop/rock band to allow the influence of LSD, the movement's main sacrament, a central part in their output, thereby to a large extent inventing the psychedelic style in music. Though they took their visual psychedelia from artists and designers who were already working to convey the acid experience, The Beatles were the first to use the panoply of the psychedelic recording studio: Indian drones and scales, backwards tapes, phasing and other ideas – features soon taken up by others in the pop world (most notably by The Rolling Stones in *Their Satanic Majesties Request* – quite a departure from what had gone before).

WELL IT'S CERTAINLY NOT TOBACCO

Without any doubt, then, The Beatles helped to change the world during the psychedelic years. They did this by being open to existing elite ideas, by themselves being changed by these trends and concepts, and by almost immediately allowing these changes to affect their work. The first step in this process was their initiation into marijuana by Bob Dylan in New York in August 1964. By the time of their next project, the film and album *Help!*, they were seasoned potheads. However, they didn't begin to allow mind-expanding drugs to explicitly affect their work until after they (specifically, Lennon and Harrison) had encountered LSD in spring 1965. Starr and McCartney held off from trying acid for some while, fearing the transformative force of this powerful hallucinogenic drug. For McCartney, however, marijuana was, for the time being, quite enough in terms of inner liberation. It was through smoking dope that he came to see himself as an artist rather than as a moptop pop star – a fact which sparked his many interests in the artistic avant-garde of the mid-'60s, interests which actually ran ahead of those of both Lennon and Harrison.

THE LEAST PERSONALLY CHANGED OF THE BEATLES during 1965-67 was Ringo Starr. He was the oldest in the group and the most settled. His contributions to psychedelia – the drum and percussion parts to tracks such as Rain, A Day In The Life – were no doubt affected by the stimulus of drugs but were also evolved through interaction with The Beatles' engineer Geoff Emerick in his quest for new drum sounds. Much of the distinctive Starr drum style of the psychedelic years comes from the effects of varispeed: recording drums at a faster speed and then slowing them down, producing lower tones, greater weight, and making cymbals seem hazy and impressionistic. Yet his new-found liberation in playing came as much from him, via his drug-sensitized reactions, as it did from the requirements of the new sort of song the others were writing and from the influence of the nascent rock style.

"It was through smoking dope that Paul came to see himself as an artist rather than as a moptop pop star."

McCartney, as Barry Miles has extensively documented in Paul McCartney: Many Years From Now (1997), was the original avant-garde Beatle, long before Lennon came to occupy that role in tandem with Yoko Ono. It was Paul who first came into contact with the counter-culture and the artistic 'underground' of the time, via his contacts with figures such as the cultured family of Jane Asher, the bookish Miles, and the gallery owners John Dunbar and Robert Fraser. As such, he was steeped in Surrealism and Absurdism, in kinetic sculptures, experimental films, beat poetry, and "happenings", and in the associated anti-establishment state of mind. McCartney was well ahead of Lennon, his colleague being married and confined to his house in Weybridge while the bachelor McCartney lived it up in London's art circles. Not until early 1968 did Lennon began to fully catch up in these areas of interest.

On the other hand, Lennon and McCartney were abreast of each other in their awareness of the universal love motif associated with LSD. Though McCartney didn't take LSD until late 1966, he got the message through a combination of his own pot-smoking and listening to Lennon and Harrison. McCartney recalls Day Tripper, recorded in October 1965, as a song about tripping. Since he hadn't tried acid then, he can only be using the drug terminology of the embryonic acid counter-culture to indicate something more generalised and conceptual: the new state of mind associated with the acid revelation – the Universal Love vibe. McCartney refers to Day Tripper as "a tongue-in-cheek song about... somebody who was committed only in part to the idea – whereas we saw ourselves as full-time trippers, fully-committed

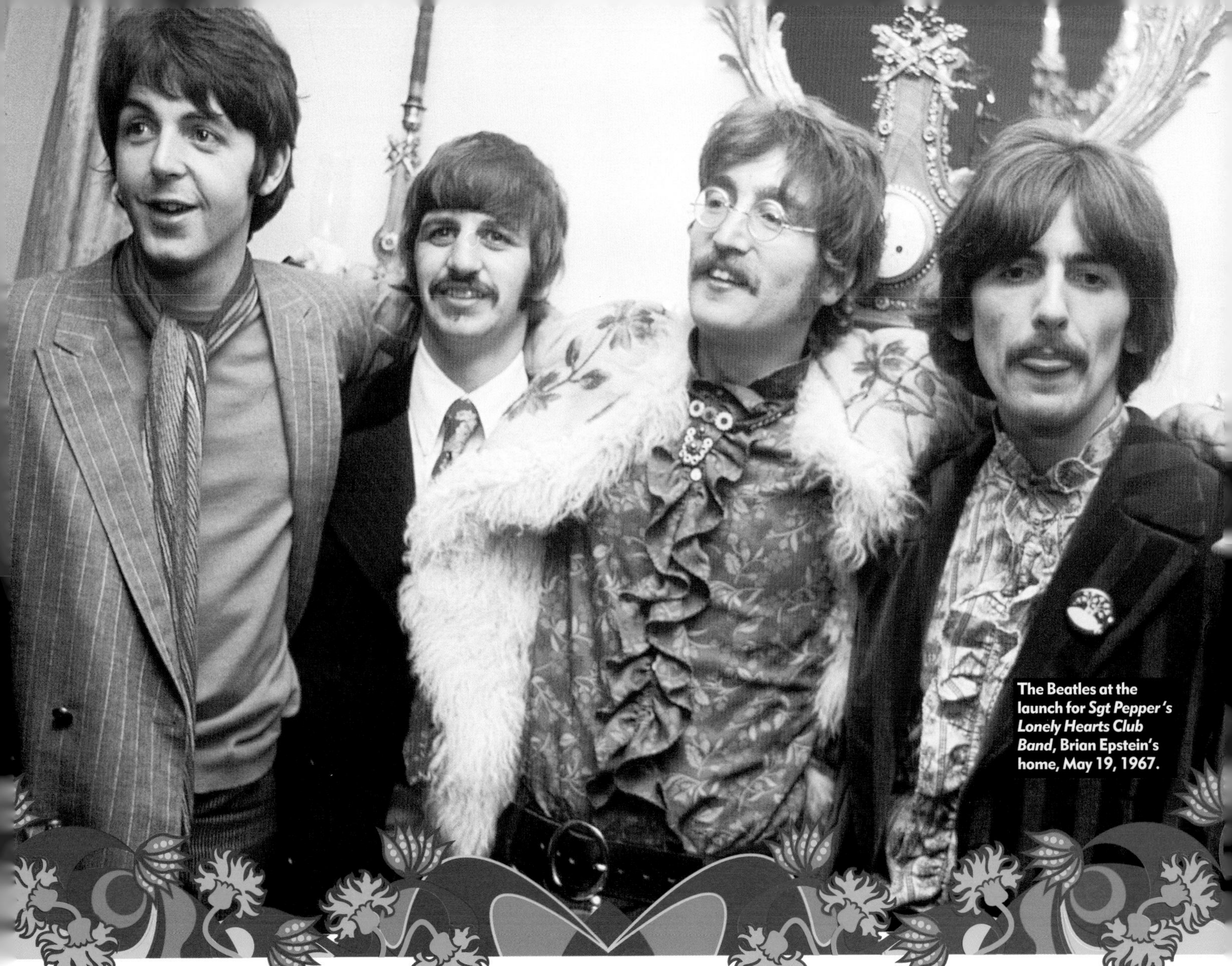

The Beatles at the launch for ***Sgt Pepper's Lonely Hearts Club Band***, Brian Epstein's home, May 19, 1967.

drivers". The subject of Day Tripper is an egoist ("a girl," explains McCartney, "who thought she was it"), egoism being the unenlightened opposite of Universal Love. A month after Day Tripper, Lennon and McCartney co-wrote The Word, celebrating it by smoking a joint and using coloured crayons to make a sort of psychedelic illuminated manuscript of the lyric with its explicit anticipation of the assertion "that love is all and love is everyone" in the acid-inspired Tomorrow Never Knows six months later.

McCARTNEY, THROUGH HIS CONTACTS WITH International Times, knew as much, if not more than, Lennon about the burgeoning counter-culture and its LSD ideology of universal love. He also knew more than Lennon about the phenomena of "be-ins" and "happenings" which formed the overlap between the acid-inspired hippies and the avant-garde artists of London and New York. McCartney was musically the most alert and inventive of The Beatles during the psychedelic period; not that any of the band's psychedelic masterpieces were primarily written by him, but that his input into them was so passionate and quick on the uptake. Good examples are Taxman and Tomorrow Never Knows, which share a remarkable McCartney guitar solo (on the latter, spooled backwards in a different key). In Taxman, the guitar solo is far beyond anything Harrison could have done in terms of content and attack in the pseudo-Indian style, while the bass part is startling in its own right and the basis of the entire rhythmic feel of the track. On Tomorrow Never Knows, McCartney takes the raw material of Mark 1, Lennon's first thoughts now available on *Anthology 2*, and turns it into a dazzling aural happening, possibly suggesting the chord change, certainly coming up with the drum pattern (and locked-in one-note/octave bass riff), adding all the celebrated tape-loops, and, as already mentioned, furnishing the guitar solo from Taxman for exploitation backwards.

One of the leading motifs of The Beatles' psychedelic period was the theme of carnival – a multicoloured explosion of street-level popular culture against which the grey establishment of the time was seen in repressive contrast. Again, McCartney was ahead of his fellow Beatles in responding to this idea, so central to the counter-culture. This can be seen in songs as various as Yellow Submarine, Good Day Sunshine, Penny Lane, Sgt Pepper's Lonely Hearts Club Band, Magical Mystery Tour, All Together Now and Why Don't We Do It In The Road. As Lennon observed, "Paul said, 'Come and see the show'; I said, 'I read the news today, oh boy'." Rightly understood in this antithesis, the "show" was McCartney's sense of the carnivalesque. (It was, after all, he who orchestrated the other Beatles into ad-libbing the as-yet-unreleased aural happening Carnival Of Light, made for a mixed media event of the same name at London's Roundhouse theatre early in 1967.)

Typical of McCartney's attitude to his cultural and pharmaceutical excursions of 1965-67 was an inquisitive and acquisitive point of view. He thirsted for new ideas and stimuli as potential new strings to his bow as an artist. A key song in this respect is Got To Get You Into My Life, which, he says, is "an ode to pot, like someone else might write an ode to chocolate or a good claret". Many of McCartney's other songs of the time – For No One, Sgt Pepper's Lonely Heart's Club Band, Honey Pie – employ novel instrumentations, all of them "acquired" as a result of his endlessly curious cultural intake. For example, he originally wanted the string arrangement of Eleanor Rigby to adopt the style of Vivaldi, to whose music Jane Asher had drawn his attention. Similarly, he requested a high trumpet for the solo on Penny Lane after hearing such a passage in one of Bach's Brandenburg concertos on television.

PHOTOS: PICTORIAL PRESS/REX/ROBERT WHITAKER/HULTON ARCHIVE

Harrison in October 1966, while painting his bungalow in Esher.

Lennon's psychedelic Rolls Royce, 1967.

"The impresario of the band, McCartney was the live wire behind most of The Beatles' psychedelic rejoicing."

Eventually, McCartney's concept of himself as an artist – able to use techniques from jazz and the serious avant-garde as well as, in true Pop Art style, the classical and music-hall references which fuse in *Sgt Pepper's Lonely Hearts Club Band* – burgeoned in his novel film-music hybrid Magical Mystery Tour, the half-dreamed semi-failure created towards the end of the Summer Of Love. The impresario of the band, McCartney was the live wire behind most of The Beatles' psychedelic rejoicing. By contrast, Lennon retained a sceptical, querying edge to his work of this period, while Harrison's deep fascination with Indian religion took him into a completely different philosophical outlook. Yet McCartney, too, looked deeper in his work of the psychedelic era – for example, in Eleanor Rigby, She's Leaving Home, A Day In The Life and The Fool On The Hill – while even a song as comfortably ordinary as When I'm 64 contains a sting in the tail in the lyric of its final verse.

If McCartney is the great celebrator among The Beatles, the great quester and questioner is usually said to be Lennon. Certainly, he is the main author of nearly all of The Beatles' psychedelic classics: Tomorrow Never Knows, I'm Only Sleeping, Rain, She Said She Said, And Your Bird Can Sing, Strawberry Fields Forever, Lucy In The Sky With Diamonds, Being For The Benefit Of Mr Kite, I Am The Walrus and Across The Universe. (He also co-composed A Day In The Life and Baby You're A Rich Man.) Although he knew less than McCartney about other musical styles, Lennon, through his sheer originality as a writer, evoked extraordinary soundscapes from his colleagues and George Martin. The classic cello-and-sitar fusion style, brought to an apogee by Harrison in Within You Without You, was invented by Martin for Lennon's Strawberry Fields Forever and recapitulated in I Am The Walrus. The calliope cut-up soundtrack of Being For The Benefit Of Mr Kite represents another outstanding feat of production wizardry by Martin in response to Lennon's imagination.

Lennon, though, was more engrossed by psychedelic drugs than McCartney. His development during 1965-67 is essentially introverted, following his inner fortunes rather than, like McCartney, extrovertedly engaging with the outside world. His encounter, at London's Indica book shop in late March 1966, with Timothy Leary's The Psychedelic Experience initiated an exploration of alternative realities which changed his character profoundly, bringing out the peaceful side of him and aligning him with Harrison's deeper and more detailed interest in Indian religion. The middle eight of We Can Work It Out shows Lennon's understanding of the link between universal love and the great Beyond glimpsed in oriental philosophy: "life is very short and there's no time for fussing and fighting, my friend". His own commitment to the idea of universal love – of being a "full-time tripper, a fully-committed driver" – is embodied most poignantly in the "I'd love to turn you on"

Performing Hello, Goodbye, Saville Theatre, London, November 10, 1967.

refrain of A Day In The Life, co-written with McCartney. Yet his sceptical, querying eye was always open, informing most of his aforementioned psychedelic classics.

In the end, although for a while he shared Harrison's interest in Indian religion, Lennon stayed the sceptic, rebounding to the opposite pole of outright dismissal of the transcendental in Sexy Sadie and his first solo LP. As such, he ended up closer to McCartney. In this respect, Lennon's belated interest in mid-'60s avant-garde London is significant in that the key to the underground outlook was that it was chiefly anti-establishment. There was not much talk about God in the English underground, which was essentially secular or Zen-sceptical in the tradition of the Beat movement. This renders Harrison's initiative into Hindu mysticism all the more unique, even though, for about six months (between Bangor and Rishikesh), all four Beatles were happy to be publicly identified with such an interest. Lennon, though he went as far as appearing on a television show with Harrison to promote Transcendental Meditation, did not retain his affiliation; indeed, he rejected it.

Despite his ever-lurking cynicism, Lennon refused to follow the Revolutionary Left in calling for civil disorder without first seeing a programme of positive action with which to balance the implied negation and destruction. He and Ono wanted to see something constructive come from the counter-culture, insisting that one must not only be *against* outmoded things but *for* something with which to replace them. His solution was the Dadaist peace-art of his post-psychedelic period. In this way, Lennon remained faithful to the abiding optimism of The Beatles' work – the "can do"/"love will conquer all" spirit which lay at the heart of the band's carnival style.

HARRISON, BY CONTRAST, STAYED TRUE TO THE precepts of Hindu religion which appear to have impacted on him with great force, probably in conjunction with LSD, early in 1965. Certainly acid endowed him with a more than conceptual experience of the Universal Love motif. Speaking about this 35 years later, Harrison recalled: "It was like a very concentrated version of the best feeling I'd ever had in my whole life. I fell in love, not with anything or anybody in particular, but with *everything*." This, perhaps, is the experience he later recorded in the grandiose Try Some, Buy Some on *Living In The Material World* (1973): "Not a thing did I have, not a thing did I see/Till I called on your love and your love came to me". Such a sweeping attitude underlies, in a fundamentally serious way, almost everything that Harrison did after late 1965. Although not all of his lyrics of 1965-73 have a transcendental twist, he speaks often in terms of profound and simple spiritual reciprocity: "My love belongs to who can see it", "The Lord helps those that help themselves/And the law says whatever you do is going to come right back on you", etc. With a few exceptions, the "you" he addresses in his songs is both God and, at least potentially, the listener. It's an impressively whole-cloth point of view with very few conceptual creases in it.

Harrison said that when he first heard Indian music it seemed somehow familiar to him. Possibly he was thinking in terms of reincarnation. Whatever the truth, it's certainly fair to say that Within You Without You, the philosophical centre-piece of *Sgt Pepper*, is a remarkable achievement for someone who'd been exposed to the conventions of Hindustani classical music for little longer than 18 months. The song's opening line (a single sentence extending over 20 bars) shows its author entirely absorbed in the idea of Karma, the Hindu law by which the soul is stubbornly bound to existence by its attachment to the things of material life (and, reciprocally, unbound by its detachment from the same things). Karma is a constant theme of Harrison's work between Within You Without You and *Living In The Material World*. So completely did he integrate Hindu religion into his life from the outset that his 1966 interview with International Times speaks of little else.

As for the psychedelic theme, Harrison ➳

PHOTOS: REX/HULTON ARCHIVE/ROBERT WHITAKER

Psychedelia found its way onto the walls of the Apple Boutique and (right) the interior of George's Esher home.

studio as part of the palette. *Revolver* was not quite the first record to do this; yet while The Beach Boys' *Pet Sounds* was arguably the first pop album to be nigh on impossible to reproduce live, *Revolver* was the first complete step into the new sound-world of studio pop/rock. It was the first Beatles album to be a unified work of art in its own right rather than merely a set of songs in various moods and styles. (This did not prevent its artistic integrity being violated in America by Capitol, who pulled three tracks off it to fill out *Yesterday and Today*.)

Notwithstanding its track-for-track quality, which these days makes *Revolver* a more common choice as The Beatles' best album than *Sgt Pepper*, it's *Sgt Pepper* that most authentically conjures up the elusive 'spirit of '67'. It contains both the more brilliantly colourful and the deeper music. There's an emotional seriousness, a weight, about songs like Within You Without You, A Day In The Life and She's Leaving Home (even With A Little Help From My Friends and Getting Better), which one finds in *Revolver* only on Eleanor Rigby, I Want To Tell You and Tomorrow Never Knows. Which is to say: there is more feeling in *Sgt Pepper* than in the quick-firing acuity of *Revolver*. Embedded in its time in a way that *Revolver* isn't, *Sgt Pepper*, appropriately approached, continues to be an active generator of "period vibes". If you want a contact high with the spirit of '67, a taste of the Universal Love vibe as it was then widely felt, *Sgt Pepper* is the place to go.

After *Sgt Pepper*, the only option left for The Beatles' psychedelic style was to continue to fill out the carnival picture, recruiting new "turns" to the performance. *Magical Mystery Tour* is perhaps a drug-inspired step too far – but only just. The best of its music compares to *Sgt Pepper* in combining dazzle-factor with depth of feeling. But what brought the band's essentially drug-based mind-expanding phase to an end was their encounter with Transcendental Meditation and the Maharishi Mahesh Yogi. First, LSD was replaced by meditation and marijuana: the kaleidoscopic quality departed to be replaced by something less starry-eyed. Second, TM was followed, in three of The Beatles, by a recoil to ordinary life. (In Harrison, meditation moved on to his experience of Krishna Consciousness in 1969.) In other words, the drug-based sense of enchantment ceased and the group awoke to its adult diversity – and an almost immediate outbreak of divisive bickering.

The Beatles' psychedelic music represents a state of mind different from ordinary reality: a magical, all-beautiful, all-loving vision in which opposites are peacefully reconciled. Whether that state of mind is ultimately a delusion is up to the listener. ■

"Revolver was the first Beatles LP to be a unified work of art rather than a set of songs in various moods and styles."

soon abandoned LSD in favour of more secure ground: meditation. It's All Too Much is a sort of farewell to acid; after that, he allowed himself no more than marijuana. In a similar fashion, Blue Jay Way is a sort of farewell to psychedelia (unless we are to include Long Long Long from the White Album). In effect, it was George Harrison who inspired the West's mainstream acquaintance with Hindu religion and created the late-'60s' so-called Spiritual Revival. While the rest of The Beatles soon passed through their Hindu phases, Harrison's allegiance was life-long. This singlehanded responsibility for such a fundamental cultural sea-change is an abiding testimony to Harrison's importance as a counter-cultural figure, albeit that he would have felt uncomfortable being described as such.

The Beatles' psychedelic era – which begins with Tomorrow Never Knows (having been previewed in outline six months earlier in The Word) and ends, more or less, with Across The Universe in February 1968 – introduced a new sort of love along with a new sort of music. Clearly, the main inspiration was LSD (or, in McCartney's case, marijuana). Mind-expanding drugs engendered a renaissance for The Beatles which they probably would not have realised so rapidly otherwise, if at all. It was not surprising that they regarded drugs as crucial. By agreement of all four Beatles, *Revolver* was originally to be called *Abracadabra*, but this was dropped when it was found that someone had already used it. The implication of this alternative title is that The Beatles plus psychedelics equalled ("hey presto") a new world of sound-feeling.

It was not surprising that the group considered *Revolver* to be a discrete step forward in their work, unlike anything they'd done before. The most obvious aspect of this was that little of the album's music could be performed live. It was, in effect, sonically *painted* using the recording

PHOTOS: REX

Magical, all loving... deluded? The Our World press call, June 1967.

Photo:Topfoto

Stretching The Boundaries

Rubber Soul was the first Beatles album to expose the band's wonderful sense of adventure. Richard Williams explains how sex, drugs and spirituality began to turn the Fab Four on.

By the winter of 1965, we were all a little bit wiser. On the face of it, *Rubber Soul* was another 'Fab Four' LP completed and released in time to catch the Christmas market, a tradition established by *With The Beatles* in 1963 and continued by *Beatles For Sale* a year later. Those albums had soundtracked the teenaged nation's winter parties. As wax guttered from candles stuck in Chianti bottles and horizontal forms littered every available surface, they tended to get left on automatic replay to repeat themselves over and over again. *Rubber Soul* took on that valuable role as a social lubricant, too, but it had something more besides.

The hint of distortion in Robert Freeman's low-angled cover portrait, echoed in the choice of proto-psychedelic lettering for the title, gave a clue to the nature of the music within, for *Rubber Soul* was the first of their albums to expose their sense of adventure to general view. Almost from the start they had been been noted for their inquisitiveness, but this was where they really started to blend their discoveries into something genuinely original, and also where they learnt to use drugs, sex and an interest in the spiritual quest as components of their songwriting – while still maintaining the brevity and clarity of the classic pop song.

To open the album, Drive My Car borrowed from impeccable sources. Guitar and bass doubled the riff under the vocal just like Steve Cropper and Donald 'Duck' Dunn were doing behind Sam and Dave in the Stax studio. The use of a tambourine to take the place of a hi-hat or a ride cymbal over Ringo's crisp backbeat rimshots was pure Motown, going all the way back to Barrett Strong's Money (That's What I Want), one of their early favourites. The lyric, however, borrowed from nobody. A dry commentary on stardom and seduction, its light irony came from deep inside a place with which only they were familiar – their own experience as the most famous, fawned-on and lusted-after entertainers on the planet.

> "The hint of distortion in the low-angled cover portrait gave a clue to the nature of the music within."

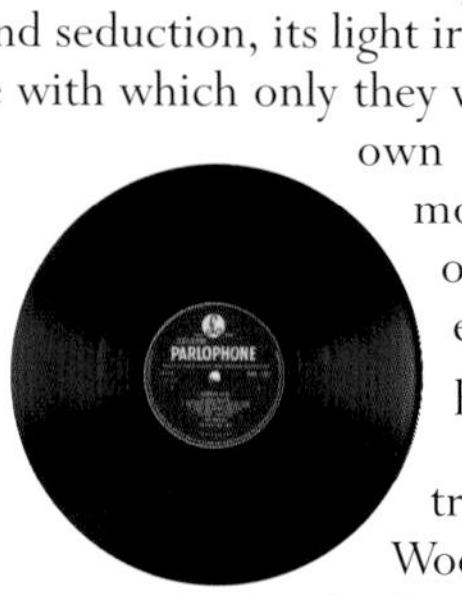

When the needle tracked to Norwegian Wood for the first time, the listener's attention was divided between its two main characteristics – the silvery twang of Harrison's sitar, used for the first time in place of a lead guitar, and the gobsmacking erotic wryness of opening line: "I once had a girl or should I say she once had me". It was obvious where the sitar was leading, particularly to anyone who had been paying attention to John Coltrane's experiments with the hypnotic, incantatory effect of Indian drones and modes. As for the vividly poetic description of the singer's slightly dazed reaction to a one-night stand, we were not to know for a while longer that John's marriage was destined for a premature conclusion.

By this time, two songs in, it was obvious that The Beatles had moved on, beyond even the primal cry of *Help!* and the poised accomplishment of Yesterday earlier in the year. You Won't See Me may be one of *Rubber Soul*'s most

PHOTO: CAMERA PRESS

All change: With Norwegian Wood, George introduced the sitar to The Beatles' sound for the first time.

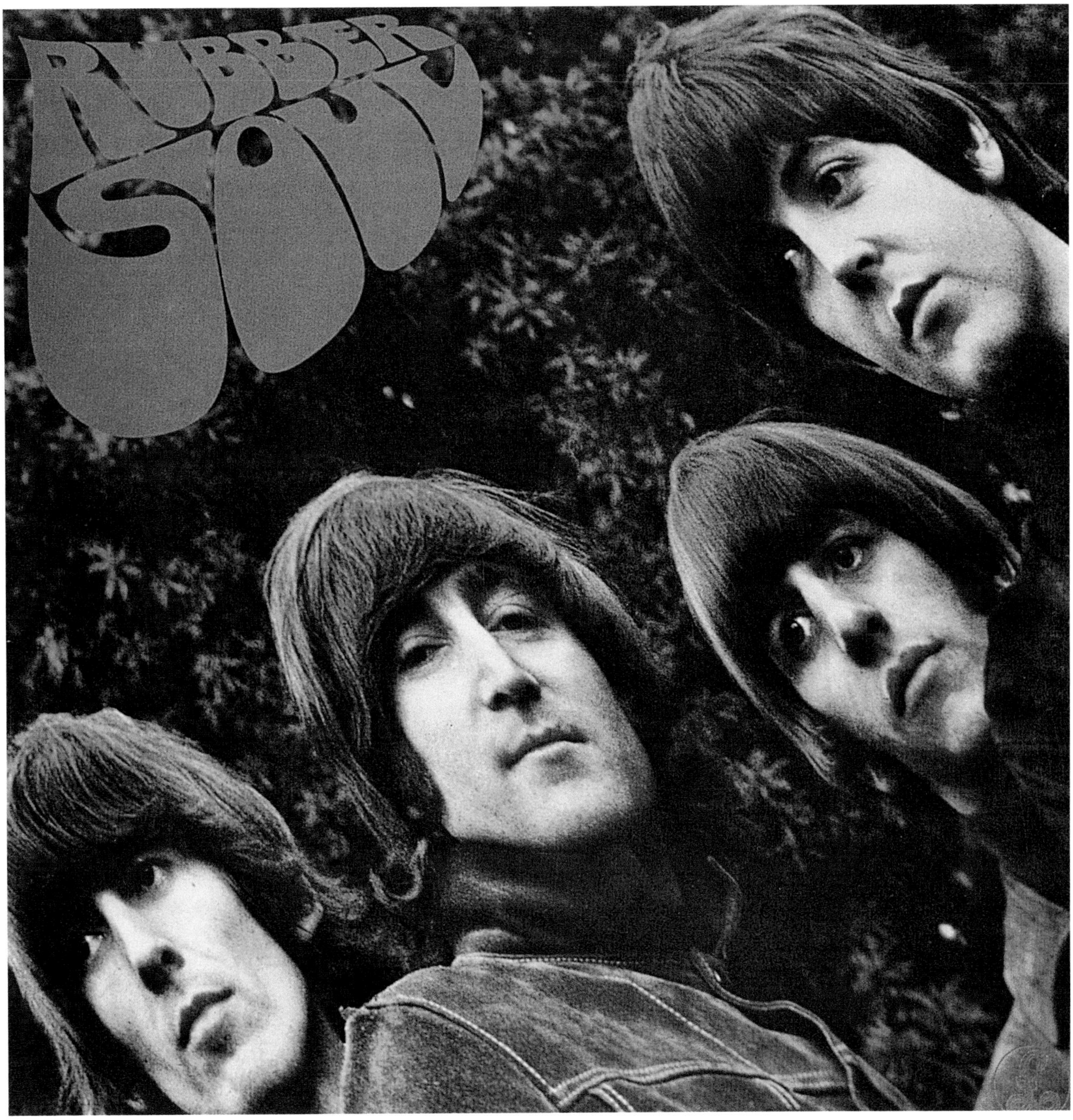

conventional tracks, but the arrangement of Paul's upbeat song of rejection is enlivened by an imaginative drum pattern that stresses their attention to every last detail of texture and decoration.

Nowhere Man's stark a cappella opening and the sober tone of John's lead vocal give the song an immediate impression of profundity. Here The Beatles were following Bob Dylan's example and beginning to function as social critics. George's brief guitar solo, doubled note-for-note by Lennon, is a fine example of his instinct for adding to the strength of the whole structure, rather than showing off.

The first of George's two contributions as a writer, Think For Yourself, is mostly notable for the use of two simultaneous bass guitar lines, one conventionally amplified and the other run through a fuzzbox. Although they sometimes

TRACK LISTING

A-SIDE

1. Drive My Car
Lennon/McCartney
Sung by McCartney

2. Norwegian Wood (This Bird Has Flown)
Lennon/McCartney
Sung by Lennon

3. You Won't See Me
Lennon/McCartney
Sung by McCartney

4. Nowhere Man
Lennon/McCartney
Sung by Lennon

5. Think For Yourself
Harrison
Sung by Harrison

6. The Word
Lennon/McCartney
Sung by Lennon

7. Michelle
Lennon/McCartney
Sung by McCartney

B-SIDE

8. What Goes On
Lennon/McCartney/Starkey
Sung by Starr

9. Girl
Lennon/McCartney
Sung by Lennon

10. I'm Looking Through You
Lennon/McCartney
Sung by McCartney

11. In My Life
Lennon/McCartney
Sung by Lennon

12. Wait
Lennon/McCartney
Sung by Lennon/McCartney

13. If I Needed Someone
Harrison
Sung by Harrison

14. Run For Your Life
Lennon/McCartney
Sung by Lennon

WHAT THE PAPERS SAID...

1965's media weren't quite ready for *Rubber Soul*.

"The new Beatles 14-track album... is not their best on first hearing. If the famous four's new one is compared with their previous LPs, it probably won't receive as much acclaim. It isn't, apparently, filled with Lennon-McCartney classics, although one or two tracks should stand out in a few months. Without a shade of doubt, The Beatles' sound has matured but unfortunately it also seems to have become a little subdued. Several of the tracks, You Won't See Me and Nowhere Man almost get monotonous – an un-Beatle like feature, if ever there was one."
Melody Maker (December 4, 1965)

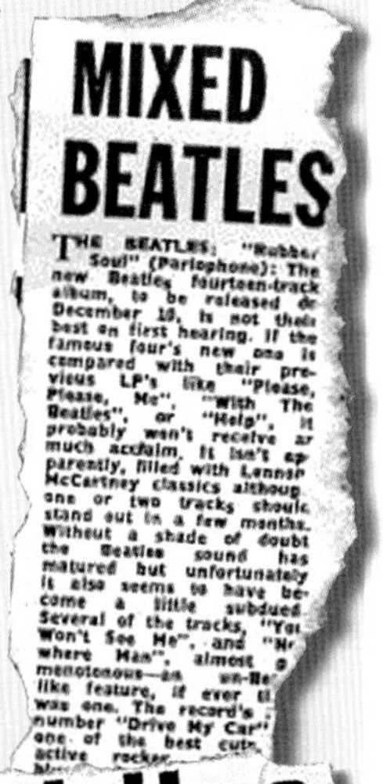

MIXED BEATLES

THE BEATLES: "Rubber Soul" (Parlophone): The new Beatles fourteen-track album, to be released on December 10, is not their best on first hearing. If the famous four's new one is compared with their previous LP's like "Please, Please, Me", "With The Beatles", or "Help", it probably won't receive as much acclaim. It isn't apparently, filled with Lennon McCartney classics although one or two tracks should stand out in a few months. Without a shade of doubt the Beatles sound has matured but unfortunately it also seems to have become a little subdued. Several of the tracks, "You Won't See Me", and "Nowhere Man", almost monotonous—an un-Beatle like feature, if ever there was one. The record's number "Drive My Car" one of the best cuts, active rocker...

"First one marvels and wonders at the constant stream of melodic ingenuity stemming from the boys, both as performers and composers. Keeping up their pace of creativeness is quite fantastic. Not, perhaps, their best LP in terms of variety, though instrumentally it's a gas."
Record Mirror (December 4, 1965)

It's Rubber Soul time

SLEEVE NOTES

How The Beatles' image was stretched to match their new sound.

The release in December 1965 of *Rubber Soul* showed the world just how much The Beatles had changed, a change even reflected in the LP's cover art – they'd never looked like *that* before. *That* was the result of a happy accident that literally gave a new slant to a moody group shot taken by photographer friend Robert Freeman in the grounds of John's Weybridge home. "For this cover I wanted another angle on the group and a different tonality – greens, browns and black, but with an almost monochrome look," explained Freeman in his book, The Beatles: A Private View. "The garden of John's house in Weybridge had the right elements. We arranged for The Beatles to wear clothes in appropriate colours, with black polo-neck sweaters or shirts. They were beginning to wear more varied clothes anyway, so uniformity was out."

Paul also saw the cover as a chance for The Beatles to progress their image – but the stretched look happened quite by chance. "Robert was showing us the slides; he had a piece of cardboard that was the album-cover size and he was projecting the photographs exactly onto it so we could see how it would look as an album cover. We had just chosen the photograph when the card that the picture was projected onto fell backwards a little, elongating the photograph. It was stretched and we went, 'That's it, Rubber So-o-oul, hey hey! Can you do it like that?' And that was it."

"I liked the way we got our faces to be longer on the album cover," recalled George in Anthology. "We lost the 'little innocents' tag, the naivety, and *Rubber Soul* was the first one where we were fully fledged potheads."

Richard Fairclough

"The desire of The Beatles to stretch out and experiment is what gives Rubber Soul a special poignancy."

duplicate the same line, McCartney's fuzz version is the more prominent and functions as a lead instrument.

The dawning of spiritual enlightenment that would reach its climax in the Summer of Love is celebrated in The Word. John's conclusion – "Now that I know what I feel must be right/I'm here to show everybody the light" – shows no sign of the cynicism that pervaded Sexy Sadie once their spiritual guide had been exposed, and the instrumental interludes form a brilliant homage to Booker T And The MG's.

By this time, the ear had become accustomed to innovation, so Michelle, ending the first side, was the biggest shock of all. In this doggedly accomplished pastiche, Paul vented all his nostalgia for a safe childhood in the 1950s, itself a decade suffused with nostalgia for the inter-war security of the '20s and '30s, the era to which this song specifically refers.

What Goes On opens the second side by evoking nostalgia for a very different kind of '50s: the decade of those yellow Sun records from Memphis. Of all Ringo's tracks on all their albums, this slice of Tennessee truckstop rockabilly is easily the least disposable.

Girl is John's Michelle, superficially lascivious (all that erotic sighing) but curiously opaque and disturbing. "Was she told when she was young that pain would lead to pleasure?" is quite a long way from "Michelle, ma belle sont les mots qui vont tres bien ensemble".

Whether or not the opening lines of I'm Looking Through You were inspired by an early experience of the effects of hallucinogenic substances, they certainly provide a good example of The Beatles' gift for oblique perception. So does In My Life, John's gorgeous ballad displaying a surprisingly mature emotional outlook, as beguilingly unexpected as the premature nostalgia of Bob Dylan's Dream was from a 21-year-old. Ringo's imaginative drumming re-emphasised the importance of all four Beatles even during moments when only one of them was taking the spotlight.

Factory records: Workers on a production line in the EMI factory at Hayes, Middlesex, with *Rubber Soul* in the final stages of production, November 25, 1965.

PHOTO: HULTON ARCHIVE

Similarly, George's use of the guitar's volume knob to soften the attack of his lead lines is the principal feature of Wait.

Written by George in response to the jingle-jangle sound of The Byrds' version of The Bells Of Rhymney, If I Needed Someone is a little gem, an early classic of power-pop which lasts not a second too long. Run For Your Life closes the album on a comparatively humdrum note, despite George's curling guitar figures. They were not quite ready to produce the sort of epic set-pieces of experimentation with which Tomorrow Never Knows and A Day In The Life concluded *Revolver* and *Sgt Pepper's Lonely Hearts Club Band*.

The first half of the '60s came to an end in the great creative explosion of 1965, the year of Like A Rolling Stone, You've Lost That Lovin' Feelin', The Tracks Of My Tears, In The Midnight Hour, Mr Tambourine Man, Nowhere To Run, Satisfaction, California Girls, Gloria, I Got You Babe, My Generation, People Get Ready and Do You Believe In Magic. The musicians were taking powers formerly held by the industry. Old restrictions were being abolished, for better and for worse. *Rubber Soul* was the last Beatles LP produced on the pop industry's traditional two-albums-a-year schedule, and the audible tension between the requirement to produce 14 three-minute songs and the desire to stretch out and experiment is what gives it a special poignancy.

SOUL MINING

For Jack White of The White Stripes, *Rubber Soul* is a fine example of natural songwriting.

"Whenever I think of *Rubber Soul*, the first thing that comes to mind is a memory of George Harrison saying in an interview that *Rubber Soul* and *Revolver* are like volumes one and two of the same album. That interested me very much for some reason. When you're young and listening to albums, you might look at all of a band's record sleeves and sort of wish there was some thing that tied them all together, like a secret code, or a record label symbol in the corner. *Rubber Soul* and *Revolver* always make me think like that.

"To be able to churn out two albums like that in a year's time is awe-inspiring to a musician. These boys weren't wasting any time, were they? What strikes me most about *Rubber Soul* is the feeling that it was 'time to make an album boys'. As if The Beatles just came in, recorded it, and went to go have dinner. It really feels that way to me. Each song is brilliant, yet I don't feel like they were in the studio for months, like the White Album feels. It just seems closer to natural songwriting. And the songwriting on the album is unbelievable. In My Life is pure genius, yes dare I say genius. Why is it that whenever Brian Wilson's name is mentioned, genius is not far behind? But that word seems to be left out of Beatles talk, almost as if, 'yeah, we all know that already'. But I think it's not fair to them.

"Drive My Car has an urgency to it, just a constant forward movement that kills me. Its monotone vocals hold on to that note until the last possible second before belting out 'But you can do something in between'. Now that's natural songwriting. And an exceptional album at that, definitely an important one to note in The Beatles' intricate structure of popularity, songwriting and attitude."

1966

In 1966, The Beatles created controversy wherever they went. They caused outrage in Japan for playing at the Budokan and were hounded out of the Philippines for snubbing Imelda Marcos. John's "we're more popular than Jesus" comments ensured an eventful US tour and by the time they arrived at Candlestick Park in San Francisco, the band had decided that this would be their final gig. It was also the year that George fell in love with India and *Revolver* was released.

Punch
AUGUSTUS 1966
75 CENT-12 FRANK
No.128-11e JAARG.
VERSCHIJNT MAANDELIJKS
1st OCTOBER 1966
208
KING SIZE FULL COLOUR PIN-UPS OF
THE MERSEYS ● ALAN PRICE ● PAUL JONES ● ALAN BALL
PLUS SECOND PART OF GIANT POSTER PIN-UP OF

Tripping the light fantastic: George runs through Paperback Writer, Abbey Road, May 19, 1966.

What: Work begins on Revolver
Where: Abbey Road, Studio Three
When: April 6, 1966

INTO TOMORROW

When The Beatles started work on the song known as 'The Void', their aim was to tear up the recording rule book. By Jim Irvin.

LATER IN 1966, PAUL McCARTNEY WOULD be interviewed by his friend Miles, for underground newspaper International Times. The 24-year-old who'd just finished *Revolver* and was about to start work on *Sgt Pepper* would betray a perhaps unavoidable mix of acute confidence – the certain knowledge that his group were way ahead of their peers – and slight disillusionment at achieving deity.

"There's no great big idols now," he'd say. "That's [the pity] about making it, you look at [people] objectively and they are no longer idols, you just see them for what they are. You lose that sort of fan thing. You lose the bit about being influenced. I think we are influenced by ourselves more and more at the moment, by what we know we could do, and what we know we'll eventually be able to do."

Other things had been having an effect on the music – and the mind-set – of McCartney. The effects of mind-altering drugs had clearly changed the way he worked. "With everything now, my aim seems to be to distort it," he told the co-founder of International Times. "The aim is to change it from what it is, and to see what it could be. To see the potential in it. To take a note and wreck the note and see what else there is in it, what a simple act like distorting it has caused... and superimpose on top, so you can't quite tell what it is any more. It's all trying to create magic."

Tuning in: the book that inspired John.

"It was implanted when we started recording *Revolver* that every instrument should sound unlike itself."

Paul had entered this spirit at full throttle during the making of *Revolver*. When newly-promoted tape-op, 20-year-old Geoff Emerick, turned up for his first session as chief balance engineer on April 6, he was immediately struck by the band's urge to distort and create magic.

"The group encouraged us to break the rules," he says. "It was implanted when we started *Revolver* that every instrument should sound unlike itself: a piano shouldn't sound like a piano, a guitar shouldn't sound like a guitar. There were lots of things I wanted to try, we were listening to American records and they sounded so different, the engineers [at Abbey Road] had been using the same [methods] for years and years."

They began with a new song by John, inspired by his experiments with LSD in January, where he'd used Timothy Leary and Richard Alpert's book The Psychedelic Experience as a guide. The book spoke of "surrendering to the void". John lifted this concept and lines such as, "Turn off your mind, relax and float downstream", directly from the book to create his impression of an acid trip. The Beatles spent five hours laying down three takes of the song – then identified simply as Mark 1 – using two guitars (one fuzzed, one through a Hammond organ's Leslie cabinet), bass, drums, organ and vocal (also through the Leslie). George Harrison provided a drone using sitar and tamboura, and George Martin added some Goons-style piano at the end.

For the drum sound, Emerick employed a Fairchild limiter – a device that prevents a signal overloading, but can produce the effect of sound fighting to break free. "It was the first time that I'd used the Fairchild on the drums," says Geoff. "I kept the bass drum separate but mixed all the rest to one track. The more bass drum that came through, the more the Fairchild would knock the other drums back, if Ringo hit a cymbal at the same time you'd get this whooshing, sucking noise of the limiter returning; that's why the drums sound backwards."

McCartney suggested that they might flesh out the track in an unusual way by using tape loops, so the following day, before starting work on Got To Get You Into My Life (Paul's own homage to discovering acid: "I was alone, I took a ride, I didn't know what I would find there..."), the band, Emerick and several other staff engineers, gathered to man the machines and be human flywheels for the lengthy loops of tape. One, featuring Paul laughing while playing his guitar, sounded like screeching seagulls when sped up; one utilised a single orchestral chord, another included a sitar sound heavily saturated onto tape by removing the machine's erase head. These effects were called up at random to punctuate the song – which was known for a while as The Void, until another of Ringo's peculiar maxims – "Tomorrow never knows!" – was appropriated by John as its definitive title.

Such experiments touched every track. A double-compressed bass sound discovered during Paperback Writer became their favoured way of recording the instrument. The fuzzed guitar solo from Taxman was spun backwards into the breakdown of Tomorrow Never Knows. The music-hall atmosphere and sound-effects of Yellow Submarine presaged *Sgt Pepper*. And then there was the haunted tea-room atmosphere of Eleanor Rigby. Curiously, in his interview with Miles, McCartney would sound equivocal about that track's fusty charms. "If it had been about anything else I think it would have been a mess, having it arranged like that. But luckily it fitted. I really can't stand that kind of classical music." Even the group themselves, it seems, were surprised by what they'd done.

Revolver took 36 days to complete, between April 6 and June 21. "I know for a fact that, from the day it came out, *Revolver* changed the way that everyone else made records," Emerick has said. "Everyone knew how we were doing those things, word would get round, but they could never quite get those sounds because they weren't using the same band!"

PHOTOS: ROBERT WHITAKER, PICTORIAL PRESS

JANUARY 66

1 Parlophone Records release *Sing A Song Of Beatles*, on which music publisher Dick James sings a medley of Beatles songs.

3 *Rubber Soul* becomes the Number 1 album in the US.

4 Brian Epstein flies to New York to negotiate details for the next Beatles tour of the States.

5 Lennon attends a party at 5 Cheltenham Terrace, London, the home of PJ Proby.

6 Day Tripper is certified as a gold disc in the US.

8 We Can Work It Out is The Beatles' first US Number 1 single of 1966. John, George and Ringo attend a party with Mick Jagger, at his home in 13a Bryanston Mews East, London.

10 Brian Epstein is appointed a director of Lennon Books Limited.

12 Ringo Starr and his wife Maureen leave the UK to holiday in Port Of Spain, Trinidad.

14 BBC TV acquires the British exhibition rights for the film of The Beatles At Shea Stadium.

21 Harrison marries Patti Boyd in Epsom, UK. McCartney is among the guests.

22 Harrison is interviewed by ABC about his marriage to Patti Boyd. George and Patti set off for their honeymoon in Barbados.

27 The Overlanders reach Number 1 in the UK with their cover of Michelle.

29 Having briefly been dislodged by Simon & Garfunkel, We Can Work It Out returns to Number 1 in the US.

31 Paul and Jane, plus George and Patti, attend the premiere of the musical How's The World Treating You, at the Wyndham Theatre, London.

FEBRUARY 66

3 McCartney sees Stevie Wonder at The Scotch Of St James, London.

4 George and Patti see the play Little Malcolm And His Struggle Against The Eunuchs, at the Garrick Theatre, London.

10 Girl, a Lennon/McCartney song recorded by St Louis Union, peaks at Number 11 in the UK singles chart.

11 Peter & Gordon release a new single, Woman, in the UK. The song is credited to Bernard Webb but, when it becomes a hit, McCartney will reveal that he wrote it.

12 George and Patti are tracked down by photographers, on honeymoon in Barbados.

13 Brian Epstein throws a party at 24 Chapel Street, with guests including Cilla Black, Gerry And The Pacemakers, John and Cynthia, Ringo and Maureen, Paul and Peter Asher.

21 A new single, Nowhere Man/What Goes On?, is released in the US.

23 McCartney attends a performance of contemporary music by Luciano Berio at the Italian Institute, London.

24 Woman by Peter & Gordon enters the UK singles chart, where it will peak at Number 28.

25 George and Patti return to London after honeymooning in Barbados.

28 Liverpool's Cavern Club, home of The Beatles, is closed due to financial problems. A hundred youths barricade themselves inside as a protest.

MARCH 66

1 The Beatles At Shea Stadium, film of the spectacular New York concert, premieres on BBC1 TV.

2 The Radio Times (left) reviews the previous night's TV broadcast of The Beatles At Shea Stadium, saying: "Superficially bracing, it was also slightly alarming as a demonstration of mass hysteria. We saw how the audience's natural excitement was increased to fever pitch by the various supporting acts. Then, in an atmosphere of frenzy and against a solid wall of sound, The Beatles came on and duly performed a selection of their best songs."

4 The London Evening Standard publishes an interview in which Lennon declares: "We're more popular than Jesus."

6 A petition with 5,000 signatures is sent to UK Prime Minister Harold Wilson, protesting about the closure of the Cavern Club.

10 The Beatles' last Number 1 EP, Yesterday, enters the British charts.

24 McCartney and Harrison attend the premiere of the film Alfie, starring Jane Asher, in the Plaza Cinema, Haymarket, London.

25 The controversial 'Butcher cover', designed for a US Beatles LP, is shot by photographer Robert Whitaker in his studio in Chelsea, London, showing The Beatles dressed as butchers holding meat-cleavers, surrounded by headless dolls and meat.

31 In New York, Brian Epstein and Tatsuji Nagashima arrange Tokyo concerts for The Beatles.

APRIL 66

3 The Beatles appear on the cover of weekly Italian magazine Ciao Amici.

5 For Jane Asher's 20th birthday, McCartney gives her 20 dresses.

6 At Abbey Road, The Beatles begin working on tracks which will become the album *Revolver*. The first song recorded is The Void.

7 Work on Tomorrow Never Knows continues at Abbey Road. They also begin Got To Get You Into My Life.

8 More takes of Got To Get You Into My Life are recorded at Abbey Road.

11 Work continues on Got To Get You Into My Life at Abbey Road. Later in the day they start the Harrison song, Love You To.

13 Love You To is completed at Abbey Road, and work starts on Paperback Writer.

14 Overdubs for the upcoming single Paperback Writer are done at Abbey Road. Work also begins on the B-side, Rain.

16 Recording of Rain continues at Abbey Road.

17 Work commences on the John Lennon song, Dr Robert, at Abbey Road.

18 The Cavern Club is sold to café proprietor Joe Davey.

What: The NME Concert
Where: Empire Pool, Wembley
When: May 1, 1966

GOING, GOING, GONE

It was supposed to be a routine show at the NME Poll-Winners' Concert, but it proved to be The Beatles' last ever UK gig. By Johnny Black.

"Those NME Poll-Winners' concerts were euphoric occasions," remembers Spencer Davis. "The nearest modern equivalent would be something like the Grammies, except we didn't have bodyguards, make-up artists and hangers-on. It was just the bands and their roadies, and we all knew each other."

Those shows represented not just the pinnacle of music business success, but the giddy peak of teen adulation, and as successful as they were, the Spencer Davis Group made only one NME Poll-Winners' Concert appearance, which was as much as any chart-topping British band of the time could dream of. Any band, that is, except The Beatles and The Rolling Stones. May 1, 1966, was the Stones' third Poll-Winners' performance, and The Beatles' fourth – and the rivalry between the two camps had never been greater. The stage was set for a clash of titans.

Other acts on the bill that year included The Small Faces, Spencer Davis Group, The Yardbirds, The Who, Walker Brothers and, lingering representatives of the old order, Roy Orbison and Cliff Richard and The Shadows. Ian McLagan, keyboardist of The Small Faces, still vividly recalls the atmosphere. "It was a big party backstage. There were so many stars that some had to share a dressing room. I walked into one where Paul Jones, Tom Jones and Cliff Richard were all elbows and bums trying to change into their stage gear. When it was our turn we walked on, the audience screamed, we played our two or three numbers and we ran offstage. I spent most of the time hanging out in the canteen with the Stones and The Who. I didn't even get to see The Beatles."

McLagan wasn't alone. Long-term Beatles aide Tony Bramwell recalls that "they were busy around that time doing the *Revolver* album, so the NME show was pretty much an in and out job for them." Little wonder that almost all Spencer Davis remembers of the Fab Four is "seeing them arrive wearing those yellow-tinted sunglasses".

But once they did arrive, battle was joined. "There was a lot of argy-bargy between [Rolling Stones manager] Andrew Loog Oldham and Brian Epstein," recalls NME news editor Derek Johnson, who was also acting as MC for the event. "It all seemed to be about who should close the show."

Indeed it was but, bizarrely, both managers were fighting to convince the NME's Executive Director, Maurice Kinn, that their band must not top the bill. Keith Altham, an NME staff writer, explains that "there was some sort of contractual dispute with ABC-TV who were filming the event, the effect of which was that the last band to play would not be filmed and thus would not appear in the TV broadcast."

Epstein and Oldham were both keenly aware that, although the glory of the occasion would go to whoever took the stage last, the potentially huge record sales generated through being seen by a TV audience of many millions meant that the financial rewards would be reaped by whoever went on second-last. As a breed, managers have never found it difficult to choose between the warm glow of glory and the cold glint of hard cash, so the war of words was long and hard-fought but, in the end, having been voted Number 1 by the readers of NME, The Beatles were obliged to take the stage after The Rolling Stones.

"Suddenly, The Beatles were there," reported Alan Smith in the following week's issue of NME, "dressed in beetle-black and standing by to give their first live performance of 1966. John stood astride in the familiar Lennon style, shoved on a pair of brown sunglasses with familiar Lennon panache, and belted straight into the vocal of I Feel Fine."

Tony Bramwell says that it was far from a classic Beatles performance. "By that time, they weren't playing as well as before, because they couldn't hear themselves through the screaming, and getting the opening feedback note of I Feel Fine always gave them trouble onstage, but luckily no one heard it there anyway."

Alan Smith's review confirms that, "the screaming seemed to reach the kind of level that only dogs and A&R men could hear."

Backstage, meanwhile, the Spencer Davis Group was facing its own dilemma. They were due to fly to Germany immediately after the gig, "But we'd never actually seen The Beatles play," says bassist Muff Winwood. "We were stuck in the dressing room, which was under the seats at the side of Wembley, and John Walters, the trumpet player of the Alan Price Set, convinced us that this was an historic occasion because we'd never see The Beatles and the Stones on the same stage again."

The NME concert's programme for The Beatles' last UK gig.

So while a Bentley, kindly loaned by Keith Richards of the Stones, stood by outside to whisk them to Heathrow, they were stacking boxes on top of the dressing room benches. Then, the entire Spencer Davis Group clambered up and peered through tiny slatted windows situated just below ceiling level. "We were actually looking through the audience," remembers Muff, "so it wasn't much of a view, but at least we did see The Beatles, even if it was impossible to hear them."

"When their set ended," notes Derek Johnson, "The Beatles did a quick bow and then, to avoid the huge amount of fans, they raced to their cars and drove off. And, of course, what none of us – not even The Beatles – realised at the time, was that it turned out to be their final live concert in the UK."

> **"The screaming was so loud it seemed to reach the kind of level that only dogs and A&R men could hear."**

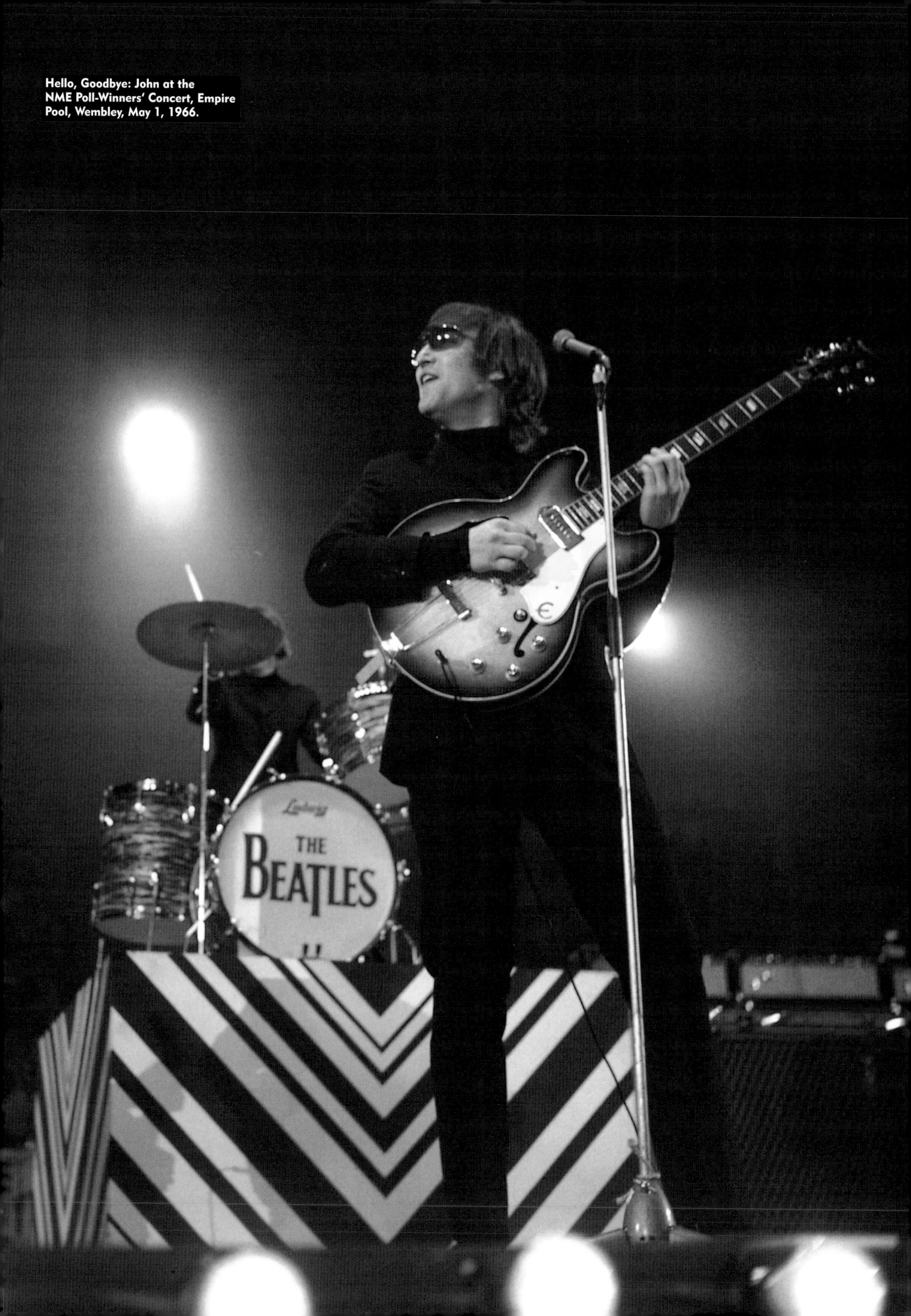

Hello, Goodbye: John at the NME Poll-Winners' Concert, Empire Pool, Wembley, May 1, 1966.

"Hey! Mind my shoes!": Lennon and a queasy Dylan are filmed being driven round Hyde Park for an American documentary, May 25, 1966.

What: Dylan meets Lennon
Where: Dylan's limo, London
When: May 25, 1966

CAR SICK BLUES

It was meant to be the meeting of two great music minds. Instead, Dylan struggled to keep from vomiting over Lennon and the limo. By Andy Gill.

Intelligence and quick-wittedness became attractive characteristics to the '60s audience, and the core trinity of pop interests – cars, girls and clothes – was suddenly expanded to include such matters as poetry, visual arts, politics, and maybe even a sketchy familiarity with the basic concepts of philosophy. Before long, a new phrase entered the language: Spokesman For A Generation, a term by its very nature applicable to only a few highly influential souls.

In fact, there were really only two serious contenders for this new position. In America, Bob Dylan had built a formidable reputation on the back of folk-protest anthems like Blowin' In The Wind and The Times They Are A-Changin'. In the UK, John Lennon had shown himself to be the sharpest Beatle, a man of acid wit whose wider ambitions were signalled by his two books of Lear- and Milligan-inspired jottings, In His Own Write and A Spaniard In The Works.

The pair had first met back in August 1964 at New York's Delmonico Hotel. Prior to that, mutual interest had been piqued by both parties' admiration for each other's music. "Anyone who is the best in his field – as Dylan is – is bound to influence people," said Lennon. "I wouldn't be surprised if we influenced him in some way." He was right, of course, Dylan being spurred to return to his rock'n'roll roots by the giant strides The Beatles were making. "I knew they were pointing the direction of where music had to go," he affirmed.

Lennon thought Dylan "the best in his field".

Both men had been driven by the unprecedented level of their fame to develop spiky, defensive carapaces which protected them from the invasive intensity of their fans' interest. So when Lennon's most obviously Dylan-esque song, Norwegian Wood, was devastatingly parodied just a few months later in Dylan's own Fourth Time Around, Lennon became all the more suspicious of Dylan's motives. "I was always so paranoid," he later admitted. "He said he wanted me to be in this film – Eat The Document – and he did just want me to be in the film, but I thought: Why? What? He's just gonna put me down."

Hence the edgy tone to Lennon's involvement in Dylan's 1966 tour "movie", commissioned (but later rejected) by ABC Television, and shot by Don Pennebaker, director of the previous year's Dylan tour documentary Don't Look Back. Dylan hadn't been entirely pleased with Don't Look Back and decided to direct the next one himself, focusing less on the performances and backstage verité material than on a series of impromptu, improvised tableaux in which members of his retinue would clamber in and out of a large hotel wardrobe, or try to interact fruitfully with innocent passers-by. One of these tableaux was supposed to be of Lennon, Dylan and his crony Bob Neuwirth being driven round Hyde Park in the back of a limousine at 7am in late May, the two superstars engaging in (hopefully) sparkling repartee.

Such, at least, was the intention, but several factors combined to capsize the idea, most notably Lennon's lingering mistrust and the sheer quantity of wine imbibed by Dylan through the previous night. The two ten-minute reels shot by Pennebaker were ignored in Dylan's own cut of Eat The Document, but as with virtually everything he said, did or touched in the '60s, they later appeared on the underground bootleg network. They offer a rare opportunity to observe a usually self-composed Spokesman For A Generation with his guard not so much down as completely demolished by drink, struggling to stay awake and – more pressingly – prevent the contents of his stomach from pebbledashing the limo's interior.

In the first reel, names are bandied about with scant concern for meaning: after promising to portray chauffeur Tom Keylock as (variously) Tyrone Power, Ronald Coleman, Reginald Young, Peetie Wheatstraw, Sleepy John Estes and Robert Johnson in his film, Dylan engages in muddled banter with a comparatively straight Lennon, the pair goading each other with mentions of Ral Donner, Barry McGuire, The Mamas And The Papas ("You're just interested in the big chick, right?" prods Dylan) and folk group The Silkie. Lennon does a decent impression of promoter Tito Burns, and Dylan complains about a pain in his side. Little of their conversation amounts to much; Oscar Wilde and George Bernard Shaw it ain't.

Dylan's condition deteriorates rapidly as nausea overwhelms him, and most of the second reel is taken up with his pathetic proclamations of sickness and increasingly urgent requests to return to his hotel. "Oh God, I don't wanna get sick in here," he moans, head in hands. "What if I vomit into the camera? I've done just about everything else into that camera, man, I might just vomit into it." Lennon looks on with a mixture of disgust and resignation as Dylan's state worsens, mocking his suffering with a gag – "Do you suffer from sore eyes, groovy forehead, or curly hair? Take Zimdon!" – to which the usually sharp-witted American, rarely lost for words, can only groan in protest.

"What if I vomit into the camera? I've done just about everything else into that camera, man." Bob Dylan

The reel ends with the hapless Dylan on the verge of puking. Whether he left his lunch behind or not, it seems likely that the short ride was a watershed in the two stars' relationship. Though they remained friends, the idealised view Lennon had held of his closest American counterpart was undoubtedly tainted by the drunken display, and his future references to Dylan in songs such as God and Serve Yourself would be more critical than reverential. As for Dylan, the occasion probably brought home to him just how damaging his current lifestyle was to his health. A few months later, his motorbike accident would provide the perfect opportunity to change his life for the better.

18 Lennon, Harrison and Eric Clapton go to see The Lovin' Spoonful at The Marquee, London.

19 Dr Robert is completed in Abbey Road Studios.

20 Work on the songs Taxman and And Your Bird Can Sing begins in Abbey Road.

22 Overdubs for the songs Taxman and Tomorrow Never Knows are completed in Abbey Road.

23 A new pop paper, Disc And Music Echo is launched in the UK. The paper has been created by merging the long-established Disc with Music Echo, owned by Brian Epstein, giving him a 50 per cent stake in the new publication. John spends the day at John's, songwriting and discussing the album.

25 Rough mono mixes of The Beatles song Got To Get You Into My Life are made at Abbey Road.

27 A lengthy Abbey Road mixing session is followed by work on Lennon's I'm Only Sleeping.

28 Recording of Eleanor Rigby begins at Abbey Road.

29 Vocal overdubs for Eleanor Rigby and I'm Only Sleeping are recorded in Abbey Road.

MAY 66

1 The Beatles play their last UK live gig at the 1966 NME Pollwinners' Concert at Wembley. Other acts on the bill include Small Faces, Spencer Davis Group, Roy Orbison, the Stones, The Yardbirds, Cliff Richard, The Shadows, The Who, Herman's Hermits, The Seekers.

2 Bob Dylan arrives in London to tour the UK with an electric band for the first time, and settles in at the Mayfair Hotel, where he meets with McCartney, Keith Richards and Brian Jones. The Beatles are interviewed for BBC radio shows Saturday Club and Pop Profile at the Playhouse Theatre, London.

4 The Japanese Finance Ministry agrees to let The Beatles perform in Japan, allowing each member to remit £10,000 of earnings from the shows overseas.

5 Backwards guitars are added to I'm Only Sleeping in Abbey Road.

6 Vocal overdubs are added to I'm Only Sleeping in Abbey Road.

7 The Beach Boys release *Pet Sounds*, acknowledged by McCartney as his inspiration to go for broke on *Sgt Pepper*.

9 Work on For No One begins in Abbey Road.

10 Mixes of Dr Robert, I'm Only Sleeping and And Your Bird Can Sing are made at Abbey Road, in order to include them on the US-only album *Yesterday And Today*.

16 Taxman is completed at Abbey Road, and various other tracks are overdubbed and mixed.

18 A 12-hour non-stop session is undertaken in Abbey Road, working mostly on horn parts for Got To Get You Into My Life.

19 Promo-clips for Paperback Writer and Rain are filmed in black and white and colour at Abbey Road.

21 After partying the night before with Mick Jagger and Chrissie Shrimpton, John and Cynthia shop at Portobello Road market, London.

25 Lennon and Dylan are filmed by DA Pennebaker during an early morning limo cruise around Hyde Park.

MAY 26 - JUNE 20, 1966

26 Bob Dylan performs at the Royal Albert Hall, London. Work starts on Yellow Submarine in Abbey Road.

27 Lennon and Dylan are filmed for documentary Eat The Document while travelling from Lennon's home in Weybridge, Surrey, to the Mayfair Hotel, London. Dylan's second night at the Royal Albert Hall, London, with John Lennon and George Harrison in attendance.

30 A new single, Paperback Writer/ Rain, is released in America.

31 Ringo is photographed at home in Sunny Heights for The Beatles Book's 'At Home' series.

JUNE 66

1 Aided by Rolling Stone Brian Jones, Marianne Faithfull and others, The Beatles dub sound effects onto the song Yellow Submarine in Abbey Road Studios. In the evening George Harrison goes to see Ravi Shankar at the Royal Albert Hall.

2-3 George Harrison's song I Want To Tell You is recorded in Abbey Road.

4 An interview with The Beatles is broadcast on the 400th edition of BBC Radio show Saturday Club.

5 Promo clips for Paperback Writer and Rain are shown on the Ed Sullivan Show in America.

6 As the day ends, McCartney does a final vocal overdub onto Eleanor Rigby in Abbey Road.

8 Work on Good Day Sunshine begins in Abbey Road.

9 Recording of Good Day Sunshine is completed.

10 A new single, Paperback Writer/ Rain, is released in the UK.

13 Johnnie Stewart, producer of Top Of The Pops, writes to Brian Epstein, asking if the group will consent to playing live on the show in four days' time.

14 The first of three days of recording Here, There And Everywhere begins at Abbey Road.

15 *Yesterday And Today*, with the 'Butcher' sleeve (right), is released in the US. American record shops refuse to handle the LP because of its notorious sleeve. The album is withdrawn from sale.

16 The Beatles appear live on Top Of The Pops for the first time (above), miming first to Rain then Paperback Writer.

17 Work continues on Here, There And Everywhere and Got To Get You Into My Life, in Abbey Road. It is reported in The Times that McCartney has bought a farm on the Mull Of Kintyre, Scotland.

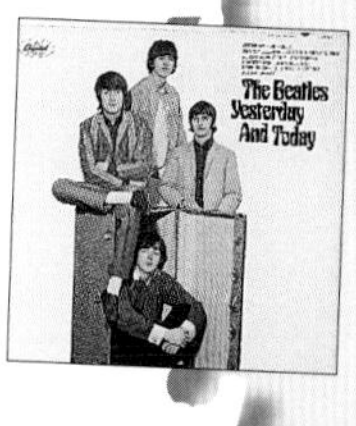

20 *Yesterday And Today* is released in the US with a new sleeve (right).

What: Yesterday And Today released
Where: America
When: June 15, 1966

MEAT IS MURDER

The infamous 'Butcher' cover shot was too much for Capitol Records, and an America who liked their Fabs nice and clean. By Bill DeMain.

"IT WAS A CONSIDERED DISRUPTION OF THE conventions surrounding orthodox pop star promotional photography," says Robert Whitaker of his most infamous creation, The Beatles' 'Butcher' sleeve.

The Aussie photographer arrived at the session in the spring of 1966 bearing a load of props that could've come from Salvador Dali's basement. "I'd brought false teeth, dolls' eyes, a set of white coats, hammers and nails, a birdcage and a box that I stuck Ringo's head in. I was going to make him into alabaster, and I wrote on the box, '2,000,000', so that he would be one in a series of two million people. I brought along a couple of strings of sausages and the raw meat. The dolls came straight from a factory in Chiswick. They've been described as being dismembered. They hadn't been. It's just exactly how they came – heads, bodies, arms. I just tipped the box on the floor and they started playing with it like that."

And how did The Fabs react to this surreal carnage? "George hated it," Whitaker says. "But I only got that reaction later from the Disc & Music Echo, where he was interviewed. I think at that stage he was becoming a vegetarian and was becoming more interested in the Holy Grail. John was really happy that we weren't just doing four people sat round looking glamorous with white teeth. Paul was open to it. Ringo, I'm not sure how he felt."

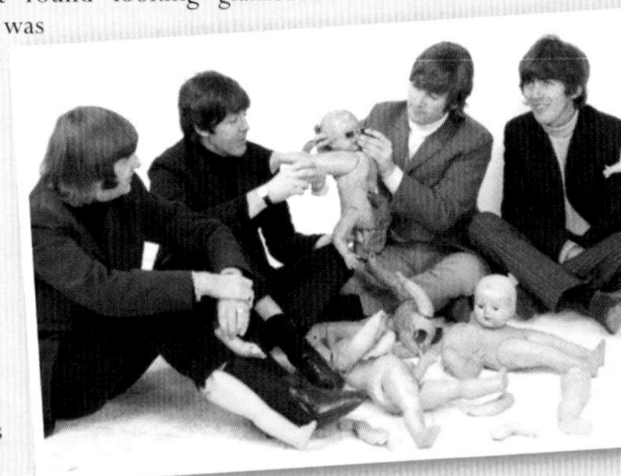

"I don't know how we ended up sitting in butchers' coats with meat all over us," Ringo said in The Beatles Anthology. "If you look at our eyes, you realise none of us really knew what we were doing. It was just one of those things that happened as life went on."

What's long been misunderstood, Whitaker says, is that the Butcher photograph – or 'Somnambulant Adventure', as he dubbed it – was not intended as a cover image. "It was meant to be on the back cover of a gatefold sleeve. It would've only been two-and-a-quarter inches square in the centre of a 12-inch sleeve. Around their heads there would've been silver halos with precious stones and then the whole of the rest of it would've been like a Russian icon – silver and gold, so that I've sort of canonised them and put them into the church. The meat is meant to represent the fans, and the false teeth and the false eyes is the falseness of representing a god-like image as a golden calf. The front cover was to be a picture of them holding two strings of sausages coming out of the nether regions of a lady. The sausages are meant to be an umbilical cord. And then that image was going to be inset inside a pregnant woman's womb, and there was going to be an illustration of a breast with a nipple and a big womb, and the four Beatles laying inside her tummy all connected to an umbilical cord.

"Capitol just got the Butcher picture," he continues. "They didn't have the other pictures – the keys to unlock it. So it was a cock-up, and I guess it upset a lot of people."

"I looked at it and thought, What in the hell is this? How can I put this out?" recalls Alan Livingston, President of Capitol Records at the time. "I showed it to our sales manager and a few other people and they turned green. So I called Brian Epstein in London, and he said The Beatles were insistent about the photo. So I said, OK, let me test it."

The album, *Yesterday And Today*, was cobbled together by Capitol to keep the American market flooded with Beatle music. Consisting of songs shaved from the UK version of *Rubber Soul*, plus film soundtrack extras and the single Yesterday, it was one of those hotchpotch collections that John Lennon said "used to drive us crackers".

Some 60,000 copies went out to radio, media and Capitol branch offices, who showed it to retailers. "The reaction came back that the dealers refused to handle them," Livingston says. "So I called London and we went back and forth. My contact was mainly with Paul McCartney. He was adamant and felt very strongly that we should go forward. He said, 'It's our comment on war'. I don't know why it was a comment on war or if it would be interpreted that way. Finally, they gave in and sent a new cover."

"They stuck an awful-looking photo of us looking just as deadbeat but supposed to be a happy-go-lucky four-some," John Lennon said in Anthology. 'Stuck' is the right word. Working overtime one weekend, Capitol employees glued the new photo – the boys around a steamer trunk (see below left) – over the top of the offensive Hard Day's Slaughter shot.

"I don't know how we ended up sitting in butchers' coats with meat all over us. It was just one of those things."

"It was a matter of economics," Livingston says. "I'm not a record collector, so it never entered my head for a minute what the value of the original albums would be, or the paste-overs."

The filet mignon of collectibles among Beatlephiles, nowadays a Butcher cover can fetch over $1000. The paste-over covers go for about $300.

And as for the original visionary photographic concept, well, we might see it yet. "I do still have all the pieces," says Whitaker, "and I intend to finish the artwork and one day publish it."

Until then, the somnambulant adventure continues.

PHOTOS: ROBERT WHITAKER/LONDON FEATURES INTERNATIONAL

"The cover was to be a picture of them holding sausages coming out of the nether regions of a lady." Robert Whitaker's studio, King's Road, Chelsea, March 25, 1966.

“I never saw them more contented than at this time.” Lennon relaxes in between shows, Tokyo, 1966.

What: First Japanese tour
Where: Tokyo
When: June 29-July 3, 1966

DIFFERENT STROKES

The Beatles' first trip to Japan was made more interesting thanks to an enterprising promoter and a box of paints. By Jim Irvin.

TWELVE DAYS AFTER THE BEATLES departed Japan, Dudley Cheke, a *chargé d'affaires* at the British Embassy in Tokyo, sent a lively despatch to his superiors in London reporting on the visit. "The group arrived in Tokyo at dawn [of June 29], immediately after an exceptionally heavy rainstorm," he wrote, "and it was as 'the Beatles Typhoon' that they swept the youth of Japan off their feet. In sober truth, no recent event connected with the UK has made a comparable impact in Tokyo – a 'Beatles mood' has gripped this city."

As ever, the "Beatles mood" comprised both delight and outrage: 209,000 applications were received for 30,000 available tickets and the papers were filled with stories about the group. One cartoon depicted Prime Minister Sato wearing a Beatles wig to win votes, while Communist paper Akahata described them as "tools of American imperialism". Japanese nationalists (see below right), meanwhile, complained about them appearing at the Budokan – an imposing 10,000-seat hall built to display martial arts at the Tokyo Olympics – claiming the venue would be "desecrated" by such a spectacle, a claim refuted by the Budokan's chairman, who noted that the boys had been decorated by the Queen and thus were models of respectability.

Business as usual then, but as it ventured further outside the West, the ability of "the Beatles Typhoon" to sweep aside any potentially dangerous cultural fall-out became less and less certain. Indeed, its arrival in Japan had sparked a major security alert. "In a country where crowds can easily become rioting mobs, they had to be protected from fans and foe alike," remarked Cheke. The policing was on the scale of the 1964 Tokyo Olympics: 35,000 officers were deployed around the city and their presence in the stadium was noticeably overstated – policemen and firemen stationed in every aisle, and several deep in front of the stage. The reason, though the group were unaware, was that there had been death threats made against the 'Biiturusu'. "Fanatical opponents of the group and of all they were supposed to stand for had threatened to have them assassinated," reported Cheke.

So The Beatles were allowed very little opportunity to venture into the city. Thanks to the massive demand for tickets, two matinee performances were added on July 1 and 2, which ate up some of their free time but, as usual, there was little else for them to do. They simply remained in their sumptuous presidential suite – Room 1005, an entire floor of the Tokyo Hilton – and conducted interviews.

Thoughtfully, promoter Tatsuji Nagashima arranged various diversions, sending along traders to proffer luxurious gifts, and even offering the services of some geisha. "The best looking crumpet in kimonos you can imagine," declared photographer Robert Whitaker, he of the *Yesterday And Today* 'Butcher' sleeve, who was documenting the trip. But all The Beatles declined.

On their second day, they managed to escape for a few hours, evading the huge crowds encircling the hotel. Paul took a stroll around Tokyo's Imperial Plaza, with Mal Evans as bodyguard, and John visited the Oriental Market and Asahi Gallery at Harajuku. But further excursions were discouraged. Instead, Mr Nagashima had some fine Japanese paper and paints sent into the suite and the boys were given the chance to create their own artwork.

A large sheet of handmade paper, about 30 inches by 40 inches, was laid out in the suite's communal lounge and a lamp placed at its centre. Working by just the light of the lamp, the group began to fill the space with colour, each of them decorating a corner with oils and watercolours, while smoking joints and listening to some acetates of their new album that had been sent over from London. It was here they decided on the name *Revolver*.

"I never saw them calmer, more contented than at this time," Whitaker recalls. "They were working on something that let their personalities come out. I think it's the only work they ever did all together that has nothing to do with music. They were very harmonious and happy, calling their wives and girlfriends, commenting on the music, all the time doing this painting. They'd stop, go and do a concert and then it was, 'Let's go back to the picture!'"

In all, it took two evenings. Paul's section was vaguely psychedelic and roughly symmetrical. John's was more sprawling, with thick oils and a large, dark centre. George applied less paint and opted for bright, busy colours. Ringo's corner was vibrant and graphic, almost cartoon-like.

Emperors' new clothes: John and Ringo get kimonoed-up.

"Opponents of the group and of all they were supposed to stand for had threatened to have them assassinated."

Each section flowed into a vivid red surround. "There was no comment between them about what they were painting," Whitaker remembered. "The end result, and how it all joined up, just happened naturally."

When it was complete, each of The Beatles signed the circle where the lamp had stood. Mr Nagashima suggested they sell the painting for charity (it was purchased by a cinema manager who ran a fan club. After his death, in the mid '90s, it was sold for 15 million yen, to a dealer from Osaka. Its current whereabouts are unknown).

When "the Beatles Typhoon" moved on, Cheke reported that apart from complaints about the hefty security and the brevity of their appearances, the Japanese press expressed "a strong undercurrent of admiration and approval for The Beatles and their achievements".

Whitaker described the mood within the group during those few days as "a crescendo of happiness". A few days later, however, their interest in remaining on the road would be gone for good.

PHOTOS: ROBERT WHITAKER/TOPHAM/ASSOCIATED PRESS

21 The Beatles record She Said She Said in Studio Three, Abbey Road, London.

22 Final mixing sessions for *Revolver* are held at Studio Three, Abbey Road. A new disco, Sybilla's, opens in London. It is owned jointly by Harrison and Sir William Piggott-Brown. Sundry Beatles and Rolling Stones attend the opening.

23 The Beatles fly out of the UK to begin a brief German tour. On arrival in Munich, they check in to the Hotel Bayerischer Hof.

24 The final world tour opens at Circus-Krone-Bau, Munich, West Germany.

25 Paperback Writer reaches Number 1 in the UK and America simultaneously. John Lennon said at the time: "We were getting into all kinds of jiggery-pokery in the studio, turning tapes backwards. On the B-side of Paperback Writer, Rain, we turned my voice around and it sounded amazing. George Martin said it sounded like Russian!" The Beatles play a live concert at Grugahalle, Norbertstrasse, Essen, West Germany.

26 The band return to Hamburg, Germany, for the first time since 1962, in an eight-car motorcade, to play two shows at Ernst Merck Halle. Emotionally overwrought fans hurl tear-gas canisters at police barricading streets around the hall.

27 The Beatles fly back from Hamburg to London, then set off again later in the day for Tokyo, Japan.

28 To avoid Typhoon Kit over Japan, The Beatles' plane lands in Anchorage, Alaska. The band's chauffeur, Alf Bicknell, remembers: "We got off the plane and there was chaos and pandemonium everywhere. They had no idea The Beatles were coming to town. We spent 24 mad hours there and got drunk as skunks. When the storm eventually died down we flew on to Tokyo."

29 The Beatles land in Tokyo, where strict police measures mean that they are met at the airport by only 20 fans.

30 The Beatles play the first of three nights at the Budokan, Tokyo. The Budokan was a cultural centre for Japan that housed sumo wrestlers, and there was an enormous protest by the public (see above) because a pop group was entering the imperial palace of sumo. The organisers had to make the stage eight-feet high so the crowds, if they did break through, couldn't get to them. The floor of the arena was all police, right round the stage, and a few cameramen were present with tiers of people above. Alf Bicknell reflects: "We met these sumo wrestlers and there was a little bit of friction about playing there. We had a police and soldier escort for two miles, all the way to the stadium, but once we got into the show, it was great, and the Japanese were so kind to us."

What: Controversy in the Philippines
Where: Manila
When: July 3-5, 1966

KILLER IN MANILA

The Beatles often turned down invitations from the rich and famous. But when they said no to Imelda Marcos, they were in *real* trouble. By Jim Irvin.

WHILE IN JAPAN, public disquiet had been kept from the group, but in the Philippines, then under martial law, it erupted in front of them. From the moment they touched down in the sticky heat they felt vulnerable. Normally, as visiting VIPs, they'd be rushed through diplomatic channels, but in Manila they were met by an armed man who ordered them to drop their bags and get into his car.

"Everywhere else – America, Sweden, Germany – even though there was a mania, there was always respect because we were famous showbiz personalities," George recalled, "but in Manila it was a very negative vibe. We were being bullied for the first time. We got in the car and the guy drove off leaving Neil [Aspinall] behind. Our bags were on the runway and I was thinking, This is it, we're going to get busted." They had reason to worry – the briefcases contained their stashes of grass.

"They took us away and drove us down to Manila harbour, put us on a boat, took us out to a motor yacht and put us in this room," George recalled in the Anthology series. "We were all sweating and frightened. For the first time ever in our Beatle existence, we were cut off from Neil, Mal [Evans] and Brian Epstein. There were cops with guns lining the deck around this cabin. We wished we hadn't come."

Quick-thinking Aspinall had scooped up the abandoned briefcases and followed the boys in a limo, realising that they'd been appropriated by some kind of gang who wanted The Beatles on their boat as a status symbol. Eventually, Brian arrived with promoter Ramon Ramos, who was fuming about the kidnap, and got the group off the boat.

The following morning, Paul and Ringo slipped away for some sightseeing and found themselves in Makati, the financial district, where Paul took pictures highlighting the contrast between the area's opulence and its adjoining cardboard city. When they returned to the hotel there was a panic. "Somebody came into the room and said: 'Come on! You're supposed to be at the palace'," recalled George. The TV was switched on and there was Imelda, wife of the country's despotic president Ferdinand Marcos, awaiting the group's arrival. The boys watched themselves not arriving at the Malacanang Palace. As ever, Brian had turned down all requests for political meet'n'greets, but this time someone had clearly refused to take no for an answer. To save face, rather than say it was a mere oversight, papers sympathetic to Marcos spun stories declaring that the boys' no-show was a deliberate snub.

Meanwhile, there were the gigs: two performances in the massive Rizal soccer stadium which held over 50,000 people, among them 14-year-old fan Charlie Santos.

The Beatles hot-tail it out of Manila airport.

"There were chairs set up on the field to accommodate more people and the mood was charged-up in anticipation. The crowd wasn't rowdy, there was no hint of the 'snub'; we didn't hear about it until the next day, in the newspapers." The show started with Chuck Berry's Rock And Roll Music. "As soon as the first chords were struck, everyone in the field section rushed towards the stage, others stacking up chairs so they could get a better view," says Charlie. "What sticks in my mind was when Paul sang Yesterday solo, I remember thinking, It sounds just like the record. After the show, everyone [said] they sounded even better live."

Brian attempted a TV press conference to smooth things out that night, but it was mysteriously foiled by a power-cut. The next morning hell broke loose when the papers came out. Suddenly, public officials turned on them. "It was an absolute disgrace," says Charlie. "The 'royal family' didn't get to meet The Beatles so they let their goons loose to rough them up. Not everyone was supportive of the actions of Marcos."

"As the boys crossed the tarmac, an angry mob started chanting, 'Beatles alis dayan!' – 'Beatles go home!'"

Promoter Ramos withheld the band's money. Ringo recalls that room-service food was suddenly inedible and drivers refused to take them to the airport, where Paul remembers someone shutting down the escalators as they struggled with their luggage, and policemen trying to punch them. The group took refuge near a bunch of nuns, figuring this was the safest place to be in a Catholic country. Everywhere they turned, thuggish men carrying guns were pushing and kicking them.

"When they started on us, I was petrified," John remembered later. "I thought I was going to get hit, so I headed for the nuns. 'You treat like ordinary passenger, ordinary passenger,' they were saying. We said: 'Ordinary passenger? He doesn't get kicked, does he?'"

As the boys crossed the tarmac, an angry mob started chanting, "Beatles alis dayan!" – 'Beatles go home'. Any sense of sanctuary once on the airplane was short-lived when Neil, Brian and publicist Tony Barrow were recalled to the airport. The Beatles feared that they'd never get away. Brian was forced to hand over a massive, hastily-invented 'tax' before they were allowed to take off.

Within minutes, Marcos finally released a statement confirming that The Beatles had not deliberately slighted the first family, but it came too late to save their nerves. Though 100,000 fans had welcomed them warmly, their 48 hours in the Philippines more or less rid The Beatles of any remaining appetite for live appearances. Back home, the usually benign George calmly suggested that an atom bomb ought to be dropped on the place.

PHOTOS: REX, ROBERT WHITAKER

JULY 66

1 The Beatles play two shows on their second night at the Budokan, Tokyo, Japan. City authorities in Munich, Germany, begin an action to get an 'entertainment tax' from The Beatles, relating to their recent concerts in the city. Music is normally exempt from tax in Germany, but the authorities claim that The Beatles' music is "incidental to the shouting and stamping of the audience, which it is designed to achieve."

2 The Beatles play two shows on their third night at the Budokan, Tokyo, Japan.

3 Flight from Tokyo to Manila in the Philippines.

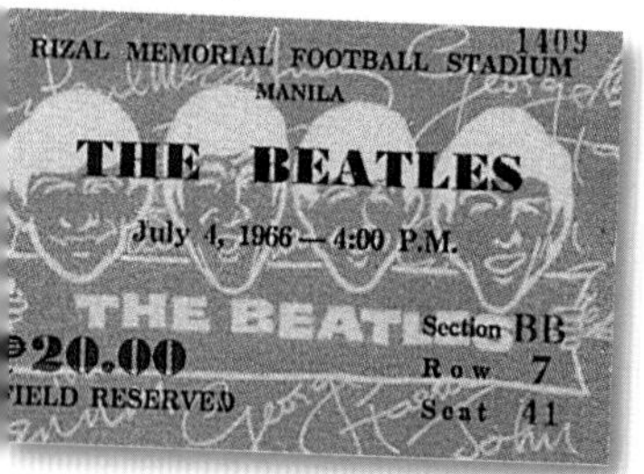

4 Angry crowds attack The Beatles in Manila, after they unwittingly snub the wife of President Marcos, Imelda. Nonetheless, The Beatles play Rizal Memorial Football Stadium (see above).

5 Flight from Manila via Bangkok to New Delhi, India.

8 The EP, Nowhere Man is released in the UK.

9 Having been ousted by Frank Sinatra's Strangers In The Night, Paperback Writer regains the US Number 1 single slot.

12 Lennon and McCartney win two more Ivor Novello Awards, when Yesterday is declared the Outstanding Song Of 1965, and We Can Work It Out has the Highest Certified British Sales. Aided by Paul McCartney, Cliff Bennett And The Rebel Rousers begin recording their version of Mccartney's Got To Get You Into My Life at Abbey Road.

13 McCartney completes work on Cliff Bennett's version of Got To Get You Into My Life.

14 US TV rock show Where The Action Is features Petula Clark performing I Want To Hold Your Hand; Marianne Faithfull performing Yesterday; Paul Revere And The Raiders performing I'm Down. (All three songs are written by The Beatles).

15 Klaus Voormann is released from his NEMS contract by Brian Epstein so that he can join Manfred Mann as bassist.

23 Liverpool's Cavern Club is re-opened; PM Harold Wilson and Ken Dodd (above) are among the guests. The Beatles cannot be present but send a 'good wishes' telegram.

"Manila? Drop a bomb on the place!" Lennon safely back home at a press conference, London Heathrow Airport, July 8, 1966.

DJs Tommy Charles (left) and Doug Layton of radio station WAQY smash Fabs records on air, Birmingham, Alabama, July 1966.

What: "We're more popular than Jesus!"
Where: Evening Standard, London
When: March 4, 1966

THE HOLY WAR

How an innocent comment about religion by Lennon brought widespread hatred of The Beatles in America. By David Fricke.

On March 4, 1966, John Lennon invented rock journalism as we know it – simply by opening his mouth. That day, the Evening Standard published Maureen Cleave's account of her visit to Lennon's home in Weybridge. Lennon spoke freely to Cleave about his life away from Beatlemania, especially his private investigations in literature and philosophy. He gave Cleave a guided tour of his pop-star lair, and Cleave made special note of the way Lennon "paused at objects he still fancies", which included a large crucifix and a huge Bible, probably antique, that he bought in Chester. "He is reading extensively about religion," Cleave wrote, and Lennon proved it with aggressive candour.

"Christianity will go," he told Cleave. "It will vanish and shrink. I needn't argue about that; I'm right, and I will be proved right. We're more popular than Jesus now; I don't know which will go first – rock'n'roll or Christianity. Jesus was all right, but his disciples were thick and ordinary. It's them twisting it that ruins it for me."

The sky did not fall; pulpits did not crumble. Lennon's comments aroused no special furore in Britain. And no one in America saw a word – until July 29, when the US teen magazine Datebook syndicated Cleave's story with the blazing cover headline "I don't know which will go first – rock'n'roll or Christianity".

That sentence, yanked out of context, was the least contentious thing Lennon said that day. It can easily be read now as evidence of Lennon's shaken trust not just in organised religion but in rock'n'roll itself. But many people never got past Datebook's headline. On July 31, a radio station in Birmingham, Alabama staged a public bonfire of Beatles albums and souvenirs. Twenty-two stations, mostly in the ferociously conservative South, banned the group's music from the air; some held their own record burnings. In Mississippi, an imperial wizard of the Ku Klux Klan announced that The Beatles were "brainwashed" by the Communist Party. The fire and brimstone so rattled Beatles manager Brian Epstein that he considered cancelling the band's summer US tour.

He didn't. Instead, on August 11, the day before the first show in Chicago, Lennon – flanked by his fellow Beatles – gamely defended himself in a nationally broadcast press conference at the city's Astor Towers Hotel. He apologised only for the manner, not the meat, of what he said: "I never meant it to be a lousy anti-religious thing, Christianity just seems to me to be shrinking, to be losing contact."

Lennon also called time on the antique etiquette of the rock'n'roll interview – idiot questionnaires on dating preferences, etc. With The Beatles' unprecedented success had come unexpected responsibility: the role of oracle, the representative voice of a restive baby boom. "We've been mushroom-grown," Lennon said, "forced to grow up a bit quick, like having 30-to-40-year-old heads in 20-year-old bodies." The people paid to ask the questions, Lennon felt, had to respect, report and live with the answers. "You hope that if you're truthful with somebody, they'll stop all the plastic reaction and be truthful and it'll be worth it."

'Jesusgate' destroyed a core fantasy of early rock celebrity – that stars only had hits, not informed opinions. If Presley believed in anything other than God, motherhood and cheeseburgers, his manager, Colonel Parker, ensured that nobody knew it. Bob Dylan was too maliciously cryptic to incite a meaningful revolution in journalistic exchange: He didn't answer questions; he mocked them. Epstein was a paragon of English politesse. Smacked sideways by Beatlemania and desperate not to offend, he naively tried to prevent The Beatles from publicly discussing drugs or America's involvement in Vietnam. He was doomed to fail. The Beatles had been gulping pills since Hamburg. And at one of The Beatles' early US press conferences, a reporter asked, "Do you plan to record any anti-war songs?" "All our songs are anti-war," Lennon shot back.

The most openly combative of the four Beatles, Lennon was poised to trip someone's wire someday. His big mistake was the choice of subject. A central paradox of American democracy is that one of our most cherished liberties – freedom of worship – is often the root cause, or fuel, of our most destructive arguments: from patriotism and gun control to abortion and stem cell research. It was bad enough, fundamentalists believed in '66, that The Beatles incited Teenage USA to extremes of idolatry. Such provocative godlessness, from a foreigner no less, was intolerable.

In Chicago, Lennon refused to play the good ashamed son, effectively setting a new standard for quality and truth in rock'n'roll reporting and, by extension, criticism. It was no coincidence that in that same year, a 17-year-old student at Swarthmore College in Pennsylvania, Paul Williams, founded the first serious journal of rock opinion, Crawdaddy. In November, 1967, a new bi-weekly, Rolling Stone, published its first issue – with Lennon on the cover. Today, pop writing is a career and an industry; Lennon, who had no shame about exploiting his fame in the service of his peace work, would surely laugh at the manipulative games that even junior stars play with the press now and the promotional hagiography that often passes for objective reporting.

But at its best, music journalism still has the capacity to excite and surprise, to crackle with contention, revelation and the sense of mission that Lennon believed – in his heart and conversation – was the essence of his chosen faith: rock'n'roll.

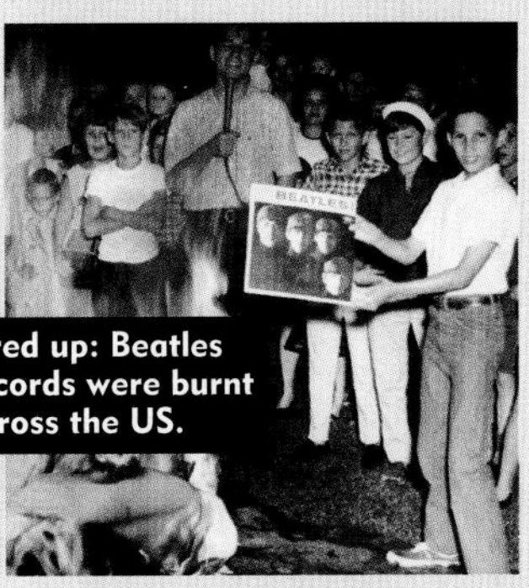

Fired up: Beatles records were burnt across the US.

"I never meant it to be a lousy anti-religious thing, Christianity just seems to me to be shrinking."

PHOTOS: TOPHAM PICTUREPOINT/CORBIS

29 US magazine Datebook reprints Lennon's London's Evening Standard "more popular than Jesus" interview. The Beatles decline to sign a contract requiring them to tour in South Africa, because the country's apartheid policy would prevent blacks from attending concerts.

30 *Yesterday And Today* hits Number 1 in the US.

31 Citizens of Birmingham, Alabama and other US cities, hold public burnings of Beatles records and artefacts, as an angry response to Lennon's Jesus comments.

AUGUST 66

1 McCartney records an appearance on the BBC radio show David Frost At The Phonograph in Studio 15B, Broadcasting House, London.

3 Following the anti-Beatle demonstrations in America, South Africa bans sales of their records.

4 A number of US radio stations announce that they will no longer be playing records by The Beatles.

5 A new album, *Revolver*, and single, Eleanor Rigby/Yellow Submarine are released in the UK.

6 Lennon and McCartney are interviewed at Paul's home in Cavendish Avenue, St John's Wood, for a special hour-long BBC radio programme, The Lennon And McCartney Songbook. Paul's interview, recorded a week earlier, for the BBC radio show David Frost At The Phonograph, is broadcast. Brian Epstein flies to New York, where he holds a press conference intended to defuse the Jesus controversy.

7 In Harrisburg, Pennsylvania, US Republican Senator Robert Fleming announces a campaign to prevent The Beatles from playing in Pennsylvania.

8 The new LP, *Revolver*, and single Yellow Submarine/Eleanor Rigby are released in the US. In Johannesburg, South Africa, the South African Broadcasting Corporation announces a ban on the playing of Beatles records.

9 Fearing that their upcoming US tour might be dangerous to The Beatles in the wake of recent protests, UK fans raise a petition to ask the band not to go.

10 A side effect of the banning of Beatles records is seen on the stock market when the price of shares in their US label, Capitol Records, drops sharply.

11 With their fourth US tour about to start, a press conference is hastily convened in Chicago, to counter the damage being done by Lennon's Jesus comment.

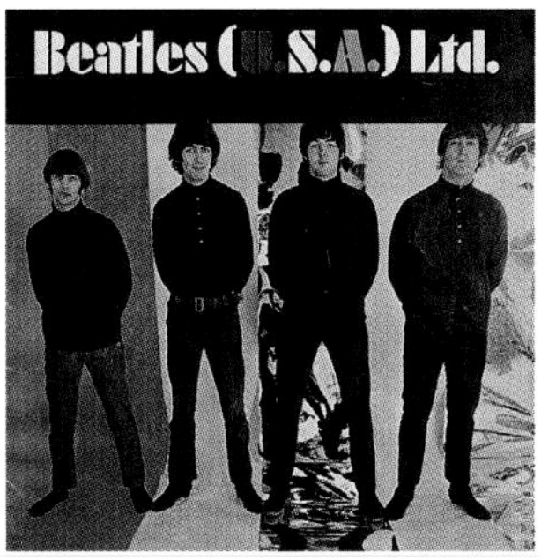

12 The tour begins at the International Amphitheater, Chicago, Illinois. (See tour programme above).

13 *Revolver* tops the UK album charts on the same day that The Beatles play Olympia Stadium, Detroit.

14 The Beatles play Cleveland Stadium, Ohio. Roman newspaper L'Observatore Romano runs an item accepting Lennon's apology for stating that The Beatles were "bigger than Jesus".

15 The tour continues at DC Stadium, Washington DC.

16 John F Kennedy Stadium, Philadelphia, Pennsylvania.

17 The Beatles play Maple Leaf Gardens, Toronto.

18 The double-A-sided single Yellow Submarine/Eleanor Rigby, reaches Number 1 in the UK, as the group play their final New England show at Suffolk Downs Race Track, Boston, Massachusetts. Barry And The Remains open the concert.

19 In the afternoon before a concert in Memphis, Tennessee, Lennon goes in search of Elvis Presley. That evening's concert at Mid-South Coliseum is delayed by a bomb threat. When the band do eventually take to the stage, they are pelted with rotting fruit and other rubbish because of John's allegedly anti-Christian views.

20 The show at Crosley Field, Cincinnati, Ohio is cancelled because of heavy rain, and re-scheduled for the next afternoon.

21 Two shows in one day. First is the delayed Crosley Field gig (above), then, in the evening, Busch Stadium, St Louis, Missouri, 341 miles away.

23 Shea Stadium, New York City. Surprisingly, the show does not sell out – 11,000 seats remain empty.

24 The Beatles arrive in Los Angeles for a one-day break in their Benedict Canyon house.

25 The Beatles play at the Coliseum, Seattle.

26–27 The Beatles enjoy two days of rest and recreation in Benedict Canyon.

28 Dodger Stadium, Los Angeles, California.

29 The last gig of the US tour, at Candlestick Park, San Francisco, later proves to be their last concert ever.

31 The Beatles arrive back in Britain.

What: The Beatles' final gig
Where: Candlestick Park, San Francisco
When: August 29, 1966

THANKS, GOODNIGHT

Against a backdrop of banners pronouncing 'Lennon Saves' and fans dashing at the stage, the Fabs' last ever gig was a triumph. By Dawn Eden.

ON AUGUST 29, 1966, WHEN THE BEATLES' US tour reached San Francisco – its final destination – the road-weary Fabs could breathe easy on one account. Of all the tour cities they'd visited, this was the one least likely to trouble them about John Lennon's "bigger than Jesus" remarks. The locals' sentiments were best expressed at the Candlestick Park concert in a banner that a group of fans hung from the front row: 'Lennon Saves'.

The Beatles flew in that afternoon from Los Angeles, minus Brian Epstein, who had opted to stay behind. According to biographer Ray Coleman, Epstein sensed that it would be the group's last show and was unable to bear the emotions of the event. On The Beatles' chartered plane, they enjoyed a special candlelit meal in honour of the tour's end. George Harrison commented to Barry Tashian, who fronted the Boston-based Remains, one of their opening acts, that he was glad the tour was almost over. "The vibe from the boys was one of anticipation of the final show," Tashian says. "They looked visibly relieved to know they'd be on their way home soon."

The Beatles' plane reached the San Francisco Airport at about 5:30pm. Unlike their previous visits, no cheering crowd awaited them. As Eric Lefcowitz wrote in Tomorrow Never Knows: The Beatles' Last Concert, they instead faced "a wall of grim-faced cops and 50 or so members of the local press". But that was nothing compared to the welcome The Beatles got when their bus reached Candlestick Park only to find the front gate locked. "All of us in the bus were laughing like crazy," recalls Tashian. "The driver headed to the outermost perimeter of the parking lot and began driving faster and faster around the park to escape the fans. Suddenly, in an attempt to get away from a growing convoy of fans following the bus, he exited the parking lot and drove around the neighbourhood near the park."

The 20-minute detour seemed right out of A Hard Day's Night. "We were cruising around tiny residential streets, nearly getting lost," Tashian says. "Finally we re-entered the park and drove through the newly-unlocked gate to the dressing-rooms area."

Backstage, after The Beatles had dinner, they were joined by reporters and guests, including Joan Baez and her sister, Mimi Fariña. One reporter asked if The Beatles were borrowing ideas from Baroque composers. John Lennon replied, "I don't know what a baroque is. I wouldn't know a Handel from a Gretel."

At 8pm, the crowd of 25,000 stood while a hired band played the national anthem. Then The Remains took the stage, which, in a security measure, had been set up 200 feet from the crowd and was surrounded by a security fence. After The Remains' brief set, they backed Bobby Hebb on his hit Sunny and three other numbers, and then The Cyrkle took the stage. Cyrkle member Tom Dawes says that the audience's energy was palpable. "I remember that it was a shining night. The flash cameras going off, the floodlights on, the roar of the crowd... the whole tour had been thrilling, and this was the capper."

The Ronettes (minus Ronnie Spector, who had withdrawn from the tour) followed, backed by the hard-working Remains. Then, at 9.27pm, a local DJ finally introduced The Beatles, who walked across the field to the stage, carrying their guitars and drumsticks.

Dressed in dark green Edwardian suits and flowered silk shirts, The Beatles opened with an abbreviated version of Rock And Roll Music, followed by She's A Woman. After their next number, If I Needed Someone, John Lennon announced a tune "about the very naughty lady called Day Tripper." Then came Baby's In Black, during which five boys dashed towards the stage, only to be stopped by security guards. The Beatles played on, perhaps comforted by the knowledge that their getaway car was nearby. The driver had been instructed to keep the motor running throughout the show, just in case. I Feel Fine followed, then a strained version of Yesterday, and I Wanna Be Your Man. During Nowhere Man there was another security breach, as more boys ran towards the stage and were stopped. The group, clearly annoyed, followed with a sloppy take on Paperback Writer.

Even with the rough edges, the show was one of the best of the tour, according to Tom Dawes. He remembers that their last number, Long Tall Sally, was a showstopper. Afterwards, attentive listeners heard Lennon strum the intro of In My Life before the group got into their car...

The flight back to LA was filled with what Tashian describes as "an air of lightness and celebration". George Harrison, who along with Lennon, had been the least fond of touring, announced: "So it's all over. I can stop pretending to be a Beatle now, people!"

Upon landing in LA, the entourage came off the plane first while the Beatles stayed on board. Before Barry Tashian departed, he timidly asked for autographs. "John said: 'Be sure and look us up if you're within a hundred miles'," Tashian recalls. "I said goodbye and walked on down the steps of the plane back to this life."

For Tom Dawes it was also a tough comedown. "In Candlestick Park, I got up and waved, and 14,000 people went, 'Aaaaaah!'" Dawes says, mimicking the crowd noise. "Three nights later, we were playing a gig at a Catskills hotel where there were 13 people eating dinner, banging their forks on their glasses and telling us to turn it down."

"The flashes going off, the roar of the crowd... The whole tour had been thrilling, and this was the capper."

Park strife: Fans attempt to storm the stage. (Right) the official poster.

PHOTOS: CORBIS

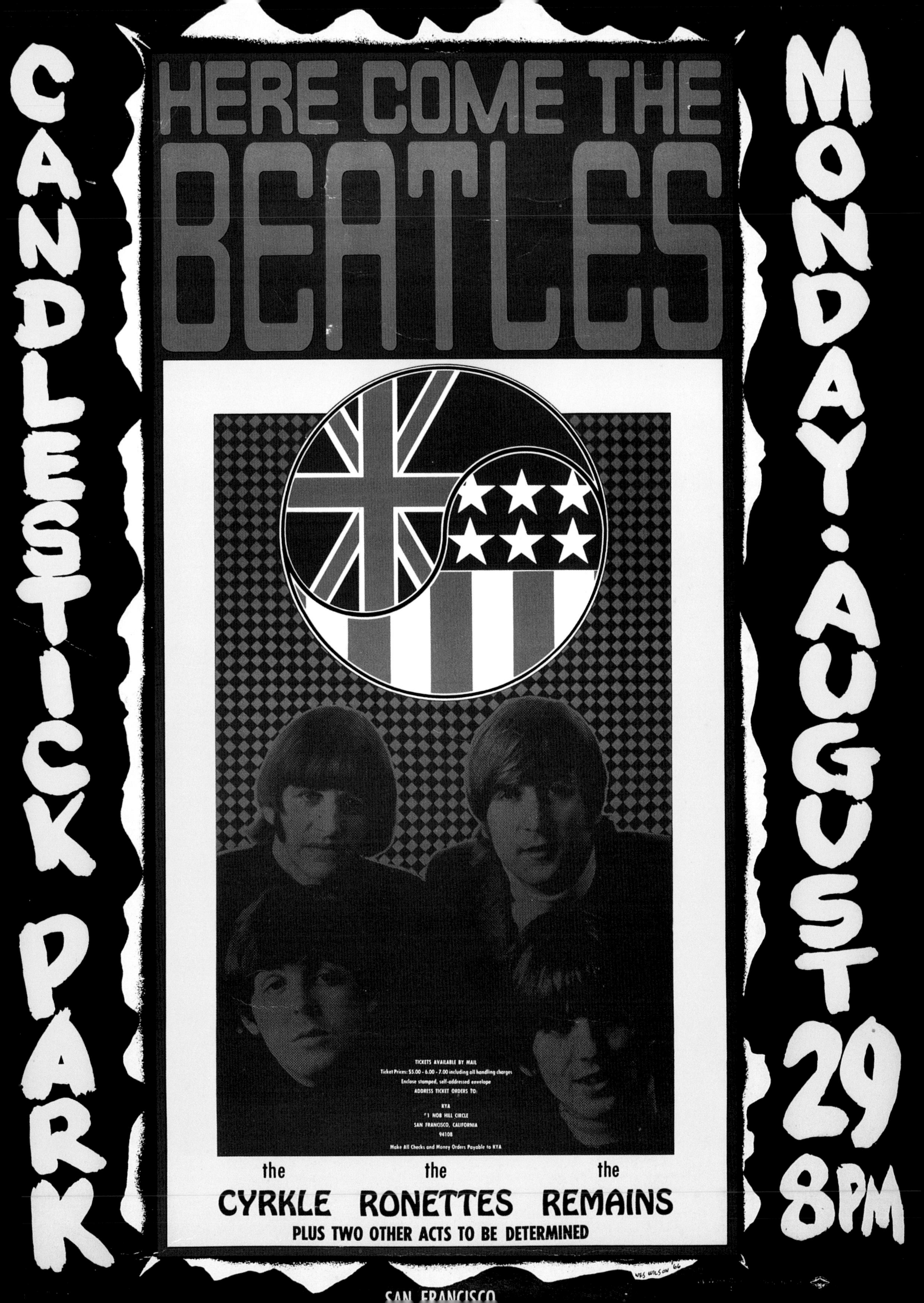

HERE COME THE
BEATLES
TICKETS AVAILABLE BY MAIL
Ticket Prices: $5.00 - 6.00 - 7.00 including all handling charges
Enclose stamped, self-addressed envelope
ADDRESS TICKET ORDERS TO:
KYA
#1 NOB HILL CIRCLE
SAN FRANCISCO, CALIFORNIA
94108
Make All Checks and Money Orders Payable to KYA
the CYRKLE
the RONETTES
the REMAINS
PLUS TWO OTHER ACTS TO BE DETERMINED
CANDLESTICK PARK
MONDAY·AUGUST 29 8PM
SAN FRANCISCO

"One Last Question...

The day before their last ever gig, at Candlestick Park, The Beatles gave their final press conference as a touring band. And the Fab Four were in a very sarcastic, yet playful mood.

On August 28, 1966, The Beatles arrived at Capitol Records Tower, just off the corner of Hollywood and Vine in Los Angeles for a press conference, before that evening playing in front of 45,000 uncontrollable fans at the Dodgers Stadium. At 5.45pm the next day, The Beatles would touch down in San Francisco for their last ever concert, at Candlestick Park, where they would leave as quickly as they arrived – without facing the press.

The Beatles had not only tired of the touring, but they were worn down by the ever more inane questioning at the hands of the press. In LA, they demonstrate the wit of old, but they are also a band who know they will no longer have to do such testing PR duties again. In front of the assembled LA press corps, and in front of a smattering of friends and celebrities like David Crosby of The Byrds and actor Robert Vaughn, The Beatles gave their last press conference as a touring band.

PHOTO: CHUCK BOYD/REDFERNS

Facing the music: The Beatles take on the US media at Capitol Records Tower, LA, August 28, 1966.

Q: What will the next movie project be for The Beatles?
George: Well, somebody has given us an idea and he's working on the script. And if the script's nice then we may do it.
Q: One question we'd like to know in Hollywood, we'd like to know how you compare movie working to, say, the concert tour or recording sessions.
John: We don't compare it much.
Q: One of your countrymen was here yesterday or the day before, and he said that he thought American women were out of style for not wearing mini-skirts, and that their legs were ugly. I'd like to ask you what you think about American women's legs.
Ringo: If they don't wear mini-skirts, how does he know their legs are ugly? (*Laughter*)
Q: On the album cover that was banned here, the one with the dolls and meat – whose idea was it?
John: The photographer who took it.
Q: What was it supposed to mean?
John: We never asked him, you know.
Q: John, why did you decide to make How I Won The War?
John: Uhh, because he [*Dick Lester*] just asked me. And I just said, Yes. And it was just like that.
Q: Do you consider that now since you've been here in the United States for almost a week, that this religious issue is answered once and for all? Would you clarify and repeat the answer that you gave in Chicago?
John: I can't repeat it again because I don't know what I said, you know.
Q: Well, would you clarify the remarks that were attributed to you?
John: You tell me what you think I meant, and I'll tell you whether I agree or not.
Q: Well, some of the remarks attributed to you in some of the newspapers... the press here... concerning the remark that you made comparing the relative popularity of The Beatles with Jesus Christ... and that The Beatles were more popular. This created quite a controversy and a furore in this country, as you are obviously aware.
Paul: Did you know that, John? You created a furore.
Q: Would you clarify the remark?
John: Well, I've clarified it about 800 times. I could have said TV or something else... and that's as clear as it can be. I just used Beatles because I know about them a bit more than TV. But I could have said any number of things. [*Jokingly*] It wouldn't have got as much publicity though.
[*Paul laughs*]
Q: My question is directed at all of you. Do you think this controversy has hurt your careers or has helped you professionally?
Paul: It hasn't helped or hindered it, I don't think. I think most sensible people took it for what it was... and it was only the bigots that took it up and thought it was, you know, on 'their' side... thinking, Aha! Here's something to get them for. But when they read it, they saw that there was nothing wrong with it really. It's just that they thought that by John saying that we were more popular than Jesus they thought, Ah, he's bound to be arrogant. Did you see the fella on telly last night? He said it... on the Tonight Show.
Q: John, who is your favourite group in the United States?
John: I've got a few, you know. Byrds, [*Lovin*] Spoonful, Mamas and Papas, I suppose... on that side of it.
Paul: Beach Boys.
John: And Miracles etcetera, on the other side of it.
Q: I was wondering if you still have an arrangement with the US Internal Revenue Department to pay your taxes through England to them. Another part of the question is, how much have you grossed on your current US tour and is it true that you lost...
George: We don't know about that.
Paul: We don't know about all that. We don't do the money side of it, you know.
George: And we don't particularly worry about it.
John: They just tell us what we get in the end, you know.
Q: The tax thing...
George: We pay tax and things but we don't know how much, or how much we've made or anything, you know, because if we were gonna worry about that we'd be nervous wrecks by now.
Q: I'd like to direct this question to Messrs. Lennon and McCartney. In a recent article, Time magazine put down pop music. And they referred to Day Tripper as being about a prostitute...
Paul: [*Nodding jokingly*] Oh yeah.
Q: ...and Norwegian Wood as being about a lesbian.
Paul: [*Nodding*] Oh yeah.
Q: I just wanted to know what your intent was when you wrote it, and what your feeling is about the Time magazine criticism of the music that is being written today.
Paul: We were just trying to write songs about prostitutes and lesbians, that's all.
[*The room erupts with laughter and applause*]
John: ...quipped Ringo.
Paul: [*Chuckles*] Cut!
John: You can't use it on the air, that.
Q: Will you be working separately in the future?
Paul: All together, probably.
Q: Yeah, but aren't... John Lennon, aren't you doing a picture alone?
John: Yeah, but I mean that'll only be on the holiday bit – in between Beatle...
Q: Fred Paul from KAXK. First of all I'd like to say Hi to you all again, it's really good to see you. I'd like to ask a question that

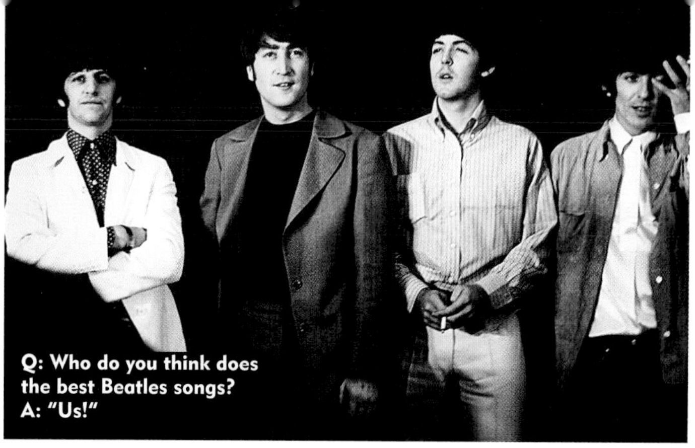

Q: Who do you think does the best Beatles songs?
A: "Us!"

you've never been asked before.
John: Oh no.
Q: What are you going to do when the bubble bursts?
Beatles: [*Laugh*]
John: That's a personal in-joke. He used to ask it at every press conference we entered, to keep the party going.
Q: Do you think we'll have another tour again next year?
John: Ask Brian. Could be.
Paul: Could be, Fred. Brian does all that.
John: OK, Fred?
Q: Outside of Hollywood tonight you had to arrive in an armoured truck, and the truck was swarmed by adoring fans. What is the situation wherever you go? Do you have an opportunity to walk out in the street without being recognised, or can you walk into a theatre to see a movie by yourselves?
John: If you go in when the lights are down you can go in.
Paul: We can do that in England. It's easier in England than it is here. And it's mainly because we know England better.
Ringo: It would also be easier to do it if we weren't on tour, you know. Because we're on tour, people know where we are. That's why we have a crowd.
Paul: [*Joking amazement to Ringo*] Oooo. Oooo!
Ringo: Yes! Yes! I worked that out!
[*Laughter*]
Q: Paul, many of the top artists and musicians in the pop field today have said The Beatles have been a major influence in their music. Are there any other artists who have an important influence on you?
Paul: Oh yes. Nearly everyone, you know. We pinch as much from other people as they pinch from us.
Q: May I ask about the song Eleanor Rigby? What was the motivation or inspiration for that?
John: Two queers.
[*Room erupts with laughter*]
John: Two barrow boys.
Paul: Oh, it's getting disgusting, this press conference...
Q: John, did you ever meet Cass of the Mamas and Papas?
John: Yes, and she's great, and I'm seeing her tonight.
Q: Good.
John: Yeah, she's good.
Q: Have you ever used or trained Beatle doubles as decoys on a...
Ringo: No.
John: No.
Paul: We tried to get Brian Epstein to do it... he wouldn't do it.
[*Laughter*]
Q: Ringo, one question – how much did you contribute to What Goes On and are you contributing to any other Lennon/McCartney compositions?
Ringo: Umm, about five words to What Goes On. And I haven't done a thing since. [*Laughs*]
[*Laughter*]
Q: I'd like to address this to John and Paul. You write a lot of stuff that other people steal from you, and also purchase from you. And different arrangements – Ella Fitzgerald and Boston Pops and stuff like that. When you listen to this on the radio or records and stuff, how do you feel about them using your pieces and changing them around to suit their styles?
Paul: The thing is, they don't steal it.
Q: No. I know that.
Paul: Well, you just said they did!
Paul: Really I mean, you know, it's... once we've done a song and it's published anyone can do it. So, you know, whether we like it or not depends on whether they've done it to our taste.
Q: Well then, let's ask it this way. Who do you think does it the best... The Beatles' songs?
John: Us.
[*Laughter*]
Q: Who?
John: Us.
Q: For those of us who have followed your career from the early days of Liverpool and Hamburg, and the pride in you being awarded the MBE, and the dismay of the unwarranted adverse publicity of late, the question is: individually, what has been your most memorable occasions, and what has been the most disappointing?
Paul: Whew!
John: No idea.
Ringo: You know, there's so many.
George: I think Manila has been the most disappointing.
John: The most exciting is yet to come.
Ringo: ...maybe the most disappointing.
Q: Gentlemen, there was quite a laugh when you went on the stock market with your stock. How is your stock doing?
John: Fine, thanks.
Ringo: Well, it went down, but it's coming up again.
George: It's gone down.
Ringo: Same as any other stock, you know. Up and down.
John: It goes down every time the LPs drop out. They all think they're buying bits of records.
Q: Leonard Bernstein likes your music. How do you like him?
Paul: Very good. He's, you know, great.
John: One of the greats.
Q: I'd like to direct this question to George Harrison if I may.
John: [*Jokingly to George*] What's your new address?
[*Laughter*]
Q: George, before you left England you made a statement that you were going out to America to be beaten up by Americans. Do you mean to say in so many words that you feel the American fan is more a hostile fan than Britain?
George: No! Not at all.
Q: ...or more enthusiastic?
George: Actually, I said that when we arrived back from Manila. They said, 'What are you gonna do next?', and I said, We're gonna rest up before we go and get beaten up over there. Merely... beaten up is... really we just got sort of shoved around.
John: Jostled.
George: Jostled around in cars and in planes, so you know, that's all they did.
Q: Well, do you think that's more an enthusiastic fan than a hostile fan?
George: Uhh, there's definitely more enthusiastic fans. We've, I think...
Paul: But if anyone beat us up, it's not the fans, you know.
George: Yeah. The fan thing... I think they proved it themselves after this. We found out that there are a lot of the fans that are great. And all the ones we lost, I think, we don't really mind anyway. Because if they can't make up their minds... who needs 'em?
Q: I wanted to ask you all about your image. How has your image changed since '63? Is it a little more... uhh... is it the same, or...?
George: An image is how 'you' see us, so you know, you can only answer that.
John: You're the only one that knows.
Q: Who's that?
John: It's you.
Q: Oh, well. No, I want to get your opinion. Is it a little tarnished now? Is it more realistic, or what would you say it is? I know I have my opinion.
John: We're attacked for our opinions.
Paul: We can't tell you our image, you know. We can only... our image is what we read in the newspapers. We know our real image, which is nothing like our.... image... [*Looks confused by his own words, then laughs*].
[*Laughter*]
Paul: [*Laughing*] Forget it.
[*Laughter*]
Q: Who is the young man with the lengthy haircut to your right, rear?
John: That's good old Dave, isn't it?
Paul: Where is he?
[*A young David Crosby, who had been standing with Brian Epstein, suddenly disappears behind a curtain to avoid attention.*]
John: That's Dave from The Byrds. A mate of ours. Ahoy maties.

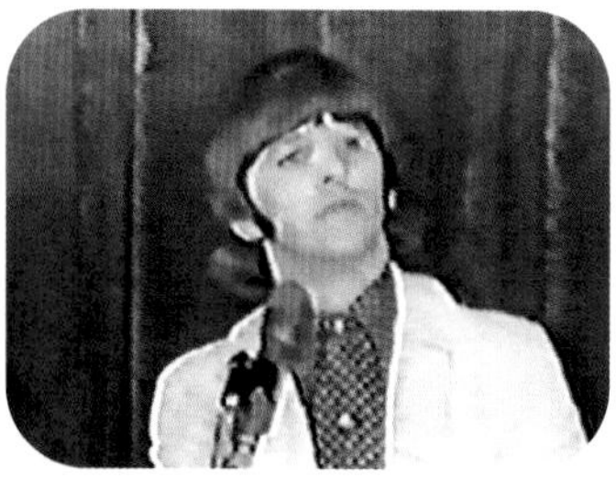

Q: "What was the motivation or inspiration behind Eleanor Rigby?" "Two queers. Two barrow boys." Lennon

Paul: Shy. He's shy.
Q: Do you ever plan to record in the United States?
Paul: We tried actually, but it was a financial matter. Hmmm! A bit of trouble over that one. No, we tried but uhh... it didn't come off.
Ringo: It entailed politics.
Paul: Hush, hush.
John: No comment.
Q: Mr Lennon, is it true that you're planning to give up music for a career in the field of comparative religions?
John: [*Laughs*] No.
[*Laughter*]
John: Is that another of the jokes going round?
Q: I'm sure you've all heard of the many Beatle burnings and Beatle bonfires?
John: We miss them.
Q: ...and I was wondering if you think American girls are fickle.
Ringo: All girls are fickle.
[*Laughter*]
John: Well, the photos we saw of them were, sort of, middle-aged DJs and 12-year-olds burning a pile of LP covers.
Q: This question is directed to Paul and John. You have written quite a few numbers for Peter and Gordon and I understand they don't like it because they think that it's you writing the song that makes it popular. Do you plan to write any more songs for them?
Paul: They, you know... if we write songs for... they ask us to write songs for them – if we do it. I mean, they don't mind it. They like it. But it's... people come up and say, 'Ah, we see you're just getting in on the Lennon/McCartney bandwagon'. That's why they did that one with our names not on it – Woman – because everyone sort of thinks that's the reason that they get hits. It's not true really.
Q: Gentlemen, what do you think would happen to you four if you came to an appearance without the armoured truck and without police?
Ringo: We'd get in a lot easier.
[*Laughter*]
John: We couldn't do it.
Paul: It depends, you know. Sometimes we could have easily made it much better without the armoured truck. But today, probably we wouldn't have.
Q: Do you think you'd be physically harmed?
Paul: Oh. Yeah, probably.
John: What do you think?
Q: Yes, I think so.
Paul: Could be.
Q: The New York Times magazine of Sunday, July 3 carried an article by Maureen Cleave in which she quotes The Beatles, not by name, as saying: 'Show business is an extension of the Jewish religion'.
Paul: Did she say that?
Q: Would you mind amplifying that?
John: Uhh, I said that to her as well. No comment.
Paul: Ahhhhh. Come on, John. Tell 'em what you meant.
John: I mean, you can read into it what you like, you know. It's just a little ol' statement. It's not very serious.
MC: Want to make these the last three questions.
Q: I was wondering, under what condition did you write In His Own Write. That, sort of, wild... those kicky words... I mean, how did you piece them together?
John: I don't know. I can't answer that. You know, it's just the way it happened. I didn't think, Now, how can I do this?
Q: I mean, did you sit down as an author and uhhh...
John: Just like an author.
[*Laughter*]
Q: John, I understand there's a suit pending against The Beatles by Peter Best who claims to be a former member of The Beatles. Is that true?
John: I think he's had a few, but we don't bother with those.
Q: Is this the last question? Are all of your news conferences like this?
John: No.
Paul: [*Laughs*] That's not the last question.
Q: Well, I'm talking about all of the reporters, or would-be reporters and semi-reporters that show up. Are you besieged by these kind of people throughout the tours that you travel here in the United States?
John: You can't always tell the would-bes from the real thing.
[*Laughter*]
Q: Is it this way when you travel in Europe?
John: Yes.
Paul: But what's wrong with them? What's wrong with the crowd?
Q: Nothing. I'm just wondering if you have this many reporters everywhere you go.
Paul: No.
Ringo: Not always.
George: Some of them are just onlookers.
MC: This is the last question.
Q: Tomorrow Never Comes is the last song on the second side, right?
George: Tomorrow Never Knows.
Q: Tomorrow Never Knows. Thank you. Could you give me a vague idea of some of the tape manipulation you used when your voice drops into the track, John. Is that sung backwards by any chance, and recorded forwards?
Paul: No, it's not sung backwards. It's just, umm, recorded pretty straight. There's tape loops on it, which are a bit different. The words are from The Tibetan Book Of The Dead, so there.

With the Press Conference at an end, The Beatles gave a short interview for ABC's Where The Action Is before pulling back some red curtains to unveil a huge blow-up of the front cover of *Revolver*. They were then presented with four gold discs from the Recording Industry Association of America.

The Beatles would not face the press again as a band for another nine months, until they invited a select group of journalists to Brian Epstein's Belgravia home on May 19, 1967, a couple of weeks before the release of *Sgt Pepper*.

"We can't tell you about our image. Our image is what we read in the newspapers. Our real image is nothing like our image."

The Fabs show off their gold discs against a backdrop of a huge *Revolver* sleeve.

PHOTOS: CHUCK BOYD/REDFERNS

Here, There & Everywhere

Photographer Robert Whitaker travelled all over the world taking the most memorable and controversial images of The Beatles. Here, he recounts the tales behind the remarkable shots he took from 1965-66.

When Brian Epstein saw the portrait of himself taken by the then 23-year-old Robert Whitaker in Melbourne, Australia in 1964, he immediately commissioned the photographer to come to London and work with him and The Beatles.

The images created by Whitaker between 1964 and 1966 remain some of the most memorable, enduring and controversial photographs of this pivotal time in The Beatles' career, encapsulating the rapidly-changing ideas of how a pop group could be portrayed. Uninterested in the conventional shots required by most art directors of the time and aware of The Beatles' boredom and frustration by the process, Whitaker involved the band in collaborations that ranged from 'pop art' to 'surrealism'. The notorious 'butcher sleeve' sessions from 1966 are a case in point. The shoot began with the Fabs smartly dressed staring blankly at the lens (the required shot) and ended a few hours later with them wearing white coats, draped in cuts of meat and playing with false eyes and a box full of broken dolls, laughing wildly (see page 50).

With unrestricted access during this period, Whitaker's reportage photos of the band's last tour show life on the road as it really was. And while his work may have come to a natural conclusion with the end of touring and the death of Brian Epstein, in 1967, the pictures here will remain a perfect visual testament to the Fabs at their most exciting.

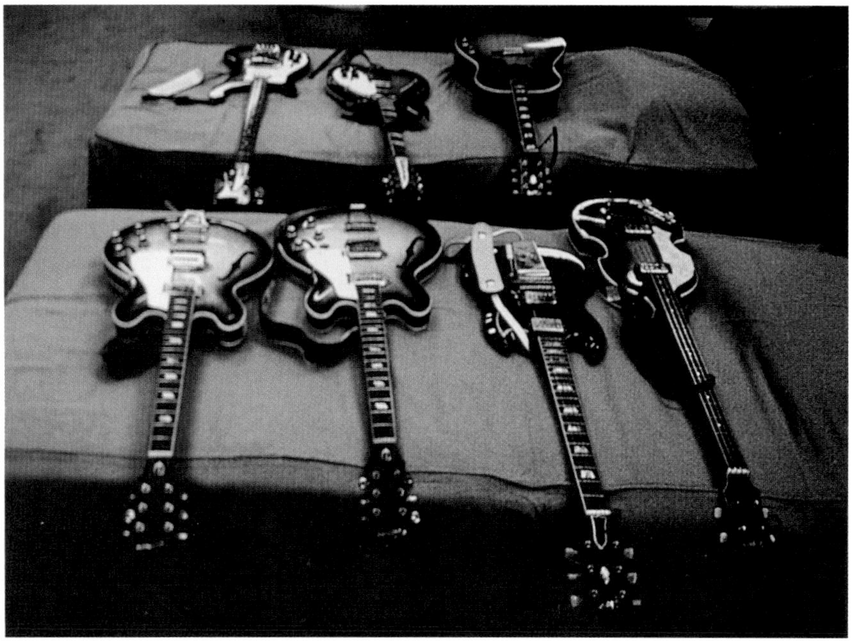

◀ **GUITARS**
TOKYO, 1966

"When I saw all those guitars on a bed in Tokyo, I thought to myself, There is a major set of instruments for a major band, all beautifully put together by Mal Evans or Neil Aspinall. I once put that print into Sotheby's and [Steven Maycock] said that, 'That is probably the most expensive line-up of guitars you'll ever see in your life as far as memorabilia is concerned'."

▶ **GEORGE**
CHISWICK PARK, 1966

"I'm pretty sure it's May '66. It's one of my favourite pictures of George, basically because it really does encapsulate an era, with the 'Way Out' sign behind him, and puffing away on a cigarette, and a bunch of fans in the back-ground. I just turned around and saw him there – I've actually put the focus on the kids – and thought, Wow! I knew that I'd got myself an amazing picture – one that I could not get from a studio. I'm told that somebody at the University of Sussex is supposed to be writing a 6,000-word dissertation about the picture."

WAY
OUT

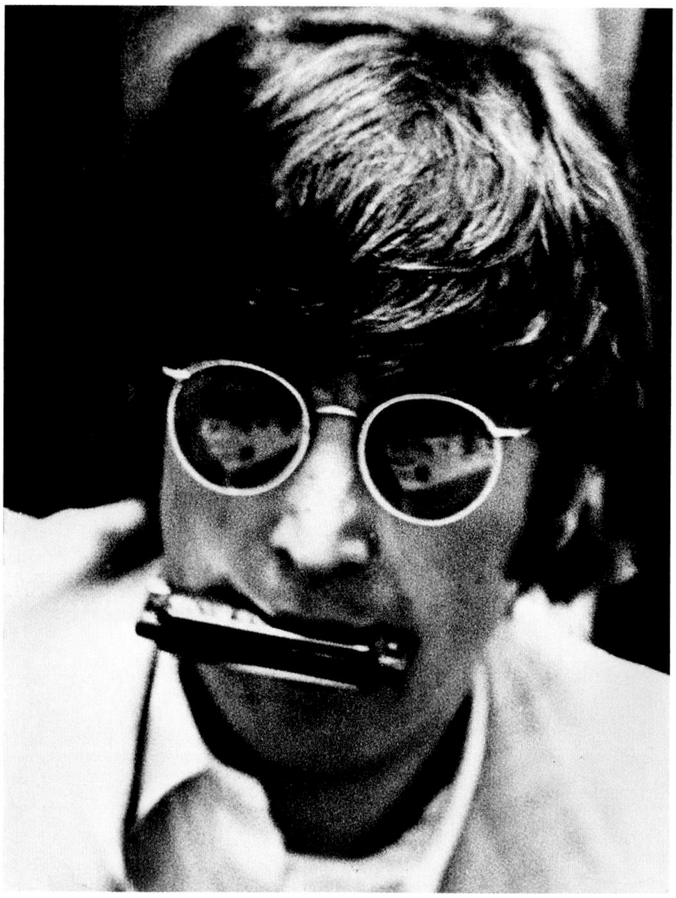

▲ **JOHN WITH HARMONICA MUNICH, 1966**

"There was a walloping great grain through the whole thing and it just floats, that picture. It's tuning-up, again, in the dressing room area and it actually reminded me of Dylan, playing guitar and harmonica at the same time. I love the whole picture, it sits on the page beautifully and graphically illustrates John very well at that period in time. What most people wanted was four people and I was invariably photographing one person so that I wouldn't encroach on their time by saying, 'Come and stand in this silly idiot's position'. I just photographed what I saw. It took a long time for them to realise that I was trying to do my best not to get in their way if I could help it."

▶ **DRESSING ROOM MUNICH, 1966**

"Every now and again I'd get these little private concerts just for me. This was one of them, with them all tuning-up, just making sure it was all correct before they went onstage which was always a great pleasure for me to hear. They would always make sure their voices were as right as rain... not that anyone could ever hear them. I'm pretty sure it's Munich '66."

▲ GEORGE AND JOHN CHELSEA, 1966

"It's part of what I wanted to be on the inside of the *Yesterday And Today* cover that I wanted to design, but ended up basically being a Capitol cock-up because they never asked me what my ideas for the design were. John would actually have had a transparent film of wood grain over his face so that he looked like a wood block, which gives some explanation for why George is banging nails into his head. There would also have been a horizon with the sky where the water should be and the water where the sky was. The idea was partially after Man Ray."

◀ JOHN WEYBRIDGE, 1965

"This is one of my favourite pictures. John and I had been through quite a lengthy conversation about what is 'solid', basically, so we thought that flowers growing out of your eyes, and things like that, could easily be an illusion that you could bring into reality just by making it happen. We were doing a series of pictures based around Narcissus and I have a feeling the flower had something to do with Euripides, who I was partially studying at the time. Somewhere or other I think that Euripides refers to flowers in people's eyes." ⋙

◀ **JOHN WITH GUITAR**
JAPAN, 1966

"The promoter was very kind and said, 'Whatever equipment you want, you can have it'. One of the lenses I was given was one of the first Nikon 21mm lenses which had a little viewfinder that went with it and, as soon as I looked through it, I thought, Here's my new world. Everywhere I looked, I had the most amazing images. This picture was exactly a part of what I wanted to look at and show people. So I was really delighted to get hold of that lens."

◀ **HOTEL**
JAPAN, 1966

"Again, it's with that 21mm lens. You can get so much in, and the detail and depth of field are amazing. The Beatles couldn't leave the hotel, and they were very keen to see as much of the best arts that they could, which was obviously difficult. They were interested in majorly exotic pieces to take back as presents. A whole bunch of people were invited, again by the promoter, to bring in a series of the beautiful *objets d'art* of Japan. That's a picture of some of the pieces that were brought in for them to purchase and, yes, they did buy some of them."

◀ **BIRDCAGE**
CHELSEA, 1966

"This is based around the lyrics for And Your Bird Can Sing. I think I discussed quite a lot of ideas with John, I was pissed off with just taking pictures for the press office... all squeaky clean, just four heads. I just got bored with it and, frankly, I wasn't terribly good at doing pictures like that, yet they seem to grace the covers of lots of magazines to this day."

▶ **JOHN WITH MASK**
TOKYO, 1966

"This is one of the art pieces that was brought in. John was really very amused by these things and he kept looking at me and making this face. Then, all of a sudden, he shoved it in his coat and I just took him over to a window where I had a bit of light and made that picture of him trying to look Japanese. I think, also, that it was at the stage when John was becoming quite interested in the oriental female. He met a lovely girl in Sydney, in '64, called Jenny Keyes whose father was Italian, I think her mother was Chinese." ■

REVOLVER

Talking About A Revolution

For a band who had only just given up touring, *Revolver* is an extraordinary sonic adventure. By Charles Shaar Murray.

Well, you say yes, we say no. The Beatles themselves saw *Revolver* as an extension and consolidation of the studio experimentation with which they'd leavened its predecessor: indeed, they saw their entire studio career as, essentially, an ongoing process. The former Black Panther Party leader David Hilliard once observed that "Revolution is a process rather than an event" and – in artistic terms, at least – The Beatles would surely agree.

Nevertheless, though *Rubber Soul* was an undeniable part of the process (and a hugely enjoyable and rewarding work in its own right), it was *Revolver* which was the event. And the differences between the two albums are at least as significant – if not more so – than their similarities.

The difference between *Rubber Soul* and *Revolver* is the difference between 1965 and 1966; between the end of the early '60s and the beginning of the late '60s, and – most crucially – the difference between a group who still considered themselves to be live performers cutting records which related to the instrumentation and structure of their in-concert incarnation, and a studio collective whose recorded sonic and musical range was limited only by their own imaginations. 1966 was a culturally pivotal year – Hendrix came to London, Star Trek hit US TV screens, bands were splintering and regrouping all over the place – and *Revolver*, The Beatles' 1966 album, was their pivotal recording, the definitive turning point between the Moptop Era and the Beardy Years. The gap between the two albums was bridged by a crucial non-album single, Paperback Writer/Rain, which clearly 'belongs' to *Revolver*. Both cuts sound like rock and roll, not least because of Paperback Writer's crunching riff and Paul McCartney's personal-best bass playing on both sides, but there was so much multi-tracked vocal layering on Writer and backward vocals and guitars on Rain that they found it an embarrassment when they attempted to play Writer live on their final US tour.

> "Revolver was the first album on which the only criterion was: how good can we make it sound here?"

Indeed, the gilt had already worn off their live gingerbread even before the disastrous experience in the Philippines – Marcoses 4, Beatles 0 – which turned them off touring for good. They prided themselves on being musicians, and good ones, but their shows had less and less to do with music. The underpowered, monitorless PA systems of the time were completely inadequate in the enormous stadia where they played, using less amplification than today's bands would haul into a good-sized club. Their music was inaudible to players and to audiences alike: the audiences might not have cared, but The Beatles did. Ringo Starr, particularly, felt that his playing was actually deteriorating: when they played in Japan, where cultural tradition

PHOTO: ROBERT WHITAKER APPLE/HULTON ARCHIVE

John and George filming Paperback Writer's promo – done during the middle of *Revolver* – May 19, 1966.

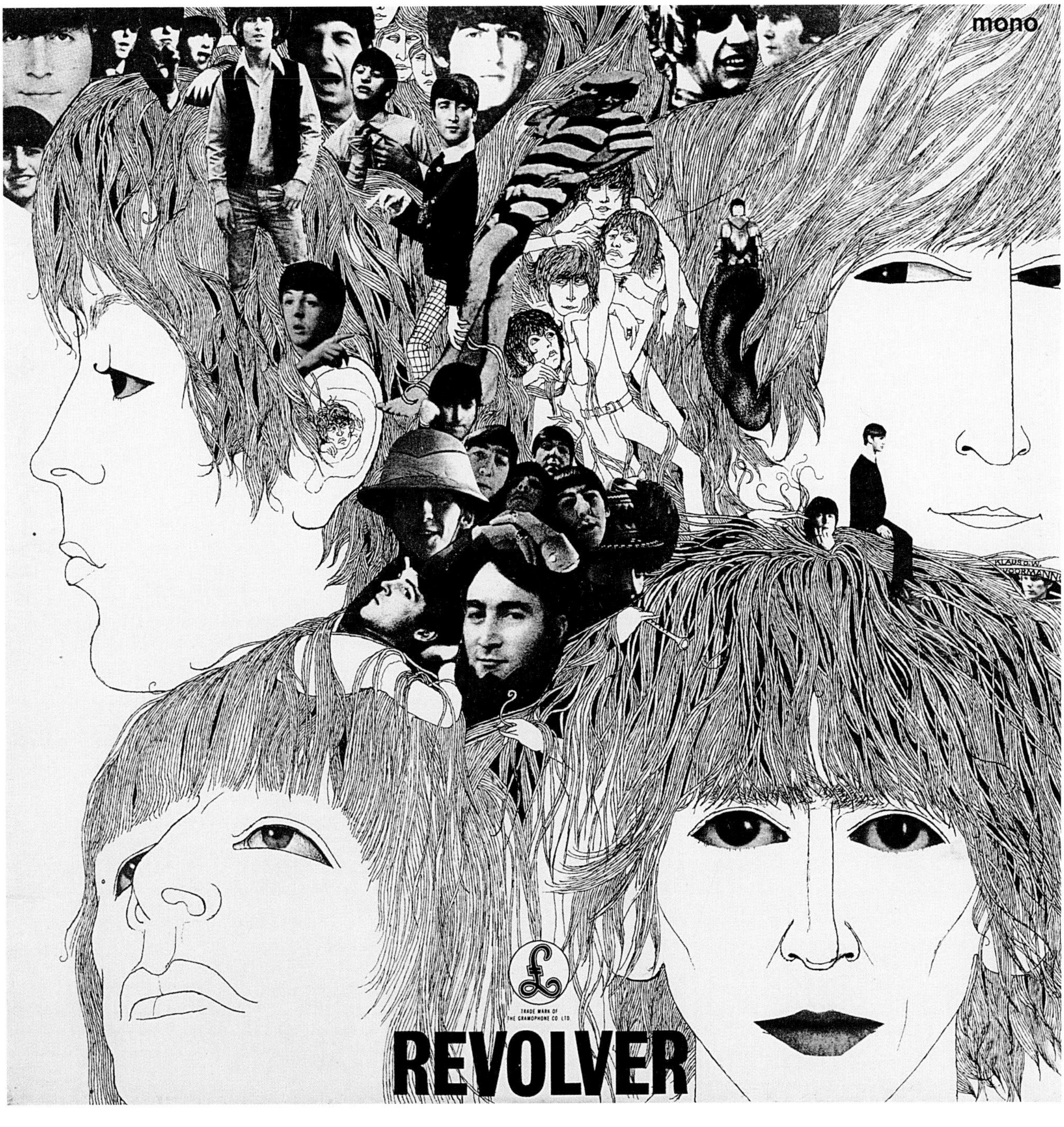

and stern security precluded the screaming which normally masked their performances, they were shocked by how ragged they sounded. The studio must never have seemed so welcoming. Their last official live performances took place after the recording and release of *Revolver*, but those were contractual obligations: they were now, for all practical purposes, a studio group and *Revolver* was the first album on which the only criterion was: how good can we make it sound here?

Revolver divides up, fairly neatly, into what sound like rock-band performances – though most of them are so studio-enhanced that it's hardly surprising that The Beatles considered them impossible to perform live – and soundscapes entirely unrelated to the band's live

TRACK LISTING

A-SIDE

1. Taxman
Harrison
Sung by Harrison

2. Eleanor Rigby
Lennon/McCartney
Sung by McCartney

3. I'm Only Sleeping
Lennon/McCartney
Sung by Lennon

4. Love You To
Harrison
Sung by Harrison

5. Here, There And Everywhere
Lennon/McCartney
Sung by McCartney

6. Yellow Submarine
Lennon/McCartney
Sung by Starr

7. She Said She Said
Lennon/McCartney
Sung by Lennon

B-SIDE

8. Good Day Sunshine
Lennon/McCartney
Sung by McCartney

9. And Your Bird Can Sing
Lennon/McCartney
Sung by Lennon

10. For No One
Lennon/McCartney
Sung by McCartney

11. Doctor Robert
Lennon/McCartney
Sung by Lennon

12. I Want To Tell You
Harrison
Sung by Harrison

13. Got To Get You Into My Life
Lennon/McCartney
Sung by McCartney

14. Tomorrow Never Knows
Lennon/McCartney
Sung by Lennon

WHAT THE PAPERS SAID...

1966's music rags were blown away by *Revolver*.

"The latest Beatles album, *Revolver*, certainly has new sounds and new ideas, and should cause plenty of argument among fans as to whether it is as good as or better than previous efforts. One thing seems certain to me – you'll soon all be singing about a Yellow Submarine... Love You To is an oriental sounding piece, with George joining with Anil Bhagwat to play some sitar jangles, and George singing a Kama Sutra-type lyric... Tomorrow Never Knows is John's vocal, telling you to turn off your mind and relax and float downstream. But how can you relax with the electronic, outer-space noises, often sounding like seagulls? Even John's voice is weirdly fractured and given a far-away sound. Only Ringo's rock-steady drumming is natural."

Allen Evans, NME (July 29, 1966)

Beatles create a new nursery rhyme

says Allen Evans

REVOLVER

New single from LP, too

THE latest Beatles album, "Revolver," certainly has new soun and new ideas, and should cause plenty of argument among fan s to whether it is as good as or better than previous efforts. One thing eems certain to me — you'll soon all be singing about a "Yellow ubmarine." This has been chosen as one "A" side (on Beatles singles both sides are "A," of course) to be released as a 45 next week, along with the ballad, "Eleanor Rigby."

Here is the track by track breakdown of this remarkable LP:

XMAN† is a fast, rocking song, with twangy guitar and vocal by George Harrison, singing a lyric about dealings with the tax inspector, something near to all wealthy Beatles' hearts.

ELEANOR RIGBY—a folksy ballad sung with very clear diction by Paul McCartney, telling the wistful tale, complete with violins in backing, of Miss Rigby being buried with no one there to see it and asking where do all the lonely people come from.

I'M ONLY SLEEPING is a very human lyric about having to get up in the morning and not wanting to. Has two catchy false-endings and good bass playing.

LOVE YOU TOO† is Oriental sounding piece, with George joining with Anil Bhagwat to play some sitar jangles, and George singing a Kama Sutra type lyric.

HERE, THERE AND EVERYWHERE is a slow, soft, wistful song by Paul McCartney, double tracking.

YELLOW SUBMARINE proves a straightforward tune and lyric that should become a nursery or sing-song

them. There's a lot more fooling around behind. As this has been picked for the single, too, it should be a household favourite soon. Words are crazy, like John's poetry.

SHE SAID SHE SAID—high, nasal tones of John Lennon ... this song, about a girl with morbid thoughts being put right by boy.

GOOD DAY SUNSHINE—Paul McCartney does a great vocal job on this bright, airy, light-hearted love song, with piano and drums intro.

AND YOUR BIRD CAN SING—strident, vigorous guitars, then high-pitched, raving vocal, led by John. Lyric is philosophical.

FOR NO ONE—Paul McCartney sings about a girl who has given up a boy who won't believe it. Good horn sound by Alan Civil.

DR. ROBERT. John Lennon's tribute to the medical profession, about a doctor who does well for everyone. Straightforward beat song.

I WANT TO TELL YOU.† Boy wants to tell girl, but can't, how much he likes her. An everyday occurrence, neatly lyriced. George lead vocal, with other wailing ... Guitars and drums ...

GOT TO GET YOU ...

"Paul was right – they'll never be able to copy this one! Neither will The Beatles be able to reproduce a tenth of this material on a live performance. But who cares? Only a handful of the 14 tracks are really Beatle tracks. Most are Paul tracks, John tracks, George tracks, or, in the case of Yellow Submarine, Ringo's track. There are still more ideas buzzing around in The Beatles' heads than in most of the pop world put together. John, Paul, George and Ringo are obviously enjoying the heady freedom of being able to translate their every whim onto record... a brilliant album which underlines once and for all that The Beatles have definitely broken the bounds of what we used to call pop."

Melody Maker (July 30, 1966)

SLEEVE NOTES

What do you give a revolutionary album? An equally stunning cover.

The Beatles were reunited with artist Klaus Voormann for the cover of *Revolver*. A friend of the group since the Hamburg days, Klaus was poised to step into the Swinging London music scene as the new bassist with Manfred Mann. Voormann was asked to come up with a concept for the front of *Revolver* after a circular collage of shots of the band's faces by Robert Freeman was left unused.

Klaus's inventive combination of drawings and photo collage (using a variety of old Beatle stills, including some from the previous LP), perfectly complemented the explosion of musical ideas on *Revolver*, bravely stating its intent in simple black and white (for the first time since *With The Beatles*) – a bold move in the face of the emerging psychedelic scene.

"We were all very pleased with it," recalled Paul in Anthology. "We liked the way there were little things coming out of people's ears, and how he'd collaged things on a small scale while the drawings were on a big scale. He also knew us well enough to capture us rather beautifully in the drawings. We were flattered."

John's friend Pete Shotton remembers The Beatles' original input into the cover. "John, Paul and I devoted an evening to sifting through an enormous pile of newspapers and magazines for pictures of The Beatles, after which we cut out the faces and glued them all together. Our handiwork was later superimposed onto line drawings by Klaus Voorman."

By tucking a small picture of himself next to his signature on the right of the LP, Klaus Voormann became the first person outside of the group to appear on one of their album covers. Voormann's sleeve design picked up the award for Best Album Cover at the 9th Grammy Awards in 1967.

Richard Fairclough

> "Revolver is the album which finds The Beatles building on the foundations of the band they were to become."

sound. "The technology we were now using on records," recalled Harrison, "didn't allow us to play a lot of songs live on tour. We were just a little dance band and we never really thought of augmenting ourselves. We thought, We'll do it to the best of our ability until the point where we can't really do it, and then we'll miss it out."

Thus Taxman – hip, crisp mutant-funk groove, Macca's storming faux-rage guitar solo, and George's lyrical index of the extent to which he was still living in the material world – still sounds like The Beatles live in a way that the real Beatles couldn't. The 'rock' portions of the album are stuffed with guitars: from Harrison's eerie, serpentine backward lines on Lennon's I'm Only Sleeping through to the glorious cascades of jangle, marking The Beatles' take on what The Byrds had done with the Fabs' own proto-folk-rock sound on *A Hard Day's Night* which glisten through Lennon's Doctor Robert, And Your Bird Can Sing and She Said She Said or Harrison's own I Want To Tell You.

And if those rock-guitar pieces were a hassle to approximate live, what of a song like For No One, in which the dominant instruments are piano and french horn? Let alone Eleanor Rigby, scored for string quartet and mass-overdubbed McCartney and Lennon voices. Or George Harrison's Love You To – what was he going to do? Sit cross-legged on the stage with the sitar which, at that point, he could barely play a tune on? Or Good Day Sunshine, with McCartney's rolling piano well to the fore and that climactic hall-of-mirrors fanfare of multi-tracked filtered voices? Or Yellow Submarine, spattered as it is with Goon Show sound effects and even a brief intervention from a brass band?

And then there was Tomorrow Never Knows, the first indication of the intoxicating and terrifying wonderments which lurked in the further reaches of Lennonland. Where previous Beatle epics had dazzled with the beauty and ingenuity of their chord changes and harmonic progressions, this was a one-chord (oh all right, two, but the undercur-

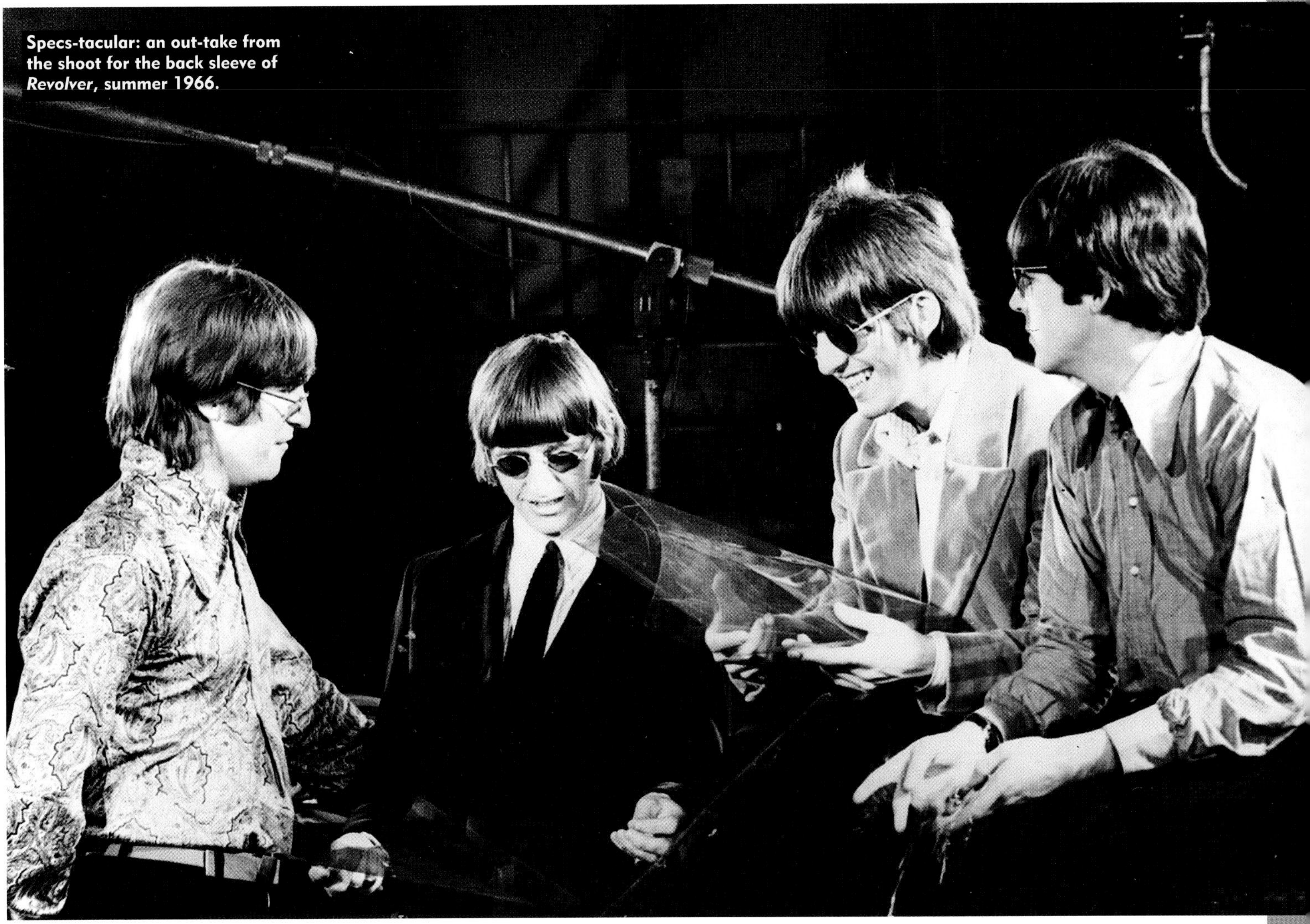

Specs-tacular: an out-take from the shoot for the back sleeve of *Revolver*, summer 1966.

PHOTO: ROBERT WHITAKER

rent remains the same) drone for tamboura, tape-loops and vocal processing which was revolutionary for one of the best studios in the world, let alone any extant performance technology. Like nothing else on this extraordinary album, it depicts The Beatles stunning themselves with the possibilities of their new capabilities, and points the path to *Pepper*.

"You could do it now – have all the loops up there on the keyboards and emulators," Harrison remarked. "You can have as many keyboard players and drummers and orchestras and whatever as you want, but back then that was it."

Revolver is such an extraordinary sonic adventure that it almost distracts attention from the magnificent song-writing from which those soundscapes grow. Remember: Eleanor Rigby, Here There And Everywhere, For No One, Got To Get You Into My Life, I'm Only Sleeping – even Taxman provided grist to Stevie Ray Vaughan's boogie mill, and Yellow Submarine became a perennial childrens' favourite.

Revolver was indeed part of The Beatles ongoing project. But, more so than any of the other recordings, it's the one which finds them building on the foundations of the band they were to become, the band they, and no one else, could be. It was where they set out on their second five-year mission: to explore strange new worlds and boldly go where no band had gone before.

I WANT TO TELL YOU

For The Dandy Warhols' Courtney Taylor-Taylor, *Revolver* is the very definition of psychedelia.

"Three years ago I had a *Revolver* freak-out for six or seven months. I didn't listen to anything else. For me, that record is what psychedelic is. It's not all the way hippy, with like, a million fucking sitars. It's just hypnotic, elasticy, boingy instruments. You use the chords and the harmonies and the melodies to create what's surreal and trippy about it. It was pretty cool that they did that sort of stuff. *Revolver* sounds like a rock band that's discovered pot.

"*Revolver* was the biggest influence on me in that it was something I could understand, it hadn't got too sophisticated. It was people from another reality. The songs were like tiny little psychedelic rock trips. They hadn't gone all the way over to Gilbert and Sullivan, which is something that so many British bands do.

"Tomorrow Never Knows – fuck. They were heading towards dirty guitar tones before that, but the only place you might have heard stuff like that was weird orchestral shit, where the oboe parts might sound backwards – one of those Russian composer trip-heads. Those fucking compressed-to-hell drums, and the cymbals that just go schwoooooo... it's super-rock. That must have freaked the fuck out of people.

"That guitar line on She Said She Said, after 'And she's making me feel like I've never been born' – that's one of the most 'me' things I've ever heard. The first time I heard it, the rest of the song didn't even matter to me. It was just waiting for them to do that bit again.

"It's hard choosing your favourite Beatles album, because it depends what time of the day it is. Maybe my favourite Beatles album is the one that's playing."

Tom Fordyce

Eastern Rising

George Harrison's 1966 trip to Bombay gave him a brief respite from Beatlemania. More profoundly, it would also influence the future of Western culture, argues Neil Spencer.

HE'D THOUGHT THE TACHE HAD DONE THE TRICK. It had been Ravi Shankar's idea – "Disguise yourself. Grow a moustache and cut your hair" – so before George Harrison got on the plane to Bombay on September 14, 1966, the mop got a chop and the tache had appeared. More than a disguise, the moustache was groovy. Patti loved it. Too bad that it hadn't fooled the bellboy of the Taj Mahal Hotel, who knew a Beatle when he saw one, even if he and his glamorous wife were checked in as Mr and Mrs Sam Wells. Once the 'lift operator' in question had reported his sighting, news that the hotel was hosting the Harrisons had spread through Bombay faster than a speeding auto-rickshaw.

Within hours, Bombay had its own outbreak of Beatlemania, as the gracious Edwardian battlements of the Taj was besieged by thousands of teenagers, yelling "George! George! Ravi Shankar! Bring George!"

In the musicians' suites upstairs, telephones rang constantly. One caller claiming to be 'Mrs Shankar' demanded to speak to George but changed her mind when the real-life Mr Shankar took the call. After a couple of days, with the police ineffectively shooing the kids away, it was clear that, as Ravi Shankar put it, "I couldn't teach and George couldn't practise". At a hastily convened press conference, the classical star explained that George Harrison had come to India "not as a Beatle but as my disciple", and asked for the pair to be left to work in peace.

PHOTO: TOPHAM PICTUREPOINT

George and his musical and spiritual guru, Ravi Shankar, relax backstage at the Hollywood Bowl, August 4, 1967.

"NOT AS A BEATLE!" HOW THOSE WORDS MUST HAVE echoed in George Harrison's ears. He yearned for escape from the gilded cage of Beatledom. His threat to quit the group meant The Beatles had already played their last concert. Over the next six weeks, 24-year-old George would discover, for the first time since he was 15, how it felt not to be a Beatle. Isolated in the foothills of the Himalayas or submerged in the dusty, crowded bustle of Indian life, Harrison discovered himself anew. His second Indian encounter – earlier in the year, there had had been a four-day stop-over in Delhi, en route from the Fabs' Manila debacle, when he had bought himself a proper sitar – was to shape the rest of Harrison's life, The Beatles' subsequent career, and influence the shape of western popular culture for decades to come.

After autumn '66, after Harrison has fallen in love with the bustling, mystical chaos of Mother India, after that comes the deluge: The Beatles in Indian drag, togged out in kaftans and Nehru suits. Meditation. The Beatles in India, up a mountain and up a gum tree with Sexy Sadie. Hendrix cast as Hindu deity on the *Axis: Bold As Love* cover. Sitars and velvet loons over the home counties. The Moody Blues chanting "Om". Cheesecloth. Hare Krishna in the hit parade. All Things Must Pass. Instant Karma. The Concert For Bangladesh.

But first came India itself, which, once George and Ravi had moved to quieter quarters outside Bombay, came crowding in on the young multi-millionaire with unexpected force. After years of stockbroker belt living and hiding in hotel rooms, the experience was overwhelming. "It's unbelievable; you can go down the street and there's somebody driving a bus or a taxi or riding a bicycle and there's a chicken and a cow, and someone in a business suit with a briefcase, and an old sannyasi with a saffron robe. All mixed together. It's an incredible place with layers and layers of sounds and colours and noises, and it all bombards your senses," George recalled later. "I felt as if I was back in time. It was the first feeling I'd ever had of being liberated from a Beatle or a number. It comes back to Patrick McGoohan in The Prisoner: I am not a number."

Study under Ravi proved rigorous – "the first time I'd approached music with a bit of discipline". There were hours of scales to learn, and enough yoga to be able to hold the unwieldy sitar in the correct position while sitting happily cross-legged for hours on end. Most of the direct teaching came not from Shankar himself but from his first lieutenant, Shambu Das, with whom Harrison quickly struck up a close relationship.

To go with the ardours of studentship there were excursions, experiences, highs to rival anything from George's dalliance with pot and acid (in India he had to clean up his act). Harrison had come to India with his head full of yogis: "stories about old men who were hundreds of years old, levitating yogis and saints who were able to be buried for weeks and live. I wanted to see it all for myself." His hosts took George to the ancient temple town of Benares, where thousands of holy men had gathered for the Ramlila festival; "all kinds of groups of people, a lot of them chanting, a mixture of unbelievable things, with the Maharaja coming through on the back of an elephant, with the dust rising. It gave me a great buzz."

Ravi Shankar: "George had come to India not as a Beatle, but as my disciple."

Later, after sightseeing and temple visits, there was more sitar practice; in beautiful, sacred Rishikesh (where the Maharishi's compound would later play host to The Beatles), and in the lofty heights of Kashmir, where Harrison lived with Shankar and his students on a houseboat moored on an Himalayan lake. It was an idyllic setting, which, 30 years on, Harrison would recall sweetly. "They'd wake us up before the sun and give us tea and biscuits, and you'd see boats going by pulling these floating gardens, and next door I'd hear Ravi doing his morning practice. It was a very privileged position."

By then Harrison knew that in Shankar he had found not just his musical guru but, since Hindu thought holds music as "a godly thing", his spiritual guru. And, as the world soon found out, George had found God, a way to make sense of what he and Lennon had glimpsed on their acid trips, "the dental experience" as the in-joke had it.

When Harrison arrived back in London with Patti in late October, he was a completely changed man. He was, for a start, a more focused musician, albeit one who would barely pick up a guitar for the next couple of years, so keenly did he pursue his sitar studies. Great songs now started to flow from Harrison – from here on, he would always have more material than The Beatles' albums could accommodate.

India also gave Harrison his own oeuvre; John had his artiness and surrealism; Paul had his music hall and avant-garde dabblings. Now George had his own thing to add to the party, something that would enable the Baby Beatle to step out of the shadow. It wasn't just India, its

Bombay mix: (left) George with a tourist guide and (right) with Patti on arriving at the Taj Mahal Hotel, Bombay, September 14, 1966.

"In Bombay I felt as if I was going back in time. It was the first feeling I had ever had of being liberated from a Beatle or a number."

music, and his new-found enthusiasm for religion and philosophy. Now he knew how it felt not to be a Beatle. None of the others had that.

To the other Beatles and their entourage it must have seemed their kid brother had 'gone troppo', lost his senses in the Tropic of Cancer . A few days after his return, Ravi Shankar also touched down in London, and was met at the airport by George, still wearing his skimpy Indian clothes. Ravi arrived wearing a crisp, European suit.

Looking back, Harrison realised that the Indian connection had been set out like a trail. The plotline for Help! – a cartoon-like tale of thugees dedicated to the dark goddess Kali chasing a magic ring – had led to his first encounter with the sitar in a restaurant scene for which Richard Lester had hired Indian musicians. The tremulous coda for Norwegian Wood had duly followed, picked out on a tourist-level sitar purchased from Indiacraft on Oxford Street.

Then there was the book. On George's 22nd birthday, on the set of Help!, an Indian had cycled up to The Beatles out of nowhere and pressed a book about Indian religion on each of them. None had given it more than a glance, but now Harrison realised that this, too, was a clue directing him to The Path. Harrison was far from the only one hearing the call of the East.

Earlier in the summer of 1965, The Kinks' See My Friend had droned its way across the river and up the charts, born on the sitar-like twang of Dave Davies' beat-up Framus 12-string, and composed by brother Ray after an Indian pit-stop en route to an Australian tour.

Ray had sniffed something on the ether, something more than the curry houses rapidly becoming a feature of mid-'60s Britain. The West was about to enter one of its periodic love affairs with the sub-continent. Ever since Madame Blavatsky had awakened interest in Hinduism and Buddhism a century earlier, Indian mysticism had been seeping into Western intellectual circles. There were successive generations of devotees to the Eastern mysteries, among them poet and magus WB Yeats, psychedelic pioneer Aldous Huxley and beat daddy Allen Ginsberg. If you listened hard enough, you could already detect finger cymbals and the chant of 'Hare Krishna' on the ether from New York, where Ginsberg had become an enthusiastic supporter of the Krishna Consciousness movement that a few years later would scoop up George Harrison and influence him for the rest of his life.

Most of the Eastern breezes wafting into the chic flats of Chelsea and the dope dens of Notting Dale blew from Buddhist Nepal or hash-laden North Africa, but no one was fussy about cultural purity. The Tibetan Book Of The Dead (inspiration for Tomorrow Never Knows), the beat zen of Jack Kerouac, the North African interiors of Stones favourite Christopher Gibbs, Chinese divination with the I Ching, Sufi love poetry, ancient Indian Vedas: all the exotica and esoterica of the Near, Middle and Far East was tumbled together, mixed with tobacco and Nepalese Temple Balls and smoked until senseless. Harrison's fascination for India fitted in seamlessly.

When The Beatles got into the East, so did everybody else. As ever, they crystallized the incoming mood first. It was the same with the ➾

PHOTOS: ASSOCIATED PRESS/REDFERNS/CORBIS

Flower power: The Beatles and partners' meeting with the Maharishi, Bangor, August 1967.

PHOTOS: REX/HULTON ARCHIVE

moustaches – no one could quite remember who'd started them off. One minute everyone was clean shaven, the next they were trying to out-Zapata each other.

Norwegian Wood set sitar strings stirring. The Stones, never afraid to follow where The Beatles had led, soon had their own shimmering through Paint It Black. Traffic kept one in their Berkshire cottage. Harrison, for his part, had already written an entire song, Love You To, on a sitar. Even if you couldn't play one, it was cool to own one.

Throughout the winter of 1965 and 1966, Harrison kept hearing a name he should check out: Ravi Shankar. David Crosby of The Byrds had mentioned him, for California, too, was experiencing its own Eastern dawn – guitarist Paul Butterfield, for example, was working on a blues raga written after listening to a Shankar record on LSD. George bought some of Shankar's records and was smitten. "It just called on me. The pure sound of it and what was playing just appealed to me so much." When Shankar next visited Britain, in 1966, it seemed everyone was keen that the two men should meet. Yet Harrison was loath to meet Shankar on terms defined by the press – 'Star of India meets mystic moptop'. That was no way for a humble student to approach a master. Harrison already had friends in London's Asian Music Circle. Discreet soundings were made, an encounter arranged.

There are at least two versions of the pair's initial meeting. Harrison recalls it being at dinner at the house of Peter Sellers, a friend since Beatlemania days. Britain's leading comedy actor was an old India hand who had entertained troops in the Eastern empire during the Second World War, and whose impeccable Indian accent had been put to use in the Goons and on his Goodness Gracious Me hit with Sophia Loren.

Shankar recalls the encounter being hosted by the Circle. Over dinner, Harrison told Shankar about Love You To, which he'd recently cut with members of the Circle. Shankar remembers the occasion as something of an embarrassment: "I was somewhat oblivious to the scale of the star. I felt ashamed because I didn't know how popular he or his group was."

Within days Shankar was down at George's in Esher to give a personal performance and teach him about the instrument. Harrison was overwhelmed. "I felt I wanted to walk out of my home that day and take a one-way ticket to Calcutta. I would even have left Patti behind in that moment," he said. Later, Shankar, complete with tabla player, staged a personal show for George, John and Ringo. George learnt one lesson early: putting down his sitar to answer the phone, he received a sharp crack to the leg for stepping across his sitar, and failing to "show respect for the instrument".

On the outside, the relationship that unfolded between Harrison and Shankar was one of ascetic Eastern master and pampered Western pop star. In fact, Ravi and George had more in common than might first appear. Both were the youngest siblings of their large families. As a young man Shankar, too, had enjoyed a privileged life which mixed showbusiness, music, art and glamour. His eldest brother, Uday, was a celebrated dancer and choreographer who had worked with Russian ballet icon Anna Pavlova and whose own Indian dance troupe wowed first Europe then the States in the 1930s. It was a family affair, with Uday's mother and two grown-up brothers on board, and little Ravi along for the ride. Ravi's teenage years were spent in Paris, sneak-reading comics hidden in the textbooks of his Catholic lycée, and later, in New York, watching gangster movies and even checking out Harlem's Cotton Club. Meanwhile, he gained his own spot in the troupe's performance.

It was only after some anguish that Ravi had renounced all this to follow his own musical guru, sarod player Ustad Allauddin Khan. Even after Shankar had emerged as a sitar star of independent India in the 1940s and 1950s, he'd raised ruffles in Indian classical circles by writing film music and collaborating with Westerners like violinist Yehudi Menuhin and jazz musicians like Bud Shank. His association with Harrison and the emergent force of rock would likewise make Shankar many enemies at home in the years to come, while winning him a huge young Western audience.

Ravi's relationship with the hippies was bumpy from the start. When he played the Monterey festival in the summer of 1967 he was appalled to find the place awash with spaced-out people. Shankar refused to play between rock acts and offered his fee back. By way of appeasement, the organisers handed him the whole of Sunday afternoon, which became a communal bliss-out, after which Shankar watched in shock as first Jimi Hendrix and then The Who destroyed their guitars. Music was meant to be a godly thing.

By summer 1967, the Indian bug was everywhere, not least because of Within You, Without You on *Sgt Pepper*, which Harrison recorded with members of the Asian Music Circle. Most of these were part-time musicians; store salesmen by day, Beatle sidekicks by night. To this day, no one knows the name of the sitar player on the track, which was widely assumed to be Harrison at the time. The song, the result of a late-night conversation between Harrison and friend Klaus Voorman, and composed initially on harmonium, was melodically beguiling – it was based on a sargam Harrison had been practising, one of the melodies that are the basis of the classical ragas. Instead of Harrison's usual sourpuss lyrics, it was warm in tone, if preachy and elitist ("If they only knew!"). George's involvement with *Pepper* was otherwise minimal beyond a few guitar parts and nominating a bunch of gurus for the cover (George Martin recalls him as "the Lone Ranger" at the time). The flippant Only A Northern Song spoke volumes about his new attitude to The Beatles and his place within them.

The group's power balance was to tip dramatically after Patti Harrison persuaded the group to attend a lecture by the Maharishi Mahesh Yogi in Bangor, August 1967. George's interest in the Maharishi's promise of meditational bliss without drugs had been spurred by a recent bad acid trip in San Francisco (he'd been gobbling LSD all year). He was in California to talk-up Ravi Shankar's show at the Hollywood Bowl on August 4, and had decided to check on the new utopia unfolding up the coast in Frisco – "you're gonna meet some gentle people there". Dropping a tab and going walkabout in Haight-Ashbury to meet the flower children, the Beatle instead encountered a crowd of panhandling drug casualties. He and his minder Derek Taylor quickly took their expanded consciousness back to the limo, but the trip got worse, ending in a wretched air flight back to Blighty.

"George met Ravi at Heathrow airport wearing his skimpy Indian clothes. Shankar arrived wearing a crisp, European suit."

Six months later, The Beatles and their wives were in Rishikesh, now playing out George's version of The Beatles as mystic messengers. In retrospect, it was amazing that John, Paul and George stuck out their retreat as long as they did (two months), though India did offer, if not enlightenment, a chance to detox, learn meditation, write the next album, and actually find out what George was on about.

Their disenchantment with the Maharishi, who was soon found to have carnal and pecuniary ambitions unbecoming to a holy man, didn't dent Harrison's fascination for India (indeed, he was inclined to give the Maharishi the benefit of the doubt), or even that of Lennon, who had written the deadly Sexy Sadie during an interminable wait for the taxi to take him, Cynthia, George and Patti from Rishikesh. A year later, when Swami Prabhupada, the founder of the International Society for Krishna Consciousness, touched down in London, John Lennon's Rolls Royce was there to whisk the elderly guru to Tittenhurst Park, where he stayed for several weeks.

"Where's the roadies?" Shankar in London, '67.

Soon the chant of 'Hare Krishna', which Prabhupada had brought to the West as a short cut to enlightenment, was ringing from the charts courtesy of Apple. Not everyone was pleased to hear it. Many of those in the would-be 'alternative society' of the late '60s were desperate to liberate themselves from the strictures of religion, wherever it came from, and were unmoved by the Krishna's sect regime of strict vegetarianism, no alcohol, no drugs, and no sex.

John Lennon's search for truth soon led him to another mantra: 'No guru', which he barked out on *Plastic Ono Band*. Later, in his bread-baking years at the Dakota, Lennon would amuse himself with vinegary send-ups of his Indian guides and 'The Great Wok' (see The Rishi Kesh Song and You Gotta Serve Yourself, both on *Anthology*, the latter written after Dylan had embraced Christianity).

Harrison's interest in Indian religion never wavered, though he admitted he often found it hard to practise what he preached. Still, after a long, long, long time he had found his sweet lord in Krishna, the beautiful, musicianly-favoured son of the Hindu pantheon and its most Christ-like figure. When George bought a lavish rural headquarters for the Krishna Consciousness movement, he put his money where his mouth was, though mainstream Hindus wondered why the generous young Beatle had gotten himself mixed up with the Hindu equivalent of the Jesus People. Sometimes it seemed Harrison's idealism came liberally laced with the naivety of the rich and remote. It was all very well for George to extend the hospitality of Apple to the Hell's Angels he befriended in California – he wasn't the one having to deal with the mayhem they caused during their stay. "People, when we were pleasant, were pleasant back," recalled Derek Taylor. "They were not pleasant."

The contradictions of George, the meditating gardener with a fast-car fixation, ran deep. In the late '60s he wrestled with the problems of attaining "the complete, whole universal consciousness that is devoid of duality and ego". On I Me Mine, Harrison also saw The Beatles' success as divinely inspired. Speaking to Hunter Davies for The Beatles' official biography, Harrison reflected on the book pressed on him by the Indian cyclist back on the Help! set. "I now know it was part of a pattern. It was all planned that I should read it now. It all follows a path, just like our path... we were made John, Paul, George and Ringo because of what we did last time, it was all there for us, on a plate. We're reaping whatever we sowed last time.

"I'll tell you one thing for sure – once you get to the point where you're doing things for truth's sake, then nobody can ever touch you again, because you're harmonising with a greater power. The farther into spiritual life I go, the easier it is to see that The Beatles aren't really controlling any of it, but that something else has now taken us firmly in hand." ■

In the army now: "John's character, Gripweed, was a slimy, servile little person – a working-class ex-Fascist, no less."

What: How I Won The War
Where: Hanover, Germany
When: September 5, 1966

PRIVATE ON PARADE

After The Beatles quit touring, John Lennon needed some time away from the band. He decided to make a satirical war movie. By Jon Savage.

FIVE DAYS AFTER RETURNING FROM THE Beatles' final paying concert at Candlestick Park, John Lennon flew out to Germany for his next role – as Private Gripweed in Dick Lester's How I Won The War. The next day, his coiffed hair was brutally cut to just over army regulation length: a drastic new look that, together with the granny glasses that he assumed for the role and would retain thereafter, marked the psychic and emotional changes occurring within.

If 1966 was the crux year for The Beatles, then Lennon's assumption of a comparatively minor role in a satirical war movie was an act both out of character and born of desperation. As he revealed in 1980, "I was always waiting for a reason to get out of The Beatles from the day I made How I Won The War in 1966. I just didn't have the guts to do it, you see. Because I didn't know where to go. I did it because The Beatles had stopped touring and I didn't know what to do."

Indeed, How I Won The War remains better-known for its part in The Beatles' story than as a piece of cinema. Lester's film, written by the Help! screenwriter, Charles Wood, attempts to harness fast-cutting surrealism to hard-hitting war protest with unhappy results. The point about the absurd illogic of war is quickly made, while the episodic script, the endless speeches to camera and the military-decibel voices remove any sense of involvement or enjoyment.

Lennon is a pleasure, as always, but the script does not give him much to do. Gripweed is a slimy, servile little character – a working-class ex-Fascist, no less – which must have been satisfyingly iconoclastic for the man who played him. He gets off a few good lines and hisses "bastard" at all the right points, but when he gets blown up by a mortar shell at the film's climax, you don't really care. After all, the script takes care of that: "I knew this would happen," Gripweed moans, holding his stomach. "You knew it would happen, didn't you?"

Place it within the context of its times, however, and you can give all concerned a medal for bravery. In 1966, Britain was still awash with films celebrating the war; criticism only became acceptable at the box office with Richard Attenborough's 1969 Oh! What A Lovely War – which took several pointers from Lester's effort. As much to the point is the fact that it occurred at the point where The Beatles, and John Lennon in particular, were at their most explicit about their opposition to war – especially the rapidly escalating American involvement in Vietnam. Interviewers had asked The Beatles about military matters during their early tours of the US, but they usually parried the topic. There would be occasional asides – like John's 1964 comment, "all our songs are anti-war" – but, under advice from Brian Epstein, they avoided direct confrontation.

Sometime in late 1965, according to Barry Miles, Paul McCartney went to see the philosopher, veteran pacifist and CND avatar Bertrand Russell who alerted him to the fact that "Vietnam was a very bad war, it was an imperialist war". The first overt statement comes with John Lennon's retort to the banning of the 'Butcher' sleeve in spring 1966: it was "as relevant as Vietnam". There were also some sharp exchanges in the June 30 Tokyo press conference. When asked, "How much interest do you take in the war that is going in Vietnam now?", Lennon replied: "Well, we think about it everyday, and we don't agree with it and we think it's wrong. That's how much interest we take. That's all we can do about it... and say that we don't like it."

Interviewed by Look Magazine on the set of How I Won The War, Lennon said he wanted to do the film "because of what it stands for". The report catches a nervous young man out of his usual environment: the other actors find it difficult to relate to him and he is not sure about his own abilities. He is also under no illusions about the new youth community: "If they said, Fight the war now, my age group would fight the war. Not that they'd want to. There might be a bit more trouble getting them in line because I'd be up there shouting, Don't do it."

John shows off his new barnet, September 1966.

How I Won The War took eight weeks to film, during which Lennon visited Hamburg and Paris, smoked marijuana, got very bored and wrote Strawberry Fields Forever. Save some post-production dubbing, that was the limit of his involvement until the film's premiere on October 18, 1967. The experience gave him an enforced detox from Beatle life which offered him a chance to refill the creative well and acquire some perspective: his comments about British society in the Look interview prefigure his infamous 'Lennon Remembers' rant.

How I Won The War stands with the 'Butcher' cover and the Jesus controversy as marking the moment – and the year, 1966 – when The Beatles stepped out from behind the boy band image and started to talk about what was really on their minds and in their hearts. As beneficiaries of the decision to stop National Service in the UK, The Beatles, at first intuitively and later ideologically, rejected militarism past (all those war films) and present (Vietnam). In doing so, they helped to influence successive generations against, as Derek Taylor later wrote, "war and violence as a means of dealing with the problems that politicians had allowed to get out of hand."

"I was always waiting for a reason to get out of The Beatles from the day I made How I Won The War in 1966."

PHOTOS: REX, PICTORIAL PRESS, TOPHAM PICTUREPOINT

SEPTEMBER 66

5 Lennon flies to Germany to begin filming his role as Private Gripweed in the film, How I Won The War.

6–14 Lennon continues filming in Germany (below).

8 Cliff Bennett And The Rebel Rousers achieve their highest-ever UK singles chart position when their cover of Got To Get You Into My Life peaks at Number 6.

12 Eleanor Rigby/Yellow Submarine is certified as a gold disc in the US.

13 Otis Redding records Day Tripper for Volt Records.

14 Harrison flies to India with Patti. While there, he takes sitar lessons from Ravi Shankar.

15 Lennon, having completed filming of How I Won The War, travels by train from Germany to Paris, France, to join McCartney and Brian Epstein.

17 Lennon and McCartney remain in Paris for the weekend, with manager Brian Epstein.

18 Lennon flies to Spain, for further filming on How I Won The War. While there, he writes Strawberry Fields Forever. Ringo sets up his own construction company, Bricky Builders, which will handle the renovations on his house.

20 In Bombay, India, Harrison becomes the first Beatle to meet with the Maharishi Mahesh Yogi. George is interviewed about his interest in Indian music and culture. The interview will be broadcast during December by BBC radio programme The Lively Arts.

27 Brian Epstein enters the Priory hospital in Roehampton, London, for rest and medical checks.

OCTOBER 66

8 Ringo and Maureen fly to Malaga for a holiday.

11 John and Cynthia see Ben E King at the Scotch Of St James.

14 It is announced that McCartney is composing the score for a new Hayley Mills movie. Provisionally titled Wedlocked Or All In Good Time, it will eventually reach the screens as The Family Way.

15 McCartney is among the guests when upcoming psychedelic bands Pink Floyd and Soft Machine perform at the launch party for London-based underground newspaper International Times (left). Despite still living with Chrissie Shrimpton, Mick Jagger turns up with his new girlfriend Marianne Faithfull.

17 The album, *The Amazing Beatles* is released in the US on Clarion Records.

22 *Revolver* is certified as a gold disc.

26 Alma Cogan, with whom Lennon was rumoured to have had an affair, dies from cancer at the Middlesex Hospital, London. Ravi Shankar arrives from India and George goes to meet him.

27 Brian Epstein, who has been in the US with Georgie Fame on a business trip, returns to England.

28 Brian tells Sid Bernstein that there are no plans for another American tour by The Beatles.

31 Stereo mixing for Paperback Writer takes place in Abbey Road.

NOVEMBER 66

6 McCartney leaves the UK with Jane Asher, for a holiday in Kenya, via France and Spain.

7 Stereo mixing for I Want To Hold Your Hand takes place at Abbey Road Studios.

9 Lennon meets Yoko Ono (above, centre) at the Indica Art Gallery in London (right: the exhibition's catalogue).

10 Newly issued photographs show The Beatles with moustaches and beards for the first time.

11 The Beatles and Brian Epstein donate £1,000 to the Aberfan disaster fund.

13 The Sunday Telegraph reports that two Beatles have approached entrepreneur Allen Klein through a third party. Epstein dismisses the story.

14 At Northern Songs' annual meeting, Epstein denies rumours that the group is splitting up.

15 Epstein makes further public announcements denying that The Beatles are breaking up.

19 Mellow Yellow by Donovan, with McCartney singing back-up vocals, enters the US singles chart, where it will peak at Number 2. Paul and Jane return to the UK from their holiday in Kenya.

24 The Beatles start recording the album that will become *Sgt Pepper's Lonely Hearts Club Band* at Abbey Road.

25 The Jimi Hendrix Experience play at a press reception at The Bag O'Nails, Kingly Street, London, with Lennon and McCartney in attendance. The Beatles record their 1966 Fan Club Christmas Record, Pantomime: Everywhere It's Christmas – at the London home of publisher Dick James.

What: Paul experiments musically
Where: Royal College Of Music
When: September 15, 1966

GOING UNDERGROUND

At the height of The Beatles' creativity, it was Paul McCartney who would frequent the avant-garde 'happenings' of London, recalls Barry Miles.

In 1965, the cutting edge of experimental music was represented by AMM, a free-improvisation music group headed by composer Cornelius Cardew, a former assistant to Karlheinz Stockhausen. Cardew had worked with John Cage in Europe and was the leading advocate of Cage's ideas in Britain. He held weekly sessions with AMM in the basement of the Royal College Of Music on Prince Consort Road, where he was a professor of composition.

Early in 1966, I attended one of the events with Paul McCartney. We arrived late and the 'music' had begun. Cardew was a multi-instrumentalist but on this occasion he sat by the piano. About 20 people sat around on the floor, facing AMM who were making noises on instruments ranging from tenor saxophone and violin to various percussion instruments and wind instruments. A number of transistor radios stood among the instruments but were only rarely turned on, usually to provide a more dense layer of sound if several players were performing at once – channels of static or distorted music from far-away stations were preferred.

Cardew sometimes tapped the piano leg with a small piece of wood. Once or twice he leaned inside the piano, to pluck a string, tap the frame or lid, but at no point did he actually play a note. There was no melody, no rhythm, just noises or 'notes' in relation to one another, the performers listening intently, responding to the textures and pace of the progression of sounds. The audience was encouraged to contribute: Paul ran a penny along the side of an old-fashioned steam radiator and, after the break, used his beer mug as an instrument to tap. Though Paul did not find the evening satisfying musically – "It went on too long" – he said that you did not have to like something in order to be influenced by it.

It was Paul's involvement in this type of event that John Lennon envied but did not participate in until he got together with Yoko, years later. In the meantime, Paul would report the latest fantastical hash-induced ideas to him and John would encourage him excitedly: "Do it! Do it!" But Paul was cautious. He was very conscious of bringing Beatles fans along with them slowly, rather than alienating them with too much weirdness. Paul did contemplate a solo album and even had a title for it, Paul McCartney Goes Too Far, but nothing came of it.

In the mid '60s, Paul patrolled London with his antennae out, omnivorous, wide open for experience. Through Jane Asher he met playwrights, actors and film directors: Bernard Miles, Harold Pinter, Arnold Wesker; through art dealer Robert Fraser he met David Hockney, Andy Warhol, Jim Dine, as well as Michelangelo Antonioni, whom Paul screened his experimental home movies for at half speed. He commissioned pop artists Peter Blake and Richard Hamilton to design Beatles album sleeves and as he was the only Beatle living in London, it also fell to him to supervise their production.

His taste was eclectic and each week was crammed with events: a lecture by Luciano Berio (see below); Cliff Richard in concert; Ubu Roi by Alfred Jarry. He would sit on the floor at the UFO Club, listening to The Soft Machine and The Pink Floyd (the only Beatle to go there) and the next night watch a cabaret at the Blue Angel. He hung out at the Indica gallery, helped to lay out International Times, Britain's first underground paper, and got very involved in the underground scene. At John Mayall's house he enlarged his knowledge of blues and R&B, and at my flat he listened to Albert Ayler, William Burroughs cut-ups and John Cage, particularly Indeterminacy, where electronic sounds and piano sometimes drown out the Zen-like stories Cage recounts. Paul was intrigued by Cage's ideas: that you can play anything – a screwed up ball of paper can be flattened and used as a score; all sound is potentially musical.

All this was dissected and processed, to finally emerge unrecognisable, in Beatles music. The best example is A Day In The Life, beginning with the lyrics which were partly found by John and Paul pulling phrases from a copy of The Daily Mail to which they added a fragment that McCartney had already written. The music was constructed like a building; Paul had roadie and friend Mal Evans count off 24 bars out loud and then ring an alarm clock. Paul: "It was just a period of time, an arbitrary length of bars, which was very Cage thinking."

The 24 bars were recorded with ever-increasing reverb so there was a tremendous echo on it towards the end. The tape was left for a week while Paul decided what to do next. His idea shocked George Martin but was loved by Lennon: 41 players were hired from the New Philharmonia and instructed to play as one instrument. Paul: "I told the orchestra, There are 24 empty bars. On the ninth bar the orchestra will take off, and it will go from its lowest to its highest note. You start with the lowest note in the range of your instrument and eventually go through all the notes of your instrument to the highest. But the speed at which you do it is your own choice. So that was the brief, the little avant-garde brief."

"Paul was very conscious of bringing Beatles fans along with them slowly, not alienating them."

Above: Paul next to Miles at a Luciano Berio lecture. Left: Cornelius Cardew.

PHOTOS: IAN MACMILLIAN/LENONO PHOTO ARCHIVE/PETER'S EDITION/ ATLANTIC SYNDICATION/CAMERA PRESS

Paul in his St John's Wood garden, London, being interviewed for ITN News about his admission in Life magazine that he has taken LSD, June 19, 1967.

All white on the night: Yoko practises her Sicilian Defence at the Indica Gallery, November 1966.

What: John and Yoko's first meeting
Where: Indica Gallery, London
When: November 6, 1966

YOUR MOVE, YOKO!

It was another 18 months until they were a couple, but John first met Yoko Ono at the preview of her debut British exhibition. By Barry Miles.

YOKO ONO ARRIVED IN LONDON IN September, 1966, to participate in DIAS – the Destruction In Art Symposium – organised by Mario Amaya, editor of Art And Artists. She was invited as an active member of Fluxus, the radical, multi-media art movement founded in 1960 by George Maciunas, which, in addition to producing magazines, posters and boxes filled with inexplicable objects, used guerrilla theatre, street events and concerts of electronic and experimental music to shock the complaisant public.

Yoko featured heavily in Fluxus publications and, as a classical pianist, she was also involved with the concerts, though it was her singing voice, not her ability to play the keys, that was called upon when John Cage stretched her half across a piano keyboard in one famous performance. Fluxus always had a close connection to music: New York police arrested Charlotte Moorman for playing a cello recital topless; Nam June Paik often used music in his happenings; LaMonte Young was involved with the early Velvet Underground; and, less directly, Al Hansen's grandson Beck became a successful rock'n'roller.

When John Dunbar, Peter Asher and I started Indica Books and Gallery in January 1966, we naturally stocked Fluxus material, including a number of copies of Grapefruit, Yoko's privately published first book. The gallery was run by John Dunbar and, unlike the commercial Cork Street galleries, John preferred not to schedule shows very far ahead. This enabled him to show new artists shortly after he discovered them, in the first flush of excitement and enthusiasm. Yoko's Unfinished Paintings And Objects opened on November 7, 1966, less than two months after she first arrived in Britain.

Yoko could be quite forceful at times, but she was mild compared to her husband Tony Cox, who, along with their daughter Kyoko, had accompanied her to Britain. On one occasion John had to eject him from the gallery because he was shrieking and hyperventilating, the result of strenuous arm-flapping exercises conducted in the gallery to the astonishment of visitors.

All the objects in the show were either white or transparent, with one exception: Add Colour Painting, where the viewer was allowed one colour to add to the painting. A white chair was provided with the painting to hold the paints and brushes. Apple consisted of an apple on a transparent Perspex stand and the catalogue featured a photograph of John Dunbar eating it; the apple was replaced daily. The show also contained a 1964 piece called Pointedness, consisting of a small sphere on a perspex stand. The most popular piece in the show was an all-white chess set: the board squares and chessmen were all white, set on a white table with two white chairs. Actress Sharon Tate and film director Roman Polanski visited the show several times, late at night, to play long games but did not buy the piece. The gallery kept normal business hours, but as it was next door to the Scotch Of St James's, at that time the 'in' club for Swinging London, John and his then wife, Marianne Faithfull, often found themselves in the club late at night and John would open the gallery to anyone he liked the look of.

Indica Books started on the ground floor of 6 Mason's Yard, with the gallery in the basement, but by September the bookshop had moved to Southampton Row, allowing the gallery to expand. Visits from The Beatles were frequent: Paul had helped to originally build the place, putting up shelves and painting the walls, and John had found the line: "Turn off your mind, relax, float down stream" in the introduction to Tim Leary's The Psychedelic Experience while flopped out on the settee that we had in the bookshop. Lennon was a good friend of Dunbar – they took a lot of drugs together – so it was not unusual when he showed up as we were hanging the exhibition.

The show was hung on November 6, the day before the opening party. Tony Cox was there, watched warily by Geneviève Morgan, the gallery manager. Yoko had also brought Tony McAulay, a student at Liverpool College of Art and Design, to help with the work. I was there with my then wife Sue Miles, and there may have been others around. John Lennon was there too. "I got there the night before it opened," he said. "I went in – she didn't know who I was or anything – I was wandering around, and I was looking at it and I was astounded. There was an apple on sale there for two hundred quid, I thought it was fantastic – I got the humour in her work immediately..."

In Yoko's official version of the meeting she claimed that she did not know who The Beatles were when she met John. However, by 1966 the downtown Manhattan art world was fully aware of The Beatles, to the extent that one of the first things that Yoko did on her arrival in Britain – weeks before her show – was to approach Paul McCartney for an original manuscript to add to John Cage's Notations collection of contemporary music scores. Paul refused and suggested she contact John for one.

"I was astounded, it was fantastic. I got the humour in her work immediately."

Lennon described their meeting at the gallery. "She came up and handed me a card which said: 'Breathe' on it, so I just went... [pant]. This was our meeting." What confirmed his interest was Ceiling Painting, a canvas with a word on it, so small the viewer had to climb a stepladder and use a magnifying glass to read it. John was relieved that it said "Yes" rather than "Piss off".

Yoko had taken John's arm to show him around the exhibition, and when it came time for him to leave, she insisted that he take her with him, and even tried to climb into his Mini. John was intrigued by her but managed to extricate himself and it was to be another 18 months before they finally got together as a couple.

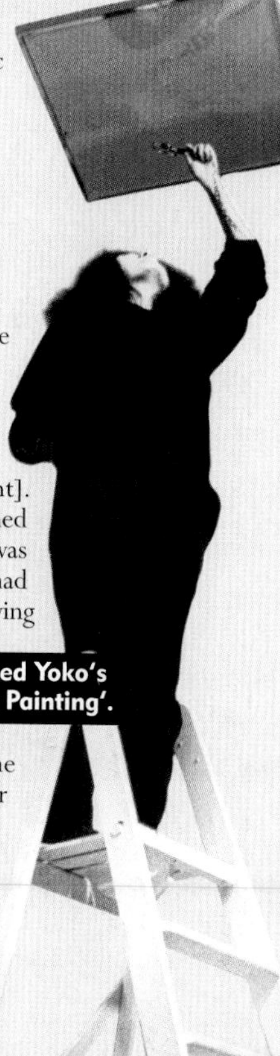

John liked Yoko's 'Ceiling Painting'.

PHOTOS: GRAHAM KEEN/REX FEATURES

NOV 27 - DEC 13, 1966

27 Lennon is filmed in Broadwick Street, London, for satirical TV show Not Only... But Also, starring Peter Cook and Dudley Moore.

28–29 Recording of Strawberry Fields Forever continues at Abbey Road.

DECEMBER 66

6 The Beatles begin recording When I'm 64 at EMI Studio 2, Abbey Road.

8 Paul McCartney overdubs his lead vocal onto When I'm 64 at Abbey Road Studios. George Martin (below with Paul): "I like to experiment with voices and you can hear it clearly on

When I'm 64. If you listen to it in stereo, you'll find that there's only an accompaniment on one of the tracks. This boomeranged on me as some foreign copies of the album were pressed that only had this track on the record, which meant that Paul's voice wasn't there. It taught me a lesson and nowadays I always put the voice in the centre."

9 The Beatles do overdubs onto the song Strawberry Fields Forever in EMI Studio 2, Abbey Road, London. Stopgap compilation album, *A Collection Of Beatles Oldies* (right), is released in the UK.

10 UK pop paper the NME publishes its annual readers' poll. The winners include:
World Vocal Group: The Beach Boys
British Vocal Group: The Beatles
World Male Singer: Elvis Presley
British Male Singer: Cliff Richard
World Musical Personality: Elvis Presley
British Vocal Personality: Cliff Richard
World Female Singer: Dusty Springfield
British Female Singer: Dusty Springfield
British Instrumental Group: The Shadows
British R&B Group: Spencer Davis Group

11 BBC radio show The Lively Arts broadcasts an interview with George Harrison about his interest in Indian music and culture, conducted in Bombay during September.

13 John Lennon is featured on the front cover and interviewed in today's edition of Look magazine. Lennon says in the publication: "I don't want people taking things from me that aren't really me. They make you something that they want to make you, that isn't really you. They come and talk to find answers, but they're their answers, not us. We're not Beatles to each other, you know. It's a joke to us. If we're going out the door of the hotel, we say, 'Right! Beatle John! Beatle George now! Come on, let's go!' We don't put on a false front or anything. But we just know that leaving the door, we turn into Beatles because everybody looking at us sees The Beatles. We're not the Beatles at all. We're just us."

15 Trumpets and cellos are added to Strawberry Fields Forever in Abbey Road. A new club, The Speakeasy (above) opens in London. It will become a favourite haunt of The Beatles. Bee Gee Barry Gibb said of the niterie: "The only people who knew of or got into it were the top end of British pop – The Beatles, The Rolling Stones, The Who. It was set like a 1920s funeral parlour; a coffin door would open, and suddenly there were the Stones and The Beatles sitting round inside."

16 The latest festive fan club record, Everywhere It's Christmas, is put out.

18 Guinness heir and socialite Tara Browne, a friend of The Beatles, is killed when his car crashes in West London. The coroner's report of his death, in the Daily Mail on January 17, will inspire John Lennon to begin writing A Day In The Life. Said Paul McCartney about Lennon's song: "A brilliant track. Basically John's song, but I worked on it with him from the start. He told me his idea, which was basically to base the lyric on newspaper articles, so we flipped through the newspaper and found little articles, like one about holes in the street in Blackburn, Lancashire, and another one about the Albert Hall, and John cleverly linked the two things together with 'now you know how many holes it takes to fill the Albert Hall', which got us banned, because the BBC thought we were being rude, which we weren't."

21 Work continues on When I'm Sixty-Four and Strawberry Fields Forever at Abbey Road.

22 Two different takes of Strawberry Fields Forever are spliced together by George Martin in Abbey Road.

23 The film soundtrack album, The Family Way, composed by McCartney, is released in the UK.

26 Lennon appears as a men's toilet attendant (above) on the satirical BBC TV show Not Only... But Also, starring Peter Cook and Dudley Moore.

29 McCartney begins work on Penny Lane in Abbey Road.

30 Work continues on Penny Lane and When I'm Sixty-Four at Abbey Road.

31 Harrison is refused entry to Annabel's nightclub, London, for not wearing a tie. Undeterred, he and Patti, plus Brian Epstein and Eric Clapton celebrate the New Year at a Lyon's Corner House restaurant in Coventry Street.

What: Work begins on Sgt Pepper
Where: Abbey Road Studios
When: November 24, 1966

"TAKE 137!"

Gone were the days of recording an album in just two weeks. *Sgt Pepper* was an unprecedented four months in the making. By Martin O'Gorman.

Time away from The Beatles and Britain had prompted both Lennon and McCartney to recall their childhood in Liverpool. Lennon used Strawberry Field, a Salvation Army orphanage near his home in Woolton, as a springboard for a trip into his psyche, while McCartney composed a song about Liverpool's Penny Lane because he "liked the poetry of the name". Reconvening at Abbey Road Studios on November 24, 1966, the group found the lack of deadlines liberating – as McCartney says, "Instead of looking for catchy singles, it was more like writing your novel".

So when Lennon was unhappy with the ethereal atmosphere of the first recording of Strawberry Fields Forever, the group scrapped the take for a heavily-scored remake with manic drumming from Starr. Unhappy with this version too, Lennon persuaded George Martin to combine both takes by slowing down the first to the correct tempo and key and splicing them together. For Penny Lane, McCartney told Martin, "I want a very clean recording... Maybe a Beach Boys kind of thing." He intended The Beatles should "answer" *Pet Sounds* and proposed a themed LP on childhood. However, the idea foundered when Strawberry Fields and Penny Lane became The Beatles' first single of 1967.

Energised by the UK avant-garde scene, McCartney added colour to a new Lennon song, which started out as a bleak meditation on newspaper stories, including a mention of the recent death of Guinness heir Tara Browne. Significantly, when Lennon first played A Day In The Life to his partner, the two looked at each other on reaching the line, "I'd love to turn you on". "We said, We know what we're doing here, don't we?" recalls McCartney. The BBC certainly did – they banned the song for its "drug" references. Plugging a gap with one of his own unfinished ideas, McCartney proposed they join the two parts with an exercise similar to work by artists such as John Cage – 24 bars of a huge orchestral glissando. A 40-piece orchestra in fancy dress arrived at Abbey Road on February 10, as did Mick Jagger, Keith Richards, Donovan and various others. The recording of the "musical orgasm" was the first major "happening" of the Summer Of Love.

The other genuine Lennon/McCartney collaboration was With A Little Help From My Friends, the obligatory "Ringo song", but inspiration came more easily to McCartney than his partner. "Paul would suddenly say, 'It's time to go into the studio, write some songs,'" Lennon complained later. "On *Sgt Pepper*, I came up with Lucy In The Sky and Day In The Life in only 10 days." Nevertheless, McCartney was "on fire" and when George Martin couldn't score the strings for She's Leaving Home immediately, the Beatle quickly drafted in arranger Mike Leander. "I minded like hell," says Martin.

Much of Lennon's work on *Pepper* was lacklustre – his stifling suburban life and a Kellogg's Corn Flakes TV ad prompted Good Morning, Good Morning, while Being For The Benefit Of Mr Kite! was lifted from an antique circus poster and given life through Martin's cut-up collage of steam organ effects. However, Lucy In The Sky With Diamonds evoked a genuinely surreal scenario that appointed Lennon as an avatar of the psychedelic experience. Inspired by a painting by his son Julian, Lennon alluded to "the female who would someday come and save me. It turned out to be Yoko..."

Having spent a month in India, Harrison also found it difficult returning to work. "It felt like going backwards," he said. Yet his inclusion on the album, Within You Without You, demonstrated the clarity of thought Harrison's Indian sojourn had taught him with his lyric evolving from a typically weighty discussion with musician Klaus Voormann.

McCartney, meanwhile, had come up with a nostalgic fantasy, Sgt Pepper's Lonely Hearts Club Band. He suggested that if the others didn't want to be Beatles, why not adopt the persona of this fictitious group and promote the LP as an imaginary show? As Lennon later pointed out, most songs on the LP had nothing to do with the "concept". According to Starr: "We got as far as Sgt Pepper and Billy Shears, then everyone said, Sod it."

"Paul, I feel oddly perky yet focused." Martin and Macca.

As the sessions ground on, the long hours took their toll. The group found themselves relying on uppers. When George Martin later complained to Harrison about *Pepper* being considered a "drugs album" even though he himself didn't partake, the Beatle confessed that they used to slip some in the producer's coffee to keep him awake. Perhaps the only time LSD entered the studio was when Lennon accidentally dosed himself with acid. "I got scared on the mic," he remembered. "I thought I was cracked. George Martin was looking at me funny. Then it dawned on me..." "John pointed to the ceiling and said, 'Look at that!'" says engineer, Geoff Emerick. "George didn't know what was going on. He took John to the roof, thinking he was a bit faint. When George told the others, they rushed upstairs to grab John, obviously."

"Harrison confessed to Martin that they used to slip uppers in his coffee to keep him awake during recording."

As the sessions wound up in late March, Beatles aide Neil Aspinall suggested that if Sgt Pepper were to introduce the LP, he ought to close it, too. The "concept album" was complete, having taken an unprecedented four months to make. Although inspired by the LSD experience, the album was as much the result of hard work as any instant psychedelic revelation. As ever, The Beatles had caught the spirit of the times and had made a quantum leap in record production techniques. And McCartney knew it; *Sgt Pepper* would silence the critics. "The music papers said, 'What are The Beatles up to?'" he recalls. "Drying up, I suppose. It was nice making *Pepper* and thinking, That's right..."

PHOTOS: REX, FRANK HERMANN, CAMERA PRESS/ TOPHAM PICTUREPOINT, PICTORIAL PRESS

John and Ringo enjoy a takeaway while recording *Sgt Pepper*, 1967.

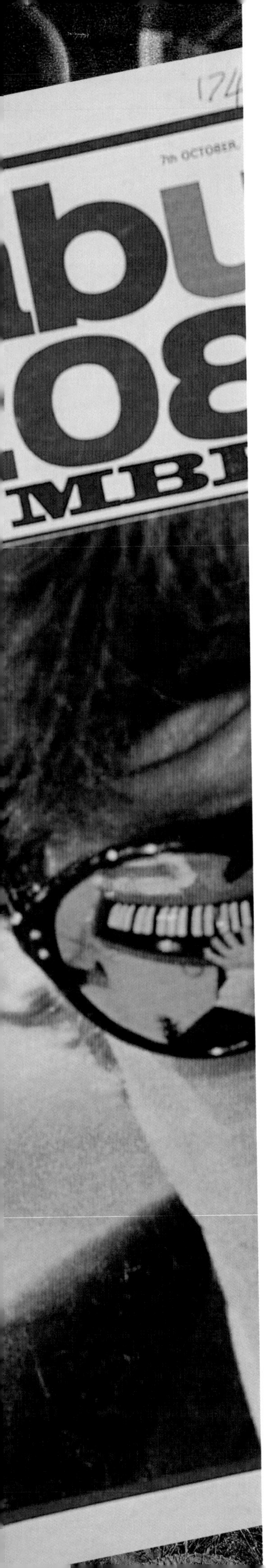

1967

In 1967, The Beatles blew away all of their competitors with the release of *Sgt Pepper's Lonely Hearts Club Band*. They founded Apple Corp with high ideals and sang to the world with the global satellite broadcast of All You Need Is Love. But it was also the year when they lost both Brian Epstein and their golden touch, with the critical failure of *Magical Mystery Tour*.

LONG JOHN: f
TOM JONES o
SCAFFOLD get
STONE goes s
BEATLES P
N TV VIEWE
6th MAY, 1967
Fabulous
208
MAY-POLL AWARDS
EVERY WEEK THE MONKEES WRITE FOR YOU—THIS WEEK MICKY DOLENZ
DOUBLE PAGE COLOUR PIC OF THE WALKER BROS • PLUS KING SIZE COLOUR
PIN-UPS OF THE MONKEES • CAT STEVENS • DAVY JONES • ENGELBERT
HUMPERDINCK • CILLA BLACK • Also your Radio Luxembourg programmes from 2nd–8th May
MBER, 1967
1/-
ulous
GROOVIN'
LOUR PICTURE OF TRAFFIC
ARUM • PAUL & BARRY RYAN • JULIA FOSTER
PIX OF MIKE NESMITH & MICKY DOLENZ
ES FROM 12th DECEMBER TO 18th DECEMBER • • •
TOP PO
Highest sale of any FULL CO
Pic: CHRIS WALTER
Miranda with Beatles on lo
HAZEL
IN COLOUR
£50,000 after

The write sound: Hunter Davies (below, left, with Neil Aspinall) listens in during the *Sgt Pepper* recording sessions, Abbey Road, 1967.

What: The Beatles' biography agreed
Where: Brian Epstein's house
When: January 27, 1967

PAPERBACK WRITER

When Hunter Davies put himself forward to Paul McCartney to write the first authorised Beatles biography, he didn't expect it to also be the last.

I GOT TO DO THE BEATLES BIOGRAPHY because I asked. In September 1966, I went to see Paul at his house in St John's Wood because I loved Eleanor Rigby – the tune, the words, the whole idea. I was writing the Atticus column in the Sunday Times at the time. Early on in my Sunday Times career, one hadn't been allowed to write about such common, working class, Northern persons; we had to do dreary bishops and who would be the next head of some boring Oxbridge college, but it had all changed, around the mid '60s.

I came from Carlisle, brought up on a council estate, like Paul's, went to a grammar school, just like Paul's, John's and George's, was roughly the same age, and had identified with them, and their music, from the beginning.

I'd had two books published by then, one of them a novel, Here We Go Round The Mulberry Bush which was bought to be made into a film. The director, Clive Donner, had this idea that Paul might do the theme tune, as he'd written a few, so I went to see Paul again, this time with my screenwriter's hat on.

Paul didn't write any music for the film, but while talking to Paul I said what about a proper biog of The Beatles. There had been only two books about them, both paperbacks, neither substantial. I said if I did a proper biog, doing the whole story, it would mean when asked the same old questions, he could say that it was all in the biog.

He thought it a good idea and straight away helped me write a letter to Brian Epstein. Brian arranged a meeting, then cancelled, several times, for reasons I later discovered (hung over, drugged, out on the town) but I eventually saw him at his Chapel Street, Belgravia, house on January 27, 1967.

We agreed a contract. Brian gave me exclusive access to The Beatles, and promised he would not allow another authorised biog for at least two years (in the event, there never was another). The advanced payment from Heinemann was £3,000, shared with Nemperor Holdings, one of Brian's companies.

It was quite a reasonable advance at the time, but nothing startling. I was thrilled, but there was no real excitement in the publishing world, no sense of having got a coup. One Heinemann director thought The Beatles bubble would soon burst, a common feeling at the time. He said pop music biogs did not sell.

I spent most of the first six months not interviewing them, just hanging around. I wanted to pick up names of relations, friends, contacts, places, people from the past, go out and see them, fill in the background, then come back and properly interview each Beatle. So I went off to Liverpool, Hamburg and New York.

In Hamburg, trying to piece it all together, I worried that I had got the sequence of events all wrong. It was all relatively recent, in 1967, and they had hardly been back very long, but they couldn't remember very much. One thought they had been there three times, another four. John could remember almost nothing.

In the end, I did get the Hamburg sequence right – but in the first edition of the book, in 1968, I made one appalling mistake about something more important. I said the day Paul met John at the Woolton Fete was in the summer of 1956. I got it wrong by a whole year (it was, of course, July 6, 1957). That's what John and Paul told me, but I am to blame for not having checked it out. My excuse is that back in 1968, there was no interest in memorabilia, no Beatles brains, no researchers. People at Woolton at the time had probably still not realised the significance. Now we have people who know more about The Beatles than The Beatles know about themselves.

The second best thing about doing the book was meeting their mums and dads, caught in fly traps, dazzled by the fame of their sons, who in a sense had turned into monsters. They had been uprooted from their homes, from their cultural and social roots, and didn't quite know what had happened to their sons, or themselves.

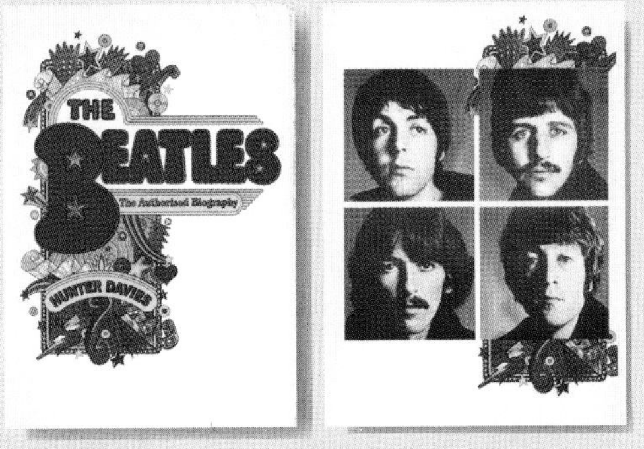

"I like to think it was all true, but most of all, it captured them as they were."

The best thing was, of course, being with The Beatles at the height of their powers, watching them compose and create, seeing how songs began, in their own homes, in their own heads, then in the studios at Abbey Road.

I used to think that if the whole project collapses, if for some reason I get chucked out of the studio while they were making *Sgt Pepper*, or when they read the final manuscript they won't like it, I will at least have been there, seen them at work.

None of them, in the event, had any problems with it. Only Aunt Mimi moaned on about the bad language, then moaned at John, who moaned at me to go and keep her happy, which I did – not by taking anything out, but putting in an extra sentence saying that "John was as happy as the day was long".

When published, critics thought it was a revelation, as I did have bad language, mention of drugs, stealing, Epstein described as gay (though it was still a code word), but, of course, compared with what came later, it was pretty mild.

I like to think it was all true, if not the whole truth, but most of all, it captured them as they were, as it was happening, without the benefit of hindsight. It could have been better written, but now it has become a prime source, which people lift chunks from, as if they themselves had been there. It's nice to know that I was...

The Beatles by Hunter Davies is still in print, now in a new, illustrated edition, published by Cassells.

PHOTOS: FRANK HERRMANN, REX

JANUARY 67

4 Work continues on Penny Lane in Abbey Road.

5 The Beatles create 14 minutes of electronic sound collage for the Carnival Of Light Rave, an underground happening set for January 28 and February 4 at the Roundhouse, London.

6 Overdubbing of instruments onto Penny Lane continues at Abbey Road studios.

7 At his home in Weybridge, Surrey, Starr is served with a writ by his landscape gardener.

8 McCartney (above) and Lennon are in fancy dress at the Cromwellian Club, London, with Georgie Fame (above, left), at the 21st birthday party of Fame's fiancée, Carmen Jiminez.

9 Flutes, trumpets, piccolos and a flugelhorn are overdubbed onto Penny Lane at Abbey Road.

12 While watching TV at home, McCartney sees a performance by the New Philharmonia of Bach's Brandenburg Concerto Number 2 on the BBC2 series Masterworks. He decides to ring the trumpeter, David Mason, and ask him to add a part to Penny Lane. Yet more classical instruments (trumpets, oboe, cor anglais and double bass) are added to Penny Lane at Abbey Road.

17 The coroner's report of Tara Browne's death appears in The Daily Mail, inspiring Lennon to write the "I read the new today, oh boy" opening to A Day In The Life. In Abbey Road, David Mason adds the finishing touch to Penny Lane – a piccolo trumpet. He is paid £27.10s.

18 McCartney is interviewed at Granada Television, Upper James St, London, for a regional TV special, Scene Special – It's So Far Out, It's Straight Down, about the underground scene in the UK.

19–20 Two days of working on A Day In The Life at Abbey Road studios.

21 NEMS Enterprises, owned by Brian Epstein, merges with the Robert Stigwood Group, bringing artists including The Cream, Merseys and Crispian St Peters into Epstein's stable.

24 Playwright Joe Orton meets McCartney at Epstein's home in Chapel Street, London, while discussing the possibility of scripting a Beatles film.

27 Brian Epstein signs a deal allowing Sunday Times newspaper journalist Hunter Davies to write an authorised biography of The Beatles. McCartney oversees a new mono mix of Penny Lane at Abbey Road. A new nine-year worldwide recording contract with EMI is signed by Epstein and The Beatles.

30–31 Promos for Strawberry Fields Forever are filmed in Knole Park, Kent.

FEBRUARY 67

1 Work starts on what will become the title track to the album *Sgt Pepper's Lonely Hearts Club Band* in Abbey Road.

2 Recording continues on the song Sgt Pepper's Lonely Hearts Club Band in Abbey Road.

3 Overdubs are added to A Day In The Life at Abbey Road.

4 At the Carnival Of Light Rave, an underground happening in the Roundhouse, London, some of the entertainment is provided by a 14-minute long electronic sound collage especially created by The Beatles.

5 In Angel Lane, Stratford, London, The Beatles film parts of a promo clip for Penny Lane.

7 Mickey Dolenz of The Monkees (above) arrives in the UK for a promotional visit, and meets up with McCartney. Further filming is undertaken in Knole Park, Sevenoaks, UK, for the Penny Lane promo. This includes more horse-riding and candelabra scenes.

8 Work starts on a Lennon song, Good Morning, Good Morning, at Abbey Road.

9 For the first time since signing to EMI Records, The Beatles record at a studio other than Abbey Road, making three takes of Fixing A Hole at Regent Sound Studios, Tottenham Court Road, London.

10 The orchestral sections of A Day In The Life are recorded in Abbey Road.

12 George and Patti leave Rolling Stones guitarist Keith Richards' home, Redlands, in West Wittering, two hours before a police raid. That subsequent raid sees Richards and Mick Jagger charged with drug offences.

13 Strawberry Fields Forever/Penny Lane, is released in the US. Harrison's Only A Northern Song is recorded in Abbey Road.

16 Bass and vocal overdubs are added to Good Morning, Good Morning at Abbey Road. Top Of The Pops shows the Penny Lane and Strawberry Fields Forever promotional clips.

17 Penny Lane/Strawberry Fields Forever is released in the UK. The recording of Being For The Benefit Of Mr Kite! starts at Abbey Road.

19 When Chuck Berry performs at the Saville Theatre, Lennon and Starr are in attendance.

20 George Martin prepares "circus atmosphere" tapes for Being For The Benefit Of Mr Kite!, at Abbey Road.

21 Work on Fixing A Hole is completed in Abbey Road.

22 The massive piano chord which closes A Day In The Life is recorded at Abbey Road.

23-24 The recording of Lovely Rita takes place at Abbey Road Studios.

What: Release of Strawberry Fields
Where: Forever and Penny Lane
When: February 17, 1967

STRANGE FRUIT

The Beatles had a new image and a new sound – but was the world ready for Strawberry Fields Forever and Penny Lane? By Martin O'Gorman.

On December 10, 1966, EMI issued a compilation album called *A Collection Of Beatles Oldies*, which neatly closed the Beatlemania years. Tapping into the then-current vogue for I Was Lord Kitchener's Valet-style nostalgia, the LP's sleeve featured a mop-topped 1920s gent, clad in Day-Glo striped trousers and a garishly patterned tie. Unwittingly, EMI's art department had predicted The Beatles' new image – as well as the multicoloured garb, Harrison had grown a moustache as a disguise while in India and the others soon followed suit. As David Mason recalled, when he arrived at Abbey Road in January 1967 to play piccolo trumpet on Penny Lane, "they all wore candy-striped trousers and floppy yellow bow ties… I asked if they'd been filming, because it looked like they'd just come off a film set. John Lennon said, No mate, we always dress like this."

The group's silence since the end of their US tour had caused much speculation in the press with headlines such as 'Twilight Of The Beatles?'. Their new image was eventually revealed to the world when ITN doorstepped the group at Abbey Road Studios in December. "I could see us not working together for a period," commented Lennon, "but we'd always get together for one reason or another." McCartney explained that recording would replace touring permanently: "Now our performance is the record."

It was into this atmosphere that the double-A side of Strawberry Fields Forever and Penny Lane was released, on February 17, 1967. The tracks had been culled from the new album sessions because, says George Martin, "Brian was frightened that The Beatles were slipping and wanted another single out that was a blockbuster." Packaged in a picture sleeve for the first time, the two nostalgic songs are complemented on the back cover by four photos of the band as babies.

Following the success of earlier clips for Paperback Writer and Rain, a promotional film accompanied the single. Directed by Peter Goldmann, the films avoided the Musicians' Union ban on miming on TV by presenting non-linear, abstract images to complement the music. Penny Lane was the more straightforward of the two, featuring shots of Liverpool buses and busy streets, growing more surreal when the group sit down at a table in the middle of a field for a meal.

The Strawberry Fields Forever clip was more experimental. Filmed at Knole Park in Kent, Goldmann uses techniques that mirrored those being used by The Beatles in the recording studio – backwards film, shots in negative, subtle changes of light. The winter sunset and a peculiar object constructed from a piano, string and lights add to the eerie and oppressive tone. Even The Beatles themselves look odd. Starr, clad in red military tunic and brown cord cap, looks like a Victorian Hansom Cab driver, while Harrison's thick balaclava and beard seem more suited to a mountaineer.

The critics were divided over the single. Penny Lane predictably gained most praise, but the unearthly Strawberry Fields perplexed many. George Martin's graft of two different versions of the track meant that the opening segment was reduced in pitch – the quavering Mellotron intro and the slow motion Lennon vocals indicated this was something out of the ordinary. "Certainly the most unusual and way-out single The Beatles have yet produced," commented a confused NME. "Quiet honestly, I don't know what to make of it."

"What's happening to The Beatles?" pondered The Daily Mail. "They have become contemplative, secretive, exclusive and excluded – four mystics with moustaches." Author Greil Marcus put it more succinctly: "If this extraordinary music was merely a taste of what The Beatles were up to, what would the album be like?"

Ever since musicologist William Mann praised the "Aeolian cadence" of Not A Second Time in 1963, the broadsheets had regularly dissected the current state of the Top 40, placing it in its appropriate context within pop culture. "Penny Lane looks back to the days when parochialism was not an attitude to be derided," stated The Times in April 1967. "While it may seem that the commonplace suburb is a pleasanter source of inspiration than a psychedelic ecstasy, it might be that the song is instinctively satisfying a youthful appetite for simplicity."

However, the single got stuck behind Englebert Humperdinck's Release Me making it the first Beatles single in four years not to make Number 1. "There's room for everything," said an indifferent Lennon, the pressure off at last. The Sun offered a back-handed compliment: "For years The Beatles have been dogged by instant success. The group have now arrived in the 'quality' field."

"Brian was frightened The Beatles were slipping and wanted another single out that was a blockbuster."

No matter. The Summer Of Love lay ahead and The Beatles were at the forefront.

As William Mann wrote in his *Sgt Pepper* review, "From The Beatles came the current preoccupation with electronically-manipulated clusters of sound… In some records, it is just a generalised effect. But in Strawberry Fields, it was poetically and precisely applied. The vogue word for this is 'psychedelic' music."

PHOTOS: JANE BOWN/CAMERA PRESS/PICTORIAL PRESS/MIRRORPIX.COM

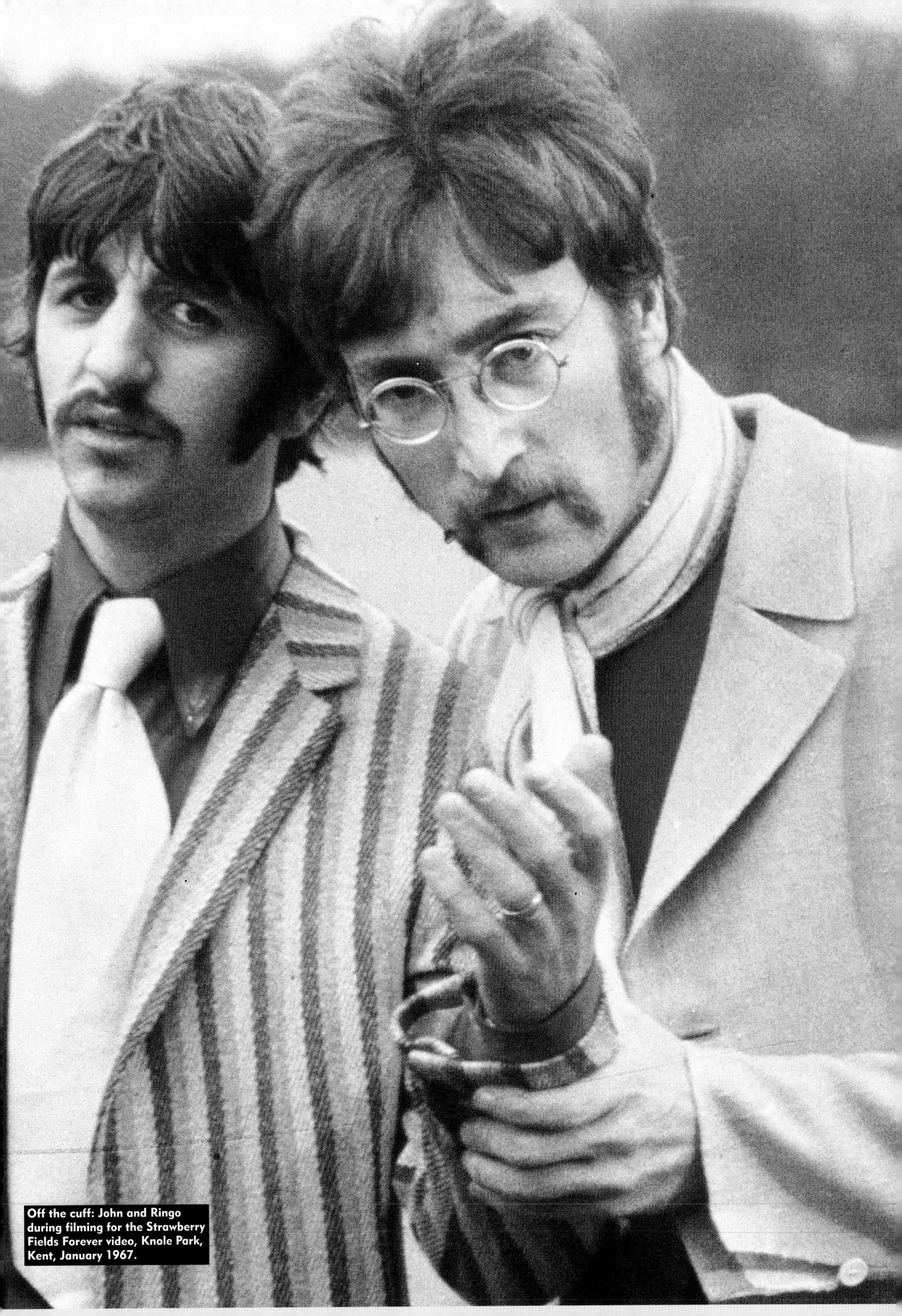

Off the cuff: John and Ringo during filming for the Strawberry Fields Forever video, Knole Park, Kent, January 1967.

"John, that outfit just won't work!" Peter Blake tries to persuade John Lennon to get into his *Sgt Pepper* uniform.

What: Shooting Sgt Pepper sleeve
Where: Michael Cooper's studio
When: March 30, 1967

PICTURE PERFECT

When it came to shooting the *Sgt Pepper* sleeve, not everyone got their way. After all, John wanted Gandhi and Hitler! By Patrick Humphries.

ON ITS RELEASE, *SGT PEPPER'S LONELY HEARTS Club Band* was hailed as a musical masterpiece, but it was also a triumph of packaging. Pepper was the first pop album to feature its lyrics; it was the first to have a gatefold sleeve; and even today, 35 years on and reduced to fit in a CD jewel case, the iconographic impact of that sleeve is undiminished: a stained glass window of the 20th century.

After four months of recording, The Beatles, George Martin, Brian Epstein and EMI knew that *Sgt Pepper* was an extraordinary achievement – and one that demanded special wrapping. A psychedelic cover by The Fool was quickly rejected, and then Paul McCartney's chum, art dealer Robert Fraser, suggested the pop artist Peter Blake.

Sgt Pepper had started out as a "concept album" centred around The Beatles' Liverpool – and in keeping with their childhood memories, they planned to dress in Salvation Army uniforms. But with psychedelia high in the air, the Salvation Army soon went out the window and instead The Beatles became enchanted with the idea of hiding themselves – both on record and on the sleeve – in Sgt Pepper's band. McCartney: "Originally, the cover was going to be us dressed as this other band in crazy gear".

Peter Blake, who received a flat fee of £200 for his work on the *Pepper* cover, suggested taking the idea a step further: "I offered the idea that if they had just played a concert in the park, the cover could be a photograph of the group just after the concert with the crowd who had just watched the concert, watching them. If we did this by using cardboard cut-outs, it could be a magical crowd of whom-ever they wanted". With the help of Blake and Robert Fraser, The Beatles began to make a list for the cast of the world's best-known album cover.

The pick'n'mix nature of the cover ensured its eclecticism: by and large, John and Paul suggested the authors (HG Wells, Aldous Huxley, Dylan Thomas); Robert Fraser, the contemporary artists (Larry Bell, Richard Lindner); and Peter Blake threw in a few personal favourites (Tony Curtis, WC Fields).

John wanted Hitler, Gandhi and Liverpool footballer Albert Stubbins (he remembered his dad talking about him). EMI were worried about losing sales on the Indian sub-continent, so out went the Mahatma. Hitler was excluded on grounds of taste, although he can be seen hovering on the sidelines in the CD booklet. Dion and Bob Dylan were the only representatives of rock'n'roll, there was no Chuck Berry, no Carl Perkins and no Elvis.

Peter Blake spent a fortnight constructing the collage and then, on the evening of Thursday March 30, 1967, the four Beatles convened at photographer Michael Cooper's studio in Flood Street, Chelsea. Here they clad themselves in colourful costumes supplied by Berman's, the theatrical costumiers, and over the course of three hours, the brightly-coloured world of Sgt Pepper gradually came to life. However, EMI's Sir Joseph Lockwood was already becoming seriously concerned, both about the spiralling cost of the sleeve – in excess of £2,868/5/3d! – and the possibility of litigation. Despite McCartney's breezy assurance that the cover stars would "love it, they'll do anything to please us", Lockwood remained unconvinced and notified McCartney that EMI would require an indemnity to the value of £50million to protect them against any legal action arising from the album cover – a figure that would be deducted from future Beatle earnings!

In the end it was thought safest to approach everyone who was to appear and seek their permission. Brian Epstein's former assistant, Wendy Hanson spent day after day tracking down the pot-pourri who would made up Sgt Pepper's world: the great, the good and the rest…

Fred Astaire was flattered; Mae West demanded to know what she would be doing in a lonely hearts club, although a letter signed by all four Beatles persuaded her; and Shirley Temple asked to hear the finished LP before she consented. The only person actually cut out was Bowery Boy Leo Gorcey, who insisted on a fee of $500 and, as a result, found himself airbrushed out of history.

The problems didn't end when The Beatles quit Michael Cooper's studio: for years, rumours abounded that the *Sgt Pepper* cover featured marijuana plants, which was not true. The sleeve was subject to endless scrutiny, although it still took many years before everyone in the collage was officially identified. When the "Paul Is Dead" rumours surfaced in 1969, everyone went back to *Pepper* and found proof aplenty – on the rear McCartney has his back to the camera; on the inner sleeve the patch on his arm reads OPD (Officially Pronounced Dead); the hand over his head on the front is an Indian sign of death, while flowers marked his grave!

It was a heady blend, but by the time *Sgt Pepper* hit the shops The Beatles were off again, with two EPs and five exclusive singles to record before their next official album. The minimalist wrapping of Christmas 1968's 'White Album' was a direct reaction against the psychedelic extravaganza that had draped *Pepper*. But for a taste of that brief shining moment when England swung like a pendulum – and a reminder of exactly who was "in" back then – just look at Sgt Pepper's Lonely Hearts Club Band, look at that cover, and marvel again at the world The Beatles created, with a little help from their friends.

"Hitler was excluded on grounds of taste, although in the CD booklet you can see him hovering on the side!"

An early Peter Blake sketch.

25 The film clips made for The Beatles' Penny Lane and Strawberry Fields Forever are shown in America for the first time on the Hollywood Palace TV show.

26 Brian Epstein buys a manor house in Rushlake Green, East Sussex, UK, at a cost of £35,000.

28 A new Lennon song, Lucy In The Sky With Diamonds, is rehearsed in Abbey Road.

MARCH 67

1–2 Lucy In The Sky With Diamonds is recorded in Abbey Road.

2 At the Ninth Grammy Awards, The Beatles earn three Grammies, for Michelle, Eleanor Rigby, and Klaus Voormann's artwork for the album *Revolver*.

3 A lead guitar part is overdubbed onto Sgt Pepper's Lonely Hearts Club Band in Abbey Road.

6 Sound effects are recorded for Sgt Pepper's Lonely Hearts Club Band in Abbey Road.

7 Harmony vocals and effects are overdubbed onto Lovely Rita, in Abbey Road.

9–10 Getting Better is recorded in Abbey Road.

11 It is revealed that Yesterday has become the most covered number ever, with 446 recordings by different artists.

13 Brass parts are overdubbed onto Good Morning Good Morning at Abbey Road.

14 Carla Thomas (left), in the UK as part of the Stax/Volt Soul Concert Sensation '67 package tour, plays a warm-up gig at The Bag O'Nails, London, where she meets McCartney.

15 Work starts on the Harrison song Within You Without You, at Abbey Road.

17 Mike Leander's orchestral backing for She's Leaving Home is recorded in Abbey Road.

18 Penny Lane/Strawberry Fields Forever reaches Number 1 in the US, for just one week.

20 The Beatles are interviewed in Abbey Road by BBC DJ Brian Matthew. Later, they complete work on She's Leaving Home.

21 While overdubbing vocals onto Getting Better in Abbey Road, Lennon suffers a bad acid trip.

22 Work continues on the Harrison song Within You Without You, in Abbey Road.

23 Vocal overdubs are added to Getting Better in Abbey Road.

25 The Beatles receive Ivor Novello Awards for Michelle and Yellow Submarine.

27 McCartney is in the audience when Fats Domino makes his live UK debut at the Saville Theatre.

28 Lennon records his lead vocal for Good Morning Good Morning, in Abbey Road.

29 Work on With A Little Help From My Friends starts in Abbey Road.

30 Artist Peter Blake's living collage, assembled for the cover of The Beatles' *Sgt Pepper's Lonely Hearts Club Band* album, is photographed by Michael Cooper, in Chelsea, London.

31 Overdubbing and mixing is carried out on With A Little Help From My Friends and Being For The Benefit Of Mr Kite, in Abbey Road.

APRIL 67

1 Sgt Pepper's Lonely Hearts Club Band (Reprise) is recorded in Abbey Road.

3 As Paul McCartney jets off to America, George Harrison is in Abbey Road, finishing off Within You Without You.

5 McCartney flies to Denver, Colorado, to be with Jane Asher at the Quorum Restaurant on her 21st birthday.

6 In Abbey Road, a master tape of the album *Sgt Pepper's Lonely Hearts Club Band* is compiled.

7 In Abbey Road, work begins on creating stereo mixes for the *Sgt Pepper* album. While in Denver, McCartney has an idea to create a TV film about a madcap bus journey, which will eventually emerge as Magical Mystery Tour.

9 McCartney flies from Denver to Los Angeles in a Lear Jet owned by Frank Sinatra. While there, McCartney is invited to join the advisory board planning the Monterey Pop Festival. His first recommendation is to book Jimi Hendrix.

10 McCartney visits a Beach Boys studio session, and reportedly participates in the recording of Vegetables for the album *Smile*.

11 While flying back to the UK from America, McCartney scribbles down ideas and song lyrics for Magical Mystery Tour.

12 McCartney lands in Heathrow Airport, London.

14 "The most significant talent since The Beatles" is the phrase used when Polydor Records releases New York Mining Disaster 1941, the debut single by The Bee Gees.

19 The Beatles become a corporation, registered officially as The Beatles & Co.

20 In Abbey Road, work starts on Only A Northern Song.

21 The final snippet of recording is done for *Sgt Pepper's Lonely Heart's Club Band* – strange noises, gibberish and a high-pitched whistle – to be used in the side two run-out groove.

24 All four members of The Beatles go to see Donovan at the Saville Theatre, London. The McCartney-penned song Love In The Open Air is released by George Martin & His Orchestra in the US.

25–27 The Beatles spend three days recording Magical Mystery Tour in Abbey Road.

29 John Lennon attends the 14-Hour Technicolour Dream event at Alexandra Palace, north London. Yoko Ono was performing but they did not meet.

30 Six weeks after having purchased it, Lennon visits the island of Dorinish off the coast of County Mayo, Ireland.

What: 14-Hour Technicolour Dream
Where: Alexandra Palace, London
When: April 29, 1967

DREAM ON!

Paul might have been the most likely Fab to attend a 'happening', but it was John who went to the 14-Hour Technicolour Dream. By Joe Cushley.

APRIL 29, 1967 WAS THE NIGHT THAT THE freaks came out to play. Some 10,000 of them descended on the Alexandra Palace in sleepy North London to experience a swarm of bands, including The Move, Pretty Things, Soft Machine, The Creation. There were poets, dance troupes and visual artists too, such as the Binder, Edwards and Vaughan team who customised Lennon's Roller and Macca's flower-power piano. There were films, light shows and, of course, 'happenings'. Many revellers discovered for the first time that they weren't the only ones to find 'straight' life in '60s Britain a trifle stifling.

The 'Ally Pally' was an appropriate venue for such multifarious goings-on. Built in 1873 and dubbed The People's Palace, it boasted a library, funfair, concert halls, art galleries, and 196 acres of park. This combination of arts, rural Arcadia and Victorian amusement arcade chimed sweetly, if slightly ironically, with many of the interests of the '60s underground and its favourite musicians – Strawberry Fields Forever was in the charts; The Beatles had just recorded their paean to 19th century circus acts, Being For The Benefit Of Mr Kite; while event headliners The Pink Floyd were also at Abbey Road making their pan-galactic, pastoral masterpiece, The Piper At The Gates Of Dawn. And, after all, Lewis Carroll was both Queen Victoria *and* Lennon's favourite author.

Barry Miles was co-owner of the Indica art gallery and bookshop, home of the fringe arts and politics paper, International Times. Both Indica and IT had been helped by donations from McCartney. "The police raided the office with an Obscene Publications warrant. The only reason I could think of was that we'd published remarks by Dick Gregory [black activist and comedian] about 'white mother-fuckers', without asterisks. Hoppy [John Hopkins, founder of both IT and the pioneering music venue, UFO] left the paper to set up this fund-raising gig."

"John Lennon went around relatively unaccosted. A lot of the hippies were like, 'No Beatlemania here, dear'."

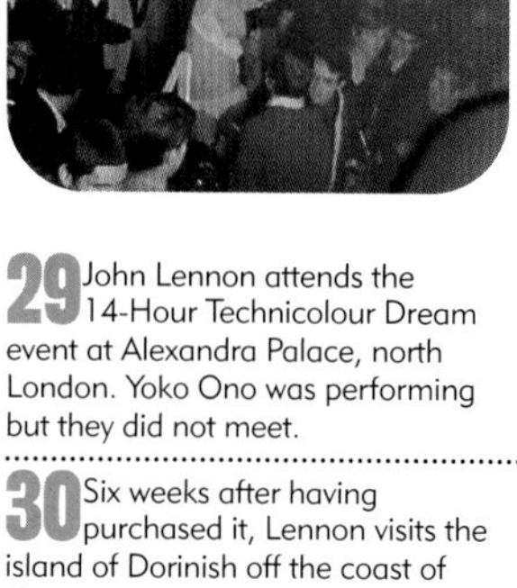

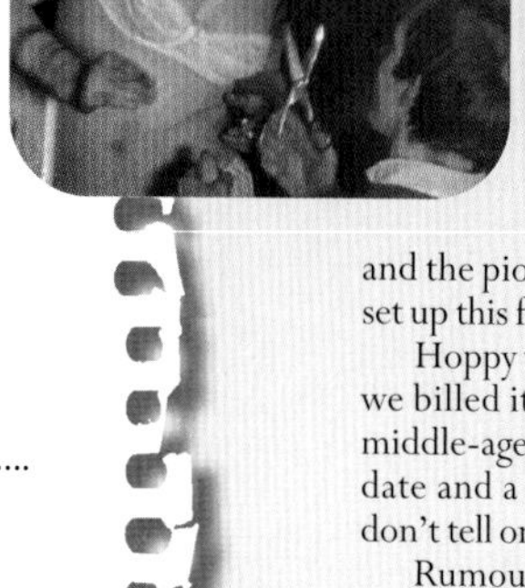

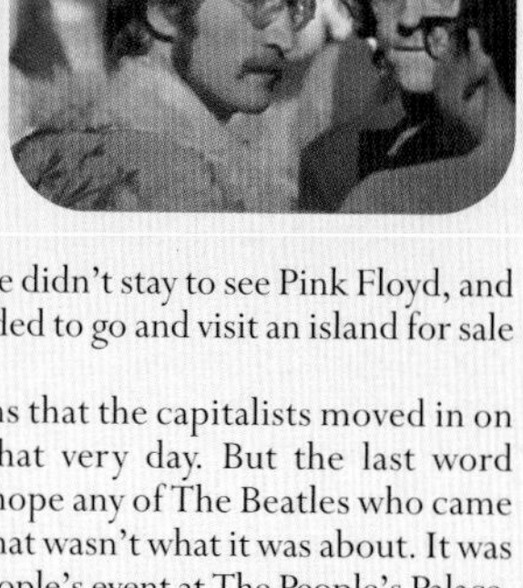

Hoppy takes up the story: "I conjured up the title and we billed it as a 'Free Speech Benefit'. There were two middle-aged gents in tweeds at the Ally Pally. We agreed a date and a fee – which I don't think ever got paid, but don't tell on me! That was the easy part."

Rumours abounded that The Beatles would top the bill, but John was the only Fab to bowl up on the day. He was accompanied by Indica gallery co-owner John Dunbar and chauffeur, Terry Doran. However, the artist – Yoko Ono – to whom Dunbar had introduced Lennon the previous November *was* appearing, though, contrary to some reports, they did not meet at 'the Dream'.

Until early evening on the April 29, John was at home in Weybridge ingesting Owsleys and cocaine with Dunbar, who recalls... well, very little, unsurprisingly. "We saw something on the television about the event. So we thought fuck it, let's go. I remember bumping into Denny Laine, who'd lost his band, and the stars behaving like fireworks... And everyone was looking at us because it was John. Was Yoko there? I don't remember that."

Film-maker Peter Whitehead's footage of the event – incorporated into his Pink Floyd: London '66–'67 video – shows the granny-glassed, Afghan-jacketed Lennon going about relatively unaccosted. Mick Farren – IT editor, UFO doorman and leader of the opening act, The Social Deviants – agrees that "a lot of the hippies were like, 'No Beatlemania here, dear'." He makes an intriguing further observation of Lennon's visit. There were two stages in the hall, and bands played simultaneously. Somewhere in the middle the sounds met. "I swear I saw Lennon standing in [the] zone of dissonance," he recalls, "moving forward and back looking quite fascinated."

As stoned as he was, this was all new for John. As Mick Farren explains: "You've got to remember that Paul was into this scene. He bought books *and* read them. He went to UFO and to art galleries. But this was the first time I'd seen John out. I think he felt he had some catching up to do. What with the noise, and the drugs and all the people, perhaps I Am The Walrus came out the other side." (It's interesting to note that 10 days later The Beatles recorded a cacophonous 16-minute instrumental track).

Joe Beard of The Purple Gang, who also played that night, saw Lennon sitting and smoking in the park a little later, but the entourage didn't stay to see Pink Floyd, and the next day they decided to go and visit an island for sale off the Irish coast.

Farren still reckons that the capitalists moved in on the counterculture that very day. But the last word belongs to Hoppy. "I hope any of The Beatles who came had a good time, but that wasn't what it was about. It was a people's event." A people's event at The People's Palace. Power to the people, right on!

PHOTOS: BBC PICTURE LIBRARY

Mick Farren: "Paul was into this scene, but this was the first time I'd seen John out. I think he felt he had some catching up to do!"

"Do you come here often?" Linda and Paul meet for the second time at *Sgt Pepper's* launch, Brian Epstein's house, 24 Chapel St, May 19, 1967.

What: Paul meets Linda
Where: The Bag O'Nails, London
When: 15 May 1967

FANCY THAT!

Paul was watching Georgie Fame play, Linda was on a night out with The Animals – but their eyes met in The Bag O'Nails club. By Phil Sutcliffe.

"THE BAG O'NAILS WAS A SOUL CLUB REALLY, but when the hippies started coming down it was like having a hundred Quasimodos in – you couldn't hear the band for all the fucking bells," says John Gunnell, co-owner of the Kingly Street watering-hole-to-the-stars – the place where Paul McCartney met Linda Eastman.

So Gunnell banned the bells. "These people would come jangling up to the door and we'd say, Sorry, no bells, and, nice as you like, they'd go back to their cars and put their normal gear on."

By November 1966, when Gunnell and his partners bought 'the Bag', Swinging London was shading into Psychedelic London. But rather tentatively. Although the Beat Boom bands had embraced flowery shirts and the antiseptic reek of patchouli, in off-duty hours they sought the members-only haven of what long-time Beatles staffer Tony Bramwell calls "these gentlemen's youth clubs", sanctuaries they shared with well-heeled businessmen, tourists and footballers (the Bag O'Nails became the Frank McLintock-era Arsenal hang-out). In turn, these 'straights' remained unruffled because no conspicuous consumption of psychedelics occurred in front of them – fear of US visa deprivation ensured that most drug use, even pot smoking, remained ultra-covert at the time.

Before Gunnell bought the place, since Victorian times it had been an upper-class 'hostess' joint. He retained the long, narrow cellar room's harem-style silk drapes, flock wallpaper and booths along the walls, cleared a small dancefloor and installed a bandstand and DJ turntables. For some months, former account customers would ring in vain for "a bottle of Dom and a couple of dolly birds" to be home delivered.

But there again, *plus ça change*. In Barry Miles's Many Years From Now, Paul McCartney said that, basically, he went to his "favourite club" on the pull – as he would tell John Lennon, he wasn't married to Jane Asher and, anyway, that winter she toured America for six months with the Bristol Old Vic company. "We were young, we were looking pretty good and we had all this power and fame and it was difficult to resist playing with it," he said. "Now I recall, I might have got asked for money one night after pulling some bird. I wouldn't pay, though."

A regular, he came for DJ Al Needles's choice soul selections and live acts including Sam & Dave, Junior Walker and John Lee Hooker. Plus, the crack, of course. Always friendly with the staff, from manager Joe Van Duyts to Spanish cook Manuel, no matter what time of night he arrived he could always rustle up one of his Scouse favourites, a chip buttie or a spam sandwich (this predated by a few months what '60s scenesman Jeff Dexter dubbed the 'macroneurotic' movement).

With work on *Sgt Pepper's* finished, on May 15, 1967, he took off on one of his solo club crawl nights before ending up at The Bag O'Nails. He joined Bramwell, already ensconced, for his usual, Scotch and Coke. A booth or two nearer the band – Georgie Fame, that night – sat Linda Eastman with Eric Burdon and Chas Chandler from The Animals, whom she'd photographed several times in America.

If the Earth moved nobody noticed, but some snapshot memories of the quietly fateful occasion remain. Linda recalled an 'our eyes met' moment. Bramwell says McCartney went over to her table. The late Chandler always insisted he made the introduction. Conversely, McCartney says she was actually leaving when he "accidentally" stepped in front of her and delivered his "big pulling line", asking her to come on to The Speakeasy with him. They both remembered what Georgie Fame was playing as they spoke: a Billy Stewart song, Sitting In The Park.

With Burdon, Chandler and Bramwell, they drove the half-mile to Margaret Street where they enjoyed the house staple, plates of peppersteak and chips with chef Enzo's special mushy peas à la fried onion. But for Paul and Linda the more abiding memory was the DJ's pre-release unveiling of A Whiter Shade Of Pale. They thought it was wonderful and that it must be Traffic. In remarkably delayed-action fashion, it became "their song".

Macca's favourite haunt, 'The Bag', 1967.

"Paul says Linda was leaving when he 'accidentally' stepped in front of her and delivered his 'big pulling line'."

They met again at Brian Epstein's house four days later – Linda establishing her professional credentials by shooting the *Sgt Pepper's* press launch. After that, they didn't see each other again for almost a year while McCartney helter-skeltered through his internationally scandalous LSD confession to Life magazine, Brian Epstein's death, the Maharishi, the Magical Mystery Tour and a forlorn last try of an engagement to Jane Asher.

Then, in May and June 1968, he met Linda for an hour in New York and three days in Los Angeles. Three months on, he rang and asked her to come over and stay with him. She arrived on the night The Beatles finished recording Happiness Is A Warm Gun, September 25.

John Gunnell says the day before they married, March 12, 1969, McCartney came down to The Bag O'Nails and invited the entire staff to the wedding (which none of the other Beatles attended).

But, the night they met, did Paul pull after all? Well, he drove Linda back to his house in Cavendish Avenue. And Linda, with either enduring American innocence or acquired British relish for the double entendre, later reported, "I was impressed to see his Magrittes".

PHOTOS: HULTON ARCHIVE/PICTORIAL PRESS

MAY 67

3–4 Overdubbing and mixing sessions for *Magical Mystery Tour* are undertaken at Abbey Road.

5 McCartney shaves off his moustache.

7 Starr is in the audience when The Jimi Hendrix Experience play at The Saville Theatre, London.

9 Mick Jagger is present when an untitled instrumental jam is recorded at Abbey Road.

11 Baby You're A Rich Man is recorded at Olympic Studios, Barnes, London.

12 All Together Now is recorded at Abbey Road.

15 McCartney meets photographer Linda Eastman for the first time in London's Bag O'Nails club.

17 You Know My Name (Look Up The Number) is recorded at Abbey Road.

18 At a Rolling Stones recording session in Olympic Studios, Barnes, London, Lennon and McCartney contribute backing vocals to We Love You.

19 Brian Epstein hosts a launch party for the *Sgt Pepper's Lonely Hearts Club Band* album at his Chapel Street, London, home (above).

20 John Lennon, Paul McCartney and Ringo Starr are heard in an interview with DJ Kenny Everett on the BBC Light Programme radio show, Where It's At.

24 The Beatles go to see Procol Harum play at the Speakeasy.

25 Lennon takes delivery of his celebrated psychedelic Rolls Royce Phantom V. On the same day, work starts on It's All Too Much in De Lane Lea Recording Studios, Kingsway, London.

27 A Day In The Life is banned by the BBC because of its drug references.

29 McCartney goes to Heathrow Airport to meet Jane Asher on her return from a US tour with the Bristol Old Vic Company.

31 Work on It's All Too Much continues in De Lane Lea Recording Studios, London.

JUNE 67

1 The LP, *Sgt Pepper's Lonely Hearts Club Band* is released in the UK.

2 *Sgt Pepper* is released in the States, with the same track-listing as the UK release.

3 *Sgt Pepper* enters the UK album chart at Number 1.

4 The Jimi Hendrix Experience play at the Saville Theatre, London, which McCartney, Jane Asher, Harrison and Patti Boyd attend. The post-gig party is held at McCartney's home.

The Complete Picture

When The Beatles released *Sgt Pepper's Lonely Hearts Club Band* in June 1967, they knew that they had something really special. Mark Ellen analyses the impact of their most famous album.

We all now know, of course, that The Beatles left Abbey Road at dawn one Sunday in May, 1967 with an acetate version of the finished album, and that its public premiere was two hours later, on a cloudless spring morning, roaring across the rooftops from speakers in the window of 'Mama' Cass Elliot's Chelsea flat to the incalculable delight of all those in earshot.

I'd have given anything to have known that at the time. Or that it had a virtual monopoly – a wall-to-wall playlist – on American radio. Or that one of the songs would have 40 session musicians on it. Without access to that kind of information, we consumed the record in spellbound isolation, aware only that it had taken a stupendous length of time to construct and cost an arm and a leg. We hadn't the faintest idea what to expect, too young in my case to sit Buddha-like on a scatter cushion speculating on its layers of hidden meaning but old enough to instantly recognise it needed approaching from another angle. Instead of auditioning it as usual for new favourite tracks, your own fantasy singles collection, it was obvious these polished and scintillating tunes, no matter how diverse, somehow hung together in the same sonic universe. Indeed, Geoff Emerick had spent hours taping microphones deep inside the bells of brass instruments and gently compressing snare-drum tones as his employers wanted everything to sound different before they even started recording.

"Sgt Pepper seemed to be pasted together out of the dazzling primary colours of its cover."

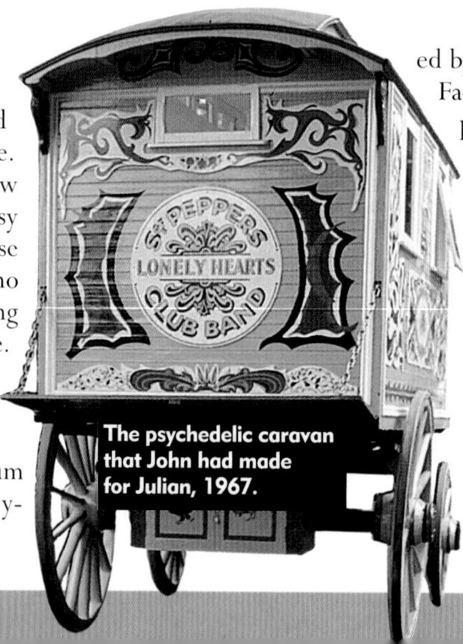

The psychedelic caravan that John had made for Julian, 1967.

We hadn't a clue, either, that all the reference points had changed. By an organic shift rather than strategic design, Stockhausen, The Beach Boys and Lewis Carroll were being ushered in the front door while Elvis, Buddy Holly and Carl Perkins were shuffled out the back. Apart from a McCartney knees-up in an idealised suburban future, all the songs were in the present tense, all emphatically *now*, and none of them subscribed to the boy-meets-girl romantic axis that had been the staple of their compositional landscape since the beginning, including a good 50 per cent of *Revolver*. They were songs with very little emotional depth but vast imaginative possibility. And with the exception of George's, they weren't about the authors' real lives – they were either fantasies (Sgt Pepper, Good Morning, Mr Kite, Fixing A Hole, Lucy In The Sky, A Day In The Life) or fictions (She's Leaving Home, Lovely Rita, Getting Better). They had a childlike charm and naivety about them roughly in tandem with the work of the Pink Floyd, who were recording next door, a stoned and dreamlike attention to detail soon to be adopted by Donovan and Traffic and The Small Faces among others, and ultimately worn paper-thin by countless psychedelic voyagers to follow.

And never before or since had an album's artwork so conditioned your approach to the music. *A Hard Day's Night* you can visualise in black and white, *Revolver* in a hazy duotone, but *Sgt Pepper* seemed to be pasted together out of the dazzling primary colours of its cover, like a watercolour daubed from a jam-jar. It was buffed up and shining and full of echoes of an uncomplicated past, sepia images of

PHOTO: REX

The Beatles' youth, a sparkling pantomime world of brass bands and tea-garden orchestras and music-hall radio hits of the '40s and '50s.

There were further surprises: we'd never seen printed lyrics before, never heard a hidden message in a run-out groove and never been offered a Beatles album without spin-off singles or EPs. None of these songs had a life outside the record, which cemented the notion that it worked as a whole. When I discovered years later there *had* been two singles but that George Martin – in "the biggest mistake of my professional life" – had allowed them to be sliced off early and released as a double-A-side back in March to satisfy the panicking EMI heads of state, I began rather pathetically to fantasise a reworked running-order and the songs I would drop to include them – Rita obviously, and probably

TRACK LISTING

A-SIDE

1. Sgt Pepper's Lonely Hearts Club Band
Sung by Lennon/McCartney

2. With A Little Help From My Friends
Sung by Starr

3. Lucy In The Sky With Diamonds
Sung by Lennon

4. Getting Better
Sung by McCartney

5. Fixing A Hole
Sung by McCartney

6. She's Leaving Home
Sung by Lennon/McCartney

7. Being For The Benefit Of Mr Kite!
Sung by Lennon

B-SIDE

8. Within You Without You
Sung by Harrison

9. When I'm Sixty-Four
Sung by McCartney

10. Lovely Rita
Sung by McCartney

11. Good Morning, Good Morning
Sung by Lennon

12. Sgt Pepper's Lonely Hearts Club Band (Reprise)
Sung by Lennon/McCartney

13. A Day In The Life
Sung by Lennon

All songs by Lennon/ McCartney except Within You Without You by George Harrison

SGT PEPPER'S LONELY HEARTS CLUB BAND

Finished symphony: The Beatles at the launch of *Sgt Pepper*, May 19, 1967.

PRODUCING PEPPER

George Martin ponders how *Sgt Pepper* would have turned out if it'd been made with today's technology.

"It would probably have been easier today to make *Sgt Pepper*, but it probably wouldn't have turned out as well. I think the discipline of four-track recording in 1967 made us do things that you wouldn't do today. And it made The Beatles perform better.

"There wasn't the luxury of saying, well, we can patch that later. We just couldn't do that; we had to work things to a conclusion as we went along. Particularly when you're mixing down from one four-track to another, you solidify everything that has gone before. You couldn't go back, otherwise you'd destroy everything that you were doing. I think that discipline, and that forward-thinking, was part of the success of *Sgt Pepper*.

"Having to do that worked out very much in our favour. It sounds as though we chose to do that, but of course we didn't. We only used the tools that were available, and that's all that was available. I think if I'd had 72 tracks in those days, I would have used them. But I'm not sorry that I didn't!"

Phil Ward

The two Georges: Martin with Harrison, Abbey Road, 1967.

Within You Without You, which I listened to intently for only the second time this morning, though to lose it would detach a spiritual dimension that seems so central to the package.

I'll never forget the release of this record. You could hear it everywhere you went. I remember leaving a friend's house and going next door to find the next track was playing, as if the sound was radiating from one giant Dansette. And here's a thing: *parents* seemed to like it and nobody minded. Your Kinks, Stones and Dylan records you played alone in a bedroom, dark, difficult works that would be destroyed if a shaft of adult light were let in on the magic. But *Sgt Pepper* came so charged with optimism and possibility that its appeal couldn't be contained. I remember seeing men who smoked pipes and women who looked like Penelope Keith – people in their *30s* for crying out loud! – tapping a toe to it and warbling its catchphrases ("Good morning!", "Getting better!") and somehow this didn't seem appalling. Parents had gone off The Beatles when they'd become gaunt and enigmatic, but these clean-cut satin-suited masters of ceremony clutching French horns and piccolos were embraced, without a trace of irony,

PHOTOS: PICTORIAL PRESS, REX

SLEEVE NOTES

Peter Blake goes on the record about his ground-breaking cover.

"Paul's initial concept for the artwork had The Beatles standing in an Edwardian lounge in front of a large wall covered with framed photographs of their heroes. One of his original pen and ink sketches had the four of them holding brass band instruments and wearing marching band outfits resplendent with epaulettes. There was a pin up poster of Brigitte Bardot stuck to the wall behind them along with various trophies and shields.

"Getting a professional fine artist to design a record cover hadn't happened before. Paul commissioned Dutch designers Marijke Koger, Jos Je Leeger and Simon Posthuma but Robert Fraser didn't like their original design. He realised that in years to come it would be seen as just another psychedelic cover so he suggested me to redesign it. It was Jann's [Haworth, pop artist and Peter's then wife] idea to have an imaginary audience watching The Beatles play. Lists were compiled of who should appear. Paul's list included Fred Astaire and William Burroughs, George wanted 12 Indian gurus and Ringo said he'd just go along with everyone else's list. As for John, his list included Jesus based on the problems he had previously experienced with his 'We're more popular than Jesus' claims. He also chose Hitler. We actually did a cut out of him. He's there, but covered by The Beatles. On some of the outtakes you can see him behind them. Neither of them were really heroes of John's. Their inclusion was just a joke, a social comment.

"EMI were horrified when they received the final bill for the sleeve – £2867.25s.3d. They usually budgeted for £25 a photograph and they probably expected to go up to £75 for a band of The Beatles' calibre. I was paid £200 but I was happy with that. At the end of the day, it was just a job like any other. It was nothing special but I guess the sleeve captured the moment as it's still revered today."

Lois Wilson

WHAT THE PAPERS SAID...

'67's press found the LP peppered with hot tracks.

"Trust the Beatles to come up with something different! Whether the album is their best yet, I wouldn't like to say after one hearing. Whether it was worth the five months it took to make, I would argue. But it is a very good LP and will sell like hot cakes. No one can deny that The Beatles have provided us with more musical entertainment, which will be both pleasant on the ear and get the brain working a bit, too."

Allen Evans, NME (May 20, 1967)

"An LP which has many brilliant highlights, seems well worth the wait and it is the sort of popular music which will exercise the brain cells as well as the entertainment tissues. Packaged in a good full-cover sleeve, with lyrics and with a cardboard cut-out slip including a picture of Sgt Pepper himself, and his three stripes! Tongue-in-cheek and clever. Not TOO clever, you understand, but once or twice right on the borderline."

Peter Jones, Record Mirror (May 27, 1967)

"Whatever the influences at work on The Beatles band, the lads have brought forth yet another saga of entertainment and achievement so solid and inspired that it should keep the British pop industry ticking over securely for another six months at least. Already several of the tracks on this 13-song album are being feverishly covered by other artists. It's all presented like one of those phoney 'live' LPs with dubbed applause and laughter coming in at the oddest moments, but the effect is used with subtlety and is not allowed to spoil the musical content."

Chris Welch, Melody Maker (June 3, 1967)

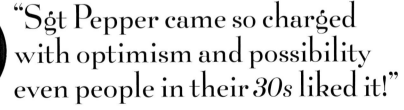

your copy of th
of wisdom by CHRIS W
t Pepper. And don't forg

Now let boring controversy begin!

WHO are the Beatles' greatest influences? Some might consider them to be William Byrd, Richard Strauss and Ravi Shankar. We humbly guess at George Formby, Lonnie Donnegan and an elderly lady schoolteacher image, locked deep in the Beatles' collective childhood memory.

The Beatles have always loved telling a tale, sometimes sadly, sometimes with wry humour, often mixing deressing sentiments with a chirpy bounce in the grand music hall tradition. And odd women constantly crop up in Beatle song themes. It was Eleanor Rigby on the classic "Revolver" album.

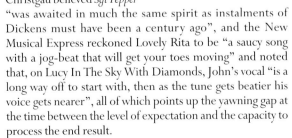

as the very family favourites they'd sought to satirise, and their music had even filtered through to the kitchen.

In fact, the New York critic Robert Christgau believed *Sgt Pepper* "was awaited in much the same spirit as instalments of Dickens must have been a century ago", and the New Musical Express reckoned Lovely Rita to be "a saucy song with a jog-beat that will get your toes moving" and noted that, on Lucy In The Sky With Diamonds, John's vocal "is a long way off to start with, then as the tune gets beatier his voice gets nearer", all of which points up the yawning gap at the time between the level of expectation and the capacity to process the end result.

"Sgt Pepper came so charged with optimism and possibility even people in their *30s* liked it!"

The 'concept', we're now aware, was little more than a happy accident and the product of some visionary sleeve design – in fact, When I'm Sixty-Four was a hastily retooled instrumental they used to kick around at soundchecks in The Cavern. Thirty-five years later the album still works sublimely as a whole but would you ever pull down an individual track and stick it on a car tape? Newsweek rightly elevated A Day In The Life from the rest of the pack, comparing it to TS Eliot's The Wasteland, yet none of these compositions ever seem to work out of context. There's simply no equivalent of Here, There And Everywhere or In My Life, recordings that stood outside of the albums that delivered them. Magnificent as they are, it's as though these 13 songs will always belong together, the soundtrack to the movie of a time when anything seemed possible, when the Us And Them divide was briefly dissolved, when you could be fined by a meter maid and then seduce her 10 minutes later, and when all thoughts were directed straight through the back of the wardrobe.

7 More instrumental jams and parts for You Know My Name (Look Up The Number) are recorded at Abbey Road. The animated Yellow Submarine film is announced.

8 Paul invites the Stones' Brian Jones to attend the recording session at Abbey Road. Jones plays a sax solo for You Know My Name (Look Up The Number).

9 You Know My Name (Look Up The Number) is edited and mixed at Abbey Road.

10 New York Mining Disaster 1941 by The Bee Gees enters the US Top 40 singles chart – having gained many radio plays because DJs believed it was The Beatles under an assumed name.

14 Work on All You Need Is Love starts at Olympic Studios, London.

16 The Beatles appear on the cover of Life magazine – inside, McCartney reveals that he's taken acid.

19 In UK tabloid newspaper The Daily Mirror, McCartney admits publicly to having taken LSD. Vocals, drums, piano and banjo are overdubbed onto All You Need Is Love in Abbey Road.

21 A mono mixing session for All You Need Is Love is held at the Abbey Road studios.

23 Orchestral overdubs are done for All You Need Is Love at Abbey Road.

24 The Beatles hold a late morning press conference at Abbey Road to discuss the Our World TV satellite broadcast scheduled for the next day. Later, there are camera rehearsals, and overdubbing for All You Need Is Love.

25 All You Need Is Love is performed on the BBC's international TV broadcast, Our World Live (above). Lennon's psychedelic Rolls Royce is entered in a Concours d'Elegance competition at an Oxfam rally in Battersea Park, London.

26 Finishing touches are added to All You Need Is Love at Abbey Road.

28 Harrison is fined £6 for speeding in his black Mini Cooper.

JULY 67

1 *Sgt Pepper's Lonely Hearts Club Band* reaches Number 1 on the US album chart. The BBC's Where It's At show broadcasts a pre-recorded interview with Paul talking about All You Need Is Love.

2 Harrison's wife Patti is introduced to Eric Clapton at a party in 24 Chapel Street, the home of Brian Epstein.

3 Promoter Vic Lewis throws a party for The Monkees at London's The Speakeasy club. Guests include Lennon, Paul and Jane, George and Patti, Eric Clapton, Procol Harum and Dusty Springfield.

5 John and Cynthia go and see The Marmalade at The Speakeasy, London.

What: Our World broadcast
Where: Abbey Road Studios
When: June 25, 1967

UNIVERSAL LOVE

For the first live worldwide broadcast, The Beatles penned All You Need Is Love. The song became the anthem of the times, writes Keith Badman.

SGT PEPPER'S LONELY HEARTS CLUB BAND was almost one month old by the time The Beatles took part in their latest musical adventure; a worldwide, live television extravaganza called Our World, billed by the BBC as "For the first time ever, linking five continents and bringing man face-to-face with mankind..."

Over 18 TV stations around the world, including Australia, France, Japan, the USA and West Germany, participated in this global event, which featured diverse activities such as opera and circus performances. Representing the British TV leg of the proceedings were The Beatles, who decided to showcase John Lennon's recently composed anthem, All You Need Is Love.

The man behind the decision to feature the Fab Four was Derek Burrell-Davis from Our World. At the time, Paul McCartney told this story of how they came to be involved: "A fellow from the BBC asked us to get together a song for this show. We said, We'd get one together with nice easy words, so that everyone can understand it. He said, 'Oh, all right then'. So we went away, and we just played Monopoly for a bit and then the fellow said, 'Now, where's the song?' So we said, Ah, don't worry Derek. So John and I just got together and I wrote one and John wrote one. We went to the session and we decided to do his first. By the time we had done the backing track for John's, we suddenly realised that his was the one."

Beatles manager Brian Epstein announced that, just like Burrell-Davis, he too once had reservations about The Beatles' appearance. "Time got nearer and nearer [to the show] and they still hadn't written anything. Then, about three weeks before the programme, they sat down to write and the record was completed in 10 days." In charge of the recording was The Beatles' regular producer, George Martin, who recalled, "When it came to the end of their fade away at the end of song, I asked them, How do you want to get out of it? 'Write absolutely anything you like, George,' they said. 'Put together any tunes you fancy, and just play it out like that.'" Martin chose Greensleeves and In The Mood. George Harrison admitted that Paul thought of singing She Loves You at the end of the song at the time of the recording.

The setting for this historic Our World performance was Studio One at EMI's Abbey Road. Rehearsals for the show began on Saturday, June 24, 1967 – the day before transmission. To accompany the Fabs' television performance, it was decided that a motley crew of friends, fellow pop celebrities and known faces from the London scene should surround The Beatles, many of which were in fact pulled into the proceedings by NEMS employee, Tony Bramwell. "On the Saturday evening I went off to find guests for the next day," he recalled. "You could find nearly everyone down The Speakeasy, The Cromwellian, The Bag O'Nails and The Scotch Of Saint James. I got Eric Clapton, Mick Jagger and Marianne Faithfull. I found Keith Moon in The Speakeasy, absolutely enjoying himself, throwing peanuts everywhere. I said to him, 'Ere, you, there's a party tomorrow. Two o'clock, EMI, and he said, 'Right, I'd better go home then, and his chauffeur took him home."

On the day of broadcast, the studio at EMI had been decorated with brightly coloured floral displays and balloons. The friends and celebrities were told to sit around where The Beatles' instruments had been set up. Rolling Stone Keith Richards ended up sitting next to Ringo. But, in truth, everyone fought to be next to John Lennon, as he was the lead vocalist and most likely to get the best camera shots.

Just before the live broadcast was due to begin, there was panic in the control booth, as The Beatles' recording engineer, Geoff Emerick, recalled. "We went on air about 40 seconds early. George Martin and I were having a glass of Scotch when we got word over the intercom that transmission was starting. There was a big panic to hide the bottle and the glasses. We ended up shoving them under the mixing console."

Also among the star-studded audience was Mike McGear, singer with The Scaffold pop group and Paul's brother. "When the 'live' button was pressed," he recalls, "I did my best to liven things up by throwing streamers and holding up cue cards with 'Smile' and 'Laf Now' written on them." The performance, watched by an estimated 500 million people, was a success, though George Harrison remarked after the broadcast, "We were trying to make it into a recording session and a good time but the BBC were trying to make it into a television show. It's a constant struggle now to get ourselves across through all these people, who are all hassling."

Aside from George's mild dissatisfaction, it was still a monumental and historic event in The Beatles' career and perfect for the impending Summer Of Love. Brian Epstein said afterwards, "For me, All You Need Is Love is the best thing they've done. They wrote it because they really wanted to give the world a message." He rang The Beatles' former publicist, Derek Taylor, and gushed down the line, "It was their finest." Paul McCartney was in agreement. "All You Need Is Love was perfect if you're going to say any message," he said. "That's a fine and wonderful message to say, really."

"All You Need Is Love was perfect if you're going to say any message. It's a fine and wonderful message to say."

PHOTOS: REX

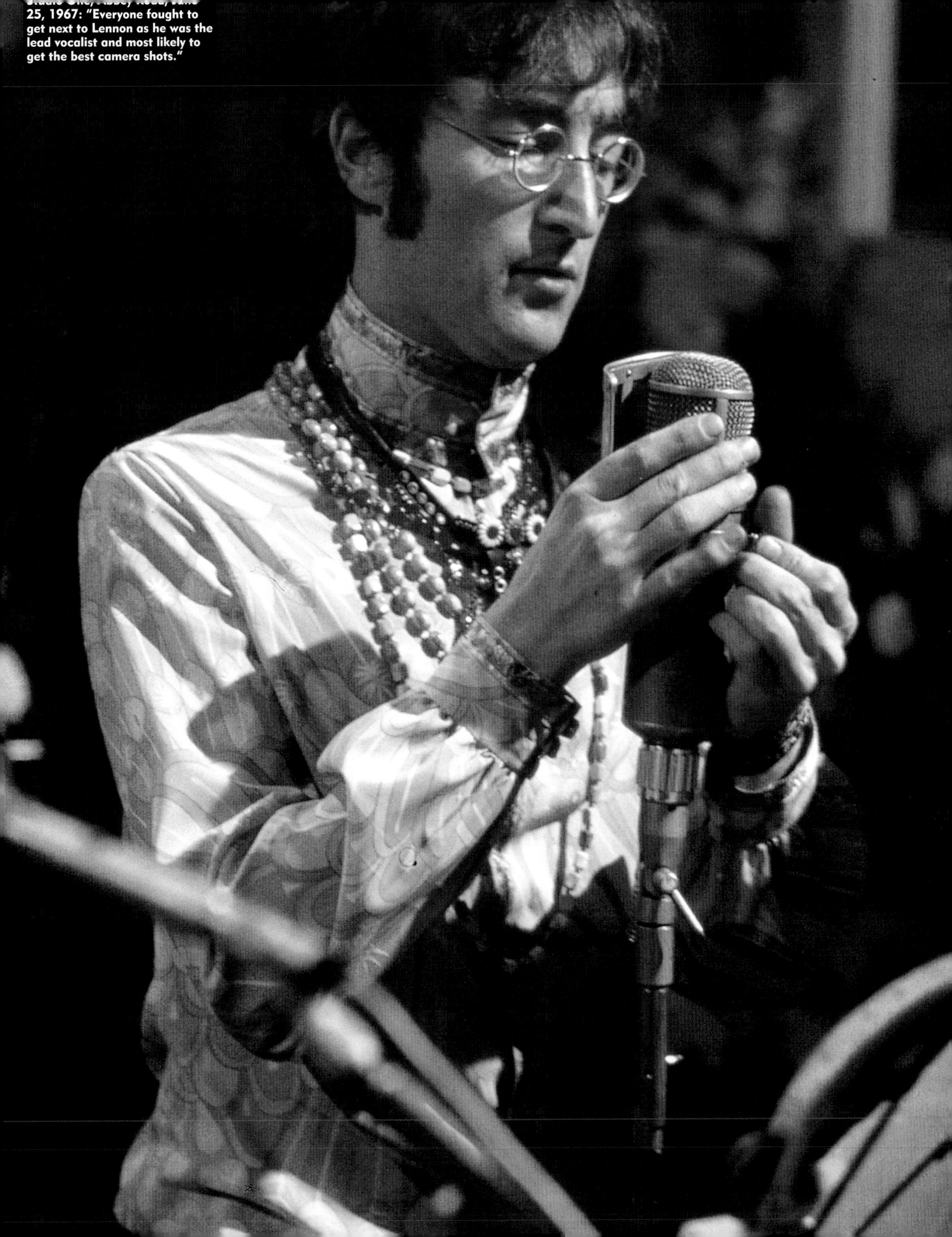

Studio One, Abbey Road, June 25, 1967: "Everyone fought to get next to Lennon as he was the lead vocalist and most likely to get the best camera shots."

What: Buying a Greek island
Where: Leslo
When: July, 1967

FANTASY ISLAND

John Lennon had a vision that The Beatles could all live on a Greek island together. So they all went looking for one in a boat. By Chris Hunt.

AT THE HEIGHT OF THE SUMMER OF LOVE, The Beatles were on a high. All You Need Is Love was Number 1 and *Sgt Pepper* was on a 23-week run at the top of the album charts. There was a belief The Beatles could achieve anything, that they knew no creative boundaries other than those imposed by their own limitless, drugged-fuelled imaginations. This climate of creative madness was at its zenith when, weighed down by life in the constant spotlight of their own notoriety, they decided they wanted to get away from it all and live on an island. In the words of Peter Brown, it was a time when it was becoming harder to tell what part of the madness was drug induced and what part was pure whimsy.

Sitting in the studio one night, John suggested the idea of an island retreat, where the band could create a kingdom for their families and friends, and where they could even build the best studio that money could buy. By no means sold on the idea, McCartney recalls it as "a drug-induced ambition", not unlike many of the schemes that would later drive Apple.

John Alexis Mardas – 'Magic Alex', as Lennon dubbed him because of his supposed genius with electronic gadgetry – suggested his native Greece, where he said they were "virtually giving islands away". Alex and the band's own 'Mr Fixit', Epstein's assistant Alistair Taylor, were dispatched to find an island. "We went off for about a week and we shortlisted three," recalls Taylor. "I reported back and they said 'right, let's go out there'."

"Yeehah!" John in Greece, July 1967.

Given the ongoing political situation, Greece seemed the least likely destination for The Beatles. Just three months earlier the country had been taken over by a fascist military junta who had not only suspended democracy, but had banned rock'n'roll and long hair. Lennon seemed unphased. "As long as it doesn't affect us," he told Hunter Davies, "I don't care if the Government is all fascist, or Communist. They're as bad as here."

Of the properties shortlisted, the most likely was Leslo, an island of 80 acres, with four idyllic beaches and four smaller habitable islands – one for each Beatle. It came with 16 acres of olive groves, which Taylor calculated would pay back the £90,000 price tag in just seven years.

On July 20, George, Patti, Ringo and Neil Aspinall flew to Athens, where they were met by Alex and his father, a major in the Greek secret police. Paul, Jane, John, Cynthia and Julian flew out two days later, with Mal Evans, Taylor and Patti's 16-year-old sister, Paula. Despite being included in John's sketchy vision for communal island living, Brian Epstein was not among the party – his father had died days earlier and he was still 'sitting *Shiva*', observing the Jewish faith's week-long period of mourning. On the day The Beatles' yacht finally arrived in Athens – it had been delayed by a storm until July 25 – Brian was still at his mother's home in Liverpool, from where he wrote to his New York based business partner, Nat Weiss. He sounded less than enthused by the scheme. "The boys've gone to Greece to buy an island," he wrote. "I think it's a dotty idea but they're no longer children and must have their own sweet way."

While waiting for the yacht, The Beatles spent time sightseeing, but their plans were frustrated by crowds who seemed to appear in advance of their every move. 'Magic Alex' had struck a deal with a Greek government official – the band would not be searched at the airport and in return Alex kept the Ministry of Tourism aware of every photo opportunity. Diplomatic immunity had been exchanged for an endorsement of the Junta – but it also meant they could arrive with whatever drugs were needed to make the trip worthwhile!

As the yacht prepared to sail, Ringo flew home to his pregnant wife, accompanied by Neil Aspinall. The remaining party spent their time swimming, sun-bathing and taking LSD, as they cruised the Aegean without a care. Sitting on deck until late into the night, they would sail towards the moon, singing hare krishna to the accompaniment of George's ukulele.

When they arrived at Leslo, "the boys just fell in love with it," recalls 'Mr Fixit'. "They took it in turns to cruise around the island in the little boat that we had on the yacht." Everyone was delighted and Alistair was sent home to make the necessary arrangements. Because of currency restrictions in operation in Britain at the time, taking large sums of money abroad was difficult and a direct appeal was made to Chancellor of the Exchequer, James Callaghan, pointing out The Beatles' contributions to British exports. The treasury gave special dispensation, but £95,000 was the absolute limit allowed. At the bottom of his letter, James Callaghan added by hand: "But not a penny more… I wonder how you're going to furnish it."

"I don't care if the Greek government is all fascist, or Communist. They're all as bad as here." John Lennon

Furnishing requirements were not front of mind for The Beatles, and their accountants were instructed to purchase the necessary 'property dollars' from the government. But all this was taking far too long and interest had waned. "Having been out there I don't think we needed to go back," recalls Paul. "Probably the best way to not buy a Greek island is to go out there for a bit."

The property dollars were sold back at the new rate of 37 per cent, making a profit of £11,400 on the deal. "It was the only time The Beatles made any money on a business venture," joked George in Anthology. "It came to nothing. We didn't buy an island, we came home," recalled Ringo. "We were great at going on holiday with big ideas, but we never carried them out… It was safer making records, because once they let us out we went barmy."

PHOTOS: TOPHAM PICTUREPOINT, HULTON ARCHIVE, CORBIS

7 The new single, All You Need Is Love/Baby, You're A Rich Man, is released in the UK.

17 All You Need Is Love/Baby You're A Rich Man, is released in the US.

20 George Harrison and Ringo Starr arrive in Athens, Greece, amid reports that The Beatles have bought an island in the northern Aegean for £150,000.

22 All You Need Is Love reaches Number 1 in the UK.

23 The Beatles drive from Athens, Greece, to Delphi, to see a performance of Agamemnon by the Oxford University drama company, but are forced to turn back when their car is assailed by crowds of fans and journalists.

24 The Times runs a full-page ad advocating the legalisation of marijuana, signed by all four Beatles and many other celebrities.

26 Because Maureen is heavily pregnant, Ringo cuts short his stay in Greece, and returns to the UK.

30 George and Patti return from their trip in Greece.

31 Ringo records a farewell message for UK pirate radio station Radio London, at their Curzon Street, London, premises. Like all pirates, it is shortly to be forced to cease broadcasting.

31 Lennon and McCartney return from Greece.

AUGUST 67

1 George and Patti move into a rented house on Blue Jay Way, above Sunset Strip, Los Angeles.

4 Harrison sees Ravi Shankar (below) play at the Hollywood Bowl, LA.

7 Harrison meets up with Ravi Shankar again in Hollywood, LA.

8 Harrison (with former Beatles press officer Derek Taylor – below, to George's left) pays his first visit to Haight Ashbury in San Francisco.

9 Harrison flies back from the United States to London.

18 The single We Love You by The Rolling Stones, with backing vocals by Lennon and McCartney, is released on Decca.

19 All You Need Is Love reaches Number 1 in the US singles chart, as Maureen Starkey, wife of Ringo, gives birth to their baby boy, Jason (below), in Queen Charlotte's Hospital, Hammersmith, London. On the same day, KNOW radio in Denver bans all Beatles records because they apparently advocate 'trip-taking'.

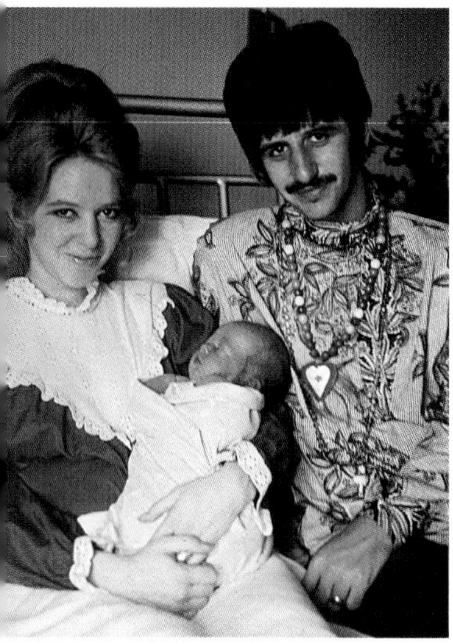

22–23 Two days of recording Your Mother Should Know at Chappell Recording Studios, Maddox Street, London.

24 The Beatles (minus Ringo), Mick Jagger and Marianne Faithfull attend a lecture in the Park Lane Hilton, London, by Maharishi Mahesh Yogi.

25 The Beatles travel to Bangor, Wales, to study Transcendental Meditation with the Maharishi.

26 While The Beatles are still in Bangor, Brian Epstein attends a meeting at his Warbleton, Sussex house.

27 Brian Epstein dies of a drug overdose in bed at his home in Chapel Street, Belgravia. The Sunday Express reveals that former Beatles drummer Pete Best is earning £18-a-week, working in a bakery.

28 Brian Epstein's death makes front page news in virtually all UK newspapers.

29 Following Brian Epstein's death, over £250,000 is wiped off the market value of shares in their publishing company, Northern Songs, but the shares rally again by the end of the day.

30 The inquest into Brian Epstein's death opens at Westminster Coroner's Court, and is adjourned until September 8.

31 The Times reports that The Beatles have announced, in the wake of Brian Epstein's death, that they plan to manage their own affairs.

SEPTEMBER 67

1 The Beatles hold a planning meeting at Paul McCartney's home in London, and decide to press on with Magical Mystery Tour.

2 The Times reports experts from the Applied Psychology Research Unit in Cambridge believe that The Beatles' "eccentric articulation" in *Sgt Pepper's Lonely Hearts Club Band* might help specialists to detect heart disease.

5 Sixteen takes of I Am The Walrus are recorded at Abbey Road.

What: The Stones' 'We Love You'
Where: The UK
When: August 18, 1967

BANDING TOGETHER

The Stones had outraged 'the establishment', and in a show of support, Lennon and McCartney lent their voices to We Love You. By John Harris.

ON FEBRUARY 5, 1967, THE NEWS OF THE World carried a story headlined 'The Secrets Of The Pop Stars' Hideaway'. Its text purported to be founded on a conversation between Mick Jagger and two undercover journalists at Blases, one of the London clubs whose fragrant murk hid all manner of rock aristocrats. The man they took to be the singer with the Rolling Stones casually necked a number of benzedrine tablets, showed off a lump of hashish, invited the journalists back to his house for a smoke… and thereby sealed his fate.

There was but one small snag: 'Mick Jagger' had actually been Brian Jones. Jagger prepared to issue the newspaper with a libel writ – and thus began one of the most pivotal sagas of the era. Two weeks later came the infamous bust at Keith Richard's country seat, the consequent demolition of Jagger's legal actions, and the delivery of the Stones' scalps to the establishment. The Beatles were tied into the brouhaha from the off: George Harrison had been among Richard's guests, but had departed a mere 90 minutes before the arrival of the cops (indeed, the notion that police waited for him to leave has long been built into the Stones' myth).

The Beatles/Stones relationship was at its closest during 1967. That year's run of events speaks for itself: five days after the News Of The World appeared, Mick Jagger and Marianne Faithfull visited the climactic session for A Day In The Life; nine days after that came the bust; and on May 18, as if to put their regal seal on the upsurge of solidarity around Jagger and Richard, Lennon and McCartney added their voices to We Love You, the single that dramatises the Stones' experiences to heart-stopping effect. Less than a month later, Brian Jones leant into an Abbey Road microphone, and provided the tongue-in-cheek saxophone solo on You Know My Name (Look Up The Number). On June 24, Mick and Marianne were in Abbey Road's Studio One for the Our World broadcast of All You Need Is Love. And five days after that, Jagger and Richard were driven to their respective jails, after a three-day trial that ended in guilty verdicts and howls of incensed protest.

The treatment of The Stones wrenched the English counter-culture out of its Through-The-Looking-Glass state of innocence, and plunged it into a new generational war. John Lennon, still in the midst of what amounted to a two-year acid trip, suddenly seemed to leave behind Mr Kite and Lucy In The Sky, and speak with a new vituperative edge. "Look what they do here," he said in the summer of '67. "They stopped Radio Caroline and tried to put the Stones away while they're spending billions on nuclear armaments, and the place is full of US bases that no-one knows about." Within these words lurk not only a hint of psychedelia morphing into the seditionary anger that would surface in 1968, but the first stirrings of the New Left radicalism that would fleetingly define Lennon in the early '70s.

In the meantime, Jagger and Richards lodged successful appeals and were released. Thus, We Love You – released on August 18, as the aftershocks of the case still registered – was a perfectly-timed blast of defiance.

In his book, The Stones, Philip Norman writes that "We Love You is a single that loses all ironic point in its feeble attempt to echo The Beatles' summer anthem All You Need Is Love". Fortunately, nothing could be further from the facts. Its charms are legion: Nicky Hopkins' beautifully mesmeric piano, its opening chorus of sarcastic falsetto voices, mellotron passages – from 3:46 until the song's end – whose eeriness cannot help but evoke the idea of a conspiracy.

The presence of two Beatles is not initially obvious, although in the call-and-response sections that end both the middle eight and announce the song's final passages, one can clearly make out John Lennon's gloriously nasal vowels. Whatever, it still stands as the one moment that psychedelia united both groups at a moment of absolute brilliance; a token of how far each had come since John and Paul handed The Rolling Stones' I Wanna Be Your Man in 1963.

We Love You? Tell it to the judge, Keith!

There were further murmurings of joint action that summer. For a couple of months, the two groups even discussed the possibility of opening a jointly-run recording studio; plans got as far as the buying of a plot of land next to the Regents Park Canal. "We'll need a hotel as well," said a very excited Paul McCartney, "so that the groups will have somewhere to stay when they're recording. And we'll also build a heliport, so that foreign groups can land at Heathrow and be brought straight here..."

The project soon foundered, while beads, bells and their common sense of psychedelic purpose tipped both Beatles and Stones towards disaster. *Their Satanic Majesties Request* appeared in December, with a sleeve featuring The Beatles' faces, and songs that – with a couple of exceptions – suggested little more than a harried attempt to ape *Sgt Pepper*. Weeks later, Magical Mystery Tour arrived, and the curtain was drawn on psychedelia as rudely as Jagger and Richard's jail doors had been slammed shut.

"We Love You still stands as the one moment that psychedelia united both groups at a moment of brilliance."

PHOTOS: REX, CAMERA PRESS

After Paul and John had lent their vocal support to We Love You, Mick Jagger returned the favour by joining The Beatles for their Our World satellite broadcast of All You Need Is Love.

"Didn't we have a wonderful time the day…" George and the Maharishi aboard the 'Mystical Special' from Euston to Bangor, August 25, 1967.

What: Meeting the Maharishi
Where: Bangor, Wales
When: August 25, 1967

END OF THE LINE

How The Beatles joined the Maharishi on the 'Mystical Special' to Bangor – and heard tragic news when they got there. By Alan Clayson.

A DECISION BY THE BEATLES TO BOARD A train from London to Bangor in late August was as abrupt as it was seemingly spontaneous. The trip was traceable to the previous February when Patti Harrison had attended a lecture entitled 'Spiritual Regeneration' at London's Caxton Hall. The doctrines advanced that evening were imperatively appealing, although the orator had stressed that his words were but a pale sketch onto which his guru, Maharishi Mahesh Yogi, could splash more vivid hues.

Born plain Mahesh Prasad Varma, the silver-bearded Maharishi – 'Great Soul' – had founded a British branch of the International Meditation Society in 1959. He had worked up around 10,000 converts by the time Patti – and George – relayed to the rest of the gang the sweet verbal flowers from the lips of the robed and ascetic Varma: that through brief daily contemplations, all vices would be eradicated bit by bit until a pure state of bliss was achieved. Moreover, such washing of spiritual laundry was possible without forsaking material possessions (bar the Society's membership fees).

This seemed an excellent creed to The Beatles as all but Ringo (whose second child, Jason, had just been born) stole into the Hilton's hushed functions room to hear his Divine Grace speak. Indeed, he so lived up to the Harrisons' spiel that, directly afterwards, John, Paul and George wound up promising to journey to Bangor that very weekend, where they would undergo the Society's initiation course, conducted by the 'Great Soul' himself, the Maharishi. Once, it might have been the last bolt-hole where anyone might have expected to find them, yet fans and media homed in on the mid-afternoon Bank-Holiday train from Euston to Bangor – described by Fleet Street as the 'Mystical Special'.

While packing, they rang others who might want to go – boarding the 'Mystical Special' too would be Mick Jagger, Marianne Faithfull and Patti's sister, Jennie. Waylaid by "What's the Maharishi like?", "Do you reckon you'll all be changed by next Tuesday?" and further bellowed questions from the press, Jagger dismissed the outing straightaway as "more like a circus than the beginning of an original event". Unable to shove through the mob, Cynthia Lennon missed the train – and one of the last opportunities to save her deteriorating marriage.

The rest of the party crammed into the same carriage as the Maharishi who, in the uproar at Euston, had realised what a catch he'd made. Previously, he'd been unaware of The Beatles' stature, but he made a mental note to try to insert quotes from their lyrics into his talks.

In The Beatles, the Maharishi might have found eager listeners, but other artists in the Brian Epstein management stable were more inclined to Jagger's view. To Cilla Black, for instance, meditation was "somebody who goes to the loo with a big pile of papers, and sits there and reads them all". Another Epstein artist found himself in the vicinity of the Welsh seaside town that weekend, but Gerry Marsden wasn't there for the 'Great Soul' – it just happened to be a short drive from his recently-purchased holiday cottage in Anglesey. "It didn't register that they were only a few miles away with the Maharishi – but I wasn't interested in all that," recalls Marsden.

Brian Epstein wasn't sure about all that either – and, in the end, neither were his principal clients. A cynical comment – "He's only after your money, lad" – from one of Ringo's uncles would reinforce misgivings, but not as much as the argument that The Beatles ought to tithe part of their income to the Swiss bank account of the mere mortal that Private Eye was to lampoon as 'Verichi Lotsamoney Yogi Bear'.

His Grace also treasured pious hopes of a successful recording career, having negotiated the forthcoming release of an eponymous spoken-word album on Liberty Records.

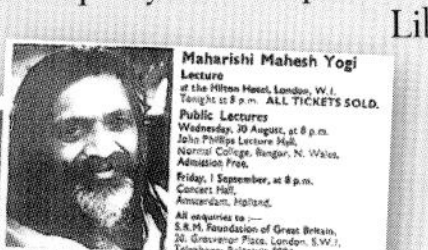
Maharishi Mahesh Yogi
Lecture
at the Hilton Hotel, London, W.1.
Tonight at 8 p.m. ALL TICKETS SOLD.
Public Lectures
Wednesday, 30 August, at 8 p.m.
John Phillips Lecture Hall,
Normal College, Bangor, N. Wales.
Admission Free.
Friday, 1 September, at 8 p.m.
Concert Hall,
Amsterdam, Holland.
All enquiries to :—
S.R.M. Foundation of Great Britain,
20, Grosvenor Place, London, S.W.1,
Telephone: Belgravia 8994

Yogi exercises: the Fabs with the 'Great Soul', August 1967.

As pop stars who'd lived in more of a world of illusion than most since 1963, the trip to Bangor was perhaps too much of an adventure. Hard cash had become as unnecessary to them as eyesight to a monkfish, and they were at a loss the following night when handed a bill in a Bangor restaurant. George was the first to realise why the waiters kept hovering around the table, and it was he who settled the matter with a few banknotes he chanced to have – as you do – in one of his shoes.

"For Cilla Black, meditation was 'Somebody who goes to the loo with a pile of papers, sits there and reads'."

Neither this incident nor the hard mattresses in the student hostels on the campus were as disconcerting as the press conference that Varma's public relations team had set up in the main hall – where nearly all newshounds appeared to regard The Beatles' preoccupation with meditation as flippantly as Cilla did. A few sick jokes circulated among the press corp when Brian Epstein didn't arrive in Bangor after all – his lonely life having ended suddenly in London the night before.

Inside the college, the 'Great Soul' was consoling his famous devotees. "We mustn't let it get us down," sighed Ringo, "because Brian will be able to feel our feelings in his spiritual state."

All the same, as twilight thickened, The Beatles brushed past a pitiless *woomph* of flashbulbs as they walked from the university building into a black Rolls Royce. For all the dicta they'd just absorbed that trivialised death, they were visibly shaken. "We didn't know what to do," shrugged George, "we were lost."

PHOTOS: REX

SEPT 6 - OCT 4, 1967

6 Mixing and overdubbing of I Am The Walrus continues at Abbey Road. Work also starts on Blue Jay Way.

7 Work on Blue Jay Way continues at Abbey Road.

8 The Beatles' instrumental, Flying, is recorded at Abbey Road.

11 The Magical Mystery Tour bus departs from Allsop Place, London.

12 The Magical Mystery Tour bus becomes stuck on a bridge on Dartmoor, en route to Widdecome, causing a traffic jam.

13-14 Filming of Magical Mystery Tour continues around Newquay, Cornwall.

15 Further Magical Mystery Tour filming is undertaken in Taunton, Somerset, before the bus returns to London.

16 A new, more forceful, version of Your Mother Should Know is recorded at Abbey Road.

18 Filming for Magical Mystery Tour resumes at the Raymond Revue Bar, Walker's Court, London.

19 Further filming for Magical Mystery Tour begins at West Malling Air Station, Maidstone, Kent.

20 At a business luncheon in London, Dick James, chairman of Northern Songs, reports that The Beatles have earned between £25m and £30m for Britain, during the past five years.

20-24 Filming of Magical Mystery Tour continues at West Malling Air Station, Maidstone, Kent.

25-26 Two days are spent recording The Fool On The Hill in Abbey Road.

27 Orchestral and vocal overdubs are added to I Am The Walrus in Studios 1 and 3 at Abbey Road.

28 Mixing and overdubbing is undertaken on the tracks I Am The Walrus and Flying in Abbey Road.

29 Lennon and Harrison appear on UK TV late-night chat show, The Frost Programme, speaking about Transcendental Meditation.

30 Starting around midnight, The Beatles work until the early hours of the morning in Abbey Road, mixing I Am The Walrus. They also do further work on Your Mother Should Know.

OCTOBER 67

1 Further scenes for Magical Mystery Tour are filmed at West Malling Air Station, Maidstone.

2 Work starts on Hello, Goodbye at Abbey Road.

3 Scenes for Magical Mystery Tour are filmed in the garden of Ringo's Weybridge home, Sunny Heights.

4 Lennon and Harrison appear for the second week running on The Frost Programme (below), speaking about Transcendental Meditation.

The Death Of Brian

Did The Beatles dream go wrong because Brian Epstein died or did Brian die because The Beatles dream was going wrong? Jim Irvin investigates.

Mourners (left) read the papers outside Brian's home after his death; (right) posing in the Cavern Club, early '60s.

PHOTOS: DAVID STEEN, CAMERA PRESS/HULTON ARCHIVE

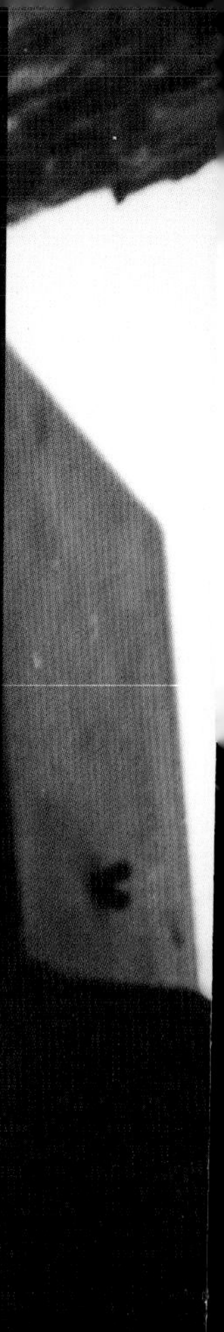

THERE'S A STORY, PROBABLY apocryphal, concerning John Lennon during his infamous 'lost weekend', the period in the mid-'70s when he split from Yoko and devoted himself to booze and carousing. One night, a fan came across John and his pals tying one on in a nightclub and stopped for a chat with his hero. John seemed only too happy to answer questions about The Beatles. One of them concerned the fan's favourite song.

"Is it true that Hey Jude was about Julian?" the fan asked.

"Actually, that one's about Brian Epstein," said John, looking deadpan, "Originally it was called Gay Jew."

Epstein with the Fab's debut LP, *Please Please Me*, 1963.

The whole table broke into a spontaneous rendition of the chorus: "Lah lah lah la-la-la lah, la-la-la-lah, Gay Jew!" At which point John apparently burst into drunken tears and shouted at the ceiling.

"Stupid fucking sod!"

The story rings true because Lennon's spiky affection towards his lost mentor sounds typical. At the Christmas before his death, Brian Epstein received a card that read: "Happy Christian Brian, from John".

Though he apparently had a rare knack for recognising what records would sell in his Liverpool store and maintained a photographic memory for catalogue numbers and trivia, Brian Epstein was never really a pop fan. He started writing a record column for Mersey Beat in August 1961 and sold the paper in the shop, but didn't seem especially aware of the scene The Beatles emerged from. In fact, according to Alistair Taylor – Brian's assistant at North End Music Stores and the man who accompanied him to the show where he first saw The Beatles at The Cavern on November 9, 1961 – Brian was under the impression that they were German, as all the flyers read 'Direct From Hamburg' and their My Bonnie single was a German import. It was only when they ambled onstage that he realised that these boys had been customers at NEMS.

"In the same way Brian foresaw that The Beatles would explode, it feels like he knew that they were poised to implode too."

Yet, despite his ignorance of their origins, Taylor and others remember Brian declaring, almost immediately, that these scruffy kids from up the road would soon be "bigger than Elvis". So what sparked his all-consuming enthusiasm for this group?

Brian was gay, but any sexual interest they may have aroused in him doesn't entirely explain it, as it wasn't their rough-and-ready, leather-clad look – which Brian certainly responded to – that he intended to sell to the world. His belief went deeper than that. When you consider how often his entreaties were rejected by the London music business, Brian's certainty of the importance of "his boys" feels vaguely supernatural. When he approached George Martin at Parlophone, it ought to have been with all the enthusiasm of a last resort. But Martin has stated on several occasions that while he found the music indifferent (listen to the 'Decca demos' and its hard to disagree with him), Brian's energy and belief made him curious to meet this group, and once he had, he too recognised their star quality. It's as if Brian, a lone believer at the heart of a soon-to-be-exploding universe, instinctively understood that he was the catalytic material from which the big bang would emanate, that when he and The Beatles came together there'd be a starburst which would reverberate for as long as pop music lasts.

The chilling part about Brian's demise was that in the same way he foresaw that The Beatles would explode, it feels like he knew that they were poised to implode too. The verdict on his death was that it was accidental, and all the facts point that way. But it came after months of withdrawal, depression and turmoil that suggest that Brian was retreating from a horde of demons, any one of which might have tipped him into suicide. An inescapable question arises: did The Beatles dream go wrong because Brian Epstein died or did Brian die because The Beatles dream was going wrong?

MEETING THE BEATLES HAD been Brian's salvation. He'd led an oddly directionless life until that day. Born in Liverpool on September 19, 1934, the first child of businessman Harry Epstein and his wife Malka (who, because Malka means 'queen' in Hebrew, was known to everyone as Queenie) he grew up as a well-to-do but restive suburban Jewish boy. Never particularly happy at school during the war, he was bored working in the family's furniture store from 1950.

Conscripted into National Service two years later, he lasted only 10 months before being discharged as "emotionally and mentally unfit to serve". Another spell in the family business was interrupted by a sudden urge to enter showbiz and he won a place at RADA in 1954 to study acting, but quickly dropped out. His homosexuality almost certainly exacerbated his sense of not quite fitting in anywhere, as did the expectations he felt as the eldest son in a Jewish household.

Though he seemed to blossom when he was put in charge of the music department of the family's electrical goods store, NEMS, Brian never shook off his unease. But when he saw The Beatles, he discovered a previously unimagined purpose, a world that chimed with so many things he'd been unable to express: music, rebellion, theatricality, freedom, humour, creativity, youth. Perhaps this explains his unshakeable belief in their importance. Their arrival in his life changed, positively, the way he felt about himself, why shouldn't the rest of the world have the same response?

Incredibly, it did. Two years after taking them on in December 1961 with the promise to raise their Cavern earnings from £5-a-time to £10, Epstein was steering the most astonishing entertainment phenomenon Britain had ever seen, with over £6 million worth of records sold. The Beatles pervaded the culture, first in the UK and then around the globe. Think of the astounding ubiquity of Harry Potter and then multiply that by four, everyone from schoolgirls to presidents felt that to move in the world they had to have an opinion on The Beatles, and then voice it.

To control such power and influence, Brian had to rapidly construct an empire. Guiding a roster of Liverpool acts who totally annihilated the rest of the pop business in 1963 – Gerry And The Pacemakers, Cilla Black, Billy J Kramer – the demands on Epstein's time were tremendous. With Liverpool associates like Taylor and Peter Brown, he moved NEMS to London, where they quickly outgrew their Argyll Street offices next to the London Palladium. Soon, Brian was delegating all but Beatle business to his staff.

Brian operated from the inner circle, as a trusted confidant of the Fab Four. When he moved into a modern block, Whaddon House in Williams Mews off Lowndes Square, George and Ringo took a flat in the same building, and they would often socialise together. Though his public image was as a straight-laced young entrepreneur, Brian was also revelling in the offstage party that accompanied the group's fame. In 1970, John Lennon told an interviewer that he felt responsible for introducing Brian to the pills that began to dominate his life and his moods. "I introduced Brian to pills, to get him talking, to see what he was like – which gives me a guilt association with his death."

In August 1964, when The Beatles were introduced to Bob Dylan by Al Aronowitz and Dylan in turn introduced them to marijuana, Brian was not slow to join in. Dylan passed around a skinny joint of pure grass. By the time it was Brian's turn to turn on, everyone was feeling the effects and found the image of their refined manager toking on the tiny roach, like a tramp sucking on a discarded fag butt, to be among the most hilarious things they'd ever seen. "We were all in hysterics," McCartney told Barry Miles in Many Years From Now. "Then Brian was pointing at himself and going, 'Jew! Jew!', and it was hilarious! We couldn't believe this was so funny. It may not seem the least bit significant to anyone else, but in our circle it was very liberating."

Derek Taylor spoke of Brian as "immensely cheerful and buzzy" and others remember that when The Beatles and their manager entered a room, Brian had as much charisma and charm – and as wicked a sense of humour – as his charges. But Brian also had a morbid side that his closest associates knew well, which was rarely seen by the outside world. "He was definitely mercurial," recalls Alistair Taylor. Brian's American business partner, attorney Nat Weiss, noted his recklessness; Brian liked to flirt with danger. After a holiday in Spain, he developed a great passion for bullfighting. "I think his fascination for bullfighters had something to do with his strange preoccupation with death," Weiss told the makers of the BBC's Arena documentary. Socially, Brian seemed as comfortable among the high-society crowd frequenting casinos and gentlemen's clubs like Curzon House or the Clermont (where Lord Lucan was a member), as he was in seamier parts of town where he'd go to pick up rough trade. Careful not to mix business with his private life, he nevertheless had run-ins with potential blackmailers and there were occasions when he was beaten up by some of his dodgier conquests.

"This was a repeat pattern which he brought on by living too dangerously and drinking too much," Derek Taylor told Arena, "and there were certainly some pills knocking about." By 1964, Brian was collecting regular prescriptions for sleeping tablets and amphetamines and entering the classic 'pills to wake, pills to sleep' trap that has claimed so many. The Beatles' foreign tours, movies, records, merchandising and legal issues all clamoured for his attention; the workload required superhuman stamina. Under such pressure, it was perhaps inevitable that Brian would occasionally lose his cool. His usually calm presence could be demolished by ferocious tantrums at the smallest provocation, often some tiny detail that was meaningless to anyone else.

Brian's private life didn't exactly help him relax, and he never really found a steady relationship. "The people he was attracted to were not the kind of people you settle down with," says Peter Brown. Brian thought he'd found true love when he met Diz Gillespie, a neat young Californian, who moved temporarily into Whaddon House. But Diz was bisexual and upset Brian by bringing women back to the flat and causing scenes in public, once in front of Brian's parents; their doomed relationship dragged on for too long and clearly made him miserable.

IN MOST POP CAREERS, THE public's moral outrage comes first and the cosy approval arrives later. With The Beatles, it happened in reverse. There was a moment, somewhere in 1965, when the whole world knew and approved of the Fab Four, seated at the 'toppermost of the poppermost' that they'd famously aimed for. From that summit the only possible direction was down. Once the screamers paused for breath, the dissenters could get ➳

IVE WRITTEN A VERY LOVELY SONG ID LIKE YOU BOYS TO SING

Oz magazine's Martin Sharp added this caption to Whitaker's photo of George, Brian and John resting after the concert at Essen, June 1966.

PHOTOS: REX FEATURES/ROBERT WHITAKER

a look in; and when thousands dissent, it's a political act. With Britain and America conquered, and the records selling everywhere from Finland to Borneo, it seemed like a nice gesture to pay a visit to some remoter places, but the mere presence of The Beatles in a country was starting to generate the sort of uproar that implied they were an invading cultural force to be vanquished. Suddenly 'the public' was not a single acquiescent organism, content to be charmed and entertained, now it was a many-headed beast, showing its teeth. John's infamous "bigger than Jesus" statement in March 1966 had turned the tide in America; by the time of the tour that took in Japan, India and the Philippines, the public mood had definitely soured. The confinement to hotel rooms, the pointlessness of playing to crowds who drowned out the music with hysteria, the combative press conferences, the public burnings of their records, the very real chance of physical danger, all these took the shine off being Beatles.

In Many Years From Now, Paul recalls the moment on August 21, 1966, when, after a miserable, wet and potentially dangerous outdoor appearance in St Louis, Missouri, he finally snapped. "We did the show in the rain and piled into one of those chrome-lined panel trucks, this terrible empty space, on this tour which had become spiritually rather empty, and this empty playing, and on that one occasion I let off a bit of steam, swore a bit and said, Oh well, I really fucking agree with you. I've fucking had it up to here too. And the guys said, 'We've been telling you for weeks, man'. But finally they had my vote."

"When Brian saw The Beatles, he discovered a world that chimed with so many things he'd been unable to express."

The decision to stop touring was one that Brian couldn't influence. He saw the sense in it and he respected the boys' feelings, but some part of him felt that, if they weren't going to go out in public again, he was effectively being made redundant.

As the final date – at Candlestick Park in San Francisco on August 29, 1966 – approached, Brian told Nat Weiss that this would be The Beatles' last ever tour. The night before, at LA's Dodger Stadium, Brian's errant lover, Diz Gillespie, showed up unexpectedly. Brian was delighted and thought it proved Diz's love for him, but Weiss believed the suave young man was a hustler, only interested in taking money from his rich gay prey. Sure enough, after the final performance, it was discovered that Diz had vanished and taken briefcases belonging to both Brian and Weiss. Brian's contained pills, contracts and material he was embarrassed about becoming public, so he decided not to pursue the matter. Weiss, however, wanted his case returned, so alerted the police. Gillespie was picked up and the cases and their contents recovered, but realising that he'd been duped by someone he trusted – coinciding with the last performance by his boys – seemed to tip Brian into despair. "That accounts for his first major depression," says Weiss. "That was the beginning of Brian's loss of self-confidence."

"Brian was always subject to mood cycles," Geoffrey Ellis, NEMS' CEO told documentary-maker Deborah Geller. "He would be high from time to time, people would take problems to him and he'd say, 'We'll resolve this, don't worry, everything will be fine'. Other times he would retreat to his home and not come out, just refuse to take calls and refuse to attend meetings."

Brian began to conduct all his business from his new house in Chapel Street, Belgravia, dealing mostly with his assistants Wendy Hanson and, later, Joanne Newfield. The latter recalls starting work at 10am and frequently finding notes from Brian saying "Wake me up with breakfast at 3pm". Brian would be putting in late nights at his favourite casinos, fuelled by amphetamines. Paul McCartney recalls seeing Brian losing thousands at chemin de fer or baccarat. "The jaw would be grinding away, Brian would be, 'Ugghhh, the pills'."

Towards the end of 1966, Brian entered into negotiations with Robert Stigwood, the capable Australian manager of The Bee Gees and Cream, to come on board as co-managing director of NEMS. "This wasn't a popular move among the NEMS staff," Geoffrey Ellis told Geller, "because it meant we'd lose Brian as the constant presence and mentor, and he was very well liked." Stigwood was to be assigned everything except The Beatles and Cilla Black, but was also offered an option to pick up a controlling interest in the company for £500,000.

"I wasn't terribly happy about it and The Beatles weren't at all happy about it," says George Martin, "they didn't want to work with anybody except Brian."

The Beatles held a meeting with Brian, insisting that they refused to be sold to anybody. They were happy for Brian to carry on managing them, but if he sold his interest in them to Stigwood without their permission they would, to quote McCartney: "Record God Save The Queen for every single we make from now on. And we'll sing it out of tune. So if this guy buys us, that's what he's getting." As far as they were concerned, the matter was closed.

With the group busy in the studio, Brian realised he needed to concentrate on other aspects of their career. He was particularly keen on setting up another feature film, commissioning hot, young –

John and Brian enjoy James Thurber on the train to Hamburg, June 1966.

George, Brian and John, Tokyo, July 1966.

and gay – playwright Joe Orton to write an original script. (Orton delivered a first draft called Up Against It, a brave effort defeated – as Charles Wood had been on Help! – by having to concoct a plausible story with four heroes. Orton's awkward solution was to cast the four Beatles as different aspects of a single character.) Brian also re-entered into discussions with King Features, holders of the rights to animate the Beatles, about a full-length cartoon.

"I had several meetings with The Beatles, while they were going to Harrods to buy the gear for their [Indian] trip," remembers Yellow Submarine producer Al Brodax. "We talked a lot and we got along very well when Brian was out of the room. [He] was difficult." But if Brian was tough to deal with it was because he'd learnt his lesson over the debacle with American merchandising. In 1965, realising that they'd entered into a very poor deal for all The Beatles' US spin-offs – the wigs, lunchboxes, bubblegum cards et al – Epstein and his lawyers sued the American company, Seltaeb. Now, in January 1967, after a protracted and expensive suit and counter-suit, The Beatles had finally secured a fairer deal, though it came too late to save the revenue generated at the height of Beatlemania. Perhaps feeling guilty at having sanctioned such a poor deal, Brian paid the legal expenses out of his own money.

He soon had a chance to make amends, though. The Beatles' 1962 contract with EMI included three renewable one-year options and a miserable penny-per-single royalty. Renegotiating the terms in 1963, Brian could offer just one further option, because his own contract with the group only extended to 1967. This meant that, as The Beatles became preoccupied with *Sgt Pepper's Lonely Hearts Club Band*, their EMI contract was about to expire. Visiting America, Brian thought he'd shop around. He went to CBS, who told him The Beatles had peaked, and stormed out; he spoke with RCA, who seemed happy to coast along with Elvis releases – he thought they were "cabbage-heads"; he may also have talked briefly to Ahmet Ertegun at Atlantic. Finally, he simply agreed to re-sign to EMI, but requested separate contracts with Parlophone UK and Capitol US. A huge deal was agreed, securing the group, collectively and individually, until 1976, with a massive $2 million bonus received from the US alone. The group also won a nine per cent royalty, a major coup in the age of three and four per cent deals.

Having set all this in motion, Brian took a break, visiting friends in New York and travelling to Spain for the bullfights. He also pursued a recently discovered interest in LSD – "I think LSD helped me to know myself better and helped me to become less bad-tempered," he told Melody Maker in May 1967 – which he gleefully added to his intake of booze, amphetamines and barbiturates. His holiday ended several weeks later in the Priory drug-rehabilitation clinic in Roehampton.

He emerged just in time for the release of *Sgt Pepper* and the massive Our World global live TV broadcast of June 25, where The Beatles performed All You Need Is Love. It had been a triumphant period: a lucrative new contract, a hugely successful album, an epochal new single unveiled in front of the largest TV audience ever known. Brian had every right to feel good about the way things were going, but just a few weeks later, his father suddenly died, and Brian's equilibrium was rocked yet again.

ON WEDNESDAY AUGUST 23, BRIAN VISITED London's Chappell Studios to chat to the boys as they worked on Paul's song, Your Mother Should Know. He'd already spent some time sketching out budgets and production requirements for the Magical Mystery Tour during a previous meeting with Paul, but was now firming-up plans for the filming. George, John and Paul had tickets to see a lecture the next day by the Maharishi Mahesh Yogi at the Hilton Hotel (Ringo was visiting his wife Maureen, and their new baby, Jason, in hospital). They were so impressed by the Maharishi's talk that they decided to travel to Bangor in Wales to attend a seminar he was conducting there over the weekend. The boys invited many friends and associates to join them on the train journey to Wales on Saturday, but Brian had planned to spend the weekend with friends in his

PHOTOS: ROBERT WHITAKER

Sofa so good: Maureen, Ringo, Brian, George and Patti relax on Epstein's balcony, 1965.

country house, Kingley Hill in Sussex. However, he said he'd join The Beatles for the final day of the seminar, August Bank Holiday Monday.

Friday was a warm, sunny day and Brian was in a good mood when he left his house in Chapel Street after work and drove down to Sussex in his convertible Bentley Continental. He'd invited Geoffrey Ellis and Peter Brown to join him for the weekend, but had also been hoping to see the young, gay manager of The Yardbirds, Simon Napier-Bell, whom he'd first met a week earlier. Bell, however, had other plans and, despite Brian's insistence that he break them, declined the offer to visit Kingley Hill. Brian had also been turned down by his assistant Joanne and her best friend, the singer Lulu, who both had previous engagements. By the time Ellis and Brown arrived at the house, Brian was impatient for some company. He'd invited some other friends too but, when they hadn't shown up by dinner time, Brian apparently decided that a quiet weekend in the country with two people from NEMS wasn't what he wanted, and declared that he was returning to London in search of entertainment. Ellis and Brown tried to dissuade him – he'd had rather a lot to drink at dinner – but Brian was adamant and said he'd be back in time for breakfast. Ironically, shortly after he left, a taxi pulled up outside and deposited four tardy friends who were surprised to find that their host had gone.

"I introduced Brian to pills, to get him talking, to see what he was like – which gives me a guilt association with his death." Lennon

At lunchtime on Saturday, Ellis and Brown were alone again, and went to a nearby pub for lunch where they called Brian at the Chapel Street house. He called back later and said he was tired and going to stay in bed to rest. By the following day, they were beginning to feel a bit awkward about enjoying Brian's hospitality without him. They called Chapel Street again to persuade him to come back for the remainder of the weekend, and spoke to Brian's butler, Antonio, who said Brian was home but had locked the hall door which led to his room. Ellis and Brown returned to the pub for Sunday lunch.

Shortly afterwards, Joanne Newfield received a call from the distressed Antonio, who said that he was worried about Brian. She wasn't especially concerned, as she was used to Brian's 3pm breakfasts, but, after eating her lunch, she decided to drive round and check on him. He still hadn't appeared, and between the bedroom and the locked hall door there were two sets of doors and a dressing room, so rousing him was tricky. She went to her office and tried the intercom that Brian had installed between their rooms, but there was no reply. She began to wonder why Brian was here anyway and called Peter Brown to ask why Brian had left Kingley Hill. He told her the story. She told him she was going to break down the doors but he advised against it, as Brian had been furious after a previous false alarm. Unable to contact Brian's doctor, Joanne asked Brown if he knew of anyone. He suggested his own doctor, John Galway. She rang Dr Galway, who agreed to come over, and then called Alistair Taylor, who, reluctantly – because he'd experienced similar, pointless missions, and had, literally, only just returned from LA – agreed to come to the house. He sensed a particular unease in Joanne's voice which he could not ignore. Dr Galway arrived and, with Antonio, broke down the doors to Brian's bedroom.

The curtains were drawn. On the bed was some correspondence, a plate of chocolate digestive biscuits, a glass and half a bottle of bitter lemon. On the bedside cabinet were about eight bottles of tablets, but none of them empty and all with the lids firmly replaced. In the bed was Brian, apparently asleep. Dr Galway examined him. He was dead.

The Beatles heard the news in Bangor. John took the call and went white. "Brian's dead," he told the disbelieving room of Beatles and their partners. Yet, hearing the news at this spiritual retreat helped cushion the blow. As they left, George declared to the waiting press: "There is no such thing as death. It is a comfort to us all to know that he is OK." In footage of their departure, John looks completely disorientated. "I can't find words to pay tribute to him. It's just that he was loveable, and it is those loveable things that we think about now."

The Beatles were never the same again. In fact, very little in the organisation survived intact. Robert Stigwood had indeed exercised his option on NEMS and now offered his services as The Beatles' manager, but was turned down, and left the company, taking his artists with him. NEMS entered a steady decline. All Brian's clients suffered personally or professionally.

NOT SURPRISINGLY, THE RUMOUR-MILL immediately considered suicide. Motives put forward included the forthcoming end of Brian's management contract with The Beatles and possible doubts about its renewal and insecurity at the sudden appearance of the Maharishi. Some say that The Beatles were already rocky, their desire for Beatledom waning, what with Ringo's family commitments, George's spiritual quest, John's insatiable appetite for drugs and Paul taking charge of *Sgt Pepper*; hence Brian felt sidelined and powerless to halt a decline. Others wondered if Brian had simply felt tremendous loneliness after being unable to persuade friends to join him at Kingley Hall and was disconsolate over his loveless life. Simon Napier-Bell, returning from his weekend away to find several slurred answer-phone messages from Brian, even briefly wondered if Brian had actually killed himself just to spite him, as if in the ultimate tantrum.

The coroner's inquest found that Brian Epstein had died accidentally of Carbrital poisoning. The most likely scenario seems to be that he had taken barbiturates to get to sleep. In the middle of the night he'd awoken, woozily imagined he'd not had his sleeping tablets, and then taken two more. Mixed with the alcohol he'd ingested earlier, and perhaps because he'd been inactive during most of the day, these two pills were enough to prove fatal.

Suicide was ruled out. The evidence against it rested chiefly on the amount of barbiturate found in his body and the state of the pill bottles in his bedroom; if he'd seriously intended to overdose he could have taken many more pills. There was also no note. Friends also knew that in previous weeks, he had been full of ideas and projects he seemed very excited about. He was also concerned about his mother's welfare following his father's death.

But rational justifications for living wouldn't necessarily occur to a depressed, suicidal person such as Brian. For Brian had intentionally overdosed before, on at least two occasions. The worst time, when he was discovered by Peter Brown and chauffeur Bryan Barrett, he even left a goodbye note. He was saved by a stomach pump in the Priory. Another time, he rang Barrett and told him what he'd done; the chauffeur raced round and made him vomit with salt water. And, on two other occasions, he'd threatened to end it all on the telephone to Alistair Taylor.

Joanne Newfield had once asked Brian's doctor why her boss kept slipping suddenly into deep depressions: "He told me, 'Brian's on a collision course. We all have an in-built ability if we're depressed to try to rise above it or waylay it. But Brian heads straight towards it and collides with himself'."

Some weeks after his death, Joanne returned to Brian's house for the first time, to collect some paperwork for his brother Clive, who had inherited the business. "I didn't want to go back," she said. "The staff had gone and the house was empty. I was really spooked about being in Brian's room. All I wanted to do was put everything in bags and get out. Then I found a book that I used to leave letters in for Brian to sign. I opened it and, to my absolute horror, I found two suicide notes. One to Clive and one to Queenie. But they were dated much earlier, some seven or eight weeks before he died, saying something to the effect of: 'Don't be sad. I'm OK. Take good care of yourself. I love you'. They were very short. Maybe they'd been there ever since he'd written them and he'd never looked in that book again, I don't know. I think Brian was obviously contemplating suicide. Then [his father] died and he changed his mind. He couldn't do that to his mother."

It appeared that Brian Epstein had not intended to die – this time – but was loitering near the slipway to oblivion, when he tripped. He was 32 years old.

Of course, since his death there have been murmurings that Brian Epstein wasn't a very good manager. But at least three things suggest he was brilliant. First, he was the original. There were no precedents for a pop group on The Beatles' scale, yet he made it happen, and ran it as smoothly as anyone could have at the time. Second, the suited and booted, mop-topped Fab Four – the first globally-recognised pop group – were Brian's vision. These days a committee of overpaid stylists and marketing execs would shape that image. And get it wrong. Brian did it alone. Lastly, there's The Beatles' loyalty to his memory. They have always admitted that their amazing story could not have happened without Brian, whom they loved; and that unity became impossible after his death, that when he'd gone they felt bereft in ways beyond mere business guidance. There are very few groups who'd speak in those terms about their management, however good the deals. They've always insisted that they would have renewed their contract with Brian. The Beatles had been a Pandora's Box of possibilities. Only Brian carried its key. ■

The Beatles in Bongor on the day they found out Brian was dead August 27, 1967. Below, at Brian's funeral, Abbey Road's New London Synagogue, October 17, 1967.

PHOTOS: ROBERT WHITAKER/HULTON ARCHIVE

6 A cello part is overdubbed onto Blue Jay Way in Abbey Road.

7 New York promoter Sid Bernstein offers The Beatles $1m to perform live again at Shea Stadium.

11 An exhibition, Yoko Plus Me, opens at the Lisson Gallery, London. The show is funded by Lennon, who is also the 'Me' of the title.

12 In Abbey Road, Lennon assumes the role of producer for the first time, working on tracks for Magical Mystery Tour. The main track recorded is Shirley's Wild Accordion performed by Shirley Evans, Reg Wale, Paul and Ringo.

13 To promote the film How I Won The War, United Artists Records release a single, How I Won The War, credited to Musketeer Gripweed and The Third Troop. The implication is that this is a solo single by Lennon, who played Gripweed in the film. In fact, Lennon's voice is heard in a two-second long dialogue excerpt from the soundtrack. The Times reports that informal discussions have taken place between The Beatles and The Rolling Stones "on possible business projects" involving both groups, but these are later dismissed as insignificant.

17 All four Beatles attend a memorial service for Brian Epstein at the London Synagogue, St John's Wood.

18 The movie How I Won The War, featuring Lennon , opens (above) at the Pavilion Theatre, London.

19 Guitars and vocals are overdubbed onto Hello, Goodbye at Abbey Road Studios.

20 Flutes are added to The Fool On The Hill and a viola is overdubbed onto Hello, Goodbye at Abbey Road. The Chris Barber Band releases a new single, Cat Call, composed by McCartney.

25 McCartney overdubs bass onto Hello, Goodbye in Abbey Road.

27 At Twickenham Film Studios, The Bee Gees are asked if they would consider composing a soundtrack to the film Wonderwall. The job eventually goes to Harrison.

29 Additional filming for Magical Mystery Tour takes place in Acanthus Road and Lavender Hill, London.

30–31 McCartney spends two days filming The Fool On The Hill sequence of Magical Mystery Tour, in Nice, France.

NOVEMBER 67

1 Mixing sessions for Hello, Goodbye and The Fool On The Hill take place in Abbey Road.

2 McCartney overdubs a second bass guitar part onto Hello, Goodbye at Abbey Road.

What: I Am The Walrus recorded
Where: Abbey Road studios
When: September 5, 1967

THE EGGMAN COMETH

I Am The Walrus was meant to show the meaninglessness of analysing pop music – but it became Lennon's most-studied lyric, says Johnny Black.

JUST FOR A MOMENT, IMAGINE THERE'S A heaven. It's easy if you try. And then imagine John Lennon up there. He's laughing, isn't he? That's because, 30-odd years after he cobbled together I Am The Walrus, we're still trying to analyse what it means. Yet Lennon himself made it crystal clear in 1980, during a Playboy interview, that his most deliberately meaningless song came about shortly after he noticed how, sometimes, "Dylan got away with murder. I thought, I can write this crap too."

As a psychedelic classic, the combination of words and music in ...Walrus is devastatingly powerful but, as a lyric, it works only because Lennon's skilfully compiled hodgepodge of surreal images and literary references can be interpreted in countless ways, each as right as all the others.

Musically, the song's first inspiration was the distinctive two-note siren-wail of a police car passing Lennon's Weybridge home while he was tripping one weekend. The words, "Mis-ter, ci-ty, policeman, sitt-ing, pre-tty..." fitted nicely, and more was added a week later, under the same chemical.

Simultaneously, he'd been noodling with a brace of unconnected ideas. First was the more pastoral melody that carries the lyric, "Sitting in an English garden...", and second was the phrase, "sitting on a cornflake".

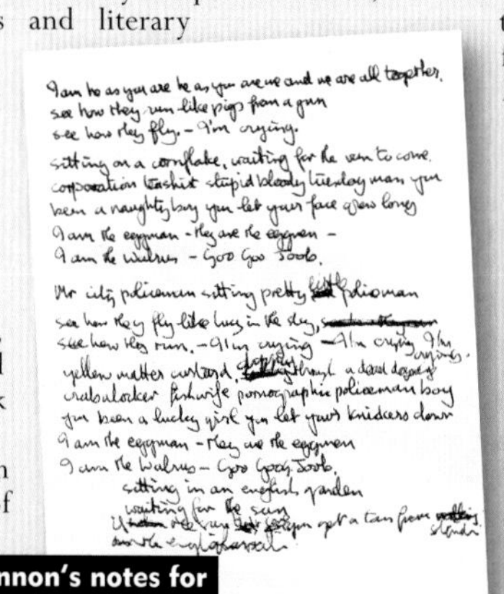
I am he as you are he as you are me and we are all together.
see how they run like pigs from a gun
see how they fly. – I'm crying.
sitting on a cornflake, waiting for the van to come.
corporation teashirt stupid bloody tuesday man you been a naughty boy you let your face grow long
I am the eggman – they are the eggmen –
I am the walrus – Goo Goo Joob.
Mr city policeman sitting pretty little policeman
see how they fly like lucy in the sky,
see how they run. – I'm crying – I'm crying I'm crying.
yellow matter custard, dripping from a dead dog's eye
crabalocker fishwife pornographic policeman boy
you been a lucky girl you let your knickers down
I am the eggman – they are the eggmen
I am the walrus – Goo Goo Joob.
sitting in an english garden
waiting for the sun

Lennon's notes for I Am The Walrus.

> **"Lennon hoped to provoke scholars into interpreting his gibberish as pearls of Beatle-esque wisdom."**

In his book, John Lennon: In My Life, Lennon's lifelong friend Pete Shotton revealed the catalyst that brought all those parts together. During a visit to Weybridge, the pair had "howled with laughter" on learning that Beatles songs were being analysed in classes at their old school, Quarry Bank. Lennon was immediately determined to write something as meaningless as possible, purely for the fun of provoking scholars, critics and musicologists into interpreting his gibberish as pearls of Beatle-esque wisdom.

Lennon then asked Shotton to remind him of a scabrous verse they had sung as schoolboys. He obliged...

"Yellow matter custard, green slop pie,
All mixed together with a dead dog's eye,
Slap it on a butty, ten-foot thick,
Then wash it all down with a cup of cold sick."

Seizing the moment, Lennon adapted the verse, added the freshly minted image of a "semolina pilchard climbing up the Eiffel Tower", and the song was under way. Well satisfied, he turned to Shotton and said, "Let the fuckers work that one out."

The titular Walrus came later, drawn from Lewis Carroll's poem, The Walrus And The Carpenter, in Alice Through The Looking Glass. Continuing in Carroll's absurdist vein, Lennon spiced up his lyric with several newly created words – 'crabalocker', 'snied' and 'texpert'.

On September 5, 1967, recording of the rhythm track started in Studio 1, Abbey Road, with Lennon completing a piano/vocal demo the following evening.

George Martin then came up with one of his most memorable orchestrations, although McCartney insists that, "John told him very specifically what the orchestration should be on I Am The Walrus, sang to him how he wanted the strings." However the work was shared, Martin's arrangement is a key element in the track, a masterful blend of eight violins, four cellos, three horns and a clarinet. Martin also brought in the Mike Sammes Singers who, more used to crooning easy-listening standards, sound as if they relished the rare opportunity to extend their range by chanting, "Got one, got one, everybody's got one" and "Oompah, oompah, stick it up your jumper!"

One final surreal touch came on September 29, when random lines from a BBC Third Programme radio production of King Lear were added – the radio being tuned by Ringo, while John worked the mixing desk.

Coupled with McCartney's Hello, Goodbye, I Am The Walrus was released in the UK on November 24, hitting the shelves in America three days later. It also appeared on the British Magical Mystery Tour EP, and its album-length American equivalent.

Within days of release, the BBC had banned the track because of its use of the deeply offensive word 'knickers', but that didn't stop it reaching Number 1 in the UK singles chart on December 6, where it remained for seven weeks. Three weeks later it hit Number 1 in the US for the first of three weeks.

Just as Lennon had hoped, successive generations of scholars have outdone each other in efforts to imbue the song with precisely the kind of significance he set out to avoid, pointing out, for example, the relevance of the fact that Chapter 6 of Through The Looking Glass, "deals with the inherent meaninglessness of words, the arbitrary assignment of semantic content."

And even Lennon fell into his own trap. In the afore-mentioned Playboy interview he offered an explanation of the term "elementary penguin", saying, "All these people were going on about Hare Krishna, Allen Ginsberg in particular. The reference to elementary penguin is the elementary, naive attitude of going around chanting 'Hare Krishna', or putting all your faith in any one idol."

Whatever it may or may not mean, I Am The Walrus remains an undisputed, trail-blazing psychedelic masterpiece, as profound in its influence on popular music as Alice In Wonderland was on fantasy literature.

Lennon filming Magical Mystery Tour at West Malling Air Station, September 19, 1967.

'The High Priestess Of The Happening' at her Half-A-Wind Show, Lisson Gallery, October 1967.

What: Yoko's Half-A-Wind opens
Where: Lisson Gallery, London
When: October 11, 1967

THE OTHER HALF

Yoko Ono and John Lennon's world became one when she invited the Beatle to invest in her latest art project. By Peter Doggett.

IN 1967, YOKO ONO WAS THE MOST notorious avant-garde artist in Britain. Virtually exiled from New York by disputes among her peers in the Fluxus Group, Ono was adopted by the British media as the token weirdo of an already weird year – dubbed 'The High Priestess Of The Happening'.

The Tracey Emin of her era, Ono collected more column inches than the rest of the artistic community combined. Her Film No. 4 (Bottoms) scandalised and titillated London society in equal measure. Her conceptual and mostly silent concerts of Music Of The Mind provoked fierce debate in the fledgling underground press. Wrapping Piece, in which she covered the Trafalgar Square lions in rolls of paper, made the pages of the London dailies.

Since their meeting at the Indica Gallery the previous autumn, Ono had maintained regular contact with John Lennon, aware that such a prestigious admirer could secure endless financial and publicity benefits for her work. In early September 1967, she made one of her occasional visits to the Lennons' house, catching John unawares in the wake of Brian Epstein's death. He agreed to subscribe to her forthcoming 13 Days Do-It-Yourself Dance Festival, price £1. More importantly, Yoko persuaded him to sponsor her next art event, a show billed as 1/2 Life at the Lisson Gallery in Marylebone.

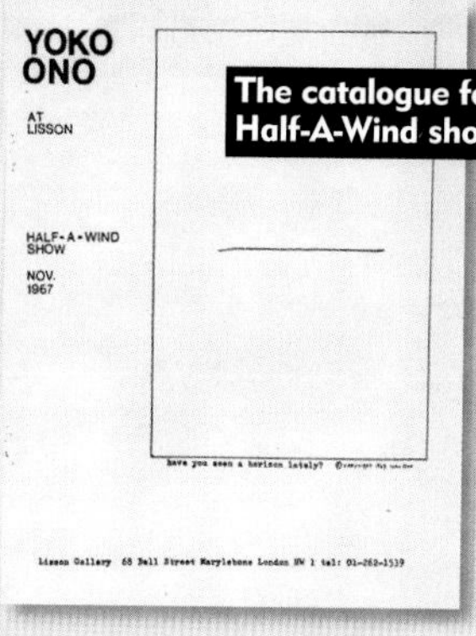
YOKO ONO

AT LISSON

HALF-A-WIND SHOW

NOV. 1967

have you seen a horizon lately?

Lisson Gallery 68 Bell Street Marylebone London NW 1 tel: 01-262-1539

The catalogue for the Half-A-Wind show.

"Lennon stayed away from Yoko's exhibition. But his mind couldn't help but respond to Yoko's ideas."

Though she had written earlier in the year that "men have an unusual talent for making a bore out of everything they touch", she was eager to obtain Lennon's backing. He agreed on the condition that his name didn't appear in the publicity. But, accidentally on purpose, Ono added a blatant reference to the Beatle into her programme notes, and let slip to the press that the event's subtitle, 'Yoko Plus Me', was a subtle reference to a famous millionaire pop star.

Meanwhile, daily postcards from Ono tripped through Lennon's letterbox in late September and early October. Her Dance Festival comprised a series of 13 instructional cards, bearing messages such as "Draw a large circle in the sky" and "Boil water and watch until it evaporates". While Cynthia Lennon lampooned the Festival as a joke, Lennon was intrigued. Coincidentally or not, the Dance Festival was timed to end on his 27th birthday.

Two days later, Ono's event – now retitled Half-A-Wind Show – opened at the Lisson. One room was entirely devoted to items of furniture and household appliances, all painted white and chopped in half. "I was feeling like a half at the time," she explained later. "The other side of me was empty. The piece was a reflection of the metaphysical room within me." To the press at the time, she noted merely that "everything we see is just the tip of the iceberg", and "I think of this show as an elephant's tail". In the programme notes, she enlarged on her theme: "Somebody said I should also put half-a-person in the show. But we are halves already."

The show gave Ono a second chance to exhibit some of the pieces which had intrigued Lennon at the Indica – the apple on a stand, the box of smiles. The other major exhibit was The Stone, another starkly white room made of shoji, a fragile and transparent form of paper manufactured in Japan. Lights beyond the walls slowly brightened and then dimmed, condensing a year in the life of the earth, revolving around the sun, into a few minutes. Not that participants were aware of the luminosity or otherwise of their surroundings, as they were asked to climb into black bags, into which no light passed. "When you are inside the bag," Yoko explained, "you are observing yourself going from dawn into night. It is as if you are experiencing a highly abstract life process."

Embarrassed at being linked with this strangeness, and uncertain about the nature of his feelings for Ono, Lennon stayed away from the Lisson Gallery while the exhibition was being staged. But his mind couldn't help but respond to Yoko's ideas. During one of their regular phone calls, he suggested that she should sell a range of empty bottles, under the premise that they contained the missing and therefore invisible halves of the furniture from the Half-A-Room. "It was such a beautiful idea," Ono crooned, "I decided to use it, even though it was not mine."

Slowly, John and Yoko's worldviews were edging closer together. It was not so far from Lennon's "turn off your mind, relax and float downstream" to Ono's conviction that "what art can offer is an absence of complexity, a vacuum through which you are led to a complete relaxation of mind... Make yourself dispensable, like paper. See little, hear little and think little". The Half-A-Wind Show was their first public acknowledgement of a shared artistic identity. Any closer union would have to wait six months, until Lennon's wife Cynthia was out of the country and two misunderstood artists could be reborn as virgins.

Yoko: "I was feeling like a half at the time."

PHOTOS: TONY COX/LENONO PHOTO ARCHIVE/HULTON GETTY

3 Harrison is filmed for the Blue Jay Way section of Magical Mystery Tour at Starr's home, Sunny Heights.

6 The Beatles oversee mixing sessions for various Magical Mystery Tour tracks, at Abbey Road.

7 In Abbey Road, McCartney adds new vocals and effects to Magical Mystery Tour.

8 Cynthia Lennon divorces John. How I Won The War has its US premiere in New York.

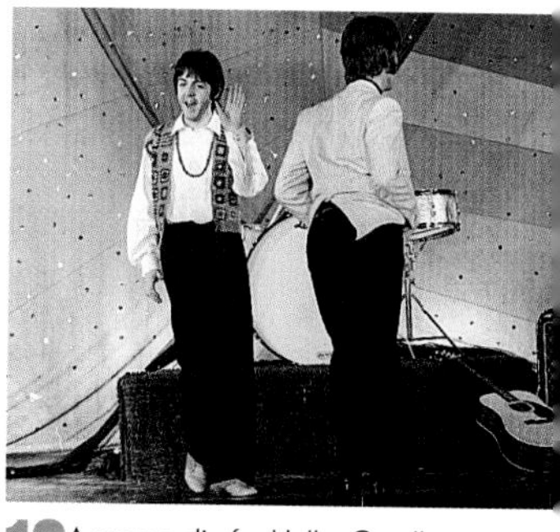

10 A promo clip for Hello, Goodbye is filmed at London's Saville Theatre (above).

15 In a vain attempt to circumvent a new Musicians' Union rule forbidding miming on UK TV, George Martin removes the violas from a mix of Hello, Goodbye, and dubs the result onto the group's promo clip for the song. This is because no viola players are seen in the film, and it is hoped that no one will notice that The Beatles themselves are miming in the clip. The deception fails, however, and the film is not shown on British TV.

17 A new mix of I Am The Walrus is prepared at Abbey Road.

19 McCartney is present when The Bee Gees play at the Saville Theatre, London.

21 The Beatles are filmed by a camera team from Top Of The Pops at Norman's Film Productions, London. The plan is to use the footage to mask the most obvious miming in their promo clip of Hello, Goodbye.

22 Harrison is in Abbey Road working on his soundtrack to the film Wonderwall. Because of the Musicians' Union rule, tonight's edition of Top Of The Pops cannot show the promo clip for Hello, Goodbye. The song is shown instead over a background of scenes from A Hard Day's Night.

24 Hello, Goodbye/I Am The Walrus, is released in the UK.

25 Lennon is interviewed on the BBC Radio 1 programme, Where It's At, speaking about the Magical Mystery Tour EP.

26 The promo film for Hello, Goodbye has its first US showing, on the Ed Sullivan Show.

27 Hello, Goodbye/I Am the Walrus is released in the US. Magical Mystery Tour is released in the UK, as a double EP in a gatefold sleeve; an album-length version is released in the US, with the augmented tracklisting featuring five extra tracks taken from singles, including Strawberry Fields Forever and All You Need Is Love.

28 The final Beatles Fan Club record, Christmas Time Is Here Again!, is recorded in Abbey Road.

29 The Scaffold, featuring McCartney's brother Mike McGear, enter the UK Top 30 with their single Thank U Very Much.

DECEMBER 67

3 Ringo Starr flies from Heathrow, UK, to Rome, Italy, to begin filming his role in Candy, based on the Terry Southern novel.

4 In Rome, Ringo Starr is fitted for his costume for the film Candy. He also has his hair dyed black for the role as a gardener, and is coached in speaking with a Mexican accent.

5 Lennon and Harrison represent The Beatles at a party to mark the next day's opening of the Apple Boutique, in 94 Baker Street, London.

6 Hello, Goodbye begins a seven-week run at Number 1 in the UK.

7 The Apple boutique opens at 94 Baker St, London.

9 A Whiter Shade Of Pale by Procol Harum is voted Best British Single of The Year by readers of NME, some 1,200 votes ahead of The Beatles' All You Need Is Love.

9 Starr films interiors for Candy, on a sound-stage at Incom, Rome, Italy.

11 The final Beatles Fan Club Record, Christmas Time Is Here Again, its sleeve a montage in *Sgt Pepper*-style, is mailed out.

12 Starr continues filming interior scenes for Candy in Rome.

13 The Times reports that, following critical letters received at Westminster City Hall, The Beatles are to be asked to submit a formal application for planning permission relating to the brightly coloured psychedelic designs painted by The Fool on the exterior of their Apple Boutique, on Baker Street, London. The Town Planning Committee will then decide whether the designs contravene the Control of Advertising regulations and, if so, they will have to be removed.

14 Starr films a motor-cycling sequence for Candy in Rome.

15 Shooting begins on the film Wonderwall, for which Harrison is composing the soundtrack.

16 In Rome, Starr does has his last day of filming for Candy, while Lennon and McCartney fly to Paris for a UNICEF gala.

17 Lennon and Harrison host a Magical Mystery Tour party for the Fan Club Secretaries at the Hanover Grand Film and Art Theatre, London. Beatles & Co becomes Apple Corps Ltd.

20 Ray Charles enters the UK singles chart with his version of Yesterday, which will peak at Number 44, as Paul McCartney and Jane Asher return from Campbeltown to London.

21 The Beatles hold a party in the Royal Lancaster Hotel, London, to launch their TV film, Magical Mystery Tour.

25 Paul and Jane announce their engagement, but the news is kept strictly to family and close friends.

26 Magical Mystery Tour is screened by the BBC, to almost universally bad reviews.

What: Apple is born
Where: London
When: November 17, 1967

THE BIG APPLE

The Beatles were advised to spend some money before the tax man got it. Thus the seeds of Apple Corps were sown. By Harry Shapiro.

SOURCES DIFFER AS TO EXACTLY WHEN The Beatles started Apple, but on November 17, 1967, The Beatles partnership, Beatles and Co, changed its name to Apple Corps Ltd and the holding company was born. Flip back to April 1967, in the run-up to the Summer of Love. London was wreathed in dope smoke and incense, but serious financial matters were afoot with The Beatles. Crippling taxation of anything up to 96 per cent was threatening to bang a black hole in their individual wealth and unless they wanted to hand over three million large ones in tax, the advice was to invest in related music activities to catch whatever tax breaks were going.

From their existing company Beatles Ltd, Apple Corps was formed, which was to manage a new partnership called Beatles and Co. Apple would own 80 per cent of the partnership with the individual Beatles owning 5 per cent each. The first thought was that there should be a chain of Apple Record shops, not so much because they wanted to sell records, but because prime retail sites would be bought up for the chain. But the idea was ditched as too commercial for The Beatles. Apple needed to reflect the spirit of the age and instead of real estate, the ideas for the company ballooned to incorporate music, film-making, publishing, design and electronics. This was revolutionary stuff for the times – a band, even a band as big as The Beatles, having some control over their finances. But while the financial imperative for Apple may have been obvious, what motives drove the The Beatles?

John Lennon was a changed man after meeting Yoko Ono and under her influence he metamorphosed from a scally rough-house into an eager supporter of 'causes' and creative guerillas like Yoko, whose avant-garde art was savaged by the critical establishment. McCartney's consciousness had been expanded too, not only by drugs but by his first solo trip to the USA in April 1967. And like John, Paul had a philanthropic vision, but he came at it from the more traditional perspective of upper middle class patronage than a benefactor of underground radicalism. Paul had lived at Jane Asher's parent's house and was captivated by their cultured social milieu – acting, classical music, stimulating after-dinner conversations. Once the Beatles stopped touring, Paul busied himself improving his education – reading, watching foreign movies. It was the Magritte's big green apple painting, 'The Guessing Game' lying around Paul's flat, that inspired the company logo and Paul added 'Corps' for a joke.

Paul with 'Magic' Alex, the MD of Apple Electronics.

More than the others, Paul was becoming dissatisfied with the way Brian Epstein was managing their affairs. In January 1967, Epstein secured a much more favourable contract from EMI than the risible royalty they had 'enjoyed'. Paul was scathing of the new deal, pointing out that the Rolling Stones were earning more money even though they sold fewer records. Once The Beatles came off the road, Epstein felt increasingly remote from the band, became even more insecure and upped his intake of drugs. In a self-fulfilling prophesy, he was now less able to hold the reins of his business empire and made the unpopular decision to sell a controlling interest in NEMS to Robert Stigwood who became co-managing director. Paul had further grounds for dissent when a court case revealed that Epstein had signed away 90 per cent of their US merchandising rights. The agreement to form Apple was made in April 1967, but the whole process was accelerated by Brian's death on August 27.

Paul said in 1967: "Apple is not in competition with any underground organisations, rather it exists to help, collaborate with and extend all existing organisations, as well as to start many new ones". So far so good, but then a comment which showed the advice to invest was being taken as a brakes-off clarion call to spend "The profits go to the combined staff (of the different divisions) so that everyone who needs a Rolls Royce can have one..."

The terms of the partnership agreement which seemed fine for the 'Summer of Love' became germane to the 'Winter of Discontent' when Paul tried to dissolve the partnership through the courts in January 1971. Apart from pooling all the income for their creative efforts into one pot, under the Partnership Act the partnership could act on a majority decision – one of the most controversial being to appoint (against Paul's wishes) Allen Klein to handle their affairs. However, the judge ruled that while the April '67 deed allowed the appointment of 'agents' to act for Apple, a manager was more than an agent, and to appoint Klein without Paul's agreement was a breach of the 1967 deed of partnership.

Early beneficiaries of the Beatles initial £800,000 investment revealed everything that was right and wrong with Apple. 'Magic' Alex Mardas was a Greek student who passed himself off as an inventor and electronics genius. At John's insistence, he was made head of Apple Electronics, but his inventions like a voice-activated phone and 'wallpaper loudspeakers' didn't work. Simon Posthuma, Josje Leeger and Marijke Koger were Dutch designers who shipped up in London after their Amsterdam boutique Trend collapsed in debt. Calling themselves The Fool, they approached The Beatles about a boutique project and from there the expenses went into orbit.

"Unless they wanted to hand over three million large ones in tax, The Beatles were advised to invest."

So the Beatles, led by Paul, were genuinely keen to promote new talent. Trouble was, owing to an extended stay on the planet Zog, either they failed to spot con artists or they were taken advantage of by the likes of The Fool, whose notion of their own importance and ability entirely outstripped reality. And as we know, it all went horribly wrong, collapsing in Richard Neville's words "in a confusion of crooked accountants, straw-clutching stunts, snivelling celebrity fuckers".

PHOTOS: REX, PICTORIAL PRESS, HULTON ARCHIVE

Until a permanent home was found for Apple Corps in 1968, they used the top floor of the Apple Boutique in Baker Street as an office.

All Aboard The Magic Bus

Magical Mystery Tour isn't simply a sensational soundtrack to the weird and wonderful film that it was written for, but for those revolutionary times that existed when it was released, argues Charles Shaar Murray.

OK, THIS IS A TEST. HANDS UP ALL OF those whose reaction to the death of George Harrison was to pull out some Beatle records and dance to a tune that was a hit before Hear'Say's mothers were born. Yeah, me too. And yet, funnily enough, The Beatles album we kept coming back to round our house wasn't one of The Beatles' acknowledged masterpiece albums. In fact, on its original UK release, it wasn't an album at all. *Magical Mystery Tour*, the soundtrack to The Beatles' late '67 movie of the same name, was originally issued in the UK as a strange hybrid: a 'double EP' in a gatefold sleeve containing the six new tracks developed for the project.

In the US, however, it was expanded into an album via the simple process of including five tracks from uncollected singles: five rather than six because I Am The Walrus had appeared on the flipside of Hello, Goodbye as well as on the double EP (swizz!). Beatles fans have, over the years, rightly railed at the American '60s practice of cutting up Brit albums and salting them with singles in order to squeeze more product out of a single body of work, but in this particular instance, the Yanks got it right. The British mania for excluding previously released singles from albums had thereby left several crucially important tracks floating around loose on 45, scattering a vital era of Beatlework to the (fab) four winds. With Strawberry Fields Forever, Penny Lane, All You Need Is Love, Baby You're A Rich Man and Hello, Goodbye now reunited with their long-lost siblings, a startling album emerges. Or rather, the other half of an already startling album.

> "The US Mystery Tour LP is the other half of the double-album that Sgt Pepper should have been."

If we consider The Beatles' recordings from late '66 to late '67 as a single project, a single body of work – which, in experiential terms, it was – then the US *Magical Mystery Tour* LP becomes the other half of the double-album that *Sgt Pepper* should have been. Strawberry Fields and Penny Lane were among the first three tracks cut during the sequence of sessions which generated *Sgt Pepper*: a single was needed, so those two epochal pieces were split off from the ongoing project to go their own way on 45 (and then it was kept off the top spot by Engelbert Humperdinck. Laugh? I almost stubbed out my spliff). All You Need Is Love, Marseillaise quote and all, was as much a part of the soundtrack of the summer of '67 as the magisterial album alongside which it marched into the stores. And I Am The Walrus is an awesome bookend to Strawberry Fields as an index of the extraordinary soundscapes of Lennonland: both of them belong as close to A Day In The Life as packaging and programming can bring them.

So what of the rest of the *MMT* album? Specifically,

Recording the promo film for Hello, Goodbye at London's Saville Theatre, November 10, 1967.

PHOTO: APPLE-HULTON ARCHIVE

what of the original songs cooked up for the incoherent but charming film project with which The Fabs occupied their autumn? The songwriting score was three-in-one in favour of McCartney: the ringer being the collectively-credited instrumental Flying, which sounds like Booker T & The MGs after (a) an intensive course of TM; (b) a serious acid trip, or (c) a prefrontal lobotomy. Lennon fielded I Am The Walrus, an exhilarating and evocative splatter of imagery and wordplay which benefits immensely from no attempt to shovel the glimpse into the ditch of what each line 'means'. My Sweet George contributed the eerie, serpentine Blue Jay Way, a fine and worthy companion for *Pepper's* Within You Without You.

Macca, for his part, weighed in with Your Mother Should Know (no generation warrior he – this warm, yeasty slice of music-hall rooty-tooty mines the same rich

TRACK LISTING

A-SIDE

1. Magical Mystery Tour
Lennon/McCartney
Sung by McCartney

2. The Fool On The Hill
Lennon/McCartney
Sung by McCartney

3. Flying
Harrison/Lennon/McCartney/Starkey

4. Blue Jay Way
Harrison
Sung by Harrison

5. Your Mother Should Know
Lennon/McCartney
Sung by McCartney

6. I Am The Walrus
Lennon/McCartney
Sung by Lennon

B-SIDE

7. Hello, Goodbye
Lennon/McCartney
Sung by McCartney

8. Strawberry Fields Forever
Lennon/McCartney
Sung by Lennon

9. Penny Lane
Lennon/McCartney
Sung by McCartney

10. Baby You're A Rich Man
Lennon/McCartney
Sung by Lennon

11. All You Need Is Love
Lennon/McCartney
Sung by Lennon

MAGICAL MYSTERY TOUR

WHAT THE PAPERS SAID...

The press loved the magic touches of the new EP.

"The Beatles are at it again, stretching pop music to its limits on beautiful sound canvasses, casting wonderful spells beyond the clouds to turn the dullest plastic disc into a magical mystery tour of sounds fantastic, sounds unbelievable! The four musician-magicians take us by the hand and lead us happily tripping through the clouds past Lucy in the sky with diamonds and The Fool On The Hill, into the sun-speckled glades along Blue Jay Way and into the world of Alice in Wonderland, where the walrus softly croons, I am the Eggman, and Little Nicola cries back, No, no you're not. This is The Beatles out there in front and the rest of us, a cast of millions, in their wake. This is *Sgt Pepper* and beyond, heading for marvellous places."

Nick Logan, NME (November 25, 1967)

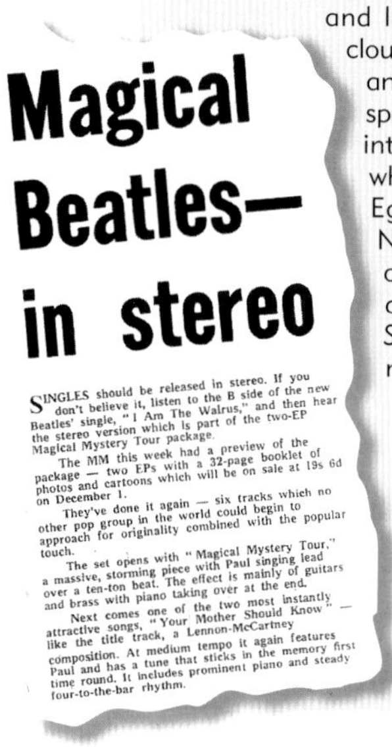

Magical Beatles—in stereo

SINGLES should be released in stereo. If you don't believe it, listen to the B side of the new Beatles' single, "I Am The Walrus," and then hear the stereo version which is part of the two-EP Magical Mystery Tour package.

The MM this week had a preview of the package — two EPs with a 32-page booklet of photos and cartoons which will be on sale at 19s 6d on December 1.

They've done it again — six tracks which no other pop group in the world could begin to approach for originality combined with the popular touch.

The set opens with "Magical Mystery Tour," a massive, storming piece with Paul singing lead over a ten-ton beat. The effect is mainly of guitars and brass with piano taking over at the end.

Next comes one of the two most instantly attractive songs, "Your Mother Should Know" — like the title track, a Lennon-McCartney composition. At medium tempo it again features Paul and has a tune that sticks in the memory first time round. It includes prominent piano and steady four-to-the-bar rhythm.

"They've done it again – six tracks which no other pop group in the world could begin to approach for originality combined with the popular touch."

Bob Dawbarn, Melody Maker (November 25, 1967)

SLEEVE NOTES

With its colourful book, *MMT* was certainly a pretty picture.

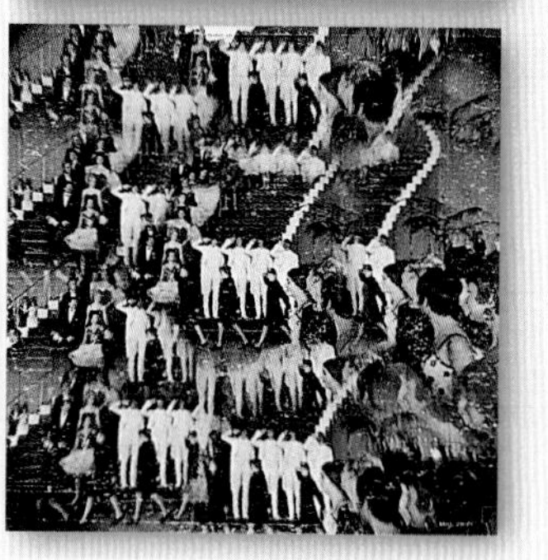

As with *Sgt Pepper's Lonely Hearts Club Band*, The Beatles treated the release of *Magical Mystery Tour* as an event. Emerging in the UK as a revolutionary six-track double EP, expanded to an LP for the American market, the lavish package included a 28-page colour booklet. Like *Sgt Pepper*, printed lyrics were included (for the film songs only in the US), alongside John Kelly's wonderful movie stills and Bob Gibson's whimsical illustrations, which told the Mystery Tour tale in cartoon form, complete with suitably 'storybook' annotations.

It was yet another new look for The Beatles – the front cover didn't even feature the faces of the group, they instead appeared masked, donning animal costumes in a still from a break in filming the I Am The Walrus sequence at West Malling Air Station in Maidstone, Kent.

Richard Fairclough

> "This is the sound of a time when society still seemed to be opening up rather than closing down."

vein of nostalgia for the pre-rock, pre-war years as *Pepper's* better-known When I'm 64), the rhapsodic acid pastoralism of Fool On The Hill, and the title tune, wherein his lead vocal at its richest and most 'blaring' meets Lennon's filtered, vinegary backing part in one of the most inspired juxtapositions of Britain's two most distinctive rock voices. The sheer enthusiasm and excitement with which the song welcomes an uncharted but benign future represents the same archetypal '60s vision which informed the original Star Trek: that there is a better world ahead, and that it's gonna be *fun*.

Obviously they were wrong, but what do you expect? They were just pop singers. They were caught up in the intoxicatingly euphoric vortex of an epochal cultural moment. In their work they articulated and cheered its most positive aspects, and by adding their energy to it, they massively increased its momentum and power. Nobody thought that Baby You're A Rich Man was about money. And how *did* it feel to be one of the beautiful people? When we listened to The Beatles, we all were. And would that we all could be again. This music was nothing if not inclusive. A splendid time was guaranteed for *all*.

But these are, as Lou Reed pointed out, "different times". Nowadays, the announcement that "The Magical Mystery Tour is waiting to take you away" seems more like a threat than a promise.

So listen up, bredren and sistren. I'm serious about this. Some of us take it for granted that the music of this period represents a creative peak in the history of post-war pop. Others believe, with equal passion and commitment, that this idea is simply the reactionary nostalgia of senescent baby-boomers unwilling to let go of their (middle) youth and concede that the torch passed long ago. Ultimately, whichever side of this argument you notionally consider yourself to be on is unimportant as long as you take the next chance you get to hear some of the music of this era with fresh ears and an open mind. Don't

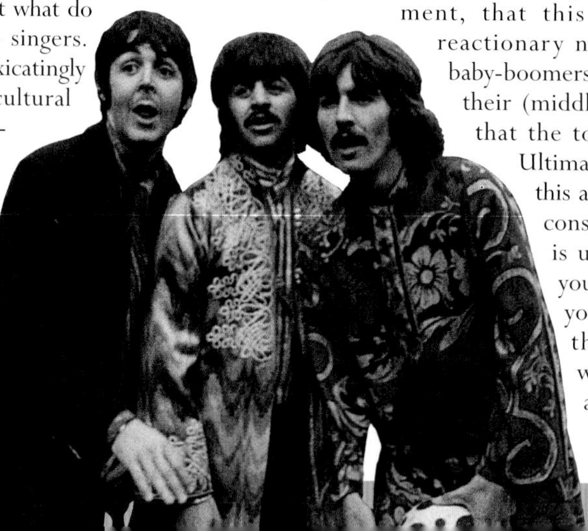

PHOTOS: APPLE-HULTON ARCHIVE; REX

Animal magic: the Fab Four in their I Am The Walrus costumes for the record's covershot.

listen to it as nostalgia or retro, an evocation of your youth or your parents', but try to hear it as living music, speaking to you now, in your present. Doesn't matter if it's *Otis Blue* or *My Generation*, *A Love Supreme* or *Are You Experienced?*, *Live At The Regal* or *Highway 61 Revisited*, *Lady Soul* or *Rubber Soul*, *Ogden's Nut Gone Flake* or *Dear Mr Fantasy*, *Disraeli Gears* or *Eight Miles High*, *Pet Sounds* or *Les Filles De Killimanjaro*.

What is overwhelmingly apparent from each and every grove is that this is the sound of a time when society still seemed to be opening up – "I got to admit it's getting better, getting better all the time" – rather than closing down; when what Patti Smith called "the sea of possibilities" stretched to the furthest horizon. It's not all peace-love-and-bananas-man by any means: there's real rage in much of this music, particularly the black music, as well as the starry-eyed Fool On The Hill optimism, but it's a rage that's going somewhere, rage as an energy dedicated to fuelling a generation's cultural and spiritual journey towards a better place and time.

Just try to hear it for what it was and what it meant and it'll break your fucking heart. Or mend it. In Do You Believe In Magic, The Lovin' Spoonful cajoled us to "believe in the magic that can set you free". Even if only for the duration of a particular song, it still can.

TALKING 'SHOP

Tjinder Singh of Cornershop talks about why *Magical Mystery Tour* really is magic!

"I got into The Beatles quite late in the day. Unlike most people I didn't have parents with Beatles albums in their record collections to play. It wasn't until I was 18 and bought up an old boss of mine's record collection that I discovered the *Magical Mystery Tour* LP. What can I say? It's sheer brilliance from start to finish.

"While the film lost a lot of its psychedelic impact when it was first shown on TV in black and white, the album itself is faultless. I Am The Walrus – you can't knock it. The songwriting, the rough and ready production – it's so in-yer-face. There's just nothing to criticise. They wrote the script with this for all future recording and production techniques. It's the typification of attitude and power – the power of the song rather than the power of the music. It's four people really going for it. Lennon's guitar playing is astounding but Ringo is a star too. He plays a real simple beat. You could say he's the pioneer of the hip hop beat. There was a time when the common consensus was that Ringo couldn't play. What's that all about? He's totally unique, a one-off and hip hop has a lot to thank him for.

"All You Need Is Love is the culmination of all their influences, which had gone before them. It has a real Eastern feel to it, a religious feel with all the mantra chanting on it. It's beautiful music and a great sentiment too. Strawberry Fields Forever is fantastic, Paul McCartney's vocals on The Fool On The Hill... I love it. They covered so much ground with just this one album. Remarkable!"

ROLL UP, ROLL UP FOR THE MYSTERY TOUR

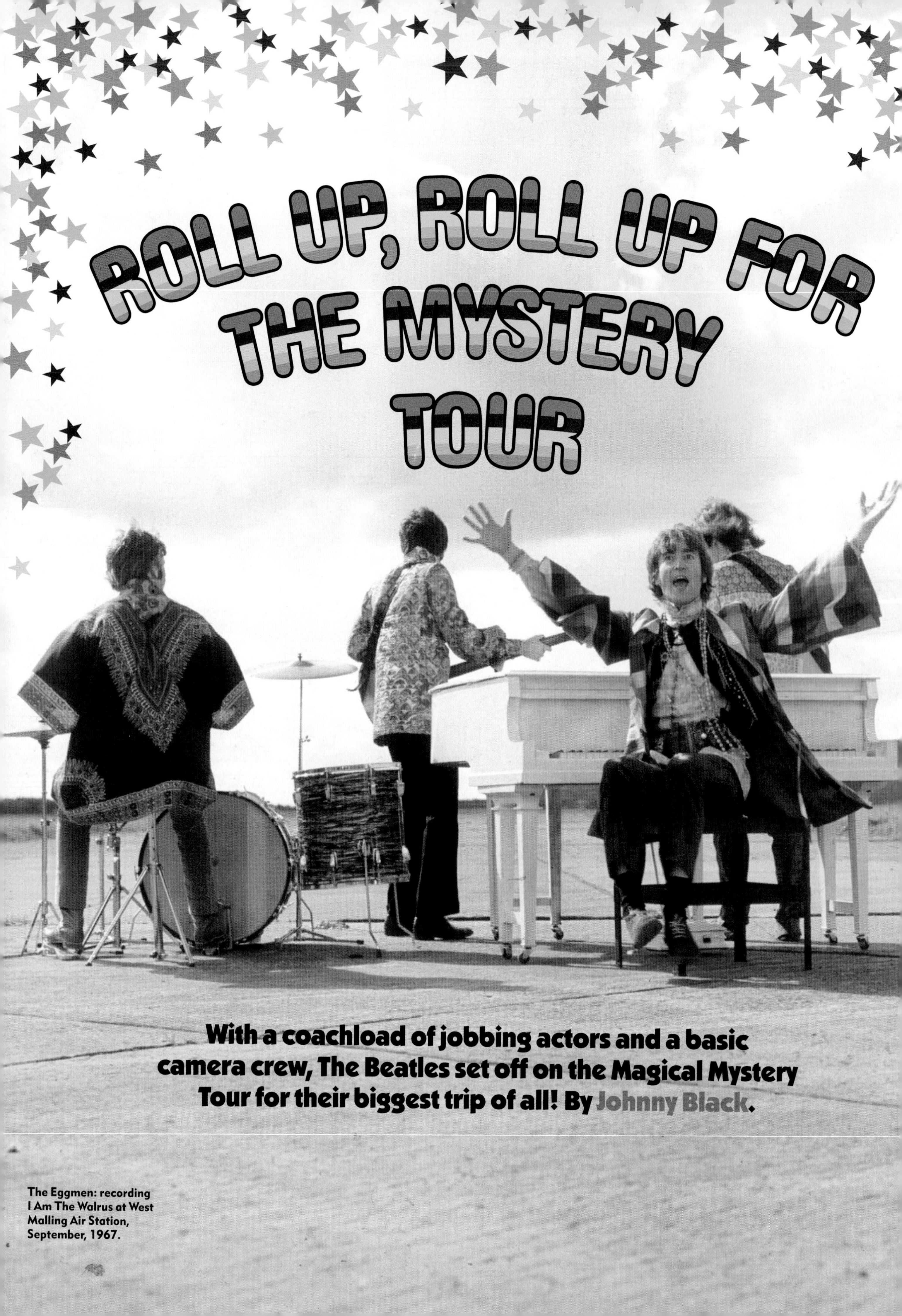

With a coachload of jobbing actors and a basic camera crew, The Beatles set off on the Magical Mystery Tour for their biggest trip of all! By Johnny Black.

The Eggmen: recording I Am The Walrus at West Malling Air Station, September, 1967.

If The Beatles' career was laid out in the form of a massive Blackpool rollercoaster, Brian Epstein would be seen to meet his maker just as the carriage hit the top of the highest point on the track. There were peaks still to come, but the general direction from that moment on was downhill, and the biggest, most stomach-churning drop of all was imminent. It was while barrelling down into that dip that Paul McCartney sold the other three Beatles their tickets for the Magical Mystery Tour.

On April 7, 1967, two days after joining his girlfriend, the actress Jane Asher, for her 21st birthday party at The Quorum Restaurant in Denver, Colorado, McCartney began to reflect on the stories he'd been hearing about California's acid-guru Ken Kesey and his hippy cohort, the Merry Pranksters. Their crazed bus-to-nowhere adventures were fast acquiring the status of modern myths, and McCartney reasoned that a similar trip, translated into the somewhat more British context of a Mystery Tour by coach, might serve as a good basic structure for The Beatles' next project.

High over the Atlantic on a return flight to London on the April 9, McCartney borrowed a pad of scrap paper from a stewardess and used it to scribble down some of his rough ideas and started working out the title song, Magical Mystery Tour. By the time the Beatle stepped off the plane at Heathrow he had sketched out plan for a 60-minute TV show, described by Ringo as "one sheet of paper with a circle drawn on it, and it was marked like a clock, except there was only one o'clock, five o'clock, nine o'clock and 11 o'clock. The rest, we had to fill in."

Lennon, perceiving himself as at least an equal partner in The Beatles, didn't take it well when Paul offered him a segment and instructed him to write something for it. In Lennon's own words, "I thought, Bloody hell!" Although he and Harrison grumbled openly about the project, Lennon felt that the band "owed it to the public to do these things" and buckled down to work.

Before the month was out, work had started in Abbey Road on recording Magical Mystery Tour but, before much could be done, a more pressing project took precedence. John and Paul had both written songs to be used on a history-making BBC world-wide satellite broadcast, Our World, in late June. John's contribution, All You Need Is Love, was deemed ideal for the broadcast, leaving Paul's offering, Your Mother Should Know, up for grabs. Almost inevitably, it was incorporated into the Mystery Tour soundtrack.

Between promoting All You Need Is Love, taking summer holidays and hanging out with the Maharishi, The Beatles made little further progress on Mystery Tour before Brian Epstein died on August 27. Then, just five days later the quartet came together at McCartney's St John's Wood home, to discuss the way forward. McCartney seized the moment to convince the others that they must maintain their momentum, and that the way to do it was to press on immediately with Magical Mystery Tour.

Whether the others liked it or not, Paul was now running the show, although Denis O'Dell, the associate producer of Lennon's solo film project How I Won the War, was drafted in to look after the nuts and bolts. From the start, the production was notable for its lack of not only a script but anything resembling a coherent vision of what it should be. Richard Lester (who had directed both A Hard Day's Night and Help!) recalls how, "I would hear Denis on the phone to Paul, saying, I've found a great place… we're going to film it all in an old off-shore military fortification tower. Then it would be, We're going to Egypt to shoot it in the Pyramids. Then, the next day, they would change their minds. He went crazy. From the moment that they finally decided to make it till the time the first shots were made was only two weeks. It went off totally unprepared and half-cocked."

A cast was rustled up by the simple expedient of rummaging through the actors' directory, Spotlight, a process Ringo described as saying, "Uh, we need someone like that and someone like that, and we needed the large lady as my auntie [Aunt Jessie] 'cause I was gonna play this person with this auntie."

McCartney was also making efforts to involve other like-minded bands in the project, including Traffic and the Jimi Hendrix Experience. "Paul McCartney told me about this little scene he had," said Hendrix, a few years later. "He wanted us to be in this film. We weren't known when McCartney asked us. He was trying to help us, but we got a nice break before they got the movie together."

Traffic got a little bit further down the line, going so far as to film a performance of Here We Go Round The Mulberry Bush, plus sequences in which they chased a globe of the world down a hillside, but their footage ended up on the cutting room floor.

The gaily re-decorated coach, hired from Fox's of Hayes, Middlesex, by NEMS executive Alistair Taylor, set off from Allsop Place, London, on Monday September 11 with a total of 43 persons on board, including a minimal shooting crew of three cameramen and one soundman, for a five-day shoot in Cornwall. Trailing behind came what Beatles' publicist Tony Barrow has described as "an entourage following the coach. Half of Fleet Street took to cars and drove down to the West Country."

It was perhaps symbolic that the tour ground to an unexpected halt the very next day. En route to the first proposed filming location, the annual Widdicombe Fair on Dartmoor, driver Alf Manders took a shortcut along minor back roads which resulted in the bus becoming stuck on a narrow bridge. With the day wasting away, tempers began to fray, but the bridge proved impassable. Manders and the 20-car entourage were obliged to reverse for half a mile before they were able to turn and re-join the main A38.

"It was symbolic that the tour ground to a halt with the bus stuck on a bridge."

With the Widdicombe Fair sequence reluctantly abandoned, the coach pressed on via Plymouth to the Atlantic Hotel at Newquay in Cornwall, which would be their base of operations until Friday morning. Given that the first two days had achieved virtually nothing in the way of completed scenes, the next three really had to make up for lost time.

Covering the story for short-lived rock weekly Top Pops was Miranda Ward, who had followed the coach since it left Allsop Place. She recalls the next day (Wednesday) as a frantic burst of activity ➳

PHOTO: APPLE/HULTON ARCHIVE

Multi-coloured Beatles: in their I Am The Walrus costumes; and (below) Paul from the recruitment officer scene.

during which McCartney directed humourist/poet/musician Ivor Cutler in a charming romantic interlude with Ringo's 'Aunt Jessie' on nearby Tregurrian Beach, while Lennon took charge of filming comedian Nat Jackley in pursuit of bikini-clad wenches around the hotel swimming pool and along the Cornish clifftops. Neither sequence, however, made it to the version of the film that was first shown on British TV. Indeed, Jackley became one of Mystery Tour's fiercest critics, fuming, "I thought it shocking! I couldn't make head or tail of it. All my comedy stuff – 20 minutes – was cut out."

Ivor Cutler, on the other hand, in the role of the tour guide Buster Bloodvessel, still seems to relish his fleeting association with the Fab Four. "John was the one I found easiest to get along with and I suspect it was mutual. Paul was a very intelligent, shrewd man. His mind was really keen, very much a seeker after information, very aware and alive but, and this is not meant as a criticism, with a mind rather like a machine in some ways, busy synthesizing and correlating all the time."

"Paul had a mind like a machine, always busy correlating & synthesizing."

Miranda Ward, meanwhile, remained at the Atlantic Hotel, where she secured an interview with George for BBC radio, using a reel-to-reel tape machine with which she was completely unfamiliar. "We went to his room and sat cross-legged on the bed. After a couple of false starts George took over the tape machine, set the levels and held the microphone. I kept fluffing my questions. He, with great patience kept re-winding to record over all the fluffs thus giving me the best chance of getting a good interview for broadcast. He was determined that I make it as professional as possible. He also spoke over my voice at times and used my name directly. This, he explained, was to reduce the possibility of the interview being broadcast with my voice cut out and some other DJ 'dropping' questions in to make it sound as if they had done the interview."

Harrison and Ward then sat on the lawn and took afternoon tea for a photo call to accompany the interview. As the photo-session progressed, Harrison kept inviting more and more fans to join them. "He ordered extra pots of tea, poured it himself for the fans and signed autographs for all of them."

By now, an evening routine was beginning to evolve, during which Paul held meetings with the film's technical director, cinematographer Peter Theobalds, and the cameramen. "I ended up kind of directing it," he said later, "even though we said The Beatles had directed it at the end. Just because I was there most of the time and all the late night chats with the cameramen about what we were going to do tomorrow would tend to be me more than the others."

But once again, despite all the activity, by the end of the day there was very little useable footage actually in the can, except for an argument between Ringo and Aunt Jessie, and some shots of Paul cycling on Porth Beach.

On Thursday, a sequence showing the entire cast piling into one very small tent was successfully completed in a field near Newquay and, that evening, a completely serendipitous filming opportunity fell into their lap. McCartney had always hoped that, in the course of their travels, The Beatles and their attendant throng would make chance encounters which would throw up opportunities to create interesting footage. On this day, by just such a chance, they met Spencer Davis of The Spencer Davis Group.

"I was having a holiday," recalls Davis, "staying with my wife and daughters at the Tywarnhale pub in Perranporth, which was owned by the parents of our roadie, Alec Leslie. I knew The Beatles quite well,

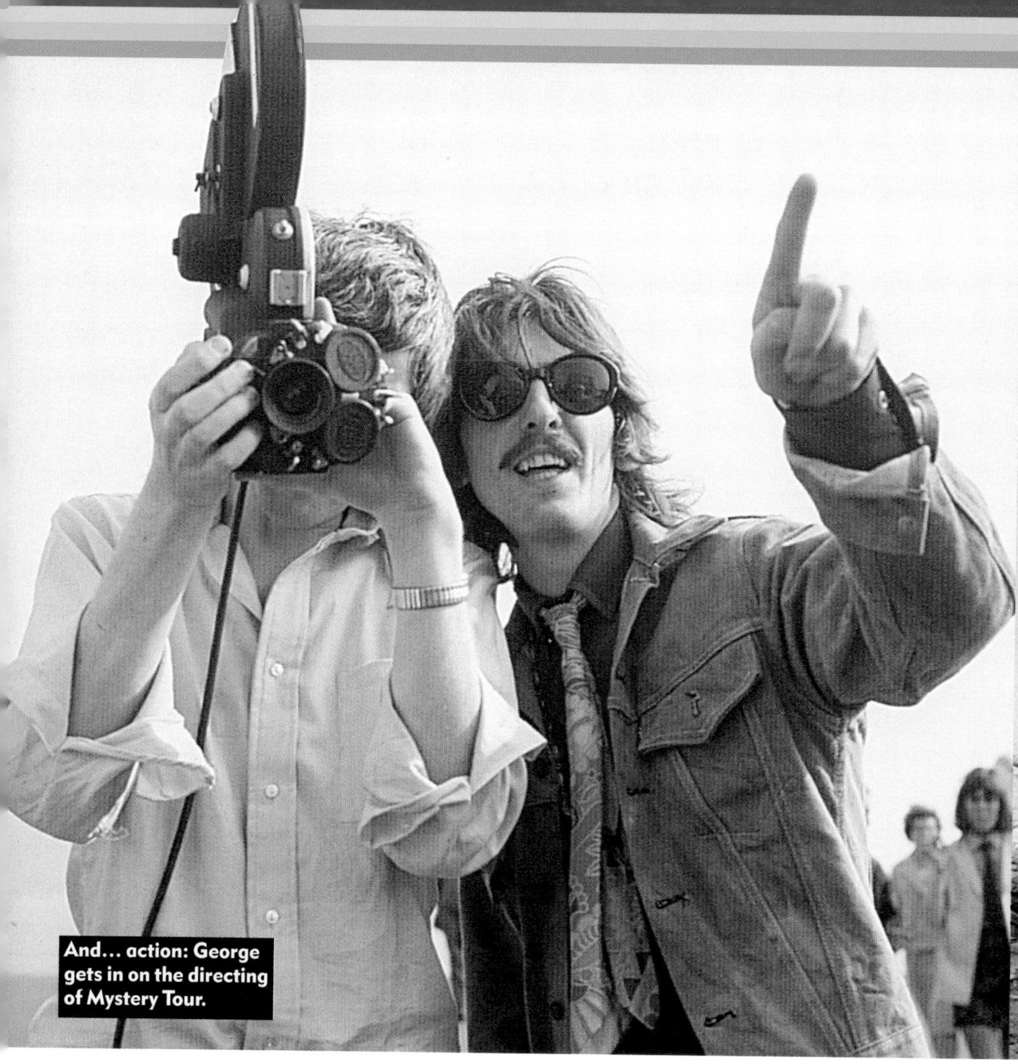

And... action: George gets in on the directing of Mystery Tour.

Shore thing: John tries to pretend he's not noticed the camera.

so when I heard that they were filming in Newquay I called up and asked their roadie, Mal Evans, what was going on."

Mal immediately invited Spencer over and, while chatting, he invited Paul back to the pub in Perranporth for a drink. "So that night, I'm sitting in the bar when in walks Paul and Ringo. The punters in the pub just couldn't believe it. Ringo stationed himself at the bar, but Paul, being the sort of character he is, just grins at everybody and shouts out, Evening all. He stuck a pint of beer atop the piano and said, I'm the pub pianist and I'm taking requests. Then he sat belting out pub songs all evening with everybody singing along until about two in the morning. But, needless to say, McCartney's free concert for the locals was not committed to film.

Before heading back to London on Friday morning, a crowd sequence was filmed on the steps of the Atlantic Hotel. "It really was a case of the left hand not knowing what the right was doing," recalls Miranda Ward. "The crowd had to give three cheers, but the production had run so over time that the sound man had been obliged to return to London. So I got pressed into service, unpaid of course, to hold up a microphone and record the sound for that little scene."

Filming on the trip back to London provided many yards of footage unused in the finished film, including the band eating fish suppers in a Taunton chippery, but shots of accordionist Shirley Evans entertaining the coach travellers with a selection of singalong favourites did make the final cut.

Back in Abbey Road, the weekend was taken up with further recording of Your Mother Should Know, but filming resumed on Monday, September 18, in a Soho strip joint, the Raymond Revuebar. Beatles aide Tony Bramwell was charged with the task of booking strippers and recalls "spending the afternoon watching one particular girl take her clothes off time and time again while the Bonzo Dog Doo Dah Band played Death Cab For Cutie. John and George sat there ogling her."

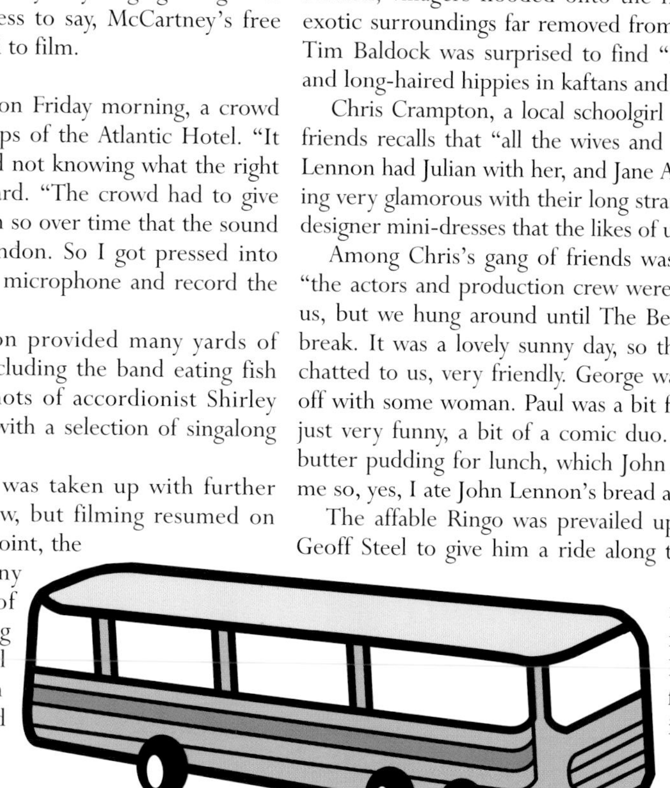

The second major chunk of Mystery Tour location shooting began the next day, in and around Hangar No2, at West Malling Air Station, Maidstone, Kent. Just as it had in Cornwall, The Beatles' arrival excited much interest among the locals. "I saw the bus arriving in the village," recalls businessman Tim Baldock. "Ringo and Maureen came to my menswear shop and he bought a mauve and pink round-necked collar shirt for £1.50."

Taking advantage of an almost total lack of security at the Air Station, villagers flooded onto the field, and found themselves in exotic surroundings far removed from the daily routine of rural life. Tim Baldock was surprised to find "flower-painted cars and buses, and long-haired hippies in kaftans and sandals everywhere."

Chris Crampton, a local schoolgirl playing truant with a bunch of friends recalls that "all the wives and girlfriends were there. Cynthia Lennon had Julian with her, and Jane Asher and Patti Boyd were looking very glamorous with their long straight hair and wearing expensive designer mini-dresses that the likes of us could only dream of."

Among Chris's gang of friends was Gill Skinner who found that "the actors and production crew were quite snooty, wouldn't talk to us, but we hung around until The Beatles came out for their lunch break. It was a lovely sunny day, so they sat on the grass lawns and chatted to us, very friendly. George was a bit reserved, and he went off with some woman. Paul was a bit flirty, but John and Ringo were just very funny, a bit of a comic duo. They'd been given bread and butter pudding for lunch, which John hated, so he passed it over to me so, yes, I ate John Lennon's bread and butter pudding."

The affable Ringo was prevailed upon by 13-year-old schoolboy Geoff Steel to give him a ride along the runway in his Mini which "had more sound equipment in that tiny space than I had in my room." Local reporter Peter Rimmer, however, didn't fare so well. "My attempt to interview George Harrison ➻

PHOTOS: APPLE-HULTON ARCHIVE/REX/REDFERNS

"It was chaotic to start with because there had been no script, no continuity notes."

Tickets to ride: a crowd sequence was shot outside the Atlantic Hotel, before getting back on the bus, September 15, 1967.

was brief and to the point. George just looked at me and said, Get a proper job! End of interview."

Despite such distractions, West Malling turned out to be a productive location, providing such scenes as the Magicians' Laboratory, the Recruiting Office, the Tug Of War and the Runway Marathon, although the best-loved segments by far are the two songs, I Am The Walrus and Your Mother Should Know.

"When they filmed I Am The Walrus," says Tim Baldock, "they somehow got up on top of the blast wall which had been built to protect the airfield from attack during the war. Those walls were 30 feet high, solid concrete, so it must have been pretty precarious up there. Paul spent much of the time in a chair on the end of one of those hydraulic lifting arms, shouting directions through a megaphone."

Harrison's favourite scene – "the one of John shovelling the spaghetti on the fat woman's plate" – was shot the same day. Like everything else in Mystery Tour, it had come about in a totally spontaneous fashion. As Paul recalls it, John had "come in and said, Hey, I had this wild dream last night, I'd like to do it. I'm a waiter...' you know? So we just put them in, you know, and it was very haphazard."

The Monty Pythonesque recruiting office sequence, featuring The Beatles' actor friend Victor Spinetti as a crazed army sergeant who ends up shouting at a papier-maché cow, was put in the can on Friday. More significantly, the film's opening shot, in which Ringo buys a Mystery Tour ticket from John, was done at local newsagent Stanley Brown's shop in West Malling High Street. After initially rejecting their request because he was busy, Brown relented and allowed them to return at closing time. "They made a very good impression on me," he says. "They were very polite, and left the shop as they found it." There was no offer of payment but, "as they packed up to leave, somebody handed me a fiver to buy myself a drink."

To Brown's surprise, however, the shop did profit on the deal. When Ringo had paid John in the scene, it was with real money, so, "when we checked the takings at the end of the day, we were thirty bob better off from the ticket money."

The film's big production number, Your Mother Should Know, was done over the weekend. "We had hired dancers from the Peggy Spencer Dance School, and sea cadets," recalls Tony Bramwell. "I had to get a staircase specially built, it was all resting on scaffolding, and the day was spent with The Beatles endlessly going up and down that staircase, miming to the music on loudspeakers, in their white suits."

Maurice Gibb of The Bee Gees still reckons that, "McCartney saw a show of ours at the Saville Theatre, during which I was all in white, you see, and that's where he got his idea to have the guys in white tails for Your Mother Should Know."

Chris Crampton and her friends were roped in to add more bodies into the finale. "Either side of the staircase were two stages," she remembers, "and we were taught a little dance to do in time to the song. When it ended we had to jump down and run after The Beatles. We were instructed not to get in front of them, but we wanted to be sure we were filmed, so some of us ran ahead."

Tim Baldock and his cronies went one better. "We worked out that if we jumped into the air on every third step, we'd be on camera, and you can see us doing that in the film."

With the bulk of the filming now completed, editing began the next day at Norman's Film Production, in Soho's Old Compton Street. Film editor Roy Benson was initially dismayed by the Herculean task ahead of him. "It was chaotic to start with because there had been no script, and they had no continuity notes, so I was simply presented with hours and hours of film and told to get on with editing it. It took about a week on my own to get the film into ➳

PHOTO: REDFERNS

"The film's participants seemed to be taking a trip rather than making a tour."

"Where's this bus going, mate? It's a mystery to me."

some sort of order, then we started work mainly with Paul and John, both of whom were very interested in the technical side of it."

Norrie Drummond, sent along by the NME to report on this process, delivered a vivid word picture. "The room was hot and smoky. Long strips of film hung from steel coat racks, and dozens of LPs lay scattered around the floor. Empty coffee cups were dotted everywhere and ashtrays spilled over with cigarette butts. John and Ringo were sitting on a table watching the film through a viewfinder, while Paul was synchronising the sound of a barrel organ."

Another visitor to Norman's was Lennon's old school chum, Pete Shotton, who recalled in his 1983 book John Lennon – In My Life that John was in a particularly good mood. "He even called out the window to an elderly drunk we heard singing in the street and invited him to join us. The drunk duly shambled upstairs, bottle in hand, to lead John, Paul, George and Ringo through round after round of old drinking songs such as There's An Old Mill By The Stream. He seemed totally oblivious to the identity of his new friends."

Simultaneously, the lavish packaging for the Magical Mystery Tour record release was being readied. "Paul and I were in another little room getting that book together," remembers Tony Barrow. "He spent a lot more time on it than I ever imagined. It pleased me greatly because I thought that he would lose all interest after they'd finished filming because there were so many disasters on that. But Paul saw it through to its conclusion."

As if this wasn't enough, The Beatles were also working on Fool On the Hill, I Am the Walrus, Blue Jay Way and the instrumental Flying, in Abbey Road.

A brief return to West Malling became necessary at the start of October, because they'd forgotten to film pick-up shots with the coach, and other scenes were tacked on during the month in the garden of Ringo Starr's Weybridge home, Sunny Heights, and in Acanthus Road and Lavender Hill, London.

It's indicative of the general lack of organisation that, towards the end of October, another bombshell hit the production. "It was realised that nothing had been shot for Fool On The Hill," explains Tony Bramwell, "so Paul set off for France one day, going back to a hill above Nice which he'd seen on a previous visit. Of course, because The Beatles had become so used to operating with assistants and minders, it never occurred to him to take his passport. Usually someone else would do that for him. When he got to customs he told them his passport was already in France, and when he got to France he told them it was following on from England. I think they were only too happy to let him in."

Although McCartney had steered The Beatles through Mystery Tour, he showed little interest in taking over the day-to-day managerial functions that had been Epstein's province. Others, however, did have their eyes on that job. The notorious Allen Klein was already expressing an interest and there had been one evening after Mystery Tour filming had wrapped for the day, when Epstein's partner Robert Stigwood had come to visit the band. "We were in a hotel having dinner," says their loyal lieutenant Neil Aspinall, "and Robert was intimating that he was now The Beatles' manager because he'd been Brian's partner." The Beatles made it clear, there and then, that whatever stake Stigwood might hold in NEMS, he was not their manager. Given the apocalypse that followed after Klein was invited in by Lennon, Harrison and Starr, it's not difficult to wonder if Stigwood might not, at the very least, have been the devil they knew.

Magical Mystery Tour was released as a uniquely packaged double EP in the UK on 27 November and, with the addition of recent singles and B-sides, as an equally lavish album in the US. In either format, the music represented another high water mark for the band, but the film itself was not to be so well received.

Having bought screening rights for £10,000, the BBC first transmitted it on Boxing Day, December 26, attracting 20 million viewers and almost universally bad reviews.

"Realities are annihilated by cinematic devices," wrote Henry Raynor of The Times, "few of which seem particularly new, and a sort of well-meaning, good-humoured anarchy prevails." Raynor also noted wryly that the participants seemed to be "taking a trip rather than making a tour".

McCartney leapt to his baby's defence on the following day's Frost Programme, explaining that "We tried to present something different for the viewers but, according to the newspapers, it did not come off. We thought we would not underestimate people and would do something new. It is better being controversial than purely boring."

In later years, he began downgrading it with remarks such as, "It was alright, you know, it wasn't the greatest thing we'd ever done. I defend it on the lines that nowhere else do you see a performance of I Am The Walrus. That's the only performance ever. So things like that, I think, are enough to make it an interesting film."

Even though Steven Spielberg has described Magical Mystery Tour as a film that he and his generation of film-makers took note of while learning their craft, some of McCartney's most recent pronouncements see him consciously distancing himself from it. "I'm not sure whose idea Magical Mystery Tour was," he says in the Anthology book, "It could've been mine, I'm not sure whether I wanna take the blame for it, you know. Umm, we were all in on it, but a lot of that stuff at that time could've been my ideas 'cause I was coming up with a lot of, sort of, concepts."

Maybe it's time for him to come up with the concept that it's OK to fail every once in a while. After all, even if no respectable film critic would claim any great artistic merit for Magical Mystery Tour, its quirky charms have been lent a rosy glow by the passage of the years. To the world's legions of Beatlefans, it's the home movie we all wish we could have made.

Thanks to John of Platt Comstock Lode; Sandy Brown of Disc; Jimmy Shapland of the Cornish Guardian; Vernon Leonard of The Grapevine; Mick Newton. ■

"I Was There"

She was an eyewitness to The Beatles' turbulent psychedelic years. Marianne Faithfull remembers the triumphs and heartaches.

Legends, as can be the case, are sometimes true and often wonderful. I don't know about the LSD bit – everybody kept it back around me because I was so much younger, a little angel on my pedestal – but I do know that one day, quite early on, The Beatles met Bob Dylan whilst changing planes, and the rest is history. Because before that the drug of choice had been alcohol and maybe speed. The Beatles, I remember, always drank the same thing, rum and coke, and they took reds, whatever they were. And then psychedelia happened. One minute it was just there, and it blew everyone – everything – away.

Apart from The Beatles being the greatest rock'n'roll band in the world, I was very lucky to have known them when I did, because it was just at a time when I was starting to learn my craft. My apprenticeship was spent going to sessions like Lovely Rita and A Day In The Life – and many other great sessions. In spite of all the competition that went on between bands – and still does – they were always dropping into my sessions and I into theirs. Because I was a girl and was not considered serious, I was actually free to move around, and of course I did. I went to sessions by The Who, I went to a lot of the Stones' sessions, but the ones that were the most fascinating – until a little bit later on when *Beggars Banquet* started to get really interesting – were The Beatles' sessions. They were doing things that really hadn't been done before. They were looking *forward* like nobody else. And I would just sit there and watch.

"Those were interesting times and psychedelia was an interesting movement. The Beatles did it really well, better than the Stones, I'm afraid."

I was particularly good friends with Paul. I even managed to get on quite well with John – he was very angry and a little bit frightening to me because I was only young. But Paul was extremely kind to me. Paul and John were the first Beatles I met; my boyfriend John Dunbar knew Jane Asher's brother Peter, of Peter And Gordon. And I loved Yesterday and wanted to do it – looking back on it, my version is probably too grandiose, but that's life.

In those days it was like a village – we were all friends, everybody knew everybody – and so of course I was in the crowd for All You Need Is Love. You can hardly see me but I was there, just a little twinkling presence. And, of course, I was there with everybody for A Day In The Life. On Yellow Submarine I was doing backing vocals, and making noises; John would be going, 'Come on, no shyness, just do it!' But then you would do anything for them. They were The Beatles.

I remember us all getting onto a train and going to Bangor to see the Maharishi, rather like a school trip. And, as it happened, this conference was being held in a school that was closed for the summer holidays. Paul was very cynical, but Patti and George were the real spiritual seekers. John, too, in his own way. When we got to the school what really annoyed me, I recall, was that Mick [Jagger] and I weren't allowed to sleep together because we weren't married, and since we were passionately in love at the time, we thought this was a very poor show.

I remember very little about the Maharishi because the weekend was so traumatic – it was there that the news came that Brian Epstein had died. It was simply terrible how lost, how heartbroken, The Beatles were. They kind of went into close family mode from the sorrow and pain. And Mick and I did what we felt was the best thing to do, which was to say very little, just try to support our friends. It was terrible. But even more terrible was to see how the Maharishi tried to come straight in there and say, 'Oh well, Brian Epstein's dead, I'll do it for you' – and they were so vulnerable that they fell for it. But then we were all very, very young.

It's hard to describe exactly how The Beatles changed in those few years when you are changing so much yourself.

I would say that they became much more peaceful, community-centred, much more full of love. John stopped drinking so much. There was much less aggression. As for the music, I don't know if it necessarily got better, because the pre-psychedelic records are absolutely wonderful. It got different. Those were very interesting times and psychedelia was an interesting movement, and The Beatles did it really well – I have to say, to be fair, better than the Stones, I'm afraid.

The Beatles weren't that different stoned and they weren't that stoned, really; they were like everyone else in London at the time. They turned it into great art.

Marianne Faithfull
London
February 2002

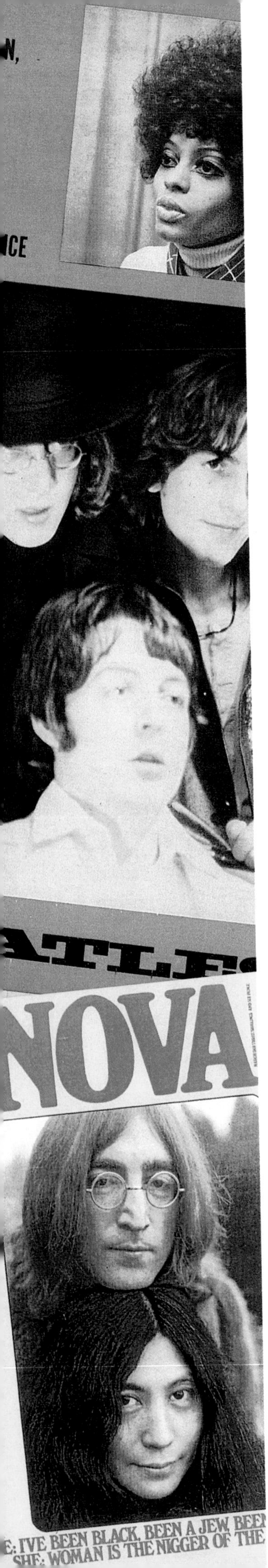

1968

In 1968 The Beatles, directionless since the death of manager Brian Epstein, kicked back with the Maharishi and stocked up on songs for what would become the White Album. Returning to take charge of their own destiny with the launch of Apple Records, they went and made Hey Jude, their biggest selling single ever. It was also the year they made a guest appearance in their own film, Yellow Submarine, and John Lennon hooked up – then stripped off – with Yoko Ono.

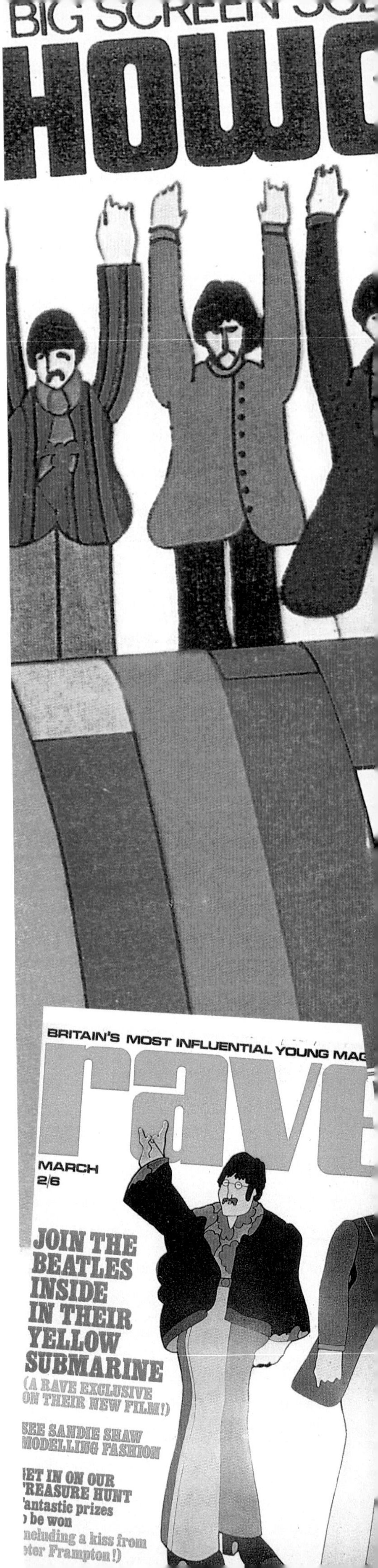

UIDE
RECORD MIRR
Largest selling colour pop
Every Thursday. Week ending September 14th, 1968
PRIVAT
No. 179
Friday
25 Oct. '68
It's no good, officer. It wont stand up in court
Member of the British Empire
SWINGING SAGA
16 NEW POP ALBUMS
12" LPS
THIS IS THE MAGIC MIXTURE
The Magic Mixture
IRELAND AGOGO
tles
ave
2/6 JULY
ck
ut
he
oms
h The
eatles
SUSS OUT
The Saturday Evening Post · May 4, 1968
POST
3/6
Here's the scene:
THE BEATLES
MIA FARROW
and a Post reporter
all gather in India
to meditate
with
THE MAHARISHI
MAHESH YOGI

A Passage To India

After Brian Epstein's death and the Magical Mystery Tour débâcle, The Beatles needed a new direction. Travelling to Rishikesh, India, they hoped the Maharishi might slip them 'The Answer'. By Mark Paytress.

It hadn't seemed very long ago that John Lennon had declared, casually but catastrophically, that religious disciples were "thick and ordinary". Now, in mid-February 1968, a stunned world looked on as pop's reluctant anti-Christs found themselves chasing a self-proclaimed guru halfway across the globe in search of spiritual guidance. Their potential guide and master was the self-styled Maharishi Mahesh Yogi who, on his first meeting with The Beatles at the Hilton Hotel in London in August 1967, had told them: "The kingdom of heaven is like electricity. You don't see it – it is within you." To four young men who'd lived their lives in public for the past five years, his words came as a revelation.

With that in mind, Rishikesh, in a remote corner of northern India, seemed a particularly long way to go, given that the wisdom they expected to unfold was under their noses all along. But The Beatles' unlikely sojourn to India was always more than a simple tale of four fabulously famous musicians forsaking wealth and ego under a hot sun. Sandwiched between the death of Brian Epstein and the public unveiling of Apple, this seemingly karma-filled episode in the band's story packed one or two killer punches.

After their ignominious return several weeks later, The Beatles' public standing never really recovered from the suspicion that they'd become faddists tipped into eccentric habits by unfathomable fame. Worse still, any inner peace gained through the Maharishi's regime of Transcendental Meditation appeared to come at the expense of the band's collective consciousness. When that was usurped, The Beatles' future was always going to be in jeopardy.

Just as LSD had done, and £sd was soon to do, Rishikesh unmasked The Beatles as individuals more concerned with their own well-being than group affairs. But however likely it is that the Maharishi experience hastened the band's demise, that's no reason to denigrate it. In fact, peel away the scandalous – and, as we shall see, dubious – conclusion that has always overshadowed the liaison in the history books and the hitherto tragicomic trip to Rishikesh re-emerges as as one of the most inspirational episodes in The Beatles' career. Viewing film footage shot in India several months afterwards, Paul turned to John and laughed: "We should have called it What We Did On Our Holidays." But the gurning faces and exotic costumes disclose little of the true story of The Beatles' appointment with a truly alternative way of life.

Ever since the band joined the Maharishi for a much-publicised weekend seminar in Bangor, north Wales, in late summer 1967, the press nicknamed him – with typical condescension – 'The Giggling Guru'. To many among the Love Generation, though, this tiny man with unkempt hair, sing-song voice and far-out wardrobe personified ancient wisdom.

"He was awe-inspiring. Hearing him speak was the most profound experience I'd ever felt," says Beach Boy and fellow Rishikesh initiate Mike Love, recalling his first encounter with the man known to his aides as His Holiness. "And the practice of meditating was so simple, yet so powerful. It seemed obvious that if everyone did it, it would be an entirely different world out there – relaxed and peaceful."

Peace and relaxation had been rare commodities in The Beatles' lives since 1962. "It was time for us all to drop out for a while," recalled Cynthia Lennon. "The years of fame and fortune had taken their toll on our nerves and minds." Maharishi's enthusiasm was infectious, his panacea perfect. "I feel a great promise for the younger generation," he remarked within hours of his first meeting with the group. "Because if The Beatles take up this Transcendental Meditation, that will really bring up the youth on a very good level of understanding and intelligence... They seem to me very intelligent and alert."

But, for John Lennon and George Harrison at least, the Maharishi experience was more about personal growth than cultural responsibility. As Harrison later admitted, meditation was in many ways an extension of the band's experiments with drugs. "Up until LSD, I never realised that there was anything beyond this state of consciousness. First time I took it, I had such an overwhelming feeling of well-being, that there was a God and I could see Him in every blade of grass."

Prior to this revelation, George – the first Beatle to take a keen interest in Indian music, culture and thought – was, remembered Cynthia Lennon, "the most tactless, blunt and often pig-headed" band member. She wasn't alone in hoping that the projected three-month sojourn in the Maharishi's secluded retreat overlooking the sacred River Ganges would have a similarly positive effect on the rest of the band and its entourage. And so, she recalled, "We set off with great optimism..."

The Beatles left London for India in two separate convoys. Revealingly, John and George, the two most desperately seeking salvation, travelled first, flying out from London Airport with Cynthia, Patti Boyd and her sister Jenny on February 15, 1968. Paul and Ringo followed three days later with their partners, Jane Asher and Maureen Starkey, finally touching down on February 20 with rather less lofty expectations. "John and George were going to Rishikesh with the idea that this might be some huge spiritual lift-off and they might never come back if the Maharishi told them some really amazing thing," remembered McCartney in Many Years From Now. His own attitude was, he asserts, rather more "pragmatic".

There was, of course, more than a whiff of the absurd to the entire venture. As the plane roared off the runway, even George was moved to crack a joke. "It will probably turn out like a Billy Butlin holiday camp!" he quipped; a comment later picked up and elaborated on by Ringo Starr. Donovan, who followed the group to Rishikesh several days later, remembers being tickled by the in-flight entertainment.

"On the plane there were three classically tall Indian ladies in saris pretending to be stewardesses," he says. "The first-class cabin windows of the Boeing 707 were framed in the manner of Muslim temples, and the walls were paisley-patterned."

The 150-mile trip from Delhi to Rishikesh was a mystery tour packed with considerably more magic than The Beatles' recent and critically lambasted stab at psychedelic cinema. Their taxis, groaning under the weight of £20 worth of excess baggage, passed through villages that

A taste of India: (top) the ashram entrance and (above) a view of the Rishikesh compound from the Ganges.

PHOTOS: HULTON ARCHIVE (PREVIOUS PAGE) MIRRORPIX

"Do you know any Ravi Shankar?" John takes requests with the Maharishi, Rishikesh, February, 1968.

betrayed a strange simplicity about the way of life there. "Scents of incense and sewage, gorgeous, kohl-eyed children and hideously deformed beggars," Donovan remembers, "visions that were both medieval and fascinating."

Reaching the temple-rich town of Rishikesh, the visitors first glimpsed the Maharishi's ashram from across the river, partially visible through the forest-covered hillside. The fenced compound, set back on a plateau 150 feet above the Ganges, was accessed through a white picket gate beside which was a one-room 'Inquiry Office'. The 15-acre site housed several bungalow-style blocks (or puri), each with around half a dozen self-contained rooms for accommodation, the Maharishi's residence situated near the cliff's edge, a two-storey lecture-hall and, towards the rear of the site, a kitchen and dining area. Generously carpeted with well-tended flowerbeds, including an abundance of outsized, blood-red hibiscus blossoms, the ashram's privacy was assured by the teak, sissoo and guava trees that hugged its perimeter.

"The place was idyllic," says wandering student and rookie photographer Paul Saltzman. "It was an extremely relaxed and simple existence, which is what ashrams are supposed to be about. Everything was focused on meditation and being at ease. There was no hurry. Life there was full of joy and humour." With only peacocks and monkeys punctuating the blissful sounds of silence with their exotic cries, it was as if The Beatles had landed in some Rousseau-inspired back-to-nature paradise.

The Beatles wrote so many songs at the ashram that George complained: "We're not here to do the next album, we're here to meditate!"

The group's split-shift arrival – celebrated by welcoming garlands of red and yellow flowers – further elevated the mood. "The ashram, up to this point, was a strange, colourless place where meditation was the sole focus," remembered actress Mia Farrow, who'd arrived a couple of weeks earlier with her brother John and sister Prudence. "We moved as if in a dream and spoke only where necessary, in the respectful, hushed tones of visitors to a graveyard." The Beatles, she said, brought an "element of normalcy" to the place.

At first, that normality meant press photographers scaling trees beyond the compound in a bid to peer into The Beatles' privacy. However, a compromise was soon reached with Mal Evans dispatched to utter perfunctory daily reports at the ashram gates. When his mantra-like regular updates – "food, meditation, sleep" – began to show little sign of changing, the press packed up and left.

Life at the ashram was anything but normal – at least by The Beatles' standards. Their rooms were comfortable but spartan, each furnished with a firm bed and a chest of drawers, a dim lamp and heat provided by a steaming bucket of water left by an aide outside the door. Meals were communal, usually taken in the open-air at a long table, adorned by a plastic tablecloth held down by jars of jam and fruit bowls. The Western diet, largely based on meat and fish, was replaced by strictly vegetarian fare, invariably lightly spiced curries.

The visitors' Carnaby Street glad rags were packed away, replaced by kurta tunics and Nehru jackets for the men, embroidered silk saris for the women. "We began to realise that we needed very little to find contentment," remembered Cynthia.

Ostensibly, The Beatles had been invited to join the Maharishi at his Academy Of Transcendental Meditation to complete a three-month

PHOTOS: PHOTODISC, PICTORIAL PRESS

Teacher Training course. This loosely consisted of two 90-minute lectures, at 3.30 and 8.30, with question-and-answer sessions afterwards. Plus, of course, as many hours of meditation as possible. But it soon became apparent that the main rump of students there – "All lovely people bent on a vision of becoming better equipped to cope with life," said Cynthia – were a class apart from the Maharishi's celebrity guests. "He treated The Beatles totally differently," confirms Paul Saltzman. "I don't even think they were on the main course. They received individual attention."

"The purpose of the course was to become teachers of Transcendental Meditation," insists Mike Love, "but I remember Paul telling me that becoming a teacher 'wasn't the lads' cup of tea'. It was obvious that Maharishi was happy to have a few celebrities along in the hope that they might understand the benefits of TM and spread the word."

Going solo: John became evermore distant from Cynthia.

"Every morning John would be up and out saying he was off to meditate alone. I realised later he was collecting Yoko's mail." Cynthia Lennon

The moment no initiate can forget is the act of being inducted into meditation. Seated cross-legged and face-to-face with the Maharishi in a quiet room, the student would hand him a bunch of cut flowers in exchange for a 'secret' mantra which it was expressly forbidden to divulge.

"I checked later with John," says Apple director Denis O'Dell who visited the group in Rishikesh at the start of March, "and I'd been given the same mantra as he had!" Mia Farrow was less lucky still. Sneezing at the exact moment of disclosure, she politely requested Maharishi to repeat her mantra. He wouldn't, and from that moment on, she was "never 100 per cent sure if I was doing it right".

If the secret mantra was a marketable slice of jiggery-pokery, the effects of daily meditation – whether done 'properly' or not – were soon felt. One afternoon, while meditating on one of the many flat roofs on the site, Paul was overwhelmed by the experience. "It appeared to me that I was like a feather over a hot-air pipe. I was just suspended by this hot air, which was something to do with the meditation. And it was a very blissful thing."

Bliss of a momentary kind was never going to be enough for George Harrison. Within minutes of his arrival, Denis O'Dell remembers George hustling him into his bungalow "where he told me he could now levitate. I thought, That is a most extraordinary thing to do! He demonstrated it, but whether he did levitate an inch or two I cannot say because I was so astounded by what I was seeing. I realised that this was a very devout man."

Invariably, the most complex response to the regime of meditation came from John Lennon. One day, at a private audience with Maharishi, Lennon admitted: "Whenever I meditate, there's a big brass band in me head". "John was a sincere man, and I enjoyed hearing him and George putting questions to Maharishi," says Mike Love. "But remember he went from Transcendental Meditation to heroin. He definitely had some issues. I'm not a psychologist, but he was abandoned by his father and hurt as a child. Meditation obviously helped him a bit..."

"John and George both took meditation seriously," remembers Paul Saltzman, who soon found himself among The Beatles' entourage. "George seemed to find what he was looking for, in essence, but John was looking for something in – and I don't mean this rudely – a more adolescent way. He was looking for 'The Answer'. Well, there isn't The Answer." According to Mia Farrow, "John seemed to see everything on a mystical plane. He thought of Maharishi as a kind of wizard."

Denis O'Dell is not convinced by the idea that Lennon was in search of a father-figure ("We used to talk a lot, and it never struck me that he ever needed any advice"), though he does remark on an added strain on Lennon's life during this period. "One was aware that his marriage wasn't going well. John spent a lot of time in isolation, and you could sense that something was wrong even though he maintained that he needed solitude for the purposes of meditation. He and Cyn were in the process of splitting up; there was no question about that."

"Every morning he would be up and out of our room before me, saying he was off to meditate alone," remembered Cynthia Lennon. "The first week he was fine, but after that he cut me off... I put it down to being away, his changed attitudes to meditation and the beauty that there were now no drugs. I realised later that he was going to collect the morning mail..."

There, Lennon would excitedly prise open the latest missive from Yoko Ono that would invariably contain a magical instruction such as: "I'm a cloud. Watch for me". John did, and as the weeks went by, those clouds seemed ever closer to him.

"These crazy letters kept coming, driving me mad," Lennon remembered. There was "nothing in them that wives or mothers-in-law could have understood", but their cryptic, philosophical nature were perfectly in tune with his state of mind.

One day, after hearing Paul Saltzman's tale about being dumped by his girlfriend, Lennon told him, "Love can be pretty tough on us. But eventually you get another chance, don't you?" "I realise now that he was talking about his own situation," Saltzman says. He was right. "In India, I started thinking of [Yoko] as a woman, not just an intellectual woman," Lennon later admitted.

Together, and with time on their hands, it was inevitable that after the initial flourish of devout meditation The Beatles would turn to their guitars. "I had my guitar with me and they had their Martin D-28 acoustics," remembers Donovan. "While George was content with the Chet Atkins style of picking, John saw me playing finger-picking style and he wanted me to teach him the technique. He was a fast learner – he got the patterns in two days." Two Lennon originals, Julia and Dear Prudence, both written in Rishikesh, owe an obvious debt to John's newly acquired skill.

Meditation may have fed The Beatles' heads with a growing sense of maturity and control, but the impact of the Rishikesh experience on the band's music turned out to be doubly dramatic. Much of the White Album and *Abbey Road* was written out there in what was undoubtedly the most fertile bout of songwriting in the group's career. More significantly still, the lavish, studio-enhanced productions that had climaxed with *Sgt Pepper* the previous summer were largely consigned to the past. After India, The Beatles' music began to mirror the quest for simplicity that had prompted their journey there.

"We wrote *tons* of songs in India," said Lennon. So many, in fact, that at one stage, George Harrison was moved to complain: "We're not fuck-

PHOTO: TOPHAM PICTUREPOINT

Man in the hills: Maharishi Mahesh Yogi, 1968.

ing here to do the next album, we're here to meditate!" In truth, few of the songs written out there – with the obvious exception of Mike Love's Transcendental Meditation – were overtly associated with the experience, though Lennon's songs especially were characterised by a certain tempo that reflected what Denis O'Dell has called the "slow-motion" sensibility of life on the ashram.

If The Beatles usually wrote alone, they would often congregate to develop material, sometimes with each other, occasionally with whoever was close by. "I remember Paul McCartney coming to breakfast one morning with his acoustic guitar," says Mike Love. "He was playing what turned out to be Back In The USSR. I told him it was cool, but I said, You gotta talk about the girls in Russia. Of course, he needed no help in writing a song, but he later acknowledged that I helped him out on the bridge. A tape still exists of he and I playing around with the song."

Cynthia, John and Mike Love, February, 1968.

Only marginally less obvious than The Beach Boys' influence on Back In The USSR is the impact of Donovan's finger-picking technique on Paul McCartney's Blackbird. "He peered over my shoulder a few times to get the style and absorbed it in his talented way," Donovan says. It wasn't all one-way traffic, though. "George helped me write Hurdy Gurdy Man out there," the singer continues. "And the tamboura George gave me out there ended up on the song, too."

Into the mystic: the Maharishi and the Fabs with Donovan (far right) and Mia Farrow (third right).

That The Beatles ended up working on so many songs in India was especially surprising given that the sole creative project in their minds when they arrived in Rishikesh was a vague notion of a documentary film about the Maharishi. Once there, the idea took on a more serious dimension, and the band requested assistance from London. "When the cable came, I was absolutely amazed that they wanted to do something on TM with the Maharishi," remembers Denis O'Dell, who'd been recruited to head up the new company Apple's film division. "I thought, I must get out there to stop that." Besides, he had another project in mind for them.

"When I got there and told them about the Lord Of The Rings idea I'd been discussing with United Artists in New York, the Maharishi film was quickly forgotten. Almost instantly, they started casting themselves in roles, and John told me that he could literally write a double album around it." O'Dell's idea was to have the four Beatles inhabiting Middle Earth, find a suitable role for Donovan,

PHOTOS: MIRRORPIX, HULTON ARCHIVE, TOPHAM PICTUREPOINT

add a supporting cast of seasoned English actors and get David Lean to direct it. The project was stillborn, but it did put a stop to Maharishi – The Movie.

O'Dell cannot recall any business meetings with the Maharishi and his eagle-eyed lawyer about the proposed documentary. However, a well-worn story emanates from Apple director Neil Aspinall, who recalled a meeting in the Maharishi's bungalow where "suddenly, this little guy in a robe who's meant to be a Holy Man starts talking about his two-and-a-half per cent". It's odd that such a tale has been widely used as damming evidence of the Maharishi's supposed avarice. As head of a humanitarian-based organisation that relies on funds in order to grow, it's self-evident that there would have been a fiscal element to any negotiations. And besides, even before The Beatles set off for India, hadn't Lennon rebutted earlier suspicions with a curt, "So what if he's commercial? We're the most commercial group in the world!"

Paul Saltzman reckons that The Beatles harboured doubts about the Maharishi from the start. "Mal said that the guys were unhappy with Maharishi on two points. They didn't like him using their name for publicity and had spoken to him about it: I think an LP of his lectures had already come out billing him as 'guru to The Beatles'. Mal also told me they were not happy about the money issue. He said Maharishi had asked for 25 per cent of their net earnings."

For the time being, though, The Beatles were more concerned with saving their souls than hanging on to their savings. Apart, that is, from Ringo, who, with his wife Maureen, beat a hasty retreat back to London on March 1 after little more than a week of ashram life.

"If everyone in the world started meditating, then the world would be a much happier place," he declared on his arrival back home. But bliss was never on the agenda for Ringo or Maureen. They pined for their infant son, Jason, Maureen detested the insects and Ringo's dodgy stomach couldn't handle the unfamiliar food.

Denis O'Dell inherited the couple's living quarters. "Ringo said he'd left a present for me – and behind the door was about 28,000 cans of baked beans." O'Dell wasn't feeling too good himself a few days later...

Neither was Mia Farrow's 19-year-old sister Prudence. "If we'd been in the West, they'd have put her away," Lennon quipped years later. Luckily for 'Pru', it was March 1968 and her 'team buddies' were George and a rather more charitably disposed John. Despite the support of the two Beatles, who paid her regular visits to check on her well-being, Prudence steadfastly refused to come out to play. "I just wanted to meditate as much as possible," she explained years later. But at the time, her behaviour – refusing to attend lectures and only accepting food from a plate left outside her door – was a genuine cause for concern.

The remaining trio of Beatles cooked up a unique remedy. Picking up their guitars, they stood outside her window and started to play a new song Paul had written, Ob-La-Di, Ob-La-Da. "They were trying to be cheerful," Prudence remembered, "but I wished they'd go away. At first, I don't think they realised what the training course in meditation was all

PHOTO: PICTORIAL PRESS

"Anyone fancy an Indian?" Accusations of sexual impropriety began to surround the Maharishi.

about. They were just having fun." Lennon famously immortalised the episode on Dear Prudence, another White Album song written in Rishikesh.

"We're leaving," said Lennon. "But why?" asked the puzzled Maharishi. "If you're so cosmic, you'll know why," deadpanned John.

Just as the rainy season had, during February, given way to balmy evenings and perfect sunsets, the old competitiveness between The Beach Boys and The Beatles defrosted in the Himalayan humidity. Altruism was in the air, and before Mike Love headed back to California, his English rivals joined the Maharishi in giving him a fine birthday send-off on March 15. "Maharishi threw a great party with musicians, magicians and fireworks, and The Beatles gave me a painting of Maharishi's master, Guru Dev." They also recorded a special song for him, Happy Birthday Mike Love. Mike Love still treasures the song on cassette.

The real turning-point at Rishikesh came with another departure: that of Paul McCartney, who left for London with Jane Asher and Neil Aspinall on March 26. With so many of his playmates now gone (even Mia Farrow had left, choosing instead to explore the hippy hideaways at Goa and Kathmandu), John Lennon too began to show signs of restlessness. Enter Alexis Mardas, the Greek technical whizz earmarked to head Apple's new Electronics division. Summoned to India by John Lennon and George Harrison, ostensibly to build the world's smallest radio transmitter thus enabling Maharishi to beam his message across the world, 'Magic Alex' soon sullied the gracious vibe with his unrestrained scepticism.

"I never saw a Holy Man with a bookmaker!" he joked when the subject of the Maharishi's money was raised. Looking around at the other students, he disparaged them as "mentally ill Swedish old ladies… and a bunch of lost, pretty girls". And, when Cynthia and Patti casually lamented the lack of home comforts, Alex magically smuggled in playing cards, cigarettes and on one occasion a bottle of potent local wine to remind them of life beyond the strict regime of Transcendental Meditation.

According to Cynthia, John and George "did not imbibe". However, the occasional flush of doubt that the pair did their best to ignore was proving increasingly difficult to suppress. What if it was all one big con-trick? Was the Maharishi, who used The Beatles' name to sell his own records and television specials, really so naive? And why, Lennon asked himself, hadn't the Wise One slipped him 'the secret' when he joined the Maharishi for a ride in his private helicopter?

There were other factors, too, that began to cast shadows over the golden garden. While The Beatles had gone cold on their projected Maharishi film, an American conglomeration headed by TM enthusiast Charles Lutes had flown over to reactivate its own film project. The presence of the film cameras upset John and George, who did their best to stay out of view – a matter made worse by the increasingly humid spring temperatures. And still the band's other guru, Magic Alex, had yet to work wonders with his electronic pulpit.

"If we drop a stone in a pond, the ripples begin to move over the whole pond, reaching all the extremities," said the Maharishi on his 1967 spoken-word album. The idea that one individual's ability to shake the entire universe was central to the Maharishi's Vedic-inspired knowledge. Unfortunately, if that individual's intent was negative, then the results could be catastrophic. "It was obvious to me that Alexis Mardas wanted out," remembered Cynthia Lennon, "and more than anything, he wanted The Beatles out as well."

April 12, 1968 had been a stiflingly hot day at the ashram. Maharishi's customary mid-evening lecture had drawn to a close a little earlier than usual due to a power failure. The 50 or so students returned to their quarters, from which the welcome sound of gentle rain could be heard, and settled down to reflect on the day's teachings. Alex Mardas had other ideas.

A couple of weeks earlier, Alex had hooked up with an American woman in her late twenties who'd grown disenchanted with the course, but couldn't leave prematurely due to restrictions on her airline ticket. The pair had spent several evenings together bemoaning their situation, and one day, she claimed that the Maharishi had fed her some forbidden chicken during a private chat. More sensationally, she then suggested that he'd made a sexual pass at her after first holding her hands in a bid to intensify a spiritual union. When the rumour reached Cynthia and Patti, they wept tears of disbelief.

That was nothing compared to the reaction on this particular night when John and George were awoken by a wildly animated Alex. It was true, he said; he'd witnessed a similar situation with his own eyes while secretly observing Maharishi with the woman through a window. John Lennon recalls "a big hullabaloo"; Cynthia that "a night was spent trying desperately to sort out what to believe". It got worse. "Out of confusion and accusation came anger and aggression," Cynthia continued. The critical moment came when George Harrison, the Maharishi's most loyal Beatle, began to waver. "I thought, well, if George is doubting him, there must be something in it," said John.

Early the next morning, John, George and Alexis confronted the Maharishi over breakfast. "We're leaving," said Lennon. "But why?" asked the puzzled guru. "If you're so cosmic," John deadpanned, "you'll know why." After eight weeks of love, peace and understanding, Lennon had rediscovered his cruel sense of humour to shocking effect.

Not everyone was convinced by the claims, nor that what the remaining Beatles were about to do was right. "I have never packed my belongings with such a heavy heart," said Cynthia. "I felt that what we were doing was wrong, very, very wrong." As they waited for the taxis – ordered by Alex – to arrive, John felt moved to pen some instant karma. "Maharishi," he began. "You little twat/Who the fuck do you think you are/Oh, you cunt." Disillusionment was a bitter pill for the impulsive Beatle to swallow.

The unity of master and students, of East and West, and of ancient wisdom and contemporary culture had been ripped apart. As The Beatles' entourage waited for their cars, the Maharishi's aides shuffled uncomfortably some 100 yards away. One of them walked over in a futile bid to heal the rift.

"It was so sad," said Cynthia. "The Maharishi looked very Biblical and isolated in his faith." The taxis arrived. "Poor Maharishi," thought Jenny Boyd. "I remember him standing at the gate of the ashram, under an aide's umbrella as The Beatles filed by, out of his life." As John and George passed through the picket gate to begin the long journey back to London and the madness of their pop lives, the Maharishi made one last plea. "Wait," he said, his tiny voice inflected with hurt. "Talk to me." But The Beatles were no longer listening. ■

Mac to basics: Paul McCartney in 1969.

What: Lady Madonna is released
Where: UK
When: March 15, 1968

BACK TO THE FUTURE

Lady Madonna was a turning point for The Beatles, as they left psychedelia behind and embraced the emerging roots revival. By John Harris.

THERE ARE NO SHORTAGE OF BEATLES songs that sit in a pivotal place as regards both the group themselves and wider musical developments: I Want To Hold Your Hand, Help!, Tomorrow Never Knows, Strawberry Fields, Hey Jude… you name them. However, in most accounts of their progress, precious little importance has been accorded to the two-and-a-bit minutes that both wrenched the group away from psychedelia, and laid one of the foundation stones for a roots rock revival that would take hold within a year of its release.

The song in question was Lady Madonna, Paul's clipped salute to the can-do spirit of motherhood. But its lyrics form but a tiny aspect of its significance. In re-acquainting The Beatles with '50s rock'n'roll and featuring embellishments no more grandiose than four saxophones, it informed the world that it would soon be time to discard beads and bells, forget about backwards guitars and six-minute mini-operas, and go back to the source. A clutch of American albums – among them Creedence Clearwater Revival's self-titled debut and The Band's *Music From Big Pink* – have been credited with way more importance in this sea-change, but The Beatles unquestionably knew which way the wind was blowing. "It's not outright rock, but it's that kind of thing," Paul explained at the time. "We think the time is right."

"I describe it as 'rockaswing'," reckoned Ringo, before dispensing a mind-boggling bit of humility. "We've been trying to make a decent rock'n'roll record ever since we started, and, as far as I know, we haven't done a decent one yet. This is another bash; it's pretty near it. If we get together for a jam session or something… we invariably start playing the basic rock chords and rhythms as soon as we pick up our instruments."

The jumping-off point for Lady Madonna was Humphrey Lyttelton's Bad Penny Blues, originally put to tape in 1956. One only need play the two songs back to back to hear Paul McCartney's borderline pilfering of the Lyttelton tune's gloriously nimble piano part, and its walking bassline in particular – although he used it as only one aspect of the song's downhome alchemy. In the scat harmonies that arrive at 1:02, one can discern the influence of The Mills Brothers, the Ohio-born vocal quartet who attracted acclaim on account of their camped-up impressions of brass instruments. Perhaps most importantly, in Paul's lead vocal, there lurks the clear wish to salute Elvis Presley – whose leather-clad comeback, launched eight months after Lady Madonna's release, was another key factor in music's sudden re-kindling of its love affair with primal rock.

In keeping with the song's stripped-down aesthetic, Lady Madonna was recorded over two sessions, on February 3 and 6, 1968. It was during the latter that Paul McCartney belatedly realised what the song was lacking: a stampeding brass part. Four saxophonists – among them Ronnie Scott – were hastily summoned to Abbey Road studios, only to find that the usual session etiquette had been ignored, and they were expected to come up with their own parts. "Paul McCartney went through the song on the piano and we were each given a scrap of manuscript paper and a pencil to write out some notes," recalled one of them, Bill Jackman. "Had there been music, we would have been in and out in about 10 minutes. As it was, it took most of the evening." One of the saxophone players in particular was none too pleased: in Ronnie Scott's furious solo, one can hear the anger that comes from being detained against one's will.

The man with the horn: Lady Madonna soloist, Ronnie Scott.

Upon completion, Lady Madonna was scheduled for release on March 15, by which time The Beatles would be perfecting their meditational skills in India. In that sense, its timing was perfect: if their spell with the Maharishi represented their last, ill-fated flirtation with psychedelia-inspired mind-expansion, Lady Madonna proved that they were already mapping out another route. The song's B-side fits the picture: The Inner Light, begun in Bombay and completed in London, may represent George's loveliest addition of Indian music to The Beatles' repertoire, but it was also his last.

"It's not outright rock, but it's that kind of thing. We think that the time is right." Paul McCartney

Lady Madonna duly went to Number 1 in the UK and Number 4 in America. Within 18 months, The Beatles' implied re-embracing of rock's founding values was de rigueur. The Stones had released *Beggars Banquet*, and begun their turbo-charged rock'n'soul'n'blues phase. Having decided that the era of Cream's virtuoso head-rock had passed, Eric Clapton would soon fall in with the Southern musicians with whom he would form Derek And The Dominos. The Who were covering Eddie Cochran and Johnny Kidd And The Pirates; Chuck Berry and Little Richard were back on the rarefied pedestals where the British Invasion groups had originally placed them.

Meanwhile, as if to confirm Lady Madonna's rock'n'roll credentials, no less a figure than Fats Domino had recorded a version, included on 1968's *Fats Is Back*. The greatest accolade, however, came with the 1995 release of Elvis's *Essential '70s Masters*: though his rendition was never completed, on May 17, 1971, Presley had run through the song in the studio. Given his regal stature, that fact alone confirms Lady Madonna's place in The Beatles' myth.

PHOTOS: CAMERA PRESS, REDFERNS, HULTON ARCHIVE, MIRRORPIX

JANUARY 68

1 Paul McCartney visits his family in Liverpool with girlfriend Jane Asher.

5 John Lennon has a meeting with his estranged father, Freddie, at Kenwood, Weybridge, during which they reconcile some of their differences.

6 *Sgt Pepper* is finally knocked off the UK Number 1 slot by the equally innovative *Val Doonican Rocks But Gently*.

7 George Harrison flies to Bombay, India, to work on the soundtrack for the film Wonderwall.

11 In Bombay, George records the backing track for his song The Inner Light.

17 John, Paul and Ringo, plus Jimi Hendrix and Rolling Stones guitarist Brian Jones, attend a launch party in London for The Grapefruit (above) who have just been signed to Apple.

20 Jimi Hendrix records guitar parts for the album, *McGough And McGear*, under the supervision of Paul McCartney, at De Lane Lea studios.

21 John Fred And His Playboy Band are at Number 1 in the US Top 40 singles chart with Judy In Disguise (With Glasses) – a parody of Lucy In The Sky With Diamonds.

22 Paul McCartney, Cliff Richard, Cat Stevens and Michael Caine are in the audience for the first night of The Supremes' show at London's Talk Of The Town. Apple offices open at 95 Wigmore St, London.

25 The Beatles film their live insert to the Yellow Submarine movie at Twickenham Film Studios.

27 John Lennon is interviewed at home in Surrey by BBC Radio 1 DJ Kenny Everett.

28 Paul rehearses his song, Step Inside Love, with Cilla Black (above), who will use it as the theme for her upcoming TV series.

30 George Harrison completes recording of the Wonderwall soundtrack at Abbey Road, London.

FEBRUARY 68

1–2 Ringo has rehearsals in West London for an upcoming appearance on Cilla Black's BBC TV show, Cilla.

3 Work begins on Lady Madonna at Abbey Road.

Baby's in black: the promo clip for The Ballad Of John And Yoko, featuring the eponymous couple, 1969.

What: The latest Beatles promo airs
Where: Top Of The Pops
When: March 14, 1968

BOYS ON FILM

The unsung pioneers of the pop video, for The Beatles the 'promo film' was just a means of avoiding going into TV studios. By Joe Cushley.

IT WAS THE STRANGE CASE OF THE Madonna and the Bulldog – when millions of viewers were hoodwinked by The Beatles. The public assumed they were watching a tape of the boys they trusted, nay, loved, performing their latest single, Lady Madonna on Top Of The Pops, on March 14, 1968, but actually they were watching the bounders record a new track, Hey Bulldog. Welcome to the era of the pop video – where nothing is real (and nothing to get hung about).

The Beatles had long since used the medium of 'promo films' to sell their singles, the demands on their time meaning that as soon as the technology became available, they would try to get away with appearing on film rather than in the studio. Indeed, The Beatles appeared 'live' on Top Of The Pops just once – miming to Rain and Paperback Writer in 1966. And even then, in the weeks before and after, the beautiful, colour promos for those songs – filmed by Michael Lindsay-Hogg – were shown on Top Of The Pops in monochrome.

These promo films already represented a major advance on the 10 video clips taped by Joe McGrath at Twickenham Studios in November, 1965. The technology was in its infancy then, and those videos were, by all accounts, the first recorded by a pop group. They included Day Tripper, with Ringo sawing through the train carriage scenery, and Ticket To Ride, in front of placard-sized tickets.

The Beatles had decided to take this filmic route to promotion to lessen their workload. "It was a great ruse," said Ringo. "It was to save us going round the TV shows and saying, Hello, yet again to Cathy McGowan." In the process they, as Harrison would later suggest, "invented MTV".

By the time of Strawberry Fields/Penny Lane, these promos had become mini-epics. "It was a proper little movie," Tony Bramwell, a general troubleshooter at NEMS remembers. "It was all done in that bloody field [Knole Park, Sevenoaks]. After that, it was me and Andrew Gosling in the editing suite for 36 hours, getting all the dissolves, and opticals, which cost a lot of money." The mad music professors' outdoor seminar of Strawberry Fields, and the Lewis-Carroll-goes-to-Liverpool of Penny Lane are paragons of the promo-maker's art.

Two slightly less triumphant filmic excursions followed – Magical Mystery Tour, slammed after its Boxing Day 1967 showing on the BBC, and the video for Hello Goodbye, unused by the Beeb because of its lip-synching rules. Neither Bramwell, nor his boss, Denis O'Dell – head of the newly formed Apple Films – recall there being a definite decision to abandon the gnomic psychedelica of recent work, but that's exactly what the studio-bound Lady Madonna video looks like. "It was just a question of getting a few shots of fab mop-tops," quips Bramwell, the nominal director. "They'd do anything you wanted them to do, as long as it was our little mob filming them." Apart from running through a song they'd already recorded it seems…

"I wasn't that experienced in promos," recollects Denis O'Dell, associate producer on A Hard Day's Night, "so I'd spent a few days coming up with ideas for Lady Madonna. When The Beatles wanted to get on with recording Hey Bulldog, all that went out the window!"

The band may have focused on recording their new song, but the frenetic editing and The Beatles' own joyous performance still carry the day. Lady Madonna? Who cares that they were singing a completely different song!

O'Dell is more sure of his contribution to their next outing, Hey Jude, filmed at Twickenham Studios (during the same filming session they also made a promo for Hey Jude's B-side, Revolution). "I liked the song enormously, and it had this great singalong quality. I thought it would be marvellous to see The Beatles playing together again in front of an audience – but in a controlled way, to get the atmosphere of a live performance."

"To give them some measure of security, I had these rostra built so they'd be above the audience," says O'Dell. Tony Bramwell recalls McCartney's drawing for the set: "It was piano, there; drums, there; orchestra in two tiers at the back. Paul's ideas were usually attainable. John's were generally unattainable, and when Yoko turned up it was, 'Let's film John's cock'."

Doing it for the vids: the Revolution promo clip, 1968.

"John's promo ideas were generally unattainable, and when Yoko turned up it was, 'Let's film John's cock'."

The different levels of the podia gave the band the air of an organic entity, a Mount Rushmore of rock – and when the audience climb up to join them, the effect is exhilarating. "Afterwards, they said, 'Denis, we're delighted with the way it's gone, let's do another live show along those lines'," O'Dell remembers. "That's what sparked off the 'Get Back' sessions and *Let It Be*."

The documentary that followed at Twickenham was not an experience that The Beatles enjoyed, but their climactic roof-top performance gave them more than enough footage for the splendid promotional video for the single Get Back – and clips from this period also backed the promos for Let It Be and The Long And Winding Road.

However, the films for Something and The Ballad Of John And Yoko, well-made as they are, serve as a barometer of a band in its final throes. Ballad… follows John and Yoko on the trip painted by the lyrics: Amsterdam, Heathrow, Paris, etc. Something shows The Beatles with their ladies of the moment, larking about in their respective gardens; or, in Paul's case, farm. In neither clip do you see them together as a band.

O'Dell adds a poignant footnote to the Fabs' promo filmology. "You can see my young son standing behind Ringo in the Hey Jude clip. He died of cancer the following week, but he was so happy at that moment." The Beatles did that for people.

PHOTOS: HULTON ARCHIVE, VIN MAG ARCHIVE LTD, MIRRORPIX

4 The Beatles start work on John's song Across The Universe in Abbey Road. Fallout, the last episode of cult UK TV series The Prisoner (above), is transmitted in the London area. The Beatles are watching because their song All You Need Is Love is used on the soundtrack. Impressed by the directing skills of the show's star, Patrick McGoohan, they resolve to ask him to write and direct a movie for them, but the project never gets off the ground.

5 In the Royal Garden Hotel, London, Paul lends his presence to a press conference for the Leicester Arts Community Festival.

6 Ringo guests on the Cilla Black Show (above) on UK TV, and they perform a duet on Act Naturally.

8 The Beatles finish work on Across The Universe in Abbey Road.

9 Apple begins a series of media ads to publicise The Beatles' new enterprise.

10 The Beatles move all their business affairs from NEMS to their own newly-formed company, Apple.

11 The Beatles are filmed at Abbey Road, recording Hey Bulldog.

15 John and George fly to India to spend time with the Maharishi Mahesh Yogi. The final mono remix of Lady Madonna is produced.

18 Paul is interviewed by the London Evening Standard.

19 Paul and Ringo fly to India to spend time with the Maharishi Mahesh Yogi.

24 Paul's recent London Evening Standard interview is published, in which he states that The Beatles now have all the money they will ever need.

MARCH 68

1 Disenchanted with the Maharishi, Ringo and his wife Maureen leave the Academy Of Transcendental Meditation's compound in Rishikesh, India, and begin the journey home.

3 Ringo and Maureen land at Heathrow Airport.

9 *Sgt Pepper's Lonely Hearts Club Band* wins four Grammys: Best Album, Best Contemporary Album, Best Engineered Album and Best Album Cover. Cilla Black releases her new McCartney-penned single, Step Inside Love.

13 Ringo is interviewed by Alan Smith of the NME.

14 Lady Madonna gets its first UK TV airing on Top Of The Pops.

15 Lady Madonna is released in the UK.

Working flat-out: John Lennon gets experimental on Revolution 1, Abbey Road studios, June 4, 1968.

What: Work begins on the White Album.
Where: Abbey Road
When: 30 May, 1968

DOUBLE TROUBLE

The White Album was supposed to be an opportunity to pull together, but soon the four Beatles were working separately. By Martin O'Gorman.

WHEN THE PHOTOGRAPHER FROM Beatles Monthly arrived at Abbey Road to document the early sessions for the group's new album, he wasn't aware of the explosive situation he was walking into. It was traditional for the magazine to snap "the boys" getting back down to serious business, but on this occasion, he only had time to fire off a few pictures before being abruptly asked to leave by the group's assistant, Mal Evans. Unwittingly, amid the shots of the unusually sour faces of the Fab Four, he'd captured delicate evidence of The Beatles' rapidly changing personal lives, because lurking in the background were McCartney's latest conquest Francie Schwartz and Lennon's new obsession, Yoko Ono.

McCartney's romance with Jane Asher was still officially on, but after Schwartz arrived from New York to pitch a film script to Apple, it became common knowledge among the group's inner circle that she'd been a guest at the Beatle's Cavendish Avenue home while Asher was away working. Even more scandalously, it was only a matter of days since Lennon and Ono had finally consummated their burgeoning relationship, but as far as the world at large was concerned, John was still happily married to Cynthia.

Behind closed doors at Abbey Road, Ono had installed herself firmly at Lennon's side. To keep herself occupied while The Beatles worked on the first song for the new album, Revolution, she carried a portable tape recorder into the control room and began a rambling commentary on the session. Although Lennon tried to give her attention, he would be repeatedly dragged back to work. "Jooooohn," Yoko says into her microphone after one brief conversation with her lover. "I miss you again…" It was only a matter of time before Ono decided she didn't want to be left on the sidelines and began to add her own input to The Beatles' recordings. It was here that, as Harrison would later comment, "the rot set in".

The group had become insular and increasingly treated Abbey Road as sanctuary from the outside world.

But sessions for what was to become the White Album should have been a gloriously creative time. The two months spent in Rishikesh with the Maharishi had refreshed the group and prompted Lennon, McCartney and Harrison to compose dozens of new songs. The Beatles congregated at George's house in Esher in late May to tape demos of an impressive 23 tracks, including compositions such as Junk and Not Guilty that would be held over for future solo albums.

Magi mix: Paul shows off to George Martin and Ringo Starr, Abbey Road, '68.

However, despite the positive attitude in India, the group had become even more insular thanks to their shifting personal and professional lives and increasingly treated Abbey Road as sanctuary from the outside world. They block-booked Studio 2 from 2.30pm until midnight, but sessions frequently dragged on into the early hours of the following morning. Additionally, The Beatles reverted to some of the undisciplined plodding of the previous summer, which saw the birth of some of the group's most sonically intriguing, but unfocused tracks, such as It's All Too Much and Baby You're A Rich Man. "For a lot of the recordings, they would have a basic idea," says George Martin. "Then they would have a jam session to end it, which sometimes didn't sound too good."

Revolution was a case in point. The original album version of the song was a straightforward blues riff dressed with a daringly political lyric. On one take, the song evolved into a 10-minute marathon as the band played the same two chords over and over, like a mantra. Meanwhile, Lennon repeatedly screamed the word "Alright!" and gibbered nonsensically in a fair approximation of Yoko's freeform style. Putting the song to one side for brass overdubs, Lennon would later take off the last six minutes for his avant-garde experiment, Revolution 9.

The Beatles then tackled Starr's first solo composition, the country-flavoured Don't Pass Me By, which had been knocking around for at least five years. It was, as Lennon told DJ Kenny Everett when he visited the session on June 6 for his Radio 1 programme, "composed in a fit of lethargy". Again, the basic track was recorded before being left for overdubs from session musicians, this time a suitably hoedown violin solo.

Despite such disjointed work patterns, Harrison saw the new album as an attempt for The Beatles to work as a proper unit again, following the laborious piecemeal approach that spawned *Sgt Pepper*. "The new album felt more like a band recording together," he later explained. "There were a lot of tracks where we just played live. There was also a lot more individual stuff, and, for the first time, people were accepting that it was individual."

This was apparent when Harrison and Starr made the unprecedented move of taking a trip to America in early June, while sessions carried on without them. As Lennon and McCartney continued working at Abbey Road, not only did they carry on without the drummer and the lead guitarist, they were working on two entirely separate tracks – Lennon tinkering with his expanding collection of Revolution 9 tape loops and McCartney perfecting the acoustic Blackbird.

Things became even more fragmented when McCartney left for America on Apple business at the end of the month, leaving Lennon and Harrison to put the finishing touches to Revolution 9 without the bassist's watchful eye on proceedings. At one point, Lennon commandeered three separate studios at once to accommodate his tape loops. As the sessions stretched out over the summer and into autumn, each Beatle began to closely guard his own corner and material. It was only a matter of time before they realised the freedom that being a solo artist would give them.

PHOTOS: TONY BRAMWELL, LINDA McCARTNEY, TOPFOTO

18 Lady Madonna is released in the US.

23 Lady Madonna enters the US Top 40 singles chart, where it will peak at Number 4.

26 Paul McCartney flies back to London from India.

27 Under the patronage of John Lennon, UK band Grapefruit make their debut performance at the Royal Albert Hall, London, supporting The Bee Gees.

30 The Beatles hit the UK Number 1 slot again with Lady Madonna.

APRIL 68

2 The Beatles inaugurate a new publishing company, Python Music Ltd.

8 Grapefruit film a promo-clip for their upcoming single, Elevator, in Kensington Gardens, London, with Paul as director.

12 John and George are the last of The Beatles to leave the Maharishi Mahesh Yogi's Academy of Transcendental Meditation compound in Rishikesh, India.

16 The Beatles start yet another company, Apple Publicity.

17 George is filmed playing sitar with Ravi Shankar in Madras, India, for the documentary film Raga.

18 US record company Bell Records is launched in London, with John and Ringo among the guests.

20 Apple Records advertises in the UK music press, asking aspiring pop stars to send tapes to the company.

21 George arrives back in London from Madras.

MAY 68

5 Mary Hopkin, a young Welsh singer, appears on TV talent show Opportunity Knocks. She is seen by top model Twiggy, who will recommend her to Paul.

9 A meeting is held at Apple, with John and Ringo in attendance, to discuss the possibility of starting an Apple-funded school for children.

11 John and Paul fly to New York to launch Apple in the US (above).

12 In a Chinese junk sailing round the Statue Of Liberty, John and Paul hold a business meeting with the head of Apple Records in the US.

13 In the St Regis Hotel, New York, John and Paul give interviews to US media.

14 John and Paul hold a press conference in New York to announce the formation of Apple. McCartney again meets up with Linda Eastman, who gives him her telephone number.

Midsummer Madness

For photographer Tom Murray it was a dream come true… spending the day hanging out in London with The Beatles and documenting their "crazy" antics. By Lois Wilson.

Tom Murray got to shoot The Beatles quite by chance. Don McCullin may have been a renowned photojournalist and one of the most respected and revered war photographers in the world but when it came to shooting pop groups, he didn't have a clue. McCullin had a session lined up for July 28, 1968 and needed some assistance. Murray, then a photographer for The Sunday Times, got the call: "Don asked me if I fancied helping him out one Sunday as he wasn't sure about this band he'd been asked to cover. We arrived at a rehearsal studio and I heard Hey Jude coming out of it. As I walked through the door there was Paul McCartney sat at the piano playing the song. I couldn't believe my luck!"

Alongside McCullin, Murray was one of the select few people given carte blanche to snap The Beatles in 1968 – a year when they kept themselves away from photographers as much as possible.

"They were fed up of having pictures taken," remembers Murray, "so they decided to do one final day of what they called 'mad' photography. They hired Don to capture their antics in black and white and I was left to my own devices to shoot whatever I liked. It really was a dream come true."

Murray had landed his job at The Sunday Times on a recommendation by Lord Snowdon no less. "I'd been working for five years on the Zambia News And Times in Africa. When I returned to England I sent my portfolio to a few photographers – David Bailey, David Montgomery and the like, and Lord Snowdon was the only one who got back to me."

Since then Murray has snapped such luminaries as actress Anjelica Huston, director John Schlesinger and actors Michael York and Dustin Hoffman. He's also had a private audience with the Royal Family and is the youngest person ever to be commissioned by them.

"The Queen Mother was great," he recalls. "Because I looked like a little kid, my camera was bigger than I was, so she'd say, 'Let that young man to the front', and I always got the best shots." There was a downside to this however. "I did get chicken pox from Princess Margaret's kids. That'll teach me to get too close!"

Getting close to The Beatles, however, posed no such problems. "It really was a perfect day. Getting to hang out with one of my favourite bands and take pictures was sensational. Were they really mad? Well, you know what pop stars are like. They're always running around doing crazy things. That's what makes them so interesting."

◀ **THE BEATLES, ST PANCRAS OLD CHURCH PARK AND GARDENS**

"We were originally heading for Highgate cemetery but it was locked so we found this little park instead. It was an ideal location, the hollyhocks were in full bloom and the boys just ran into the flowerbeds and started to pull poses. It was indicative of the whole day. Just them jumping in their Mercedes Pullman and me in my Jag following them and stopping off wherever we fancied to take a picture. It was so off the cuff and relaxed – I think that shows in the pictures."

▶ **THE BEATLES WAPPING PIER HEAD**

"It was my suggestion to stop off at Wapping Pier Head. I thought the backdrop of the river, the cranes and the buildings made a perfect setting. We were in a very nice Georgian square, which is open at the dockside. The group had their own preconceived ideas as to what made a good photo and I just followed their lead and took the shot. John lay down and I took my opportunity. He thought it would make a good photo and he was right."

▲ **THE BEATLES
SWAIN'S LANE, HIGHGATE**

(Top) "We were driving along Swain's Lane when The Beatles stopped outside this house. They'd brought along some rosettes as a prop so I suggested they put them on so it looked like they were canvassing the area. They liked the concept, got out of the car and posed. I've no idea why they picked that house or whose house it was."

▲ **THE BEATLES
OLD STREET STATION ROOF**

(Above and left) "They're just play-acting. Paul really was falling off the edge of the roof and John was holding on to him. It was a sequence of four shots and took about an hour. I'd been following them in the car and lost them and I ended up going the wrong way down a one-way street at 80mph to catch up. The other shot (left) is the band pretending to be horses!"

▲ **PAUL**
ST JOHN'S WOOD

"This is one of my favourite pictures. It's such a fabulous profile of Paul. We were sitting in the dome of his house in St John's Wood. He'd locked all the others downstairs so we wouldn't be disturbed. The photo had to be cropped slightly because it got damaged on one side."

▶ **THE BEATLES**
ST KATHERINE'S DOCK

"John suddenly lay down and closed his eyes. I've no idea why he decided to pretend to be dead but it made a great photo. George immediately put his glasses on and Ringo felt his forehead. It literally took about three seconds in all. I really don't think they had rehearsed it beforehand. The band were getting on really well that day. I know it's reported at the time that they weren't but all I saw was four boys having a great time. Yoko was just out of shot and joining in with the japes too."

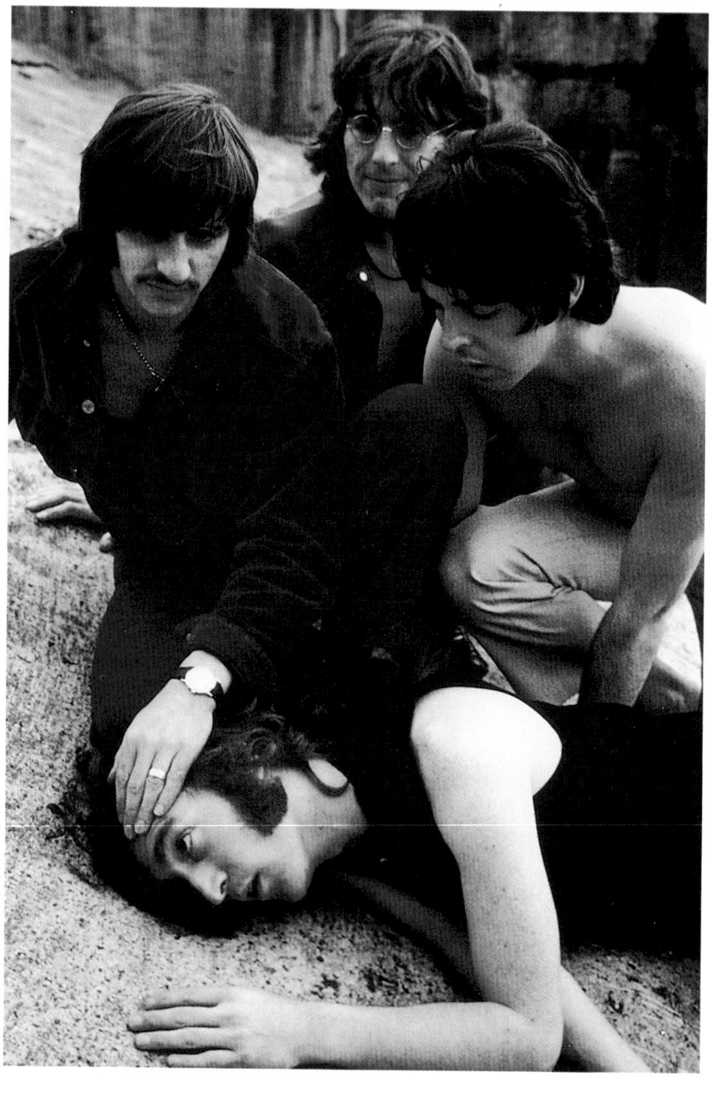

▲ **THE BEATLES ST KATHERINE'S DOCK**

"I just liked the shape of this photograph and the way they stood. I liked having George in the foreground. I was just trying to capture a split second, a moment. It's a nice contrast with the background and we had perfect light, which was fortunate, as I had no flash. It's like the perfect holiday snap. It captures the band's camaraderie."

◀ **PAUL, ST PANCRAS OLD CHURCH PARK AND GARDENS**

"Paul and I had a game. He'd check I was watching then pull some silly face or make a pose. I spent the whole day watching him like a hawk. When he realised I was taking a shot of him at the water fountain he sprayed the water out of his mouth at me. We were outside the park just having a breather. It was a tiring day."

PAUL
ST KATHERINE'S DOCK

"We were by the docks. Paul saw the chains, took his shirt, socks and shoes off and ran down to the water's edge. He looked round to check I was ready to capture the moment then wrapped himself in chains. The band got caught up in the whole excitement of the day and rushed from one location to the next pulling interesting poses. It helped that I'd turned up with just my Nikon F and two rolls of film. I didn't even have a flash with me. But being unprepared it made me think on my feet. There was no time to shoot reels and reels of film. I only had a split second to react and that made the better picture. It also meant that the boys didn't have to wait for me to set up each time. I just blended into the background."

▶ GEORGE
ST KATHERINE'S DOCK

"I knew this was going to be a fabulous picture when I took it. It just captures George perfectly. He really was the Quiet One. He didn't chit-chat but spent the whole day looking pensive. We're down by the Thames here and the light reflecting off the water was lovely. It's what we called a Kodak cloudy bright day. The sun was just peaking through the clouds. There's a slight blue tint to the photos and that's because they were shot on Kodak Ektachrome."

◀ PAUL, RINGO AND MARTHA
ST JOHN'S WOOD

"Paul was sat with his dog Martha in the dome in his back garden. When we pulled up outside his house there were seven or eight girls waiting by the door and when they saw all the boys turn up they went hysterical and started crying and screaming. Paul was the perfect host. He was very polite and made us a cup of tea and offered the biscuits around. He posed for this shot. It was just Paul, Ringo, the dog and myself in the room. All the others were in a different room and as the dog looked one way and Ringo the other, I snapped. I only took one or two frames. Why take 10 when one will do?"

16 John and Paul fly back into London from New York, where they were promoting Apple.

17 Ringo and his wife Maureen (above), with George and Patti, attend the Cannes Film Festival to watch the Wonderwall premiere, which boasts a George Harrison soundtrack.

19 John Lennon invites Yoko Ono to his home in Kenwood, Surrey, while his wife Cynthia is away on holiday.

21 Andy Williams plays at the Royal Albert Hall, London, with Paul in the audience.

22 A second Beatles-funded boutique, Apple Tailoring, is launched on the King's Road, Chelsea. George and John attend the opening.

23 Paul and Ringo are filmed in Abbey Road studios for an upcoming TV documentary entitled All My Loving.

26 Cynthia Lennon returns from a holiday in Greece and finds that Yoko Ono has moved into Kenwood, the home she shared with John in Weybridge.

30 The Beatles start work on what will become the double album, *The Beatles*, better known as the White Album. Yoko Ono is present in the studio.

31 Work continues in Abbey Road on John's song, Revolution 1.

JUNE 68

4 The Beatles continue work on Revolution 1 at Abbey Road.

5 Work starts on Ringo's composition Don't Pass Me By at Abbey Road.

6 John begins to compile the material that will form the basis for Revolution 9 at Abbey Road.

7 George and Ringo fly to LA where George is to make another appearance in Ravi Shankar's film Raga.

11 Paul McCartney records Blackbird at Abbey Road, London.

13 On their Californian visit, George and Ringo jam with David Crosby and Peter Asher at the Willow Glen, LA, home of The Monkees' Peter Tork.

15 The Beatles renounce the Maharishi as "a public mistake". John and Yoko stage an 'Acorn Event' in Coventry Cathedral, during which they plant acorns to symbolise the coming together of East and West.

16 Paul McCartney and Mary Hopkin are recorded at InterTel Studios, Wembley, for a David Frost TV special.

18 In His Own Write, a stage adaptation of John Lennon's book, opens in London.

19 John lunches with actor Victor Spinetti and Apple press officer Derek Taylor, to hold a post-mortem on the launch of In His Own Write.

What: John starts recording Revolution 9

Where: Abbey Road studios

When: May 30, 1968

THE MAGIC NUMBER

After John Lennon met Yoko Ono, his music changed. In fact, in some ways, Revolution 9 didn't even sound like music. By Mark Paytress.

REVOLUTION 9, THE PENULTIMATE track on the White Album, is the most unpopular piece of music The Beatles ever made. In many ways an apocalyptic response to the nursery-rhyme naivety of All You Need Is Love, this eight-minute-plus sonic collage managed to offend Paul and Ringo as much as it did many fans. To John Lennon, it marked a new beginning. "This is the music of the future," he claimed. "You can forget about all the rest of the shit we've done – this is it! Everybody will be making this stuff one day. You don't even have to know how to play a musical instrument to do it!"

The predicted deluge of musical miscreants never quite happened (few punk-era bands besides Throbbing Gristle sounded this peculiar), and even Lennon later rescinded his faith in avant-garde work of this sort. Despite this, Revolution 9 remains one of the most enduring – and relevant – recordings in The Beatles' catalogue. Providing a shop window for musical experimentation, it went where *Sgt Pepper* (and Paul McCartney – whose own sound-painting, Carnival Of Light was recorded a year earlier, but not released) feared to tread. Sounding as fresh as it did back in June 1968 when it was assembled, and as visceral as it is cerebral, Revolution 9 is music to put fire in your belly *and* light fires in your mind. The most extraordinary Beatles recording ever? Most definitely.

While the piece was Lennon's, from conception through to the final mixing and editing stages, Revolution 9 owed much to two key external influences: Yoko Ono, and the social disturbances that had flared up in the days before it was written. The source for such a radical departure in sound can be traced back to the night Lennon attended a preview of Ono's work in November 1966, and found himself atop a stepladder staring at a piece of paper fixed to the ceiling. Its message – 'Yes' – liberated him from his struggle with the avant-garde, which he'd regarded as "French for bullshit". After his relationship with Ono was consummated, creatively and physically, on the night of May 20, 1968, John Lennon was ready for anything.

Revolution 9 was, in many ways, an extension of the experimentation that had produced *Two Virgins*, the result of John and Yoko's cataclysmic union in the company of a tape-recorder and a battery of effects. But while that set, issued shortly after the White Album, had been throat-clearingly unfocused, Lennon's new piece resolutely pursued its theme. "I spent more time on Revolution 9 than I did on half the other songs I ever wrote," he remembered, adding that "it was an unconscious picture of what I think will happen when [a revolution] happens."

Surprisingly, perhaps, the piece began not at home but in the studio on the first day's sessions for what would become the White Album. The group had spent much of May 30, 1968, perfecting a new Lennon song, Revolution, his guarded response to the recent tide of political activity among the young. By take 18, the group stretched the song for 10 minutes, the last six "pure chaos", according to Beatles historian Mark Lewisohn. This provided the basis for Revolution 9, and more dramatically still, ushered in a new era in Beatles history. For amid the howl of feedback and Lennon's catatonic cries of "Alright!" was a new voice, Yoko Ono's, moaning and volunteering that infamous piece of ego-shedding wisdom, "You become naked".

Her presence marked a significant breach of Beatle etiquette, and though Lennon later jested that "she forced me to become avant-garde", it was obvious that he regarded her as his new musical collaborator. "Once I heard her stuff – not just the screeching and the howling but her word pieces, the talking and breathing and all this strange stuff – I thought, My God! I wanted to do one."

During June, Lennon – with more than a little help from his friend – amassed a number of tapes, from home and from EMI's archive at Abbey Road. On June 20, he constructed a series of tape loops from this raw material, which were fed into the original backing track and then mixed live. "Yoko was there for the whole thing, and she made decisions about the loops to use," Lennon happily admitted. Paul McCartney, meanwhile, was on a plane somewhere over the Atlantic.

Over 100 fragments lifted from classical and opera music, impromptu spoken-word asides from John, George and Yoko, and assorted 'found' sounds such as applause, gunfire and an oddly serene choir, can be heard on the recording. One particular extract, an effervescent male voice uttering, "Number nine", lifted from a Royal Academy Of Music examination tape, was utilised extensively and gave the piece its title. "I was born on 9 October. I lived at 9 Newcastle Road," Lennon later explained. "Nine seems to be my number so I've stuck with it… It's just a number that follows me around."

"I spent more time working on Revolution 9 than I did on half the other songs I ever wrote." John Lennon

Loop guru: Yoko Ono, the inspiration for Revolution 9.

By the early '70s, Lennon had dropped impressionistic music-making in favour of pointed political anthems, and he rejected the thinking behind the piece. "I thought I was painting in sound a picture of revolution, but I made a mistake," he insisted. "It was *anti*-revolution." Beatles scholar Ian MacDonald concurs, calling it "a revolution in the head". It's tempting to suggest that the real mistake is underplaying the connection between the piece's terror-filled sounds and the explosive atmosphere in which it was conceived, proof that Lennon was becoming an acute – if apocalyptic – observer of social change. Who's to say that his findings might not yet turn out to be prophetic?

PHOTOS: TOM HANLEY, RETNA, HULTON ARCHIVE

For reel: John Lennon, Abbey Road studios, 1968.

"Altogether now! We all live in a…": The Beatles, with Anita Pallenberg and Keith Richards (second row), 'enjoy' the Yellow Submarine premiere, London Pavilion, July 17, 1968.

What: Premiere of Yellow Submarine
Where: London Pavilion
When: July 17, 1968

BEATLES FOR SAIL

During the Summer of Love, every talented animator in town was press-ganged to bring the Fab Four to life for the big screen. By Jim Irvin.

CANADIAN GEORGE DUNNING, co-founder of small Soho animation house, TVC, had doubts about the offer to make a full-length cartoon feature for The Beatles. It came from Al Brodax, producer at King Features, the American company which had employed TVC to work on their Beatles TV series. George was worried that there wasn't much steam left in the frolicsome boys who'd peopled their cartoons. While the project was being discussed, George Martin invited him and TVC partner John Coates to Abbey Road to hear the album The Beatles had just completed. One listen to *Sgt Pepper's Lonely Hearts Club Band* was all it took to convince George of the project's viability.

Pepper tipped them off that this film could and should be more ambitious than anything they'd attempted before. The Beatles themselves expressed anxiety about the project. They didn't want a cartoon bearing their name to be twee or to smack of Disney. TVC agreed. Not that a Disney-scale production was an option. By the time the contracts had been signed, there were only 11 months left to complete the film – the night of the premiere had been booked for July 1968 – with a budget of $1million dollars, just £385,000.

Absorbed in *Sgt Pepper*, The Beatles had had no time to be involved in the film's genesis. Brodax's search for a suitable screenplay writer unearthed one Lee Minoff, whose main qualification for the job seemed to be that he was young and trendy. The Beatles met him and approved his ideas, but when his fairytale script was delivered it didn't have the groundbreaking feel or the kind of humour everyone was expecting. Subsequently, around 40 writers contributed to the script. Among them was Liverpool poet Roger McGough, a colleague of McCartney's brother Mike in The Scaffold, who was hired to provide credible Liverpudlian dialogue.

The producer reckons about 13 babies were conceived during the making of Yellow Submarine.

Brodax then approached Erich Segal, a young American classics professor, to be script doctor. At the time, Segal was working with composer Richard Rogers and would go on to write the hit film, Love Story. However, he wasn't particularly conversant with The Beatles and didn't want the job. Brodax informed him that *Sgt Pepper* had just sold three million copies. "I said Mrs Pepper must be very happy," recalls Segal. Brodax thought this hilarious. "That's John Lennon's humour! You got the gig." A final script wouldn't be assembled until the film was complete, a few days before the premiere.

Meanwhile, TVC began work anyway. Dunning was the director, Coates was producer and a team of Britain's best animation directors was hired to tackle separate sequences – the concept of animations for various songs being linked by a storyline having already been established. Work began on some of the musical numbers, but the appearance of The Beatles themselves hadn't been finalised.

Special effects director Charlie Jenkins suggested calling Heinz Edelmann, the gifted Czech art director on trendy German magazine Twen. TVC told Edelmann they needed to see some ideas for how The Beatles' cartoon selves would look. A week later, a package arrived stuffed with drawings that stunned them. Recognisably the Fabs, the figures perfectly captured the spirit of the time with their vivid colours and soft, balloonish graphics.

A few weeks into production, Brian Epstein died. The Beatles withdrew and were unavailable to provide the voice-track the animators needed to begin shooting group scenes. TVC found actors who could simulate their voices. Among them was Geoffrey Hughes, later famous as Eddie Yates in Coronation Street, who played McCartney. Casting Harrison proved harder until Dunning heard a young Liverpudlian man at the bar of TVC's local pub. The mysterious Peter Batten accepted the job of voicing George and hung around the production until some military police turned up and arrested him for desertion from the army.

Almost every young animator in London was employed on the film. TVC's Dean Street offices held only 40 people, and more space was found in Soho Square to accommodate all the tracers, colourists and background artists. A special nightshift of cel painters was bussed in from London's art schools; an extra 160 people. Such a concentration of bright young things in the Summer of Love had inevitable results. John Coates reckons about 13 babies were conceived during the making of Yellow Submarine.

The interest of The Beatles themselves grew as they saw the quality of the rushes and agreed to be filmed for the closing sequence. However, the last of their contracted four new songs was delivered late. The Hey Bulldog sequence was shot in the final weeks of production (after the UK premiere it was decided that the ending dragged and the slapstick Bulldog sequence, the closest in spirit to the TV series, was removed before the US premiere, consequently baffling purchasers of the soundtrack album).

Perhaps its psychedelic mood already seemed dated by July 1968, perhaps United Artists' marketing of the film as a children's cartoon was misguided. Whatever, the film was not a great success in Britain. But a few decades' hindsight has allowed its value as a delightful document of the year it was conceived to shine through.

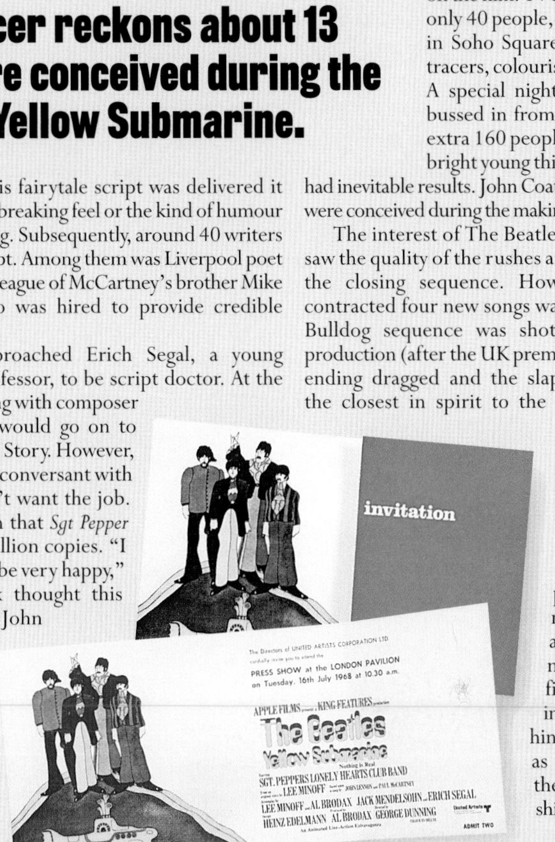

PHOTO: REX/LFI

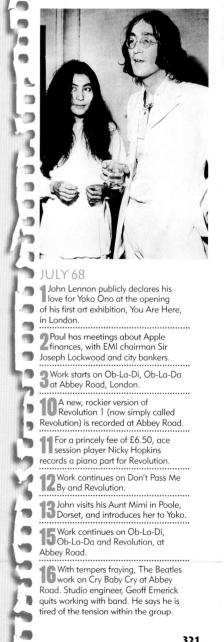

20 Paul flies to Los Angeles on Apple business.

21 John finishes work on Revolution 1 at Abbey Road. Paul announces to a Capitol Records sales conference in LA that all future Beatles records will appear on Apple, although the group are still technically on EMI/Capitol.

22 The Beatles purchase a house at 3 Savile Row, London, for around £500,000. It will become the headquarters of their Apple organisation.

24 Outside his Los Angeles hotel, Paul busks his way through several new Beatles songs much to the delight of a group of fans.

25 George works on the Jackie Lomax song, Sour Milk Sea, at Abbey Road.

26 Work commences on Everybody's Got Something To Hide Except Me And My Monkey, at Abbey Road.

27 Work continues on Everybody's Got Something To Hide Except Me And My Monkey, at Abbey Road.

28 The Beatles record Good Night at Abbey Road.

30 On his way home from Bradford, where he has been recording with the Black Dyke Mills Band, Paul stops in the village of Harrold, Bedfordshire, and entertains patrons in the local pub by singing and playing the piano.

JULY 68

1 John Lennon publicly declares his love for Yoko Ono at the opening of his first art exhibition, You Are Here, in London.

2 Paul has meetings about Apple finances, with EMI chairman Sir Joseph Lockwood and city bankers.

3 Work starts on Ob-La-Di, Ob-La-Da at Abbey Road, London.

10 A new, rockier version of Revolution 1 (now simply called Revolution) is recorded at Abbey Road.

11 For a princely fee of £6.50, ace session player Nicky Hopkins records a piano part for Revolution.

12 Work continues on Don't Pass Me By and Revolution.

13 John visits his Aunt Mimi in Poole, Dorset, and introduces her to Yoko.

15 Work continues on Ob-La-Di, Ob-La-Da and Revolution, at Abbey Road.

16 With tempers fraying, The Beatles work on Cry Baby Cry at Abbey Road. Studio engineer, Geoff Emerick quits working with band. He says he is tired of the tension within the group.

17 With John, Paul and George in attendance, Yellow Submarine premieres at the Pavilion in London. Other guests include Mick Jagger, Donovan, Sandie Shaw, Twiggy, PJ Proby, Clem Curtis of the Foundations and Tony Blackburn.

18 The Beatles begin recording Helter Skelter in Abbey Road.

19 Recording of Sexy Sadie begins in Abbey Road.

20 Jane Asher announces that her engagement to Paul is off.

22 Don't Pass Me By is completed at Abbey Road.

24 Work on Sexy Sadie continues at Abbey Road.

26 John and Paul complete the writing of Hey Jude at Paul's house in St John's Wood, London.

28 The Beatles have an all-day photo-shoot around London with war photographer Don McCullin.

29 Work begins on Hey Jude at Abbey Road.

31 When The Beatles close their unsuccessful Apple Boutique, giving everything away to passers-by, the last item to go is a naked female dummy labelled 'For the attention of John Lennon'. While working on Hey Jude, The Beatles move to Trident Studios, St Anne's Court, London, for the first time. The bill for use of the studio between 2pm and 4am is £416.

AUGUST 68

1 Work on Hey Jude continues in Trident Studios, London.

3 Paul spends the evening at the Revolution Club, London, with his new girlfriend, Francie Schwartz.

4 The film Yellow Submarine goes on general release in the UK.

6 John attends a fashion show at London's Revolution Club where he is interviewed for BBC Radio show Late Night Extra.

7 In Abbey Road, work continues on George Harrison's song Not Guilty, which will never be released as a completed track.

8 In Abbey Road, mixing sessions are held for Hey Jude and Revolution.

9 Paul starts work on Mother Nature's Son in Abbey Road.

10 Paul is interviewed by Alan Smith of NME.

11 The Beatles launch Apple Records and declare National Apple Week.

What: Apple shop closes down
Where: 94 Baker Street
When: July 31, 1968

THE FABS SELL OUT

When the Apple shop had finally cost The Beatles too much money, they threw the mother of all closing-down sales. By Bill DeMain.

AND IN THE END, THEY EVEN TRIED TO take the carpet. The ravenous mob who tore through the Apple shop on July 31, 1968, had snatched up everything else, from psychedelic frocks and inflatable chairs to store fixtures and hangers. The prices were certainly right. The Beatles had decided to abruptly end their eight-month experiment in retail with an everything-is-free blowout.

"We came into shops by the tradesman's entrance but we're leaving by the front door," the group said in a press statement. "I suppose what we're really doing is spring cleaning in mid-summer. The amazing thing is our giving things away. Well, it was much funnier to give things away."

Funnier perhaps, but with all the £10,000 of merchandise given away fully subjected to British tax law, this was but the last in a series of whimsical decisions that brought down what Paul McCartney had dubbed the "beautiful place where you can buy beautiful things".

Why did The Beatles open a shop in the first place? It was partly on the recommendation of their accountants. By investing in related businesses, the boys could ease their tax situation. But more than that, they wanted to share their Pepperland-ish sense of style with the world.

"We were all very much like a clique, the people who were *aware*," says Jenny Boyd, who was a salesgirl at the boutique and younger sister to George's wife Patti. "Part of that awareness did have something to do with smoking pot and trying mind-expanding drugs. There was a real feeling of fellowship and camaraderie and it felt like it was us and *them*. When The Beatles opened the boutique it was about making that available – some of the fun and the stuff that we'd experienced – to them."

A Dutch quartet known as The Fool, who'd impressed the Fabs by painting trippy designs on John's piano and dressing the band's wives and girlfriends in a kind of Middle Earth chic, was given £100,000 to produce an exclusive line of garments and accessories (that the hippy artistes' previous shop in Amsterdam, The Trend, had gone belly up because of extravagant overspending didn't seem to worry anyone at Apple).

To set the boutique apart, The Fool covered the entire face of 94 Baker Street with a psychedelic mural, finished in time for the opening night party on December 5, 1967. The mural – a three-storey bearded mystic floating among moons and stars – defied a warning from Westminster City Council and angered conservative neighbours, who petitioned and had it removed within the month.

"Trying to influence people and doing things like painting the Apple shop was all just part of the Teddy boy in us," recalled George in Anthology. "The Teddy boy theme of 'We'll show them'… Once we were told to get rid of the painting, the whole thing started to lose its appeal."

From the beginning, the shop was a money pit. Simon Posthuma of The Fool went on a buying trip to Morocco that turned into an expensive opium holiday, with most of what he purchased later "lost in the post". He also insisted, against the protests of store manager Pete Shotton, on having pure silk labels woven into all Apple clothing. According to Shotton's book, John Lennon: In My Life, when Pete complained to his old Liverpool mate, the response was, "'Oh, just do it the way he wants. We're not business freaks, we're artists… If we don't make any money, what does it fucking matter?'"

"No, it's mine!" Two rozzers argue over an Apple handbag.

Then there was the shoplifting. Not only did The Fool have to be continually reprimanded for skimming choice items for themselves (they eventually fell out with The Beatles and moved to America to become a singing group), but every day customers were taking advantage of the shop's lack of supervision to help themselves.

Jenny Boyd, who today works for the Cottonwood rehab treatment centre in Tucson, Arizona, recalls with a chuckle, "I wouldn't have got into that bit *[shoplifting]*. I was definitely a sort of flower child. I was interested in talking to people and trying to convert them. There was a good friend of mine called Amos who worked there, and Amos and I would find a little bit of hash most days and put it in a cup of tea, and just really enjoy the day."

"We're not business freaks, we're artists. If we don't make any money, what does it matter?" John Lennon

By June 1968, the boutique had lost over £200,000. When a newspaper column criticised The Beatles for having turned into shopkeepers, that was the last straw. John and Paul decided to liquidate. But not before the band had their way with the stock the night before (according to Peter Brown in The Love You Make, it was Yoko who grabbed the most, carrying a huge bundle that made her look like an "Oriental Santa Claus").

At the closing, the police did finally prevent the mob from prying up the carpet. The next week, the whited-out shop windows became an advertisement for The Beatles' single of Hey Jude and Revolution. For Apple, it was on to 3 Savile Row and equally money-draining ventures.

If the whole boutique episode seems hard to fathom today, with pop groups being ultra-business-savvy and corporate sponsored, Boyd puts it in perspective: "We felt that anything was possible. We believed in magic. We were so gullible, but in a lovely way."

PHOTOS: HULTON ARCHIVE, CAMERA PRESS, VIN MAG ARCHIVE

Core values: crowds queue for some Apple shop goodies, 94 Baker St, July 31, 1968.

Julian Lennon: "Paul and I used to hang out a bit – more than dad and I did." McCartney and 'Jules' on holiday in Greece, 1967.

What: The Beatles record Hey Jude
Where: Trident Studios, London
When: July 31, 1968

HERE COMES THE SON

Despite clocking in at over seven minutes in length, Hey Jude became The Beatles' biggest selling single of their career. By Chris Hunt.

IN LATE JULY 1968, WITH WORK ON THE White Album well underway, Paul McCartney sidetracked The Beatles with the recording of what he intended to be the band's next single. Written the previous month while driving to Surrey to visit freshly estranged Cynthia Lennon, the song was inspired by Paul's sudden feelings of sympathy for the children of divorce, more specifically by the plight of his songwriting partner's five-year-old son, Julian. McCartney later switched 'Jules' for 'Jude', because it "sounded a bit better", but other than that the song arrived with all its basic elements in situ.

In the month between writing and recording, with the song in need of just a little refinement, McCartney opted to test his latest composition on anyone too polite to refuse. And that meant *everyone*. The Bonzos recall Paul bashing through Hey Jude when he should have been hard at work producing I'm The Urban Spaceman. "He was just enjoying singing and playing it, like you do when you first write a song," recalls Neil Innes. "You want to go through it in public to see if there might be something else in there. It was at that demo stage." The Barron Knights, too, remember the Beatle interrupting their session at Abbey Road: "He said, 'I've just written this song, would you like to hear it, it's hopefully going to be our next single'," says Pete Langford. "He actually forgot the words too." Badfinger, meanwhile, were treated to a performance just the day after they signed to Apple as The Iveys. "Paul walked over to the grand piano and said, 'Hey lads, have a listen'," remembered bass player Ron Griffith. "He sat down and gave us a full concert rendition of Hey Jude. We were gobsmacked."

With his ad hoc market research complete and the recording just a weekend away, McCartney spent a day polishing the song with Lennon, whose enthusiasm for the lyric far outweighed Paul's own uncertainties. After a two-day test run at Abbey Road, The Beatles relocated to the eight-track luxury of Trident Studios. With the basic rolling rhythm track nailed in just four takes, a 36-piece orchestra was ordered to flesh-out McCartney's grand vision, the musicians not only asked to play their simple scored parts, but to down instruments and contribute to the singalong extended coda – clapping too, if they would be so kind. For a double fee all but one happily obliged.

EMI studio engineer Ken Scott had worked on the song's initial run through at Abbey Road but hadn't heard it again until the mix. In the thoroughly modern surrounds of Trident, through the loudest monitoring system he had experienced, Scott was "absolutely blown away". But back at Abbey Road, while observing the tapes being transferred to acetate, something began to trouble him. "There was no high end on it, the sound muddy," he thought, confiding as much to George Martin. Minutes later, the first Beatle arrived. "Ken thinks it sounds like shit," was Martin's greeting. After a few tense moments The Beatles concurred and the remainder of the session was spent fixing the track to everyone's satisfaction. Except, of course, for a pretty obvious expletive – "fucking hell" – uttered by Lennon and hidden in the bridge to the extended ending, but completely audible if you had the ears to spot it.

"I was told about it at the time but could never hear it," says Ken Scott. "But once I'd had it pointed out I can't miss it now. I have a sneaking suspicion they knew all along, as it was a track that should have been pulled out in the mix. I would imagine it was one of those things that happened – it was a mistake, they listened to it and thought, 'doesn't matter, it's fine'."

Lennon, not always the first to praise a McCartney tune, pronounced it the best song his partner had ever written. His judgement may well have been coloured by the fact he mistook the lyric for McCartney's tacit approval of his relationship with Yoko Ono, but he still didn't plan to let the song get in the way of a prize much coveted – the A-side of the first release on Apple.

Despite its epic proportions, McCartney had always viewed Hey Jude as a single, but it still had to pass The Beatles' stringent in-house quality control test, to be rated worthy of release by the remaining Fabs. Lennon was doggedly fighting the corner of Revolution, but with Harrison, Starr and George Martin siding with the more obvious commercial appeal of Hey Jude, the McCartney song got the nod.

Lennon, not always the first to praise McCartney, pronounced it the best song his partner had ever written.

"And this is a G..." John and Julian do a spot of bonding.

Hey Jude went on to become The Beatles' biggest selling single, topping the charts in 11 countries and selling 7.5 million copies. But while the world has spent decades celebrating the reassuring emotional clarity of this monumentally uplifting song, it wasn't until 1987 that Julian and Paul, after a chance meeting in a New York hotel, discussed it for the first time. "He told me that he'd been thinking about my circumstances all those years ago, about what I was going through," says Julian. "Paul and I used to hang out a bit – more than dad and I did. We had a great friendship going and there seem to be far more pictures of me and Paul playing together at that age than there are pictures of me and dad."

Indeed, when McCartney's scribbled recording notes for the song came up for auction in 1996, it transpired that Julian Lennon was the anonymous bidder who paid £25,000 to secure what, along with some of his father's former possessions, he described as "family heirlooms". McCartney, too, has never forgotten the inspiration for The Beatles' most successful single. "Every birthday and every Christmas, he sends a card," says Julian. "He's never missed. I find that amazing."

PHOTOS: HULTON ARCHIVE, CAMERA PRESS, REX

12 In Abbey Road studios, work continues on vocals for George Harrison's song Not Guilty.

13 In Abbey Road, work continues on Sexy Sadie and Yer Blues.

14 In Abbey Road, work continues on What's The New Mary Jane and Yer Blues.

15 In Abbey Road, work starts on Rocky Raccoon.

16 In Abbey Road, work continues on George Harrison's song While My Guitar Gently Weeps.

17 Publishers McGraw-Hill rush Hunter Davies' biography of The Beatles to bookshops ahead of schedule to prevent loss of sales to Julian Fast's unauthorised The Beatles: The Real Story (left). Fast admits to never having met Lennon, McCartney, Harrison or Starr.

20 With George Harrison having left for a visit to Greece, the other three Beatles are in Abbey Road. John and Ringo are in Studio 3 completing Yer Blues. Paul is in Studio 2 working on Mother Nature's Son and Wild Honey Pie. When John and Ringo visit Paul, the atmosphere is strained.

21 Sexy Sadie is completed at Abbey Road.

22 Ringo quits The Beatles in the middle of an Abbey Road recording session. After his departure, the others record Back In The USSR with Paul on drums. Meanwhile, John is sued for divorce by Cynthia on the grounds of his adultery with Yoko.

23 The Beatles, minus Ringo, are in Abbey Road, completing Back In The USSR.

24 John Lennon and Yoko Ono are interviewed live on David Frost's UK television programme Frost On Saturday (below), which broadcasts from Wembley.

26 Apple Records release their first four singles, including Hey Jude by The Beatles and Those Were The Days by Mary Hopkin.

27 On a visit home, Paul goes to see Liverpool play Everton.

28 The Beatles, minus Ringo, are in Trident Studios, London, working on Dear Prudence.

29 The Beatles, minus Ringo, are in Trident Studios, London, overdubbing vocals, handclaps, tambourine, piano, and flugelhorn onto John Lennon's song Dear Prudence.

30 The completed Dear Prudence is mixed. Paul attends the wedding of Beatles staffer, Neil Aspinall, in Chelsea. The single, Sour Milk Sea, which was produced by George, is released in the UK.

WE ARE NOT AMUSED!

CRUEL BRITANNIA

For years The Beatles had been the darlings of the British establishment. Then in 1968, "The Man" started to turn on them. By John Harris.

Help! may be The Beatles movie in which, to use John Lennon's words, the group became "extras in their own film", but some of its scenes act as neat encapsulations of the strange point at which they had arrived circa 1965. Harried by Leo McKern's sacrificial sect, the Fabs are soon afforded the highest level of protection by the British state, whose representatives eventually decide to billet them to the most secure quarters imaginable: Buckingham Palace.

Although the episodes in question were actually filmed in Cliveden (the Home Counties seat at which John Profumo had first made the acquaintance of Christine Keeler), the scenario would soon be replayed for real, when The Beatles were ushered into the Palace to be awarded their MBEs. In the movie, one of the tensions implied by such a turn of events becomes obvious: as evidenced by the bleary-eyed recital of their lines – and, in the Anthology videos, admissions of multiple retakes – The Beatles were stoned out of their minds. That they have long been alleged to have repeated the trick during the official trip to Buck House only reinforces the point: though the British establishment was still fond of The Beatles, they were indulging in habits that would soon drive a wedge between the group and their more haughty associates.

For the moment, this most fragile of relationships remained intact. Their investiture was the climax of two years during which the social stratum then known as "The Ruling Class" had recurrently expressed the view that The Beatles were probably A Good Thing: Prince Philip was heard to mention that he considered The Beatles to be "good blokes"; Field Marshal Montgomery expressed the wish to invite them to his home for the weekend "to see what kind of fellows they are". Politicians queued up to try and grab some reflected glory: though Harold Wilson was the most successful candidate, the scramble for electorally useful Fabness had actually been started by the Conservatives' Bill Deedes. The British press, meanwhile, recurrently hailed The Beatles as the vanguard of a social change that seemed to suggest nothing more threatening than an upsurge of funny haircuts and skyrocketing consumer spending.

However, by 1966, it was starting to become clear that The Beatles perhaps represented something a little more unwelcome. In both Britain and the USA, the same young people whose worlds had been lit up by The Beatles' success were moulding a belief in personal freedom, an appetite for recreational drugs and hostility to authority into what we now know as "the counter-culture". As evidenced by much of their music, The Beatles were keenly aware of such developments, and subtly aligned themselves accordingly. Rain amounts to John Lennon's dazed acknowledgement of the divide between groovers and squares; in Love You To, George Harrison bemoans "people standing round/Who'll screw you in the ground/They'll fill you in with all the sins you'll see".

In 1971, John Lennon looked back on the schizoid existence The Beatles were consequently forced to endure. Though their minds were being galvanised by psychedelics, their music was being pushed into experimental places, and their worldview was more riven than ever by an Us/Them division, they were still occasionally forced to share the company of the squarest people on earth: politicians, royalty, police chiefs. ➳

They're out to get us, part 2: Patti and George leave Esher and Walton Magistrates' Court, March 31, 1969, convicted of cannabis possession.

They're out to get us, part 1: John and Yoko leave Marylebone Magistrates' Court, charged with cannabis possession, October 19, 1968.

"FOR ONE OF THE BEATLES TO GET BUSTED WAS VERY SERIOUS BECAUSE THEY WERE USED TO BEING UNTOUCHABLE. NOW THINGS WERE GOING WRONG." DEREK TAYLOR

"I was very miserable," he said. "At first, we had some sort of objective, like being as big as Elvis. Moving forward was the great thing, but actually attaining it was the big letdown. I found I was continually having to please the kind of people I'd always hated when I was a child."

The tensions between The Beatles' self-image and the company they were forced to keep were usually smoothed over by Brian Epstein – but by 1966, even his emollient presence couldn't work its usual wonders: in retrospect, John's claim that the group had become bigger than Jesus was a clumsily-worded attempt to finally achieve the kind of public honesty that he had long been denied. In 1967, with the counter-culture at its zenith and Brian ailing, things only became more fractious: when, in June of that year, Paul informed Life magazine that he had taken LSD, he prompted exactly the kind of furore that Epstein had long managed to avoid. In the wake of Brian's death, one of the consequences of his sudden absence from The Beatles' lives became obvious: from now on, The Beatles camp would not be nearly as worried about the views of the rich and powerful.

By then, of course, they had heralded a new phase of their lives by starting their relationship with Maharishi Mahesh Yogi – exactly the kind of figure who might convince The Beatles' one-time admirers within the establishment that the group's lives had taken a rum turn. In September 1967, the Queen held a reception at Buckingham Palace for the Council Of Knights Bachelor, whose number included Sir Joseph Lockwood, the Chairman of EMI. When the latter caught Her Majesty's eye, she uttered eight withering words: "The Beatles are turning awfully *funny*, aren't they?"

The Queen seems to have been simply bamboozled. However, by the end of 1968, it had become obvious that some sections of the British state were turning horribly hostile. If Help! had found the establishment allowing The Beatles to shelter from a crowd of exotic oddballs, three years later, the scenario was well on the way to being completely reversed.

In the mid '60s, British popular culture had been underpinned by a surprising level of generational harmony. Even the demonisation of The Rolling Stones usually saw them portrayed as little more threatening than a gang of pantomime villains; for the most part, the new innovation of globally successful British rock music was successfully incorporated into the patchwork of UK showbiz. Tours were promoted by the Arthur Howes Organisation; songs were published by middle-aged men with offices on Denmark Street; the popular press gleefully championed the new crop of groups in the knowledge that they would assist circulation figures. The Beatles were all this in excelsis: happy to do the rounds of provincial Gaumonts and Odeons, contractually bound to the likes of Dick James, on good terms with the journalists who enjoyed their hospitality.

In 1967, however, all this began to unravel. Musicians were increasingly surrounded by strange aromas, wrapped in freakish clothes, and in implied revolt against showbiz etiquette. The Daily Mail's response to *Sgt Pepper* hinted at a new unease: "What's happened to The Beatles? It's now around four years since they happened, and since the early days of 1963, The Beatles have changed completely. They rose as heroes of a social

PHOTOS: HULTON ARCHIVE, MARY EVANS LIBRARY

revolution. They were everybody's next door neighbours; the boys whom everybody could identify with. Now, four years later, they have isolated themselves, not only personally, but also musically. They have become contemplative, secretive, exclusive and excluded." The Mail's problem, it seemed, was that The Beatles had ceased to be everymen: they were now proudly placed in the elite of London's counter-culture, and were thus the focus of a mixture of envy, bafflement and suspicion.

In early 1967, Paul McCartney, ever the group's diplomat, attempted to sound a note of generational détente. "I really wish the people that look in anger at the weirdos, the happenings and the psychedelic freak-out, would just look with nothing, with no feeling, and be unbiased about it," he implored. "They really don't realise that what these people are talking about is something that they really want themselves. It's something that everyone wants… it's the personal freedom to be able to talk and be able to say things, and it's dead straight. It's a real sort of basic pleasure for everyone, but it looks weird from the outside."

Not entirely surprisingly, those who thought that Britain might be about to fall victim to a new degenerate menace were not convinced. Paul's own admission of LSD use, which crash-landed in the headlines in the wake of *Sgt Pepper*'s release, must have increased their ire yet further – and if some of the UK's more conservative elements were soon calling for counter-cultural scalps, by the end of the summer, they would be satisfied. The police raid of Keith Richards' Sussex home, which led in turn to the brief imprisonment of both him and Mick Jagger, marked a watershed for those who wanted rid of rock groups and their degenerate habits, and the musicians themselves. Suddenly, the Alice-In-Wonderland worldview of English psychedelia looked laughably irrelevant: as the Stones' experience proved, there was a war on.

Stones lore has long held that, though George Harrison was one of Richards' house-guests, he received a tip-off about the bust and therefore cut short his visit. The truth, it seems, is more innocent: George and Patti simply decided to go home. Whatever, in the wake of the Stones' arrest, prosecution and imprisonment, The Beatles rallied to their cause: by way of support, John and Paul added their vocals to the Stones' single, We Love You, and The Beatles' rhetoric was now infused with a new anti-establishment anger.

From now on, Lennon would recurrently voice the kind of sentiments that had always been ruled out during The Beatles' apolitical mop-top years.

In July, the band travelled to Greece, to investigate buying a small island; just before they left, John was asked about his take on the country's authoritarian regime. "I'm not worried about the political situation in Greece, as long as it doesn't affect ⋙

PHOTO: TOPFOTO

us," he shot back. "I don't care if the government is all fascist, or communist. They're all as bad as here – worse, most of them. I've seen England and the USA, and I don't care for either of their governments. They're all the same. Look at what they do here: they stopped Radio Caroline and tried to put the Stones away while they're spending billions on nuclear armaments and the place is full of US bases that no-one knows about."

If sections of the establishment were likely to respond to such words by doing their best to put The Beatles back in their place, one factor stood in their way. For all the signs that the group were sailing away from the mainstream, The Beatles seemed as infallible as ever: success, for the moment, proved to be a potent deterrent to any hostility. All that changed however, with the deluge of criticism heaped on to the Magical Mystery Tour movie. "The bigger they are, the harder they fall," said The Daily Express's James Thomas. "The whole boring saga confirmed a long-held suspicion of mine that The Beatles are four rather pleasant young men who have made so much money that they can apparently afford to be contemptuous of the public."

"Whoever authorised the showing of the film on BBC1 should be condemned to a year squatting at the feet of the Maharishi Mahesh Yogi," said The Daily Sketch. Suddenly, it seemed, The Beatles were no longer the nation's favourites: placed in the same odious bracket as – to use Paul's words – the weirdos, the happenings and the psychedelic freak-out, they seemed newly vulnerable. By way of adding their voice to the anti-Beatle chorus, the BBC swiftly banned I Am The Walrus, for both the line, "Boy you been a naughty girl, you let your knickers down" and its supposedly euphemistic reference to "yellow matter custard".

However, the group were hardly contrite.

"I thought John's line about taking her knickers down in I Am The Walrus was great," said George. "Why can't we have people fucking as well? It's going on everywhere, all the time. So why can't you mention it? It's just a word. Keep saying it – fuck, fuck, fuck, fuck. See – it doesn't mean a thing, so why can't you use it in a song? We will eventually. We haven't started yet."

"Room service, we seem to be missing our Gideon Bible..." the Amsterdam Bed-In, Hilton hotel, March 27, 1969.

Get sack: John and Yoko explain Bagism to the nation on Thames TV's Today programme, April 1, 1969.

Carry on campaigning: John and Yoko support James Hanratty's parents, 1969.

JOHN LENNON NOW VOICED THE KIND OF SENTIMENTS THAT HAD ALWAYS BEEN RULED OUT DURING HIS APOLITICAL MOP-TOP YEARS.

The last sentence seemed to imply that, if Magical Mystery Tour had sent Britain's squares into a fit of pique, the group might be about to annoy them all the more – and with the entry into The Beatles' world of Yoko Ono, their tempers became very frayed indeed.

In the wake of The Beatles' return from India, Yoko Ono's introduction to the British public was couched in terms that were bound to antagonise. Firstly, her relationship with John was bound up with such taboos as marital breakdown and imminent divorce: when the couple arrived at the opening night of the staging of In His Own Write in June 1968, journalists greeted John with a distinctly moralistic challenge – "Where's your wife?" Inflaming the hostility yet further, the couple went on to announce their bond via the age-old British bugbear of avant-garde art. To cap it all, Yoko was Japanese. The hardcore disciples who trailed The Beatles around London regaled her with such affectionate words as "Chink" and "yellow"; sections of the press, though their vocabulary was a little more measured, seemed hardly more friendly.

Not that John and Yoko were in any mood to tone their public activities down. Over the summer of 1968, they came up with an enterprise that would cause a very British upsurge of puzzlement and anger: *Two Virgins*, the borderline unlistenable result of their first joint creative endeavours, which was wrapped in a monochrome shot of the couple *sans* clothes. The sleeve was duly delivered to the office of Sir Joseph Lockwood, who later recalled his displeasure. "What on earth do you want to do it for? I asked them. Yoko said, 'It's art'. In that case, I said, Why not show Paul in the nude? He's so much better-looking. Or why not use a statue from one of the parks?" In the end, *Two Virgins* became the first work by a Beatle to appear on a label not owned by EMI: in the US, it appeared on an obscure imprint called Tetragrammaton, while British copies were pressed up by The Who's label, Track.

In The Beatles' own reading of their history, *Two Virgins* marked the point at which, as far as the UK's authorities were concerned, open season was declared on John and Yoko. "I knew it [the sleeve] was shocking,"

PHOTOS: HULTON ARCHIVE, LFI

Paul McCartney later reflected, "but I'm not sure whether us lot were too shocked by it – we just knew he'd have a lot of flak. Obviously, the minute the newspapers saw that, they were going to be on the phone. I knew John was inviting a lot of that. In the end, he'd invited a lot more than they wanted and they started to get busted and things. Quite an oppressive campaign started against them and it probably began with that cover."

In fact, John and Yoko were busted just over a month before the album appeared, though the fact that the resultant case came to court one day before *Two Virgin*'s release ties both events together in a pivotal moment: essentially, the point at which the establishment blackballed John Lennon once and for all. "For one of The Beatles to get busted was very, very serious because they were more or less used to being untouchable… and now things were going wrong," Derek Taylor later recalled.

The bust was the work of a five-man squad led by Detective Sergeant Norman Pilcher, a puritanical figure with an apparent mission to fine, imprison and therefore crush the morale of London's most notable musicians, whose actions also seemed to be indicative of a new establishment antipathy towards The Beatles. "I guess they didn't like the way the image was looking," John later reflected. "The Beatles thing was over: no need to protect us for being soft and cuddly, so bust us! That's what happened." On account of the apparent discovery of one and a half ounces of cannabis, John was fined £150 and ordered to pay 20 guineas costs, though the experience perhaps exacted an even graver toll: as John's solicitor told the court, in the wake of the police raid, Yoko had suffered a miscarriage.

Looking back, it seems truly remarkable that in response to such events, The Beatles' music did not seem to take on any sense of radical anger. Late 1968 saw the release of the Stones' Street Fighting Man: a tribute to the student revolts of that spring and summer that derived much of its force from their experiences the previous year. For all their public rhetoric, The Beatles' songs, by contrast, seemed to speak the language of peace and goodwill. Notwithstanding John's rather lame "Count me out/in" addition to Revolution, it still stands as a song of pacifist liberalism rather than politicised aggression; *Abbey Road* and *Let It Be* are festooned with words – on such songs as The End, Because, Two Of Us and Dig A Pony – that emphasise such abiding themes as nostalgia, redemption, individual transcendence and the universal potency of love. Even when backed into a corner, The Beatles carried on smiling at their foes.

In 1969, unfortunately, the sense that they were experiencing the wrath of the establishment was hardly diminished. In March, Sergeant Pilcher performed his second Beatle bust, raiding the home of George and Patti on the day that Paul married Linda. The police – seemingly believing that the kind of people who smoked cannabis were also chronically untidy – claimed to have found a large block of dope lying on a carpet. "I'm a tidy person," said George. "I keep my socks in the sock drawer and my hash in the hash box. It's not mine." Two decades later, he was in little doubt as to what had inspired the bust. "We were outspoken, " he said, "and the Cromwell figures in the establishment were trying to get their own back on us." Pilcher, at least, would eventually get his just desserts: in 1972, he was jailed for four years after being found guilty of conspiracy to pervert the course of justice and sentenced to four years in prison.

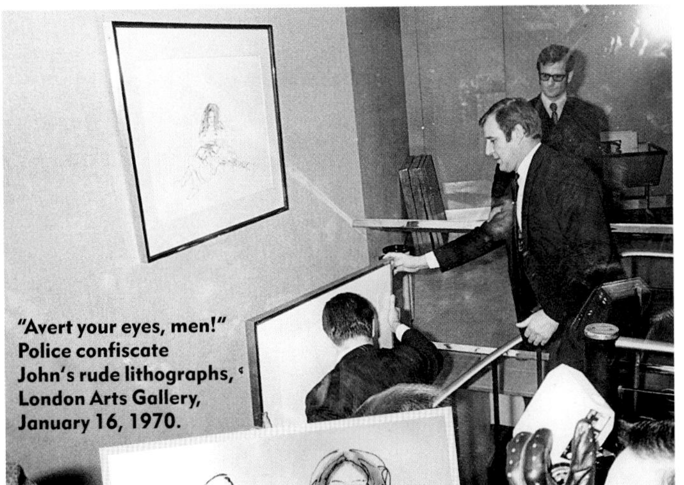

"Avert your eyes, men!" Police confiscate John's rude lithographs, London Arts Gallery, January 16, 1970.

Predictably, although John and Yoko were advocating their own version of the peace'n'love credo that informed The Beatles' music, their public activities continued to confuse and annoy. The first Bed-In began on March 25 in Amsterdam. Later that year, the newly married Lennons would demonstrate their support for the posthumous pardoning of James Hanratty, the last British man to be hanged, as well as attempting to popularise the notion of "Bagism": neutralising human prejudice via the expedient of hiding in a white sack. They also launched their career as film-makers, via such works as Apotheosis (a 16-minute piece shot from a hot air balloon) and Self-Portrait (a study of John's penis, both in semi and full erection). If the Queen had expressed the opinion that the 1967-period Fabs had turned "awfully strange", by now it must have seemed as though they had relocated to another planet. Other sections of the establishment, meanwhile, were voicing sufficient opposition to the Lennons' agenda that the couple started to feel rather embattled: though The Ballad Of John And Yoko is characterised by knockabout camp, its hookline – "They're gonna crucify me" – was surely rooted in genuine anxiety.

Still, John and Yoko did not exactly go to ground. On November 25 came the stunt that neatly illustrated the difference between 1969 and 1965. John's MBE, which had spent the previous four years perched atop Aunt Mimi's television set, was returned to Buckingham Palace, with a note protesting British support for Vietnam, the UK's involvement in the "Nigeria-Biafra thing" and "Cold Turkey slipping down the charts". The latter point was intended to sound a note of bathos – "to stop it sounding like another stupid letter to the Queen from some loony colonel," said John – though it rather couched the gesture in an unbecoming silliness. The Queen, as is her way, refused to comment, though censure came from a source rather closer to home. "He broke my heart over that," Mimi said some years later. "And also, he didn't tell me first why that medal was being taken away."

At 1969's end, the BBC broadcast a 35-minute documentary entitled The World Of John And Yoko. Among its viewers was the political diarist Richard Crossman, then Secretary Of State For Social Services. Although he and the Lennons were the occupants of worlds that stood in polar opposition, it was to Crossman's credit that he saw beyond the idea that the Lennons were lunatic degenerates, and hailed them as representatives of something altogether more praiseworthy.

"Some days ago, I saw an extraordinary interview with John Lennon, who is now a kind of Jesus Christ figure," he wrote, with no little understatement. "Here he was again and, do you know, he was the only person who said that it hadn't been a bad decade, that we'd made enormous advances, and that a lot of people were happier than ever before. In their own way, he and The Beatles were saying, 'We disown the whole establishment, not out of utter desperation and pessimism, but because we are confident of the future and that we can take over and create a world of peace and amity.' In his strange fashion, looking through those spectacles, with his beard and his odd Japanese wife, he was, I must admit, the only person in all these programmes with a gospel, a hope and a belief."

At the time, it seemed that precious few people were attuned to such sentiments. However, 34 years later John Lennon finished eighth in the BBC's ranking of Great Britons, wedged in between Nelson and Elizabeth I, and just two places away from – oh, the irony – Oliver Cromwell. To all intents and purposes, he had posthumously been allowed back in the Palace: divested of his more troublesome aspects, and once again ushered into the company of "the kind of people I'd always hated as a child". Strange days indeed… ■

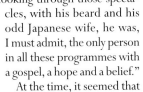

PHOTOS: REX, POPPERFOTO

"He is healed!" John lays hands on press officer, Derek Taylor, as the head of Apple Records, Ron Kass (back, right) looks on, 1968.

What: Apple Records launched
Where: UK
When: August 11, 1968

STRANGE FRUIT

Within a couple of months of launching Apple Records, the label had scored two chart-toppers, but its success was short-lived. By Barry Miles.

OF ALL THE BUSINESSES launched under The Beatles' Apple imprint, Apple Records was the one closest to their hearts. Launched on August 11, 1968 with 'National Apple Week', the press received the first four releases in a promotional pack labelled 'Our First Four'. It was an immediate success, with two chart-toppers – The Beatles' Hey Jude and Mary Hopkin's Those Were The Days – among the 'first four'.

First bite: the initial Apple press release for Mary Hopkin.

The original idea of having your own record company was that you could release any artist you liked. They had immediately approached Donovan and there had been talk of joining together with The Rolling Stones to form a company independent of the major record labels, but though there were meetings between Paul and Mick Jagger, about a jointly financed recording studio, the idea was impractical.

"The thinking behind it was very excited," recalls Paul McCartney. "If we get Donovan, and we've got The Beatles, and we get James Taylor, and then maybe the Stones might even want to come on. And what if some of the really cool American bands like The Byrds want to come, because we're good friends with them? We figured all our friends would eventually join us. It would be a revolution in the recording business. It was enough for me to be enjoying what we were doing, to be making good music, making good friends, and just getting on. If we had a hit, great."

John and Paul placed ads in the papers and went on television in New York announcing Apple's launch and inviting people to send in tapes and ideas. They should have known better – there was no-one to listen to the sacks full of cassettes, the vast majority of which were never opened. In fact, none of the acts released by Apple Records came to The Beatles this way. Mary Hopkin, for instance, came

"We figured all our friends would join us. It would be a revolution in the recording business." Paul McCartney

through Twiggy, who saw her on TV show Opportunity Knocks and telephoned Paul McCartney. Those Were The Days, arranged and produced by Paul, went to Number 1, replacing The Beatles' own first single release on Apple, Hey Jude, which was itself their biggest-selling single ever.

They had known Jackie Lomax from Liverpool days when he was a member of The Undertakers. His Sour Milk Sea was written and produced by George Harrison. And Paul had always fancied making a brass band record, and as The Black Dyke Mills Band were the "best band in the land" he got them to record one of his own compositions called Thingumybob as one of the first four Apple singles.

Peter Asher, Apple's newly appointed A&R manager, brought in James Taylor, whose band The Flying Machine used to back Peter & Gordon on their US tours, and Beatles roadie Mal Evans discovered The Iveys. Paul encouraged them to change their name, which they did, calling themselves Badfinger – but only after Apple had released their first album, *Maybe Tomorrow*. Badfinger's first record with that name was Come And Get It – written, produced and arranged by Paul who made them a demo on which he played all the instruments. Paul: "I said to Badfinger, You should copy this slavishly and they said, 'But we'd like to change it a little bit'. I said, No, it's the right arrangement. Change all the other stuff on the album, but please don't change it. I guarantee it's a hit." He was proved right when it reached Number 4 in 1970.

George produced *That's The Way God Planned It*, an album by his old friend Billy Preston, and brought in Hare Krishna devotees to make a single and album, stretching the abilities of Derek Taylor in the press office whose job was to promote them. Ringo's contribution was a young classical composer called John Taverner whose composition, The Whale, was the hit of the 1968 Proms. The only Beatle who took no part in the early years of Apple was John. He was only interested in Yoko Ono, and acting as William Randolph Hearst to Yoko's Marion Davies, he produced a stream of her records, none of which sold.

At first it was fun: in a way, they were playing at running a record company. And the success of Those Were The Days and Hey Jude did show that McCartney, at least, had sound commercial instincts. There were some mistakes: George Harrison fell in love with Delaney & Bonnie's first LP, and wanted it for Apple. Copies were pressed and awaiting delivery of the sleeves before anyone realised they didn't have the rights – the record belonged to Elektra, who had them under contract. Copies of the junked record with the green Apple still show up at record fairs.

The actual head of Apple Records was Ron Kass, whom they headhunted from Liberty Records. Kass, who later married Joan Collins, had little say over what was released – that was The Beatles' choice; but he oversaw the technical problems of shipping tapes, sleeve translations, artwork and publicity to all the overseas countries where Apple records were released. In theory, a new Beatles single would go on sale simultaneously in 30 countries, and Apple employed multilingual translators to deal with the problems inherent in such an ambitious plan.

The initial enthusiasm palled as The Beatles began to break up, the splits between them being echoed in Apple. The company continued to make money. The income generated by the White Album alone would have sustained a small country, but unfortunately 3 Savile Row was a den of thieves and money poured out of the door. The office boy was even caught stealing the lead off the roof.

Apple still exists, controlled by an appointed board of directors, and makes more money than ever: the Anthology CDs, videos and book made millions and the recent *1* CD was Number 1 in 28 countries, just like the old days.

SEPTEMBER 68

3 Ringo rejoins The Beatles at Abbey Road.

4 Fifty Beatles fans are special guests in Twickenham Film Studios at the live recording of single, Hey Jude on the TV show Frost On Sunday, hosted by David Frost. Mary Hopkin enters the UK singles chart with Those Were The Days, which peaks at Number 1.

5 Work continues on While My Guitar Gently Weeps at Abbey Road.

6 Recording of While My Guitar Gently Weeps is completed at Abbey Road, with a guitar solo by Eric Clapton. The Black Dyke Mills Band release a new single in the UK, Thingumybob, written by Lennon & McCartney.

8 Hey Jude gets its UK TV premiere when the promo film is shown on Frost On Sunday.

9 George Martin's assistant Chris Thomas takes over as producer of The Beatles at Abbey Road while Martin is on holiday.

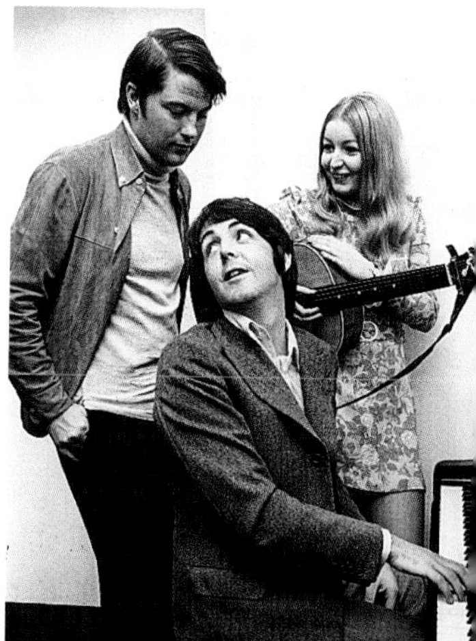

10 Paul appears on UK children's TV show Magpie, with Mary Hopkin (above right).

11 Running for seven minutes and 10 seconds, Hey Jude becomes the longest ever UK Number 1 single.

12 The Beatles are at work on Glass Onion in Abbey Road.

13 Work continues on Glass Onion at Abbey Road.

14 Hey Jude enters the US Top 40 singles chart, where it will peak at Number 1.

16 Work begins on Paul's song I Will, in Abbey Road.

17 I Will is completed in Abbey Road.

18 Birthday is recorded at Abbey Road.

19 In Abbey Road, work begins on basic tracks for the song Piggies.

20 In Abbey Road, Piggies is completed.

22 Apple Records announces that the next album by The Beatles will be a two-LP set.

23 In Abbey Road, work commences on John's song, Happiness Is A Warm Gun.

24 In Abbey Road, work continues on Happiness Is A Warm Gun.

25 Mary Hopkin starts a six-week run at Number 1 in the UK singles chart with Those Were The Days.

26 The Beatles are in Abbey Road, London, mixing several tracks for what will become the White Album.

PHOTOS: HULTON ARCHIVE/TOPFOTO

28 Hey Jude hits the Number 1 spot in the States. It will stay at the top for nine weeks.

30 The Beatles (left), an authorised biography by Hunter Davies, is published.

OCTOBER 68

1 While The Beatles are in Trident Studios, London, recording Honey Pie, American songwriter Jimmy Webb drops in to meet them.

2 With A Little Help From My Friends, a Lennon-McCartney song covered by Joe Cocker, enters the UK charts on its way to Number 1.

3 The Beatles are in Trident Studios, working on the George Harrison song Savoy Truffle.

4 At Trident Studios, Paul McCartney records Martha My Dear, possibly the definitive musical statement of a rock star's affection for his old English sheepdog.

5 The Beatles are in Trident Studios, working on overdubs for the songs Savoy Truffle and Honey Pie.

7 In Abbey Road, work begins on a George Harrison song, Long, Long, Long. In a laborious session, 16 hours are spent on the rhythm track alone.

8 I'm So Tired and The Continuing Story Of Bungalow Bill are recorded in Abbey Road.

9 Paul records the basic track for Why Don't We Do It In The Road in Abbey Road.

10 Why Don't We Do It In The Road and Glass Onion are completed. George starts up a new publishing venture, Singsong Ltd.

11 The Bonzo Dog Doo-Dah Band (above) release a new single, I'm The Urban Spaceman, in the UK. The producer credit is shown as Apollo C Vermouth, but is actually Paul.

13 John records his song Julia in Abbey Road alone without the help of the other Beatles.

14 Ringo flies to Sardinia for a two-week holiday.

16 George flies from London to Los Angeles, leaving John and Paul to complete work on the White Album in Abbey Road.

18 John and Yoko are arrested for drug possession at their flat in Montague Square. The flat, owned by Ringo Starr, had recently been occupied by Jimi Hendrix.

19 John and Yoko appear in Marylebone Magistrates' Court, London, where they are remanded on bail.

20 Paul flies to New York for a short holiday with girlfriend Linda Eastman.

What: Recording While My Guitar Gently Weeps
Where: Abbey Road
When: September 6, 1968

GUN FOR HIRE

When Eric Clapton guested on While My Guitar Gently Weeps, he helped out a friend and kept The Beatles on their toes. By Ashley Kahn.

FRUSTRATION...FRUSTRATION...TRANSCENDENCE. That pretty much sums up the three-month creative process that brought a delicate George Harrison ditty ruminating on spiritual disconnection up to the sound and status of an enduring rock ballad. And, contrary to the possessive in the title, the irony of While My Guitar Gently Weeps is that the featured instrument belongs to another. In 1968, Eric Clapton's brilliant, sticky-fingered blues solo was the uncredited coup de grâce that made this White Album track a classic. Today, it stands as the most celebrated performance on any Beatles record by a non-Beatle: a melancholy reminder of a band falling out of harmony, and of a friendship that outlasted a legendary love triangle.

For the group, the end of summer '68 was a pressure-cooker schedule crammed with TV appearances, film shoots, arguments and sessions for their as-yet unnamed next album. Little surprise then that While My Guitar... was largely ignored by the other Beatles, who were more focused on material such as John's Dear Prudence and Paul's Helter Skelter. "They were not interested in it all," said Harrison.

Early that summer, the conception of While My Guitar... began with an experiment inspired by the "nothing-is-coincidental" philosophy held within the I Ching. "When I visited my parents' house I decided to write a song based on the first thing I saw upon opening any book," Harrison explained in I Me Mine. "[I] saw 'gently weeps', then laid the book down again and started the song."

George's first draft included a list of alliterative words ("Tampering, tapering, tempering... Wandering, watering, wavering") and a gelling theme of universality ("I look at the world and I notice it's turning... with every mistake we must surely be learning"). Recording began on July 25, eight weeks into the sessions for the White Album, with George first tracking an airy, mostly solo acoustic demo. Now featured on *Anthology 3*, his vocal and solo guitar were spiced by a subtle organ overdub, an extra last verse and little hint of the more robust version to come.

The EMI studio logs show The Beatles as a whole approaching While My Guitar... six weeks later. On three separate days, an eventual 44 takes brought the song to its fleshed-out maturity. "George wanted to get the sound of a crying guitar, but he didn't want to use a wah-wah pedal," stated Abbey Road technical engineer Brian Gibson. "We spent a whole night trying to get it to work."

By 3.45am on the morning of September 6, The Beatles stopped and take 25 was deemed the best performance. But George returned to his Surrey home less than enthused. "It wasn't happening," he remembered. "So I went home that night thinking, Well, that's a shame."

Later that same day, George found what he needed in the driver's seat. Grabbing a lift to the studio with Clapton, he had a flash of inspiration, turned to the fellow guitarist, and said: "We're going to do this song. Come on and play on it." Clapton objected, "I can't do that. Nobody ever plays on Beatles records." But George's insistence trumped any reservation; and there was another thing. "Look, it's my song, and I want you to play on it."

That settled, Clapton stepped into the studio, unpacked his Les Paul and quietly joined the group to slight surprise, but no objection. "We'd had instrumentalists before," recalled Paul, "but we'd never actually had someone other than George – or occasionally me or John – play guitar." Clapton's presence added an important element beyond the musical; he put the lads on point. "Eric came in and the other guys were good as gold because he was there," confirmed George. "Paul got on the piano and played a nice intro..."

Paul's percussive attack sounded a funky, bell-like opening to a tune that built on the best take from the day before, adding overdubs of a new lead vocal, fuzz bass, vocal harmonies, percussion and organ. And, of course, Clapton's vibrato-rich, impromptu solo. "His style fitted well with the song," was Paul's ultimate judgement.

Cream of the crop: Fab session man Eric Clapton.

But there remained a slight problem, recalled George. "We listened to it back... it [was] not Beatley enough. So we put it through the ADT [automatic double tracking] to wobble it a bit." The effect remains one of the song's most distinctive aspects, enhancing the song's lugubrious aspect.

Thirty-five years on, While My Guitar... has become a tuneful symbol of the connection between the two guitarists, a friendship that began during the 1964-65 Christmas season when The Yardbirds featured on the bill of The Beatles' three-week stand at the Hammersmith Odeon. "That's the first time I met him," remembered Harrison. "Then somehow Brian Epstein was managing The Cream and The Bee Gees and... that's when I really got to know him quite a bit, it must have been 1966."

"We'd never had someone other than George – or occasionally me or John – play guitar." Paul McCartney

Much has been made of the role of George's first wife Patti Boyd, of the songs she inspired both guitarists to write (Something, Layla) and of Clapton's long-frustrated attraction to Patti. George himself remained unaffected by the whole affair. "I think that deep down inside [Eric] wishes that it really pissed me off," he stated only a few years ago. "But... I was happy that she went off, because we'd finished together and it made things easier for me."

In truth, the Harrison/Boyd union survived a few years (11 legally – 1966-77 – but less in reality) while the Clapton/Boyd marriage lasted nine years (1979-88, though they were together from 1974). What endured the longest was the Harrison/Clapton partnership. Again and again, they met and performed: Concert for Bangla Desh, in 1971; The Prince's Trust, '87; Japan, '90. As the years progressed, those performances grew rarer, always marked by the tune that had become *their* song: While My Guitar Gently Weeps.

PHOTOS: BARRIE WENTZELL/STARFILE

You looking at my bird?" "Yes."
ric Clapton (left) and George Harrison.

25 John and Yoko announce that Yoko is pregnant.

28 Ringo returns from his holiday in Sardinia.

31 Paul's girlfriend, Linda Eastman, moves in with him in London.

NOVEMBER 68

1 George releases Wonderwall, the first solo album by a Beatle. It will one day provide the inspiration for an Oasis song title.

3 In Los Angeles, George records an electronic piece, No Time Or Space, with synthesizer guru Bernie Krause of experimental duo Beaver And Krause.

4 Worried that she might lose her unborn child, doctors admit Yoko to Queen Charlotte's Hospital, London.

5 Paul and Linda drive north to Paul's farm near Campbeltown, Scotland.

6 I'm The Urban Spaceman by the Bonzo Dog Doo-Dah Band, enters the UK singles chart, where it will peak at Number 5.

8 Cynthia Lennon (above) is granted a divorce from John.

9 The new Number 1 single in the UK is With A Little Help From My Friends by Joe Cocker.

11 John and Yoko release the album *Unfinished Music No 1 – Two Virgins*, whose cover shows them naked, in the US.

13 The Beatles' full-length cartoon movie, Yellow Submarine, opens in the US.

15 George records an appearance on The Smothers Brothers' Comedy Hour, at CBS TV Studio, Los Angeles.

19 Ringo and his family move from Weybridge to a new home, Brookfields, in Elstead.

20 Paul is interviewed by Radio Luxembourg at his house in Cavendish Avenue, London.

21 Yoko Ono suffers a miscarriage at Queen Charlotte's Hospital.

22 *The Beatles*, more commonly known as the White Album, is released in the UK.

24 After an unsatisfactory relationship, Grapefruit quit Apple Records.

25 The White Album is released in the US.

28 John pleads guilty to possession of marijuana at Marylebone Magistrates' Court and is fined £150. The conviction later hinders him from getting a Green Card to live in the States.

What: Wonderwall album released
Where: UK
When: November 1, 1968

OFF THE WALL

George Harrison's "challenging" soundtrack to the Wonderwall movie was effectively the first Beatle solo album. By Alan Clayson.

GEORGE HARRISON'S WONDERWALL soundtrack long-player marked a double first for The Beatles. Not only was it the first album release on the nascent Apple Records, but, more importantly, it was the first solo LP by a Beatle. However, the film that inspired Harrison to go it alone is now more noted for the fact that its soundtrack was composed by a Beatle.

The film itself concerns an elderly academic who spends his leisure hours spying on the antics of a young model in the flat next door. The erotic mirror-posing, wild parties and athletic sex that he sees are so alien to him that reality dissolves – as does the storyline – until his fantasies become concrete and he saves the girl from suicide.

The girl was played by Jane Birkin, who would later become famous with the 1969 chart-topper Je T'Aime… Moi Non Plus, her duet with Serge Gainsbourg. Birkin was present at the Cannes Film Festival on May 17, 1968 when Wonderwall received its world premiere. Also in attendance were George, Ringo and their wives.

At an Apple board meeting the following week, George's emotions were mixed about a proposal that Zapple, its subsidiary label, should issue an interview LP with Daniel Cohn-Bendit, a prime mover in the political unrest that had hit France that summer. After all, it was Cohn-Bendit who had stoked up the political rally that had disrupted the screening of Wonderwall. George's big moment had been blighted too by the attitude of many critics who slayed the film. The Times correspondent's verdict that it was "a right load of old codswallop" proved to be a typical assessment.

Since this was his first time as director of a major film, Joe Massot was an obvious sitting duck. At the start of the decade, the New Yorker had been mainly shooting documentaries for the Castro government in Cuba. However, shortly before the 1962 missile crisis, Massot fled the political unrest on the island and ended up in London. Here, he entered the orbit of Roman Polanski's scriptwriter, Gérard Brach. Brach had come up with the story for Wonderwall and offered Massot the chance to direct it.

To create the centrepiece of the film – the "wonderwall" itself – Massot hired The Fool, four Dutch designers whose colourful and vaguely medieval fancy dress matched their style and trade name. The Fool, however, weren't as daft as they looked. Worming their way into The Beatles' court, they'd obtained commissions to paint both the bodywork of John Lennon's Rolls-Royce and the outer walls of the Harrisons' home in Esher. "I don't know how we met them," recalled Patti Harrison. "They just appeared."

The Fool were also given £100,000 with which to decorate and stock Apple's "head shop" on Baker Street. At its opening on December 7, 1967, Joe Massot sounded out George Harrison about providing the Wonderwall music. In fact, Massot had approached The Bee Gees first, but they had turned him down. Aware of the publicity that Beatle involvement would generate, the film's investors felt that anything merely functional would suffice so long as the words "George Harrison" could be printed on the credits.

Harrison was far more impressed with the film than The Bee Gees had been, and began his task by timing each sequence with a stopwatch. Barely able to sight-read, he would next sing his ideas to transcriber John Barham. Barham was a classically educated Londoner who had assisted Ravi Shankar with the scoring of incidental music for the 1967 TV version of Alice In Wonderland.

Armed with Barham's manuscripts, as well as demo tapes, George would repair to Abbey Road to "make 35 seconds, say, of something, mix it and line it up with the scene". Within these strictures, he compiled a soundtrack that many would cite as Wonderwall's saving grace. One glowing review – in Films And Filming – commented on how "the Harrison music replaces dialogue, waxing almost vocal like a cinema organist from the silent days".

The album was, therefore, worthy in its own right. This is despite Harrison's later dismissal of the soundtrack as "loads of horrible mellotron stuff and a police siren" – by which he probably meant the evocative mouth organ blowing of Tommy Reilly, more renowned for his theme to BBC TV's Dixon Of Dock Green police drama series.

On Party Seacombe, George's Liverpool Institute school chum, Colin Manley, even got a look-in playing wah-wah guitar. Under George's supervision, further contributions from Manley – and from more famous players such as Eric Clapton and Ringo – were taped at Abbey Road, while Guru Vandana and Gat Kirwani came from an EMI studio thousands of miles to the East.

Wonderwall's investors felt anything would suffice so long as the words "George Harrison" were on the credits.

On the top floor of the Universal Building in Bombay, Harrison had toiled for an intensive five days with antiquated mono equipment and soundproofing so poor that it was impossible to record during the late afternoon rush hour without picking up outside traffic noise. Still, these were fruitful sessions for the musicians assembled by Shambu Das, another Ravi Shankar protégé. Fascinated, they obeyed the visiting Beatle's Western rules of harmony as they made their contributions to a film most of them would never see.

"I was getting so into Indian music then," George would recall, "that I decided to use Wonderwall as an excuse for a musical anthology to help spread the word."

Harrison's Beatle status also guaranteed this challenging soundtrack album some additional attention. But the elevation of such an oddball work into the US Top 50 – just – was testament to something more substantial than just the influence of a famous name.

PHOTO: RONALD GRANT

Going to the 'Wall: the film's star, Jack MacGowran, realises that drugs may have been used in the making of this movie.

In the altogether now: John and Yoko pose for the *Two Virgins* album cover, 1968.

What: John & Yoko release Two Virgins.
Where: US
When: November 11, 1968

PRIVATES ON PARADE

Talked about more for its cover than for its content, *Two Virgins* proved that John Lennon hadn't lost his knack to shock. By Dave DiMartino.

"IT WAS A GREAT EVENT." SUCH IS ONE OF five pithy comments made by Yoko Ono via e-mail in January 2003 regarding the release of *Unfinished Music No 1: Two Virgins* – or, as some would have it, that unlistenable album where John and Yoko bared all. Or at least much more than any of us had asked for. Ranking very highly as the most infrequently listened to and least purchased Beatle-related album, *Two Virgins* made those who heard it wonder precisely what the pair might do to actually *finish* what they themselves admitted was incomplete. The simple addition of a brass band wouldn't quite do it.

Released first in America on November 11, 1968, and in the UK on November 29, 1968, a mere week after the White Album hit the shops – certainly time enough for ardent fans to get a sample of the coming weirdness via Revolution 9 – *Two Virgins* was very definitely a statement of some sort. Purported to be recorded on the night before John and Yoko first made love, Lennon later described it to Rolling Stone's Jonathan Cott as "a music metaphor for two persons seeing each other for the first time and then seeing what's there".

Two sides, roughly 15 minutes apiece, of whispering, whistling, giggling and random electronics.

All well and good, but what does that mean for the casual listener? Two sides, roughly 15 minutes apiece, of whispering, whistling, giggling, reverbed guitar and piano, and random electronics. Sort of like those transitional moments on *The Faust Tapes*, but without the German accents.

What was the most daring aspect of its release? "The fact that we were naked, on many levels," says Yoko today. And indeed, this is true. Both front and backsides! Surely there are other levels to examine – but the means by which the pair of photos decorating this memorable package were obtained is interestingly quaint: after a photographer set up a camera with a remote shutter switch, Lennon and Ono asked those present to depart; thereafter, the pair de-clothed, posed, snapped, turned, snapped, and the dirty deed was done. In complete privacy. Just the pair of them – and countless thousands of record sleeves to be shipped to every corner of the world.

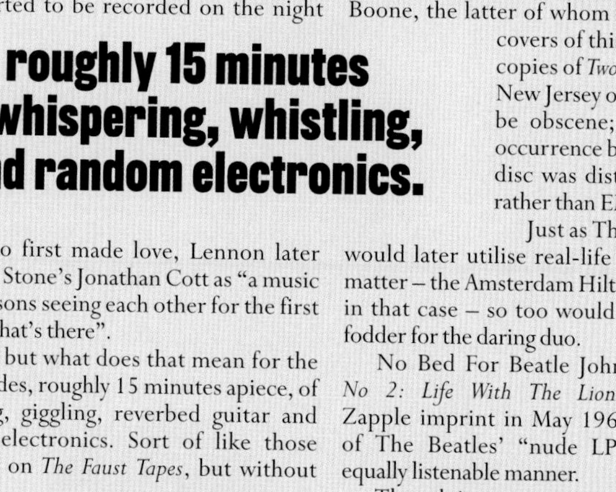

Released just three weeks after Cynthia Lennon filed for divorce because of her husband's adulterous behaviour with Ono – of which album photos like these might be considered a prime example, one supposes – *Two Virgins* did not exactly sail out of the shops. For that matter, it barely sailed *into* them. "We had to fight for it all the way," says Yoko, who with Lennon faced resistance from many quarters, including band members and record labels mildly reluctant to distribute product that might be deemed pornographic by those unused to full-frontal album cover nudity.

There was one solution to the dangling participle-factor that, in a way, made *Two Virgins* that much more of a prurient affair: the album was encased in a brown paper sleeve that showed only the duo's heads, allowing potential consumers to only imagine – as Lennon himself would have it – what lay underneath.

"It's the reflection of our society," Yoko notes today. In the States, Capitol Records wouldn't distribute it; honours instead went to Tetragrammaton Records, the Bill Cosby-funded venture which broke Deep Purple Stateside and released other albums by Biff Rose and Pat Boone, the latter of whom was rarely linked to album covers of this sort. Within two months, copies of *Two Virgins* were confiscated by New Jersey officials who felt the cover to be obscene; this was not an isolated occurrence by any means. In Britain, the disc was distributed by Track Records rather than EMI.

Just as The Ballad Of John And Yoko would later utilise real-life experience for its subject matter – the Amsterdam Hilton "bed-in" of March 1969 in that case – so too would *Two Virgins* provide lyrical fodder for the daring duo.

No Bed For Beatle John – from *Unfinished Music No 2: Life With The Lions*, released on the new Zapple imprint in May 1969 – draws from accounts of The Beatles' "nude LP" controversy in, er, an equally listenable manner.

Though in retrospect it may seem a complete sales non-event, famous only for its cover and the controversy that would follow, *Two Virgins* was more successful than you might think. In America it spent two months on the Billboard album chart, peaking at Number 124 – beating both its avant-sequels, *Life With The Lions* (Number 174) and *Wedding Album* (Number 178 and off the chart in three weeks). Some might say this illustrates the principles of a consumer learning curve – but that would not explain the Top 10 appearance of The Plastic Ono Band's *Live Peace In Toronto*, issued just a month after *Wedding Album*.

John Lennon once described *Two Virgins* as a "sophisticated multi-media" package, and in retrospect, he was completely correct. It had a profound impact – whether people heard it, saw it wrapped in brown paper at the shops, or merely read that the man who said The Beatles were more popular than Jesus was now granting us a viewing of his private parts. Detractors may have called it a stiff, but photographic evidence proves otherwise.

29 *Unfinished Music No 1 – Two Virgins*, is released in the UK.

30 It is reported that Hey Jude is approaching a worldwide sales figure of six million copies.

DECEMBER 68

2 George's Wonderwall soundtrack is released in the US.

4 George memos the staff of Apple, advising that 12 Hells Angels will be stopping off at the office en route to Czechoslovakia. He suggests: "Try to assist them without neglecting your Apple business and without letting them take control of Savile Row."

6 James Taylor releases his eponymous debut album in the UK, on Apple Records.

7 The White Album hits Number 1 in the UK.

9 Newsweek reports that after only five days on sale, the White Album has sold 1.1 million copies in America.

10 John and Cynthia's home in Weybridge is put up for sale. Meanwhile, John and Yoko attend rehearsals at InterTel Studios, Wembley, London for the next day's filming of The Rolling Stones' Rock'n'Roll Circus. The concert features the Stones and various guests including Taj Mahal, Jethro Tull, The Who and Marianne Faithfull.

11 The Rolling Stones continue filming Rock'n'Roll Circus (above) at InterTel Studios. John makes his first solo appearance, singing Yer Blues. His backing band consists of Keith Richards, Eric Clapton and Mitch Mitchell.

12 The Rolling Stones complete filming of Rock'n'Roll Circus.

14 Lily The Pink by Scaffold is the new Number 1 single in the UK. The White Album enters the US album chart, where it will peak at Number 1.

15 British lawyer David Jacobs, whose clients included Brian Epstein, hangs himself in the garage of his home in Hove, Sussex, aged 56.

17 A year after being shown on British television, the Magical Mystery Tour film receives its theatrical premiere in America when it is screened at the Savoy Theatre, Boston, Massachusetts.

18 John and Yoko appear inside a voluminous white bag at a happening, An Alchemical Wedding, in London's Royal Albert Hall.

20 The Beatles' 1968 Christmas Record – a free annual flexi-disc – is mailed out to the band's UK fan club members.

23 A party for children of staff and friends is held at the Apple Building in London. John and Yoko both appear as Father Christmas.

25 George spends Christmas in Woodstock, New York State, with Bob Dylan, while the other Beatles remain in the UK.

28 The White Album reaches Number 1 in America, a position it will hold for nine weeks.

White Riot

Five months in the making and an incredible 95 minutes in length, the White Album remains The Beatles' most original work. Ian MacDonald examines the wealth of riches within.

After the high psychedelic noon of *Revolver*, *Sgt Pepper* and *Magical Mystery Tour*, the long slow afternoon of The Beatles' career unfolds in the eccentric, highly diverse, and very variable quality of *The Beatles*, aka the White Album, issued in late November 1968. There's a casually liberal attitude to the White Album, as though the main work of the group is over and relaxation and individualism are the order of the day. The Beatles made the album in a state of mind different from that of their astonishing peak in 1966-7: a feeling that something was over and that no revelation of anything substantial to replace it had arisen. Essentially, the band had begun to disintegrate in the wake of the comedown from their major drugs period. It wasn't a group effort any more, but an association of former colleagues co-operating.

Despite this – and the fact that around a third of it is forgettable by The Beatles' high standards – the White Album continues to command a Top 10 placing in most "All-Time Best Album" lists. This is despite the misgivings of George Martin, who produced most of the White Album and thought it would have been better to have edited it down to a single album rather than include more or less everything the group recorded between May 30 and October 13, 1968. Whether or not The Beatles chose the double album option the quicker to fulfil the terms of their recording contract, it's fair to say that a single album version wouldn't have had room for the best of what they had on offer in 1968. In any case, the double album has something extra which wouldn't have been there had it been edited: a sense of character derived from the sheer variety of its material, the compendious air of a world of its own.

Until July 1968, when Family released their debut, *Music In A Doll's House*, The Beatles' first title for what became the White Album was *A Doll's House*, supposedly after Ibsen's play. This was a pity because the concept of a doll's house, with its motif of objects collected into various rooms, was a

> "Flawed and bulked out with filler material the White Album may be, but it has a unity to it."

TRACK LISTING

SIDE ONE

1. Back In The USSR
Sung by McCartney

2. Dear Prudence
Sung by Lennon

3. Glass Onion
Sung by Lennon

4. Ob-La-Di, Ob-La-Da
Sung by McCartney

5. Wild Honey Pie
Sung by McCartney

6. The Continuing Story Of Bungalow Bill
Sung by Lennon

7. While My Guitar Gently Weeps
Harrison
Sung by Harrison

8. Happiness Is A Warm Gun
Sung by Lennon

SIDE TWO

9. Martha My Dear
Sung by McCartney

10. I'm So Tired
Sung by Lennon

11. Blackbird
Sung by McCartney

12. Piggies
Harrison
Sung by Harrison

13. Rocky Raccoon
Sung by McCartney

14. Don't Pass Me By
Starkey
Sung by Starr

15. Why Don't We Do It In The Road?
Sung by McCartney

16. I Will
Sung by McCartney

17. Julia
Sung by Lennon

SIDE THREE

18. Birthday
Sung by McCartney

19. Yer Blues
Sung by Lennon

20. Mother Nature's Son
Sung by McCartney

21. Everybody's Got Something To Hide Except Me And My Monkey
Sung by Lennon

22. Sexy Sadie
Sung by Lennon

23. Helter Skelter
Sung by McCartney

24. Long, Long, Long
Harrison
Sung by Harrison

SIDE FOUR

25. Revolution 1
Sung by Lennon

26. Honey Pie
Sung by McCartney

27. Savoy Truffle
Harrison
Sung by Harrison

28. Cry Baby Cry
Sung by Lennon

29. Revolution 9

30. Good Night
Sung by Starr

All tracks by Lennon/McCartney unless otherwise specified.

good model for the double album, in particular in its associations with childhood and private fantasy games. Cry Baby Cry, held back until almost the last, before the sound fantasia of Revolution 9, sums up the prevailing mood of the White Album: half-charming, half-sinister, tinged with obscure childhood memories, and primarily introspective.

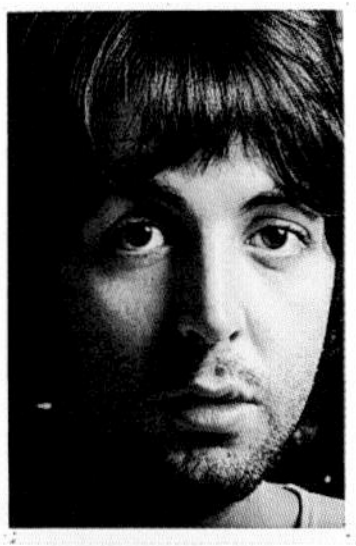

Had the White Album been called *A Doll's House*, what else would have been different about it? For a start, Richard Hamilton, if asked, wouldn't have been able to get away with the modish minimalism of a perfectly blank canvas distinguished only by a supposedly unique edition number embossed in one corner. Family's LP took the concept of the doll's house literally, which might have suited Peter Blake had The Beatles wished to use the same idea. Instead, they – and we – are stuck with what is arguably the greatest cop-out by an artist of repute in the annals of 12-inch album design. Did Hamilton hear the music before he submitted his solution? It seems unlikely since its mood-movement from lazy afternoon to dreamlike darkness, its associations of

THE WHITE ALBUM

WHAT THE PAPERS SAID...

The press liked the White Album's mixed bag.

"The most important musical event of the year occurs today. It is, of course, the publication of the new two-disc album from, by and simply entitled *The Beatles*... The poetic standard varies from inspired (Blackbird) through allusive (Glass Onion) and obscure (Happiness Is A Warm Gun) to jokey, trite, and deliberately meaningless. There are too many private jokes and too much pastiche to convince me that Lennon and McCartney are still pressing forward... but these 30 tracks contain plenty to be studied, enjoyed and gradually appreciated more fully in the coming months."

William Mann, The Times, November 22, 1968

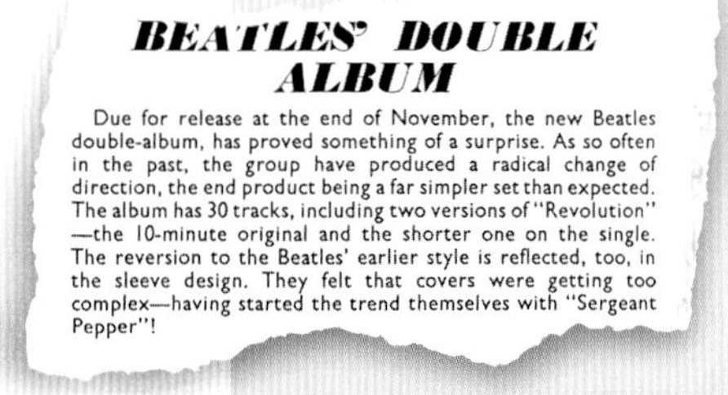

BEATLES' DOUBLE ALBUM

Due for release at the end of November, the new Beatles double-album, has proved something of a surprise. As so often in the past, the group have produced a radical change of direction, the end product being a far simpler set than expected. The album has 30 tracks, including two versions of "Revolution" —the 10-minute original and the shorter one on the single. The reversion to the Beatles' earlier style is reflected, too, in the sleeve design. They felt that covers were getting too complex—having started the trend themselves with "Sergeant Pepper"!

"The new Beatles album has proved something of a surprise. As so often in the past, the group have produced a radical change of direction, the end product being a far simpler set than expected... The reversion to The Beatles' earlier style is reflected, too, in the sleeve. They felt covers were getting too complex – having started the trend themselves with *Sgt Pepper*!"

Beat Instrumental, November 1968

"Of course the new Beatles double LP... is the best thing in pop since *Sgt Pepper*. Their sounds, for those open in ear and mind, should long ago have established their supremacy... They have misses, but there aren't many. It is a world map of contemporary music, drawn with unique flair. Musically, there is beauty, horror, surprise, chaos, order. And that *is* the world; and that is what The Beatles are on about. Created by, creating for, their age."

Derek Jewell, Sunday Times, November 24, 1968

SLEEVE NOTES

Paul wanted a stark contrast to the *Sgt Pepper* cover. He got it.

Most assume that the stark white cover artwork that adorns The Beatles' eponymous ninth LP was the brainchild of Yoko Ono or John Lennon. Its minimalist and conceptual art influence was definitely in step with the pair's avant-garde leanings. Lennon had utilised both a white canvas and white balloons in his You Are Here exhibition held at the Robert Fraser Gallery in July of that year. Yet, according to the LP's designer, Richard Hamilton, it was Paul McCartney who made the initial request for a sleeve in complete contrast to the Day-Glo explosion of *Sgt Pepper*.

Hamilton, a British pop artist, had landed the job via mutual friend and gallery owner Robert Fraser. In the early stages of design, he had proposed that the white of the sleeve be augmented with a coffee cup stain, but that was deemed "too flippant". Then he suggested that the cover be impregnated with apple pulp, in homage to The Beatles' company Apple, but that was too impractical.

In the end, they settled on a plain white cover. Alongside the embossed band's name, the first two million copies of the LP also had an individual edition number. John got 00001, "because he shouted loudest", Paul recalled.

Such was the revolutionary nature of the artwork that it led to the record being renamed the White Album.

The inner-sleeve, however, was far more conventional with its collage of snapshots and contact sheets put together by Hamilton, plus its portraits of each member. As the music contained within was less a collaboration and more the result of three distinct songwriters in John, Paul and George, so the composition focused on The Beatles as individuals rather than a group in its utilisation of solo shots of the band members.

Lois Wilson

> "Some hold Helter Skelter to be a thunderous masterpiece and others hear it only as a flailing noise."

guarded privacy and locked doors, are so tangible. The White Album is anything but minimalist and its chicly empty cover and consequent nickname are essentially irrelevant to its ethos.

If Richard Hamilton's cover for The Beatles is one of the laziest ways iconic status has ever been achieved, the double album itself represents a lot of hard work done over a considerable period of time, much of it turned to superlative effect. The opener, Back In The USSR, is especially galvanising with its breakneck pace, incident-packed design, witty lyrics, and screaming jet-engine effects. Dear Prudence is the first of a series of delicate finger-picked songs created on acoustic guitars in Rishikesh under the influence of Donovan, who taught The Beatles various finger styles. Blackbird and Julia are two other outstanding songs in this mode, while the same method appears in Happiness Is A Warm Gun, the strikingly obscure song which brings down the curtain on Side One. Here, Lennon can be heard becoming more adult in feeling, while struggling lyrically to keep up with himself (or perhaps to sustain the original inspiration for the song, its opening line, "She's not a girl who misses much").

Other tracks of high quality include I'm So Tired, Mother Nature's Son, Revolution 1, and Harrison's sighing reconciliation with God, Long Long Long. Most of the material for the White Album was written in Rishikesh in an atmosphere of communal sing-song and rather too many of the record's tracks are, in effect, jokes which wear thin rather rapidly. The best of these is McCartney's Birthday (not a Rishikesh song, being quickly assembled in the studio). Among the less tolerable are Wild Honey Pie, The Continuing Story Of Bungalow Bill, Rocky Raccoon, and Why Don't We Do It In The Road?. Lennon's Yer Blues is a more serious form of joke, deeply felt at the same time as it is conceptually arch.

The shallow end of McCartney's brilliant fluency can be heard on Ob-La-Di, Ob-La-Da, Martha My Dear, I Will and Honey Pie. Harrison's weighty While My Guitar Gently Weeps makes rather a meal of its message and rhyme-scheme. His Savoy Truffle is an efficient *jeu d'esprit*, while Piggies is a nasty piece of work, the only song on the White Album which

"...And if we just turn Ringo down a little bit more..." Paul and John, Abbey Road studios, 1968.

PHOTO: LINDA McCARTNEY

Charles Manson didn't completely misinterpret. Lennon's Sexy Sadie, mocking the Maharishi, justifies its presence with its sliding harmonic scheme, while his Good Night, stylistically far from anything else he ever did, works well as a closer. Starr's Don't Pass Me By, on the other hand, is amiably disposable.

The two most controversial tracks on the White Album are McCartney's Helter Skelter, which some hold to be a thunderous masterpiece and others hear only as a flailing noise, and the long excursion into tape-looped random anarchy, Revolution 9. Apart from being the most widely distributed piece of genuine avant-garde art in history, Revolution 9 is arguably the heart of the White Album, drawing together all its dreamy, disruptive, secretive and searching impulses. Only The Beatles could have got away with making Revolution 9 the climax of their 95-minute double album. Rarely has anyone else in the pop/rock business gone further out than Revolution 9, which is The Beatles' high-water mark as experimentalists.

Flawed and bulked out with filler material the White Album may be, but it has a unity to it, imparted to a large extent by the sequencing of the tracks, an effort of compilation which took an unprecedented 24-hour session to accomplish. More than that, the record has a capaciousness, an all-inclusivity, which establishes an atmosphere and a space in which the listener's mind can wander with the music. For all these reasons, it remains among the The Beatles' most original work.

TALKIN' 'BOUT A REVOLUTION

Linda Thompson believes that the *White Album* is The Beatles' greatest long-player.

"I first saw The Beatles back in 1964 when they played in Glasgow, and it was my epiphany with music. Watching them onstage that night I suddenly saw the light.

"For me, their greatest album was always the White Album. There was something for everyone on that and there still is. It really is an album that has stood the test of time. Perhaps that's because it is just so diverse in both its lyrical content and musical style. Back In The USSR has the greatest production. It's just so clever, and the lyric is so wacky as well. While My Guitar Gently Weeps is *the* perfect song. George Harrison, who was always my favourite of The Beatles, sings in such a soothing, lilting way. His voice is just so comforting and melancholy. He lulls you into this false sense of security and the next thing, you'll get a song like Why Don't We Do It In The Road?, which was extraordinary for the time when it came out and genuinely shocking as well. Nowadays people really do 'do it in the road', but it was enough to just sing about it in those days. That song really was very avant-garde.

"Paul McCartney also comes up with the goods on I Will. That song has such a great lyric, "For if I ever saw you/I didn't catch your name/ But it never really mattered/I will always feel the same". The words are so ambiguous that the listener doesn't know if McCartney is addressing a girl or God in the song.

"I think that the whole of the White Album is very underrated. It's definitely one that holds your attention and makes you think."

Lois Wilson

Behind The Shutters

As a member of staff at Apple, photographer Tony Bramwell had unique access to The Beatles. Lois Wilson gets a glimpse of the band's inner sanctum in 1968.

Tony Bramwell never set out to become head of Apple Promotions. All he was interested in was getting to see The Beatles play live for free. "I used to carry their equipment so I could watch their gigs," he explains. "I'd seen The Quarrymen, but when they turned into The Beatles they were phenomenal. There'd only be 15 to 20 people watching, but it was such an atmosphere. So exciting!"

Bramwell had first met George Harrison when the pair were in their teens. "The Beatles used to introduce me as George's friend, but then that's what I was, George's friend. We used to go on bike rides together and George was impressed when I told him I'd met Buddy Holly when he came to play in England. I used to lend him my records and we played them so many times that in the end we had to throw them away because they were so scratched."

When The Beatles signed to Parlophone, Bramwell was put on the payroll too. First as an office boy at NEMS, later as the stage manager at Brian Epstein's Saville Theatre. When Epstein died, Bramwell joined Apple, "helping out here and there. I ran the film company Subafilms, was the label's radio plugger and finally took over the promotion."

It was during Bramwell's time at Apple that he found himself in the enviable position of being able to visually document The Beatles. "I loved taking photos, but only as a hobby mind you. I used to carry my camera – a Nikon Nikkormat – with me everywhere. My constant snapping just became a part of the background. I took some press shots of Apple artists like Mary Hopkin and pictures of The Beatles for the Beatles Monthly magazine. But the majority of the snaps I took were just for personal use. At the time I thought nothing of it. That was the way I lived my life but now I realise just how special it was. Half the world would have given an arm and a leg to have been in my position."

▶ GEORGE
APPLE SALON, KING'S ROAD, LONDON

"The hairdresser in this photo is Leslie Cavendish. He ran Apple's hairdressing salon on the King's Road. It didn't matter where The Beatles were or what they were doing, if they wanted their hair cutting he'd do it. There's another picture from this session where George has this huge smile on his face. The group never minded me taking photos of them. I took literally hundreds over the years. They were used to me always being around."

◀ THE BEATLES AND GEORGE MARTIN
ABBEY ROAD STUDIOS, LONDON

"This is taken from the control room at Abbey Road. I was looking down on the four of them discussing production techniques with George Martin. I think the photo sums up their working relationship. In the early days George Martin was far more involved with the making of the records. By this time it was the band that had control, especially Paul who had acquired a lot of production skills over the years. But George Martin played a necessary role. He kept the balance steady within the group."

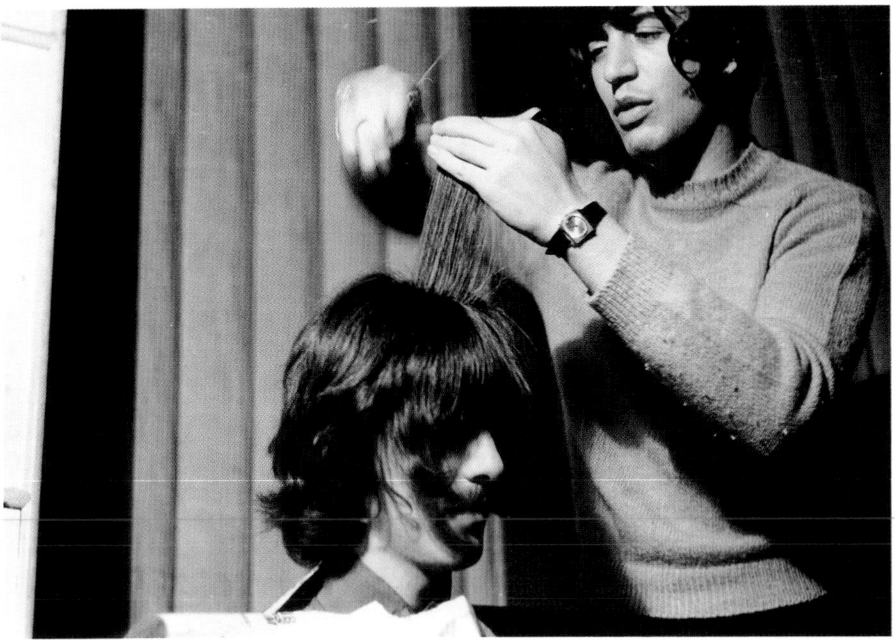

▲ **PAUL, TRIDENT STUDIOS, LONDON**

"This shot was taken during the recording of Hey Jude in Trident Studios. I wanted to catch Paul at work in the studio and this picture did just that – it's a very groovy snap. Paul was totally animated when at work. He was always concentrating really hard, always the most dominant person in the studio. He could play all the different instruments as well as the others and spent much more time in the studio than the others too. Because he lived so close to Abbey Road, when he got bored he'd pop in and fiddle about with tracks. A couple of the shots from this roll got published in the Beatles Monthly magazine. That's where a lot of my pictures ended up. I was responsible for keeping the fan club up to date with all the news and Beatles' goings-on."

▶ **THE APPLE GIRLS**
APPLE OFFICES, SAVILE ROW, LONDON

"Debbie, Frankie and Chris were three of the girls who worked in the Apple office. Here they are sat in the lobby. Debbie was English, while Frankie and Chris were Americans. Chris is mentioned in one of George's songs – Miss O'Dell. She was Miss Chris O'Dell. She went on to marry Lord Russell."

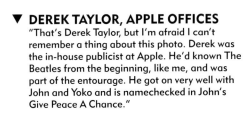

▼ DEREK TAYLOR, APPLE OFFICES
"That's Derek Taylor, but I'm afraid I can't remember a thing about this photo. Derek was the in-house publicist at Apple. He'd known The Beatles from the beginning, like me, and was part of the entourage. He got on very well with John and Yoko and is namechecked in John's Give Peace A Chance."

◀ **JOHN AND YOKO, ROYAL LANCASTER HOTEL, LONDON**

"We had a reception on the top floor of the Royal Lancaster Hotel to launch Apple Records. All the top executives from EMI and Capitol Records from all around the world came to meet The Beatles and have a cup of tea with them. We were all hanging around just waiting for them to arrive. I decided to take a couple of shots of John and Yoko using the reflection of the mirrored wall. I just thought it was an easy way to capture them in a different light. It was nothing fancy. That's me with the camera in the photo. We played the executives bits of the White Album. It went amazingly well. Anyone who met The Beatles in those days was always impressed."

▼ THE BEATLES TWICKENHAM STUDIOS

"You can just see Peter Asher's shoulder in the front of this photo. Here, the band is rehearsing for the Hey Jude video in the Twickenham Studios. That's what all the cameras are there for. They were also rehearsing the song for the David Frost programme they were appearing on a few days later. They loved playing. Paul could never leave a piano alone. If you went into a pub and there was a piano there, he'd start playing and singing. We often did that – impromptu singalongs in the pubs."

▲ **JOHN, PAUL AND GEORGE**
ABBEY ROAD STUDIOS, LONDON

(Top) "They've just tried out Hey Jude here and Paul's looking to see the response. The Beatles would come along with ideas and bits of songs and it would look like they were just sitting around doing nothing for days on end and then suddenly this song would appear. It was very different to the early days when they came into the studio with 12 songs all thoroughly rehearsed and would record their album in two days flat. After *Sgt Pepper* they'd take months."

▲ **JOHN AND YOKO**
ABBEY ROAD STUDIOS, LONDON

"It was the first time that anyone had ever come between the four members of the band. It wasn't that we didn't get on with Yoko, it was more that no-one was used to having someone else constantly there. Friends and girlfriends would pop by but they wouldn't comment on the music and make contributions. Here the pair are listening to the playback of Hey Jude. I just liked the way they were concentrating so hard."

1969

In 1969, The Beatles began work on what would become known as *Let It Be,* only to go and release *Abbey Road* first. Meanwhile, many were claiming Paul was dead. Undeterred, John spent much of the year in and out of beds and bags, before getting married, writing a hit single about it, and deciding to quit The Beatles. Taking the hint, Ringo started to make his first solo record.

NTAL
STUDIO
special inside
FILM STARR
Stones fever: concerts sold out!
JAGGER: in New York
THE WORLD OF RECORDING SOUND
The Studio Revolution: What Modern Electronics Can Do
Cassette or Reel-to-Reel? A Guide Through the Tape Maze
Don Schlitten: An Independent Jazz A & R Man
The Jazz Reissue Bonanza: A Survey by Dan Morgenstern
db music workshop
Dr. Wm. Fowler's ℞ For Jazz Guitarists
Electronics in the Rock Group: A Do-It-Yourself Project, Part II
record mirro
Review of Rolling Stones' new LP
The Hollies: good guys of pop
TREMELOES BEHIND T
IRON CURTAIN: exclusi
No. 455 Week ending November 29th 1969. A Billboard Publication
Changing fac
of Beatle Joh
ECORD
IRROR
selling colour pop weekly newspaper
424. Every Thursday. Week ending
1969.
NSIDE THIS
EEK'S R.M:
TREMELOES
TELL OF THEIR
BIG MISTAKE
EW
YLAN & CASH
LBUM!
JOHNNY NASH
NINA SIMONE
MERRILL MOORE
& R.M's LAUGH IN!
HOPKIN &
CLODAGH
COLOURS
THE BEA
once again sto
charts- 'GET
to reach the
DISC
and MUSIC ECHO 1s
MAY 10, 1969
EVERY THURSDAY
Is this
man
sick ?
'PINBALL WIZARD' STORM: BACK PA
Beatles' album delayed
IS CARNABY STREET SWINGING OR HAS

Film On Four

The 'Get Back' documentary began life as a reason for The Beatles to pull together. But by the end of the project all four of the band just wanted to Let It Be. Martin O'Gorman watches a band disintegrate.

There's an infamous photograph of The Beatles taken in January 1969, which accurately sums up the mood of the group as they teetered on the verge of breaking up. Gathered around a mobile recording desk in the basement of the Apple offices at Savile Row, the four are pictured listening to an obviously underwhelming playback of the track they've just recorded; The Beatles caught in, as John Lennon later described, "the most miserable sessions on earth".

On the far left of the photograph sits George Harrison, eyes shut, a look of absolute pain on his face. To his left is Ringo Starr, wearing his standard-issue look of gloom while staring into the middle distance. Next to him is John Lennon, feet on the mixing desk, a tight-lipped expression of intense indifference on his face; behind him, as ever, is Yoko Ono. On the far right of the photo is Paul McCartney, leaning forward and frowning, his hands gripping the mixing desk as if he were holding onto the group's future for dear life. Bad times, indeed.

But the situation The Beatles found themselves in at the beginning of 1969 arose for the best reasons – they were intending to end the decade with a monumental live show that would mark their return to the stage for the first time in nearly three years. The show was to become a TV extravaganza which would depict the band embracing the simple stagecraft that had made their name, by forsaking the studio trickery they had pioneered on *Sgt Pepper's Lonely Hearts Club Band*. In the words of an Apple press release for the aptly-named Get Back single, the project was to feature, "The Beatles as live as can be in this electronic age – The Beatles as nature intended."

Unfortunately, the lack of decent material and the rapidly worsening relationship between the four members meant that the 'Get Back' sessions actually depicted The Beatles breaking up before the cameras; the sad end to a glorious career amid a tortuous month of bickering, infighting, bad attitudes and sloppy work. But oddly enough, the sessions were free of any violent confrontation. While their contemporaries – The Who and The Kinks particularly – were brutally forthcoming with their opinions, The Beatles were more like a dysfunctional family, preferring to let their resentment simmer. Rather than throwing punches, they would lapse into uncommunicative silences or revert to their trademark in-jokes, preferring to suffer in sulky silence.

Creatively frustrated and sick of being a sideman, Harrison finally cracked and walked out on the sessions for a week, brooding long enough to make his feelings clear. Similar frustrations had seen Starr leave the band briefly the year before and with his movie career burgeoning, The Beatles had become a chore for the drummer. Lennon's obsession with Yoko Ono achieved a new intensity that saw the lovers descend into their own pit of heroin-dulled misery, prompting John to psychologically withdraw from the group and allow his new partner to speak on his behalf.

"The 'Get Back' sessions actually depicted The Beatles breaking up before the cameras – the sad end to a glorious career."

The key player: Paul, the mastermind behind the Let It Be film and album.

Stuck in the middle, McCartney was keen to build bridges, withdrawing when he overstepped the mark with Harrison and making allowances for Lennon's relationship with Ono, despite its detrimental effect on the band's morale. "They're going overboard about it," McCartney reasoned. "But John always does. It's going to be such an incredible, comical thing, like, in 50 years' time… for people to say, 'They broke up 'cos Yoko sat on an amp'."

It was McCartney who prompted the 'Get Back' sessions in the first place, feeling that the "live" approach would inspire The Beatles to work together properly again, like they did in the old days. Despite the personal friction that blighted the recording of the White Album, they had enjoyed moments when they operated as a tight unit, particularly on straightforward rock tracks such as Yer Blues and Birthday.

"I thought it was a great idea," says producer George Martin. "They said, Let's rehearse all the stuff we're going to do for the album, get it really well organised as a band, record it live before an audience and issue that. Nobody had done a live album of completely new material before, and I was all for it."

The "live" aspect would hone their skills as musicians. The overdub-heavy recordings of *Revolver* and *Sgt Pepper* had seen The Beatles become lazy, but McCartney felt that with the right motivation and the right project, they could still cut it. He suggested The Beatles make their comeback with three shows at the Roundhouse in North London beginning December 15. Or December 16, no-one was quite sure. "Mary Hopkin and Jackie Lomax will also appear," gushed an Apple press release on November 7, 1968. "The concerts will benefit charity and a one-hour TV spectacular may be built around the shows."

"These concerts will be a mindbender," enthused Apple's Jeremy Banks in the NME. "Negotiations for the Roundhouse are at an early stage, but they will be completed this week." Despite the venue being unconfirmed, tickets were given away through the fan club magazine The Beatles Book. Unsurprisingly, the projected date came and went with no action from the Beatles camp, but just before Christmas 1968, Apple's press guru Derek Taylor told reporters that The Beatles were seeking suggestions for where they should hold a single concert, which was now pencilled in for January 18, 1969.

It was now decided that there should be two one-hour TV specials. The first instalment would be a documentary on The Beatles rehearsing their act. The second night would be the live special. Ever the intellectual, McCartney was particularly inspired by a recent TV documentary on Pablo Picasso, which showed the painter building up a piece of work before the cameras – Paul thought that The Beatles' documentary could show the same development. "I remember I had an idea for the final scene," says McCartney, "Which would be a massive tracking shot, forever and ever and then we'd be in the concert."

A veteran of Ready Steady Go, American film director Michael Lindsay-Hogg was brought in to steer the project, following his work on The Rolling Stones' Rock'n'Roll Circus and The Beatles' own Hey Jude and Revolution promo clips. Apple Films producer Denis O'Dell had booked Twickenham Studios' Stage One from the beginning of January 1969 to shoot Ringo Starr's forthcoming movie, The Magic Christian, and found that by delaying filming by three weeks, he could fit The Beatles into the space. When the three weeks' rehearsals were up, they'd be ready for the live show, which would take place somewhere visually impressive. O'Dell liked the idea of an abandoned flour mill by the Thames that he'd found, but Lindsay-Hogg became obsessed by an idea that had been suggested to him by Mick Jagger's assistant, Peter Swales.

The concept was that The Beatles would begin to perform somewhere exotic, such as a Roman ampitheatre or a desert. Then, as the show pro-

PHOTOS: ATLANTIC, MIRRORPIX

"The most miserable sessions on earth", Apple offices, January, 1969.

Film Starr: Ringo keeps up the jolly vibe during filming, January, 1969.

gressed, the venue would slowly fill with an audience comprising people from all nations, races and creeds.

The only hurdle was that neither Harrison nor Starr wanted to travel abroad, but the idea stuck and Lindsay-Hogg's pursuit of the idea and impractical suggestions began to grate with McCartney, who thought he could do a better job himself. When the director suggested that the band begin to play without announcing the show, hoping that the venue would spontaneously fill up with people, Paul's reply was suitably blunt: "Inane, I'd call that, straight off the top of my head. Inane and imbecilic." Despite this response, a three-day reconnaissance trip to Africa was planned and even an on-site caterer booked.

Although plans for the show were still undecided, rehearsals began at Twickenham on January 2, 1969. With three weeks to rehearse the hour-long show, the tight schedule was punishing for The Beatles, who had got used to pleasing themselves in the studio; at one point during the rehearsals, Lennon marvelled, "We've never learnt so many numbers at once, have we?" Handling the audio side of the project was Glyn Johns, who had also worked with the Stones and done the honours on the 1964 TV special, Around The Beatles. Johns was at Twickenham to oversee the technical side. The live sound and subsequent album of the event would be produced, as usual, by George Martin.

"George would phone in every now and then," says Johns, "but I was left entirely to my own devices and was used by the band as the producer in George's absence. I found it embarrassing, because as far as I was concerned, George Martin was their producer."

Although nothing was officially recorded at Twickenham, the film cameras captured the sessions on audio tape for inclusion in the documentary, and it is these recordings that have formed the basis for the hundreds of bootlegs that have appeared since. The tapes capture the group running over and over their pool of new songs, off-the-cuff improvisations, jokes, parodies and a selection of covers from The Beatles' old live repertoire, including tracks by Elvis (I Got Stung), Dylan (Rainy Day Women Nos 12 & 35), Buddy Holly (Crying Waiting Hoping) and sundry rock'n'roll standards (Lawdy Miss Clawdy, Be-Bop-A-Lula, Whole Lotta Shakin' Goin' On). There is also the odd dip into the vintage Lennon and McCartney songbook, with prehistoric excavations like One After 909, Too Bad About Sorrows, Hot As Sun and I Lost My Little Girl. Additionally, there were also some works in progress – Lennon's Give Me Some Truth, Child Of Nature and a fragment titled Watching Rainbows that features the "shoot me" refrain that would ➳

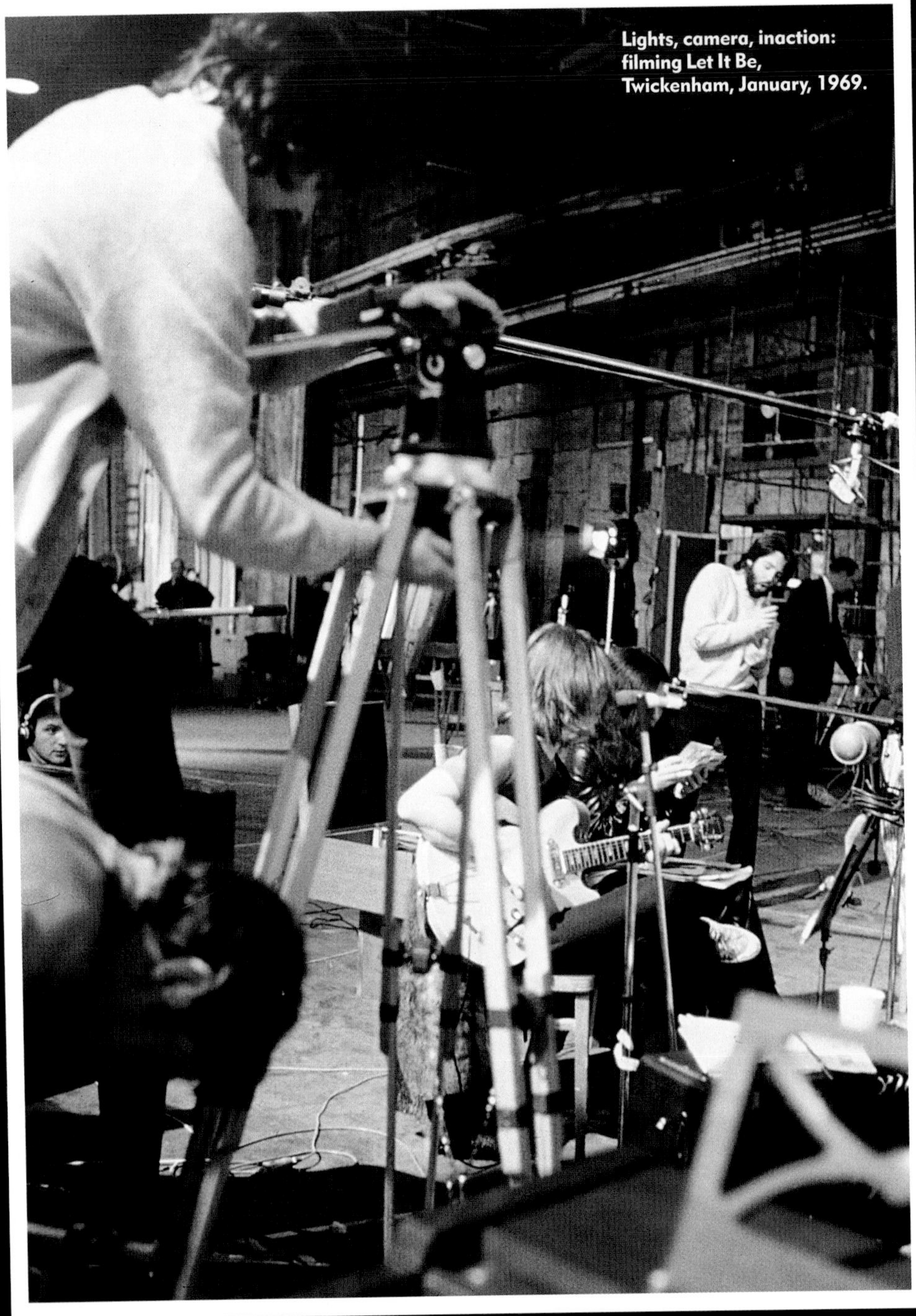
Lights, camera, inaction: filming Let It Be, Twickenham, January, 1969.

I didn't hit him and I don't know why." Now pushed beyond the simple first flush of love, John and Yoko had settled into a routine of TV, sex and heroin abuse, arriving at a state of "total communication" in which they didn't feel it necessary to verbalise their feelings because they felt they were on the same wavelength. For the forthcoming Beatles rehearsals, this was disastrous.

Lennon's problems had also affected his creativity. Since the end of the White Album recordings, he'd written very little new material – there were embryonic versions of Dig A Pony and part of what would become I've Got A Feeling, an unfinished sketch titled A Case Of The Blues and a rough version of Child Of Nature (which later became Jealous Guy). He even made another attempt on his 1968 recording Across The Universe, but his most complete composition was Don't Let Me Down, whose stark honesty impressed Paul. "I think it was a genuine cry for help," McCartney says today. "It was saying to Yoko, 'I'm really letting my vulnerability be seen, so you must not let me down'." Even so, McCartney had to help Lennon arrange the separate fragments of the song into one coherent whole.

Lennon had taken the opposite stance to McCartney's boundless enthusiasm and, in between sarcastic comments and shoddy attempts to teach the others his songs, lapsed into an almost comatose boredom with the situation. His ennui is evident in one revealing moment that was eventually included in the film Let It Be, as McCartney explains at length that The Beatles' problems may be simply down to unfamiliarity with the territory. Lennon stares past his colleague, shuffling in his seat and grabbing hold of his arm like a fidgeting child.

For his own part, McCartney was coming up with new compositions at an astonishing rate. He arrived at Twickenham with several songs

eventually resurface in Come Together, plus McCartney's Back Seat Of My Car and Another Day.

But despite the amount of material tinkered with, it became readily apparent that the atmosphere in the studio wasn't conducive to creating polished new material. "You couldn't make music at eight in the morning or 10, or whatever it was," Lennon told Rolling Stone the following year, "in a strange place with people filming you and [with] coloured lights. It was a dreadful, dreadful feeling in Twickenham Studios, being filmed all the time. I just wanted them to go away."

Lennon was not in the best frame of mind; the previous six months had seen John's personal life take a downward turn. In October 1968, he and Yoko had been arrested for possession of cannabis resin. Lennon was fined a mere £150, but the stress of the event caused the pregnant Ono to lose her baby the following month. These traumatic incidents, coupled with the general animosity directed towards the "weird" Japanese artist from both the public and members of The Beatles' inner circle, had prompted the couple to seek solace in heroin.

"I didn't even give a shit about anything," Lennon confessed. "I was stoned all the time on H. You sit through 60 sessions with the most bigheaded, uptight people on earth and see what it's fuckin' like. And be insulted just because you love someone. George insulted [Yoko] right to her face in the Apple office at the beginning and we both sat through it.

ready to rehearse, including I've Got A Feeling, Two Of Us, She Came In Through The Bathroom Window and Oh! Darling, plus the winsome Teddy Boy and the twee Maxwell's Silver Hammer.

The most promising new track was based on a nimble bass riff that was playing on his mind during one morning session. It eventually mutated into Get Back, a simple rocker that acquired an off-the-cuff lyric inspired by headlines concerning the ongoing fallout of Enoch Powell's controversial "rivers of blood" speech of 1968, in which the MP claimed that Britain would be overrun by immigrants within 20 years. With a lyric that initially took the deliberately provocative stance of "Don't dig no Pakistanis, taking all the people's jobs," McCartney later modified the line to avoid misinterpretation. It became "Too many Pakistanis living in a council flat", but feeling the word "Pakistanis" didn't scan well enough and wanting to avoid any controversy, he dropped the idea, later explaining, "The words were not racist at all. They were anti-racist."

McCartney was obviously pleased to be back at work and energised by the prospect of playing live again, but he secretly harboured a growing unease over the future of The Beatles. "Personally, it was a very difficult time for me," he recalls. "I think the drugs, the stress, tiredness and everything had really started to take its toll." The tension manifested itself in a moving dream in which he saw his mother Mary, who had died in 1956 – she told young Paul not to worry about things so much and to

PHOTOS: CAMERA PRESS

"let it be". The experience prompted McCartney to write the song that would eventually become the title track of the project and, ultimately, The Beatles' epitaph.

McCartney also admits that The Long And Winding Road was prompted by his feelings over the group, Apple and his personal life, which had lost focus since his split with Jane Asher and had only started to get back on track after meeting Linda Eastman several months earlier. "I was a bit flipped out and tripped out at that time," he explains. "It's a sad song because it's all about the unattainable; the door you never quite reach."

Paul McCartney wasn't the only one feeling the tension. Harrison had spent a pleasant Thanksgiving in Woodstock with Bob Dylan and The Band and experienced the unexpected joy of being allowed total creative freedom. According to Apple executive Peter Brown, Christmas 1968 had been a pretty glum affair for George, who allegedly spent New Year's Eve arguing with wife Patti. Now, Harrison wanted to bring some of the positive attitude from the US back to The Beatles' "winter of discontent". "I can remember feeling quite optimistic," he later admitted. "I thought, OK, it's the New Year and we have a new approach to recording." He was to be disappointed.

Always the junior partner, Harrison brought numerous beautiful songs to Twickenham, but they received derision and indifference from Lennon or heavy-handed interference from McCartney. Isn't It A Pity, Let It Down and Something were all passed over, while only For You Blue and I Me Mine were given any attention by The Beatles. All Things Must Pass was also heavily rehearsed by the band, but Harrison was unhappy with McCartney's interference in its arrangement (although one attempt endearingly features Lennon, McCartney and Harrison taking it in turns to sing a line from the first verse). At one point, George admitted he'd rather play his songs solo rather than have the band mess up his material.

It was such a conflict over working methods that caused the bitterest moments at Twickenham. During one frustrating afternoon, Paul and George disagreed over how to learn the song. Paul was concerned with ironing out problems with the details as they came up, while George favoured the ensemble approach to playing the whole song through and getting an overall impression of the composition – something he'd obviously enjoyed doing with The Band. "Paul had fixed an idea in his brain as to how to record one of his songs," remembered Harrison. "He wasn't open to anybody else's suggestions and it became stifling."

By the start of the second week, Harrison's frustration boiled over. Despite announcing that he'd written a new song over the weekend, Hear Me Lord, he was ignored by Lennon and McCartney and debuted the song alone, while the other two are fooling about at the other end of the studio. Musing aloud that maybe they should cancel the idea of the live show, Harrison finally lost his temper with McCartney during a dull rehearsal of Two Of Us. "I'm trying to help you, but I always end up annoying you," said McCartney, trying to remain reasonable. "I'll play whatever you want me to play," replied Harrison through gritted teeth. "Or I won't play at all. Whatever it is that will please you, I'll do it."

"I think George got pissed off with me coming in with ideas all the time," a rueful McCartney remembers. "I think to his mind it was probably me trying to dominate. It wasn't what I was trying to do. I started to feel it wasn't good to have ideas." While it was this celebrated incident that the surviving Beatles remembered as the cause of Harrison's departure during the 'Get Back' sessions, in reality the guitarist didn't jump ship until four days later. The actual argument that tipped George over the edge remains obscure, but contemporary rumours claimed that Lennon and Harrison "came to blows" during the lunch-break on January 10. Existing tapes don't reveal anything about the impending loss of a Beatle, but it's long been thought that there was a fair degree of upset over Lennon's comments in that week's Disc And Music Echo that Apple was in financial trouble and would be "broke in six months".

In the event, Harrison came back from lunch after an apparent argument with Lennon and told the others that he was leaving straight away, even suggesting that they advertise in the NME for his replacement. He departed with the immortal words, "See you 'round the clubs" and headed for home in Esher. The whole incident had given him a headache, which he immortalised in the song Wah-Wah. Lennon's opinion of George Harrison's discontent was that, "It's a festering wound, and yesterday we allowed it to go even deeper and we didn't give him any bandages. This year, he's suddenly realised who he is."

Tellingly, despite George's departure, the session continued, indicating that the others did not take his threat too seriously. Instead they indulged in a vicious, bluesy, feedback-laden jam with plenty of shrieking from Yoko, who finally moved centre-stage to join The Beatles. Lennon was certainly less than impressed by Harrison's actions. When Lindsay-Hogg asked what their next move should be, John deadpanned, "We split George's instruments." He then, in all seriousness, added, "I think if George doesn't come back by Monday or Tuesday, we ask Eric Clapton to play. We should just go on as if nothing's happened."

Lennon's uncommunicative and condescending attitude had riled Harrison. At the meeting at Ringo's house that Sunday, George once again stormed out when he discovered that John would rather have Yoko speak for him than add anything constructive to the discussions, which were now based around the survival of The Beatles. McCartney recalled that, "Yoko was saying, 'This is my opinion how The Beatles should be'." Returning to Liverpool, Harrison left the others to spend two more unproductive days at Twickenham before the sessions were cancelled, pending an Apple board meeting on Wednesday, January 15. After this five-hour marathon session, George agreed to return to the fold, but only if certain demands were met and plans for the live TV show were cancelled. To save The Beatles, the other three agreed.

With the TV show idea dropped (much to Lindsay-Hogg's chagrin), the sessions moved to the Apple offices at 3 Savile Row in London with the ➛

"It's going to be such an incredible, comical thing, in 50 years' time… for people to say, 'They broke up 'cos Yoko sat on an amp'." Paul McCartney

"Erm, Yoko, fancy climbing back inside your bag for an hour or two?"

purpose of finishing the album, while still shooting a "behind-the-scenes" documentary. Despite problems with the in-house studios that "Magic" Alex Madras promised The Beatles (what little equipment he'd built was unusable, causing the project further delays), the environment was much more comfortable. The basement featured a plush apple-green carpet and a roaring log fire (which was not used during recording, causing consternation throughout the rest of the building).

To alleviate potential friction, Harrison was still open to ideas that would bring some levity to proceedings. The solution appeared when he saw Ray Charles play at the Royal Festival Hall, with Billy Preston on organ. The Beatles had first met Preston in Hamburg in 1962 and George invited him to come to Savile Row and come and sit in, "Because they're acting all strange". "I hadn't seen them in a while," remembers Preston, "but they didn't seem to have changed from their Hamburg days. They made me feel so comfortable and they let me play whatever I wanted to play. I didn't realise what they were going through until much later."

"He got on the electric piano and straightaway there was 100 per cent improvement in the vibe in the room," recalled Harrison. "Billy didn't know all the politics and the games that had been going on, so in his innocence, he got stuck in and gave an extra little kick to the band." By the second week at Apple, The Beatles had Get Back and Don't Let Me Down in a good enough state to reel off the takes that became the band's next single. As Starr admitted, "When you were working on something good, the bullshit went out of the window." "They were in extremely

PHOTO: HULTON ARCHIVE

High times: the finale of Let It Be, the roof of Apple headquarters, Savile Row, January 30, 1969.

good spirits," recalls Glyn Johns. "I don't think they were aware of it themselves. I was blown away by what was going on, particularly after their paranoia about their ability to actually play live was displayed to me on several occasions."

However, it was still McCartney's intention that The Beatles were rehearsing for a climactic "live" show. With considerable resistance from Harrison and Starr (whose shooting schedule for The Magic Christian was due to begin in a matter of days), it seemed the only option would be to perform on the roof of the building they were recording in. It wasn't the Roman ampitheatre Lindsay-Hogg was after, but if The Beatles could stop the Savile Row traffic at lunchtime, that'd do. The day for the "show" was set for Thursday, January 30.

The Beatles, with Billy Preston in tow, took to the roof of 3 Savile Row for what was to be their last public performance, played to an audience of Apple staff, reporters, local office workers, businessmen and passers-by. And, for three-quarters of an hour, The Beatles actually gelled as they blasted their phenomenally loud, rockier numbers into the icy London air. McCartney was proved right; the four musicians enjoyed themselves as they ran through several takes of Get Back, Don't Let Me Down, Dig A Pony, I've Got A Feeling and One After 909. Tellingly, none of Harrison's songs were performed.

Local businesses were variously delighted, confused or offended: "It's The Beatles? Christ, it doesn't sound like them," said one man. "You call that a public performance? I can't see them!" asked a woman. "This kind of music is alright in its place, but I think it's a bit of an imposition to absolutely disrupt the business in this area," complained a businessman. The impromptu concert was brought to a premature end by local police after the manager of a nearby bank complained about the breach of the peace. Although no arrests were made, it was as dramatic as they could manage. Afterwards, The Beatles felt the elation of the live performance. "The whole scene is fantastic," beamed Lennon.

The following day, The Beatles returned to the Apple basement to reel off the songs that weren't suited to the open air for the benefit of the cameras – The Long And Winding Road, Let It Be and a rather stilted version of Two Of Us. With that, the project was put to bed and Lindsay-Hogg began the laborious process of editing the footage. However, none of the group could stand to listen to the tapes. With Lennon off on his peace campaign and a full-scale business row brewing with the appearance of Allen Klein on the scene, the project was handed over to Glyn Johns, who had already mixed some of the tracks for The Beatles' own perusal. Although Apple had confidently pencilled in a March release date for the album, it wasn't until the 10th of that month that Johns got round to compiling a loose collection of tracks.

Police stop Beatles raising the roof!

Big guard ready for LSE protest

500 ON PATROL

STUDENTS DEFIED

EX-CIA CHIEF DULLES DIES

KENT TAKEOVER

£50,000 raid

High and low tides

AT COLCHESTER . . .

AT CAMBRIDGE . . .

Containing plenty of audio verité chat and even a take of I've Got A Feeling that broke down halfway though, Johns claimed, "I thought it would make the most incredible Beatles album ever, because it was so real." The Beatles didn't agree and rejected the LP. Johns had another try in May 1969, compiling a collection that took its name from the band's last single, Get Back, and was intended to have a cover that parodied The Beatles' first album *Please Please Me* (an idea of Lennon's). Despite Apple sending out promo copies of the LP which were broadcast on several US radio stations (thus spawning dozens of bootlegs), the 'Get Back' project didn't progress any further, because The Beatles had – unexpectedly – agreed to record some more material together, which ultimately became *Abbey Road*.

As the release date for 'Get Back' was pushed back through the summer and autumn of 1969, it was even suggested that the new material be accompanied by an album of covers recorded during the sessions. But this was thinking of the most wishful kind. The 'Get Back' project had become an embarrassing thorn in The Beatles' side; a crack in the façade that should have been covered up. It was only after Phil Spector's arrival that anything was made out of the lacklustre material – certainly, none of The Beatles could have faced dealing with the tapes. As Lennon said, "Up until then, we believed intensely in what we were doing. Suddenly we didn't believe. It'd come to a point where it was no longer creating magic." ■

YELLOW SUBMARINE

Underwater Treasure

A contractual obligation album in every way, *Yellow Submarine* still showcases some fascinating Beatle moments. Peter Doggett goes in search of neglected gems from the 1969 cartoon soundtrack.

John Lennon was mortified by *Yellow Submarine*. "It's a whole sort of joke," he complained. "George Martin is on one side of our album." In his notorious 1970 interview with Rolling Stone, Lennon had demanded sarcastically: "Show me some George Martin music. I'd like to hear some." All he had to do was play Side Two of *Yellow Submarine*.

If ever a Beatles album screamed "contractual obligation", this was it. The cartoon itself was a compromise solution to the group's unwillingness to appear in a third feature film. The contract Brian Epstein negotiated with the animators, King Features, stipulated: "Three other songs [besides Yellow Submarine] are to be written by The Beatles once the film treatment is complete, which songs are to relate to said story treatment".

> "It's a whole sort of joke. George Martin is on one side of our album." John Lennon

Once the deal was signed, the movie became a sour joke at Beatles recording sessions. Every time they were disappointed by a playback, Lennon would quip: "It'll do for the film". Once George Harrison's cynical Only A Northern Song was ruled out of contention for *Sgt Pepper*, for example, it was immediately earmarked for Yellow Submarine.

Yet by early May 1967, King Features' deadline was looming, and only one of the required songs had been delivered – bearing little obvious relevance to "said story treatment". At the moment when The Beatles should have been luxuriating in the imminent release of *Sgt Pepper*, they were forced back into the studio. At the same time, Brian Epstein had agreed that they would supply another tune for a forthcoming TV spectacular – and Paul McCartney was entertaining his own film plans, which soon mutated into Magical Mystery Tour.

Yellow Submarine became a reservoir for The Beatles' dregs. When All You Need Is Love was aired on Our World that July, Lennon let slip that McCartney had also concocted a suitably international song for the show. The most likely contender is All Together Now, recorded during the week that Epstein was negotiating the TV deal. Dismissed as sub-standard by the group, it was lobbed into the Submarine pot.

So was George Harrison's epic It's All Too Much, a piece of mystic yet jaded psychedelia. King Features were left to puzzle over how to translate it into kiddies' film fare. The equally oblique Baby You're A Rich Man was handed over, only for its contractual significance to be undermined when it appeared on the All You Need Is Love single.

Having apparently satisfied their obligations, The Beatles hastily forgot about Yellow Submarine until 1968. After recording Lady Madonna in February, they returned to Abbey Road to make a promotional film clip. Rather than miming for the cameras, they taped Lennon's madcap Hey Bulldog. "[King Features] wanted another song, so I knocked [it] off," he explained later. "It's a good-sounding record that means nothing."

With the premiere just five months away, King Features' team hastened to complete the animation sequence for Hey Bulldog. In fact, the initial prints circulated around America didn't contain the song, mystifying US fans when the soundtrack album was released.

But why were the film-makers demanding another song at such short notice? Because The Beatles were having second thoughts about throwing away all of their original submissions on the soundtrack LP. Already, the soundtrack was being delayed until after the official follow-up to *Sgt Pepper*. Ultimately, the White Album didn't appear until November

PHOTO: CAMERA PRESS

1968, which ended up pushing back *Yellow Submarine* until January 1969 – six months after the release of the film that it was supposed to be promoting.

During a marathon session that October, Lennon and McCartney sequenced the White Album. Among the songs considered for the double LP was It's All Too Much – presumably a sop to George Harrison, whose Not Guilty had already been axed from the project. With Harrison out of the country and unable to state his case, It's All Too Much was also rejected, and left to appear as one of four new songs on the forthcoming soundtrack album.

As the group no doubt intended, *Yellow Submarine* was completely overshadowed by the release of the White Album. Apple spokesman Derek Taylor echoed the party line: commissioned to pen liner notes for *Yellow Submarine*, he

TRACK LISTING

SIDE ONE

1. Yellow Submarine
Lennon/McCartney
Sung by Starr

2. Only A Northern Song
Harrison
Sung by Harrison

3. All Together Now
Lennon/McCartney
Sung by McCartney

4. Hey Bulldog
Lennon/McCartney
Sung by Lennon

5. It's All Too Much
Harrison
Sung by Harrison

6. All You Need Is Love
Lennon/McCartney
Sung by Lennon

SIDE TWO

7. Pepperland
Martin

8. Sea Of Time
Martin

9. Sea Of Holes
Martin

10. Sea Of Monsters
Martin

11. March Of The Meanies
Martin

12. Pepperland Laid Waste
Martin

13. Yellow Submarine In Pepperland
Martin

YELLOW SUBMARINE

WHAT THE PAPERS SAID...

The papers got all trippy for *Yellow Submarine*.

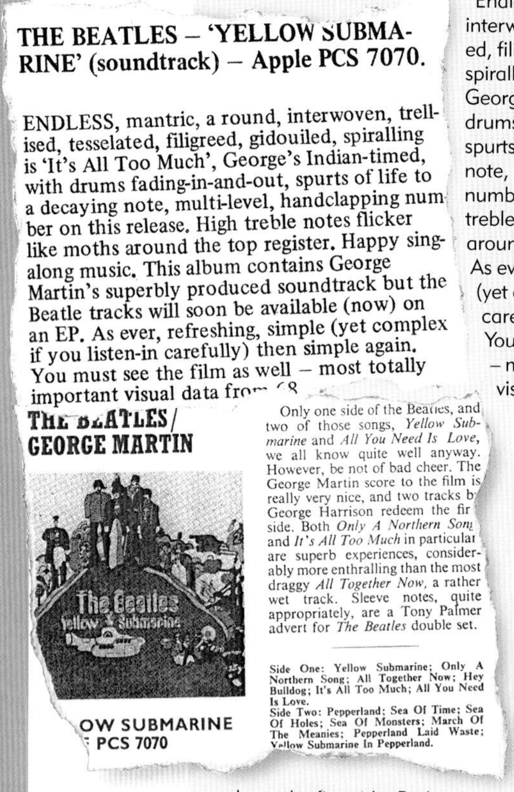
THE BEATLES – 'YELLOW SUBMARINE' (soundtrack) – Apple PCS 7070.

ENDLESS, mantric, a round, interwoven, trellised, tesselated, filigreed, gidouiled, spiralling is 'It's All Too Much', George's Indian-timed, with drums fading-in-and-out, spurts of life to a decaying note, multi-level, handclapping number on this release. High treble notes flicker like moths around the top register. Happy singalong music. This album contains George Martin's superbly produced soundtrack but the Beatle tracks will soon be available (now) on an EP. As ever, refreshing, simple (yet complex if you listen-in carefully) then simple again. You must see the film as well – most totally important visual data fro...

THE BEATLES/ GEORGE MARTIN

Only one side of the Beatles, and two of those songs, *Yellow Submarine* and *All You Need Is Love*, we all know quite well anyway. However, be not of bad cheer. The George Martin score to the film is really very nice, and two tracks by George Harrison redeem the fir... side. Both *Only A Northern Song* and *It's All Too Much* in particular are superb experiences, considerably more enthralling than the most draggy *All Together Now*, a rather wet track. Sleeve notes, quite appropriately, are a Tony Palmer advert for *The Beatles* double set.

Side One: Yellow Submarine; Only A Northern Song; All Together Now; Hey Bulldog; It's All Too Much; All You Need Is Love.
Side Two: Pepperland; Sea Of Time; Sea Of Holes; Sea Of Monsters; March Of The Meanies; Pepperland Laid Waste; Yellow Submarine In Pepperland.

...OW SUBMARINE
... PCS 7070

"Endless, mantric, a round, interwoven, trellised, tessellated, filigreed, gidouiled, spiralling is It's All Too Much, George's Indian-timed, with drums fading-in-and-out, spurts of life to a decaying note, multi-level handclapping number on this release. High treble notes flicker like moths around the top register... As ever, refreshing, simple (yet complex if you listen carefully) then simple again. You must see the film as well – most totally important visual data from '68."

Miles, International Times, February 14, 1969

"Only one side of The Beatles, and two of those songs, Yellow Submarine and All You Need Is Love, we all know quite well anyway. However, be not of bad cheer. The George Martin score to the film is really very nice, and two tracks by George Harrison redeem the first side. Both are superb xperiences, considerably more enthralling than the most draggy All Together Now, a rather wet track."

Beat Instrumental, February, 1969

SLEEVE NOTES

How The Beatles became two-dimensional caricatures.

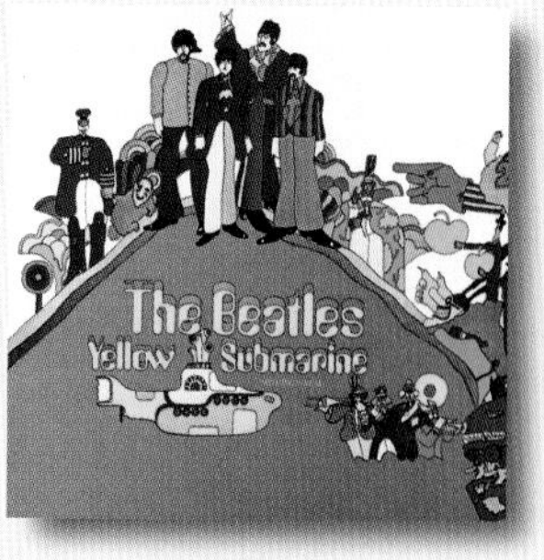

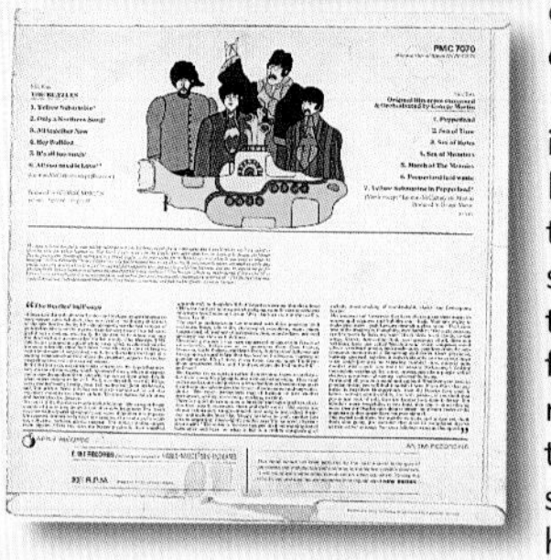

The sleeve to The Beatles' *Yellow Submarine*, like *Sgt Pepper* before it, featured the Fab Four in Pepper Band guise, yet where the latter LP's cover had actually pictured the band in fancy dress, this time, their soundtrack to the film of the same name, captured the quartet in their animated form, as seen in the flick.

Producer Al Brodax, alongside John Coates and the London cartoon company, TVC, which was behind the US cartoon series of the four-piece from 1965 to 1967, put together a feature-length animation of the band's exploits in Pepperland. The drawings were based partly on their previous cartoon and also on the poster art of Heinz Edelmann, whose garishly bright mix of art nouveau, op art, Hieronymus Bosch and psychedelic lettering was utilised to full effect on the film's land and seascapes.

The sleeve is lifted directly from the film's promotional poster and depicts the four alongside their co-stars the Blue Meanies, Jeremy, Captain Fred, Glove, the Apple Bonkers and the Snapping Turk.

Perhaps the most notable artwork feature on The Beatles' 10th album is the inclusion of Tony Palmer's review of the LP's predecessor, *The Beatles* (or the White Album), from the Observer newspaper as the album's sleevenotes, where he argues, "If there is still any doubt that Lennon and McCartney are the greatest songwriters since Schubert, then next Friday – with the publication of the new Beatles double LP – should surely see the last vestiges of cultural snobbery and bourgeois prejudice swept away in a deluge of joyous music making." Which is all very well, but he's talking about the wrong album.

Lois Wilson

> "George Martin's efforts have been derided or ignored ever since. Yet objective consideration reveals the quality of his work."

devoted the space to reprinting the Observer review of the White Album.

New York Times film critic Pauline Kael expressed her disapproval at the marketing campaign which saw American shops flooded with Yellow Submarine memorabilia. "Wasn't all this supposed to be what The Beatles were against?", she asked. "The way attacks on the consumer society become products to be consumed is, to put it delicately, discouraging."

Nothing illustrated her complaint more vividly than the *Yellow Submarine* album. Packaged not as a soundtrack but as a fully-fledged Beatles album, it featured the four new songs, the vintage 1967 title track, All You Need Is Love, as well as an entire side of George Martin's incidental music. This, too, was a contractual obligation: Martin's financial reward for services rendered.

"Brian made a mistake by letting George Martin put in all those fills on *Yellow Submarine*, the Sea Of Holes shit," Lennon noted. "He recorded all this terrible shit that went out with our album." And Martin's efforts have been derided or ignored ever since.

Yet objective consideration reveals the quality of his work, which mixed classical pastiche (several nods to Stravinsky) with a cut-and-paste playfulness of the kind exhibited on Frank Zappa's *Lumpy Gravy*. Sea Of Monsters borrowed Bach's famous Air On A G String, and then demolished it with orchestral laughter, in a moment worthy of a Tom & Jerry soundtrack (and yes, that's a compliment). Sea Of Time, meanwhile, was obviously inspired by the scoring of Harrison's Within You Without You and The Inner Light, and would have fitted perfectly on his own Wonderwall soundtrack.

In his authorised biography, Many Years From Now, McCartney allowed his Boswell, Barry Miles, to state that there were only two new Beatles songs on *Yellow Submarine*. 'Accidentally', of course, McCartney and Miles had forgotten Harrison's two efforts. Yet, alongside Lennon's edgy Hey Bulldog, Only A Northern Song and It's All Too

The Beatles in Abbey Road, February, 1968.

Much did much to rescue the album from oblivion. "I complained that it didn't really matter what I wrote," Harrison said of the gloriously ironic Only A Northern Song, "because the bulk of the money we earned was going into other people's pockets." It's All Too Much has virtually vanished from The Beatles' collective memory; it's not mentioned in their Anthology book, or indeed Harrison's I Me Mine. Yet it's one of the pinnacles of British acid-rock, its sleepwalking rhythm retaining a bizarrely contemporary feel today.

Despite its musical merits, *Yellow Submarine* was still unsatisfactory as Beatles product. The group recognised as much, and considered releasing their new songs on an EP in spring 1969, alongside the then-unreleased Across The Universe, before realising that this would alienate everyone who'd already bought the LP. Why didn't they issue the EP in 1968? Or perhaps a Beatles album of all the songs featured in the film, as provided by the *Yellow Submarine Songtrack* CD in 1999? Because both options would have denied George Martin his contractual right to appear alongside The Beatles – and robbed him of potentially the largest royalty payment of his career.

More than a year after Brian Epstein's death, the straitjacket their manager had designed left The Beatles totally unable to manoeuvre. A project that had begun in compromise ended the same way.

PHOTO: HULTON ARCHIVE

ON THE 'TOON

Bonzo Dog man Neil Innes recalls the childlike moments that made *Yellow Submarine* different.

"The story I heard was that The Beatles were not very interested in the Yellow Submarine movie at first, and so the band just gave the film-makers a few off-cuts; but then they saw some early sequences and liked it, and decided to put in a bit more. It's fair to say that a couple of the songs on it were not The Beatles' best, but there are good things too. Hey Bulldog, I really loved. The piano riff is great. Being a piano-player I thought, Oooh, that is so good. It's similar to something, but it isn't. It's got an edge to it. The thing is, The Beatles very rarely repeated themselves.

"I remember when Yellow Submarine came out and people were saying – 'Have you heard The Beatles' new single? It's a children's song!' But – without going too waffley and pretentious – we are all children, and anything that reminds us of that is good. Michael Jackson is proof of the weirdness that happens when you lose a childhood.

"We had a couple of cello players on *The Rutles* album who had worked for George Martin, and they said, 'He told us to play like this', and then they made a sound like sawing a plank of wood in two. It was George's way of getting the band to sound a bit more rock-'n'roll. That's why his orchestration fitted so well.

"All You Need Is Love is an advert for peace. I think John Lennon had seen the tricks that advertisers used to sell things such as Marmite or cornflakes and thought: 'Why not peace?' And Only A Northern Song was George Harrison realising that the music business is not a lot of fun. That's probably why we got on so well together!"

Joe Cushley

JANUARY 69

1 George Harrison returns to London from America.

2 Police in Newark, New Jersey, confiscate a shipment of John and Yoko's *Two Virgins* album because the cover is considered "pornographic". Lennon's response was: "The picture was to prove that we are not a couple of demented freaks, that we are not deformed in any way and that our minds are healthy." On the same day, The Beatles arrive at Twickenham Film Studios, Twickenham, UK, to begin filming rehearsals for a TV show which will eventually become the *Let It Be* album and documentary. The new Number 1 single in the UK is Ob-La-Di, Ob-La-Da by Marmalade.

3 The Beatles continue filming rehearsals at Twickenham Film Studios.

4 Beatles press officer Derek Taylor announces that their next album will be recorded live, possibly at Liverpool's Cavern or London's Roundhouse.

6–9 Filming of rehearsals at Twickenham Film Studios continues.

10 In a lunch break during filming at Twickenham Film Studios, George announces his intention to leave The Beatles. The same night he relents.

12 Wonderwall finally gets a UK premiere, at Cinecenta, London.

13 The *Yellow Submarine* soundtrack album is released in the US.

14 Filming of rehearsals at Twickenham continues.

17 The *Yellow Submarine* soundtrack album is released in the UK.

18 Former Beatles drummer Pete Best is awarded a settlement in his lawsuit against his old band. John tells Ray Coleman, editor of Disc And Music Echo, "Apple is losing money every week... if it carries on like this, all of us will be broke in the next six months."

20 Filming for Let It Be moves to the basement of Apple, at 3 Savile Row, London, where a new studio has been installed.

21 Ringo Starr is interviewed by Daily Express journalist David Wigg for the BBC Radio 1 show Scene And Heard. In 1976 Wigg would release all his BBC interviews with The Beatles on a double album, The Beatles Tapes. A legal attempt by the band failed to stop its release.

22 Recording sessions for the *Let It Be* album begin in the Apple Studios. George asks American keyboardist Billy Preston to play on The Beatles' sessions for *Let It Be* to help ease the tensions within the band.

23 The Beatles record Get Back at Apple Studios.

What: Billy Preston joins The Beatles
Where: Apple Studios
When: January 22, 1969

THE FIFTH ELEMENT

They first met him in Hamburg, but it was another seven years before organist Billy Preston became the "fifth Beatle". By Lois Wilson.

IF ANYONE COULD LAY CLAIM TO THE TITLE of the "fifth Beatle", surely it is organist Billy Preston. The first musician to be credited on a Beatles record – his name gets equal billing alongside the Fab Four on their single, Get Back – he contributed keyboards to their last ever live performance on the rooftop of Abbey Road studios on January 30, 1969 and their swansong album release, 1970's *Let It Be*.

Yet The Beatles first met Preston way back when both they and he were in their musical infancy. On November 1, 1962 they were supporting Little Richard at Hamburg's Star Club. Preston, aged just 15, and a veteran entertainer – he'd already performed alongside gospel legends Mahalia Jackson and James Cleveland – was a member of the rock'n'roll wild man's backing band. After the show a star-struck George went up to introduce himself.

"He was a bit in awe when he said hello but the feeling was mutual," explains Billy. "We were the youngest two there and that drew us together. He wanted to know all about America. It was a very exciting time for both of us and we immediately bonded."

Despite this it would be a further seven years before their paths crossed again, when Billy came over to Britain, this time touring with Ray Charles. "I was playing the London Palladium. George was in the audience and recognised me. He sent a message backstage asking me to come over to the Apple studio and say hello. The next day I went over and they were in the middle of filming Let It Be."

"Billy walked into the office," George recalled. "I just grabbed him, and brought him down to the studio."

However, George wasn't just eager to reacquaint himself with an old friend. He needed an ally too. By 1969 The Beatles were at breaking point. Lennon had publicly ridiculed his bandmates on the group's 1968 Christmas fanclub flexi-disc referring to them as his "beast friends". When Paul started suggesting that the band play exotic locales such as a Tunisian desert or a Roman amphitheatre, George exploded. He'd had enough of Paul's ridiculous ideas and condescending attitude, while Lennon's disinterest in the group as a whole frustrated him. Rebelling against his tag "the quiet one", he walked out.

Returning a week later with his pal Preston in tow, he prayed the atmosphere would get better. After all, getting Eric Clapton to add guitar on While My Guitar Gently Weeps during the White Album recording had helped the band get along back then, so why couldn't it happen again?

From January 22, 1969 for a total of 10 days, Preston became a part of the band. Not only were the group courteous to one another, they also rekindled some of the magic that had been missing prior to the *Let It Be* recording sessions. "Everyone was pitching in with ideas," Billy recalls, "trying different things and they just let me play whatever I wanted to play."

Billy appears on the majority of the LP, including the tracks One After 909 and Dig A Pony, both recorded during The Beatles' live rooftop concert, which was to be the grand finale to the album's accompanying film, Let It Be. But it is on the band's single, Get Back, that Billy really excels. Conceived by McCartney as a way for the group to pay their respects to their R&B roots, the song contained a visceral organ solo by Preston. "When they got to the solo part, Paul just told me to take it and I did. It was totally ad libbed. I had no idea that it was coming."

As a thank you The Beatles signed Billy to their Apple label. Over the next three years he recorded two LPs co-produced by Harrison – 1969's That's The Way God Planned It and the following year's Encouraging Words. "It was the first time that I got to sing songs that I had written. George said he'd invite some of his friends over to help out on my Apple debut and I never dreamed he meant Eric Clapton, Keith Richards and Ginger Baker."

Preston also recorded a take on the Harrison-penned My Sweet Lord. And while it may have been George who had the UK Number 1 hit in January 1971 with the song, it was Billy who recorded it first, releasing his take on the uplifting spiritual some four months earlier. "We were on tour with Delaney and Bonnie and there was a piano in the dressing room," Billy remembers. "George asked me how to write a gospel song so I started playing some chord changes. Delaney and Bonnie started singing, 'Oh My Lord, Hallelujah' and George took it from there and wrote the verses. It was very impromptu. We never thought it would be a hit."

> **"Everyone was pitching in with ideas on *Let It Be*. They just let me play whatever I wanted to play." Billy Preston**

Such was the strength of The Beatles' relationship with Billy that even when the band split up they still stayed in touch with him. He appeared on four of George's solo albums – *All Things Must Pass*, *Extra Texture*, *Dark Horse* and *33 & 1/3* – and joined him onstage at The Concert For Bangladesh and on his 1974 Dark Horse tour. He also contributed to the *John Lennon/Plastic Ono Band* LP and Lennon's *Sometime In New York City*, and teamed up with Ringo on the drummer's 1973 eponymous album and its follow-up, *Goodnight Vienna*. Five years later he played Sgt Pepper in Robert Stigwood's film, Sgt Pepper's Lonely Hearts Club Band.

Last seen in the UK performing Isn't It A Pity alongside Eric Clapton at the George Harrison tribute concert in 2002, he's also a current fixture in the guitarist's band. "I've even got George to thank for that," Billy smiles. "After all, it was he who introduced us in the first place."

"Do we have to keep mentioning my organ?" Billy Preston in Apple's press office.

PHOTOS: TOM HANLEY, VIN MAG ARCHIVE LTD

Billy Preston: "When they got to the solo part of Get Back, Paul told me to take it and I did. It was totally ad libbed."

The main manager: rock impresario, Allen Klein imagines Macca's head in 1969.

What: The Beatles meet Allen Klein
Where: Apple offices, 3 Savile Row
When: January 28, 1969

THE FAT CONTROLLER

When Allen Klein took over the management of The Beatles, he achieved a goal he'd worked towards for most of the decade. By Johnny Black.

THE LETTER WAS SHORT AND TO THE point. "Dear Sir Joe," wrote John Lennon, "I've asked Allen Klein to look after my things." Lennon's epistle to EMI Chairman Sir Joseph Lockwood sounded out across Beatledom like the bugle call of Trumpeter Landfrey, the soldier who signalled the start of the charge of the Light Brigade at Balaclava.

Lennon scribbled his note on January 27, 1969 in London's Dorchester Hotel immediately after meeting Klein for the first time, in the hope that the hard-nosed accountant might rescue him from the financial chaos that had followed Brian Epstein's death. At 9pm the next evening, all four Beatles sat down to talk turkey in the same room as Klein. George and Ringo were won over by Klein's promises to restore their fortunes by extracting them from their existing obligations to NEMS and renegotiating their EMI recording contract. Paul was unconvinced.

Klein first screamed at the world in Newark, New Jersey, on December 13, 1931. Born into an impoverished Jewish family, he spent his childhood in an orphanage, because his father could not afford to bring up three children. Never shy of work, Klein took evening classes, qualified as an accountant, and joined the accountancy firm handling rock'n'roll crooner Bobby Darin. He soon switched to publishing, looking after The Shirelles' catalogue, then moved into management with Bobby Vinton and Sam Cooke.

High-rolling: Klein with Mick Jagger in 1967.

Hitting his stride in the mid '60s, Klein set his sights on the ultimate prize – The Beatles. Realising, however, that they would not easily be pried away from Brian Epstein, he first established himself as manager of as many other British Invasion acts as he could handle, snapping up Herman's Hermits, Donovan, The Animals, Dave Clark Five and, most tellingly, The Rolling Stones.

> **"I never signed a piece of paper with Allen Klein but I'm sure he can pull one out of a drawer." Ray Davies**

Never one to slip a credit card under the latch when a steamhammer would do, Klein's management approach was to threaten to audit record company accounts, publicly revealing how much they owed their artists. Given that many companies thrived by screwing their stars, this threat shook buckets of cash out of the system. Vinton, for example, got $100,000 in "overlooked royalties".

Some of Klein's earliest clients maintain that he dramatically improved their fortunes, but others are not so happy. "I never signed a piece of paper with Klein," says Ray Davies of The Kinks, "but I'm sure he can pull one out of a drawer."

When Klein renegotiated the Stones' Decca contract in 1965, the resulting $1.25m advance somehow ended up in the coffers of a Klein subsidiary rather than in the Stones' bank account. A lawsuit ensued as the Stones tried to recover their cash while still tied to Klein as their manager.

A non-drinker, Klein had evolved into a workaholic, with no outside interests other than a lasting loyalty to his family. Clive Davis, then President of Columbia Records, characterised Klein as "a hard-working businessman, who has operated quite imaginatively in the record world". 'Imaginatively' seems a tad euphemistic. In 1967, for example, he finessed a takeover of Cameo-Parkway Records, then announced the company would be making various purchases which sent Cameo shares rocketing. Intriguingly, although fewer than a quarter of a million shares were available for public sale, more than two million were traded by February 1968 – at which point the Securities And Exchange Commission suspended trading.

Klein's route to The Beatles was made easier when, following Epstein's death, Paul assumed leadership, forging ahead with the creation of Apple. It was some months before the others realised a whole new system had grown up under McCartney's direction. Aggravation, because they didn't understand how it worked, turned to anger when that system started falling apart.

Lennon was the first to look around for a new leader. Like Klein, he had been a virtual orphan, and was an inveterate schoolyard scrapper. It's hardly surprising then that he considered the plain-talking American, "highly sensitive as well as highly intelligent".

McCartney, not solely because he was about to marry the company patriarch's daughter, was leaning toward the law firm Eastman & Eastman who had been appointed to look after The Beatles' legal affairs. He was drawn to the Eastmans because they were well-connected and gentlemanly – everything Klein was not.

It was a losing battle, however. On February 3, 1969, a decision that would in happier times have required the agreement of all four was reached by a vote of three Beatles to one, and Klein was given control of their financial affairs. McCartney's forebodings were soon made manifest. "Allen Klein had £5m the first year he managed The Beatles," he noted later. "So I smelled a rat and thought, £5m in one year? How long is it going to take him to get rid of it all?"

Klein's subsequent career has been marked by continued controversy and seemingly endless lawsuits. Following the '60s, he was involved in litigation with The Beatles, the Stones, Arhoolie Records and various other music industry stalwarts.

Although few of the lawsuits stuck, Klein did spend two months in jail during 1979 for tax evasion in connection with profits from Harrison's Bangladesh Concerts, which, it was also claimed, he had diverted into his own coffers.

These days, Klein concentrates his energies on the film world but, presumably, still manages the odd sly grin when he recalls that in 1981, George Harrison was ordered to pay $587,000 to Klein's company ABKCO, for "subconscious plagiarism" of The Shirelles' hit He's So Fine in My Sweet Lord.

PHOTOS: LINDA McCARTNEY, CAMERA PRESS, PICTORIAL PRESS

24 Recording begins on Two Of Us, Teddy Boy, Maggie Mae, Dig It, Dig A Pony and I've Got A Feeling at Apple Studios.

25 The Beatles start work on the song Let It Be at the Apple Studios.

26 At Apple Records, the idea of a live roof-top Beatles concert is put forward by John Lennon. Recording of The Long And Winding Road begins at Apple Studios.

27 John meets music business manager Allen Klein and asks him to look after his financial affairs.

28 Allen Klein meets all four Beatles. George and Ringo ask him to look at their affairs. Paul leaves the meeting.

29 The Beatles are in Apple Studios working on I Want You (She's So Heavy), One After 909, Teddy Boy and other tracks.

30 The Beatles make their final public appearance – a free concert at lunchtime on the roof of Apple HQ in London.

31 Versions of Let It Be, The Long And Winding Road, Lady Madonna and Two Of Us are recorded at Apple Studios.

FEBRUARY 69

2 Yoko is divorced from Tony Cox, and granted custody of their child, Kyoko.

3 Allen Klein, against the wishes of Paul McCartney, takes over control of The Beatles' financial affairs. Ringo starts filming at Twickenham Film Studios, on the movie version of Terry Southern's book The Magic Christian.

4 In response to the hiring of Allen Klein, Paul McCartney appoints lawyers Eastman & Eastman as general counsel to Apple Records. The firm is owned by the father of the future Linda McCartney, Lee Eastman.

5 The *Yellow Submarine* soundtrack album is certified as a US gold disc.

8 *Unfinished Music No 1 – Two Virgins* enters the US album charts at Number 158.

13 Apple Records host a party in the restaurant of the Post Office Tower, London, to launch Mary Hopkin's debut album, *Post Card*. Paul and Linda attend, as does Jimi Hendrix.

15 The *Yellow Submarine* soundtrack enters the US album chart, where it will peak at Number 2.

20 Ringo attends the European premiere of his film Candy (above), at the Odeon, Kensington.

22 I Want You is recorded again at Trident Studios, London.

25 George is in EMI's Abbey Road studios in London, starting work on recording Something.

MARCH 69

1 Mary Hopkin records Goodbye, written by Paul McCartney, at Morgan Studios, London.

2 John and Yoko perform at the Lady Mitchell Hall, Cambridge, UK, where they record side one of the album *Life With The Lions*.

4 Paul attends the London premiere of the film Isadora, about dancer Isadora Duncan.

8 The Beatles hold the top two places on the US album chart with the *White Album* and *Yellow Submarine*.

12 George Harrison is busted for drugs just before setting off for Paul McCartney's marriage to Linda Eastman at Marylebone Registry Office, London (below).

13 The Daily Mirror carries a front page banner headline – 'Beatle George And Patti On A Drugs Charge'.

14 The Beatles' film soundtrack album *Yellow Submarine* is certified as a gold record in the US.

15 As subsequently documented in The Ballad Of John And Yoko, the not-so happy couple are prevented, because of passport problems, from boarding a ferry to France at the Thorensen Passenger Terminal, Southampton.

16 John Lennon and Yoko Ono fly to Paris.

17 Cream release a new single, Badge, in the US, with contributions by George Harrison.

18 Ringo is filmed at the Star & Garter pub, Putney, London, for his latest movie, The Magic Christian.

19 George and Patti appear in Esher And Walton Magistrates' Court, Walton-On-Thames, on drugs charges, but are released on press officer Derek Taylor's surety.

20 John Lennon marries Yoko Ono in Gibraltar.

21 Jackie Lomax releases a new single in the UK, Sour Milk Sea, written by George Harrison. Lomax's backing musicians on the single include George, Paul and Ringo.

22 John and Yoko are "honeymooning down by the Seine" in Paris, France.

25 John and Yoko move to the Amsterdam Hilton, Holland, to stage their Bed Peace event.

27 In London, Ringo states that The Beatles will not play before an audience again.

28 Mary Hopkin releases a new single in the UK, Goodbye, written by John and Paul. McCartney also plays guitar on the single.

What: Filming The Magic Christian
Where: Twickenham Film Studios
When: February 3, 1969

STARRING ROLE

Despite acclaimed performances in two Fabs films, Ringo insisted he couldn't act. The Magic Christian was his first real test. By Fred Dellar.

IT WAS EVIDENT FROM THE START THAT, though John and Paul might be onstage heroes, when it came to filming, Ringo was king of the clips. That face. Hangdog and hound dog, ever woeful, ever watchable, and the deadpan voice that turned even the most mundane of phrases into something that had audiences waiting for the next earful. A Hard Day's Night and Help! – Ringo stole them both, without even trying.

The big screen beckoned and Brian Epstein was aware of the fact. Ringo recalls that Epstein helped sort out some suitable scripts. "We decided that Candy was good for me as a trial because it was only two weeks' work."

Candy, despite a cast list that included Marlon Brando, Richard Burton, James Coburn and Walter Matthau, was really no big deal for Ringo who took just a minor role. "Then The Magic Christian came in, which was also by the same writer, Terry Southern."

Southern was flavour of the era. He'd not only penned both Candy and The Magic Christian, and fashioned the screenplay for Barbarella and Dr Strangelove, but had also shaped the plot of Easy Rider, a turning point in rock movie-making. There was a madcap, almost psychedelic quality about his work that Ringo loved.

"He's fantastic," enthused Starr. Accordingly, the would-be thespian set out for Twickenham Studios on February 3, 1969 to start shooting. A role had been created for him, one that didn't figure in Southern's book. He was to become Youngman Grand, adopted son of Sir Guy Grand (Peter Sellers), a man dedicated to proving that people will do anything for money.

But Ringo was still informing anyone who would listen that he really was no film star. "I can't act, I don't know how to. I just don't do anything. I don't know, perhaps that's acting."

As filming proceeded, the cast changed almost daily. Ringo recalled that various stars would drop in to say hello and then find themselves handed a script. "The producers would come up to Terry and say: 'Terry, you'd never guess!' And he'd say 'Well, what is it?' 'We've got Yul Brynner!' So Terry would have to type something in for Yul Brynner." Raquel Welch ended up in the picture through much the same procedure. Eventually Roman Polanski, Richard Attenborough, Laurence Harvey, Christopher Lee, Dennis Price, Spike Milligan, John Cleese and Graham Chapman were also installed somewhere amid the ever-changing plot. If director Joseph McGrath was constantly bemused by all that was happening around him, it was nothing in comparison to Terry Southern's worries. "It's a giant sleeping pill," he proclaimed as he began losing count of the re-writes.

Meanwhile, Ringo and Peter Sellers proceeded on their manic way, as Sir Guy and Youngman Grand turned a rendition of Hamlet into a striptease show, ruined a grouse shoot by employing machine guns and tanks, disrupted both Cruft's and Sotheby's, causing everyone aboard an ocean liner to abandon ship by means of a take-over by Dracula, and induced a traffic warden (Milligan) to eat a parking ticket following a £500 bribe.

The two had forged something of a mutual admiration society, Sellers informing the press that "Ringo is a natural, he can speak with his eyes." But Ringo could sometimes be put out of his easy-going stride by the ex-Goon. "I know him quite well," explained Ringo, "but suddenly he was going into character and I got confused!"

Sometime in June, 1969, Rolling Stone emerged with the news that: "The Magic Christian, which will feature Ringo Starr, has a prominent scene in which a freak millionaire humiliates The American Way by sticking out for grabs a huge container of money – mixed with shit. The scene is being filmed in New York's Wall Street district, and Southern is holding out for the real shit."

It didn't happen. The film's American financiers vetoed the plan. The scene, featuring a huge vat of urine, which, onscreen, came accompanied by the sound of Thunderclap Newman's There's Something In The Air, was eventually shot on London's South Bank, near the National Film Theatre.

The gown show: Ringo and Peter Sellers in The Magic Christian.

Protests that the film was offensive were surfacing even before it was finished, but to Ringo it was all a bit of fun. "I'm sick of message films," he said. "It's about time we got back to Doris Day."

"I can't act, I don't know how to. I just don't do anything. I don't know, perhaps that's acting." Ringo Starr

The principal photography for The Magic Christian concluded, a party was thrown at Les Ambassadeurs, in London, on May 4, with both John and Paul joining Ringo in the festivities. Paul's one songwriting contribution to the film, Come And Get It, performed by Apple group Badfinger, was recorded during the summer. The group, overseen by McCartney, also fashioned two other songs for the film. There was other post-production work to be done on the film, including an audio track for the trailer. By the autumn all was complete, a Royal Charity Performance being lined up for the Odeon, Kensington on December 18. Before the Royals took their seats, John and Yoko paraded outside the cinema, waving banners that proclaimed 'Britain Murdered Hanratty'. Sir Guy Grand might well have fashioned the situation.

But even the poor reviews that followed the film's opening – one commenting that "the novel collapses as a film within the first few minutes" – failed to faze Ringo. "Nobody made me do it, I wanted to do it," he reflected. And then began musing about his next project.

PHOTOS: TOPFOTO, PICTORIAL PRESS, POPPERFOTO

"...And this is for Honey Don't!"
Raquel Welch and Ringo on the set of
The Magic Christian, Twickenham
Film Studios, February 1969.

Putting the business into showbusiness: Paul and John with Peter Brown (sitting) and Magic Alex (right) in 1968.

A SLICE OF HISTORY

George invited Hell's Angels to pop by the office, John had a room where all the furniture was half-size, and the 'house hippy' rolled joints for passing guests – there was never a dull moment at Apple… By Johnny Black.

PHOTO: TOPHAM

WHO'S WHO AT APPLE?

Neil Aspinall: Trusted former roadie who became Managing Director.
Alistair Taylor: Long-time NEMS employee, brought over as General Manager.
Ron Kass: Head of Apple Records, former VP of Liberty Records (Europe), and Joan Collins' husband.
Peter Brown: CEO, Apple Corps. Suave and erudite former NEMS director.
Peter Asher: Head of A&R. Jane Asher's brother and former member of Peter And Gordon.
Denis O'Dell: Head of Apple Films. Associate producer of John Lennon's movie How I Won The War.
Derek Taylor: Head of Press. Local newspaper journalist-turned celebrated Beatles PR guru.
Tony Bramwell: Head of Promotions, Apple Records. Trusted ex-roadie who rose through the ranks of NEMS.
Terry Doran: Head of Apple Publishing. A former partner of Brian Epstein in a car-dealership that earned him immortality as the "man from the motor trade" in She's Leaving Home.
Alexis Mardas, aka Magic Alex: Head of Apple Electronics. Greek-born electronics 'expert'.
Barry Miles: Manager of Zapple Records. Miles knew McCartney as a friend since 1965. His love of avant-garde jazz and poetry made him a natural for the Zapple gig.
Allen Klein: US music business accountant, brought in to sort out The Beatles' financial problems.
Richard DiLello: Apple's 'house hippy' and future director of public relations at the company.

Peter Brown

Ron Kass

Derek Taylor

Allen Klein and Neil Aspinall

Terry Doran

1967

JANUARY 13

Brian Epstein publicly announces a merger between his company NEMS and RSO, owned by entrepreneur Robert Stigwood.
Tony Bramwell: The merger was great from Brian's perspective because it brought a lot of new acts including The Who and Cream into the NEMS stable, but The Beatles were never keen on Robert Stigwood.
Barry Miles: They were outraged when they learned that Brian had discussed a plan to sell them to Stigwood.
Tony Bramwell: They told Brian that if he gave Stigwood any more control, they'd leave NEMS completely. It was around then, the idea of taking control of their own affairs started to come in.

JANUARY 19

At Studio 2, Abbey Road, London, The Beatles start work on A Day In The Life.
Tony Bramwell: I remember Paul saying, "A is for Apple, B is for Beatles..." around when they were making A Day In The Life. It had come from that Magritte painting he had on the shelf above the radiator in his lounge.
Alistair Taylor: Paul rang me up at the office and said he had a name for the company they wanted to start – Apple. I said, "Paul, what does that mean?" He said: "Think about it, Alistair. What's the first thing a child learns at school? A is for apple." He was convinced it would revolutionise the entire business world.
Barry Miles: There was talk of getting together with Donovan and the Stones and forming one big company, but that never got very far.

JUNE 1

***Sgt Pepper's Lonely Hearts Club Band* is released.**
Tony Bramwell: If you look at the cover of *Sgt Pepper*, you'll see a credit saying the cover was designed by "MC Productions and The Apple". That was the first time it appeared in public.

AUGUST 27

Brian Epstein dies of a drug overdose at his home in Chapel Street, Belgravia.
Alistair Taylor: I stayed on at NEMS after Brian died, but I very quickly came to hate it. There was the most dreadful in-fighting, with everybody – Vic Lewis, Robert Stigwood – struggling to take control of The Beatles.

SEPTEMBER 13

The Beatles form an electronics company, Fiftyshapes Ltd, with Magic Alex as company director. This will become Apple Electronics.
Ringo Starr: Magic Alex invented electrical paint. You paint your living room, plug it in, and the walls light up! We saw small pieces of metal as samples, but then we realised you'd have to put steel sheets on your living-room wall and paint them.

SEPTEMBER 27

With Neil Aspinall established as Managing Director of Apple, a music publishing subsidiary, Apple Music Publishing Ltd, is formed, with offices at 94 Baker Street.
Neil Aspinall: A lot of people put themselves forward to run it, but there didn't seem to be any unanimous choice. So I said to them, "Look, I'll do it until you find somebody that you want to do it."
Alistair Taylor: The point of The Beatles having a company or companies was to avoid paying too much tax. They were paying 19/6d in the pound but, if you were a company with a business plan that you could submit to the Inland Revenue, you could reduce that to 16/-. So, if you're earning millions of pounds, that represented a vast saving.

Brian Epstein's brother, Clive, came in one day with a brilliant idea for a national chain of greeting card shops. There was nothing like that back then. Clinton's didn't exist. We all loved it, but The Beatles hated it. In fact, they hated all our ideas.

Finally, Lennon came in and said, "We should start a company to help artists and creative people". So that's what we set about doing. After all, it was their money.

We started out in that tiny office in Baker Street, which later became the Apple shop. The first ideas were the publishing company, the recording studio and the record label.
Peter Asher: The idea was to create a record company that was more artist-friendly, more open to new ideas. People nowadays complain about the 'suits' who run record companies, but record companies then really were run by men in suits. If you went into the office of Sir Joseph Lockwood at EMI you almost felt you should bow.

DECEMBER 7

The Apple shop opens at 94 Baker St, London.
Tony Bramwell: That was run by The Fool, this group of Dutch hippy designers. They had some wonderful designs for clothes but there wasn't really anybody who knew anything about running a shop.
Alistair Taylor: Round about then, they asked me if I'd like to join Apple as General Manager and I was very keen. I started the next day.

DECEMBER 11

Apple Music Publishing signs its first band, Grapefruit.
John Perry (guitar, Grapefruit): I was in the Speakeasy when I bumped into Terry [Doran]. He said he had a music publishing business and gave me a card. I'd never heard of Apple and, for a couple of weeks, I didn't think about it. Then I had some songs ready that I wanted published, so I thought I may as well go and see him. By this stage The Beatles had gone 'heavy', and we got chatting about an idea of mine for a project to fill the gap they were vacating. We formed a band called Grapefruit, which was named by John Lennon.
Geoff Swettenham (drums, Grapefruit): Apple paid for our house and gave us a retainer every week. They kept us alive, basically.

DECEMBER 21

The Beatles hold a party in the Royal Lancaster Hotel, London, to launch their new TV film, Magical Mystery Tour.
Tony Bramwell: The last real NEMS event was the Mystery Tour Christmas party. Within a few days, all the people from NEMS that The Beatles wanted had moved over to Apple. That was me, Alistair Taylor, Peter Brown, Laurie the switchboard girl and Barbara the secretary.

1968

JANUARY 22

The Beatles move into new offices at 95 Wigmore Street, London. Joining them at the new premises is Apple Films, plus the accounting and administration offices.
Tony Bramwell: The Music Publishing

PHOTOS: MIRRORPIX/TONY BRAMWELL/MIRROR SYNDICATION

remained at Baker Street, and it wasn't until we moved to Savile Row in July that all of the Apple companies were under one roof.

FEBRUARY 10

The Beatles transfer all their business affairs from NEMS to the newly formed company, Apple, and Peter Asher joins as Head of A&R.

Peter Asher: Paul was aware that I had been producing records, so when he first asked me about Apple it was to see if I would be interested in producing for the label. A little later, he asked if I'd like to become Head of A&R. Apple had only one 'suit' and that was Ron Kass, formerly of Liberty Records, because we needed somebody with a good business head.

At the start, it was genuinely exciting. We felt very optimistic that we could achieve the things we were setting out to do. We had a weekly A&R meeting which always had to have a quorum of Beatles in attendance.

APRIL 8

Former Beatles PR Derek Taylor returns from Los Angeles to rejoin the Fab Four as Head of Press for Apple.

Richard DiLello: I got my job at Apple as the house hippy because I was in the right place at the right time. I knew Derek Taylor from his time in LA. I was knocking around the world in '67 and wound up in London by the spring of '68. When I saw that Derek was back with The Beatles I called and asked him for a job. I asked and I received.

MAY 3

James Taylor takes his demos to Peter Asher.

James Taylor: I had made a demo tape. Peter heard it and liked it. He played it for McCartney, who said he liked it, and suddenly I was signed.

Peter Asher: What I didn't know at the time was that James was a heroin addict. It was only while we were making his first album that I realised he was spending a lot more time in the toilets than was normal.

MAY 5

Mary Hopkin appears on TV talent show Opportunity Knocks.

Alistair Taylor: Twiggy went up to see Paul. He rang down shortly after to ask if I'd seen Opportunity Knocks the night before, but I hadn't. He said, "Twigs is here and she's seen this wonderful singer on Opportunity Knocks." So I was given the job of tracking Mary down.

Once I'd found her, we brought her to Dick James's studio in London. She only knew about four songs but, as soon as she opened her mouth, Paul and I looked at each other. He'd made up his mind.

Peter Asher: Paul had heard the song Those Were The Days, sung by two people in a nightclub in London. As soon as he heard Mary singing, he said: "We must sign her, and I know exactly what her first single will be."

Alistair Taylor: During the second song, she snapped a guitar string and then this demure little angel said, "Oh, bugger!", which completely cracked Paul and me up.

MAY 14

John and Paul hold a press conference at the Americana Hotel, New York, to announce the formation of Apple.

John Lennon (at press conference): It's a business concerning records, films and electronics. We want to set up a system whereby people who just want to make a film about anything don't have to go on their knees in somebody's office, probably yours.

Paul McCartney: We're in the happy position of not really needing any more money, so for the first time, the bosses aren't in it for the profit. If you come to me and say, "I've had such and such a dream," I will say, Here's so much money. Go away and do it.

JULY 15

Apple Corps moves to 3 Savile Row, London, purchased a month earlier for £500,000.

Tony Bramwell: The ground floor was reception, switchboard and Ron Kass's office. Magic Alex had the run of the basement. He built the studio down there, although it never worked properly. The second floor was Derek's press office, where all the craziness went on.

Derek Taylor: We never made a note. Rolled joints all day, for our guests and ourselves… and we had hundreds of people through our room. Ken Kesey wanted to recite. Or a Joe Smith or Mo Ostin from Warner Bros wanted to say, "Hi." "Put them in the back room, Ringo. Roll them a joint." Lauren Bacall's downstairs, wants to meet them. It was crowd-pleasing on a grand scale.

Tony Bramwell: Across from Derek was the main Beatles office, where Neil and Mal were also installed. The third floor was accounts, and I was on the top with Denis O'Dell, which we shared with Peter Asher.

I was taken on to be the assistant to Denis O'Dell, who was the head of Apple Films. Mostly, we were just making promo clips, so I'd also go and plug records to the BBC. One day I'd be filming Lady Madonna, next day I'd be plugging it, so I became Head Of Promotions, gave myself the job really.

JULY 17

James Taylor accompanies Mary Hopkin to the premiere of Yellow Submarine at the Pavilion, London.

Alistair Taylor: I arranged for James to accompany Mary to the premiere

"THERE WAS AN ENDLESS SUPPLY OF GREAT HASHISH, WHICH WAS PART OF MY JOB AS THE HOUSE HIPPY TO PROCURE, TO ROLL AND TO DISPENSE."
RICHARD DiLELLO

"Right, first thing on today's agenda – where's the friggin' furniture?" Apple gets new premises at 3 Savile Row, August 1968.

Feeling fruity: budding Apple entrepreneurs, Ringo, George and Paul in 1968.

"THEY WERE HANDING MONEY OUT TO PEOPLE LIKE IT WAS GOING OUT OF FASHION. PEOPLE WERE BEING GIVEN CARS AND HOUSES." ALISTAIR TAYLOR

of Yellow Submarine, and go on with her afterwards to the party in the Royal Lancaster Hotel. Half an hour later, I see Mary looking rather forlorn, standing on her own. So I asked where James had got to. "He's out on the veranda," she said. So I go out there and find him smoking a massive joint. He'd just walked off and left her. Three times that night I had to go out and drag him back inside until eventually I said, "Look, either you stop this, or you get out." Eventually, I called him a cab and sent him home. He wasn't in any fit state to get home on his own.

JULY 23

Mal Evans signs The Iveys to Apple.
Peter Asher: Each of The Beatles would come along to the weekly A&R meetings and they'd all really just be interested in their own projects. George would be talking about Jackie Lomax, John about some strange project he was planning with Yoko. At one particular meeting, Mal was really enthusing about a group he'd been championing, The Iveys. Paul also liked them, and John and George were quite impressed by their demo tapes, so we signed them up.

JULY 31

When the ailing Apple shop is closed, all remaining merchandise is given away to customers.
Barry Miles: The collapse of the Apple shop was an early signal of things going wrong. I think they lost about £100,000 on that, which was a huge amount of money then.

AUGUST 11

The Beatles declare National Apple Week and officially launch Apple Records.
Alistair Taylor: They were handing money out to people like it was going out of fashion. People were being given cars and houses. We had two cordon bleu cooks based in the building, a huge cabinet six-foot high full of vintage wines and champagnes. The idea was that it made sense to entertain people in the building rather than going out for expensive lunches, but it just got out of control.
Richard DiLello: There was an endless supply of great hashish, which was part of my job as the house hippy to procure, to roll and to dispense.
Alistair Taylor: I got the boys together for a meeting in about August of '68, and I told them, "Your money is flying out the window." They asked what they should do, and I told them to bring in a really good businessman. The Apple staff were good people but we were really small-town businessmen, none of us had experience of big business.

AUGUST 26

Apple Records releases its first four singles, including Hey Jude by The Beatles and Those Were The Days by Mary Hopkin.
Tony Bramwell: People often think Apple was some kind of disaster area, but the record label and the publishing division were remarkably profitable. On the publishing side, The Iveys became Badfinger and wrote Without You which was a huge hit for Harry Nilsson, and we had Gallagher & Lyle. We even had The Steve Miller Band signed for songwriting and we had their publishing.

SEPTEMBER

Barry Miles is appointed label manager of Zapple, the avant-garde/experimental subsidiary of Apple, launched in May the following year.
Barry Miles: We sent boxes of Beatles records to people like Fidel Castro and Mao Tse Tung so they could see we were a real record company, and we asked them if they'd be prepared to be recorded for the label, or let us have tapes of their speeches or whatever. We never heard anything back from any of them.

NOVEMBER 3

Crosby, Stills & Nash are in London, rehearsing their new group.
Tony Bramwell: There were some missed opportunities. The William Morris Agency was next door to Apple. The main guy there, Larry Curzon, had a mews house just off Gloucester Road, where Crosby, Stills And Nash were rehearsing. They brought their demos in to Apple and everybody loved them except John, who thought it was just twee nonsense, so they were rejected.

NOVEMBER 24

Grapefruit part company with Apple.
George Alexander (bass/vocals): [Speaking at the time] We want to lose the Beatles tag. Sure, it helped us in the beginning and everybody knew us as The Beatles' group, but we want to make it on our own.

DECEMBER 4

George Harrison memos the Apple staff, advising that 12 Hell's Angels will be stopping off at the office en route to Czechoslovakia. He suggests: "Try to assist them without neglecting your Apple business and without letting them take control of Savile Row."
Richard DiLello: Not a day went by that there was not some totally tripped-out crisis and/or triumph to deal with. How could anything this beautiful have a chance of lasting? It couldn't.

1969

JANUARY 18

John Lennon is quoted in Disc And Music Echo, saying Apple could be bankrupt within six months.
Allen Klein: I read in the press, a statement attributed to John Lennon, to the effect that if The Beatles continued to spend money at the rate at which they were doing, "they would be broke in six months". I telephoned Mr Lennon from the US and arranged to meet him in London.
John Lennon: People were robbing us and living on us. Eighteen or 20 thousand pounds a week was rolling out of Apple and nobody was doing anything about it...

JANUARY 22

Long-delayed because of Magic Alex's incompetence, Apple Studios finally opens.
Tony Bramwell: There were some very poor financial decisions, like Apple Electronics. That was John's thing. He had such absolute faith in Magic Alex Mardas that he let him run up all kinds of massive bills, and none of it ever came to anything. Alex just drained cash away.

JANUARY 27

John Lennon meets Allen Klein and asks him to look after his financial affairs.
Allen Klein: He made it clear that he was there for himself and Yoko, period. He told me that the Eastmans were handling The Beatles' financial affairs.
Peter Asher: I had already heard bad things about Klein's dealings with the Stones, so I was alarmed when I heard John wanted to bring him in. He had allegedly done great things for a string of artists he'd had before, American singers like Bobby Darin or Bobby Vinton, but there was always a suspicion that he ended up with a bigger share of their earnings and futures than was proper.
Peter Brown: Mick Jagger wanted to come around and tell The Beatles what Klein was really like. He went to John and told him, "Before you make a commitment to Klein, let me tell you my experience."
Mick Jagger: He's a person to be avoided as far as I'm concerned. He's just interested in himself.
Peter Brown: So John tells Klein that Mick was coming and when Mick arrived he was presented with not only the four Beatles but also with Klein. So there wasn't much that Mick could say. It was a very, very bizarre thing for John to have done.

FEBRUARY 3

Allen Klein is appointed to look into the business affairs of The Beatles and all their companies.
Peter Asher: Paul reacted very negatively to Klein's arrival. I remember him walking around the building looking scary in his black turtle-neck pullover. My reaction was to get out

Days in the life of Apple: (second row, right) The Iveys, soon to become Badfinger; (bottom left) Paul with one of Apple Records' first signings, Mary Hopkin.

"Joint, anyone?" Apple's press office with Derek Taylor (far right) sitting in the white chair.

"YOU COULD NO LONGER WANDER IN AND OUT OF PEOPLE'S OFFICES. KLEIN WAS VERY CONTROLLING ABOUT ANY OF US HAVING PERSONAL CONTACT WITH THE BEATLES."

TONY BRAMWELL

while the going was good. I had the luxury of resigning instead of being booted out, and I made sure I took James Taylor with me.

FEBRUARY 4

In response to the hiring of Klein, Paul McCartney appoints Eastman & Eastman as general counsel to Apple Records. The firm is owned by Lee Eastman, the father of Linda McCartney.

Barry Miles: The other three Beatles stopped coming in. John and Yoko took over. Kyoko [Yoko's daughter from her first marriage] was allowed to run riot. I remember her pulling all the plugs out of the switchboard, cutting off people in the middle of what might well have been important conversations, and when the switchboard operator objected, Yoko threatened to have her sacked. Yoko was never afraid to wield her power.

Jean Nisbet (music publisher, Apple): John had a 'half-giants' room, where all the furniture was cut in half, and a giant suit was laid out on the floor. What he and Yoko did in there, God alone knows.

MAY 1

Apple publicly announces the formation of Zapple. But it didn't last long.

Barry Miles: Right in the middle of my second trip to New York, to record Ginsberg singing William Blake's Songs Of Innocence And Experience, Klein cut the funding, and I was left stranded in the Chelsea Hotel. Ginsberg ended up financing the recording himself. I couldn't even get in touch with The Beatles, Klein made sure that nobody could reach them.

MAY 8

John, Ringo and George sign a new management agreement with ABKCO, which gives Allen Klein 20 per cent of their future earnings.

Chris O'Dell (secretary, Apple Records): He just moved in and started firing people. It took him more than a year, but in that time he got rid of everybody he could possibly clear out.

Alistair Taylor: Within two weeks of Klein arriving, I was sacked. There were 16 names on the list, with me at number one. Neil was the only survivor. He was untouchable. Klein cleaned out everybody who was close to The Beatles and from that moment I couldn't even get them on the phone. The next time I spoke to Paul was 20 years later.

Richard DiLello: Don't forget, Allen Klein had his marching orders from John, George and Ringo: "Straighten this mess out and stop the haemorrhage of money!" Fundamentally, Allen Klein did what he had to do. He just did it his way. And I think he did a pretty good job of it too. Whether or not in the end he ripped The Beatles off I don't know.

Tony Bramwell: I managed to get along with him for a while but the whole atmosphere changed right away. You could no longer wander casually in and out of people's offices. He was very controlling about any of us having personal contact with The Beatles. John was the only one who continued to support Klein. Paul and Ringo stopped coming in. George lost interest. They realised Apple was screwed.

MAY 9

John, George and Ringo confront Paul in Olympic Sound Studios, trying to make him sign the new ABKCO agreement. He refuses.

Paul McCartney: I said, "He'll take 15 per cent." But for some reason the three of them were so keen to go with him that they really bullied me and ganged up on me. It sounds a bit wimpy but, anyway, they out-voted me on these issues.

AUGUST 29

Apple Electronics is closed.

Alistair Taylor: Apple Electronics was madness, although Alex did make a few things that actually worked. I saw him demonstrate a voice-activated telephone in his little lab behind Marylebone Station. He told it what to dial and it did it, no hands required, which was amazing to see back then.

SEPTEMBER 20

During a meeting between The Beatles and Allen Klein at Apple, John Lennon says, "I want a divorce. The group is over. I'm leaving." However he agrees to keep his feelings private for the time being.

Paul McCartney: He wanted to live life, do stuff and there was no holding back with John. It was what we all admired him for. So we couldn't really say, We don't want you to do that, stay with us. You'd feel so wimpy. It had to happen.

OCTOBER 2

In an interview, John Lennon likens Apple to a big black hole sucking up all his benefits as a composer and performer.

Paul McCartney: We were great creators. But nobody had half an idea about a budget. So what we were spending, I think, was more than what we were earning.

Barry Miles: There were top executives on huge salaries flying all over the world and staying in five-star hotels. None of the people at the bottom made more than £15 a week.

Richard DiLello: I was only being paid 10 quid a week, 20 Yankee dollars. But who cared about money? It was the rush of working for The Beatles that I was after.

Barry Miles: The canteen staff were on £12, and you'd get John and Yoko coming in and ordering a £60 can of caviar that they'd sit and eat for lunch – that's five times the canteen staff's weekly wage on one lunch!

1970

FEBRUARY 12

Using the pseudonym Billy Martin, Paul starts work on an instrumental, Kreen-Akrore, intended for his solo debut album, in Morgan Studios, London.

Tony Bramwell: It got very depressing towards the end when everything was being done in secret. Paul was sneaking in and out of studios, booked under false names, working on his first solo album, and I was sworn to secrecy about it. And John would ring up and get me to do some filming for him and Yoko. He'd want a film of some crazy event, or some part of his anatomy or whatever, but I had to do it without telling the others. And I had to try to take it seriously, which was pretty hard.

DECEMBER 31

A writ issued on behalf of Paul McCartney by the Chancery Division Of The High Court, London, formally begins the legal process which will result in the dissolution of The Beatles.

Tony Bramwell: The record label wasn't wound up officially until 1975 but in my mind, the break-up of The Beatles was the end of Apple.

I stayed as long as I could, but just before Christmas a little item appeared in a gossip column saying that Harry Saltzman had offered me a job. When Klein heard about that he asked me if it was true, was I going to work for Saltzman? I said I had been offered but I hadn't decided, and Klein was just so rude and offensive that I decided to resign.

Closing time: the doorway of 3 Savile Row, 1971.

Richard DiLello: Apple was the ultimate stoner's dream come true. It was a pure, naïve, utopian fantasy brought briefly to fruition by The Beatles' genius. But, like a beautiful butterfly, it was broken on the rack of corporate reality. No-one since has ever tried to do what The Beatles attempted to achieve at Apple.

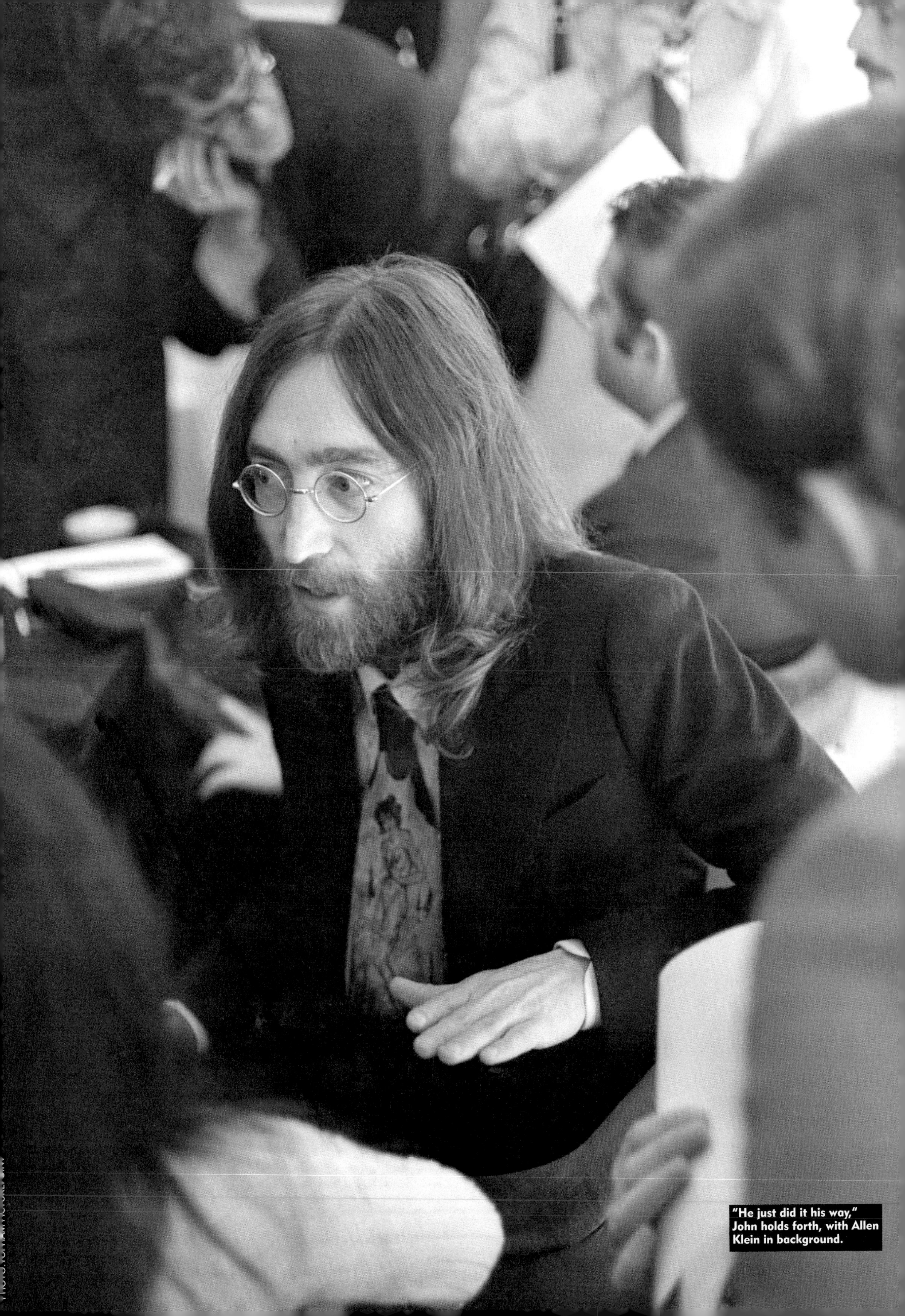

"He just did it his way," John holds forth, with Allen Klein in background.

The happy couple board a private plane to Paris after exchanging vows in Gibraltar, March 20, 1969.

What: John marries Yoko
Where: Gibraltar
When: March 20, 1969

WHITE WEDDING

John Lennon wanted his marriage to Yoko Ono to be a low-key affair – so he wrote a chart-topping song about the big day. By Chris Ingham.

WHEN LEFT STRANDED ON THE platform of Euston Station in August 1967, lost in the mêlée as The Beatles caught the train to Bangor for an audience with the Maharishi, Cynthia Lennon couldn't help but feel the moment symbolised the drift in her life with John. By the time she returned home from a holiday in May 1968 to find a blank-faced, unperturbed John and Yoko, dressing-gowned and sipping tea in the conservatory, she understood the marriage was over. "I knew immediately when I saw them together that they were right for each other," she remembered. "I knew I'd lost him."

Stumbling numbly into the arms of Magic Alex (Apple's electronics guru) for one night only, Cynthia was invited back to Kenwood for a semi-reconciliation before receiving, within weeks, a demand for divorce from John, citing her adultery. When it became clear that Yoko was pregnant, the adultery charges were reversed and Cynthia was granted a decree nisi in November 1968, accepting £100,000 a few months later as full settlement.

With Yoko already free of her husband Tony Cox and Paul McCartney having married Linda Eastman on March 12, it was suddenly imperative in mid-March 1969 that John and Yoko get hitched. "Intellectually, of course, we did not believe in getting married," Lennon said, "but one does not love someone just intellectually."

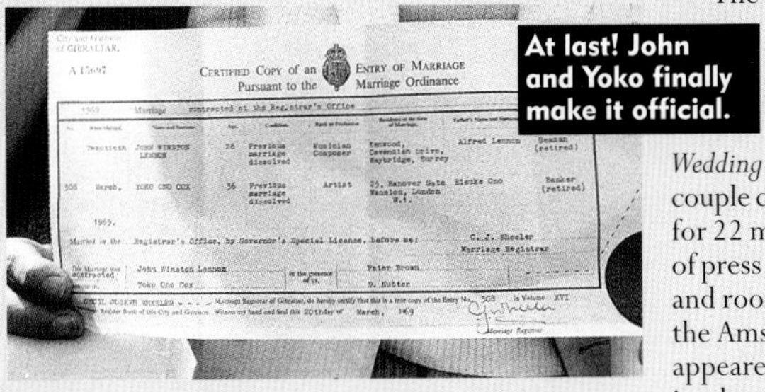

At last! John and Yoko finally make it official.

Wanting it to be a quick, private wedding, Lennon dispatched chauffeur Les Anthony to Southampton to investigate the possibility of marrying at sea. When this proved impossible, John and Yoko attempted to sail to France anyway, but were refused on the grounds that there were inconsistencies in their passports.

Still unsure where and when they could marry, the couple then chartered a private plane to Paris for a pre-wedding honeymoon before Apple employee Peter Brown informed Lennon that as a UK citizen, he could marry in Gibraltar, the British-protected island near Spain, immediately.

Lennon assigned Apple's Alistair Taylor to organise cash and transport from Paris. Taylor arrived in the private jet at Le Bourget Airport. "It was a beautiful misty morning and I saw John and Yoko, both in white, running towards the plane to meet me," he remembered. "I had laid on the champagne as always and they seemed so carefree and in love with each other." Taylor was so taken with the sentimental scene, he forgot about the £500 he had brought for them which was wrapped up in his wife's stockings and secreted in his trouser leg. Only just remembering as he waved them off on the runway, Taylor was forced to stop the plane to complete his assignment.

Peter Brown met John and Yoko at Gibraltar Airport with photographer David Nutter and the party went straight to the British Consulate building. The ceremony was performed by registrar Cecil Wheeler with Brown acting as best man and Nutter capturing the event for posterity. Returning to Paris immediately following the wedding, John and Yoko had been on Gibraltan soil for less than an hour, though Lennon was pleased with the location's resonance. "It's the Pillar Of Hercules," he enthused. "Also, symbolically, they called it The End Of The World at one period."

Though Yoko would admit that she "got so emotional at the wedding, I broke down, John nearly did too," the event was also a continuation of their intellectualised life-as-art attitude. It was "a fantastic happening" said Lennon. "We are going to share many happenings and events together," warned Yoko, "and this marriage was one of them." Indeed, while their wedding was as private an affair as they could manage, their honeymoon was a week-long media blitz as they took to bed in Amsterdam for peace.

The entire nuptial saga was celebrated with two significant artistic offerings. One was John and Yoko's third avant-garde LP, *The Wedding Album*, which featured the couple calling out each other's names for 22 minutes, plus an audio collage of press interviews, improvised songs and room service phone calls during the Amsterdam bed-in. It eventually appeared in November '69 packaged in a box with a cardboard cake, press clippings and a copy of their marriage certificate and sold in the dozens.

"We are going to share many events and happenings together and this marriage was one of them." Yoko Ono

Perhaps the more durable celebratory artefact of the event was Lennon's piece of self-mythologising rock'n'roll journalese, The Ballad Of John And Yoko, or Johnny B Paperback Writer, as he had it. Lennon brought it to McCartney in April 1969 and persuaded him to come straight down to Abbey Road to record it. Despite personal and business disagreements being at their height, McCartney agreed (one has to wonder whether Lennon would have offered McCartney the same support in a reverse situation). With George out of the country and Ringo filming The Magic Christian, it was up to just John and Paul to make the music, the first 'Beatles' session in eight weeks.

Meeting up with George Martin at the studio, John played guitars and sang, Paul sang harmony, played piano, bass and drums, "good drums" said Starr later. The results became The Beatles' summer single, hitting Number 1 in June '69, thereby linking forever the John & Yoko story with that of The Beatles. George Harrison, the most openly opposed to the John/Yoko situation, was unconcerned not to be involved. "It was none of my business," he said later. "If it had been The Ballad Of John, George And Yoko, I would have been on it."

PHOTOS: HULTON ARCHIVE, TOPHAM PICTUREPOINT

31 George and Patti plead guilty to possession of cannabis resin at Esher and Walton Magistrates' Court, and are fined £250 each, plus 10 guineas costs. On the same day, the film Rape (Film No 6), made by John Lennon, has its world premiere on Austrian TV.

APRIL 69

1 Ringo is filmed at the Theatre Royal, Stratford, East London, for The Magic Christian. On the same day, John and Yoko appear live on early evening news programme Today in London, presented by Eamonn Andrews (below). He interviews the couple about Bagism. The Daily Express publishes an off-the-record comment made by John in which he reveals: "I am back to work, recording with The Beatles. I need the money… Right now, in cash, I have about £50,000."

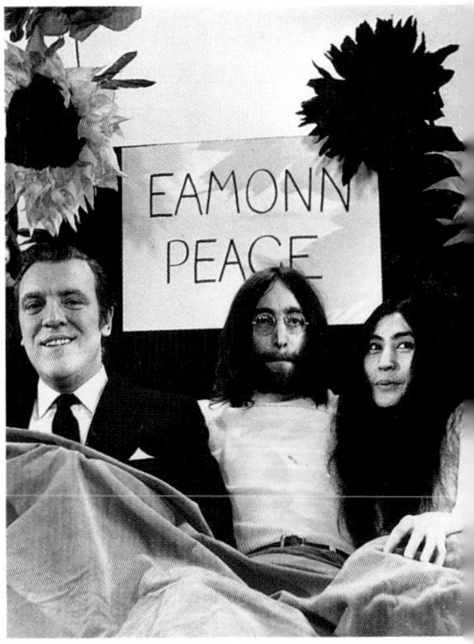

3 R&B organist Billy Preston, occasionally referred to as 'the fifth Beatle', is signed to Apple Records.

5 John and Paul reject a £9 million offer from ATV for their shares in Northern Songs.

7 Having received some adverse reactions from UK DJs, Paul remixes Get Back in Abbey Road.

9 Ringo is filmed at Barclays Bank Rowing Club, on the Thames Embankment, Putney, London, for The Magic Christian.

11 Get Back is released in the UK.

12 John and Yoko attend a financial meeting at the offices of Henry Ansbacher & Co in London.

13 A highly critical article about Allen Klein is published in the Sunday Times.

14 John and Paul record The Ballad Of John And Yoko at Abbey Road, London.

15 John and Yoko return to the offices of Henry Ansbacher & Co for further meetings, now with Allen Klein in attendance.

16 The Beatles work on Something and Old Brown Shoe in Abbey Road Studios, London.

18 The band complete the recording of Old Brown Shoe and add guitar overdubs to I Want You, in Abbey Road.

20 Work continues on I Want You and Oh! Darling at Abbey Road.

22 On the roof of the Apple building, John changes his middle name by deed poll from Winston to Ono.

24 Paul and John make a counter-offer against ATV, in order to acquire full ownership of Northern Songs Ltd.

25 John's film Rape has its European theatrical premiere at the Montreux Film Festival.

26 Get Back enters the UK singles chart at Number 1.

29 Ringo records his vocal for Octopus's Garden in Abbey Road.

30 Work continues on Let It Be and You Know My Name (Look Up The Number) in Abbey Road, the latter track having first been recorded back in 1967.

MAY 69

1 Apple announces the formation of a new label, Zapple, devoted to experimental music and spoken-word recordings.

2 An announcement by ATV that their offer for Northern Songs will remain in force for another two weeks is swiftly followed by a rise of nine pence in the Northern Songs shares.

4 Ringo and actor Peter Sellers (above) hold a party at London's Les Ambassadeurs club to mark the end of filming on The Magic Christian. Guests include John Lennon, Paul McCartney, Sean Connery, Roger Moore, Richard Harris, Christopher Lee and Stanley Baker.

5 As Get Back is released in the US, John buys an 18th-century Georgian mansion, Tittenhurst Park, in Ascot, for £150,000.

6 The band begin work on You Never Give Me Your Money, the second song of the medley on side two of *Abbey Road*. Because of his 1968 drug conviction, John's 'standing visa' is withdrawn by the US Embassy in London.

7 John and Paul, along with manager Allen Klein, meet EMI's Sir Joseph Lockwood in London, to discuss increasing royalty payments to the band. Lockwood refuses.

8 John Lennon, George Harrison and Ringo Starr appoint Allen Klein's ABKCO Industries Inc to manage their business affairs. Paul McCartney, however, refuses to sign up with Klein.

9 John and Yoko release a new LP, *Unfinished Music, No 2: Life With The Lions* (right).

10 The artist Alan Aldridge presents John and Yoko with a small statue, depicting them naked, as on the cover of *Two Virgins*. Get Back enters the US Top 40 singles chart where it will peak at Number 1.

11 Jack Bruce, of Cream, records the song Never Tell Your Mother She's Out Of Tune with George playing guitar.

13 A photographic session with Angus McBean is held at EMI's offices, Manchester Square, London, intended for the 'Get Back' LP cover.

What: The Abbey Road medley concept begins
Where: Abbey Road studios
When: May 6, 1969

THE END OF THE ROAD

After the *Let It Be* sessions, The Beatles kept on recording, but it was only with the idea of a 'medley' that *Abbey Road* took shape. By John Robertson.

A COLLECTIVE SIGH OF RELIEF MARKED the end of the tumultuous January 1969 recording sessions. After four weeks of bickering, The Beatles had succeeded in performing two sets of new songs live in front of the camera, on the Apple roof and in the basement studio.

However, none of them really believed that they had completed a satisfactory album. Apple quickly announced that the group had cut 12 new songs, but needed four more to fulfil their April 1969 release date. Apparently keen to avoid the familiar surroundings of Abbey Road, they regrouped in late February at Trident Studios in Soho. There they devoted two days to a Lennon song which had emerged during the Twickenham ordeal: I Want You (She's So Heavy).

The Beatles quickly discovered that a change of location couldn't dissolve their current ennui. The Trident dates proved simply that the entire back-to-basics project was doomed. All plans to cut four more songs were abandoned, as was the April schedule. The January tapes were passed to engineer Glyn Johns, who was instructed to rescue as much as he could.

Meanwhile, Apple spokesman Derek Taylor was encouraged to enter the realms of fantasy. He told an eager world that "around two dozen" songs were now ready for release, including Maxwell's Silver Hammer, Octopus's Garden and Polythene Pam – none of which were anywhere near completion at this point. In addition, he claimed that The Beatles had reworked three leftovers from the White Album: Not Guilty, What's The New Mary Jane and a McCartney ditty entitled Jubilee (alias Junk). It was a total invention, but it reassured their fans that The Beatles were maintaining their usual creative flow.

As late as April, Lennon still imagined they were working, in a mysterious way, towards finishing the 'Get Back' LP.

In an April interview, Lennon waxed lyrical about The Beatles' current rate of inspiration: "If I could only get the time to myself, I think I could probably write about 30 songs a day. As it is, I probably average about 12 a night. Paul, too: he's mad on it. As soon as I leave here, I'm going round to Paul's place and we'll sit down and start work."

And what kind of songs were these speedy geniuses composing? "The way we're writing at the moment, it's straightforward and there's nothing weird. The songs are like Get Back. A lot of the tracks on the next LP will be like Get Back, and a lot of that we did in one take. We've done about 12 tracks, some of them still to be remixed. All the songs we're doing sound normal to me. There's no Revolution 9 there, but there's still a few heavy sounds."

As late as April, then, Lennon still imagined that they were working, in a mysterious way, towards finishing the 'Get Back' album – despite the fact that the group had passed the project to Glyn Johns to salvage. But another interview he gave that month suggested that a quite different approach was under consideration.

"Paul and I are now working on a kind of song montage that we might do as one piece on one side," he told the NME. "We've got about two weeks to finish the whole thing, so we're really working at it."

The deadline marked the date which The Beatles had set as the end of their next batch of sessions. The montage bore no relation to the no-frills, no-overdubs ethos of the January sessions; the group were obviously now heading in a very different direction.

Intriguingly, Lennon's statement requires a radical rewriting of the group's history – or, to be more accurate, it suggests that Lennon did exactly that after *Abbey Road* was released. The lengthy medley which filled much of the album's second side has always been regarded as a McCartney invention, an idea which Lennon was only too keen to promote. Supporting this theory, Chris Thomas, who produced some of the group's late-'60s sessions, recalled: "I remember Paul sitting down in Abbey Road number three [studio], and playing me this whole thing which lasted about 15 minutes." By the early '90s, George Martin had decided to take the full credit himself: "The symphonic piece on side two was my idea, and to be quite honest, John didn't approve."

"They weren't real songs," Lennon complained about the medley in late 1969. "They were just bits and pieces stuck together." Yet two weeks before any of the songs which made up the medley were recorded, he had already told the press that this was a Lennon/McCartney project, not some lame McCartney or Martin confection he'd been forced to swallow.

On May 6, at the end of two weeks of (by 1969 standards) unusually productive sessions, The Beatles recorded the first of the songs earmarked for the medley: You Never Give Me Your Money. The next few weeks were set aside for other activities, notably the launch of Lennon's peace campaign in North America. They were scheduled to become Beatles again at the start of July. But by then, Lennon had enjoyed the taste of artistic freedom, seen the crumbling state of the Apple empire, and knew which he preferred. When he returned to London, nursing injuries sustained in a car crash, all of his enthusiasm for The Beatles had gone, and so had any interest in the 15-minute medley. In his mind, that was now a banal Paul McCartney idea – scarcely worthy of a man who had global peace in his sights.

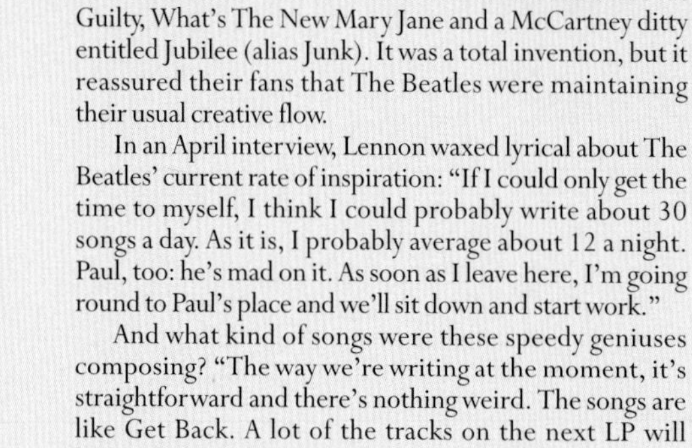

Studio lines: the *Abbey Road* medley recording sheet.

PHOTOS: LINDA McCARTNEY, MIRRORPIX

Two of us: John and Paul put aside their differences for *Abbey Road*.

DEAR PRUDENCE
JOHN LEN and PAUL McCARTNEY
GET BACK
PAUL McCART
Bid for Beatle songs
JOHN AND PAUL SAY 'NO' BUT £10 m OFFER IS ON
By TREVOR BASS
BEATLES John Lennon, still in bed wit bride and tulips in Amsterdam, ar Paul McCartney, on more convention honeymoon in New York, said No-No la night to a takeover.
They had just heard that Sir Lew Grade's Associated Television in London was going for
Shares in Northern S were first offered to the pu just four years ago at 7s. each. Last night news of takeover move sent them ing 4s. 3d. to 39s. 3d.—sli above the value of the one ATV "A"
DEMO DISC
NORTHERN SONGS
DICK JAMES
MUSIC LIMITED
45 R. P. M.
TEM. 1687/8
1610/1035
Title: DAY TRIPPER
Artist: THE BEATLES
BANK of ENGLAND
I Promise to pay the Bearer on demand the sum of
FIVE POUNDS
LONDON For the Govr and Comp^a of the Bank of England
CHIEF CASHIER
D12 715571
£5

GOING FOR A SONG

Mark Lewisohn reveals the saga behind John and Paul's music publishing deals and explains how they lost control of their songs.

In a move that has rocked the music industry on both sides of the Atlantic, Michael Jackson purchased the music publishing company ATV Music from Associated Communications Corporation on August 10 for a reported $47,500,000 (about £34 million) – thereby obtaining complete world rights to ATV subsidiary Northern Songs, the company set up in February 1963 to publish Lennon-McCartney and some other Beatles songs. Northern accounted for half of ATV's annual revenue of $15 million/£10,800,000 last year.

from the Beatles '85 news column, The Beatles Book Monthly, October 1985

Michael Jackson and Sony Music Publishing announced on November 7 a long-anticipated deal creating a worldwide music publishing joint venture, Sony/ATV Music Publishing, that combines Jackson's ATV Music holdings (including 251 Beatles songs) with Sony's. Sony said Jackson received an undisclosed amount – which industry sources pegged at from $90 million to $110 million – in the merger. Jackson's catalog is worth about $300 million, based on a valuation of 10 times its net revenue of $30 million.

from Beatlenews roundup, Beatlefan, Nov-Dec 1995

The story of how Lennon-McCartney lost their copyrights while making other people fabulously rich is a typical tale of show business shenanigans suffused with intrigue and peopled with colourful characters. It shows how wealth generated beyond wildest dreams could shift so spectacularly that the two young men whose genius made it all possible lost first the plot and then the lot. The postscript, for there's no need to wait to the end, is a deep and bitter resentment that grinds on to this day. Neither Paul McCartney nor Yoko Ono, administrating John Lennon's estate, expect to get them back.

"We actually used to think when we came down to London that songs belonged to everyone," Paul McCartney told me in 1987. "I've said this a few times but it's true, we really thought they just were in the air, and that you couldn't actually own one. So you can imagine the publishers saw us coming. 'Welcome boys, sit down. That's what you think, is it?'"

Both sides of The Beatles' first single, Love Me Do and PS I Love You, carried the words Ardmore & Beechwood Ltd on the label. This was a company allied to the American music publisher Beechwood Music Corporation; Beechwood was a subsidiary of Capitol Records, which in turn was owned by the British company EMI. So an EMI subsidiary was the first to publish a Lennon-McCartney song. Brian Epstein had chanced upon the company because its general manager, Sid Colman, kept an office above the (also EMI-owned) HMV record store on Oxford Street, London, into which he had walked during his mission to get The Beatles a recording contract.

"Plugging" was the name of the game in the British record industry of 1962 and it was the job of publishers, more even than record companies, to stir interest in a song through airplay and sales of sheet music. In Epstein's opinion, Ardmore & Beechwood did far too little to push Love Me Do. The song received virtually no BBC radio plays and was not reviewed on the important TV show Juke Box Jury. For The Beatles' second single, Please Please Me backed with Ask Me Why, Epstein wanted to take the publishing elsewhere. EMI thereby lost out on a guestimated hundred million pounds. (In 1976, Paul McCartney used the goodwill of his recording contract to buy the Love Me Do and PS I Love You copyrights from EMI. The songs are now published by his company MPL Communications, the only Beatles copyrights owned by Paul. He accounts to Yoko for John's share of the royalties.)

George Martin says that Epstein discussed vesting the two new Beatles copyrights in Hill & Range Songs, the New York company which had founded and was administering Elvis Presley Music, Inc. Martin replied that if Ardmore & Beechwood – which, though British-owned, was in certain respects an American company – had done little for The Beatles,

PHOTO: CAMERA PRESS

the London outpost of Hill & Range (address: 17 Savile Row) was unlikely to do much better. He suggested Epstein find a British publisher, one with hunger and desire. Specifically, he recommended Dick James Music.

One of Martin's former artists, Dick James had lately hung up his toupee on a moderately successful singing career and gone into publishing, working for Sydney Bron Music Company. Then, in September 1961, aged 41, James left Bron and set himself up in his own company. Start-up capital was provided by Emanuel Charles Silver, 47, a chartered accountant based in High Holborn. Silver became the silent, equal partner in Dick James Music Ltd. The company set up office at 132 Charing Cross Road, literally yards from Denmark Street, London's "Tin Pan Alley". James numerically sequenced all his company's copyrights; 001 was Double Scotch, an instrumental piece composed by George Martin.

On November 27, 1962, the morning after The Beatles recorded Please Please Me and Ask Me Why at Abbey Road, Epstein placed a couple of acetate discs in his attaché case and went out to get the publishing signed up. The story goes that he had two appointments. The first kept him waiting beyond the appointed time. Exit Mr Epstein. The second was with Dick James, already at his desk and happy to see Epstein early.

Epstein did his "they're big now in Liverpool, one day they'll be bigger than Elvis" spiel. James retorted, "What's from Liverpool?" – the perennial London-blinkered view – then put the discs on his record player and found out. Please Please Me is a sure-fire Number 1, he said, can I publish it? Ask Me Why as well?

Epstein asked what James could do to promote The Beatles where Ardmore & Beechwood had failed, and James responded with a masterstroke of salesmanship: he phoned Philip Jones, the producer of ITV's Saturday evening pop show Thank Your Lucky Stars, and played Please Please Me to him, holding the receiver next to the speaker. You'd think it corny in a Hollywood movie. Jones and James knew each other of old, back to Radio Luxembourg's golden 1940s when Jones the radio producer booked James the crooner. Jones too heard the promise in Please Please Me and offered The Beatles a spot on the show. Epstein rifled through the diary. They were free to record on January 13, 1963. The show would air on January 19, eight days after release of the single. It would be The Beatles' first appearance on national television, a major step-up.

Epstein gave the publishing rights in Please Please Me and Ask Me Why to Dick James Music Ltd, Lennon and McCartney signing the standard agreement for a 10 per cent royalty on receipts. The record came out, James plugged it for all his worth and the single shot up the charts. They were on a roll. Moreover, Epstein and James instantly liked each other. James gave The Beatles' inexperienced manager business advice that turned out to be sound. Respect formed. In his autobiography, A Cellarful Of Noise, Epstein described James as "honourable... [with] huge integrity". To The Beatles, James came across as something of an avuncular figure who turned up at recording sessions, urged them to write more great songs (he especially liked Paul's) and gave out gold cufflinks on their birthdays.

James was evidently a smart thinker. Right then, in February 1963, even before Please Please Me hit Number 1, he made a suggestion. Since it was clear that Lennon and McCartney were talented songwriters, he said, and that they had a fund of unpublished songs of great potential, they should have their own publishing company and share in the profits. A name? Well, as they came from the north it could be called Northern Songs.

This was the idea: Lennon and McCartney would assign to Northern the full copyright in all their songs published during a three-year period commencing February 28, 1963.

The company structure: 98 shares, given out "equally" – 49 "B" shares divided between John (19), Paul (20) and Epstein's company NEMS Enterprises Ltd (10), 49 "A" shares owned by James. Additionally, Dick James Music Ltd was appointed manager (administrator) of Northern Songs Ltd for a 10-year period, expiring February 1973, at a remuneration of 10 per cent of gross receipts. So, for every £100 earned, Dick James Music took £10 and the remaining £90 was split 50:50. Did Lennon or McCartney look at the small print? Did they care? It seems they were simply too busy to think much about it, and trusted that if Brian Epstein thought it a good deal then so it was, and so it appeared to be.

For me, the question of *why* Dick James suggested the formation of Northern Songs has never been adequately answered. He cannot be asked now: he died in 1986. Seven years earlier, when interviewed by Shout! author Philip Norman, James stated: "Brian said to me, 'Why are you doing this for us?' What I said to him then was the truth. I was doing it because I had faith in the songs."

Certainly, James could instead have encouraged Lennon and McCartney to tie themselves to a deal with Dick James Music Ltd on the standard 10 per cent royalty, which would have given him complete ownership, making him much more money and them far less. This is what he did when – lightning miraculously having struck him a second time a few years later – he published the songs of Elton John and Bernie Taupin. In his autobiography All You Need Is Ears, George Martin labels James's idea "very clever... because in offering as large a slice as 50 per cent he ensured that they would sign a contract for a long period of time. He wouldn't have got a deal like that had he offered them a smaller share." (Martin also revealed that James offered him a share in Northern Songs, as a thank you for establishing the connection. Feeling it would be unethical, Martin declined.)

The first Northern Songs pact between Lennon, McCartney, Epstein and James was dated February 11, 1963, the day The Beatles recorded all 10 new numbers for their debut album, and the company was officially registered with the Board Of Trade (now the Department Of Trade & Industry) on the 22nd. To show instant goodwill, James volunteered to transfer John and Paul's latest copyrights – the four new songs on the *Please Please Me* LP – from Dick James Music to Northern Songs. Only Please Please Me and Ask Me Why remained assigned to Dick James Music, reward from Epstein, said James, in recognition of his sterling work as plugger.

A total of 56 copyrights were published under this initial contract. John and Paul's royalties were paid into a private company they formed in May 1964, Lenmac Enterprises Ltd, owned 40 per cent by John, 40 per cent by Paul and 20 per cent by NEMS Enterprises.

When Britain fell to Beatlemania in 1963 and the rest of the world did likewise in 1964, The Beatles hit paydirt beyond the realm of all pop music experience. Northern Songs established a range of overseas representation, companies that published Lennon-McCartney songs in their respective territories, kept 50 per cent of the proceeds and returned the rest to Britain. Huge royalties were derived from Maclen Music, Inc, an American company set up by Dick James along similar lines to Northern Songs.

The question was, how could The Beatles, as British citizens, best shelter all this income? The personal taxation rate for high earners at this time was 83 per cent (and this under a Conservative government). Unless steps were taken to protect their money The Beatles would end up giving virtually all of it to the Inland Revenue. Of the numerous financial schemes put in place on their behalf, the most dramatic was the flotation of Northern Songs on the London Stock Exchange. The effect was to translate the company's 98 privately held shares into five million public ones. Business taxation rules then in force were such that John and Paul's instant profit would not be subject to Capital Gains Tax. They could, in effect, each derive a huge cash sum merely by restructuring their own assets.

The transfer of Northern Songs from

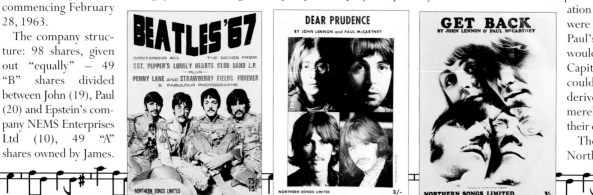

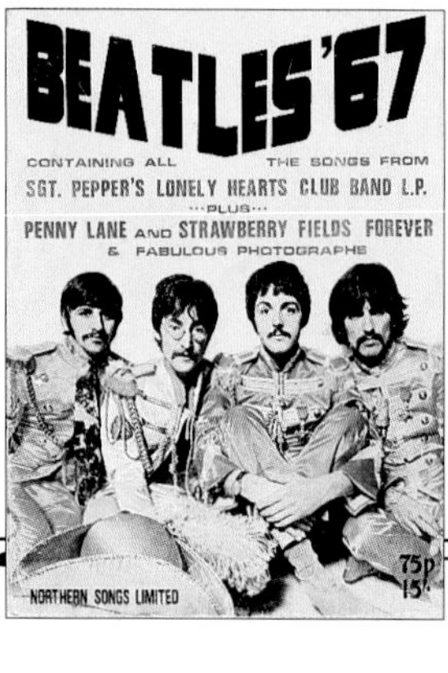

"So... anyone fancy a game of Monopoly?" The Beatles at Lennon's home, Tittenhurst Park, Berks, August 22, 1969.

"I'M NOT GOING TO BE FUCKED AROUND BY MEN IN SUITS SITTING ON THEIR FAT ARSES IN THE CITY." JOHN LENNON

private to public company was a revolutionary concept in the British music industry. Anyone could now buy a piece of Can't Buy Me Love as well as the future hits bound to flow from golden boys Lennon-McCartney. (It's a fairly safe bet that none of the investors saw Revolution 9 coming, though.) The idea that such trivial things as "pop songs" could be bought and sold as an investment caused much amusement among the pinstriped, bowler-hatted City businessmen.

In February 1965, to underline their support for the flotation, John and Paul agreed to a sweeping new agreement with Northern Songs. First they formed a new company, Maclen (Music) Ltd – owned 40 per cent by each of them and 20 per cent by Brian Epstein (later NEMS Enterprises Ltd). This company in turn assigned to Northern Songs full copyright in all Lennon-McCartney compositions, written together or as individuals, for eight years until February 1973, Maclen guaranteeing Northern a minimum six new compositions per calendar year. (The publishing royalties were split three ways: Dick James Music Ltd's 10 per cent managerial fee, 55 per cent for Maclen, 35 per cent for Northern Songs.) A year later, in April 1966, Lennon and McCartney sold Lenmac Enterprises Ltd to Northern Songs, an ill-advised move that realised them £365,000 cash but was ultimately disastrous, for when Northern eventually passed into new ownership Lenmac went with it. From that day to this, neither McCartney nor Lennon (and his Estate) have earned publishing royalties from their first 56 Northern songs, a catalogue that includes She Loves You, I Want To Hold Your Hand, All My Loving, A Hard Day's Night and all the other hits and tracks of the peak Beatlemania years.

Dick James was managing director of the public Northern Songs Ltd. Charles Silver was chairman. Together, and with a further portfolio in the name of Dick James Music Ltd, they held 1,875,000 shares (37.5 per cent). Lennon and McCartney each had 750,000 (15 per cent), George Harrison 40,000 (0.8 per cent), Richard Starkey the same. To further aid the flotation, George was persuaded to sign as songwriter to Northern for three years, even though he had just formed his own music publishing company, Harrisongs Ltd. (He owned 80 per cent of this, Brian Epstein 20.) It was only in March 1968, when his Northern deal expired, that George would be free to put his songs through his own company. Seen in this context, the lyrics, "It doesn't really matter what chords I play, what words I say or time of day it is, as it's only a northern song", have an added piquancy. Ringo formed his own wholly-owned publishing business, Startling Music Ltd, in July 1968, just in time to copyright his first song Don't Pass Me By. Until then, his co-compositions (What Goes On, Flying) were assigned to Northern.

Northern Songs shares opened on the Stock Exchange at 7s 9d [39p]. Subscription was high, and though the price fell for a while it was soon on the increase. Newspapers covered the ups and downs of Northern's price, and not just on the City pages. It rose when The Beatles released a new Number 1 single, fell when it was rumoured that they were splitting up; it tumbled dramatically – and then rallied – when Brian Epstein died.

If John and Paul still thought they owned their songs they were deluding themselves. Northern Songs now had literally thousands of owners. Moreover, it was prone to predators. Steadily, over time, an array of companies acquired reasonably large chunks of shares, risking a punt on the pop business. The foremost predator was Lew Grade, Britain's premier postwar show business impresario. He was especially keen to grab a slice of The Beatles, having wanted 'in' for years. Though details remain frustratingly sketchy, it is understood that he initially approached Brian Epstein about buying out his management in the first flush of Beatlemania in late 1963. It is part of Beatles legend that when Epstein told 'the boys' about it, asking honestly if he should accept Grade's offer, a very Lennonish "Fuck off" was heard from the leader, terminating the discussion. Lew Grade and his like, the old showbiz establishment, were literally the sworn enemy.

Five years later, with the 1960s almost over, Grade was still keen. He wanted The Beatles, and Grade usually got what he wanted. The pop business had proven to be more than a five-minute wonder and many of its great songs were sure to become "standards" and reap royalties forever. Through his company ATV, Grade had latterly made a bid for the copyrights in Chappell, losing out narrowly to Philips, and he had also bid

PHOTO: REDFERNS

for Lawrence Wright Music only to be beaten by Northern Songs, which got it for £812,500. (In addition to publishing Beatles songs, Northern had begun to acquire other catalogues; with Lawrence Wright it now had four.)

The big news story on January 1, 1969, was that Lew Grade – the erstwhile Russian immigrant Louis Winogradsky – had been knighted. Sailing on a sea of invincibility, Sir Lew Grade set determined course for Northern Songs. He and Dick James had a professional relationship dating back to January 1953, when James, the singer, signed to Lew & Leslie Grade Ltd, the talent agency. Now Grade took lunch with his former client. His timing was always faultless. James sensed trouble brewing in The Beatles and was beginning to consider his options. He told Sir Lew that neither he nor Charles Silver were interested in selling, but that if they wanted out they would give Grade first option.

Dick James had been feeling the chill since Brian Epstein's death in August 1967. The Beatles, it would have been his experience to note, had turned from arrogant young men to stroppy and arrogant young men who reckoned, with good reason, that a lot of people around them were either ripping them off, or at least making more money from their endeavours than they were themselves. John and Paul were especially irritated that they were still on what Paul called "the 1963 rate" for their Northern Songs publishing royalties. (He says he's *still* on it now, in 2003.) They handled this anger in two ways: by saying they would refuse to discuss any extension to their contract until the terms were improved, and by treating Dick James with open contempt.

WITH THE 1960s ALMOST OVER, LEW GRADE WANTED THE BEATLES, AND GRADE USUALLY GOT WHAT HE WANTED.

In the summer of 1968, James was invited to a meeting at Apple where he was put thoroughly in his place by John and Paul. Voices were raised. We know this because they filmed it. When James asked why cameras were present John told him, "It's a commercial for Apple, to be shown at a forthcoming Capitol sales conference. It's ours and you can see it if there's something you don't like in it."

The film was shown at Capitol Records' sales convention in Hollywood in June 1968. Paul even turned up in person to push the great Apple cause; it was during this trip that he re-met Linda Eastman and their relationship began. The transcript is revealing:

Dick: "...It would be very tragic if we weren't more heavily involved in the future, if we've got the respect for each other's ability and integrity. I can't think of any other requirement that business associates need." [John is drawing during the conversation. Paul looks at him, a slight conspiratorial smile plays on his face.]

Paul: "But we now..."

Dick [riled, interrupting]: "Tell me your problems."

Paul: "Dick! We think that it's time we sorted it out a bit more fairly."

Dick: "I promise you I will try to sort it out as quickly as possible, come back and sit down with you and put it on the line. If I am advised, that I were to sit with my own thoughts, that I'm not prepared to do anything I'll still come back and sit down and honestly tell you so. And that's the most pessimistic view I can take."

Paul: "So, Dick, that's it. You go away and you come back with something which you know won't start this argument again."

It is hard to believe that James would have approved the screening of this footage. He was a senior figure in the British music industry, with many American business relationships; it would have caused him acute embarrassment. He would also not have enjoyed being called "a pig" by John and George, easily within earshot, when he turned up at Twickenham Film Studios one day in January 1969 while The Beatles were filming what became the movie Let It Be.

As well as being the pariah, James had another worry. He was the managing director of a public company whose investors had become very jittery indeed. What *was* going on with The Beatles these days? It was well known now that they took drugs: John had been busted and George soon would be. Full of weird ideals and ideas, they had formed Apple and were haemorrhaging money so fast that John was telling journalist friend Ray Coleman The Beatles would be "broke in the next six months", a statement hardly likely to inspire City confidence. George had quit the group temporarily, amid (incorrect) headlines about punch-ups. Most worrying of all, John had left his wife to live with Yoko Ono, embarking with her on a long series of events viewed by the public with absolute derision, not the least of which was the *Two Virgins* nude album cover.

And there was more. Through the spring of 1969, post-Epstein business anguish was taking hold too. Linda's father, Lee Eastman, hoped to be the one to extricate The Beatles from their mess but he was firmly rebuffed by John, George and Ringo. They in turn appointed Allen Klein to look after their affairs, a man whose wheeler-dealer methods were alien to The Beatles' besuited London business associates. A fantastic duel ensued amid the fine tailoring establishments of Savile Row as Park Avenue Eastman took on New Jersey Klein, a man who only recently had been investigated by the Wall Street watchdog, the Securities & Exchange Commission. Klein won The Beatles battle 3-1, a majority but never the full complement. Paul said that group decisions had always been taken on a unanimous basis. Not any longer.

Sir Lew Grade, 1969: "Northern has first-class management plus the talent of two brilliant musicians in Lennon and McCartney."

PHOTO: HULTON ARCHIVE

The Northern Songs bomb fell on March 28, 1969. Dick James and Charles Silver sold their combined 1,604,750 shares to Sir Lew Grade in exchange for ATV shares and cash worth around £3m. With ATV's own 137,000 shareholding Grade suddenly owned 35 per cent of Lennon and McCartney's music and instantly announced his intention to bid for the rest, or at least for the 15.1 per cent that would give him control.

Grade's timing was impeccable once again. Allen Klein was taking a short holiday in Puerto Rico, John Lennon was in Amsterdam, in the middle of his honeymoon "bed-in for peace" with Yoko, talking in their bed for a week, and Paul McCartney was in America, on his honeymoon with Linda. They only found out that

Businessman Allen Klein: leader of the pack.

James (read James and Silver from here on) had sold out when journalists sought their reaction. John must have held on to every ounce of good peace karma to restrain himself when he told the Financial Times, "I'll be sticking to my shares and I could make a pretty good guess that Paul won't sell either."

When finally reached by the Daily Express, Paul's response was, "You can safely assume that my shares are not for sale to ATV."

There were yet more quotes to supplement this bountiful media story. When asked if he had told John and Paul that he was going to sell, Dick James replied, rather disingenuously, "To telephone John and Paul would have been difficult. The call would have gone through a number of people and there was a need to keep it confidential."

Sir Lew Grade, however, sat back, puffed contentedly on one of his phenomenal cigars and was effusive in victory. "Northern has first-class management plus the talent of two brilliant musicians in Lennon and McCartney. They are brilliant, have no doubts, no matter what they may do with their private lives." Northern's share price rocketed on news of ATV's move, at one point climbing to 39s 3d.

To The Beatles, John and Paul especially, James's act was a gross betrayal. He had made a personal fortune from their labour yet hadn't even offered them first chance to buy the shares. In reality, they had been sunk by the Silver phenomenon. Paul still talks about it. If James had operated alone he would have had only 17 per cent of Northern to sell to ATV, and Grade may not have been that interested. But with Charles Silver in tandem he controlled close to 35 per cent of a well-run, profitable publishing catalogue of wonderful songs. Whoever they sold to was bound to have the whip hand.

All was now far from quiet on the Northern front. The Beatles scurried from one business meeting to another, day after day, discussing their options, all while somehow managing to record a new album. Yet they were scarcely in a fit state to fight. A City investment trust had just grabbed 25 per cent of all their record royalties through to 1976 via the sale of NEMS Enterprises' share in their nine-year 1967 EMI recording contract. Every move made by Klein to claw back Brian Epstein's quarter was met by protest from Lee Eastman and his son John who felt it could be more safely achieved if things were done their way. John, George and Ringo were still on Klein's side, Paul on Eastman's. Clive and Queenie Epstein, Brian's brother and mother, wanted no part of any of this and sold out to Triumph Investment Trust in order to meet Brian's considerable death duties. One fine spring day, George "sagged off" from the endless round of meetings, sat himself in a deckchair in Eric Clapton's garden and out of sheer light-headed relief from the tension wrote Here Comes The Sun.

In conjunction with a City merchant bank, Henry Ansbacher & Co, The Beatles urgently mounted a counter-offer for Northern Songs. They owned 29.7 per cent of the shares and could find another 0.6 scattered among some of their companies, like Subafilms Ltd, which had 30,000. Paul had 751,000 (worth around £1.4m), John 644,000 (£1.2m) plus another 50,000 as a trustee, and Ringo still owned 40,000 (£75,000). George had sold his shares when his Northern songwriting contract lapsed in March 1968, but his wife owned 1000 and added these to the pot. It was then realised that a block of 237,000 Northern Songs shares, 4.7 per cent of the company, had just fallen into the lap of Triumph Investment Trust through its purchase of NEMS Enterprises Ltd; The Beatles were able to obtain an option on these. (John noticed in this count-up operation that Paul owned 107,000 more Northern Songs shares than he did. In court depositions in 1971, when Paul was trying to dissolve The Beatles' legal partnership, John declared that he and Paul had once made a verbal pact to keep their shares on an equal footing. Paul's response was "I had some beanies and wanted some more.")

The balance in the ensuing power struggle between The Beatles and ATV hinged on a consortium of brokers and investment fund managers who, together, owned 14 per cent of Northern Songs and manoeuvred themselves into the front line. This battle, between Sir Lew Grade and Allen Klein (and Lee/John Eastman), took place in the City and on the financial pages of the newspapers. It ran for 25 days, with rumours and counter-rumours flying. Suddenly there was a fear that the presence of Allen Klein, with his chequered business history, might injure The Beatles' chance of winning. The American held a press conference at Apple on April 28 in which he announced that, should they win, the experienced British music publisher David Platz would be appointed managing director of Northern Songs in place of Dick James.

John Lennon even made an appearance, telling financial journalists that the ongoing battle was "Like Monopoly, man". Two days later, The Beatles, via Ansbacher & Co, re-emphasised that Klein would be keeping his distance from Northern by placing an advertisement in four national newspapers. Its wording suggests further City concerns over The Beatles' own involvement:

"None of us intends to join the Board, nor would we interfere with the management of the Company. We recognise that our talents lie chiefly in composing and entertaining, rather than in financial management. Mr Allen Klein, who is working with us on other projects, would not become a Director of Northern Songs."

And so it dragged on, Klein and Eastman offering contradictory advice, Paul suddenly refusing to commit his Northern shares as part of the collateral for a loan necessary to finance the counter-offer. At one point Sir Lew feigned death ("ATV defeat in bid for Northern Songs" – headline in The Times, May 17, 1969), at another it looked like The Beatles stood a genuine chance of winning. Then John Lennon, who had worked hard in pursuit of a successful outcome for him and Paul, even accompanying Klein to meetings with the merchant bankers, tired of the whole business and pronounced: "I'm not going to be fucked around by men in suits sitting on their fat arses in the City".

Everyone sensed the bell for the final round. It sounded and then expired the afternoon of May 19 when, amid great drama in the Square Mile, ATV secured an option to purchase the consortium's shares. This guaranteed the company 50 per cent of Northern Songs. It was all over bar the shouting. Four months later, on September 19, the consortium capsized and ATV scooped the lot. Lew Grade had finally got his slice of The Beatles.

By an artistic miracle, The Beatles managed to finish off their album, which they called *Abbey Road*. Then they fell apart in disarray. ■

PHOTO: CAMERA PRESS

John Lennon and Yoko Ono record Give Peace A Chance, Room 1742, Hotel Reine Elizabeth, Montreal, June 1, 1969.

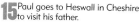

What: John & Yoko record Give Peace A Chance
Where: Hotel Reine Elizabeth, Montreal
When: June 1, 1969

BLANKET COVERAGE

Out of the 'Bedism' and 'Bagism' of their worldwide stunts for peace, John and Yoko created a new anti-war rallying cry. By Keith Badman.

ON SUNDAY, JUNE 1, 1969, IN ROOM 1742 AT the Hotel Reine Elizabeth in Montreal, Canada, John and Yoko recorded Give Peace A Chance, a song soon to be embraced as the peace anthem of our generation. Following their meeting in November 1966, John and Yoko socially hovered around each other for 19 months before becoming an item in May 1968 and entwined in marriage in March 1969. Typical of their activities at the time, the two master media manipulators chose to invite the world to their honeymoon, a 'bed-in' for peace event in room 902, the presidential suite of the Amsterdam Hilton. The press avidly pursued them, assuming that the famous nudists would make love for their cameras. Instead, the pyjama-clad newlyweds spoke out about world peace. John vocalised, "We're trying to sell peace, like a product, and sell it like people sell soap or soft drinks." The honeymoon was performance art, interlaced with a protest against the Vietnam war.

For a week, John and Yoko gave non-stop interviews, ignoring the mockery and hostility to spread their words of peace to a global audience. "It's part of our policy not to be taken seriously," John told the bewildered reporters, "because our opposition, whoever they may be, in all their manifest forms, don't know how to handle humour. We're humorists; we're Laurel & Hardy, that's John & Yoko. We're willing to be the world's clowns." As expected, the backlash from the press followed. The Daily Mirror wrote, "A not inconsiderable talent seems to have gone completely off his rocker."

The couple's next stunt was their humorous 'Bagism' activity. On March 31, at Vienna's Hotel Sacher, just hours after finishing their 'bed-in', the Lennons faced the country's press while sitting inside a large white bag. Bemused journalists fired questions to a large white sack while John and Yoko sat inside, singing and occasionally answering the questions. He explained: "Bagism? We're all in a bag, you know. Yoko and me realised that we came from two bags. I was in this pop bag going round and she was in her little avant-garde clique going round and we all come out and look at each other every now and then, but we don't communicate. We all intellectualise about how there is no barrier between art, music, poetry, but there is. You ask us what 'Bagism' is, and we say, We're all in a bag, baby! If people did interviews for jobs in a bag they wouldn't get turned away because they were black or green or had long hair, you know, it's total communication."

In mid-May, the couple planned a second 'bed-in', this time in New York. But authorities at the US Embassy in London refused to issue Lennon a visa because of his earlier marijuana arrest. So on May 24, John and Yoko flew to the Bahamas. John found the island too hot and humid to stay in bed there for a week so they abruptly left, headed north and took up residence in room 1742 at the stately Hotel Reine Elizabeth in Montreal on May 26. It is there that they staged their second, week-long 'bed-in' for peace. They climbed into the bed in the hotel room and invited the rest of the world to symbolically climb in with them and discuss the idea of world peace.

Scores of journalists and photographers besieged the hotel for a chance to meet the Lennons, who ended up playing host to visiting musicians, writers, counter-culture personalities and celebrities such as the comedian Tommy Smothers of Smothers Brothers fame. Naturally, the event received worldwide media interest, greatly helped by John and Yoko speaking to almost 150 journalists every day. In the US alone, an estimated 350 radio stations carried reports on the world's best-known peace-niks.

The nadir of the 'bed-in' was reached when American cartoonist Al Capp dropped by and assaulted the naivety of John and Yoko's non-violence campaign, claiming that 'bed-ins' wouldn't have prevented the Nazi Holocaust. "If I were a Jewish girl in Hitler's day," replies Yoko, "I would approach him and become his girlfriend. After 10 days in bed, he would come to my way of thinking." "That's stark raving madness," Capp responds, before going on to make various insults toward John and Yoko. John used every ounce of strength that he had not to lash back at him.

Increasing the peace: John and friends sing along, June 1, 1969.

On June 1, the penultimate day of their latest peace event, the call went out for some recording equipment. A guitar was found, oversized lyric sheets were pinned up on the bedroom walls and John and Yoko, along with a roomful of people that included the LSD guru Dr Timothy Leary, the poet Allen Ginsberg and Phil Spector recorded Give Peace A Chance. Members of the Canadian Radha Krishna Temple danced around the hotel room while John sat on the bed, Yoko by his side, strumming his acoustic guitar. It was a magic and memorable moment.

"We're trying to sell peace, like a product, and sell it like people sell soap or soft drinks." John Lennon

Apple press officer, Derek Taylor, who was present at the recording remarked, "Give Peace A Chance was born when the mood was right and the moon was full. That night in Montreal, 40 or more seemed to fill that room. Tim Leary, Tom Smothers, a few journalists, many friends and, dare I say, there was a member of the CIA there in drag!"

Bearing a Lennon & McCartney songwriting tag and credited to The Plastic Ono Band, it reached Number 14 on Billboard's chart and Number 2 in the UK. More importantly, though, their mission was accomplished – the track inspired a generation to chant the song of peace. John and Yoko had managed to sell the idea of peace.

PHOTOS: ALLEN RADU, HULTON ARCHIVE, TOPHAM, COOPER OWEN

15 Paul goes to Heswall in Cheshire to visit his father.

16 Ringo leaves for New York on the QE2 (above). "Inadmissible immigrant" John goes to the US Embassy in London, seeking a visa to visit the US.

17 Paul announces that his wife Linda is expecting a baby. Later in the day, they leave for a holiday in France.

19 The single Get Back is awarded a gold disc in the US.

20 John and George visit the offices of Henry Ansbacher & Co, to discuss the latest developments in ATV's bid for Northern Songs.

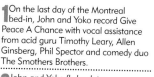

21 The Beatles formally announce the appointment of Allen Klein (left) of ABCKO as their financial manager.

22 Ringo arrives in New York City aboard the liner QEII. He undertakes some additional filming for The Magic Christian. The Beatles are given an Ivor Novello Award for Hey Jude.

24 Get Back reaches Number 1 in the US singles charts. On the same day, John and Yoko start a new company, Bag Productions, to make films and publish books. The pair also fly to the Bahamas, where they are planning another bed-in.

25 John and Yoko decide to move their proposed Bahamas bed-in to Canada, to be closer to the US border.

26 John and Yoko start their eight-day bed-in in room 1742 at the Hotel Reine Elizabeth, Montreal.

29 Ringo and his wife Maureen return to the UK from New York City.

30 The Ballad Of John And Yoko is released in the UK.

JUNE 69

1 On the last day of the Montreal bed-in, John and Yoko record Give Peace A Chance with vocal assistance from acid guru Timothy Leary, Allen Ginsberg, Phil Spector and comedy duo The Smothers Brothers.

2 John and Yoko fly back to London from Canada.

4 The Ballad Of John And Yoko is released in the US where it will eventually reach Number 8.

7 John and Yoko appear on UK TV's The David Frost Show.

12 The Ballad Of John And Yoko reaches Number 1 in the UK.

14 John and Yoko pre-record an interview for the US edition of The David Frost Show, at InterTel studios, Wembley, London.

27 Ringo and Maureen set off for a holiday in the south of France.

29 John and Yoko set off for a holiday in Scotland.

JULY 69

1 When their car crashes in Scotland, John, Yoko and daughter Kyoko are rushed to hospital to have minor injuries attended to. Sessions begin in Abbey Road, London, which will result in the *Abbey Road* album. Paul is the only Beatle present on this first day, working on the track You Never Give Me Your Money.

2 George and Ringo now join Paul in Abbey Road where they work on Golden Slumbers/Carry That Weight.

3 Paul, George and Ringo continue work on Golden Slumbers/Carry That Weight in Abbey Road.

4 Paul, George and Ringo continue work on Golden Slumbers/Carry That Weight in Abbey Road.

6 John is released from hospital in Scotland, where he has spent five days following his and Yoko's car accident.

7 The first recording session for George's Here Comes The Sun is held at Abbey Road. Meanwhile, John Lennon And The Plastic Ono Band release a new single, Give Peace A Chance, in the US. There is a press launch for the Plastic Ono Band at Chelsea Town Hall, London, but John and Yoko are unable to attend due to their injuries.

8 The second recording session for the George Harrison song Here Comes The Sun is held at Abbey Road.

9 All four Beatles start work on Maxwell's Silver Hammer at Abbey Road.

10 Work on Maxwell's Silver Hammer continues at Abbey Road.

11 Work continues on Something, You Never Give Me Your Money and Maxwell's Silver Hammer at Abbey Road.

12 The Ballad Of John And Yoko is banned by half of the Top 40 AM radio stations in America, because the line, "Christ, you know it ain't easy", is deemed blasphemous.

15 Work continues on You Never Give Me Your Money at Abbey Road.

16 The Beatles are awarded a US gold disc for The Ballad Of John And Yoko.

17 The band work on Oh! Darling and Octopus's Garden, at Abbey Road.

18 Carlos Mendez releases a new single in the UK, La Penina, written by John Lennon and Paul McCartney.

What: Manson Family killings
Where: Los Angeles
When: August 9, 1969

FAMILY MISFORTUNES

When the Manson Family went on their two-night killing spree in LA, they left a series of clues taken from Beatles songs. By Mark Paytress.

IT WAS, EXPLAINED STATE PROSECUTOR Vincent Bugliosi, "a bizarre motive". That the deaths of actress Sharon Tate and six others during a two-night spree of apparently random murder in Los Angeles in August 1969 could have been inspired by The Beatles was, surely, too ghoulish to contemplate. But when one of the most notorious criminal trials of the 20th century ended in guilty verdicts for Charles Manson, and the three young women who stood accused with him, The Beatles' White Album never sounded quite the same again.

"All that Manson stuff was built around George's song about pigs and Paul's song about an English fairground," claimed John Lennon. "It has nothing to do with anything, and least of all to do with *me*. He's barmy, he's like any other Beatles fan who reads mysticism into it... What's Helter Skelter got to do with knifing somebody?" McCartney's song, perhaps the most savage The Beatles ever recorded, had clearly been inspired by a popular fairground attraction. Manson, who understood rather less about English leisure pursuits than he did sex and control, saw it differently. This philosopher-misfit interpreted Helter Skelter as his cue to wreak havoc on the 'straight' society that created, and then oppressed him.

The evidence that linked the Manson Murders to The Beatles' White Album was gruesome yet clearly irrefutable. The killers left a series of slogans, written in their victims' blood, daubed indiscriminately on walls, doors and refrigerators. These markings – 'Pig', 'Political Piggy', 'Healter (sic) Skelter' and 'Rise' – all clear references to songs on the record, were a shocking indictment of the power of pop; so much so that many questioned the motives of those who used the case to discredit the hippy way of life. In truth, while the concept of 'Helter Skelter' was probably exaggerated for the purpose of securing convictions – there were other, more prosaic motives for the murders – there's little doubt that the union of The Beatles and their most infamous fan contributed much to extinguishing the last embers of '60s innocence.

According to Family associate Paul Watkins, "From the beginning, Charlie believed The Beatles' music carried an important message to us." Make that Manson and a few million other lost souls who, via a thrilling compound of sex, drugs and rock'n'roll, had begun to scoff at convention. During 1967, many had rallied round The Beatles' flower power anthem, All You Need Is Love. By late 1968, though, the message had become confused – and decidedly combative. The White Album, the most thrilling and bewildering in The Beatles' catalogue, was as coarse and ambiguous as *Sgt Pepper* had been lustrous and celebratory. Love had changed nothing. Neither acid nor the Maharishi had the answer. In fact, with riots and assassins seizing the headlines, the world had grown uglier still since the Summer of Love.

Manson too had "gotten the fear". Life was no longer the magical mystery tour that had been his avowed pursuit since being released from prison in May 1967. "When I met him there was no violence in the Family, no talk of Helter Skelter," Watkins recalled. "In fact it was the complete opposite. Charlie's love then was real." Happily out of step with society, Manson and his mainly female entourage soon found themselves almost pathologically so. And, increasingly, control guru Charlie's "no sense makes sense" philosophy began to blur the bounds of good and evil, and eventually, of life and death itself.

A songwriter keenly courted by The Beach Boys, Manson's happy/sad philosophy rings clear in his songs. Celebrating the Family's "garbage dump" lifestyle and ego-shedding psycho-games, he also ridiculed those in their "cardboard houses" and driving "tin can cars" whose "world is so mixed up". Stopping off at a friend's house in Topanga Canyon early in December 1968, he heard the White Album for the first time. "After that, things were never the same," claimed Watkins.

That's because Manson found literally dozens of 'messages' that chimed with his own increasingly bleak outlook on man's fate. George Harrison's Piggies ridiculed the 'straight' world and recommended, half-jokingly, that it needed "a damn good whacking!". Buried beneath the apocalyptic Revolution 9, he apparently heard the words, "Charlie, Charlie, send us a telegram", as well as several entreaties to "Rise!". But it was Helter Skelter that Bugliosi claimed reflected best Manson's paranoiac world-view. "It meant the black man rising up against the white establishment and murdering the entire white race," he claimed, "with the exception of Manson and his followers, who intended to 'escape' from Helter Skelter by going to the desert and living in the Bottomless Pit." This, said Bugliosi, was a key motive for the murders that shook the world in August 1969.

The 'Helter Scelter' (sic) door at the Family's Spahn ranch.

Helter Skelter certainly provided a backdrop to the Tate/LaBianca slayings, but it wasn't intrinsic to the transformation of the Family from free-living commune-dwellers to a pseudo-revolutionary murder cult. After Family member Bobby Beausoleil was indicted for the murder of Gary Hinman, after a row over drug money, the die was cast. One of the killers, Susan Atkins (alias 'Sexy' Sadie Mae Glutz) left the words 'Political Piggy' in blood on a wall; similar slogans at the 'copycat' murders were intended to prove the imprisoned Beausoleil's innocence – and, of course, to instill fear in the bourgeois communities that Manson despised.

"Charlie believed in The Beatles and we believed in Charlie," said Paul Watkins. It was a lethal combination. By 1971, the ex-Beatles were squaring up in court, and Manson and his acolytes were on Death Row. Help, though, was at hand from John Lennon's God, a powerful denunciation of false idols: "I don't believe in Beatles," he concluded, "just believe in me... and that's reality."

PHOTO: TOPFOTO

Manson is led to the Inyo County Court, Independence, to face minor charges though he's already suspected of involvement in the Tate/LaBianca murders, December 1969.

John Lennon's first solo gig, Varsity Stadium, Toronto, September 13, 1969.

What: The Plastic Ono Band play live in Toronto
Where: Varsity Stadium, Toronto
When: September 13, 1969

THIS BIRD HAS FLOWN

On a whim John Lennon decided to play a rock'n'roll festival in Toronto. By the time he returned he'd decided to go solo. By Paul McGrath.

KIM FOWLEY WAS TRYING TO SAFEGUARD a pay cheque when he suggested bringing John Lennon to Toronto. Fowley, the man who wrote the 1960 novelty hit Alley Oop, had been hired to MC the Toronto Rock'n'Roll Revival, mixing pioneers such as Jerry Lee Lewis, Fats Domino, Little Richard and Gene Vincent with topical acts Chicago, Alice Cooper and The Doors. Three days before the show, promoters John Brower and Ken Walker had sold 2,000 tickets to the 20,000-seat Varsity Stadium, and all agreed that only a stray Beatle could avert a complete disaster. When Brower phoned Apple, three things went his way: Lennon was there, he was just bored enough not to reject the idea offhand, and most importantly, there was someone at Apple that day who could vouch for Brower.

Before the first phone call was over, Lennon had said yes – although it's not clear he understood exactly what he'd said yes to.

"John didn't know they wanted him to play," recalls artist/musician Klaus Voormann. "When they asked him who was in the line-up, he said 'What line-up?'"

Brower insists it was Lennon who got back on the line and said he wanted not just to attend, but to perform. "Everyone was on the extensions in our office listening in, and all their eyebrows shot way up, as in, 'Holy shit, he can't be serious'. So I said, Yes, I think we can find a spot in the line-up for you, I think we can squeeze you in."

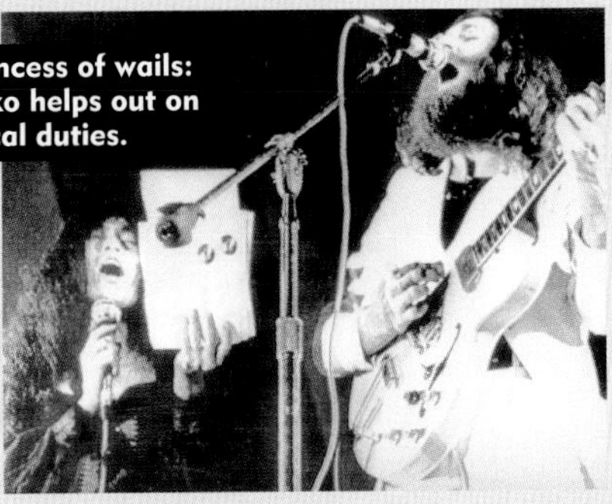

Princess of wails: Yoko helps out on vocal duties.

Lennon, George Harrison and Apple assistant Anthony Fawcett found the band: Klaus Voormann on bass and session drummer Alan White future Yes drummer. The chase was on for Eric Clapton, but he was asleep.

In Toronto, no media would believe the promoter's story. The show survived only because one Detroit DJ repeatedly played a tape of Lennon stating he was coming, which jammed both the bridge and the tunnel leading from Detroit over the border to Toronto.

Just as ticket sales were hitting 10,000, Anthony Fawcett called Brower from Heathrow. He had White and Voormann, but John and Yoko, unable to find Clapton, had already called the gig off. Just as Fawcett was telling Brower this, the news came that Clapton was available. But John and Yoko were still no-shows. Brower had one last chance. He cajoled Anthony Fawcett into giving him Clapton's phone number, and he dialled it instantly.

"Eric, you may not remember me," he said, "but I'm the promoter who lost $20,000 on your Blind Faith show last month. Please call John Lennon, and tell him he must do this or I will get on a plane, come to his house and live with him because I will be ruined."

That did the trick. Clapton called Lennon, angry at the complications. "John respected Eric and he was mortified at having pissed him off so much," says Brower. "John was shamed into coming."

One plane and an 80-motorcycle escort brought John Lennon to his dressing room. His old Hamburg friend, a shattered and dishevelled Gene Vincent was waiting at the door. "Gene was beside himself all day, excited that John was coming," says Brower. "It was kind of sad," says Larry Leblanc, then a young reporter, now Billboard's Canadian editor. "John was trying to move gently past him, Gene was saying, 'Hey John, remember Hamburg?' John was really polite but he did not want to stop. He put his arm around Gene and said, 'Hi, Gene, nice to see ya', and kept moving. The whole exchange took maybe 20 seconds."

John and Yoko stayed locked in their dressing room for three hours before their performance – and Yoko wasn't impressed with the surroundings. "I came from the avant-garde world, which is kind of like the classical world," she says. "They have lovely reception rooms, they treat you really well. We arrived in this dressing room, and it is a concrete locker room, it's dirty, it's ugly. I looked at John and he laughed and said, 'Welcome to rock'n'roll'."

Onstage, Lennon looked better than he sounded, in a sleek white suit, but artistically it wasn't anybody's best day. The Beatle tunes fared better than the old rock'n'roll numbers, and a singalong Give Peace A Chance sounded as if it would finish it all – but no-one had expected Yoko alone. Her vocal work, performed from inside a bag, is less significant than the fact that it was performed at all. From wail one, it slaughtered every rule of pop performance. Rumblings could be heard at the edges of the crowd. The biker security guards, especially, were muttering dark oaths.

The Beatle tunes fared better than the old rock'n'roll numbers, but no-one had expected Yoko alone.

Larry Leblanc was in the pit between stage and audience. "People were polite. They were bewildered, but everybody knew she was an artist, she'd taken photographs of bums and things like that. We figured whatever she was doing, eventually it would end. But it didn't fuckin' end."

She clocked in finally at 17:27, and exited quickly. It was reported locally that things had been thrown at her. "There was some booing off to the side, but anything thrown at her would have had to go over my head and hit a spot pretty close to me," says Leblanc. "It didn't happen."

Not until Beatles roadie Mal Evans came on to turn off the amps was it clear that Lennon would not return, a dismal finish to so rare and unexpected a performance. Few people were aware of just what else had drawn to a close that day. For John Lennon, this one act, this rogue performance, was the leap from imagining life as a non-Beatle, as he had done for years, to actually living it. Two weeks later he faced the others and told them it was over.

PHOTOS: ASSOCIATED PRESS, TOPFOTO, LFI

21 The Beatles begin recording Come Together at Abbey Road.

22 Work continues on Come Together and Oh! Darling at Abbey Road.

23 Work continues on Come Together, and begins on The End, at Abbey Road.

24 Paul records a demo of Come And Get It for Badfinger, and the whole group records Sun King and Mean Mr Mustard.

25 Work continues in Abbey Road on Polythene Pam, She Came In Through The Bathroom Window, Come Together, Sun King and Mean Mr Mustard.

28 Work continues in Abbey Road on Polythene Pam and She Came In Through The Bathroom Window.

29 Work continues in Abbey Road on Come Together, Sun King and Mean Mr Mustard.

31 Work continues in Abbey Road on Golden Slumbers, Carry That Weight and You Never Give Me Your Money.

AUGUST 69

1 Work begins on Because in Abbey Road studios.

2 Badfinger (above) record Come And Get It at Abbey Road, with Paul McCartney as producer.

4 Work continues on Because in Abbey Road.

5 The Beatles make their first group use of a Moog synthesizer, when George Harrison overdubs Moog sounds onto Because in Abbey Road.

6 At Abbey Road, George works on Here Comes The Sun, while Paul works on Maxwell's Silver Hammer.

7 Work continues on The End at Abbey Road.

8 The celebrated, and oft-copied, cover of The Beatles' *Abbey Road* album is photographed at 11.35am (above).

9 Actress Sharon Tate and four others are found slaughtered by Charles Manson's followers in the former Los Angeles home of record producer Terry Melcher.

11 Work continues on I Want You at Abbey Road.

14 John Lennon is interviewed in Abbey Road by Kenny Everett for the BBC Radio 1 show Everett Is Here.

ABBEY ROAD

Road To Nowhere

Despite the strife and bitterness surrounding The Beatles in 1969, *Abbey Road* became their biggest-selling album ever. David Fricke reassesses the reputation of the Fab Four's last will and testament.

The Beatles recorded their final album in January, 1969: the meagre soundtrack to a bleak documentary about how, after seven years at the top of the world, the band was struggling to make music together. They called that record, and the film, Let It Be. Even the title sounded like a death rattle. By the time the album and movie limped into stores and theatres in May, 1970, there were no more Beatles – only ex-Beatles.

But between those two black months, in the summer of 1969, John Lennon, Paul McCartney, George Harrison and Ringo Starr made one more, *real* last album. And they named it *Abbey Road* – after the address of the EMI recording studio in St John's Wood, London, that had been their working home and comfort zone since Love Me Do, the only place where they could simply be musicians, not stars.

The Beatles were breaking up that year. They didn't care to stop it. They also knew, instinctively, that it was essential to leave the way they had arrived in 1962, as the greatest rock'n'roll band in history. *Let It Be* was an obituary waiting to be printed. *Abbey Road* was The Beatles' subconscious prayer to the world: Remember us *this* way.

The album was released in the UK on September 26, 1969 and in the US on October 1. In America, it is The Beatles' biggest-selling, non-compilation album – 12 million copies, according to the Recording Industry Association of America. But *Abbey Road* is the least regarded of the Great Beatles Albums, spoken of more with respect than in the gasps of religious awe reserved for *Rubber Soul*, *Revolver* and *Sgt Pepper's Lonely Hearts Club Band* – and with understandable reason. There is no dramatic forward motion to *Abbey Road*. After the débâcle of *Let It Be* – a McCartney gamble to save the group by recreating the power and thrills of The Beatles' Cavern Club days, the simple joys of look-ma-no-overdubs rock'n'roll – *Abbey Road* was itself a retreat: to proven strengths, to the lessons learned in the EMI womb, under George Martin's paternal encouragement.

> "They named it *Abbey Road* after the only place where they could simply be musicians, not stars."

The Beatles stopped being a concert band way back in 1964; the robotic half-hour sets of 1965 and '66 were obligation, not showbiz. Instead, The Beatles turned the studio into their stage, performing exceptional feats of song construction. They were running out of reasons (musical, personal, financial) to work together by the summer of '69, but The Beatles were still a band in that they built *Abbey Road* as one. The album is not a masterpiece – there are dips and holes, but it is a triumph of immaculate, if temporary, unity.

Twelve of the 17 songs on *Abbey Road* – including McCartney's Oh! Darling and Maxwell's Silver Hammer; Lennon's Sun King and Polythene Pam; Harrison's Something and Starr's Octopus's Garden – first surfaced in some form during the *Let It Be* sessions at Twickenham Film Studios and The Beatles' recording grotto downstairs at Apple. Since *Let It Be* was McCartney's brainstorm, it is no surprise that Oh! Darling – a hot plate of Louisiana slow-dance swamp pop –

Come together: The Beatles outside Abbey Road studios, August 8, 1969.

PHOTO: CAMERA PRESS

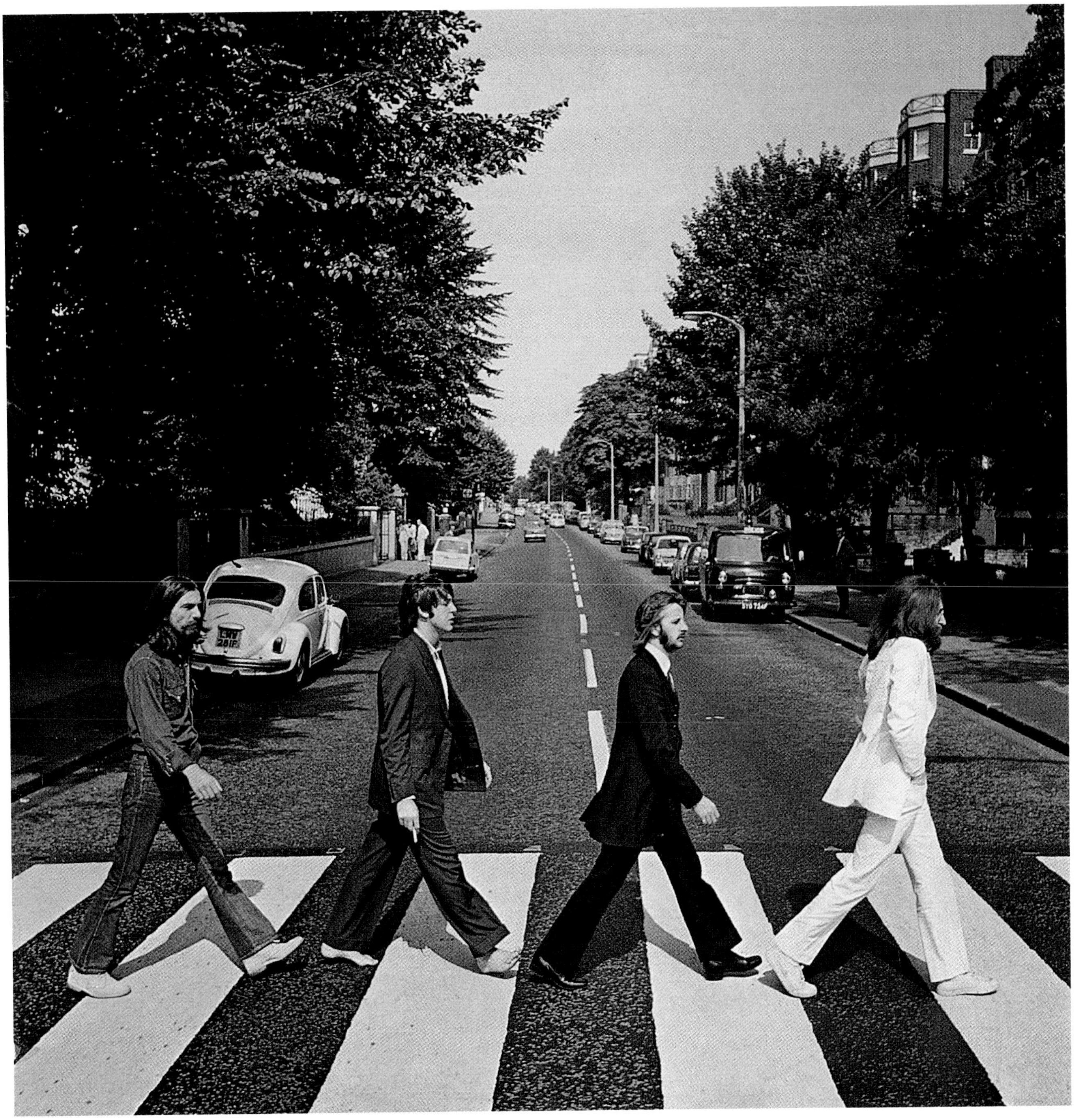

and Maxwell's Silver Hammer, a bizarre music-hall confection about a homicidal nutcase, got whole days of attention.

Yet, ironically, there is much about *Abbey Road* that is "live". Basic tracks were cut by all four Beatles, polished over take after take – like the 36 that went into You Never Give Me Your Money – then overdubbed to a blinding shine, generally under the direction of the song's composer.

The Beatles nailed the voodoo swagger of the rhythm track to Lennon's Come Together in a single day. And, after seven months of on-off labour on his greatest ballad, Something, Harrison recorded his pithy, elegiac guitar solo live with the strings, on the last day of orchestral work. Engineer Geoff Emerick later noted that Harrison's playing was "almost the same solo, note for note" as a previous, rejected take. "The only reason I feel he wanted to redo it was emotion."

TRACK LISTING

SIDE ONE

1. Come Together
Sung by Lennon

2. Something
Harrison
Sung by Harrison

3. Maxwell's Silver Hammer
Sung by McCartney

4. Oh! Darling
Sung by McCartney

5. Octopus's Garden
Starkey
Sung by Starr

6. I Want You (She's So Heavy)
Sung by Lennon

SIDE TWO

7. Here Comes The Sun
Harrison
Sung by Harrison

8. Because
Sung by Lennon

9. You Never Give Me Your Money
Sung by McCartney

10. Sun King
Sung by Lennon

11. Mean Mr Mustard
Sung by Lennon

12. Polythene Pam
Sung by Lennon

13. She Came In Through The Bathroom Window
Sung by McCartney

14. Golden Slumbers
Sung by McCartney

15. Carry That Weight
Sung by McCartney

16. The End
Sung by McCartney

17. Her Majesty
Sung by McCartney

All tracks by Lennon/McCartney unless otherwise specified.

ABBEY ROAD

WHAT THE PAPERS SAID...

The press proclaims *Abbey Road* to be brilliant.

"It teems with musical invention... and the second side is altogether remarkable. Nice as Come Together and Harrison's Something are – they are minor pleasures in the context of the whole disc... Side Two is marvellous... George Harrison's torrid Here Comes The Sun... melds into Because and its mind-blowing close harmony. Then a wistful romantic tune... that fades into a further instalment of Sun King... this blends into a whole series of rock'n'roll songs that seem to find their tunes in developments of the same musical mood and musical invention. John Lennon has said that *Abbey Road* is an attempt to get away from experimentation and back to genuine rock'n'roll. When one is as inventive as The Beatles, to try non-experimentation is a forlorn hope."

William Mann, The Times, December 5, 1969

Beatles' new LP '*Abbey Road*'

The Beatles' first 1969 album will be released in September. Titled *Abbey Road*, it will have one long 17-minute track on Side One made up of several songs plus two other new tracks. Side Two features six separate songs.

The new album is named after the road in which the EMI studios are situated—the home, of course, of the famous No. 2 studio, where most of the Beatles' big hits have been born.

It's the old team once again, with George Martin in the recording manager's chair, and red-haired Geoffrey Emerick sound balancing on all sessions.

Unlike their next release, *Get Back*, which does what the title says and has many songs treated in an early Beatles style, *Abbey Road* is progressive '69 Beatles all the way, and features lots of new sounds, many of which were created in the electronic depths of George Harrison's Moog Synthesizer, which he had specially brought into the studios.

A description of the musical scope of the Moog is given on page 46 of this issue.

"It's too early to say whether this is their best album, but it is brilliant. Parts of the medley are quite beautiful in conception and structuring... Whatever you may think of them as individuals, it is difficult not to be grateful to them for their continued efforts to produce good music."

David Connolly, Evening Standard, September 20, 1969

"*Abbey Road* is refreshingly terse and unpretentious. The attractive clarity of [The Beatles'] best melodies is now enhanced by skilful but sparing use of symphonic resources. Though I am as tired of their cod-1920s jokes (Maxwell's Silver Hammer) and of Ringo's obligatory nursery arias (Octopus's Garden) as of some of their philosophical dicta, this LP touches peaks far higher than did their last album."

Derek Jewell, Sunday Times, September 28, 1969

SLEEVE NOTES

The iconic *Abbey Road* cover took just 15 minutes to shoot.

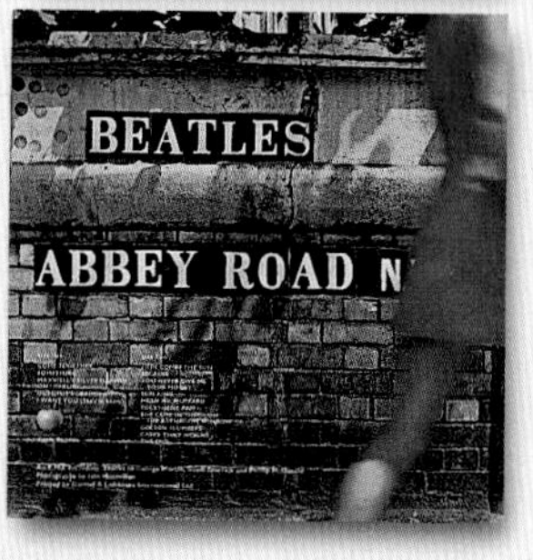

Like *Sgt Pepper* before it, the sleeve to *Abbey Road* has been much parodied. Booker T And The MGs mimicked the sleeve for their own LP, *McLemore Avenue;* the Sesame Street puppets paid tribute with *Sesame Road*, and the Red Hot Chili Peppers had the Abbey Road EP. Even McCartney got in on the act for his 1993 live LP, *Paul Is Live*. Such is the commercial clout of photographer Iain Macmillan's original snap.

Macmillan, who based the cover on a rough sketch by McCartney, had previously taken photos for Yoko Ono's 1966 art exhibition at the Indica gallery, London – where Ono had first met Lennon – and had displayed his charity money boxes in John's own You Are Here exhibition two years later. Gathering the group together on the morning of August 8, 1969 outside of Abbey Road studios, he set about capturing the band. There was little preparation for the shoot, the boys turned up in their own clothes, it was McCartney's idea to walk barefoot and Lennon's to wear his white suit. Armed with just his camera and a stepladder, Macmillan ushered the boys across the zebra crossing and back. The shots had to be taken quickly because the road was a constant stream of traffic although a passing policeman did briefly halt the cars.

The finished sleeve fuelled the ridiculous "Paul is dead" rumours that were rife in the US at the time. Lennon's suit was taken as a mark of respect to the supposed dead singing bassist, while the barefoot Paul, so the story went, was a stand-in lookalike, his bare feet a symbol of both a Mafiosa and Grecian death.

The back cover features the original Abbey Road street sign, while the blurry blob in the right hand corner is a passing girl in a blue dress who was accidentally caught in shot.

Lois Wilson

"It is hard to associate *Abbey Road* with bickering because it is a record of focused labour."

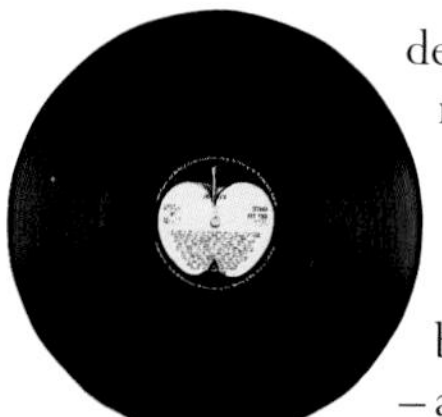

Abbey Road is actually more articulate about The Beatles' crisis of impatience and exhaustion that year than *Let It Be*. Lennon's fragmentary contributions to the Side Two medley – Because, Sun King, Mean Mr Mustard, Polythene Pam – reflect his divided attention: between The Beatles and his imminent solo life; between his addiction to heroin and his devotion to his muse and second wife, Yoko Ono. The key line in Come Together – "You got to be free" – was a bald contradiction of the title. In his best song on the LP, Lennon couldn't make up his mind which way to go. That he was running on fits and starts of inspiration was obvious, too, in the opening lyric of Come Together, borrowed from Chuck Berry's 1956 single, You Can't Catch Me. Lennon would later pay dearly, in court, for his cribbing.

The frankness of *Abbey Road* belies its gleam. Harrison wrote Here Comes The Sun, his second burst of maturation on the album, in Eric Clapton's garden, as an antidote to the depressing strain of Apple business meetings.

Paul McCartney got right to the point of his dissatisfaction with The Beatles' manager and book-keeping wolf Allen Klein – and his feeling of betrayal by the others – in You Never Give Me Your Money, a gorgeous four-minute operetta inside the longer Side Two suite. A wistful tide of voices and guitars ultimately breaks into a honky-tonk letter of resignation: "One sweet dream/Pick up the bags/Get in the limousine/Soon we'll be away from here/Step on the gas/Wipe that tear away". Several months later, in April 1970, McCartney sent the real thing, a press release announcing the beginning of his solo career and, by default, the end of The Beatles. Let It Be was the first rock'n'roll documentary about a band falling apart. On *Abbey Road*, The Beatles explained why the dream couldn't last.

Thirty-four years later, it is still hard to associate The Beatles' last album with bickering and estrangement because it is so clearly a record of focused labour and honed detail. The opening riff of Polythene Pam is right up there with The Who's Pinball Wizard in the pantheon of acoustic power-chord progressions. The melancholy cocktail of cricket noises and deep-

When it came to groupies, Ringo took what he could get: The Beatles prepare to be shot for the *Abbey Road* cover.

PHOTO: LINDA McCARTNEY, REX

throated surf guitar at the beginning of Sun King sounds like Brian Wilson producing Fleetwood Mac's Albatross.

If you don't believe Lennon's eight-minute hurricane of sexual appetite and admiration for Ono, I Want You (She's So Heavy), is bona fide heavy metal, at least note this: how Pink Floyd's Roger Waters used a variation on the closing, groaning-riff motif for his overture to *The Wall*, In The Flesh. And let's accept, for the moment, that Harrison didn't mean to lift the title of James Taylor's Apple recording, Something In The Way She Moves. Harrison's Something is the better song, and closer to white-garage R&B (choppy combo organ, Lennon's howling "I don't know" cameo in the chorus) than Frank Sinatra, one of the song's biggest fans, ever suspected.

But this is The End, and there's a song called The End to prove it: after the segue from the grand resignation of Golden Slumbers and the moral march of Carry That Weight. McCartney's lyric arithmetic in The End – "And in the end, the love you take is equal to the love you make" – was oft cited in post-mortems of The Beatles' break-up.

The real heart of the song, though, is the simple repeated chant, "Love you, love you!", under the round-table guitar solos. *Abbey Road* wasn't just goodbye. It was a thank you – from them to us, for granting the band as much in faith and licence as they gave us in art and pleasure. The Beatles gave everything they had until there was no more to give.

THE SENSIBLE OPTION

For The Damned's Captain Sensible, *Abbey Road* is an album of two halves…

"The first Beatles record I bought was a couple of years ago. I was never a fan – they were just a bit too obvious at the time. Everyone else was though. I remember having my opinion researched by some gang of thugs in the playground… 'Who's your favourite – The Beatles or the Stones?' The wrong answer would probably have earned me a dead leg or something equally unsavoury, which I escaped by spluttering 'The Hollies, actually', and legging it.

"I'm not over-fond of Side One of *Abbey Road*, which is a bunch of Lennon blues dirges interspersed with one each from the others. Harrison's sugary Something, McCartney's appalling Maxwell's Silver Hammer – and the less said about Ringo's Octopus's Garden the better. But Side Two is an altogether different affair – pop heaven or overkill depending on your taste. An amazing sequence of cracking tunes that people usually attribute to Paul, but without the efforts of the two Georges – Harrison and Martin – it would've been half-baked. Harrison's playing is sensational, and he also contributes my favourite track on the album, Here Comes The Sun, which doctors could possibly prescribe as a rival to Prozac.

"We did play a faster, gnarled version of Help! in the original Damned set which must've been pretty unrecognisable, as people would come up after the show and say that they'd seen it on the set-list and asked why we hadn't played it. Although The Beatles didn't mean much in 1977, I reckon Lennon's in-your-face nastiness would've enabled him to front a fair old punk group. Wouldn't it have been interesting if he'd been born a few years later?"

Louisa Carr

15 The Beatles oversee the recording of George Martin's orchestral backings for Something, Here Comes The Sun, Golden Slumbers/Carry That Weight and The End, at Abbey Road.

18 Paul overdubs piano onto The End at Abbey Road.

19 George Martin finishes work on Here Comes The Sun and Something, at Abbey Road.

20 All four of The Beatles are together in the studio for the last time, recording I Want You (She's So Heavy).

22 The Beatles gather at John Lennon's home in Tittenhurst Park, Berks (above), to be photographed for the cover of the *Hey Jude* US album.

24 John Lennon writes, rehearses and records Cold Turkey in Abbey Road.

26 George drives to Forelands Farm, Bembridge, Isle Of Wight, to visit Bob Dylan.

28 Paul and Linda become the proud parents of a daughter, Mary, in London. George attends an Apple press conference for Radha Krishna Temple's first recording of Hare Krishna Mantra, in Sydenham, south London.

31 John, George and Ringo attend the Isle Of Wight Festival, to see Bob Dylan.

SEPTEMBER 69

1 The day after the Isle Of Wight Festival, headliner Bob Dylan visits John Lennon's Tittenhurst Park home.

2 George drives Bob Dylan to Heathrow Airport in his Mercedes.

8 Ringo is rushed to the Middlesex Hospital, London, with intestinal trouble after being taken ill at his Weybridge home.

10 When Rape and Self-Portrait, two films made by John and Yoko, are shown at the Institute Of Contemporary Arts, London, two unidentified figures in white bags sit on the stage throughout the screening.

11 Ringo leaves Middlesex Hospital with a clean bill of health.

12 With just one day to get a band together and rehearse, John accepts an invitation to play at the Toronto Rock'n'Roll Revival Festival.

13 John Lennon's Plastic Ono Band, Chuck Berry, Little Richard, Gene Vincent, Jerry Lee Lewis, Bo Diddley, The Doors, Chicago and Alice Cooper play at the Toronto Rock'n'Roll Revival Festival at the city's Varsity Stadium.

What: US Radio show claims Paul is dead.
Where: Detroit
When: October 12, 1969

DEAD MAN WALKING

The big rumour of autumn 1969 was that Paul McCartney was dead. In actual fact, he was very much alive. By Merrell Noden.

RADIO CALL-IN SHOWS ARE CATNIP TO conspiracy theorists, so Russ Gibb, a DJ at WKNR-FM in Detroit, was not surprised when "Tom", a caller on the afternoon of October 12, 1969, dropped his bombshell. "I was going to rap with you about McCartney being dead and what is this all about?" said Tom, who identified himself as a student at Eastern Michigan University.

After allowing himself a roll of the eyes skywards, Gibb tried to reason with the young man. "Look," he said, "that story is always floating around, but it's just not true."

But Tom persisted. "There are clues to McCartney's death in the records," he told Gibb. "What you've got to do is play Revolution 9 backwards."

Humour the guy, thought Gibb. He cued the song up to the point where a voice repeats, "Number nine, number nine…" and began turning it backwards. Sure enough, a voice could be heard chanting, "Turn me on, dead man, turn me on, dead man…"

Before Gibb could get off the air, a young man who'd been listening showed up at the studio wanting him to play the end of Strawberry Fields Forever. Once more, a voice was audible, saying what sounded like "I buried Paul".

Yet another listener that day was Fred LaBour, a wise guy who had just been assigned a review of *Abbey Road* for the Michigan Daily student newspaper. Instead, he wrote the wild fiction that elevated the Paul-Is-Dead rumour beyond the world of dormitory myth. Not content with the clues Gibb had mentioned on the air, LaBour began inventing them, such as the claim that "walrus" is Greek for death. He even dreamed up a stand-in for McCartney, an "orphan from Edinburgh named William Campbell" who, after winning a Paul lookalike contest, had been secretly coached by the surviving Beatles to imitate him.

Thus began one of the stranger episodes in The Beatles' career. Coming roughly midway between the Kennedy assassination and the Watergate hearings, a certain amount of paranoia made perfect sense. A few years earlier, when Bob Dylan had vanished following his motorcycle accident, wild rumours sprang up to explain his 18-month absence, among them that the government had taken him out because he was getting too powerful.

"A lot of us, because of Vietnam and the so-called Establishment, were ready, willing and able to believe just about any sort of conspiracy," says Tim Harper, whose story in the Drake University student newspaper on September 17 was the first published discussion of the rumour. Exactly why The Beatles, who were presumably the good guys in the scheme of things, would choose to deceive their fans wasn't clear.

"When you look back on it, it all seems so silly and absurd," says Vin Scelsa, who in 1969 was just starting his career as the thinking man's New York DJ. "But the distinction you have to make between then and now is that then there was this counter-culture tied together by certain key artists, and the major ones were the lyric writers – Dylan, Lennon and McCartney, Jagger and Richards. Every song from them – starting about late 1966, became a personal message, worthy of endless scrutiny. They were more than just songs: they were guidelines on how to live your life."

Where exactly the rumour started remains a mystery and probably is destined to stay that way. It may have been the motor scooter accident McCartney suffered in December of 1965, or his rumoured car crash the following year. Harper says he heard it upon returning to college that fall. "It was the sort of thing people would sit around at night and talk about."

Very soon, every college campus, every radio station, had a resident expert. With speculation reaching a high point in November, F Lee Bailey, the renowned defence attorney, conducted a mock trial on prime time TV. Respected news anchor John Chancellor was reduced to saying, "All we can report with certainty is that Paul McCartney is either dead or alive."

The more people looked, the more clues they found. The Beatles, it seemed, were positively desperate to communicate with their fans, and almost every object, every pose, every word on those very crowded album covers and sleeves was pored over and records were spun backwards and at varying speeds.

One man claimed there was an orphan from Edinburgh, named William Campbell, standing in for McCartney.

Some of the 'clues' stood on their own, while others required a certain amount of fabrication. *Abbey Road*, with its cover photo showing the four Beatles walking across a zebra crossing, was the clincher: obviously this was a funeral procession, with minister Lennon leading undertaker Ringo, resurrected Paul and grave digger George. The licence plate on the 'Beetle' that read 28 IF? This was the age McCartney would have been if he had lived. Never mind that Paul was in fact 27 – this inconvenient fact was explained away by invoking the Hindu custom of counting babies as one at birth.

The Beatles dismissed the furore. "It's the stupidest rumour I've ever heard," said Lennon. McCartney himself was not exactly helpful in dispelling the rumour. He had married Linda Eastman in March, and with *Abbey Road* completed, he was determined to lie low and contemplate his future in a disintegrating band. When a team of journalists from Life magazine showed up at his farm in Scotland, he chased them away angrily before relenting and inviting them in for tea. The cover photo of the McCartneys – with the cover billing "Paul is still with us" – began strangling the rumour, which was soon overshadowed by the demise of The Beatles as a whole.

LIFE
THE CASE OF THE 'MISSING' BEATLE
Paul is still with us
NOVEMBER 7 · 1969

PHOTOS: CAMERA PRESS

A grave error: Paul frolics with his dog
n distinctly undead fashion, 1968.

"You can uncover your ears now…" Ringo's talent finally enjoys its full flowering for the *Sentimental Journey* promo film, shot at the Talk Of The Town nightclub, London, March 1970.

What: Ringo records his first solo LP.
Where: Abbey Road studios
When: October 27, 1969

A STARR IS BORN!

Five weeks after John announced he would be quitting The Beatles, Ringo was the first of the Fabs off the blocks. By Alan Clayson.

OF EACH BEATLE'S PREPARATIONS FOR the end, Ringo Starr's were the most pragmatic. Before *Let It Be* began its sojourn in the album lists in May 1970, he'd already struck out on his own as a recording artist. In the privacy of his home studio, Starr – with assistance from near-neighbour Maurice Gibb – had knocked together an album's worth of "experimental" woofing and tweeting on one of these new-fangled monophonic synthesizers. "They take control of you, those machines," laughed Ringo. "I turn all the dials and press buttons and get excited and put a few mics out, and put it through amplifiers into my Revox. We found this riff on the machine and I was playing with it, and he [Gibb] started humming words and read the dials, like modulator and envelope shaper, things like that." Another item featured drums with "lots of echo and it just sounds strange. I love it. Some of the tracks are just incredible".

There was talk of Starr's twiddlings being issued as his debut solo album. However, the idea was never mentioned again after the 'shock' announcement in December 1969 that three tracks were already "in the can" for an infinitely more straightforward LP, *Ringo Starrdust*. The rest would be cut in time for release in March. The provisional track-listing might have given the average Beatles fan cause for concern – the presence of Whispering Grass, Love Is A Many Splendoured Thing, Autumn Leaves and further pre-rock'n'roll showbiz evergreens showing rather idiosyncratic taste.

"I really dug all that old music," Ringo explained, "because that was the first I ever heard, and I thought my mum'll be pleased if I sing all those songs." Apparently, the notion had been fermenting for a couple of years, and, with The Beatles in abeyance, time hung heavy. Like the man who paid to conduct the London Symphony Orchestra at the Albert Hall for just one night, Ringo too had the wherewithal to fulfil a dream.

While *Ringo Starrdust* was as self-indulgent in its way as mucking around with a synthesizer, at least a Beatle was taking on 'decent' songs instead of any John-and-Yoko-ish avant-gardenings. The attention of EMI retailers could also be directed to its George Martin production as well as Starr's engagement of arrangers of the calibre of Quincy Jones, Count Basie's Chico O'Farrill, Johnny Dankworth and some of his own musical cronies like Klaus Voormann, Maurice Gibb and, for Hoagy Carmichael's Stardust, Paul McCartney. Because he'd impressed Ringo with his orchestrations on a Tiny Tim LP, Richard Perry was chosen to frame a version of Doris Day's Sentimental Journey which he invested with a new US device called a 'vocoder'.

To stress the nostalgic selling-point, the cover and full page advertisements would show a dapper Starr in front of the towering Empress pub in the Liverpool district where he grew up. The promotional short – directed by Neil Aspinall – was Ringo against a backdrop of the Empress, crooning Sentimental Journey – that had been seen to make greater sense as the album's title than *Ringo Starrdust*.

Autumn Leaves and a version of I'll Be Seeing You were also rejected. You wonder what they were like when assessing the numbers that did survive, even if the immaculate scoring may be exemplified by the few bars of fluid saxophone busking that leapt from the horn riffing on O'Farrill's Night And Day; the glissando swoops of Voormann's violins on Ted Daffan's I'm A Fool To Care – or Elmer Bernstein's witty Have I Told You Lately That I Love You leitmotifs.

"He sings better than you'd expect him to," wrote a particularly sympathetic reviewer, overlooking, say, a misjudged note on the coda of Bye Bye Blackbird and some dubious scatting on Fats Waller's Blue Turning Grey Over You. Yet while the new LP contained material tried by the likes of Crosby, Sinatra and Matt Monro, none were so deluded as to think Starr a 'quality' vocalist any more than Johnnie Ray, the half-deaf "Prince of Wails", who'd preceded Elvis Presley as a world class pop sensation, and who still drank from much the same repertory pool as Starr had on *Sentimental Journey*. After Ray appeared at the Liverpool Empire in 1955, a teenage Ringo had been among the rapt crowd watching him sip coffee in a window of the Adelphi in the city centre. "He was waving at people from big hotels," gasped Starr, "and I thought, There! That's the life for me."

Johnnie Ray was more a yardstick of style than vocation now that Ringo was rich and famous too. Nevertheless, who cares if *Sentimental Journey* isn't "real singing"? Admittedly, on more than one track, it could have been a faceless anyone but otherwise, as Ringo would assure you himself, "Once my voice comes over on the radio or record, you know that it's me!"

His humble vocal endowment with its hangdog tone, hit-or-miss pitching and untutored phrasing compounded a hypnotically hideous charm common to certain singers who superimpose a disjointed range and eccentric delivery onto a given song's melodic and lyrical grid. Starr shared this approach with other unorthodox vocalists like the asthmatic Yardbird Keith Relf, laconic Dave Berry and Reg Presley of The Troggs with his Long John Silver burr.

"Once my voice comes over on the radio or record, you know that it's me!" Ringo Starr

Nonetheless, the hoisting of *Sentimental Journey* high up Top 40s throughout the globe testified less to vocal individuality than the value of screening the title clip on programmes such as the nationally-networked Ed Sullivan Show in the States, and a comprehensive media jaunt by Ringo Starr, the soon-to-be ex-Beatle, in the flesh.

"The great thing was that it got my solo career moving," concluded Ringo, "not very fast, but just moving. It was like the first shovel of coal in the furnace that makes the train inch forward."

PHOTO: CAMERA PRESS, REDFERNS

19 ATV acquires 50 per cent of the shares of Northern Songs Ltd.

20 During a meeting between The Beatles and their accountant/manager Allen Klein at Apple Records, London, John says, "I want a divorce, just like the divorce I had from Cyn. I mean the group is over. I'm leaving." Tactfully, though, he agrees to keep his feelings private for the time being. Meanwhile, in the Melody Maker Pop Poll, The Beatles are voted best group.

22 An Illinois University newspaper hints that Paul McCartney is dead, listing clues on the cover of the *Sgt Pepper* album and the words, "I buried Paul" in the fade-out to Strawberry Fields Forever.

25 ATV acquires another 4 per cent of shares in Northern Songs, becoming the major shareholder with 54 per cent, and wresting control away from Lennon and McCartney. John begins Plastic Ono Band sessions in Abbey Road, with work on the live concert recordings from Toronto, plus an attempt at Cold Turkey.

26 The Beatles release *Abbey Road* in the UK. The cover shot of Paul, barefooted and dressed in black, sparks further rumours of his demise.

28 John Lennon records the final version of Cold Turkey, in Trident Studios, London.

OCTOBER 1969

1 *Abbey Road* is released in the US.

2 In an interview, John Lennon likens Apple to a big black hole that is sucking up all his benefits as a composer and performer.

3 Aretha Franklin (above) records Eleanor Rigby at Criteria Studios, Miami, Florida. Eric Clapton joins John and Ringo in Abbey Road studios, adding his guitar to the Plastic Ono Band track Don't Worry Kyoko (Mummy's Only Looking For Her Hand In The Snow).

4 *Abbey Road* begins an 11-week run at Number 1 in the UK.

5 John Lennon is in Abbey Road studio adding overdubs to Cold Turkey.

6 The Beatles release a double A-sided single, Something/Come Together, in the US. This is the first time a George Harrison song has been the A-side of a Beatles single.

8 George Harrison is interviewed at Apple by David Wigg for BBC Radio 1 show Scene And Heard.

12 An unnamed caller to underground American radio station WKNR in Detroit, urges DJ Russ Gibb to listen to Revolution 9 by The Beatles backwards. When Gibb plays it on air, listeners claim to hear the words, "Turn me on, dead man". This becomes a 'clue' in the 'Paul is dead' myth.

13 Paul and Ringo attend Mary Hopkin's debut live concert at the Savoy Theatre, London.

15 Ringo and Maureen fly to Los Angeles.

18 Come Together/Something, enters the US Top 40 singles chart where it will peak at Number 1.

20 When Ravi Shankar performs in London, George Harrison and Patti Boyd are in the audience.

22 Paul publicly denies rumours that he is dead.

24 Cold Turkey is released in the United Kingdom.

25 *Abbey Road* enters the US album chart, where it peaks at Number 1.

27 Ringo begins recording his solo album, *Sentimental Journey*, at Abbey Road with producer George Martin.

31 The Beatles release a new single, Something/Come Together, in the United Kingdom.

NOVEMBER 69

1 The Beatles' *Abbey Road* album hits Number 1 in the US and stays there for 11 weeks.

6 Ringo is recording Stormy Weather for his album *Sentimental Journey*, at Wessex Sound Studios, London. It is not included on the final album.

7 Paul and Linda McCartney are featured on the cover of Life magazine. John and Yoko release the *Wedding Album* in the UK.

14 Ringo records his vocals for Stardust, to appear on his album *Sentimental Journey*, at Wessex Sound.

15 Hamburg's Star Club, an early training ground for The Beatles, closes because bands have become too expensive to hire.

20 UK TV show Top Of The Pops is broadcast in colour for the first time.

25 John Lennon returns his MBE in protest against UK involvement in overseas wars.

28 Ringo is recording Blue Turning Grey Over You, for *Sentimental Journey*, at Wessex Sound.

29 Come Together/Something hits the US Number 1 for just one week.

DECEMBER 69

1 Ringo is filmed at several locations around London for a BBC2 documentary to be shown as part of the arts series Late Night Line-Up.

2 When Delaney And Bonnie And Friends (including Eric Clapton, above left) play at Colston Hall, Bristol, they are joined by George on guitar.

3 John and Yoko are filmed at home in Ascot, for a TV documentary, The World Of John And Yoko.

4 John And The Plastic Ono Band record two experimental pieces, Item 1 and Item 2, at Abbey Road, but neither will be released.

What: The release of something
Where: UK
When: October 31, 1969

SOMETHING ELSE

It was George Harrison's best song yet, and the first Beatles single to break the Lennon-McCartney monopoly. By Mark Lewisohn.

"THEY BLESSED ME WITH A COUPLE OF B-sides in the past, but this is the first time I've had an A-side. Big deal, eh?" said George Harrison to reporter David Wigg on October 8, 1969.

A big deal it was, and it's hard to imagine the situation did not stir a wry, lop-sided smile in the man who would later declare he'd been an "Economy-class Beatle". The shadow cast by John and Paul was always an imposing one – did either foresee the dark horse emerging as front runner in the final furlong?

"There was an embarrassing period where his songs weren't that good and nobody wanted to say anything," John remarked in 1974. "He just wasn't in the same league for a long time – that's not putting him down, he just hadn't had the practice as a writer that we'd had."

The "couple of B-sides", The Inner Light and Old Brown Shoe, arose in tandem with an increasingly impressive array of Harrison LP tracks in 1968–69. George's compositions had been getting more interesting over the years. Something first surfaced in September 1968 during a White Album session for Piggies. Chris Thomas, an assistant to George Martin, recalls running through that song's harpsichord part when Harrison "started playing another new song to me, which later turned out to be Something. I said, That's great! Why don't we do that one instead?' and he replied, 'Do you like it? Do you really think it's good?'"

George told Chris Thomas he would give Something to his Apple protégé Jackie Lomax to release as a single. He didn't, but gave it instead to Joe Cocker (then at Number 1 with his roaring With A Little Help From My Friends) and helped him record a demo at Apple Studios in spring 1969. Cocker's subsequent re-recording was issued in November, a month after the song appeared on *Abbey Road* and days after it was released as a Beatles 45, the group's only single not written by Lennon or McCartney.

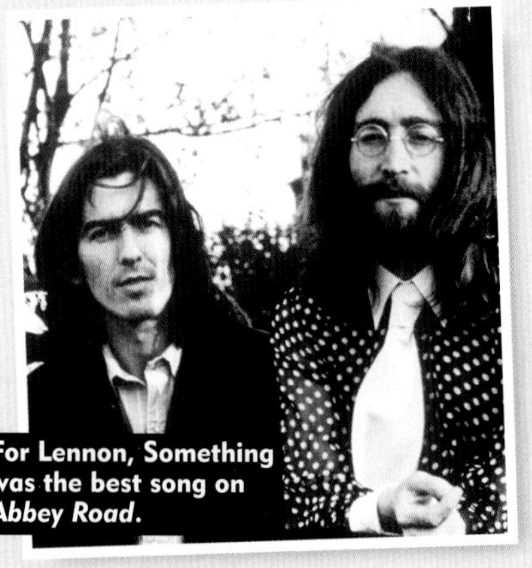
For Lennon, Something was the best song on *Abbey Road*.

Except for the bridge section, the Something melody arrived complete. The lyric took longer. Caught on tape during the January 1969 *Let It Be* sessions, George asked Paul what could follow the opening line "Something in the way she moves". "Attracts me… what?" John interjects: "Just say whatever comes into your head, 'attracts me like… a cauliflower' until you get the word." George jokes "pomegranate", but he does already have the next line, "I don't want to leave her now".

Anthology 3 features the song's first known recording, a vocal/electric guitar demo taped by George at EMI on February 25, 1969, his 26th birthday. The lyric was complete, in fact it included a counter-melody left off the finished version: "You know I love that woman of mine/And I need her all of the time/And you know I'm telling you/That woman, that woman don't make me blue". Recording proper occurred through the spring and summer – the first attempt in April, a remake in May (during which time it picked up and then lost a long instrumental coda), overdubs in July, orchestral track with tasteful guitar solo in August.

Something was instantly proclaimed a standout track on *Abbey Road* and John called it the best of the lot. As a single, it restored The Beatles to the top in America, The Ballad Of John And Yoko having fallen some way short. It didn't make Number 1 in Britain but then neither did Let It Be, the next and last single. The home release was doubly extraordinary: not only was it the first Harrison A-side, it was also the only time The Beatles issued a single from an already-released LP. The decision owed everything to Allen Klein, whose ABKCO company now "managed" Apple Corps.

In 1988, I wrote in The Complete Beatles Recording Sessions that Something was issued as a 45, "to spur George's career in giving him his first A-side [and] to bring in extra money". In direct rebuttal, Klein told me in 1990: "It *was* done on purpose, not to make money but to help the guy. Lennon wanted to help him. He knew that for all intents and purposes for a period of time they weren't going to be working together any more. Something was a great song. But to make money? Not a chance. It was really to point out George as a writer, and give him courage to go in and do his own LP. Which he did."

When the single was issued, George remarked to the NME's Alan Smith, "There's a lot of songs like that in my head. I must get them down. Maybe even other people would like to sing them." And how. Something attracted dozens of high-profile covers, including Frank Sinatra (1971 album Sinatra And Company) and Elvis Presley (1973 TV special Aloha From Hawaii). Sinatra, who had never cut a Beatles song before and long been sniffy about them, first called it a Lennon-McCartney composition and then hailed it as the greatest love song of the decade. He also added to the lyric, "You stick around, Jack, it might show". George parodied this in his own few live performances.

"At the time I wasn't particularly thrilled that Frank Sinatra did Something," George said in the Anthology book. "I'm more thrilled now than I was then. I wasn't really into Frank – he was the generation before me. I was more interested when Smokey Robinson did it and when James Brown did it." Brown's funky version was a long-term favourite: George plugged it enthusiastically during an important Radio 1 interview with Anne Nightingale in 1977 and it was on his jukebox at home in Henley.

There was a great irony in all of this. The 150-plus cover versions, the stage renditions, the strong airplay and The Beatles' own perpetual record sales resulted in a rich flow of royalties down the years. Something was published by George's own company, Harrisongs – 80 per cent owned until 1970, after that owned outright. Lennon-McCartney had just lost the tenure of their own songs, and with it the lion's share of the vast income they generated. The dark horse, whose compositions John and Paul had once found risible, had snuck up in the most artistically satisfying and remunerative canter.

PHOTOS: CAMERA PRESS, MIRRORPIX

George, 1969: "Shrink-to-fit jeans? I swear by 'em!"

"...And, while I'm at it, my old school can shove that swimming medal too!" John Lennon with his letter of protest to Harold Wilson, November 25, 1969.

What: John returns his MBE
Where: London
When: November 25, 1969

RETURN TO SENDER

When John Lennon wanted to raise publicity for his peace campaign, he used his most powerful weapon – his MBE. By Spencer Leigh.

ON NOVEMBER 25, 1969, JOHN LENNON told his chauffeur, Les Anthony, to retrieve the MBE from the top of Aunt Mimi's TV set in Poole, Dorset. "Mr Lennon said would you lend him his MBE for a while," Les told her. Mimi passed it over, just requesting its safe return.

With the medal back in his possession, Lennon prepared a letter to the Queen. "Your Majesty," he wrote on his Bag Productions stationery, "I am returning my MBE as a protest against Britain's involvement in the Nigeria-Biafra thing, against our support of America in Vietnam and against Cold Turkey slipping down the charts. With love, John Lennon of Bag."

Les drove John and Yoko to the tradesman's entrance at Buckingham Palace where they handed over the letter and the medal. A copy was also sent to the Prime Minister, still Harold Wilson, the man who had recommended The Beatles for the honour in the first place.

John had always been uncomfortable with the award. After its announcement on June 12, 1965, The Times had published letters of complaint from ex-servicemen threatening to return their decorations in protest, yet though Lennon reasoned that The Beatles had been given their MBEs for peace rather than war, acceptance still made him uneasy. He had followed Brian Epstein's wishes, but while McCartney framed his MBE, Lennon passed the award on to Aunt Mimi. He didn't anticipate that he would ever have reason to need it again.

Give peace a billboard: John's anti-war campaign kicks off, London, 1969.

John and Yoko launched a "peace offensive" and were looking for headlines where they could get them.

In 1969, however, John and Yoko Ono launched their "peace offensive" and were looking for front-page headlines wherever they could get them. Every day, newspapers reported situations that could benefit from the support of the Lennons. Civil war had raged in Nigeria since 1967, but famine in the breakaway region of Biafra had brought humanitarian protests and many felt that the UK government should do more. And in Vietnam too, there was a reason to call for peace – despite widespread opposition, President Nixon was reducing the US presence, but his forces were also attacking communist bases in Cambodia.

If Lennon could grab front page headlines by just sitting in bed, or by climbing into a bag, it was obvious that his MBE could be put to better use, a powerful weapon in raising the profile of the campaign for peace. Peace in Biafra. Peace in Vietnam. Peace everywhere.

After returning the medal, at a press conference John made it clear that he had felt the honour had been given as a political ploy. "Whenever I remembered it I used to flinch because I'm a socialist," he said. "I sold my soul when I received it, but now I have helped to redeem it in the cause of peace." His sentiments in returning the medal echoed the comments made by the Labour MP Tony Benn in 1965. "The Beatles have done more for the royal family by accepting MBEs than the royal family has done for The Beatles by giving them," Benn had commented.

John had expected criticism of his gesture, but the response in Britain was fierce. Harold Wilson regarded Lennon's behaviour as naïve and the press pilloried him, taking the flippant remark about Cold Turkey as another sign of his monstrous ego (Lennon grew to regret adding this joke, but it had initially been included "to stop it sounding like it was another stupid letter to the Queen from some boring colonel"). Even his Aunt Mimi showed her disapproval. "If I had known what John wanted it for, I never would have given it to him," she said, unhappy at the part she had unwittingly played in embarrassing the Queen. "It won't bother her a bit," John retorted of Her Majesty. "It won't spoil her cornflakes."

In response, a Buckingham Palace spokesman simply placed the gesture in its historical context: "The first MBEs to be returned were from people protesting that Mr Lennon was given the award in the first place." But elsewhere there were people who believed the gesture to have been worthwhile. "The MBE was awarded to John for peaceful efforts and it was returned as a peaceful effort," said Ringo. "That seems to be a full circle." The philosopher and peace campaigner, Bertrand Russell, agreed, telling Lennon: "Whatever abuse you have suffered in the press as a result of this, I am confident that your remarks will have caused a very large number of people to think about these wars."

The following month, John Lennon, championed on television by Desmond Morris, was voted the Man Of The Decade alongside JFK and Ho Chi Minh. The cabinet minister Richard Crossman noted in his diary: "I must admit that John Lennon was the only person in all these programmes with a gospel, a hope and a belief."

Despite the gesture, John remained an MBE – recipients can send back their medals but they cannot renounce an honour once it has been bestowed – but he appreciated the value of the publicity. "Henry Ford knew how to sell cars by advertising," he said. "I'm selling peace at whatever the cost. Yoko and I are one big advertising campaign." His messages were crisp and simple. Before returning his MBE John had offered "Give Peace A Chance", and shortly afterwards his peace campaign moved on to a fresh slogan, the Lennons bypassing the news media by buying up prime advertising space on billboards in 11 cities around the world to proclaim, "War is over – if you want it".

PHOTOS: MIRROR SYNDICATION, HULTON PICTURE LIBRARY, POPPERFOTO

6 Ringo appears with actor Peter Sellers on UK TV show Frost On Saturday, transmitted live from Wembley Studios, Wembley, London.

7 George plays with Delaney And Bonnie And Friends again, at Fairfield Halls, Croydon.

8 Ringo records a vocal overdub to the song Octopus's Garden, in Abbey Road.

10 Delaney And Bonnie And Friends (including Eric Clapton) play the first of three nights at the Falkoner Theatre, Copenhagen, Denmark. George Harrison plays guitar with them at all three gigs.

11 The Royal Charity premiere of The Magic Christian (left), Odeon Theatre, Kensington, London. John and Yoko disrupt proceedings by protesting outside the cinema over James Hanratty.

12 The World Wildlife Fund charity compilation album, No One's Gonna Change Our World, is released in the UK. It features The Beatles track Across The Universe – marking it the first time a Beatles track has appeared on a non-Beatles album.

13 The *Wedding Album* enters the US album charts at Number 182.

14 A white bag labelled "Silent Protest", possibly containing John and Yoko (above), is delivered to Speakers' Corner, Hyde Park, London, where James Hanratty's father makes a speech calling for a public inquest into his son's murder conviction.

15 John Lennon's Plastic Ono Band makes its UK debut at the Lyceum, London. George Harrison, Eric Clapton and Keith Moon are among the musicians playing with the band.

16 John and Yoko fly to Toronto, where they spend five days at Ronnie Hawkins' farm.

17 John announces a plan to hold a peace festival in Toronto.

18 At Ronnie Hawkins' farm, John signs 3,000 lithographs from his Bag One collection.

20 John Lennon and Marshall McLuhan appear together on a CBC-TV discussion programme in Toronto.

23 John and Yoko meet for an hour with Canadian Prime Minister Pierre Trudeau, in Ottawa.

27 The *Wedding Album* peaks at Number 178 in the US LP charts.

29 John and Yoko fly to Aalborg, Denmark to visit Ono's daughter, Kyoko.

31 Ringo Starr throws a New Year's Eve party in his north London house, at which the guests include George Harrison, Lulu, Kenny Everett and Michael Caine.

1970

In 1970, The Beatles (minus John) went into the studio together for the last time. Phil Spector was controversially enlisted to salvage the 'Get Back' tapes, which were then released as *Let It Be*. But not before Paul let slip that The Beatles had broken up. And that's when the fun began...

EVERY THURSDAY
USA 25c
Is the Plastic Ono Band the new Beatles?
Has Paul lost interest in Apple?
How is
DOUBLE-PAGE PIC OF BEATLES
FULL PAGES OF PAUL
THE FOURMOST
CHUCK BERRY
BILLY J. ETC.
POP
1/-
No 40
SECOND YEAR
WEEK ENDING
Paul McCartney
GREAT NEW FEATURE— "THE BEATLES IN ELVISLAND"
FAB! FAB!
SERIES BY
EDITOR OF
STEADY
GO!
DISC
and MUSIC ECHO 1s
USA 25c
EVERY THURSDAY
APRIL 18, 1970
Grate
fly in
one
Let him be!
PAUL McCARTNEY, who fled London last Friday leaving behind him a furore of doubt and rumour about his future following his "Quit The Beatles" bombshell, was back from a secret hideaway in the country on Sunday—ready to work the first project for his new company.
Paul, wife Linda, and children Heather and Mary, left their Cavendish Avenue, St. John's Wood, house in the early hours of Friday—the day the world learned, via Paul's specially-prepared handout, of the Beatle's decision to split from John, George and Ringo.
A close friend of Paul's told Disc: "He's not giving ANY interviews at the moment. In fact, fans and other people have been making his life a bit of a misery lately by 'picketing' his pad. I wish they'd let him alone to live his own life now."
Paul has — through his American lawyers, led by father-in-law Lee Eastman —bought exclusive rights to "Rupert Bear," the traditional children's story, for his newly-formed McCartney Productions. Paul plans to produce and write the music for a full-length animated cartoon film titled "Rupert."
But an Apple office spokesman told Disc: "At the moment Paul and 'Rupert' are still only in the planning stages. We have no further details."
"McCartney," Paul's first solo LP, is officially released tomorrow (Friday) and has a 19,000 advance order.
Full story behind the split and LP review, turn to pages 10 and 11.
EXCLUSIVE DISC PICTURE BY LINDA McCARTNEY
Rumours are still rife that Cream will re-form ... office remained non-committal: "It's imposs
Solo Starr
RINGO'S first solo single, "It Don't Come Easy," on which he sings and plays drums, was being recorded in London this week under George Harrison's supervision.
Harrison also plays guitar on the track, which has a country flavour.
And the Beatles drummer—pictured right with his newly-shorn early-Liverpool style hairstyle—has a Starr line-up of Paul McCartney, Maurice Gibb and Klaus Voorman involved in his first solo album.
Ringo's first LP — originally called "Ringo Starrdust" but now retitled "Sentimental Journey" — is out on April 3. Full tracks are: Sentimental Journey; Dreams; Stardust; Whispering Grass; Bye Bye Blackbird; Blue Turning Grey Over You; Let The Rest Of The World Go By; Night And Day; You Always Hurt The One You Love; Love Is A Many Splendoured Thing; Have I Told You Lately That I Love You?; I'm A Fool To Care.
Arrangements on the collection of "standards" have been specially done for Ringo by some of the giants of jazz and pop. Paul McCartney supervised "Stardust," Klaus Voorman arranged "I'm A Fool To Care," and Bee Gee Maurice Gibb was behind

JANUARY 70

3 George's song I Me Mine is recorded by himself, Paul and Ringo. Although John does not participate in the session, it is the last recording which will be released under The Beatles group name.

4 Paul, George and Ringo add vocal overdubs to *Let It Be* in Abbey Road.

8 George is in Olympic Sound Studios, adding a vocal overdub to For You Blue.

9 The soundtrack album to Ringo's movie The Magic Christian (right) is released in the UK.

14 Ringo continues to work on his solo album, *Sentimental Journey*, in Olympic Sound.

15 John opens Bag One, an exhibition of his lithographs and drawings at the London Arts Gallery.

16 Bag One is raided by police and closed for obscenity.

20 John and Yoko have their hair cut very short in Denmark – allegedly to allow them to travel without being recognised so easily.

22 John's lithographs are exhibited at the London Gallery in Detroit – this time without police interference.

27 With Phil Spector as producer, The Plastic Ono Band record Instant Karma! (We All Shine On) in Abbey Road.

FEBRUARY 70

2 Having been in the US for promotional purposes, Ringo flies back to the UK.

3 With a 16-piece orchestra, Ringo records a new version of Love Is A Many Splendoured Thing at Abbey Road, for his solo album *Sentimental Journey*.

4 John and Yoko take part in a media event with British Black Power leader Michael X in Holloway, London (above). They give him a bag containing their recently shorn locks in exchange for a pair of Muhammad Ali's boxing shorts.

6 The Plastic Ono Band release their new single, Instant Karma!, in the UK. On the same day, an article in the New York Post reveals that mass killer Charles Manson was obsessed with the lyrics of several songs on the White Album.

7 John and Yoko appear on LWT's The Simon Dee Show, at Wembley Studios, London.

11 The Magic Christian, starring Peter Sellers and Ringo Starr, opens in New York City. The Plastic Ono Band pre-records a Top Of The Pops appearance at the BBC TV centre, Shepherd's Bush, London.

12 Paul starts work on an instrumental, Kreen-Akrore, intended for his solo debut album, in Morgan Studios, London. Top Of The Pops features John and The Plastic Ono Band playing Instant Karma!.

What: The Let It Be single is released
Where: UK
When: March 6, 1970

THE FINAL CUT

A year after its recording at the height of the 'Get Back' sessions, Let It Be became the last single released by The Beatles. By Patrick Humphries.

LET IT BE WAS THE BEATLES' SWANSONG. The Apple was slowly rotting, but despite all the acrimony, the group still managed to bow out with a little of the old magic, quitting the hit parade with their prophetically titled final single.

Although it wouldn't see release for over a year, Let It Be was initially recorded in January 1969. At the fag-end of the Fabs, it was the product of a time when John was besotted by Yoko, George was chafing, Ringo wanted to be a film star, and Paul was determined to hold it all together.

The band had long since tired of the studio wizardry that they had pushed to the limit on *Sgt Pepper*, and conscious that the pressures of making the White Album had pushed the four of them even further apart, embarking on the sessions that would become *Let It Be* was a dispiriting experience for The Beatles. However, like it or not, they were committed to a film.

Nobody could really have believed that reconvening, with no finished songs, in a north London film studio on a chilly winter morning was the best way to fashion a brand-new Beatles album – but on January 2, 1969 that's what they did. And so the scene was set for all that tension, accumulated resentment and barely concealed hostility to be played out before the cameras. The only problem was, they found it impossible to make music in these alien surroundings; and within weeks they had decamped back to the Apple studios.

It was all going to hell in a handcart, Beatle-wise. But in the midst of all that turmoil, Paul had a dream... His mother had died when he was 14, before seeing any of the fame and success that had come her eldest boy's way. Now, as The Beatles sundered, Paul found solace in a dream of his mother Mary coming to visit him; calming him in time of trouble; helping him to forget his problems, to just let it be...

McCartney was at the top of his game and Let It Be was nailed in a couple of short sessions. Two versions surfaced, but the only real difference was in the tone of George's guitar solo. Lennon, however, was particularly scathing. *Anthology 3* has Paul confidently announcing, "This is one that'll knock you out", only for John to ask whether he can giggle during the solo. And, on the finished album, it is Lennon who prefaces that most beautiful of ballads with the facetious introduction: "Now we'd like to do 'Ark The Angels Come..."

Let It Be came out just a month after Simon & Garfunkel's continent-conquering Bridge Over Troubled Water, and Paul Simon acknowledged: "They are very similar songs... in their musical feel, and lyrically. They're both sort of hopeful songs, and resting peaceful songs."

But if Let It Be was a beautiful balm for turbulent times, the B-side of the single was literally the flip-side of the Fab Four. You Know My Name (Look Up The Number) sounded more like The Bonzo Dog Doo-Dah Band than The Beatles. Here they are having fun: mocking the clichéd showbiz traditions they had single-handedly destroyed, just larking about.

Out of them all – Eleanor Rigby, Fool On The Hill, Yesterday – Paul McCartney's own favourite Beatle song keeps coming up as You Know My Name (Look Up The Number). For him, it brings back happy memories of the crazy capering that was, in the early days, as much a part of the band as their life-changing, boundary-breaking music.

You Know My Name (Look Up The Number) had begun life in the wake of *Sgt Pepper*, as the group grappled with the Yellow Submarine soundtrack. After playing around with it for a while during mid-1967, Lennon and McCartney were quite chuffed with the song. It was reminiscent of the fun they all used to have making their Christmas fan club flexi-discs. As well as Rolling Stone Brian Jones on saxophone, it also featured roadie Mal Evans shovelling gravel, not to mention John and Paul giving it their best Goon Show.

Much later, as Apple floundered and relationships within the group eroded, Lennon found creative satisfaction in the immediacy of The Plastic Ono Band. In the wake of Cold Turkey and Instant Karma, Lennon had half an eye on the stoned studio doodle What's The New Mary Jane as a Plastic Ono single, with You Know My Name (Look Up The Number) as the B-side. But McCartney put his foot down, and it appeared instead as the flip of Let It Be.

You Know My Name (Look Up The Number) was a John song inspired by the slogan on a telephone directory. Lennon and McCartney soon slipped into character – Paul as the greasy crooner, John as the scampish Just William. John welcomes patrons to Slaggers, Paul croons his own musical welcome, John comes back as a ghastly Mrs Mopp, cocktail piano ushers in impenetrable Scottish nonsense... and, finally, Jones's sax brings the weirdest of all Beatle B-sides to its conclusion.

By the time of Let It Be, the '60s had been tarnished by Altamont, the Manson family and Vietnam.

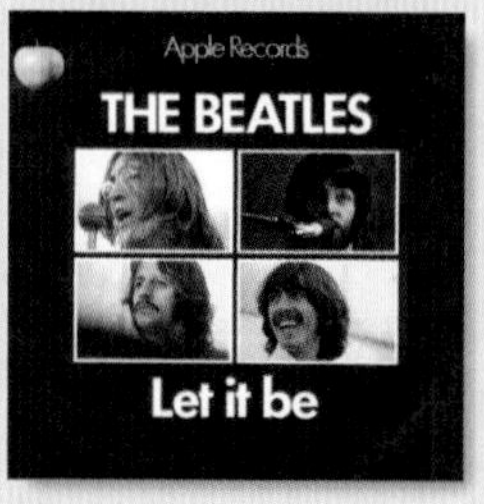

Poor Denis O'Dell, head of Apple Films, was inexplicably namechecked in the song by John, and for months after its release, he was plagued by phone calls from out-there Beatle fans: "We know your name and now we've got your number!"

Of the final seven Beatle singles, five were predominantly McCartney compositions, but even by his standards, Let It Be was Paul McCartney in excelsis. There is something stately and hymnal about the song, but above all it was a song of its times. By the time it was released on March 6, 1970, the magic of the Swinging '60s had been tarnished by Altamont, the Manson family and Vietnam.

The dream was over – and it was evident that The Beatles were no more. Their subsequent album would be heavily panned and at the British premiere of the film, there was not a Beatle to be seen. Even the single, transcendent though it was, only made it to Number 2 – kept off the top by Lee Marvin's Wand'rin' Star.

For The Beatles, it was all over. For the time being...

PHOTOS: CORBIS

And it's goodbye from them: The Beatles bid a hymnal adieu with their last single.

...And this is how it should sound: Paul was unaware of Phil Spector's work on The Long And Winding Road.

What: Reworking The Long And Winding Road
Where: Abbey Road studios
When: April 1, 1970

EXTRA-CELESTIAL

When Phil Spector introduced an orchestra and a celestial choir to the *Let It Be* sessions, it was all too much for Paul McCartney. By Merrell Noden.

THE BEATLES ALL KNEW PHIL SPECTOR long before John Lennon rang him up on January 27, 1970, to ask him to produce his quickie solo single, Instant Karma!. Spector had been with them aboard Pan Am flight 101 on February 7, 1964, when they'd flown into JFK and unleashed Beatlemania upon America. They admired his work immensely – although despite this, Lennon had once tried, unsuccessfully, to pick up Spector's wife.

If any awkwardness lingered from that breach of good manners, it was swept away the moment Lennon heard the first playback of Instant Karma!. "It was fantastic!" he recalled. "It sounded like there were 50 people playing." So, "as a gesture of gratitude", according to Apple insider Peter Brown, Lennon gave Spector the masters from the recording sessions that had been filmed throughout January of 1969 for the movie Get Back. Lennon consulted neither McCartney nor George Martin before handing the tapes over to Spector, presumably because he didn't want to risk their actually getting involved.

Whatever wonders Spector may have worked with Instant Karma!, he was an odd choice to produce this batch of Beatle songs. From the start, they had been conceived of as a radical departure from the elaborate orchestration of *Sgt Pepper* and *Magical Mystery Tour*. "It was always understood that the album would be like nothing The Beatles had done before," Martin told Rolling Stone. "It would be honest, no overdubbing, truly live... almost amateurish."

That description could not be farther from Spector's famous "wall of sound" style of production. Still only 29 years old when he began work on *Let It Be*, Spector was truly a mad boy genius. Using what he called "a Wagnerian approach" to rock'n'roll, he employed multiple overdubs to create a dense, layered sound – "little symphonies for the kids", as he put it. But after doing perhaps the best work of his career on Ike & Tina Turner's River Deep Mountain High, he had gone into a reclusive funk, hiding out in his estate high in the Hollywood hills, where, according to those who saw him, he'd grown increasingly weird and paranoid. At this point in his career, he needed The Beatles at least as much as they needed him.

To be fair to Phil Spector, he was taking on a Herculean task. None of The Beatles could face sifting through the hundreds of hours of recorded mess those sessions had produced. "They [the critics] should have listened, really listened, to what was there before," says Spector now. "Even The Beatles didn't want them out. If they had, they wouldn't have asked me to do it."

He began work at Abbey Road studios on March 23 and finished on April 2. The day before he had brought Ringo in to play drums on three tracks: I Me Mine, Across The Universe and The Long And Winding Road. That would be the last recording anyone would do as a Beatle.

By all accounts, that final day was extremely trying, as the temperamental producer worked feverishly towards the ambitious sound he wanted. According to engineer, Pete Bown, Spector "wanted tape echo on everything, he had to take a different pill every half hour and had his bodyguard with him constantly".

Beatles manager Allen Klein must have known how Spector's work would be greeted in some quarters. Along with an acetate of the record, he sent along an explanation of what had been done. It didn't begin to appease McCartney, who demanded changes.

Absolutely galling to McCartney was Spector's bombastic treatment of The Long And Winding Road. Adding 18 violins, four violas, four cellos, harp, three trumpets, three trombones, two guitarists and 14 female voices, the arrangement sounds more like the swelling climax of a bad film than the simple ballad McCartney had envisioned. "No-one had asked me what I thought. I couldn't believe it," fumed McCartney who, for some reason, fixated on the female voices, the first ever to appear on a Beatles LP. A year later, in his high court action to dissolve The Beatles' partnership, McCartney cited the song as proof that the other Beatles wanted to ruin his reputation.

Whatever he might have thought of it, the song became The Beatles' last Number 1 in America. With its poignant blend of sorrow and vague recrimination, The Long And Winding Road is one of McCartney's prettiest songs. In the movie Let It Be, he performs a simple version of the song, accompanying himself on piano, with minimal help from the other Beatles and Billy Preston on organ.

"If Paul wants to get into a pissing contest, he's got me mixed up with someone who gives a shit." Phil Spector

The choir boy: Phil Spector in 1970.

Thirty-two years on, the track still stirs hard feelings. In 2002, McCartney told USA Today that he was "going back to the original tape, before Phil Spector got hold of it".

Spector remained unrepentant: "Paul had no problem picking up the Academy Award for the *Let It Be* soundtrack, nor did he have any problem in using my arrangement of the string and horn and choir parts during 25 years of touring on his own. If Paul now wants to get into a pissing contest about it, he's got me mixed up with someone who gives a shit." But McCartney ultimately got his wish on November 18, 2003 when the tracks were re-released as *Let It Be ... Naked*. Three days later Spector was charged with murdering B-movie actress Lana Clarkson on February 3, 2003. Spector claimed that Clarkson, whom he'd met earlier in the night at the House of Blues on the Sunset Strip earlier in the night, where she worked as a hostess, may have shot herself.

PHOTOS: LINDA McCARTNEY, CAMERA PRESS, CORBIS

19 Ringo continues work on his solo album, *Sentimental Journey*, at Abbey Road.

20 Instant Karma! (We Shine On) (left) is released in the US.

21 Paul secretly switches work on his first solo album to Abbey Road.

22 Paul records Maybe I'm Amazed and Every Night, at Abbey Road.

MARCH 70

5 Learning that she is pregnant again, Yoko enters the London Clinic for observation. Meanwhile, Ringo works on the songs Bye Bye Blackbird and Whispering Grass in Morgan Studios.

6 The single Let It Be is released in the UK where it will reach Number 2.

9 Yoko's period of observation in the London Clinic comes to an end.

11 As Let It Be is released in the US, George is interviewed for a BBC Easter Monday special about The Beatles, at the Aeolian Hall, London.

14 Let It Be enters the UK singles chart.

15 Ringo films a promo-clip for *Sentimental Journey* at The Talk Of The Town, London.

16 Paul, still using the pseudonym Billy Martin, attends a secret playback of tracks from his solo album, at Abbey Road.

23 Producer Phil Spector sets to work in Room Four, Abbey Road, London, on The Beatles tapes for the album that would become *Let It Be*. Paul McCartney and George Martin are unaware of this.

25 Ringo is interviewed at Apple by David Wigg for BBC Radio 1 show Scene And Heard.

27 Ringo releases his solo album, *Sentimental Journey*, in the UK.

29 Ringo appears on UK TV show Frost On Sunday, at Wembley Studios, Wembley.

30 Phil Spector continues remixing *Let It Be*.

APRIL 70

1 In a drama-filled recording session at EMI's Abbey Road studios, London, producer Phil Spector records orchestral overdubs onto The Beatles' songs The Long And Winding Road, Across The Universe and I Me Mine. Ringo – the only Beatle involved in the session – overdubs drum parts onto the three songs. This is the last known date of any Beatles recording activity.

2 Phil Spector completes the final stereo mixes for the *Let It Be* album.

9 Paul calls John at Arthur Janov's clinic, where he is receiving treatment for heroin addiction. It is widely believed this was the moment Paul chose to tell John that he was about to publicly announce his departure from the group.

10 The Daily Mirror carries the front-page headline, 'Paul Is Quitting The Beatles'.

11 Let It Be (left) reaches Number 1 in the US Top 40 singles chart.

12 Paul starts another new company, Paul McCartney Productions.

17 Paul McCartney releases his solo debut LP, *McCartney*, in the UK where it will reach Number 2.

27 Obscenity charges brought against John Lennon's London exhibition of lithographs, Bag One, are dismissed.

29 George meets with Bob Dylan in Greenwich Village, New York City.

30 John and Yoko fly out from London en route to Los Angeles to begin further Primal Therapy treatment.

MAY 70

1 George Harrison participates in a Bob Dylan recording session for the album *New Morning* in New York City.

8 The Beatles release their final album, *Let It Be*, in the UK.

9 The Carpenters' debut single, a cover of The Beatles' Ticket To Ride, reaches Number 54 in the US charts. Ringo attends the Cannes Film Festival.

11 The Beatles release their single, The Long And Winding Road, in the US.

18 The album *Let It Be* is released in the US.

20 The Let It Be movie premieres in London and Liverpool.

26 George begins work in Abbey Road on tracks for the triple album, *All Things Must Pass*.

JUNE 70

11 John announces to the media that he intends to make New York City his new home.

13 The album *Let It Be* reaches Number 1 in the US.

28 The Let It Be movie goes on general release in the UK.

JULY 70

26 John records a demo of a new song, God, at the Primal Therapy Institute, Los Angeles.

27 Patti Harrison goes to see the revue Oh! Calcutta in London, accompanied by Eric Clapton.

31 John Lennon's ex-wife Cynthia marries Roberto Bassanini (above) in London.

AUGUST 70

1 Yoko Ono suffers her second miscarriage.

29 Melody Maker publishes a letter from Paul McCartney stating categorically that The Beatles will not get together again.

SEPTEMBER 70

24 John and Yoko return to the UK to start work on a new album.

25 Ringo releases his new album, *Beaucoups Of Blues*, in the UK.

26 John Lennon starts work in Abbey Road on the album *John Lennon/Plastic Ono Band*, with Phil Spector as producer.

27 Work continues on the *John Lennon/Plastic Ono Band* album.

What: Newspapers declare "Paul quits"
Where: UK
When: April 10, 1970

...AND IN THE END

Wary of the press, Paul McCartney interviewed himself and got the scoop of the year – it looked like The Beatles were splitting up. By Jim Irvin.

IN 1966, WHEN THE BEATLES DECIDED TO quit touring, Paul was the last one to agree to the idea. A few years later it appears he was also the last one to 'quit' the band. Unfortunately, for his part in the legend that has grown around the split, he was the one that the world first found out about, when on April 10, 1970, the Daily Mirror headline screamed: "Paul is quitting The Beatles".

"I knew at some point I had to get out," said Paul recently. "We were having heavy business meetings, not the kind of things artists want to be involved in. The word 'heavy' has never been so relevant in my life as then. These meetings were getting worse and worse. I just thought, Sod this, I'll boycott Apple, I just won't go in. This isn't me."

John had already announced to the rest of the group on September 20, 1969 – the day they signed a new contract with EMI – that he'd decided to leave. (John noted that breaking the news gave him a rush of adrenalin, like "telling Cynthia I wanted a divorce.") Susceptible to all kinds of distractions since the death of Brian Epstein, John was coming off heroin at the time. A week later, possibly in a surge of post-Beatles euphoria, he recorded Cold Turkey.

Late in October, a dazed Paul decamped to Scotland to take stock. He later described this winter as the occasion of "a near-breakdown", staying in bed, getting angry, drinking, growing a beard. Just before Christmas, however, he rallied and returned to his house in London where he'd installed a new Studer four-track tape machine. Without waiting for the mixing desk to be delivered, and with just one microphone, he set to work. Soon he was on the phone to Neil Aspinall asking for a solo album to be scheduled.

"That album came out of just trying to get out of that whole atmosphere, to get away from The Beatles and see what else I could do," says Paul.

In interviews conducted in January 1970, John, under instructions from new manager Allen Klein not to break the news publicly and spoil sales of the forthcoming *Let It Be* album, spoke as though The Beatles were still functioning, but left plenty of clues that things weren't as they had been.

On April 2, 1970, a fortnight before his solo debut, *McCartney*, was due, a disgruntled Paul told the Evening Standard that the release date that he'd been assigned was suddenly seen as ideal for *Let It Be* and Ringo had been sent round by the others to ask him to move *McCartney* to a later date. (Ringo's *Sentimental Journey* was slated for late March.)

Paul had sent his friend away with expletives ringing in his ears. "I had to get George, who's a director of Apple, to authorise its release for me," McCartney said. "We're all talking about peace and love, but really, we're not feeling peaceful at all."

The following week, promotional copies of *McCartney* were to be issued with a press release in the form of a 'self-interview' by Paul.

"I was traumatised, I suppose," says Paul. "It was getting weird for me and I didn't want to do interviews about this new album, as I knew they'd start to ask, 'What's with The Beatles?' And I didn't fancy answering that, so I said to [Apple], Just send me round some questions you think they'd want to know and I'll do it like a questionnaire – I'm boycotting Apple, remember?"

Peter Brown prepared the questionnaire.

"Peter realised the big question was The Beatles so he put in a couple of loaded questions," Paul told biographer Barry Miles. "Rather than say, I don't want to answer these, I thought, Fuck it, if he wants to know, I'll tell him. I felt I'd never be able to start a new life until I'd told people."

There were 41 questions. Number 27 was: Are you planning a new album or single with The Beatles? "No." Other questions were dealt with just as firmly…

Is this album a rest away from The Beatles or the start of a solo career? "Time will tell. Being a solo album means it's 'the start of a solo career'… and not being done with The Beatles means it's a rest. So it's both."

Is your break with The Beatles temporary or permanent, due to personal differences or musical ones? "Personal differences, business differences, musical differences, but most of all because I have a better time with my family. Temporary or permanent? I don't know."

DAILY Mirror

Lennon-McCartney song team splits up

PAUL IS QUITTING THE BEATLES

Swing to Labour .. but Tories are still in command

Clash over the running of Apple

The final question asked: What are your plans now? A holiday? A musical? A movie? Retirement? "My only plan is to grow up."

"A terse little affair," Paul says of the 'interview' now. "But some people read more into it than was intended, so it backfired a bit."

Indeed, the document was seen by journalist – and regular Beatles correspondent – Don Short of the Daily Mirror before it could be properly distributed. On April 9, Apple was forced to issue a denial that The Beatles were finished, but when the rest of the press saw the questionnaire they leapt upon its implications and by Friday, April 10, over five months after John had told The Beatles he was going, the news broke worldwide.

Derek Taylor issued one last press statement: "Spring is here and Leeds play Chelsea tomorrow and Ringo and John and George and Paul are alive and well and full of hope. The world is still spinning and so are we and so are you. When the spinning stops – that'll be the time to worry. Until then, The Beatles are alive and well and the Beat goes on, the Beat goes on."

PHOTOS: HULTON ARCHIVE, LINDA McCARTNEY

Standing alone: McCartney gets used to the solo life in Liverpool, 1970.

Can You Dig It?

It was a time of disagreements and splits – with Paul McCartney in the driving seat and Phil Spector on mixing duties. But there is a good deal of *Let It Be* that merits nothing but praise, reckons John Harris.

In retrospect, it was surely not the most inspired way to patch up The Beatles' increasingly threadbare internal relations, nor to send their musical standards flying into the stratosphere. The idea, roughly, went as follows: in early 1969, they were to temporarily abandon Abbey Road and its late-night, womb-like ambience, and instead make their music during office hours in the freezing environs of Twickenham Film Studios. To make things that little bit easier, their every cough would be recorded by a sizable film crew.

The concept was Paul McCartney's, and within a few days of the sessions beginning, even he must have been wondering what he had been thinking of. That said, the core of the *Let It Be* concept – Paul exhuming his violin bass and leading The Beatles back to basics – definitely *was* worth pursuing, both in terms of re-energising The Beatles' music, and also as regards their place at the zeitgeist's vanguard. If 1968 had seen numerous hints that rock was about to strip itself to its core values – among them, such Beatles songs as Lady Madonna, Revolution and Back In The USSR – then the following year saw the change materialise in excelsis: the Stones' *Let It Bleed*, Led Zeppelin's self-titled debut, and Eric Clapton making the acquaintance of the Southern musicians who would form Derek And The Dominos.

The early release of Get Back in April 1969 proved that, as ever, The Beatles were on the case. John, as we know, was creatively stymied by both a heroin habit, and his sneering disdain for Paul's latest project. Such is *Let It Be*'s Achilles' heel – for if he had consistently matched the quality and verve of Paul's *Let It Be* songs, the enterprise's chief aim – the Fabs restored to a potent simplicity à la 1964 – might just have been realised.

> "McCartney's work on *Let It Be* looks deeply impressive – it is clear he was in the midst of an admirably purple patch."

To begin at the beginning, take Two Of Us, McCartney's impossibly wistful paean to the long afternoons he and Linda would spend driving around Home Counties lanes, attempting to lose their way. In its own quiet way, it's among Paul's most affecting Beatles songs, suffused with both an autumnal prettiness, and a palpable sense of adulthood's inevitable corrosion of innocence. To add to its magic, the constant presence of John's counterpoint vocal refocuses the song – given its place in The Beatles' career, it acts as a requiem for Lennon and McCartney's bond: two Quarrymen warmly casting their eyes back to the '50s ("You and I have memories…"). That the album also contains One After 909, the Cavern-era rock'n'roll burlesque first put to tape in 1963, only serves to underline the point.

Pitched in the opposite ballpark, there is I've Got A Feeling: in places – particularly its bulgy-veined middle eight – the sound of the spirit of Helter Skelter being nudged away from noise-crazed nihilism, towards something altogether more euphoric. As far as its verses are concerned, it's only a

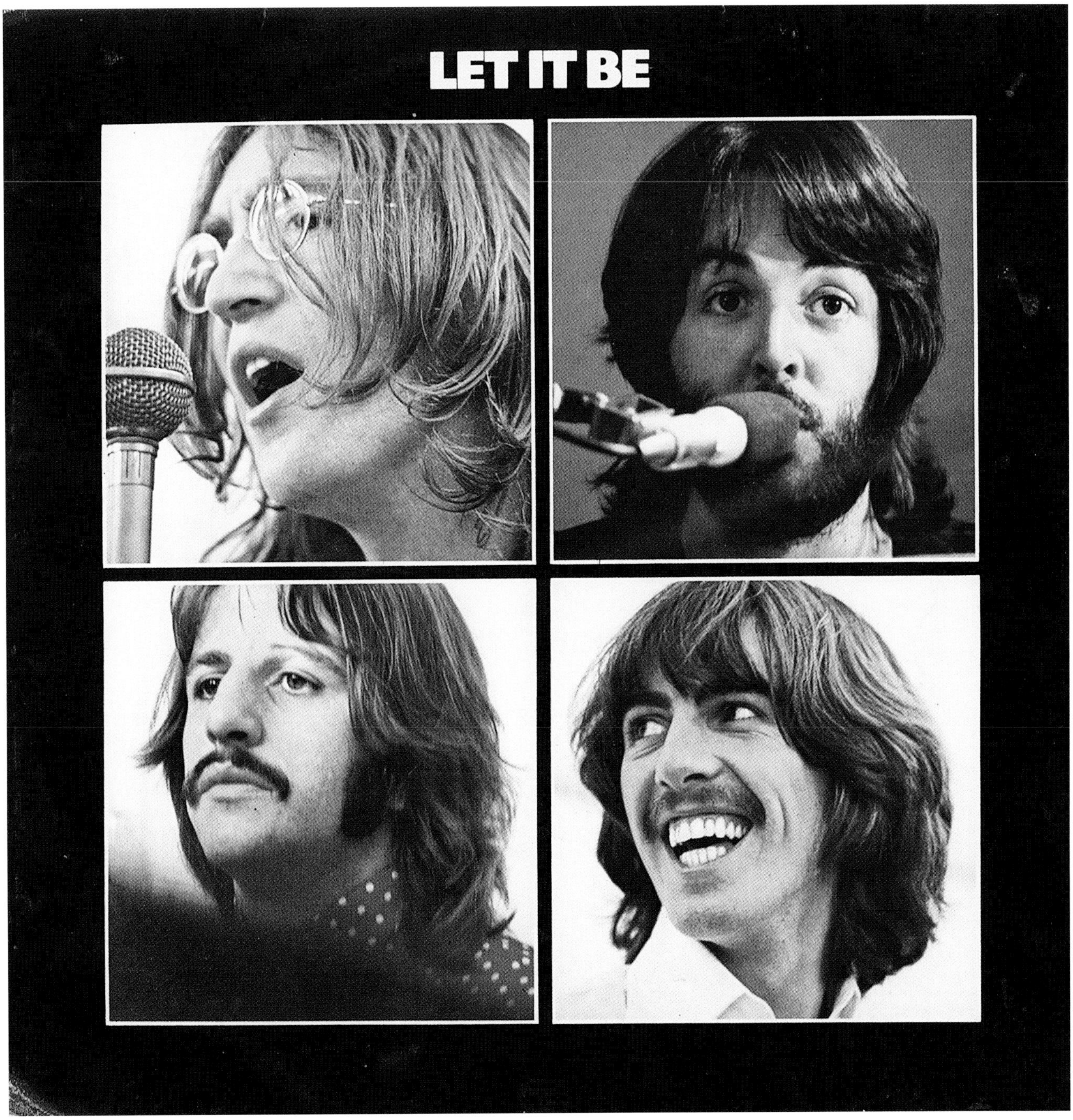

shame that Lennon didn't carry through the ad-libs heard on Anthology 3 ("I've got a feeling/Yes you have!/That keeps me on my toes/On your what?") to the finished version, though he more than redeems himself with the passages that, à la A Day In The Life, are shoe-horned into McCartney's song. If the Stones' You Can't Always Get What You Want has long stood as the most fondly-loved farewell to the '60s, Lennon's lyrics surely have a competing claim: "Everybody had a hard year/Everybody had a good time/Everybody had a wet dream/Everybody saw the sunshine..."

With the additional consideration of Get Back, essentially the compelling sound of Paul masterminding The Beatles' interpretation of the Creedence Clearwater Revival aesthetic, McCartney's work on *Let It Be* begins to look deeply impressive. Throw in Let It Be and The Long And Winding

TRACK LISTING

SIDE ONE

1. Two Of Us
Lennon/McCartney
Sung by McCartney

2. Dig A Pony
Lennon/McCartney
Sung by Lennon

3. Across The Universe
Lennon/McCartney
Sung by Lennon

4. I Me Mine
Harrison
Sung by Harrison

5. Dig It
Lennon/McCartney
Sung by Lennon

6. Let It Be
Lennon/McCartney
Sung by McCartney

7. Maggie Mae
Lennon/McCartney
Sung by Lennon

SIDE TWO

8. I've Got A Feeling
Lennon/McCartney
Sung by Lennon/McCartney

9. One After 909
Lennon/McCartney
Sung by Lennon

10. The Long And Winding Road
Lennon/McCartney
Sung by McCartney

11. For You Blue
Harrison
Sung by Harrison

12. Get Back
Lennon/McCartney
Sung by McCartney

WHAT THE PAPERS SAID...

Opinions of *Let It Be* proved to be varied.

"Ghoulish rumour-mongers are putting it about that *Let It Be* is The Beatles' last LP together... let us attend the funeral when life is pronounced extinct: at the moment the corporate vitality of The Beatles, to judge from *Let It Be*, is pulsating as strongly as ever... Not a breakthrough record, unless for the predominance of informal, unedited live takes; but definitely a record to give lasting pleasure. They aren't having to scrape the barrel yet."

William Mann, The Times, May 8, 1970

avid Skan reviews

THE LAST BEATLES LP?

the beatles were really only The Beatles when they ot themselves together on record then the end of that ttle scene isn't just nigh any more. Its arrived.

And to prove it the group's latest LP is here. Today. Listen to it and they'll be gone tomorrow. They, in the ense of The Beatles, the group, that is.

They, in the sense of the individuals, are still here. And if the LP marks the end of The Beatles (group) it urely marks the beginning of the beatles (people).

So Let It Be. Which ironic... 59s 11d album. Ironic in ...

The whole point of their songs was, eons ago, that they were THEIR songs; songs of innocence and experience. And keep your hands to yourselves!

Despite the intervention of the high priest of processing Phil Spector, who remixed the album, it has one potential standard: The Long and Winding Road, inevitably, by Paul.

It's sad and tired and beautiful and I wish I could get hold of the original version. The othe k-to-what-I-think-the-Beatles-are-all-about-track is '

on the album,

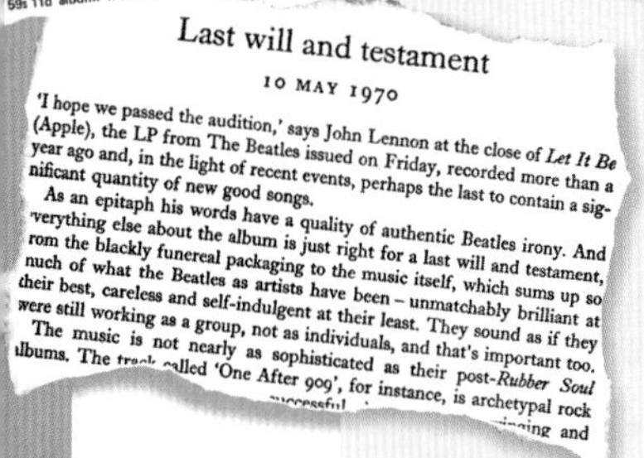

Last will and testament

10 MAY 1970

'I hope we passed the audition,' says John Lennon at the close of *Let It Be* (Apple), the LP from The Beatles issued on Friday, recorded more than a year ago and, in the light of recent events, perhaps the last to contain a significant quantity of new good songs.

As an epitaph his words have a quality of authentic Beatles irony. And verything else about the album is just right for a last will and testament, rom the blackly funereal packaging to the music itself, which sums up so nuch of what the Beatles as artists have been – unmatchably brilliant at their best, careless and self-indulgent at their least. They sound as if they were still working as a group, not as individuals, and that's important too.

The music is not nearly as sophisticated as their post-*Rubber Soul* lbums. The track called 'One After 909', for instance, is archetypal rock ...ing and

"'I hope we passed the audition,' says John Lennon at the close of *Let It Be*... As an epitaph his words have a quality of authentic Beatles irony. And everything else about the album is just right for a last will and testament, from the blackly funereal packaging to the music itself, which sums up so much of what The Beatles as artists have been – unmatchably brilliant at their best, careless and self-indulgent at their least."

Derek Jewell, Sunday Times, May 10, 1970

"If The Beatles were really only The Beatles when they got themselves together on record then the end of that little scene isn't just nigh any more. It's arrived... So *Let It Be*. Which ironically is the title of the LP. Ironic in that, that is just what wasn't done. It was tampered with, or, in the words of the sleeve, "freshened up". Some people will say castrated is a better word, because great choirs of falsetto angels have been added to some tracks along with harps, violins etc. This awful spectre, the very idea that John or Paul's songs need slick production techniques is an impertinence."

David Skan, Record Mirror, May 9, 1970

SLEEVE NOTES

The back-to-basics album came in a back-to-basics cover.

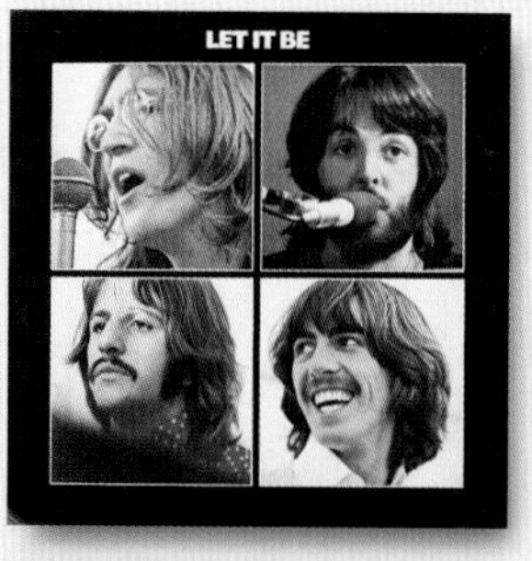

Recorded in 1969 before the *Abbey Road* LP and with the working title of 'Get Back', *Let It Be*, the band's swansong release, was originally intended in its sleeve artwork to recreate photographer Angus McBean's cover to The Beatles' 1963 LP, *Please Please Me*, which depicted a grinning Fab Four looking down from the EMI stairwell. Some six years later after the original shot was taken, on Lennon's request, the band re-enacted that famous pose for McBean once more, this time with their long hair and beards. And yet when *Let It Be* was finally released, the cover shot used was an entirely different one.

The cover itself was designed by John Kosh using photography by Ethan Russell, who had shot The Rolling Stones' Rock'n'Roll Circus TV special the previous year. The album now featured a black border – to indicate the band's imminent death – plus four head shots, one of each band member. The mainstream artwork was intended to emphasise the back-to-basics intention of the music. The LP's title sat in the middle of the top of the sleeve but, as with *Abbey Road*, there was no band name included.

Early editions of the album came in a box with a photo book. The pictures contained within had also been taken by Russell during the original recording sessions, and, because of the early print deadline, these went under the banner of 'Get Back'. Later editions of the album unfortunately came without the book.

However, Angus McBean's original photo session didn't go to waste. The updated picture was finally used on the covers of the 'red' and 'blue' compilations, *The Beatles 1962-66* and *...1967-70*, which were released in 1973.

Lois Wilson

"John was creatively stymied by both a heroin habit, and his sneering disdain for Paul's latest project."

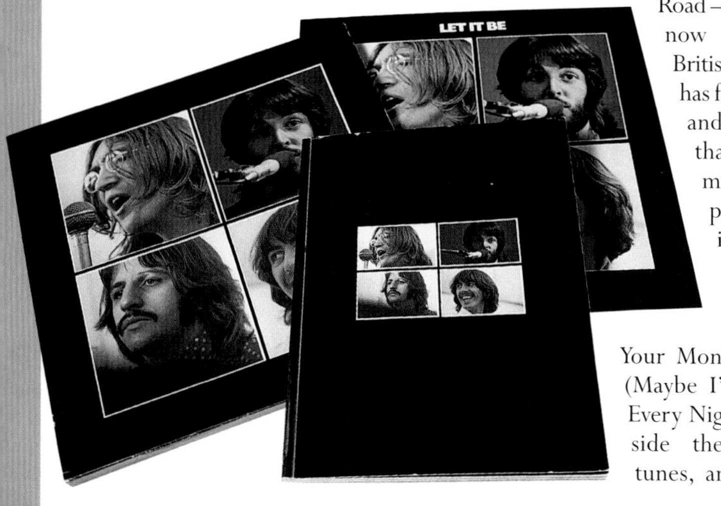

Road – both pearls, though now so stitched into British life that familiarity has faded their charms – and it becomes clear that he was in the midst of an admirably purple patch. Indeed, imagine the best Paul-driven songs on *Abbey Road* (You Never Give Me Your Money) and *McCartney* (Maybe I'm Amazed, Junk, Every Night) lined up alongside the aforementioned tunes, and you have some idea of just how astounding an early McCartney solo album might have been. The fact that his *esprit de corps* kept him throwing songs towards the increasingly ungrateful Lennon is actually quite touching; one can even detect the faint whiff of self-sacrifice.

It's sobering to consider that, aside from the makeweight Dig It, the one track Lennon brought to the *Let It Be* sessions that made it on to the finished LP was the thoroughly ignorable Dig A Pony. The inclusion of the peerless, lust-driven Don't Let Me Down would have bolstered his side of the exercise in a way that – for all the song's wonders – the hopelessly incongruous, Phil Spector-ised version of Across The Universe fails to, but even then, you're left with the image of Lennon failing to pull his weight, either gauching out behind his spectacles or cynically snickering at Paul's attempts at artistic captaincy.

Though he'd avoided the brown, George's contribution was presumably stifled by his equally sceptical take on the *Let It Be* concept. That said, his two songs are hardly disastrous. For You Blue is of a piece with Paul's

The winter of discontent: The Beatles fail to get along during the *Let It Be* sessions, Twickenham Studios, January, 1969.

desire to spiritually return to the group's beginnings – and its mesh of piano, acoustic guitar and lap steel is quietly wonderful. I Me Mine, meanwhile, contains plenty of appealing aspects: its vocal, frequently pitched just short of falsetto, is a delight, and it was also, lest we forget, the last Beatles song to be recorded, on January 3, 1970. Moreover, here, Spector's string arrangement, added even later on in April of the same year, fortuitously manages to tease out the sense of camp that underlies both the lyrics and George's delivery of them.

In 2003, of course, those who have long held *Let It Be* to their hearts were invited to hurl the original album into the historical swing-bin and make way for the belated release of the album as its authors had initially envisaged it: pared-down, pretty much live, and in implied contrast to just about everything The Beatles had put to tape from 1965 onwards. Scepticism, only fuelled by the idea of sacred artefacts being tampered with, seemed to be an irresistible response – but the rumly-titled *Let It Be...Naked* actually turned out to fulfil most of its pre-release hyberbole, managing even to feature an infinitely superior take of The Long And Winding Road, on which John Lennon's bass-playing was suddenly and miraculously in tune.

As a result, there was apparently no need for Spector's Wagnerian Sturm Und Drang. But then again...

PHOTO: ATLANTIC SYNDICATION

...BE HERE NOW

Dolf De Datsun is charmed by the honesty and "basic style" of the *Let It Be* album.

"There's always that lame question, The Rolling Stones or The Beatles? And I prefer The Beatles every time. I remember going to my parents' record collection when I was young and seeing the *Sgt Pepper* cover and thinking, Wow! What is this?! And it had the lyrics on it so you could sing along! Then my mother gave me an original Dutch copy with the cardboard cut-outs for my 21st birthday, which was cool.

"*Let It Be* is very sad, because it will always be the last Beatles album that came out, but it's still a great record. In a way, it marks how people go off to their solo careers: the McCartney piano kinda says 'Check me out', you know. And lucky George gets two songs! All Things Must Pass, which is fucking great, came straight after, and it showed how he'd been kind of bullied by the rest of the band.

"My favourite track on the album is Get Back – it just goes stomping along, with great little solos from George and Billy Preston.

"A lot of young bands say – 'Oh we want to emulate the Stones or The Beatles from this year, or do a psychedelic album', and they don't realise that those bands mastered straight rock'n'roll and R&B before they tackled the more challenging stuff. That's why I really like One After 909, because it's so straight. It's rock'n'roll. Two Of Us is good also because Macca has to reach for the vocal. Dig A Pony is totally weird, even the title is strange!

"I love the live feel of the album, because that's the way I like to record. There's something honest about that basic style. If you look at McCartney's recent stuff, that's the way he's working; just go into a room with some people, plug in and play."

Joe Cushley

FIGHT TO THE

PHOTO: TOM MURRAY

FINISH

There have been many reasons given for the The Beatles' split, but at the heart of the matter was the battle for control of the band and its destiny. By Peter Doggett.

As George Harrison discovered, you can't joke about something as serious as The Beatles. Stopped on a London street in the summer of 1970, a few weeks after Paul McCartney's announcement that he had left the group, Harrison was asked by a journalist what they would do without him. "I guess we'll have to get another bass player," George quipped.

Over the next six months, that off-the-cuff remark mutated and grew, to the point where humour became accepted as hard reality. By November 1970, the British music press was buzzing with rumours that The Beatles were about to reform, with either their old Hamburg associate Klaus Voormann or – more bizarrely, from this distance – ex-Nice bassist Lee Jackson taking McCartney's place. Eventually, Apple spokesman Derek Taylor had to be retrieved from semi-retirement to quieten down the speculation.

Meanwhile, there were other Beatles stories to conjure with. Both Lennon and Harrison had just issued solo albums. The two men met in New York in mid-December, and were briefly joined by none other than Paul McCartney, who was in town working on his second solo album. Another set of rumours began to percolate through the music business: all four Beatles were now keen to reunite. "Stranger things have happened," Harrison said carefully. Apple confirmed or denied nothing: "I can't see them doing anything official again, but they certainly seem serious about working together. There have been definite discussions in that direction."

Although McCartney had remained silent in public since his initial announcement of the split, all his former colleagues had been more vocal. Ringo Starr had never hidden his desire that The Beatles would reform, and he had already recorded (with Harrison's help) a song entitled Early 1970, which expressed exactly that hope: "When I come to town, I want to see all three."

Harrison's album was entitled *All Things Must Pass*, after a song rejected by The Beatles during the sessions for the *Let It Be* album. It included several more numbers (Wah-Wah, Run Of The Mill, Isn't It A Pity) directly inspired by the group's internal quarrels. Lennon's Plastic Ono Band record featured a more explicit statement: "I don't believe in Beatles," he sang on God. Much more pointed were his comments to Rolling Stone editor Jann Wenner, in an interview not yet published, which he carefully forgot to mention during his meeting with Harrison and McCartney.

The rosy-tinged atmosphere among the ex-Beatles was dulled forever just before Christmas, when Harrison, Starr and Lennon received official notification that McCartney's lawyers were initiating a High Court action to dissolve the group's legal partnership. The news broke on December 31, 1970; plans for a January meeting in London to discuss a reunion were scuppered. The McCartney legal team, headed by his father-in-law and effective manager, Lee Eastman, had persuaded him that nothing was important enough to delay a court action which, they claimed, was designed to prevent The Beatles from losing everything to the company owned by the group's joint manager, Allen Klein.

In the event, the amicable mood would have been shattered even without McCartney's High Court writ; that same day, the new issue of Rolling Stone magazine, which featured Lennon's explosive and often vicious analysis of his comrades, hit the US news-stands. Lennon had made it obvious that, as he reflected a year later, "We were friends and we had a function. But the function ended, and the relationship had nothing to last on except memory, and it broke down." The four Beatles never gathered together in the same room again.

It was inevitable that it should be Lennon and McCartney who ultimately decided the fate of The Beatles. From the beginning, they were not only the group's chief songwriters, but also the controllers of their destiny. To the outside world, they displayed a seamless unity which was only broken in the late '60s. Behind the scenes, however, the group's closest aides had been accustomed to seeing Lennon and McCartney jostle for position and power since the birth of Beatlemania.

"John was the noisiest of the four," says long-time Beatles press officer Tony Barrow, "and so he was accepted as being the leader. But it quickly became obvious that Paul was the most persuasive of The Beatles, and the one who wielded the real power with Brian Epstein." By accident or design, McCartney seems to have utilised a variation of the time-honoured good cop/bad cop routine. "John would make a lot of noise but not get his own way," Barrow recalls. "Paul would encourage him to nag Brian, and get nowhere. John would hurt Brian with what he said, reduce him to tears on occasion. Then Paul would go in and persuade Brian that what John had suggested was the right thing to do. He would emerge as the hero, with his more suave approach. Paul was very shrewd in the way he handled relations both inside and outside the group."

Beyond their internal business dealings, Barrow identifies another perennial struggle: "There was a permanent battle for power with The Beatles, over who was going to get the A-side of the next single – a case of 'my song, not yours'. That was purely between John and Paul. It was several years before George twigged what was going on, and realised that his songs were never coming up for consideration."

Although all four Beatles could claim equal status when it came to decision-making, Lennon and McCartney inevitably held sway, purely on the basis of their creative input. "They automatically thought that their tunes should be the priority," Harrison complained in the late '70s, "because they had such a lot of them." George Martin admitted his role in sidelining the youngest Beatle: "Possibly, we didn't encourage him enough. He'd write songs, and we'd say, 'Oh, you've got some more, have you?' The stuff he'd written was dead boring. Looking back, it was a bit hard on him, but it was natural because the others were so talented."

Once Harrison emerged as the champion of all things Indian, however, his power within the group increased. Gradually, his cultural and spiritual agenda began to shape everything from the sound of their records – encroaching sitars and tablas – to their infatuation with transcendental meditation. Harrison's emergence from his role as Paul's "baby brother" coincided with Lennon's loss of interest in the group. "I was always waiting for a reason to get out of The Beatles from the day I filmed How I Won The War," he remembered in 1980. "I just didn't have the guts to do it." While Harrison explored the reaches of the mind and the mystic East, and McCartney eased himself into Swinging London's avant-garde community, Lennon grew depressed in his stockbroker belt mansion, allowing his colleagues to set The Beatles' agenda. The arrival of Yoko Ono jolted him out of his ennui, but also cut the emotional cord that linked him to the institution that was The Beatles.

All of these threads became knotted in 1968. After one last burst of unity at the Maharishi's camp in Rishikesh, the group returned home to record the White Album, and launch their counter-culture corporation, Apple. "The Beatles weren't together," Apple press officer Derek Taylor told me. "They didn't know what they wanted out of Apple. George wanted to bring in people like the Krishnas. Paul wanted Apple to be controlled weirdness. John wanted to change the world. And Ringo was one of The Beatles, so he went along with whatever was happening. I still saw The Beatles as a tight unit, one for all and all for one. I didn't realise the tensions underneath."

Apple had been envisaged as a collective playground, in which the four-headed hydra of The Beatles could indulge their whims in the spirit of (McCartney's phrase) "Western communism". But as Lenin, Stalin and Trotsky discovered, every revolution requires a leader; and in 1968 it

"Right, whose turn is it to make the tea?": John Eastman (far left) with Allen Klein (fourth right) and Peter Howard (far right), 1969.

was Paul McCartney. "Apple was not a dream world," Derek Taylor reflected with two decades' hindsight. "I was still an employee, and the boys were still the bosses – particularly Paul, the bossiest of the bossy."

"Paul wanted to work; John hated work," Tony Barrow says. "John had a MTV-level concentration span. He got bored very quickly, and pushed things aside, whether it was a song or a business deal. Paul was a much more methodical worker. He liked the discipline of coming into the office everyday. He was the only willing commuter of the four." In Barrow's view, McCartney's dominance became plain as soon as Brian Epstein died in August 1967: "He was scared that they would be distracted by having no manager. He thought that they might go off to India and never come back and be The Beatles again. That's why he organised Magical Mystery Tour with what seemed almost unseemly haste after Brian's death. I think that, deep down, he saw the future of The Beatles as moving into the film world in a big way, and his ambition with Magical Mystery Tour was to prove himself as someone who could write, direct and produce a film. Of course, it had exactly the opposite effect."

"PAUL AND I WANT THE SAME THING FROM APPLE, BUT HOW TO ACHIEVE IT – THAT'S WHERE WE DIVERGE."

JOHN LENNON

The old balance of power was uneasily resumed when recording sessions began for the White Album in late May 1968. As ever, Harrison had to battle for space on the album, while Lennon and McCartney carved up the territory between them. Yet something had changed. "Paul was always upset about the White Album," Lennon insisted in 1971. "He never liked it, because on that one I did my music, he did his and George did his. First, he didn't like George having so many tracks; and second, he wanted it to be more of a group thing, which really means more Paul."

Ironically, the spreading tension of those epic sessions, which stretched almost unbroken until late October, was felt most strongly by the normally easy-going Ringo Starr. Frustrated by the group's lack of unity, and resentful at being given drumming instruction by McCartney, Starr walked away from the sessions for two weeks – returning only when the others reassured him that he really was still the best drummer in the world. "We'd never really argued in the studio," he said later, "that was the funny thing. We'd always sort of held back a bit. Maybe if we'd argued a lot more, then it wouldn't have got to the stage it did."

Close observers question the idea that The Beatles never argued among themselves.

"The Beatles were such profoundly artistic people that they gave themselves massive licence in other areas," Derek Taylor recalled. "They could say and do harsh things to each other, reject things in a song that were corny, and the finished work would be superb, because they had this way of dealing with each other's weaknesses." Tony Barrow notes how their vigorous camaraderie slowly soured: "They always had a very healthy rivalry, but at the end it turned vicious, more barbed. They always used to take potshots at each other and us. John vented his spleen with everyone, in and out of the group. They were like brothers: they had fierce fights, but they still loved each other. But in the late '60s, brotherly love went out of the window."

As Derek Taylor noted, an element of selfishness was part of the Apple stew. "All The Beatles could be hard to work with when they were around. But I was often unreasonable too, so I didn't mind other people being unreasonable. Unreasonableness was a way of life for me then."

Bickering and arguments could be contained within a culture of mutual respect. By the end of 1968, that essential ingredient was in short supply. One constant problem was Lennon's relationship with Yoko Ono: he began to insist that she attend recording sessions and business meetings, and by January 1969, during the ill-fated Get Back sessions, he was encouraging her to speak on his behalf, while he displayed a heroin-

PHOTO: LINDA McCARTNEY

"Let's not give peace a chance, eh?": new manager, Allen Klein, presides over the Beatles split with John and Yoko, 1969.

sedated silence. "We took heroin because of what The Beatles and their pals were doing to us," Lennon said in 1970. Around the same time, he wrote to Linda McCartney: "I hope you realise what shit you and the rest of my kind and unselfish friends laid on Yoko and I since we've been together. It might have sometimes been a bit more subtle or should I say 'middle-class' – but not often."

The January 1969 sessions found Lennon emotionally removed and artistically bankrupt; Harrison frustrated and ready to bridle at any assumed slight; McCartney walking on eggshells in his self-appointed role as group leader; and Starr dark-eyed and withdrawn, watching cagily from behind his drumkit. Provoked by Lennon's constant sarcasm about his songs, then pushed over the edge when McCartney began to criticise his playing, Harrison briefly quit the group. "I didn't care if it was The Beatles," he said later, "I was getting out." As Ringo noted, "George had to leave because he thought Paul was dominating him. Well, he *was*." A hint of Lennon's feeling towards his junior partner was provided in a 1971 interview: "There's no telling George. He's very narrow-minded and doesn't really have a broader view. Paul is far more aware than George."

Traumatic as it was, the near-collapse of The Beatles in January 1969 paled alongside the saga which was initiated in the first week of February. For several years, American entrepreneur Allen Klein had been scheming to gain some foothold in The Beatles' camp. "Klein is essential in the Great Novel as the Demon King," Derek Taylor explained nearly 20 years later. "Just as you think everything's going to be all right, here he is. I helped to bring him to Apple, but I did give The Beatles certain solemn warnings. I told them to ask around, and said that he had various reputations: that he would get them a good financial deal, but might not be someone you would want to take home to your mother."

Apple's key record promoter, Tony Bramwell, recalls: "Everyone knew that Klein wasn't a pleasant guy before he took over. Don't get me wrong, I liked Klein, and I still do. But John had this attitude of dumb blindness as far as Klein was concerned."

Both Lennon and McCartney were convinced that The Beatles would be jolted out of their creative inertia if they could find a replacement for the powerful but benign leadership of Brian Epstein. McCartney was about to marry into a family of New York show business lawyers; his future father-in-law, Lee Eastman, and his son John, were willing to offer their services to The Beatles. Lennon hadn't voiced any opposition to this plan (or, indeed, ventured any opinion at all); but then he met Allen Klein.

Brash, brazen, driven and soaked in the music that Lennon loved, Klein seemed like a Hollywood caricature brought to life. "Allen's human," Lennon explained in 1971, "whereas Eastman and all them other people are automatons. When Allen's not doing his bit, he's one of the lads. When him and his crew go on tour, they piss about like schoolkids, pretending to be deaf and dumb, whatever kind of crazy thing. He's good fun to be around, you know?"

By contrast, "Eastman wasn't a polo-neck-and-chinos kind of guy, like Allen," says Tony Bramwell. "[The Eastmans] were always in suits. But Lee wasn't totally unblemished when it came to business. He was trying to pick up publishing catalogues on the cheap, the same way that Allen would have done."

Though McCartney was impressed by Klein's energy, he was also slightly repelled by the same qualities that attracted Lennon. "The very first thing that made me suspicious about him was meeting him, because he's a bit of a boy. I put the Eastmans forward. I thought they'd be fair. For one thing, they're lawyers, they don't take percentages, they take a fee. If you don't like them, you don't pay the bill."

Lennon's infatuation was all-conquering, and he immediately informed The Beatles' business advisers that Klein was now "handling my stuff". Collectively, The Beatles continued to take direction from wherever they could find it, although Klein ensured that he was in constant attendance at Apple. An early crisis ensued when music publisher Dick James, who handled almost all of the group's self-composed songs, attempted to sell his company, Northern Songs, to Sir Lew Grade's ATV organisation without The Beatles' consent. A ferocious legal battle followed. "Businessmen play the game, we play music," Lennon said excitedly, "and it's something to see."

Klein and Eastman each suggested rival strategies; meanwhile, The Beatles were compelled to concentrate solely on finance instead of music. "We were together every day for these terrible meetings which made us uptight," Lennon explained at the end of 1969. "We got to hear how much [money] we'd wasted. That was a real bringdown. It was such a waste. I'd sooner have given it away to some deserving gypsy."

During the negotiations, Lennon discovered that his songwriting partner had been pursuing his own agenda. "Who was buying up Northern Songs shares behind my back?" he wrote accusingly to McCartney in 1971. Meanwhile, Lee Eastman pointed out apparent blunders in Klein's handling of the situation; and Northern Songs slipped out of The Beatles' grasp.

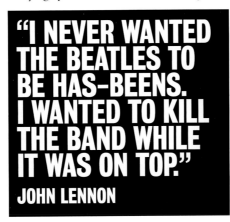

"I NEVER WANTED THE BEATLES TO BE HAS-BEENS. I WANTED TO KILL THE BAND WHILE IT WAS ON TOP."

JOHN LENNON

Through it all, the group attempted to maintain some kind of equilibrium, at least in public. "The Beatles have to be one," Harrison asserted in April 1969. "Four definite people each contribute something to make The Beatles. The trouble starts when one tries to take over. It happens all the time. But we're now at a point where we can do something to each other's individual satisfaction."

For a while, the four men carried out delicate conversations about the future of the group via the medium of the pop press. Just as John announced that he wanted The Beatles to go back on the road, Starr was quoted as saying that they'd never play live again. "I don't miss being a Beatle any more," he said. "You can't get those days back. It's no good living in the past." Harrison remained the most optimistic of the four: "We've got to a point where we can see each other quite clearly. By allowing each other to be each other, we can become The Beatles again."

That intention was carried into the making of *Abbey Road*. After the attempt to 'get back' in January 1969, the new project was a self-conscious effort to pretend that the intervening 12 months had never happened, and that a new era of *Pepper*-style unity was on the horizon. Lennon's absence from the sessions every time one of Harrison's songs was due to be recorded must have acted as a nagging reminder that the past remained elusively out of reach.

"They were much happier with themselves," George Martin said of the *Abbey Road* sessions. "Everybody seemed to be working hard and we'd got things nicely organised. It wasn't until after that that things started happening badly." The group assembled one last time for an appropriately gloomy photographic session at Lennon's house, fine-tuned the final mixes, and then searched for reasons to believe.

There were countless distractions in the air. Lennon and Yoko Ono were deep into their peace campaign, and had even issued a single, Give Peace A Chance, without the other Beatles. McCartney was anticipating the birth of his first child, and was still pondering the Northern Songs débâcle. Both he and Harrison were lending their time to other artists on the Apple label, from Mary Hopkin to Billy Preston. Harrison was looking through his sheaf of unreleased songs, and publicly discussing the idea of a solo album. Starr was considering offers of acting work.

Then there was the ongoing dilemma of what to do with the Get Back tapes from January 1969, and the accompanying feature film. Over everything loomed a potentially momentous decision about the group's management. Lennon had persuaded Harrison and Starr to back Klein. McCartney even posed for publicity photos as Apple announced that the New Yorker was now the group's sole business representative. But McCartney never signed the binding deal, and his relationship with his colleagues wasn't able to bridge the Eastman/Klein divide.

The depth of the distrust between Lennon and McCartney over their choice of manager was exposed by an open letter Lennon penned to his former partner in late 1971. "Your conceit about us and Klein is incredible," he railed. "You say you 'made the mistake of trying to advise them against him, and that pissed them off', and we secretly feel that you're right. Good God! You must KNOW we're right about Eastman." Then he added, in an aside unpublished at the time for legal reasons: "He can't even control himself in PUBLIC – even the people he buys paintings from squirm! (Shit from the inside, baby!)"

On the plane to the Toronto Rock'n'Roll Revival Festival in September, Lennon informed Klein that he intended to leave the group. Alarmed that the news might jeopardise his efforts to improve The Beatles' recording deal with EMI, Klein begged him to remain silent. In London, a few days later, The Beatles attended a business meeting at Apple. "We were discussing something with Paul," Lennon remembered, "and I kept saying no to everything he said. It came to the point I had to say something."

As McCartney recalled, "John looked me in the eye and he said, 'I think you're daft. In fact, I wasn't gonna tell you, but I'm leaving the group'. To my recollection, those were his exact words. And our jaws dropped. He went on to explain that it was rather a good feeling to get it off his chest, which was very nice for him, but *we* didn't get much of a good feeling."

"Memo: All Beatle employees must now wear moustaches..." Apple spokesman, Derek Taylor, takes dictation from George, 1969.

PHOTOS: TOPFOTO, TOMMY HANLEY

Aware of the ongoing negotiations with EMI, and perhaps hopeful that Lennon was simply shooting his mouth off in familiar fashion, McCartney entreated John not to tell the press. In a vicious missive to Linda McCartney the next year, Lennon reminded her that "Paul and Klein both spent the day persuading me it was better not to say anything – asking me not to say anything because it would hurt 'The Beatles' and 'let's just let it peter out', remember? So get that in your petty little perversion of a mind, Mrs McCartney – the cunts asked me to keep quiet about it."

Lennon did as he was told, and for the moment some of The Beatles pretended that nothing had changed. In November 1969, Harrison anticipated a forthcoming Beatles record, "an equal rights thing, so we'll all have as much [as each other] on the album". Yet the following month, Lennon came close to leaking an exclusive: "It just depends how much we want to record together again. I don't know if I want to. I go off and on it, I really do. If The Beatles never recorded together again, but each put their creative efforts through Apple, that at least it would be better than each of us having a company. Together we have that much more power."

He pinpointed the source of the problem: "Paul and I have differences of opinion on how things should be run. We both want the same thing from Apple in the end, but how to achieve it – that's where we diverge. Mainly, we disagree on the Klein bit. As far as I can see, Paul was always waiting for this guy to just appear and save us from the mess we were in. My saying it to the press enabled Klein to hear about it and come over."

The effect of the dispute on the running of Apple was obvious to Lennon: "The four of us hold different opinions on different things, and the staff don't know where they are, or who to listen to." As Tony Bramwell recalls, the actual situation was worse than that: "People like myself and Neil Aspinall and Mal Evans would constantly be getting calls from one of The Beatles, asking us to do something, but not tell the others. Paul would want us to book him a recording session at Morgan Studios, but not let John know, while John and Yoko had their own reign of terror. John got completely negative about everyone else's projects. He was only interested in him and Yoko. One week, Paul would be in the office; the next it would be John and Yoko ruling the roost. It was difficult for those of us who'd grown up being faithful to them, and who suddenly found ourselves having to play them off against each other, behind each other's backs."

To the outside world, no such difficulties were visible. *Abbey Road* had become one of The Beatles' fastest-selling albums, and the media were being titillated by John and Yoko's peace antics, and the preposterous American rumour that Paul had died and been replaced by a lookalike imposter. "It was a strange time for us then," Ringo recalled, "because we weren't doing anything. But that 'Get Back' album needed fixing."

Engineer Glyn Johns had made two efforts to salvage something releasable from the January 1969 sessions, but each time The Beatles had rejected it. Exactly a year later, The Beatles regrouped at Abbey Road to record Harrison's I Me Mine for the album – but without Lennon, who was in Denmark with Yoko's ex-husband, investigating the possibility of building a flying saucer that would operate without fuel, and making up inane ditties with his stepdaughter Kyoko Cox.

In February 1970, legendary American record producer Phil Spector was finally given the chance to fulfil his long-held ambition of working with a Beatle, after his manager – none other than Allen Klein – suggested that he should handle the session for Lennon's Instant Karma! single. Klein and Lennon then proposed that Spector should be given carte blanche to re-examine the 'Get Back' tapes. "We all said yes," Ringo explained. "At the beginning, even Paul said yes."

In the spirit of a true auteur, Spector not only edited the raw session tapes but felt free to embellish them. With Starr and Harrison in attendance – plus the inevitable Allen Klein – he added orchestral overdubs and a choir to McCartney's The Long And Winding Road, besides using his studio expertise to sharpen up the sound of other songs. Abbey Road staff were slightly alarmed by him – "He seemed to take a different pill every half-hour," one engineer recalled, "and he had his bodyguard with him" – but the sessions were completed quickly and, it seemed, successfully.

"Paul heard it," Ringo recounted in 1971. "I spoke to him on the phone and said, Did you like it?, and he said, 'Yeah, it's OK'. He didn't put it down. And then suddenly he didn't want it to go out. Two weeks after, he wanted to cancel it." But George Martin received a different story from McCartney: "He knew nothing about it, and he wrote to me to say that he was pretty appalled. When the record finally came out, I got a hell of a shock." McCartney wrote to Klein to demand the right to remix The Long And Winding Road, but to no effect.

By now, momentum was gathering for the release of the Let It Be movie and soundtrack album, and neither could be delayed any longer. Instead, Lennon, Harrison and Starr decided that McCartney should be asked to shift the release date for his forthcoming solo album, to avoid coinciding with the group's product. "They, as directors of the company, wrote to him," Starr explained, "and I didn't think it fair that some office lad should take something like that round. So I said, I'll take it round. He got angry. He told me to get out of his house. He was crazy. He just shouted and pointed at me. I couldn't believe it was happening to me. I'm very emotional: things like that really upset me." Two weeks later, McCartney announced to the world – via a self-interview issued with promo copies of his album – that he had left The Beatles.

The story broke just as Harrison and Starr were engaged in plugging Let It Be. Ringo insisted that "everything's fine" within the group, while George hymned The Beatles' "unity through diversity". But, as McCartney noted dryly, "None of us wants to admit that the party is over." He hinted at a solo tour in the near future; Apple, the company he had dreamed up as a vehicle for creative freedom, reminded him publicly that "any individual Beatle cannot offer his services, appear alone or with any other person in any branch of the entertainment industry, without the consent of Apple and the other Beatles."

"It was like a divorce," says Tony Barrow, "where you don't like what the lawyers are doing, but you have to go along with it. Lots of rash things were said and done on both sides." Tony Bramwell sees irony in the fact that "Allen Klein had achieved his ambition of managing The Beatles, but in doing so, he blew them apart".

One observer, however, had no time for regret or irony. "I never wanted The Beatles to be has-beens," John Lennon commented in 1971. "I wanted to kill it while it was on top. I know a lot of people were upset when The Beatles finished, but every circus has to come to an end. The Beatles were a monument, and had to be either changed or scrapped. Basically, we were four individuals who eventually recovered their own individualities after being submerged in a myth."

Thirty years on, his judgement seems premature. The circus may have left town, but celebrating the circus is now a worldwide industry. Lennon may have used his power to topple the Stalinist monolith of The Beatles, but even he couldn't destroy The Beatles myth. ■

PHOTO: LINDA McCARTNEY

"I Was There"

He was with them as they turned from winklepickers to love and mantras. Donovan pays tribute to The Beatles' balm for the soul.

What kind of impact did The Beatles really have on popular culture? Flashback to 1958. We were all digging roots music, albeit through the surface conduit of Elvis Presley, Buddy Holly and The Everly Brothers, to name just a few of the 'white negroes'. Underneath lay the dark and powerful elemental force of ancient black spiritual power.

Parallel, and significantly entwined with this primeval roots sound, John Lennon and Paul McCartney are songwriters of Irish descent from Liverpool – across the water from the land that has historically produced world-shattering poets. This potent mix of traditional Irish poetic power and roots healing naturally merged with a love of American pop music and bohemian 'sus' to create the most powerful vortex that the 20th century had yet to experience.

Donovan and Paul jam, March 11, 1969.

"The Beatles were, and still are, the best friends this planet ever had."

I first heard The Beatles on a trip back home from my wanderings as a beatnik folk singer. The house was empty, my mammy and daddy at the factory. I went upstairs to my bedroom, still the same with the echoes of my youthful past, the cut-out photos of 1950s Paris cafés, the dark-eyed chicks and the negro drummers. The radio was playing a 'pop' single, yet I had left 'pop music' behind when I embraced folk, jazz, blues, classical and bluebeat. The radio set was one of those plastic American Bakelite jobs, matt-black and cream, with a grill like a Cadillac. The DJ was playing a new single and when I heard two acoustic guitars, drums, bass, vocal harmonies and a harmonica I was stunned and fell into an altered state.

"Yes, pop pickers," chimed the DJ, "that was The Beatles with Love Me Do." I slumped down on the Axminster stair-carpet and heard a voice in my head say: "That's exactly what I'm going to do." I didn't quite know what 'that' was though – but 12 months later I was in the same room with them.

I first met The Beatles in 1965, after Bob Dylan, Joan Baez and I had successfully mesmerised the British public with an incredible re-evaluation of what Celtic folk music really meant. On the last night of Dylan's visit, I went to see him to say goodbye. I found myself in his dimly lit TV room at the Savoy. As I entered, my eyes slowly became accustomed to the dark and I was aware that we were not alone. Shapes appeared, on a sofa, on chairs. Four figures emerged from still corners. The one nearest leant towards and said: "Hello Donovan, howareya?"

The accent was unmistakable, the nasal drawl of the vowels. Bob stood up, switched on the light and said: "Have ya met these guys yet?" It was John and the rest of band. And that's how I met The Beatles – no fuss, no stress, accepted into the new and powerful musical centre of events.

By 1968, the 'winkle-picking' days of The Beatles were long behind them and the four guys from Liverpool and I escaped our dubious fame and left for India to the ashram of Maharishi Mahesh Yogi. We needed to learn how to really get high so that our wish to channel love and compassion would become a true expression and not just a platitude which our Christian upbringing had trivialised. All you need is love and a mantra.

There were those who thought our departure meant turning our back on the heavy realities of that violent year of 1968: the escalating disaster of the Vietnam War; the assassination of Martin Luther King; the Prague Spring that saw Soviet tanks enter the city; the rise of Black Power. In 1968, all over the Western world students and workers were dissenting. And yet, four musical heroes of the revolution decided to look for the answer deep within themselves. Obviously, those attached to outcomes saw this as indulgence. Only we who realised that all human suffering originates within each and every one of us, knew our journey to India was the only way for us. Soon, millions would 'turn on' to meditation after we popularised it.

The world looked like it was falling apart and the '60s were coming to a close. The Beatles themselves were growing into men, and by the following year they too were falling apart. The collapse of the band is so well documented I need not repeat it. Suffice to say that they had fulfilled every expectation that the Bohemian manifesto required. The great nuclear cloud still threatened all mankind, and yet, a generation had voiced its cry for sanity, compassion and love through The Beatles' music.

In times of great tragedy, it is to the poets and the artists we turn, and from out of the great heart of history, folk-blues and world music rises as a balm to soothe us, to protest against man's inhumanity to man. The Beatles were, and still are, the best friends this planet ever had.

Donovan
Cork
February 1, 2003

PHOTO: TOM HANLEY

When 1 becomes 4

In April 1970, Beatles fans were devastated to hear confirmation of the Fabs' final split. But there was consolation aplenty in the form of four solo albums to come. John Harris, Paul Trynka, Paul Du Noyer and Mat Snow assess the 211 minutes of music on offer…

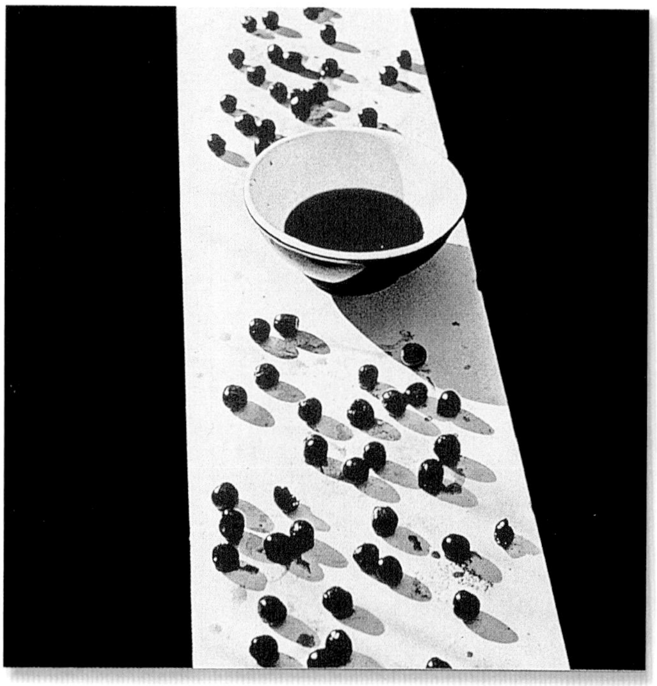

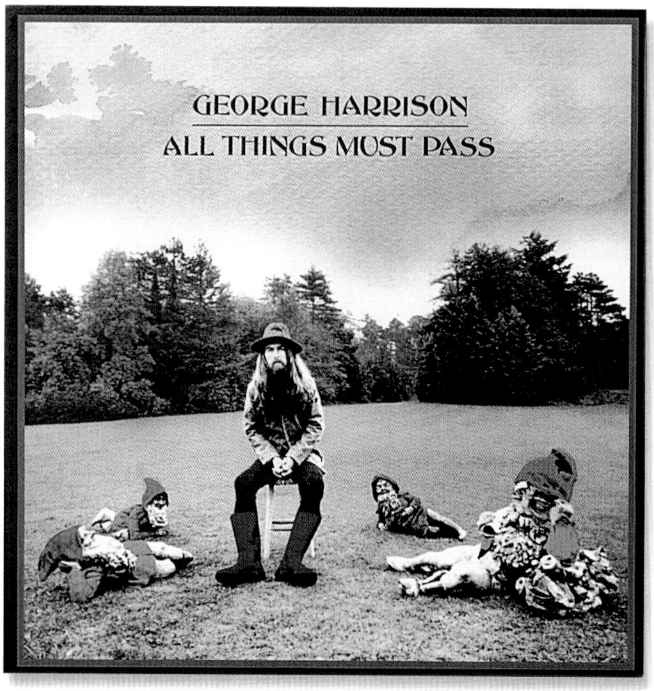

McCartney

Paul McCartney

Released: April 1970

For a man always portrayed as the ambitious, perfectionist Beatle, Paul McCartney's inaugural solo album seemed a very strange signpost for his post-Fabs future. Partly put to tape using rudimentary kit at his London home, it was proudly lo-fi, peppered with instrumentals and half-completed sketches, surrounded by the sense of its author happily retreating from the demands of his '60s life. John and George's solo debuts both oozed the creative fervour that came from being set free; the de facto chief Beatle, by contrast, sounded as if the end of the band had prompted a languid sigh of relief.

On the face of it, *McCartney* is a downhome, loose-ended album, founded on its author's new-found domesticity. Its sleeve featured Paul cradling his new-born daughter Mary. By way of announcing its abiding theme, it opened with a minute-long fireside doodle entitled The Lovely Linda. Even when he decided to rock out, the pleasures of hearth and home were never far away: Oo You, a spindly take on late '60s blues-rock, boasted that its female subject could "cook like a woman." Small wonder that, when asked about the album's underlying theme, McCartney responded, "Home, family, love."

Yet *McCartney* was altogether more complex than this suggests. By his own admission, Paul had reacted to the implosion of The Beatles by foregoing sleep and hitting the bottle. "I'd no idea what I was going to do," he later recalled. "I was *out of work*." Hence Every Night might appear to be a straightforward love song, but it contains both self-doubt and crushing lethargy ("Every night I just wanna go out/ Get out of my head/Every day, I don't wanna get up/Get out of my bed"). Man We Was Lonely sounds like whimsical country pastiche, but its title is underlined by the admission that "we was hard-pressed to find a smile." There's even a 10-second try-out of an early McCartney song called Suicide.

It's not that the self-doubt and domestic bliss aspects of the record are irreconcilable; more that McCartney convincingly documents the first being resolved by the second. In that sense, the placing of the incredible Maybe I'm Amazed towards the record's end is perfect. One minute, Paul is buckling under the strain of some unspecified trauma: "Maybe I'm a man/Maybe I'm a lonely man, who's in the middle of something/ he doesn't really understand." The next, love has worked its soul-saving wonders – though anyone who clings to the caricature of McCartney as a glib emotional simpleton should note the lines: "Maybe I'm amazed at the way you love me all the time/Maybe I'm afraid of the way I love you." That's romantic existentialism, pretty much.

For better or worse, that song is succeeded by Kreen-Akrore, a cut-and-paste experiment that stands as McCartney's most obtuse cut. Its place in the footnotes of his career is shared by a handful of the tracks here: the flatly awful Valentine Day, Hot As Sun, That Would Be Something, and the aforementioned Oo You. That said, nestling in among such long-forgotten pieces is at least one pearl: a wonderfully woozy instrumental called Momma Miss America, later included on the soundtrack to Jerry Maguire, and picked up by the DJs at the core of the short-lived British dance genre known as Big Beat.

In completely different territory, meanwhile, sit two songs whose history dates back to Rishikesh. Teddy Boy was tentatively introduced to the *Let It Be* sessions, only to founder on John Lennon's witheringly sarcastic translation of the song as a camped-up square dance. Here, it shines, a bittersweet collision of a sun-kissed arrangement and words that betray a heart-sore melancholia. Better still is Junk: in its own quiet way, one of the best songs the solo McCartney has ever recorded. It oozes a monochrome sadness, all dangling cobwebs and old photographs gathering dust. Its melody is gorgeous – so gorgeous that McCartney also included an instrumental version.

Put those two songs next to Every Night and Maybe I'm Amazed, adjust your expectations so that *McCartney*'s rough-hewn feel becomes part of its charm, and the album takes on a surprising lustre. Indeed, in a world in which countless artists – Beck, Badly Drawn Boy, The Beta Band – make a habit of retreating behind closed doors and pouring their thoughts into a portastudio, it can be retrospectively accorded a word like "Parenthetical" – and hailed as an understated delight. (JH)

> "Every Night might appear a straight love song, but it contains self-doubt and crushing lethargy."

Beaucoups Of Blues

Ringo Starr

Released: October 1970

Many of Ringo Starr's supporters concede that he wasn't the best musician in The Beatles. Some of his detractors contend Ringo wasn't even the best *drummer* in The Beatles. Yet Ringo Starr played an integral part in ensuring that, for a year at least, the solo Beatles made better music apart than they had made together.

Like John Lennon, Ringo recorded his first solo album before The Beatles officially split, although *Sentimental Journey*, a collection of '40s standards, these days probably has about as narrow a fan base as Lennon's *Two Virgins*. But as Ringo was working on George Harrison's towering *All Things Must Pass* at Abbey Road, he struck up a friendship with pedal steel player Pete Drake. Within days the two hatched a plan for Ringo to record with a stellar crew of sessioneers in Nashville.

The city was the perfect setting for the lugubrious drummer. Like the best Nashville cats, Ringo delivered downhome losers' songs with simple commitment and an absence of artifice. His face fitted, too. Like Kenny Rogers or Willie Nelson, Ringo's monumental Mount Rushmore features made him the perfect *joli laid*. His persona and voice fitted the album's songs like a glove. Ringo Starr – as train-mad toddlers would discover years later – was more narrator than singer, perfect for delivering maudlin tales of everyday tragedies – which was what *Beaucoups Of Blues* was filled with.

The title song's lilting triple-time signature and mangled French malapropisms set out the agenda: Ringo's engaging, wavering tones perfectly embody the deadbeat hero he portrays. Like Keith Richards' guitar-playing after a couple of vodka and oranges, Ringo's voice often fails the simple tests, but takes flight when the going gets tricky. For the title song's low notes, which his deep, adenoidal timbre should suit, his delivery is unsteady (cf that mooing 'town' in the opening line of Yellow Submarine). But above his natural register in the song's bridge, all his loser's charisma is on display: confident, vulnerable, the perfect example of why so many teenyboppers wanted to take Ringo home, rather than John or Paul.

The same holds true of most of the album's songs, whether he's singing about being a cuckold (Fastest Growing Heartache In The West), a john (Woman Of The Night) or other species of loser (practically every other song on the album). Of course, Ringo's reliance on the material can make for cringeworthy moments: Silent Homecoming, about a missing GI, reaches for the profundity of In The ➳

Fastest out of the gate: the Dark Horse, who led the field in the Beatles solo stakes.

Ghetto, but instead sounds like Les Dawson.

Stylistically concise, yet emotionally ambitious, *Beaucoups of Blues* built a respectable foundation for a career that scaled new heights with his next single, It Don't Come Easy. By far his best recording within or without The Beatles, it bore obvious parallels with the songs he'd recorded in Nashville. Yet it was a niftier piece of songwriting altogether, thanks to a beautifully-worked bridge, worthy of Lennon or McCartney's finest ("forget about the past, and all your sorrows"), which lifted the song onto a higher emotional plane. A well-deserved hit, it packaged everything we loved about Ringo into three minutes. Sadly, it also overshadowed everything that Ringo would do in its wake, for with the exception of 1973's memorably wistful Photograph, Ringo's career would soon wane like that of his fellow Fabs, as he descended into self-parody and his records failed to trouble the charts.

No matter. As *Beaucoups Of Blues* amply demonstrated, Ringo's persona was never about being a success. No wonder he was Marge Simpson's favourite Beatle. (PT)

All Things Must Pass

George Harrison

Released: November 1970

Its title announces the impermanence of all things – of life, love and mop-topped pop bands. So it's a little ironic that *All Things Must Pass* will probably stand as George Harrison's most enduring monument. Within its spacious acres are several of the most beautiful songs he would ever compose. His first album since leaving The Beatles, it offered dramatic proof of the Quiet One's creative liberation. In fact, for a few, heady months, it actually seemed as if George Harrison might become the most successful ex-Beatle of them all.

Nobody in November, 1970, could have mistaken the title's significance: the group had formally split six months before and this was Harrison's handful of earth upon the Beatle coffin. As if to cement the association of ideas, the wry cover picture has George in solitary splendour, surrounded by a quartet of gnomes. But there are signs on the record that George already realised there was actually no such thing as "an ex-Beatle". However much it pained him, he was doomed to remain a Fab for the rest of his days.

The title track was not new: George had tried to interest The Beatles in it almost two years earlier. But as the album took shape, the lyrics to All Things Must Pass would accrue new layers of relevance. Recording was paused for a while when his mother died; then he learned that his wife Pattie was falling for his best friend Eric Clapton. But even those events were secondary to the song's original, spiritual theme about the essential unimportance of material existence.

Fortuitously this triple long-player arrived in British shops in time for the Christmas market – back in 1970 its five pound price tag put *All Things Must Pass* firmly in the luxury bracket. In the new year it was boosted by its showcase single, My Sweet Lord, whose Number 1 showing outranked anything achieved to date by Lennon or McCartney.

A beguiling blend of black American gospel and Eastern mantra, this song was George's heartfelt call upon God to become manifest in his life. Lyrically it was a bold step to take, but My Sweet Lord's hypnotic chug would conquer all. Like a few other tracks on the album, it also introduced the swooping slide guitar that became Harrison's most distinctive style. (A rockabilly picker by background, George lacked the improvising fluency that had made guitar-heroes of his blues-based peers. But in the slide guitar he found the ideal vehicle for his melodic gift.)

Though he had made two instrumental albums while in The Beatles, *All Things Must Pass* was George's first collection of songs. Several had been written during his spell in the group, where his contributions were routinely sidelined. Not for nothing would Harrison come to dub himself the Dark Horse, for the album was a

> "His first album since leaving The Beatles, it offered dramatic proof of The Quiet One's creative liberation"

revelation of hidden talents. By hiring Phil Spector, he underlined his estrangement from McCartney, who had famously opposed Spector's involvement in *Let It Be*. And by rehearsing his solo emergence with stars such as Bob Dylan and Eric Clapton, George asserted his new status as an independent player in the global rock elite.

George was new to leadership at this point, but among the gangs assembling in the London studios were many familiar faces. Ringo Starr and Beatle confederates Klaus Voormann and Billy Preston were key players; so were the much-touted Apple signings Badfinger. Prestigious guests included Gary Brooker and Dave Mason (plus, on congas, a then-unknown Phil Collins). The sound was elegantly bulked out by Eric Clapton and the musicians he and George had met on the Delaney & Bonnie tour – a group who would coalesce in the course of these sessions to become Derek & The Dominos. In line with Spector's *modus operandi,* the record's expansive sound was obtained by using musicians in massed ranks. At certain points – Wah Wah and Let It Down being examples – the material is probably too slight to carry the colossal weight of Spector's production. Mostly, though, the effect was joyous, as if the songs were bursting with the exuberance of George's first flush of freedom.

From his friendship with Dylan came a charming co-write called I'd Have You Any Time, and the gift of Bob's new composition If Not For You. George's own song, Behind That Locked Door, was itself in the country vein of *Nashville Skyline*. Among the album's masterworks, Beware Of Darkness was characteristically spiritual, while the Hey Jude coda of Isn't It A Pity was evidence of the dead man's grip of Beatle history on George's imagination. So was the affectionate nod to Fab fans in Apple Scruffs, whilst the inspiration for Wah Wah was a latterday Beatle row. Another number, The Art Of Dying, dated back to 1966.

Despite the instant success of *All Things Must Pass*, its reputation suffered in later years. Within three months of its release, My Sweet Lord was legally ruled an "unconscious plagiarism" of The Chiffons' 1963 hit He's So Fine. It was a humiliating setback for the fledgling superstar attempting to emerge from John and Paul's shadow. Subsequently, the patchy quality of George's later albums, and their general lack of outstanding singles, led in Britain at least to a state of benign neglect. By the time of his own passing in 2001, however, the totality of Harrison's achievements was more widely recognised. And this sprawling, spirited collection is the finest way to remember its maker. (PDN)

PHOTO: HULTON COLLECTION

John Lennon/Plastic Ono Band

John Lennon

Released: December 1970

It starts with the funereal tolling of a church bell and ends with a song recorded on a child's cassette-player, called My Mummy's Dead. Even if you didn't know about John Lennon's desertion as a child by his parents and how his brief reunion with his mother ended by her death at the hands of a hit-and-run driver, the songs Mother and My Mummy's Dead that bookend and dominate the album would still be among the most harrowing in all music.

Catalysed by the Primal Scream therapy he underwent in the months before he wrote most and recorded all the songs here, the album was the by-product of his attempt to confront and so purge his feelings of unresolved grief for his mother – and also for himself, the damaged, pained human being he now accepted that he was. When *John Lennon/ Plastic Ono Band* came out, Lennon linked it back to those few personal cries for help and understanding he permitted himself to write while in The Beatles: I'm A Loser, Help!, In My Life, Strawberry Fields. "I always wrote about me when I could. But because of my hang-ups I would only now and then specifically write about me. Now I wrote all about me and that's why I like it [the album]. It's me! And nobody else."

Nor does he disguise it. Far from the phantasmagoria of even the previous year's Come Together, here the songcraft is not about weaving dreams but expressing pain, words sometimes almost failing him as they butt against a wall of feelings too deep, too dark to be contained; the lines "Mama don't go, Daddy come home" screamed ever more harrowingly a further nine times at the end of Mother are no less heart-rending than King Lear's "Never, never, never, never, never" as he cradles the corpse of his beloved daughter Cordelia.

Nowadays, we mourn the end of the '60s dream, but from the perspective of the first year of the '70s, as far as Lennon was concerned it was good riddance – spat with the venom of a man who's just realised he's been conned out of his emotional life savings. Encapsulated by the album's summation, God, the album has a consistent philosophy derived from conversations he had with Primal Scream therapist Dr Arthur Janov: that we are "born in pain" and starved of love and hope when young, and fob ourselves off with compensatory collective dreams and distractions. "God is a concept by which we measure our pain," he states and restates, before recanting a litany of false gods he's believed in, from "magic" to "Beatles". Nor, individually, does he excuse himself. John registers his self-disgust in Working Class Hero and I Found Out with only slightly less relish than his disgust with us for being fool enough to fall for the dream in the first place.

Only Yoko is saved from the savagery, alluded to as his "loved one" in Well Well Well, referred to by name in God and Hold On, and clearly present in spirit in Look At Me and Love. These last three are among the tenderest yet most elusive of his songs, yearning for inner peace in melody, words and textures as vaporously soft-focus as the sleeve photograph of the couple lying sun-dappled beneath a tree. There is a child's neediness and vulnerability about these songs that goes deeper than conventional expressions of romance and carries its own sadness: how can an adult relationship stand such an investment? Like Mother and My Mummy's Dead, we cannot – nor did Lennon intend us to – dissociate the song from the reality behind it. You cannot but hear these songs with a sigh.

Yet for all their tendresse, they share with the snarling I Found Out and the rest of the album a sound of studied rawness. Bringing in Phil Spector as the album's producer was a counter-intuitive masterstroke. Though famed for his lavish orchestrations – the last thing required here – his real ability was in microphone placement to capture the maximum impact and atmosphere from the minimum means, and as a personality to energise a creative environment. With but two sound effects (the bell on Mother and an explosion on Remember to underline the album's only joke), a strictly no-frills band (drummer Ringo, bassist Klaus Voormann, a few cameos from keyboardist Billy Preston) and Lennon accompanying his own voice live on a very dirty guitar and clomping songsmith's piano, only the Sun Studio-style slapback echo on his voice (with the exception of the sung-spoken Working Class Hero) veils his nakedness.

Released a fortnight before Christmas Day 1970, such an album could hardly be less calculated to chime with the season of mistletoe and wine, nor did it sell in anything like Beatlesque quantities. Its successor a year on, *Imagine*, was to do that – a record Lennon admitted he "sugar-coated" for mass consumption. Yet *John Lennon/Plastic Ono Band* set both the precedent and the standard for much of the intensely introspective and self-confronting rock music that has followed. Though great records since have plumbed the dark night of the soul, none have done so with such stark, unvarnished honesty. It is his masterpiece. (MS)

Linda and Paul leave the High Court, London. Inset, right, the enemy – Allen Klein.

What: Paul dissolves The Beatles
Where: High Court, London
When: 31 December 1970

SEE YOU IN COURT

As The Beatles came to an ignominious end in London's High Court, a generation of fans realised the dream was over. By Pete Doggett.

IT WAS TOO LATE TO TURN BACK. LIKE an aggrieved husband impatient for a divorce hearing, Paul McCartney had transferred The Beatles' smouldering discontent from the gossip columns to the highest legal platform in the land. The Times headline the next morning was typically low-key: "Paul McCartney Takes Court Action To Leave Beatles". But the newspaper report spelled out the end of a collective fantasy.

The decisive blow was unspectacular. On New Year's Eve 1970, McCartney's legal team simply filed a writ in the Chancery Division of the London High Court. Their client was pitted against four adversaries: John Ono Lennon, George Harrison, Richard Starkey and, just for good measure, Apple Corps. McCartney was suing not only his three best friends, but also the idealistic corporation that he had designed as a showcase for "a nice kind of Western communism".

He was seeking, so the writ affirmed, "a declaration that the partnership business carried on by the plaintiff and the defendants under the name of The Beatles And Co. and constituted by a deed of partnership dated 19 April 1967 and made between the parties hereto, ought to be dissolved, and that accordingly the same be dissolved." Additional clauses added the demand that the group's joint financial affairs should be terminated; that there should be a full investigation into the way in which those affairs had been handled; and that an official receiver should be appointed to maintain and secure the group's income and holdings.

Doorstepped at his Scottish farm the following day, McCartney explained his action: "I just want to get out of this trap. I want to dissolve The Beatles' partnership. I suppose it ceased to be a working partnership eight months ago. I left in June. The other three of them could sit down and write me out of the group, and I would be quite happy. I could pick up my cash and get out." More than anything, he asserted, "I don't want Allen Klein as my manager".

A dozen different faultlines had undermined the unity of The Beatles since the death of Brian Epstein three years earlier. But the installation of Klein as The Beatles' manager, against McCartney's express wishes, had torn a chasm between the bassist and his former bandmates. By translating that division into legal action, McCartney sealed his public image as the man who was rending the group asunder. The decision was not taken lightly: "It was murderous," he said after the action was finally settled in spring 1971. "It was a knot in my stomach all summer. You can imagine what I had to go through, suing my best mates and being seen to sue my best mates… knowing that no one would understand it, not even if I put out 50 million press releases." The subsequent backlash tipped McCartney into a depression that, he admitted later, had left him perilously close to alcoholism.

By resorting to the High Court, he not only revealed that The Beatles' arguments were beyond healing, but provided a surreal coda to a season of more optimistic tidings. Less than a month before the writ was served, McCartney, Harrison and (according to some accounts) Lennon had met briefly in America. Ringo Starr later confirmed that the entire quartet had agreed to convene in London for a summit in early January. Hints of the impending 'reunion' had reached the pop press, which in December 1970 was full of promise that talk of a split was premature. Someone described as "a friend of The Beatles" (probably press officer Derek Taylor) had told a reporter early that month: "They certainly seem serious about working together. There have been definitive discussions in that direction." Ironically, on the same day McCartney initiated his legal action, Derek left The Beatles' employment, packed off to a new job at Warner Brothers with an antique silver trinket-box and a party attended by Messrs Harrison and Starr.

The legal intervention certainly took that pairing by surprise. "I just could not believe it when I received a letter from Paul's lawyers," Harrison confessed. Starr concurred: "I was shocked and dismayed… Something serious, about which I had no knowledge, must have happened." Allen Klein was more dismissive: "(The writ) doesn't accomplish anything except bringing out into the public a lot of dirty laundry within the life that they live."

"It doesn't accomplish anything, except bring out a lot of dirty laundry into the public." Allen Klein

Klein's prediction was accurate. Ahead lay a series of hearings in which all four Beatles revealed details of their disagreements in recent years, and McCartney slipped the knife into his despised 'manager'. "Mr Klein said to me, 'The real trouble is Yoko'," he told the High Court. "I often wonder what John would have said if he had heard the remark." Now he had no choice but to hear, and so did the rest of the world.

By mid-March, McCartney would get his way, when Mr Justice Stamp appointed a city accountant, James Spooner, as receiver and manager of The Beatles' financial interests. Eventually, Lennon and Harrison's infatuation with Allen Klein would end in legally spectacular fashion. But by then McCartney would have endured years of being fingered as the catalyst for a global disaster. The Times recognised the gravity of the threat as soon as the writ was filed: "The most impressive feature in the life of young people in the past decade seems finally on the brink of dissolution." As John Lennon had astutely predicted, the dream was over.

PHOTO: HULTON ARCHIVE

OCTOBER 70

5 Ringo Starr releases a new single, Beaucoups Of Blues, in the US.

9 In EMI's Abbey Road Studios, London, George Harrison and Ringo Starr present John Lennon with a recording of It's Johnny's Birthday – a song they have written specially for him.

15 George Harrison and Phil Spector begin mixing his triple album All Things Must Pass in London.

23 It is announced that the next George Harrison single will be entitled My Sweet Lord.

27 John Lennon and Yoko Ono return to the US, having completed the album *John Lennon/Plastic Ono Band* in London.

28 George Harrison flies to New York City to complete work on *All Things Must Pass*, with Phil Spector.

NOVEMBER 70

15 Paul McCartney instructs his lawyers to instigate legal proceedings which will bring The Beatles to an end.

27 George Harrison releases his boxed triple album set, *All Things Must Pass*, in the US. Three days later, it's released in the UK.

DECEMBER 70

8 John Lennon is interviewed in his Greenwich Village apartment, New York City, by Jann Wenner of Rolling Stone magazine. The interview will be used in Rolling Stone, and will later be used as the basis of the book Lennon Remembers.

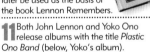

11 Both John Lennon and Yoko Ono release albums with the title *Plastic Ono Band* (below, Yoko's album).

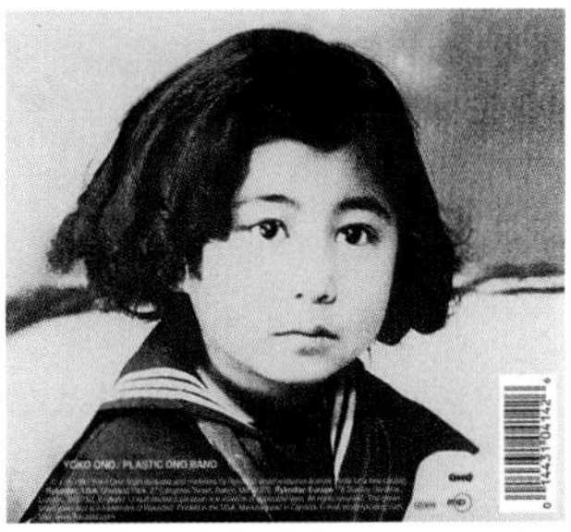

13 John Lennon does a radio interview for WABC in New York City.

14 John Lennon and Yoko Ono start work on a new movie project, Up Your Legs Forever, in New York City, finishing it two days later.

18 *From Them To You*, an LP comprising all of The Beatles' previous Christmas flexi-discs, is sent out to their fan club members in the UK.

21 John Lennon and Yoko Ono start work on another movie project, Fly.

24 John Lennon and Yoko Ono fly from New York City to London, where they will spend Christmas.

26 George Harrison becomes the first Beatle to have a solo Number 1 hit when My Sweet Lord tops the US charts.

28 John Lennon releases a new single, Mother, in the US.

31 A writ issued on behalf of Paul McCartney by the Chancery Division of the High Court, London, formally begins the legal process to dissolve of The Beatles. That evening, Ringo Starr holds a New Year party at Ronnie Scott's Club, Soho, London, where he jams with Eric Clapton, Charlie Watts, Maurice Gibb of the Bee Gees, Klaus Voormann, Georgie Fame and Bobby Keys.

Out of Time

They called it a day as the '70s opened. Was it the right decision? Nick Kent assesses how the band who'd defined the decade of love fared in the decade of decadence.

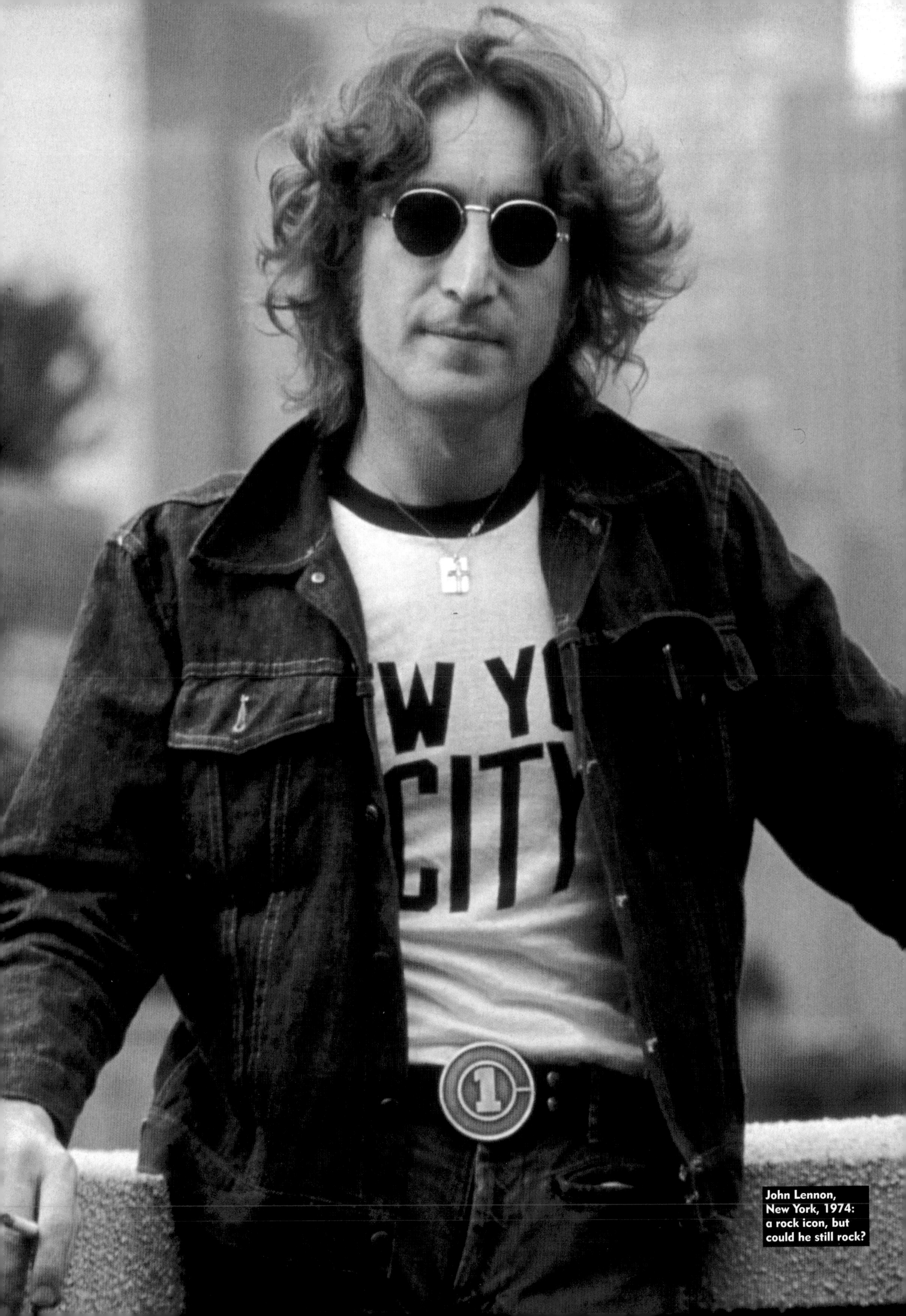

John Lennon, New York, 1974: a rock icon, but could he still rock?

BY 1970 – THE YEAR THE BEATLES OFFICIALLY broke apart – the pop culture revolution of the '60s had reached an uncertain crossroads. Over in the States, West Coast rock had lately lost its wide-eyed psychedelic sparkle and was struggling to maintain a profile as bastardised country music for cocaine users. In the UK, the prog rock tomfoolery of groups like Jethro Tull was what you'd hear being played over and over again at your local Students Union dance.

Hard rock was also much in demand, with Led Zeppelin leading the charge throughout the world, but three major acts in this genre – The Who, Jimi Hendrix and the Rolling Stones – couldn't even manage to release new studio albums in 1970, filling the gap instead with live recordings. Then, in September, Hendrix died and, two months later, so did Janis Joplin. Earlier that summer, Bob Dylan had seen fit to put out *Self Portrait,* an indigestible hotchpotch of creatively bankrupt music-making that left his audience with the sinking feeling that he was dead to the world also.

Someone once made the insightful comment that throughout the '60s Bob Dylan always managed to confuse his audience's expectations, while The Beatles usually managed to transcend the expectations of their public. With product like *Self Portrait*, and later in the '70s when he became a Born Again Christian, Dylan remained perversely consistent, if only in the sense that he continued confounding his fan-base to the point of alienation. But were The Beatles as solo artists still capable of transcending their fans' highest hopes for a new decade? As separate entities, could they hope to carry the weight of their glorious shared legacy?

While it's true that all four solo Beatles released many records throughout the '70s that hit the Top 20 charts in Britain, the US, and elsewhere, as individuals they never again managed to push the boundaries of popular music forward the way they had in the '60s. Indeed, instead of pressing ahead into the future, they often tended to look back to bygone eras for inspiration. As a solo act, John Lennon kept returning to the '50s golden age of rock for his creative stimulation, while George Harrison favoured a musical backdrop that involved blending together Phil Spector's Wall of Sound with the Band's late '60s, more textured, pastoral accompaniment. Ringo Starr's first post-Beatles recording was a George Martin-produced collection of Tin Pan Alley standards that had been popular when his mother was still a young woman, while Paul McCartney's debut found him steering clear of the ambitious song-sequences and arty experimentation of the late Beatle years in favour of more simple, sing-along material, often in the style of vintage Buddy Holly.

Another problem was that the Beatles were simply so synonymous with the '60s – they'd practically invented the decade, for God's sake – that when the 'we' decade suddenly shifted into the 'me' decade, their melodious pleas for universal harmony began to seem quaint and old-fashioned, not to mention unrealistic. "Love is the answer," Lennon continued to claim on 1972's *Mind Games,* but he didn't sound too convincing; indeed, shortly after the recording he broke up with Yoko Ono and initiated a long lovelorn drunken bachelor party for himself out in Los Angeles that made for an ideal (if mercifully brief) '70s case-history in celebrity meltdown.

The '70s were a tricky decade to live through – particularly for those who'd made their mark in the previous decade – in so far as they quickly cultivated an archly dismissive reaction towards everything that had immediately come before them. Decadence – not utopianism – was suddenly all the rage. Cocaine and downers took over from pot and acid as the hip drugs of choices. By 1977 the Clash were singing about "hate and war" with the anthemic intensity that the Beatles used to extol the virtues of peace and love 10 years earlier. Instead of "coming together," everything started to fragment. Even the music split up into conflicting little ghettoes: FM, AM, disco, country rock, heavy metal, easy listening, punk or new wave. In such a solipsistic context, a group like the Rolling Stones could still flourish even though their creative peak would be exhausted as early as 1972, with *Exile On Main Street*. The Stones understood what was involved to keep on surviving on one's own terms in a ruthless world: simply radiate a sense of 'untouchable' cool and keep aiming for the big bucks.

But The Beatles were always less about 'cool' and more about being 'kind.' They genuinely wanted their audience to share in their communal joy, not to exclude them from their in-crowd cavortings like the Stones always did. However, there was precious little to be joyful about in the '70s: indeed, voicing any kind of spiritual perspective was generally frowned upon. People preferred to listen to musicians sing about struggling with drug addiction or name-checking the walking wounded who'd once been part of Andy Warhol's fawning inner sanctum.

In such a divisive climate, a well-adjusted fellow like Paul McCartney was going to have difficulty adapting. To his credit, he remained stoically true to his former conviction that music required positive messages to win over the hearts of the greater listening public but – shorn of the creative ambition that had motivated masterpieces like *Sgt Peppers Lonely Hearts Club Band* – he quickly descended into blandness. *McCartney* – his debut release from 1970 – was a sweet, seductive, do-it-yourself album that nonetheless sounded distinctly underwhelming to anyone expecting songs as inspired as the ones he'd penned for The Beatles in the late '60s (several, like Junk and Teddy Boy, had actually been rehearsed by the Fab Four before being rejected by the other three).

Still, it sold well everywhere and generally set in motion the self-image he'd choose to promote for the rest of the decade: that of contented family man, committed music-maker, a pot of pot-head – but certainly not a 'weirdo' like John and, above all, the ultimate all-purpose people-pleaser. In 1971 he released two albums: the first, *Ram*, saw him returning to the more elaborate arrangements of his late Beatle years, but without the inspired songcraft of yore to back them up, while *Wild Life* found him fronting a makeshift group he'd named Wings and recording the most banal compositions of his entire career.

McCartney craved the companionship of being part of a group but didn't really fancy re-experiencing all the tensions of having another member challenge his musical authority, so Wings was always going to be an unequal alliance, with Paul and Linda on one side and a bunch of highly frustrated rock musos on the other.

When two members left after 1972's insipid *Red Rose Speedway,* just as McCartney, his wife and Denny Laine were flying to Nigeria to record its follow-up, the former Beatle found himself in a stressful situation that was further intensified when he and Linda were robbed at knife point in the streets of Lagos a few days after their arrival. Perhaps these traumas

"Love is the answer," Lennon continued to claim on Mind Games, but he didn't sound too convincing.

PHOTOS: CAMERA PRESS, HULTON ARCHIVES

Paul and Linda, 1970. Adversity would re-awaken his creative muse.

re-awoke his creative muse, for *Band On The Run* – the album he recorded there – became his great critical breakthrough, in 1973.

As a result of its massive global success, McCartney proved to the world he could still create new material worthy enough to stand alongside his Beatles classics. But after that, he got lazy again and his sense of quality control started to slip. In one sense, he was still prolific, recording and releasing a new album each year through the rest of the '70s, usually surrounded by an ever-shifting line-up of Wings members. He had a lot of hit records and maintained his level-headed family-man persona with great aplomb. But McCartney became lost creatively from the second half of the '70s onwards because, firstly, he did not have a force like John Lennon around to stimulate him, and secondly because he often tried to make his music sound in sync with whatever was happening in the '70s, and ended up following rather than leading the pack: a humiliating position for anyone who'd helped invent the previous decade to find himself in. He started out gamely aping glam rock with Jet in 1973, but was soon clumsily pastiching ABBA and incorporating a bland disco beat to his songs. Then in 1978 he descended to recording his own homage to punk rock – Boil Crisis. It had all gotten a bit silly by then. Maybe he was just smoking too much pot – he got busted for possession of the drug in Japan at the end of the decade and spent several days in jail. Still, McCartney remained healthy and un-bent in his messages to mankind, unlike most of his peers who spent the decade mostly scowling their way in and out of drug detox facilities. His smiling winner's face and thumbs aloft salute to the world may have made him an easy target for seething punk contempt, but it sent out a reassuring buzz to home-owners in the suburbs who appeared to become his most fervent supporters as he moved gracefully into middle age.

John Lennon's journey through the '70s would be radically different from that of his former songwriting partner though, like McCartney, he too would soon run out of championship-level creative steam. It began impressively enough with the release in 1970's early winter of his first solo album, *Plastic Ono Band*. "I don't believe in Jesus, I don't believe in Beatles… I just believe in me/Yoko and me/and that's reality," Lennon announced at the record's end, perfectly pin-pointing the zeitgeist's shift from the caring, sharing '60s, to the every man for himself 'ruthlessness' of the '70s. It didn't get any blunter than this: the dream was really over. But the record did more than just transcend its audience's expectation: it shocked them all to their very cores. *Imagine* – its more Beatles-friendly 1971 follow-up – is generally regarded as Lennon's best-loved solo work with generally good songs arranged in a more pop-conscious mode than *P.O.B.*'s Primal Scream rock. Millions consider the title track some major text of spiritual enlightenment, but personally I could never stomach the holier-than-thou tone of Lennon's voice as he sang "imagine no possessions/I wonder if you can." After that it was downhill fast, quality-wise. The politically aware *Sometime In New York City* (1972) was two albums' worth of dumb posturing; 1973's *Mind Games* was deeply uninspired. In 1974, *Walls & Bridges* found him lonely and scared, surrounded by the phoney cocaine camaraderie of top-drawer US session musicians. 1975's *Rock'n'Roll* was perhaps the most disappointing of all. Despite its title, the album of '50s covers didn't really rock – at least not with a fraction of the intensity that Lennon had brought to Twist And Shout and Money, 12 years earlier. Interestingly enough, Lennon collaborated briefly with David Bowie, the young man who most decisively helped invent the '70s the way The Beatles had defined the '60s. But the resulting track, Fame, indicated that Bowie was creatively in the driver's seat and that the former Beatle had become just a passenger. When, in 1975, Lennon abruptly retired from making music for five years, it was his wisest decision of the decade. In 1980 he and Ono returned with *Double Fantasy*, which was released just before his murder in December of that year. Due to the tragic circumstances surrounding it, the album immediately became cherished among mourning Beatles fans even though – from a more objective perspective – they could discern that Lennon was still struggling to reconnect with his muse.

George Harrison, meanwhile, became the self-appointed 'dark horse' of The Beatles breakdown. "Create and preserve the image of your choice," was a Ghandi quotation that the mystic Beatle ceaselessly adhered to throughout the '70s, single-mindedly cultivating the persona of the solemn-faced spiritual seeker who'd turned his back on the decadence of the Western world in order to devote his life to gardening, meditation and devotional music-making.

"Had they reunited in the 'me' decade, the Fab Four might have ended up sounding like ELO or Supertramp."

Harrison's first release, 1970's *All Things Must Pass*, was his masterpiece, introducing to the world a first-rate singer-songwriter who was able to channel together the penetrating lyrical insights of a wannabe Bob Dylan with delightful melodies inspired by classic tunesmiths such as Hoagy Carmichael. One song in particular, Beware of Darkness, prophesied the gloomy outcome of sinking into self-absorbed '70s solipsism with a haunting eloquence. But straight after the album's enormous commercial and critical success, Harrison started to lose his way in the world. He was taken to court and found guilty of plagiarism, once the composers of the Chiffon's He's So Fine noticed that the former Beatles guitarist had used the basic chord progression of their tune to enhance his mega-hit My Sweet Lord. Then in 1974 he embarked upon a disastrous solo tour of the States. After that, he stayed out of the spotlight, releasing new albums throughout the '70s that seemed hopelessly out of step with the mood of the times. During the '90s these same albums would be reappraised, but at the time of their release, Harrison's various heartfelt paeans to spiritual surrender sounded po-faced and bereft of humour. In addition, it was uncomfortable to listen to him – like McCartney and Lennon – struggling to incorporate synthesisers and bland reggae rhythms into the arrangements of his diminishing songcraft.

Last – and least – Ringo Starr enjoyed major success in the mid-'70s with the Richard Perry-produced *Ringo* and *Goodnight Vienna*, two light-hearted albums that managed to include cameos from all four Beatle members – though never in the same room at once. But after this high point, he quickly found himself on the losing end of the decade with a raging alcohol problem and a succession of less commercial album releases that seemed to feature every cocaine-addicted musician then resident in Los Angeles.

Once again, it should be stressed: the solo Beatles continued to sell millions of records. But the albums they released generally failed to influence what was going on around them. The group's '60s legacy, meanwhile, was being re-channelled by a number of excellent young US bands like Big Star, The Raspberries and – later in the decade – Cheap Trick. By the mid-'70s, two English bands – the Jeff Lynne-directed Electric Light Orchestra and Supertramp, a prog rock outfit smitten with the silly baroque pop of Maxwell's Silver Hammer – were even being awarded platinum discs for their own Beatles-derived pastiches. In fact, had the Fab Four decided to regroup during the 'me' decade, it's more than likely that their studio recordings would have ended up sounding like ELO and Supertramp: dweeby, positive pop drenched in radio-friendly sonic schmaltz.

Frankly, they were better off apart. The Beatles and the '70s were never going to be a marriage made in heaven because they were too hopelessly affiliated with what had just come before. Like the Brian Wilson songs they'd competed against in 1966, they simply weren't made for those times. ■

PHOTOS: REX FEATURES; CAMERA PRESS

George and, far left, Ringo in 1970. Both started their solo careers with a bang, but hit hard times in the '70s.

Hello, good buys!

Thanks to a decade of stardom, you could pack your lunch in a Yellow Submarine, hang your jacket on Ringo, or blow up a Beatle. Plus there's more typical Beatles memorabilia like ticket stubs and rare sleeves. Tom Bryant and Pete Nash consider the collectables.

Beatles Wig

Value: $650 (packaged)

Above: look like your favourite Beatle with this super-rare, mop-top toupee. A late-'60s "extra hairy" version proved too expensive for the manufacturers and was not produced.

Beatles Magnetic Hair Game

Value: $1,600

The fun that could be had with a magnet and some iron filings! This very rare 'game' is virtually impossible to find today.

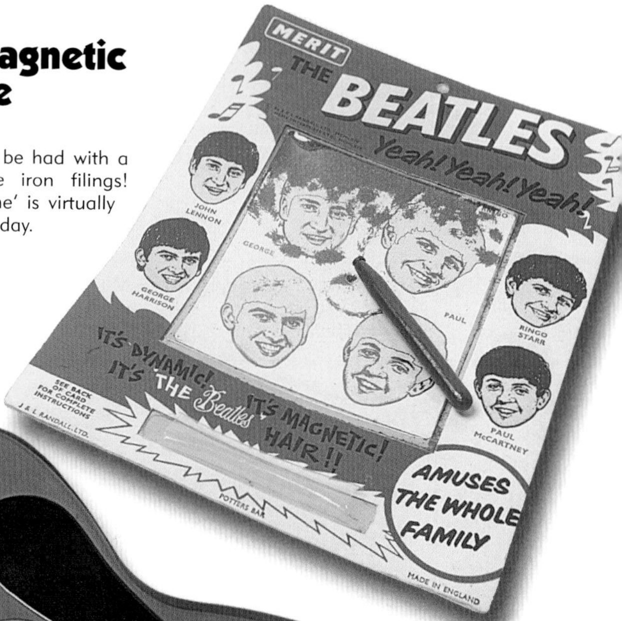

Big 6 Guitar

Value: $550 (with box), $300 (without)

It slowly dawned on Brian Epstein that The Beatles, despite being able to sell millions of records, could sell even more spin-offs and merchandising paraphernalia, so he set about licensing everything he could think of. This rare Beatles guitar (and the one over the page) were at least relevant, which is a lot more than can be said for some of the rest!

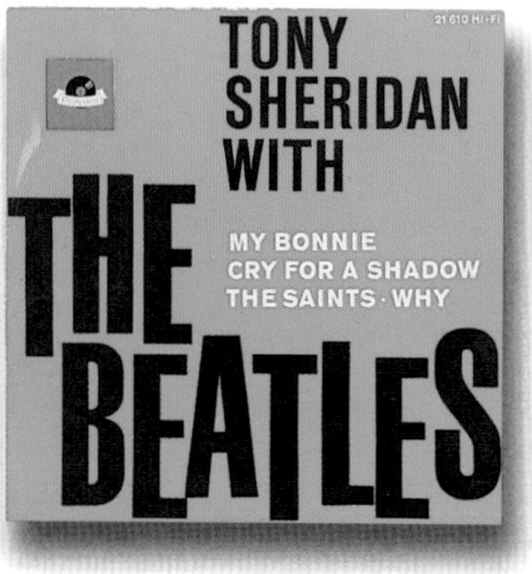

Tony Sheridan With The Beatles

Value: $90-$160

Brian Epstein was furious when The Beatles' Hamburg collaborations with Tony Sheridan were released. He claimed the recordings bore no resemblance to the mop-tops of 1964. Still, the Australian Ain't She Sweet (with John's head drawn on the cover) is now going for £60 while the British My Bonnie (with a green sleeve) now commands a whopping £100.

Beatles Cake Decorations

Value: $160

Hong Kong company Swingers noticed a gap in the market and knocked out these unlicensed cake decorations. NEMS and Seltaeb products are worth more, but these rip-offs are still highly collectable.

Beatles Nodding Dolls

Value: $1,500 (complete boxed set)
Value: $150 each

There's probably more chance of a Beatles reunion than of anyone finding a complete boxed set of these very rare items. Still, they'd look a lot better on the back shelf of your car than a nodding dog.

Record Box
Value: $275

This American Disc-Go-Case, issued by Charter Industries in 1966, will provide a loving home for your favourite Beatles singles (as long as you remove the centres).

Beatles Junior Guitar
Value: $2,500

Despite having fewer strings than the previous Big 6 Guitar, this dainty model fetches an incredible $2,500 if still in its packaging. Watch out for six-string counterfeit versions though.

Beatles Tie
Value: $240

Beatles Tie Tac
Value: $160

Before Epstein realised quite how much merchandising was worth, he struck a deal with US company Seltaeb. In exchange for 10 per cent of the profits, Epstein was happy to let the American company put out what they liked – leading to such classics as the Beatles bootlace tie and tie tac. Still, very collectable.

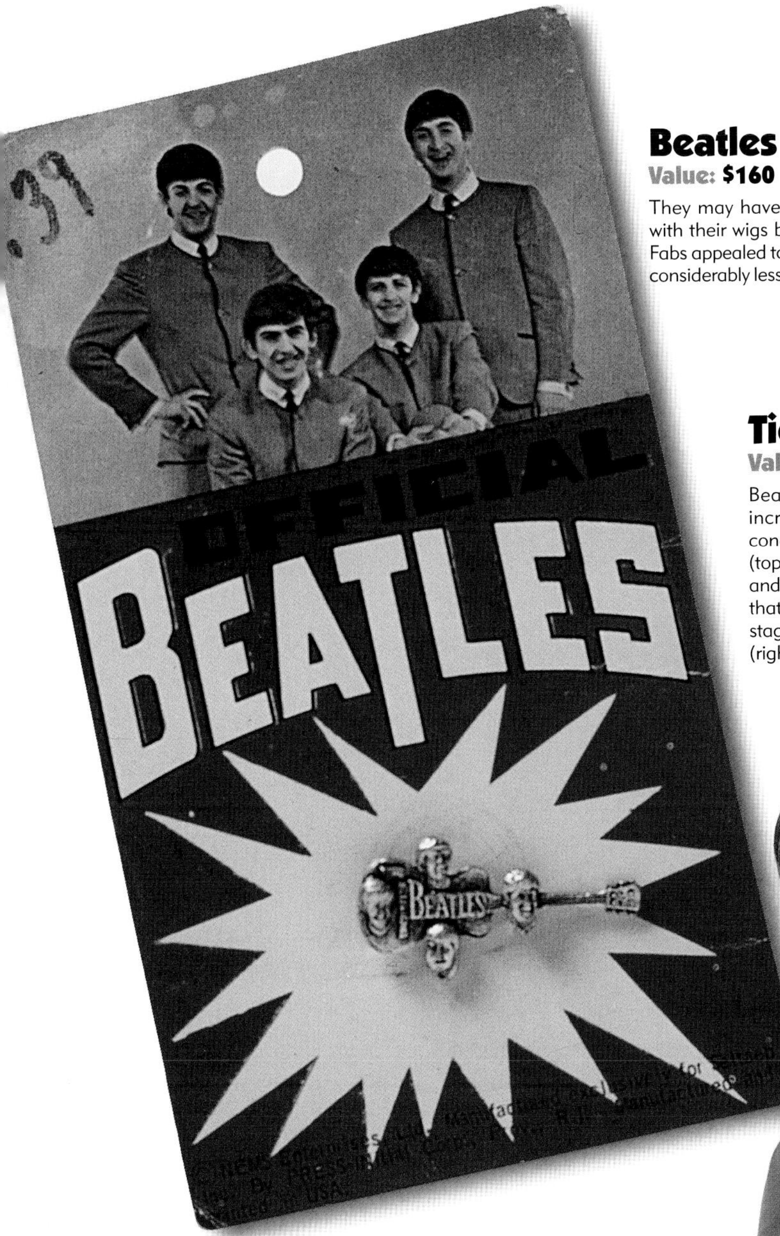

Beatles Tie Clip

Value: $160

They may have encouraged bad hair with their wigs but with this tie clip the Fabs appealed to the smarter fan. Worth considerably less without the packaging.

St. Paul's Presbyterian Church Youth Club
a'n'n'o'u'n'c'e a Return Visit of
POLYDOR RECORDING —A'R'T'I'S'T'S— The BEATLES
on Saturday 10th March . 1962 — in the Church Hall North Road
also The COUNTRY FOUR with Brian Newman
*Admittance By Ticket Only | TICKETS Five Shillings | From 7-30 p.m. to 11-30 p.m.
Right of admission reserved

Tickets

Value: $320-$500

Beatles tickets are rare and become increasingly valuable the earlier the concert. The 1962 Presbyterian Church (top right) ticket will fetch a massive $500 and proves the lads had their sights set on that "bigger than Jesus" tag at an early stage. The 1963 Baptist Youth Club ticket (right) will get you $320.

A dance promoted by the local Baptist church youth club.
BAPTIST YOUTH CLUB
PRESENTS
The Greatest Teenage Dance
FEATURING—
THE BEATLES
Supported By— THE ELECTONES THE MIKE TAYLOR COMBO THE MUSTANGS WITH RICKY DAY
IN THE CO-OPERATIVE HALL,
FRIDAY NEXT, JANUARY 25th
Non-Stop Dancing 7.30 to 11.30 p.m.
Tickets 6/. Buffet

Foreign EPs

Value: $80-$130

According to collectors, New Zealand is not generally considered a good place to sell records as it is so thinly populated – making the orange copy of A Hard Day's Night (below) fairly rare and worth $130. While The Danish EP, The Liverpool Sound (right), split with The Fourmost, will set you back $120, and the Argentinean Boleto Para Pasear (Ticket To Ride) ('Los Beatles' sleeve, below right) is worth an impressive $80.

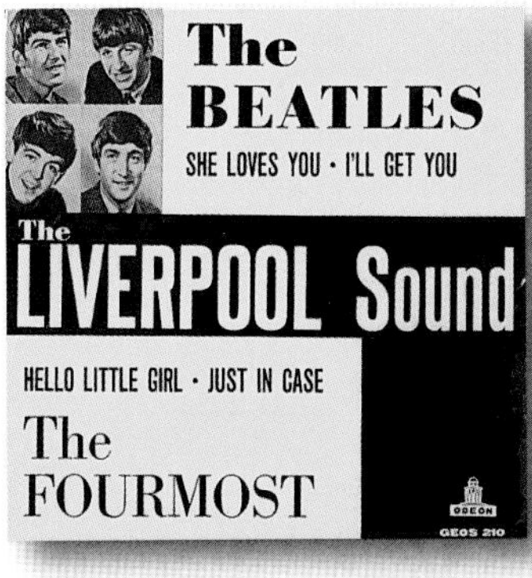

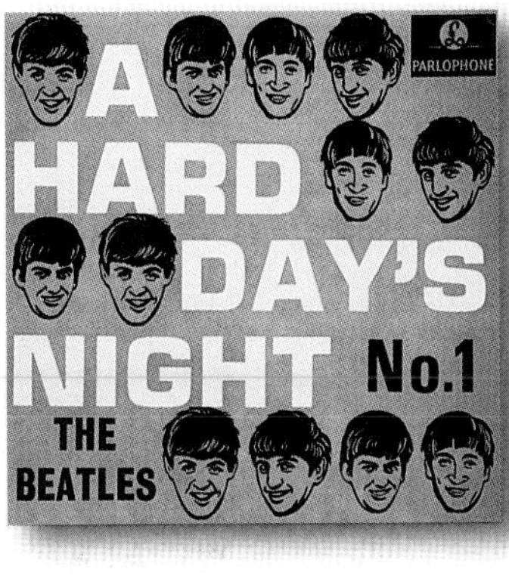

Beatles Bath Fragrance

Value: $320 (boxed)
$160 (without box)

Only Ringo and Paul bath fragrances were manufactured, making you wonder about the other two's personal hygiene.

THANKS TO PETE NASH

How I Won The War ticket

Value: $320-$400

This was issued at the UK gala premiere of John's only non-Beatle acting role. A mint specimen like this, featuring a cartoon image of the newly bespectacled Lennon, is now extremely rare.

How I Won The War book

Value: $30

This 1967 film tie-in edition of Patrick Ryan's original novel, not particularly rare, failed to go beyond a first edition.

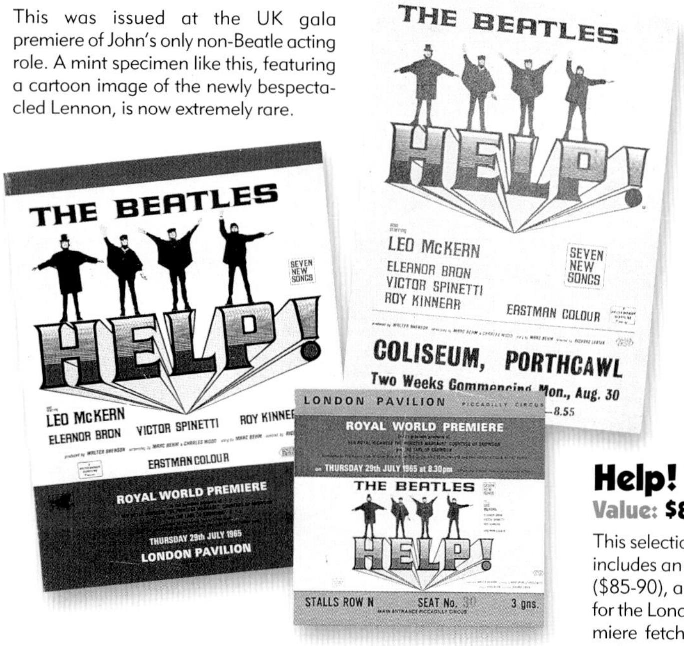

Help! items

Value: $85-$650

This selection of movie items (left) includes an original handbill postcard ($85-90), a rare-as-hens'-teeth ticket for the London Pavilion's Royal premiere fetches an amazing $600-650, and an equally coveted programme worth a whopping $500.

Beatles hangers

Value: $160-$200

This extremely rare set of coat-hangers was produced in the UK for boutiques by Saunders Enterprises in 1967. Each hanger features a 16-inch high double-sided black and white, rather dated, photo of a Beatle except Ringo, who sports his 'Our World' outfit.

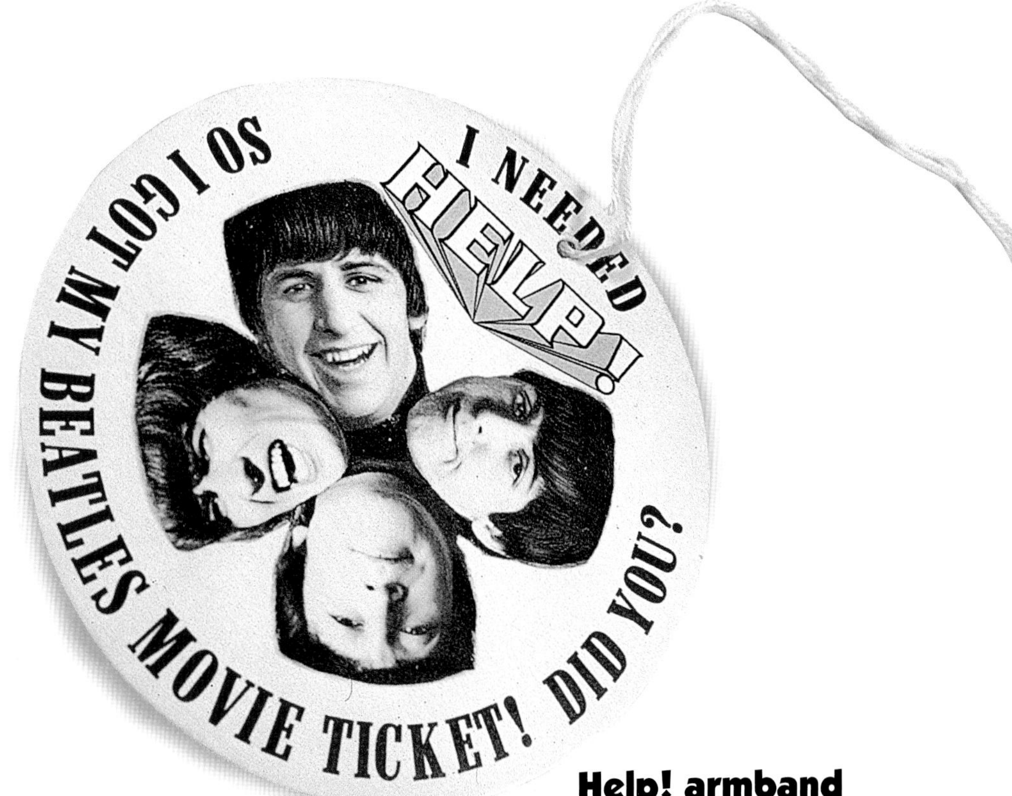

I NEEDED HELP! SO I GOT MY BEATLES MOVIE TICKET! DID YOU?

Bubblegum

Value: $8 individually; $1000 for set

Another part of the Yellow Submarine cash-in, there were 66 different packets of this bubblegum. Individually, they are fairly common but an entire set is very hard to come by. Each features a different Beatle or different picture of a Yellow Submarine moment.

Help! armband

Value: $35

Part costume jewellery, part unashamed merchandising, this armband measuring 3.75 inches in diameter was issued to American movie-goers when they bought tickets for The Beatles' second feature film, *Help!*.

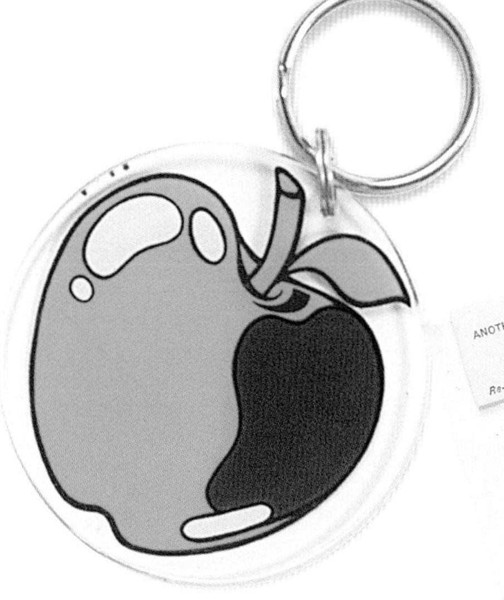

ANOTHER FANTASY PRODUCT
69 KETTERING ROAD, NORTHAMPTON, ENGLAND.
TEL. NORTHAMPTON 21343
Re-Sale Posters : Patches : Export Enquires Welcomed
SGT. PEPPERS LONELY HEARTS CLUB BAND

Sgt Pepper's badge

Value: $30

Fantasy were a popular brand of sew-on patches in the mid-to-late '60s. In 1967 they created this Sgt Pepper badge which faithfully reproduces the original artwork from the album's cut-out sheet. There are still plenty of these around, some still adhering to their original owners' clothes no doubt, although one in its original packet and in mint condition will currently fetch $30.

Tickets

Value: $30

These well-preserved tickets for the American premiere of Help! belong with the armband shown above. The original price of admittance for this event (which was not attended by The Beatles) was $1.49. An original, mint condition ticket like these is now valued at $30.

Apple key ring

Value: $125

Another Apple promo, this key ring was sent out to various lucky fans and journalists alongside the latest Apple releases. Most, though, were handed out to Beatles fan clubs who sent them on to those deemed fan-enough.

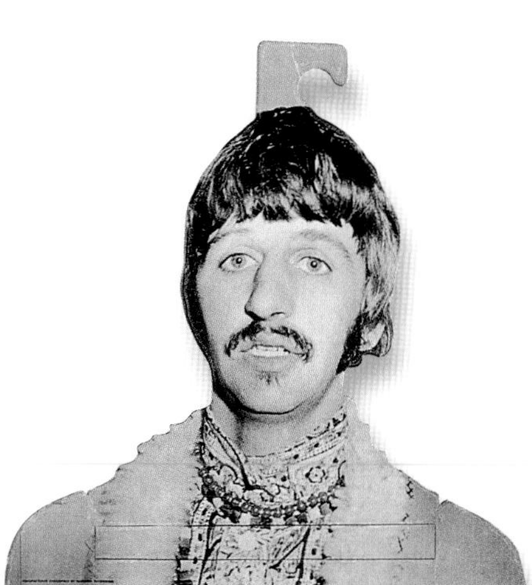

Beatles puzzles

Value: $300, Yellow Submarine picture puzzle (top); $300, illustrated lyrics puzzle (above)

Released in the UK, The Beatles song puzzle contained clues to a handful of the Fabs' songs. The idea was that, on completion of the puzzle, you could work out the names of Beatles songs from such brain-sizzling clues as a crying guitar. Meanwhile, the US-only Yellow Submarine puzzle was a much more basic affair – you simply pieced the Blue Meanies together.

Beatles coat hangers

Value: $650

By the time The Beatles geared up their marketing machine again after its 1964 heyday, most of the fans had grown up. This meant that, while the products were of higher quality and, in theory, earned the band more money, the fans were too grown up to want to buy them. A shame as many are now too rare to find.

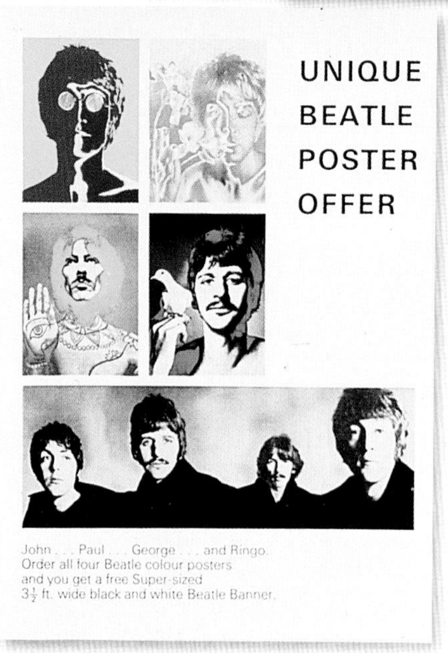

Unique Beatle poster offer

Value: $50

This Daily Express flyer was advertising an offer to buy five of Richard Avedon's classic Beatles posters. While the flyer itself is not worth much, a set of the posters will now set you back $1,500.

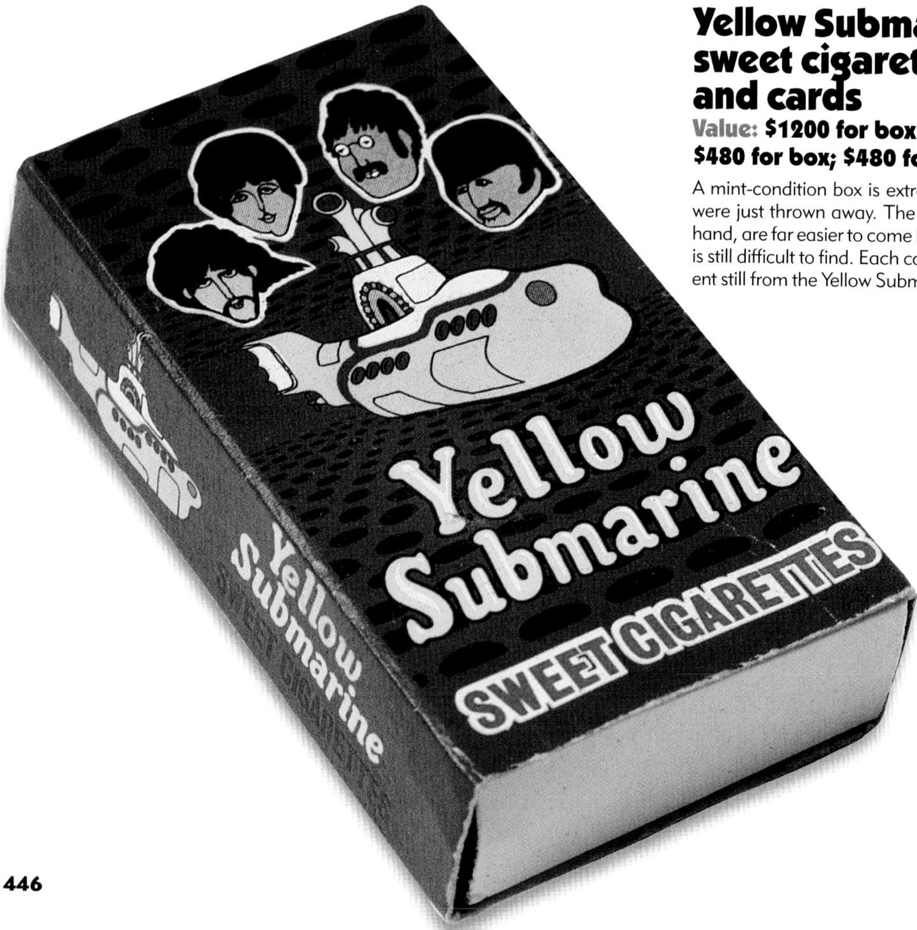

Yellow Submarine sweet cigarettes and cards

Value: $1200 for box and cards; $480 for box; $480 for set of cards

A mint-condition box is extremely rare, as most were just thrown away. The cards, on the other hand, are far easier to come by – though a full set is still difficult to find. Each card featured a different still from the Yellow Submarine movie (right).

Yellow Submarine lunch box and flask

Value: $720

Available in two different colours, this was the lunch box of choice for the psychedelic connoisseur. It's now rare to find one in mint condition as so many were battered in playground scuffles, though scratched and scraped examples are not too hard to find.

Bubblegum cards

Value: $5 each; $1050 for the whole set

Depicting individual scenes from the film, these Yellow Submarine bubblegum cards arrived inside the bubblegum packets. They were two-sided cards and, once you had them all, the reverse sides fitted together to create a poster of The Beatles and various characters from the Yellow Submarine film.

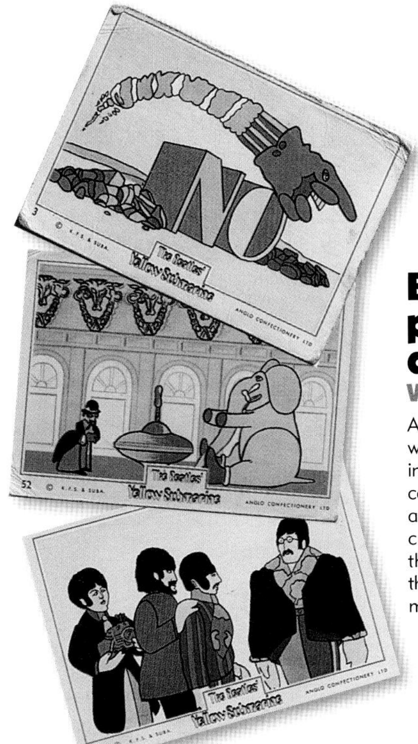

Beatles pop-out art decorations

Value: $45

An America-only release, this was a book of 20 Beatles images laid out on a perforated card page. It originally cost $1 and you could either stick the cut-outs on the wall, make them into a mobile or keep them in a box for 40 years and make a $44 profit.

Apple box-set

Value: $1600

Distributed to British radio stations and journalists, this box contained Apple's first four singles – Mary Hopkin's Those Were The Days, Jackie Lomax's Sour Milk Sea, The Black Dyke Mills Band's Thingumybob and The Beatles' Hey Jude. It also included a book profiling each of the artists.

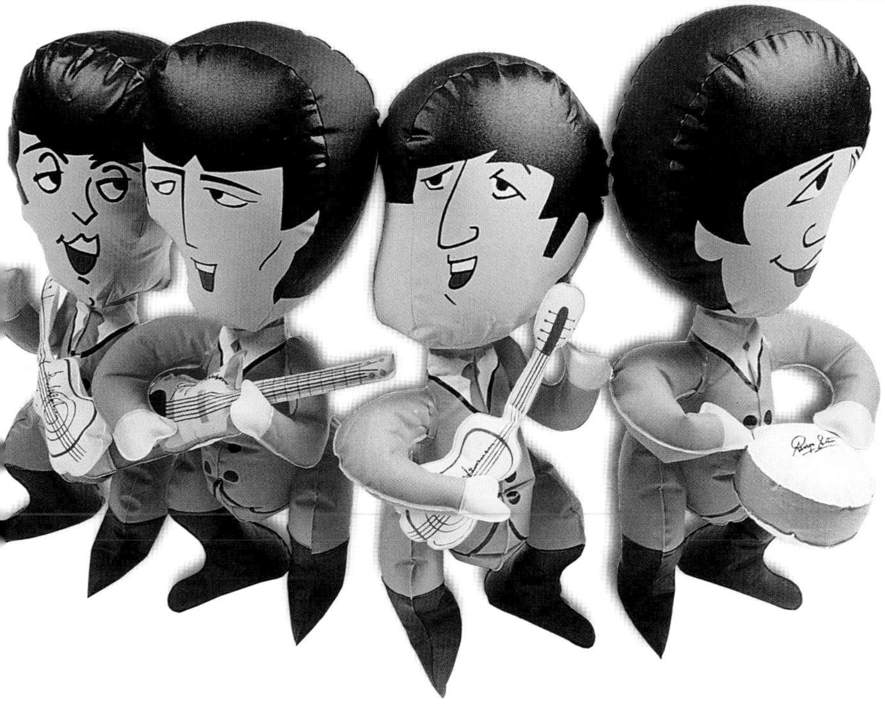

Beatles dolls

Value: $250

These mail-order inflatable dolls produced for the US market were as anachronistic in 1966-67 as the animated cartoon series on which they were based. In one episode, the series, produced by TVC Ltd, depicted these 1963-era Beatles singing Strawberry Fields Forever. Each doll is an impressive 13 inches high. A complete set would have been yours in exchange for $2 and some Nesquik or Lux soap coupons.

MEMORABILIA COURTESY OF PETE NASH, BOB KELLY AND BOB JAMES

Index

Page numbers in *italics* refer to the illustrations. Albums and films are listed under their individual titles, and songs are under the heading 'songs'.

"I like my music simple, catchy and fresh. My favourite Beatles song is Help. This is perfect pop music" **Tina Turner**

Index

D

E

F

"I love Rain. Edward Lear set to music." **John Squire**

Index

"My favourite has to be I Want To Hold Your Hand. How could the first Beatles record you heard not be an epiphanic moment?" **Todd Rundgren**

Index

"I love A Day In The Life. How could John be so in to it and so out of it?" **James Taylor**

Index

N

O

P

"Yesterday. That was one of the greatest of all time." **Steve Cropper**

Index

"Eleanor Rigby is a beautiful example of the work, at its peak, of the most sophisticated and important cultural icons of the '60s.." **Mike Stoller**

Index

"When I first heard Yesterday, I felt the earth tilt on its axis. It changed everything." **Jimmy Webb**

Index

"I Am The Walrus's 'otherness' was transporting in a way that nothing before it had ever approached." **David Bowie**

Acknowledgements

The editors would like to thank Julian Alexander, Johnny Black, Mark Bracey, Dave Brolan, David Leaf, Lora Findlay, Isabel Cruz, Murray Chalmers, Geoff Baker, Dennis Hutchins, Yoko Ono, Jason at Tracks, Robert Whitaker, Maddy Ballantyne, On The Beat, Martin O'Gorman, Reckless Records, Keith Badman, Paul Du Noyer, Mark Ellen, Jim Irvin, Spencer Leigh, Karla Merrifield, Pete Nash, Mat Snow, Chris Taylor, Barry Miles, Terence Spencer, Jane Titterington, Paul Bevoir, Genesis Publications, David Hurn, Bob Kelly, Andrew Loog Oldham, David Pritchard & Jane Roscoe.